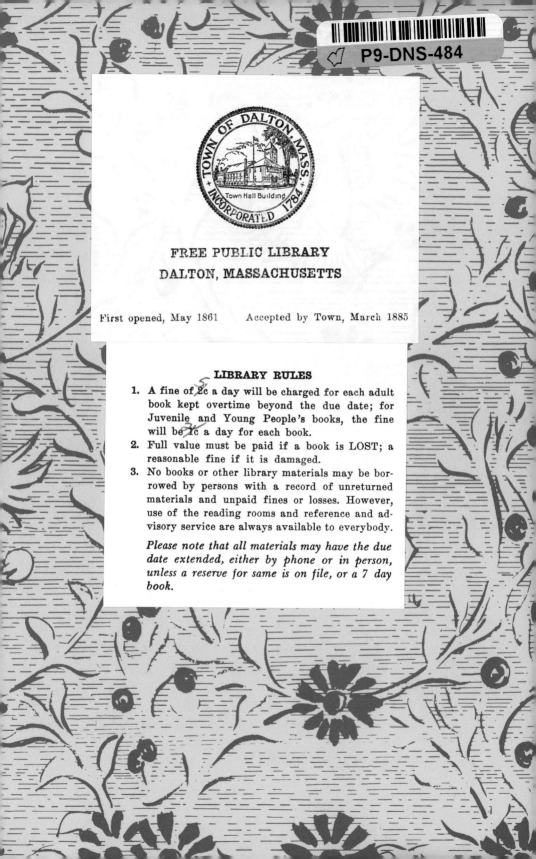

FREE PUBLIC LIBRARY
DALTON, MASSACHUSETTS

First opened, May 1861   Accepted by Town, March 1885

LIBRARY RULES

1. A fine of 2c a day will be charged for each adult book kept overtime beyond the due date; for Juvenile and Young People's books, the fine will be 1c a day for each book.
2. Full value must be paid if a book is LOST; a reasonable fine if it is damaged.
3. No books or other library materials may be borrowed by persons with a record of unreturned materials and unpaid fines or losses. However, use of the reading rooms and reference and advisory service are always available to everybody.

Please note that all materials may have the due date extended, either by phone or in person, unless a reserve for same is on file, or a 7 day book.

*The
Price of
Loyalty*

Bicentennial of the American Revolution

CONSULTING EDITORS
Richard B. Morris
Jack P. Greene
Dumas Malone
John C. Miller

PUBLISHED

Brooke KING GEORGE III: *A Biography of America's Last Monarch*

Crary THE PRICE OF LOYALTY: *Tory Writings from the Revolutionary Era*

AMONG THE PROJECTED TITLES

Beeman BIOGRAPHY OF PATRICK HENRY

Billias BIOGRAPHY OF ELDRIDGE GERRY

Bradford REVOLUTIONARY PATRIMONY: *Handbook of Sites, Structures, and Objects*

Cantor HERITAGE OF FREEDOM

Cary MASSACHUSETTS IN THE AMERICAN REVOLUTION

Ganyard NORTH CAROLINA IN THE AMERICAN REVOLUTION

Henderson PARTISAN POLITICS IN THE CONTINENTAL CONGRESS

Klein BIOGRAPHY OF WILLIAM LIVINGSTON

Syrett THE ROYAL NAVY IN THE AMERICAN REVOLUTION

Tate VIRGINIA IN THE AMERICAN REVOLUTION

Waters BIOGRAPHY OF JAMES OTIS

Weir SOUTH CAROLINA IN THE AMERICAN REVOLUTION

Narrative and Editing by
CATHERINE S. CRARY

Drawings by Cecile R. Johnson

NEW YORK ST. LOUIS SAN FRANCISCO
DÜSSELDORF LONDON SYDNEY TORONTO SINGAPORE

The

Price of

Loyalty

TORY WRITINGS
FROM THE
REVOLUTIONARY
ERA

McGraw-Hill Book Company

LIBRARY OF CONGRESS CATALOGING IN PUBLICATION DATA

Crary, Catherine S comp.
    The price of loyalty.

    (Bicentennial of the American Revolution)
    Bibliography: p.
    1. American loyalists. 2. United States—History—
Revolution—Sources. I. Title. II. Series.
E277.C72   373.3'14   73-925
ISBN 0-07-013460-X

123456789BPBP79876543

This book was set in Garamond by University Graphics, Inc. It was printed on Sebago MF medium offset paper and bound by Book Press. The designer was Betty Binns. The editors were Nancy Tressel, Judy Duguid, and Rose Arny. Joe Campanella supervised the production.

Contents

Foreword by Richard B. Morris, xxiii

Acknowledgments, xxvii

Introduction, 1

PART ONE

Bewilderment, Equivocation, and Defiance
OCTOBER 1773–JULY 4, 1776   11

1 THE MAKING OF SOME EARLY LOYALISTS   13

   1 The Tea Fracas, 13; Jolley Allen Outwits the Boston
      Committee, 14; The Faction Makes a "Tea Pot of the
      Harbor of Boston", 16

   2 The "Tide in Human Affairs": The Reverend Henry
      Caner Believes the Flame of Revolt Is Kept Alive by a
      Half-Dozen Men of Bad Principles, 17

   3 Reactions to the Boston Port Act and to the Solemn
      League and Covenant, 20; The New York Committee
      Straddles the Boycott Issue and Suggests a Continental
      Congress, 22; The Reverend Samuel Peters Describes the
      Action of the Sons of Liberty in Farmington,
      Connecticut, 23; The Quakers Protest a Sympathetic
      Boycott, 23

      The Reverend William Clarke Sees Civil War Ahead:
      "A Solemn League and Covenant . . . Is Signing about
      in the Country", 24

      William Eddis of Maryland Reports "All America Is in a
      Flame", 26

4 Audacious Proceedings: Henry Hulton Says "The Parade
   They Make Here of Resistance Is All a Flask without
   Bottom", 28

5 Westchester Protesters Declare Their "Honest Abhorrence
   of All Unlawful Congresses and Committees", 31

6 Ready-made Loyalist: Isaac Wilkins of Westchester
   Explains That He Cannot Raise His Hand against His
   King nor His Sword against His Country, 34

7 The Seizure of Skenesborough, 36;   Philip Skene
   Emphasizes the Cruelty to the Women of His Family, 37;
   The Barnes Company Tries to Capture "Lord Skene" and
   Finds a Preserved Corpse, 37

8 Olive Branches: William Smith, Jr., Advises Lewis
   Morris, Delegate to the Continental Congress, on a
   Conciliatory Answer to the King, 39

9 Taunts from the Mob: John Wetherhead Is Saluted with
   "Damn Him, Seize Him, and Drown Him", 44

10 The Brush on Breed's Hill: Dorothea Gamsby Recounts
   the Scene of June 17, 1775, to Her Granddaughter, 47

11 Flora MacDonald, Beautiful Scottish Heroine of Culloden,
   Inspires the Loyalist Highlanders before the Battle
   of Moore's Creek, 50

12 Andrew Elliot Comments That Half the Acts of Trade
   Are Improper and Keep the Merchants Cursing Them, 52

2 COMMITTEES OF SAFETY: CONFRONTATIONS, THREATS, AND
   ROUGH HANDLING   55

1 The Threat of the Tar Mop: William Aitchison of
   Norfolk, Virginia, Warns James Parker to Be on Guard, 58

2 A Dead Owl: Stephen Resco of Stockbridge Receives a Final
   Touch to His Coat of Tar and Feathers, 59

3 Join or Suffer: Janet Schaw Describes the Operations of
   the Wilmington Committee of Safety in Overcoming the
   Disinclination of the North Carolinians for Revolution, 60

4   *Recant or Hang, 62;   John Hopkins Is Ordered to "Beg All America Pardon", 63;   The Governor of Georgia Fills in a Few Details for Lord Dartmouth, 64*

5   *Temporary Accommodations: Thomas Browne of Augusta Obliges His Tormentors, 64*

6   *Dictates of Conscience: Eleazer Russell, a Quaker, Invokes His "Original Scruple" against the Shedding of Human Blood, 67*

    Colonel John Peters Recounts the Consequences in 1775 of Refusing to Oblige the King and Sign the League and Covenant, 69

7   *Deceit: Guy Johnson Misleads the Committee of Safety and Warns of the Indians' "Dreadful Revenge", 70*

8   *Bravado: "You D . . . d Rebell, . . . One Word More, I'll Blow Your Brains Out!" Sheriff Alexander White, Informed on by His Neighbors, Responds, 72;   Jellis Fonda's Testimony, 73;   William Seeber's Testimony As to White's Words, 74;   Jacob Klock's Testimony, 74*

    "The Rebellious Fourth Part . . . Had the Effrontree to Publish That They Were Unanimously Chosen by the People . . .": John Ferdinand Dalziel Smyth Tells of His Defiance of the Maryland Committee of Safety, 74

9   *Mary Watts Johnson Is Taken Hostage as a Control on Sir John's Actions, 78;   Judge Thomas Jones Describes the Incident, 79;   Mary Watts Johnson Appeals to Washington over the Head of General Schuyler, 80*

10   *A Tough Sixteen-Year-Old: Undaunted by His Tormentors, Walter Bates Refuses to Squeal on the Tories, 81*

11   *Intrepidity: The Rem Rapelje Family Are Undaunted by Persecution, 82*

12   *Abraham Gardiner of Easthampton Finds That Ambivalence Is No Protection, 84*

3   INTIMIDATION AND ABUSE OF THE ANGLICAN CLERGY   87

  1   *The Reverend Samuel Peters Tells How the "Sober Dissenters" Abused the Peterites, 90*

2 *The Plight of the Clergy in Boston, 92*

3 *Witnesses Testify to the Committee of Safety Concerning the Contemptuous Utterances of the Reverend John Rutgers Marshall of Woodbury, Connecticut, 93*

4 *The Reverend John Wiswall of Maine Describes the Outbreak of Disorder in Falmouth and the Tragedies Accompanying His Escape from the Rebels, 97*

5 *The Reverend Samuel Seabury of Westchester Protests His Arrest: Memorial to the Connecticut Assembly, 99*

6 *The Reverend Richard Mansfield of Derby and Oxford, Connecticut, Says That "No Pains Have Been Spared to Vilify and Degrade the Clergy", 103*

7 *The Reverend John Beach Doggedly Adheres to His Ordination Oath, 106*

8 *The Reverend Ebenezer Dibblee of Stamford Reviews the Wartime Tragedies to His Family, Beginning in 1775, 107*

9 *The Reverend Edward Bass of Newburyport Avows His Unshaken Loyalty to the King Despite His Middle Course during the Revolution, 109*

4 SOME FIRST EXPATRIATES   *112*

1 *Peggy Hutchinson Feels the Wrench of Parting from Family and Friends, 113*

2 *"A Few Regiments and Fleets . . . Will Sett Us Right": Cortlandt Skinner Indulges in Wishful Thinking, 114*

3 *Franklin the Archtraitor: Henry Hulton Applies a Harsh Epithet to Franklin, 116*

4 *Ahoy for Halifax: Jolley Allen and the* Sally *Founder on Cape Cod, 117*

5 *"The Cursed Rebellion": Dr. Sylvester Gardiner Is Driven from a State of Affluence to a State of Indigency, 124*

6 *The Reverend Henry Caner Departs from the Colonies*

*and Arrives in London, 126; The Reverend Henry Caner
Says He Had Only Six Hours' Notice to Prepare for
Embarkation and the Abandonment of His Parish, 127;
His Reception in London Was Characterized by "Many
Good Morrows" But Little Support, He Writes His
Friends, 128*

7 *Phila DeLancey Finds "There Is Not Such a Thing As
Disinterested Friendship" in London, 129*

PART TWO

Animosities Afire

JULY 1776–DECEMBER 1782   *133*

5 THE RUBICON: INDEPENDENCE MAKES THE DIFFERENCE   *135*

1 *Joseph Galloway Reflects on the Vote for
Independence, 136*

2 *The Loyalist Declaration of Dependence: Loyalists of
New York City Give a Lasting Testimony of Their
Fervor for British Constitutional Supremacy, 138*

3 *"[London] Is Alone a Match for Ten Americas" Henry
Hulton Exults at His Return to England, 141*

4 *"If This Be the Liberty We Are Contending For . . .":
Frederick Philipse III Is Taken from His Family into
Connecticut, 142*

5 *Roelof Elting of New Paltz, New York, Refuses
Congress Money As Good for Nothing, 145*

6 *Beverly Robinson Tells the Committee of Safety "It Is
Natural When a Man Is Hurt to Kick", 147*

7 *Beverly Robinson, Jr., Equates Freedom to Subservience
to His Beloved's Happiness, 149*

8 *Samuel Townsend Tells the New York Committee of
Safety His Toryism Is Just a Drunken Joke, 150*

9 *"What Phrenzy Possessed Your Mind?" Abel Curtiss Writes
to His Dartmouth Classmate, Levi Willard, on the Latter's
Joining the British Forces, 152*

10 *Jacob Duché Writes Washington to Urge Congress to Rescind "The Hasty and Ill-advised Declaration of Independency", 155*

11 *Goldsbrow Banyar Seeks a Compromise to the Oath and Persuades the New York Commission to Accept Compurgators, 158*

12 *Orb and Scepter: Joel Stone Determines "Sooner to Perish in the General Calamity than Abet . . . the Enemies of the British Constitution", 161*

6 RAIDS, RETALIATION, AND REFUGE   166

1 *The New York Fire, September 21, 1776, 166; The Rebels Cheer As the Trinity Church Steeple Falls, 167; Charles Inglis Acquaints the Secretary of the SPG with the Origin of the Fire, 168; Sir Guy Carleton's Commission Endeavors to Fix the Blame, 168; Dr. Mervin Nooth Testifies That the Fire Was a Deliberate Act, 170; Charles Inglis Presents His Evidence to the Commission, 170*

2 *The Burning of White Plains: A Tory Woman Helps an American Court-Martial Convict a Rebel, 171*

3 *Cowboys and Skinners, 173; DeLancey's Guerillas Effect a Coup against Rebel Outposts Near North Street, 174; Colonel James DeLancey, the Scourge of Westchester, Keeps King's Bridge "Free from the Insults of the Enemy", 175*

The Skinners Plunder and Burn the Seat of General Oliver DeLancey and Treat the Ladies of His Family Barbarously, 176

Nathaniel Underhill Evens the Score with Isaac Martling, 179

Vive le Coq's Tail! A Tory Rooster Popularizes the Drink at Elizabeth Flanagan's Tavern, July 1781, 180

4 *The Phony Tory: Enoch Crosby Infiltrates the Tory Ranks, 181*

5 Tory Hideouts: Margaret Morris Conceals Dr. Jonathan
   Odell in Her Burlington House and Deceives the
   Gondola Men, 185

   Seventeen Farmington Tories, Preferring to "Sign and
   Eat" rather Than "Fly to Starve on Loyalty," Petition the
   Assembly for Release, 187

   Hector St. John de Crèvecoeur Describes "The Grotto . . .
   the Refuge of Three Worthy Men," 189

   The Claudius Smith Gang, 194; Claudius Smith's
   Avengers Pin a Warning to the Rebels on the Murdered
   Body of John Clark, 195; William Cole Reveals the
   Hideouts of the Claudius Smith Gang, 196

6 Connecticut Whaleboaters Raid Long Island with Hit-and-
   run Tactics and Murder Isaac Hart of Rhode Island, 196

7 "Oh Thou Great Ruler": Aaron Doane, Loyalist Outlaw,
   Petitions Governor John Dickinson and the Pennsylvania
   Council for Pardon, 198

7 CRUELTIES, IMPRISONMENTS, AND EXECUTIONS   201

   1 Bryan Lefferty Sketches Conditions in the Kingston
      Jail, 202

   2 Cadwallader Colden, Jr., a Prisoner on the Fleet at
      Esopus, Records His Private Thoughts about Taking the
      Oath, 203

   3 "Let Him Starve and be Damned!": Nathaniel Gardiner
      of Rhode Island Experiences Barbarities en Route to Jail in
      Falmouth, 206

   4 Iron Fetters Torment James Moody of New Jersey in the
      West Point Prison, 208; William Buirtis Describes the
      Ordeal, 209; Moody's Description of the West Point
      Prison, 211; "Moody Is Escaped from the Provost!", 211

   5 Elijah and John Williams of Deerfield Cast Their Lot with
      the King: John Williams and Two Other Deerfield Tories
      Petition the Council for Release from Prison, 213

6   *The Black Hole of Connecticut, 216;   The Catacomb of Connecticut, 217;   Account of the Escape of Ebenezer Hathaway and Thomas Smith, Captain and Member of the Crew of the Privateer* Adventure, *from the Simsbury Mines on May 18, 1781, 218*

The Reverend Simeon Baxter Preaches a Sermon in the Simsbury Mines on "Tyrannicide Proved Lawful", 220; To General Washington, and the Congress, Styling Themselves Governors and Protectors of Thirteen Colonies, Belonging to the Crown of England 221;   To the Protestant Rebel Ministers of the Gospel in the Thirteen Confederated Colonies in America, 221;   Tyrannicide Proved Lawful by Reverend Simeon Baxter, 222

7   *The Extreme Penalty, 224*

Jacobus Rose and Jacob Midagh Are Executed at Kingston as an Example, 226;   Cadwallader Colden, Jr., Helps Rose Prepare for Martyrdom, 227;   Colden Writes John Jay That Hanging Rose and Midagh Will Not Make One Man Change His Sentiments, 228;   Petition of Jacobus Rose and Jacob Midagh for a Stay of Execution, 229

8   *The Influence of the Clergy Brings Moses Dunbar to the Gallows in Hartford, 230;   The Last Speech & Dying Wordes of Moses Dunbar Who Was Executed at Hartford on Wednesday the 19th of March, 1777, for High Treason against the State of Connecticut, 232*

9   *John Howe's* Newport Gazette *Recounts the Execution of John Hart of New York after a Sham Trial, 234*

10 *The Execution of Abraham Carlisle and John Roberts, 236;   John Roberts and Abraham Carlisle Are Executed in Pennsylvania to Appease the Extremists, 237; James Humphreys Describes the Tragic Scene for Joseph Galloway, 237*

11 *Anthony Allaire Describes the Mock Trial and Execution of Nine Tory Soldiers at Bickerstaff's, North Carolina, 238*

8 LOYALISTS ON THE NEW YORK, PENNSYLVANIA, AND
   VERMONT FRONTIERS   *240*

1 Daniel Claus Lays the Failure to Reduce Fort Stanwix to a "Want of Timely and Good Intelligence", 241

2 Hon Yost Schuyler, the Tory Half-Wit, Exaggerates "Heap Fighting Chief's" (Benedict Arnold's) Forces and Panics the Indians, 244

3 Molly Brant Is Harassed by the Oneidas and Obliged to Flee Following Oriskany, 247

4 Sarah Cass McGinn of Tryon County "Tampers" with the Indians in Favor of the British, 249

5 "Oh, Virtue, Thou, Then Really Existest!": Crèvecoeur Depicts a Frontier Hanging in the Susquehanna Valley, 250

6 Richard Cartwright, Jr., Confirms the Atrocities Charged against the Indians, Calling Them "Lurking Assassins", 252

7 Colonel Crawford Is Tortured by the Delawares in Revenge for a Massacre He Didn't Command or Countenance, 255; Simon Girty's Report of Colonel Crawford's Torture, 256; Arent DePeyster Deplores the Savage Custom of Killing Prisoners, 257; Arent DePeyster Admonishes the Indians against Barbarities to Their Prisoners, 258

8 Ethan Allen Defies Congress over the Issue of Vermont's Separate Independence: Charles Inglis Writes Galloway about the Internal Dissension, 258

9 Justus Sherwood's Journal Shows Ethan and Ira Allen Ready to Detach Vermont and Abandon the Revolutionary Cause, 260

10 "Why Do I Call the Lady Fortune by Hard Names?": Levi Allen's Letter Suggests an Answer to His Repeated Misfortunes and to His Questionable Loyalty, 265

9 THE SOUTHERN THEATER   269

1 Georgia Loyalists Take Heart, 269

Stephen DeLancey Writes His Wife That the Negroes in Savannah Are Inhumanly Treated, 270

Ann DeLancey Cruger, en Route to Savannah, Is Taken Prisoner by One of D'Estaing's Ships, 274

2 *Charleston Loyalists Are "Clamorous for Retributive Justice", 275; James Simpson Reports to Sir Henry Clinton on the Disposition of the Charleston Inhabitants toward the Crown, 277*

Whigs and Tories in South Carolina Hope the Fall of Charleston Will Bring "Respite from the Calamities of War": Robert Gray's Observations, 278

Rivington's Gazette *Publicizes the "Electrical Stroke" Which the Fall of Charleston Sparked in Europe, 280*

3 *The Carolina Backcountry: The Promised Land of Tories, 281*

King's Mountain: "Had It Not Been Covered with Woods . . .": Alexander Chesney Explains How the Trees Gave the Rebels an Advantage, 281

Levi Smith Narrowly Escapes Hanging on Rebecca Motte's Gate, 285

John Cruden of South Carolina Offers to Try Guerilla Tactics on Upriver Havens for Rebel Privateers, 291

4 *The Editors of* The Royal Gazette *Sign Off, 293*

10 LOYALISTS' REACTIONS TO EVENTS OF THE WAR   294

1 *"Oh My Poor Heart!": Edward Oxnard Agonizes over the Burning of Falmouth and Subsequent Reverses of a Destructive War, 295*

2 *"Helter Skelter Out of Town"; Peter Dubois Informs Cadwallader Colden about the Rebel Retreat from New York, 298*

3 *"O Cursed Ambition!" Washington Is Made to Exclaim in the Loyalists' Farce on the Battle of Long Island, 300*

4 *The Unlucky Hessian Affair, 302*

5 *Mrs. John Peters Is Ready to Send Six More Sons against the Rebels Despite the Bennington Defeat, 304*

6 *Lieutenant Colonel John Peters Defends the Provincials and Indians against Burgoyne's Charges of Cowardice, 306*

7 *"The* Coup de Grace *Is Given to British Glory!": Samuel Curwen Views the French Treaty with Foreboding, 309*

8 *Miss Rebecca Franks Enjoys the Gaiety of Occupied Philadelphia. She Compares Unfavorably the Ladies of New York with Those of Her Own Town, 311*

9 *"Had . . . This Been the Feast of Peace It Would Have Been Very Proper": James Parker of Virginia Recounts the Jousting of the Knights of the Mischianza, 315*

10 *James Parker and Abraham Wagg React to the Carlisle Peace Commission, 318; "Low Is the Dignity of Great Britain Fallen!": James Parker Views the Carlisle Peace Commission as Humiliating, 319; Abraham Wagg of New York Suggests to the Commission a Way to Restore Peace, 321*

11 *Grace Galloway Stages a Sit-down Protest and Charles Willson Peale Evicts Her by Force, 323*

12 *John Potts Writes Galloway of the Despondency Generated by the British Evacuation of Pennsylvania, 326*

13 *James Rivington, the Tory Printer, Proves a Double Agent, 327; James Rivington Gives His Opinion to Richard Cumberland, Secretary of the Board of Trade, That the Revolution Is on the Wane, 332; James Rivington Asks His Readers to Be Generous and Overlook Past Errors, 333*

14 *Robert Auchmuty Tells His Sister That the French Alliance Has Weaned Away America's British Friends, 334*

15 *Sylvester Gardiner Attributes Rebel Success to the "Shameful and Scandalous Conduct" of the Two Howes, 336*

16 *Benedict Arnold Feels the Rectitude of His Conduct in Revealing the State of the American Forces and Finances, 338*

"The Scoundrel Is of Great Use!": James Parker Describes
the Arnold-André Affair, 342

17 "That Memorable Night": Anna Rawle Explains the
Necessity of Illuminating the Tories' Houses on the
Reception of the News of Cornwallis's Surrender, 344

18 "The Loss of Cornwallis and 6,000 Men Is Not an
Object for Great Britain to Mourn For," John Hamilton
Tells a Friend, 346

19 Frederick Smyth of New Jersey Feels It Is High Time to
Terminate the War, 348

PART THREE

Casting Accounts
DECEMBER 1782–1800   *351*

11 THE ONSET OF PEACE   *353*

1 A Military Stratagem: Andrew Deveaux, Unaware of the
Peace, Secures New Providence (Nassau) from the Spanish
by Ingenuity, 354

2 The Spirit of Vindictiveness: Thomas Jones Records the
Merciless Treatment of Loyalists on the British Evacuation
of Charleston, 357

3 "The Mob Now Reigns": A Loyalist in New York
Appraises the Dire Situation of Refugees Both Black
and White, 359

4 "The Power Is in the Hands of the Lowest of the People":
Stephen Skinner Evaluates the Country's Plight, 362

5 "Take Your All . . . and Follow Your Friends": John
Cook of Dutchess County Gives His Information about
the Committeemen before William Smith, 364

6 David Colden Writes His Niece of the Persecution
Prevailing As Committees Reassume Extralegal Powers, 365

7   *Loyalists Inform Sir Guy Carleton of Meeting Rancor and Retribution When They Attempt to Return Home, 368; Memorial of Prosper Brown of New London, Connecticut, to Sir Guy Carleton, 370; George Beckwith [to Sir Guy Carleton], 370; Thomas Hassard of Rhode Island to Sir Guy Carleton, 371; Deposition of Isaac Foshay of Philippsburg, New York, 371; Deposition of Oliver DeLancey to David Mathews, Mayor of New York, 372; Memorial of Adam Graves, John Georg Graves, and Nicholas Andrews, of Maryland, to Carleton, 372*

8   *Sir Guy Carleton Receives Petitions for Freedom, 373; Towers Bell, Stolen in England, Indentured in Maryland, Asks Carleton to Help Him Go Home, 373; Judith Jackson, Former Slave, Refuses to Go Back to Virginia, 374*

9   *Justus Sherwood Is Convinced of the Arrogant Spirit of the Whigs, 374*

10   *Stephen Jarvis Defies the Mob to Marry the Girl for Whom He Waited Seven Years, 376*

11   *"Old Matchioavell . . . Might Go to School to the Americans," Arent S. DePeyster Comments to General MacLean, 379*

12   *Mock Money: The Counterfeiters Confess But Claim They Performed a Service for the King, 382; Memorial of John Power, a Loyalist from Massachusetts, 384; John Power's Deposition, 385*

William May's Confession, 385

12   DISPLACED PERSONS: EVACUATION, FLIGHT, AND DISPERSAL   387

1   *The Tory's Soliloquy, 391*

2   *John Piper Wants to Return to Rhode Island and Be a Good Citizen, 392*

3   *Colonel James DeLancey, "The Outlaw of the Bronx," Bids Theophilus Hunt Good-bye, 393*

4 *"This Is to Be the City, They Say": Sarah Frost's Anticipation Turns to Dismay, 395*

5 *Lieutenant Michael Laffin Tells His Brother of His Being Shipwrecked on The* Martha *Off the Coast of St. John, 397*

6 *Gregory Townsend of Boston Sends the Daniel Hubbards Glowing Reports of Conditions at Halifax, 398*

  J. Tomlinson, Jr., Finds Nova Scotia an Asylum of Freedom and Safety, 400

7 *Hannah Ingraham Recalls the Snowy Reception at Fredericton, 401*

8 *"Thirty-seven Thousand People Crying for Provisions": Edward Winslow Describes the Arrival of the Loyalists at*

9 *Settlers on the Bay of Quinte, 405; Wigwams and Tents on the Bay of Quinte. Captain Michael Grass Recalls the Scene in 1784, 407; Catherine White Remembers Her Family's Contentment Living in the Isolated Wilds along the Bay of Quinte, 407; Captain James Dittrick Describes His Parents' Ways of Surviving the Hungry Winter of 1787–1788, 408; Joseph Brant Complains of Critical Times for the Indians, 410*

10 *"The March of the Cameron Men": Nancy Jean Cameron Writes from the Mohawk Valley That Her Family Is Fleeing the Taunting Which Followed in the Wake of War, 411*

11 *James Matra Proposes New South Wales As a Refuge for the Loyalists, 412*

12 *Cat Island in the Bahamas Answers the Expectations of Oswell Eve of Philadelphia, 414*

13 EXPECTATIONS SOURED, HOPES FULFILLED   417

  1 *Memorials to Governor Parr Reveal Unnecessary Hardships, 418; Disenchantment in Nova Scotia: Memorial of Robert Ross, Samuel Campbell, and Alexander Robertson, 419*

2   Rudolph Ritzema Writes Captain Matthews He Is
    Leaving the Continent of America Forever, 420

3   Sir John Johnson Tells Robert Watts That His Prospects
    for Preferment and Compensation in Canada Are
    Bright, 421

4   Ward Chipman Writes Gloomily of the British Restrictions
    on Trade Between New Brunswick and the States, 421

5   Patrick McNiff Contends That Holding Land under a
    Seigneur Is Slavery, 423

6   John Deserontyou, a Mohawk Captain, and His Indians
    Settle on the Bay of Quinte But Soon Find That the
    Americans Threaten Their Lands "Like a Worm Which
    Cuts Off the Corn", 425

7   Black Loyalists Are Buffeted About in Nova Scotia:
    Thomas Peters Petitions for Redress of Their
    Grievances or Resettlement Elsewhere, 427

8   "The Fierce Spirit of Whigism Is Dead": The Reverend
    John Tyler of Norwich, Connecticut, Writes to Samuel
    Peters That It Is Safe to Return, 433

9   The Elting Brothers Plan Their Return Home, 436

10 John Tabor Kempe, Last Attorney General of New York
    Province, Experiences the Frustration of Securing Evidence
    from America to Support His Claim for
    Compensation, 437; John Tabor Kempe to William
    Livingston, 438; Ann Watts Kennedy to Robert
    Watts, 440

11 Martin Gay Meets with a Disagreeable Reception on
    Returning to Boston, 441

12 Chief Justice Richard Morris Suggests a Soldier's Duty
    Transcends the Dictates of the Heart in a Wartime
    Murder Case, 444

13 James Clarke Would Give His Life to Restore Rhode Island
    to Its Former Happy Situation, 446

14   *Joseph Brant Sends His Sons to Dartmouth and Requests Attention to Their Morals*, 447

15   *"Learn This of Me, Where E'er Thy Lot Doth Fall; Short Lot, or Not, to Be Content With All." —Robert Herrick,* Lots to Be Liked, *1648, 449*

16   *The Reverend John Stuart, Missionary to the Mohawks, Writes Bishop William White of Pennsylvania of His Contentment in Kingston, 452*

Bibliography, 453

Index, 469

Foreword

THE AMERICAN REVOLUTION, whose two hundredth birthday
we are about to commemorate, was a complex phenomenon. As the first
great anticolonial war of modern times, it was fought for independence and
nationhood. It was, too, a war for the overthrow of monarchy and its replacement by republican institutions broadly conceived. Moreover, as this
gripping book depicts, it was a civil war, in which at least 20 percent of the
American population, perhaps more, were hostile to the Patriot cause,
while many others managed to be neutral or remain passive spectators.
The American Revolution was not a civil war in a sectional sense like the
War Between the States. Loyalism pervaded the entire Atlantic seaboard.
Rather, it was a civil war that transcended geographical regions and class
differences, dividing the elite and bringing brother against brother and
father against son.

It is this significant minority who were loyal to King and Empire
whom the Patroits denigrated as Tories. There was a time when the Tories
or Loyalists were unmentionables. When in 1847 Lorenzo Sabine ventured
to publish his biographical sketches of the Loyalists of the American
Revolution, he suffered ostracism for his presumption. The Loyalists remained untouchables, and the Tory was traditionally assailed as one "whose
head is in England, whose body is in America, and whose neck should be
stretched." Happily, historians on both sides of the Atlantic are now

accustomed to treating that civil war among Englishmen (with due respect to other ethnic groups in America) with greater detachment than a century ago. The shared experience of fighting two world wars on the same side and the dissolution of the British Empire have removed the fangs from what to Englishmen has always been an unpleasant subject. To Americans, two centuries have brought a measure of objectivity toward the struggle, and even a certain sympathy for the underdog, the courageous Tory minority in America and chief losers in that conflict.

When historians have treated the Loyalists, however, they have generally stressed the major figures. As a result they have created a Tory stereotype—the affluent supporter of George III, usually a royal office-holder, big merchant, large landowner, or Anglican clergyman—whereas in fact, as *The Price of Loyalty* makes abundantly evident, the Loyalist party found its adherents in seaboard and back country, in the South as well as in the North, and among all classes. Two of the most moving accounts in Mrs. Crary's book concern a kidnapped servant, trepanned to Maryland, who asked General Carleton for assistance in getting back to England, and a former female slave, who sought protection behind British lines in preference to returning to Virginia and slavery. To Towers Bell, a white servant, and Judith Jackson, a black slave, the King's side meant freedom, the Patriot side bondage, the Declaration of Independence to the countrary notwithstanding. Indeed, it is the signal virtue of Mrs. Crary's account that the Tory experience is depicted mainly through the eyes of little-known, and even obscure, people, who in many cases paid a greater price for their loyalty than the rich and well-connected.

In putting the focus on the average man rather than the more prominent Tory, Mrs. Crary has succeeded in presenting a more balanced and representative account than is now available in the literature on the Tories. To do so involved the unearthing of evidence hitherto discrete and unpublished and detective work of a high order. In the unpublished Delancey Papers and the journal of Richard Cartwright, for example, she has struck rich ore. More sensational have been the results of her investigation into the career of the notorious Tory printer James Rivington. Tracking down hitherto ignored clues, she has disclosed that Rivington was in fact, in the closing years of the Revolution, a double agent working for George Washington as well as the British. This is an instance where the legend is substantiated and doubting scholars are given cause to blush.

The Price of Loyalty is replete with memorable stories and offbeat accounts of the behavior of strong individuals. Who is likely to forget the escape of Philip Skene, the upstate New York patentee, and the bizarre discovery by John Barnes's Company of the corpse of Skene's wife, beautifully preserved in a lead coffin reposing in his cellar? Did he do it to get a legacy left her and payable for each day she was above ground or until she was buried, according to gossip, or more probably to preserve her body in order to take the corpse back to Ireland or Scotland to bury her with her kindred? We shall never know. Equally memorable is the account of the legendary beauty, Flora MacDonald, who, mounted on a snow-white horse, addressed the Scottish Highlanders in Gaelic and inspired them to fight the Patriots at Moore's Creek, whence the Tories emerged, scattered, killed, or prisoners. Or the behavior of Joseph Galloway's wife, Grace, who refused to leave her Philadelphia mansion and had to be forcibly evicted by the Whig artist Charles Willson Peale? These and numerous other stories of strikingly individualistic, not to say highly eccentric, Tory behavior enliven the narrative and bring us face-to-face with the strength and determination of the Tory conviction.

The Tories mounted a serious threat to the winning of Independence. They were physically and linguistically indistinguishable from the Patriots and could move in and out of the lines almost at will, providing the enemy with invaluable espionage information, acting as scouts for British and Hessian troops, and conducting partisan warfare operations in complicity with the Indians, warfare as ruthless as any carried on by Whig partisans. The Tories had their lawless gangs ("cowboys" and "banditti") who committed numberless depredations, and in the name of the King fattened their own purses by daring highway robberies, burglaries, and a variety of other crimes for which, if caught, they could be summarily executed. More important, as long as the Tory party remained in existence in America, the British government was kept under the delusion that the Whigs were an unpopular minority who could not count on the loyalty of the countryside. Hence, after being evicted from Boston, the British army moved in on New York, Philadelphia, and the Lower South in turn—in all cases counting on Tory support, which, as the tide turned, proved more and more illusory. For their part the Tories were disillusioned by the incompetently mounted British naval and military effort, always believing that a little more force at the right place and at the right time would have ended the insurgency.

The Patriots regarded the Tories as neither meek nor passive but as posing a threat to independence, and the common man loathed them and made their lives unbearable. While we like to fancy the American Revolution as being conducted according to rules of civilized warfare and, from the Patriot point of view, as a war resting on legality, the impressive evidence Mrs. Crary marshals demonstrates that it was not always possible for the top Whig leadership, however deep its attachment to due process and its detestation of mobbism, to curb the Patriot masses or even the local leaders.

Tories were tarred and feathered, hanged in certain more notorious instances, forced into exile, or flung into black holes like the dank and abandoned Simsbury mine in Connecticut. The conditions experienced therein by wretched Tories bears comparison with the worst treatment of luckless Patriots incarcerated on British prison ships.

Both sides resorted to oaths to test the loyalty of the doubtful. Tories refusing to take an oath of loyalty to the American Congress would be summarily banished or held under house arrest. More militant Tories suffered the confiscation of their property. In most cases they were unable to recover it at the end of the war despite the provisions of the Treaty of Peace barring such confiscations, but the British government compensated its loyal sons and daughters rather generously, if somewhat capriciously. The war counted its victims on both sides; its heartaches were shared by Tories and Patriots—broken homes, wasted lives, great property loss, and, for many Tories, exile from the land they loved. *The Price of Loyalty* draws a poignant picture of the price they paid for their loyalty to King and Empire; their sacrifices serve to remind us that men and women on both sides of the great revolutionary civil war took their stands as much from principle as from self-interest.

Columbia University
Richard B. Morris

Acknowledgments

IN AN ANTHOLOGY of Loyalist stories, such as this, an editor's first indebtedness extends to the participants and sufferers who set down their experiences in journals, letters, official papers, and reminiscences. These records are so prolific that an inescapable selectivity eliminated hundreds of accounts which were nonetheless helpful in securing a well-rounded picture of Loyalist sentiments and sufferances. These records are also so scattered among well-known and minor depositories, as well as in private collections, that it would be redundant to express my appreciation to each collection by name. However, my indebtedness for their courtesy in permitting the utilization of their materials is implicit in the citation which follows each excerpt. Everywhere the staff were cooperative and often, as was particularly the case with the New York Historical Society, called attention to acquisitions which might have been overlooked. A profound tribute is given to Professor Richard B. Morris, a superb teacher, who inspired and encouraged this project and gave generously of his counsel throughout. I am also deeply grateful to Cecile Ryden Johnson for the drawings used as chapter headings, many of which she sketched at the actual historic site. Mrs. Johnson is a noted watercolorist whose work has appeared in solo shows in Philadelphia and New York and in many group shows, as well as in public collections, in *Skiing* Magazine, and in several recent books of prizewinning paintings. My appreciation extends also to many others, notably to Marguerite Hoyle Glynn of Mansfield Center, Connecticut, for a critical reading of the manuscript and to Susan Horwitz for her assistance with the bibliography and with other details of preparation of the manuscript.

My appreciation is also extended to the persons and organizations dedicated to the preservation of historic objects and sites for their courtesy in permitting the sketching and use of the following chapter-opening drawings:

Chapter 1, The Making of Some Early Loyalists
the Bevier-Elting House (The Huguenot Historical Society, New Paltz, New York)

Chapter 3, Intimidation and Abuse of the Anglican Clergy
the John Marshall Escape Hatch (The Glebe House, Woodbury, Connecticut)

Chapter 6, Raids Retaliation, and Refuge
the Tory Den (Connecticut Forest and Park Association, Map)

Chapter 7, Cruelties, Imprisonments, and Executions
the Black Hole of Connecticut (Newgate Prison, East Granby, Connecticut)

Chapter 8, Loyalists on the New York, Pennsylvania, and Vermont Frontiers
the Iroquois War Canoe (Mrs. George Stanley Smith, Sacketts Harbor, New York)

Chapter 12, Displaced Persons: Evacuation, Flight, and Dispersal
a portion of the painting, The Loyalists Landing in New Brunswick, artist unknown (New Brunswick Museum, Saint John, New Brunswick)

Chapter 13, Expectations Soured, Hopes Fulfilled
Cradling the Wheat (Upper Canada Village, Morrisburg, Ontario)

The end papers were copied from the wallpaper in the Joel Stone House, Washington, Connecticut, courtesy of Dr. and Mrs. Henry D. Fearon.

The
Price of
Loyalty

Introduction

THE STORIES TOLD in their own words by the Loyalists[1] in the following pages focus on them as individuals rather than as political or military opponents of the Revolution. The political argument which has been forcefully presented in earlier publications of Loyalist writings has been skirted in favor of reviewing the personal dilemmas which individuals encountered in the crisis and the consequences of their choice. The selections are not intended to offer merely a chronicle of mistreatment, suffering, and tribulations, but rather a sampling of assorted Loyalist experiences, both propitious and tragic, in various colonies from the time of the Tea Act (May 10, 1773) through the period of the Loyalist exodus and dispersal at the close of the war.

Limited almost entirely to their own written records, these personal experiences are of such diversity, recounting both ominous and propitious developments, and the volume of source materials so plentiful, that selectivity has brought obvious difficulties and omissions. Many of the best known and most powerful Loyalist writers, such as Thomas Hutchinson,

[1] Colonial spelling has been retained throughout, but punctuation has been modernized for ease in reading.

Introduction

Joseph Galloway, Daniel Leonard, and Samuel Curwen, many of the most
eloquent preachers, such as Jonathan Boucher and Samuel Seabury, and
many of the most persuasive pamphleteers, such as Charles Inglis and
Thomas Chandler, have been only briefly quoted or passed over entirely in
the interest of presenting the untold or less well-known accounts. The principal touchstone for the selections has been their appeal to human interest.
Thus they present a miscellany of experiences, with the common denomin-
ator only that the raconteurs either openly espoused the side of the King or
at least failed to support the Revolution. Almost invariably they felt themselves aggrieved or persecuted for their stand.

For these British subjects living on the American side of the Atlantic
the struggle was a bitter civil war with the issues cutting across lines of
family, of friendships, of neighbors, and even of husbands and wives. Some
saw the issues from Parliament's point of view, some from the radical point
of view, and a large segment from a neutral position deriving from ju-
diciousness, inertia, or a delusive hope that the storm would pass them by.
The attempt to avoid taking sides was an unrealistic position for most
colonists; in the end, as in most civil wars, almost every adult male of
consequence was obliged to reveal his choice. Two main developments
crystallized the crisis of allegiance—the action of the First Continental
Congress in setting up the Continental Association to boycott British
goods, implemented by the administration of an oath through the local
committees of safety, and the Declaration of Independence.

What influences determined the choice for each individual? What
was the main composition of the body of Loyalists? The choice of allegiance
was determined by disparate motivations—by the political argument, by
conscience, by self-interest, by opportunism. It often was contingent on a
combination of these factors plus the assiduity of the local revolutionary
committee, the military situation, and even the accident of living within
the British lines.[2] In the end the decision depended upon the kind of person
each one was, his state of mind, his experience throughout life, and his
circumstances when confronted by the rebellion. As Guy Johnson expressed the point to the Committee of Safety in Tryon County, "The present dispute is viewed in different lights according to the education and principles of the parties affected." In words which have a familiar modern

---

[2] Lt. Col. William S. Smith estimated 15,000 in this category. John Hardy, *Valentine's
Manual of the Corporation of the City of New York,* New York: 1871, p. 809 fn.

ring he furthur reasoned: "I desire to enjoy liberty of conscience and the exercise of my own judgment, and that all others should have the same privilege. . . ."[3] The rebels too wanted liberty of choice, but could not in a civil conflict permit their opponents to exercise their liberty of judgment undisturbed.

The question frequently arises why men with similar life experiences and similar life situations, such as John Jay and Peter Van Schaack, or John Adams and Peter Oliver, or even members of the same family, chose different sides when war erupted. The eminent historian Carl Becker suggests that Van Schaack's point of view was influenced by the timing of a series of family tragedies which he suffered in 1775: the death of two sons almost simultaneously in July, the ill health of his wife, and the loss of an eye and the threat of blindness. These calamities were immediate and engrossing; the country's troubles were alien and unimportant compared to his grief. He reacted to tragedy, as is often the case, by an instinctive clinging to the familiar and by an objectivity which led him to place loyalty to his own conscience above loyalty to the state. During these same months John Jay's increasing involvement with the Second Continental Congress brought his thinking more and more in line with its views. Thus Van Schaack's and Jay's experiences in life and their immediate circumstances in 1775 were divergent rather than alike, and the premise of similar life factors fails. Even brothers, brought up in the same evironment and with the same education, exhibit diverse personalities and orientation. Religious dedication, mental health, emotional makeup, and raw courage itself are factors which can determine a man's reactions in a crisis. These subtle and subconscious qualities help explain why brothers might approach the question of allegiance in a civil war differently.[4]

Generalizations about the social and economic status of those who cast their lot for George III are dangerous, for the heterogeneous composition of the Loyalists is a characteristic which stands out. They came from all walks of life and from all economic levels, from royal placemen to fugitive slaves. The categories are as numerous as man's motivations: prosperous merchants, large landowners, Anglican clergy, Highlanders, small farmers,

[3] June 5, 1775. See W. W. Campbell, *Annals of Tryon County,* New York: 1831, pp. 35–36.
[4] Carl Becker, "John Jay and Peter Van Schaack," *Quart. Journ. N.Y. State Historical Assoc.,* October 1919. See *N.Y. Hist.,* October 1969, suppl. pp. 7–8, 11.

[3]

poor craftsmen, opportunists, drifters, and scoundrels. They came from assorted geographical backgrounds. Despite many areas of concentration, such as New York City and environs, the Regulator country of North Carolina, and other frontier areas, they were fairly scattered throughout the Colonies. The Loyalists were probably strongest in New York, weakest in Virginia. In South Carolina and Georgia they may have been a majority. In Connecticut and Pennsylvania they formed small but active blocks of opposition; in Delaware, Maryland, and New Jersey there were troublesome pockets of dissidents.

Moreover, there were different degrees of Loyalism, making identification difficult and an accurate count in each province impossible. Some were out-and-out consistent Tories from the start, committed by the nature of their occupation or by conscience; some were covert; others were uncertain and vascillating; still others were moderates or semi-Tories, hoping to remain either neutral or unobtrusive throughout the rebellion. Again, others were bandwagon Loyalists, joining the British opportunely where British arms were successful, or "trimmers," as Burgoyne called them after the Bennington defeat, deserting British arms when self-interest dictated.[5] The political loyalty of Quakers and Indians would prove subservient to their religious views or their tribal ties.

However, for most of them Loyalism was an evolutionary and painful process, even as the transfer of allegiance to a new government was not easy for many rebels. Confrontation with an oath, threats of ostracism and boycott, or mob mistreatment forced many to make an early decision when they would have preferred to drift along in an ambivalent way through the years of argument, even through the years of warfare. When the port of Boston was closed, the Massachusetts charter suspended, and martial law imposed, almost all the colonists were professing loyalty to the King. The Petition to the King of the First Continental Congress (October 26, 1774) began: "Most Gracious Sovereign, . . . we wish not a diminution of the prerogative . . ." The Olive Branch Petition of July 8, 1775, disclaimed any desire for independence. In October 1775, Jeremy Belknap, chaplain to Washington's army, openly prayed for the King. Even as late as January 1776, Washington's officers toasted the King at their mess. Thus loyalty to the Crown was still the generally accepted condition through 1775, and the

---

[5] Burgoyne to Germain, August 1777. See Christopher Ward, *The War of the Revolution,* J. R. Alden, ed. New York: 1952, vol. II, p. 501.

espousal of rebellion carried the stigma of disloyalty, even treason. It was one thing to take an oath to boycott British goods until offensive measures were repealed; it was quite another matter to commit an act of treason, that is, to take up arms against one's government, to give aid to its enemies, and to support independence.

As the rift crystallized and widened during the twenty-five months from June 1, 1774, when the Coercive Acts took effect, to July 4, 1776, ambivalence, reluctance, and indecision characterized the attitude of many colonists, for their ties with England had deep roots. Open rebellion was hazardous, mob rule a likelihood, and colonial unity uncertain. Moreover, the implications of each step in severing the ties with Britain were not easily discernible to the rank and file. The Tea Party, the boycott of British goods, the extralegal meeting of the First Continental Congress, the mounting heat of the attacks on Britain in paper and pamphlet, the activities of the committees of correspondence, the indignities and injustices to outspoken friends of government—these developments might disclose that revolution was in the making but did not necessarily render a personal decision on allegiance imperative. Although resistance to the punishment meted out to Boston in June 1774 was justified as constitutional resistance to unconstitutional acts, not revolution, it presented some colonists nonetheless with the early necessity of clarifying their stand. In New York, as long as the Provincial Assembly voted down an endorsement of the proceedings of the First Continental Congress and refused to appoint a delegation to the Second Congress, as it did in January 1775, a wavering colonist could still equivocate with impunity. With Parliament debating the withdrawal of its troops and possibly recognizing the Continental Congress and the assemblies' power to tax (January 1775), it looked as if an accommodation might still be found.

Then through the late winter of 1775 the rebel movement gained momentum and positions stiffened. Into the already touchy atmosphere came the clash of arms at Lexington, Ticonderoga, and Quebec, presenting the neutral colonist with a more urgent need for decision. Still the Second Continental Congress in July sent out a feeler for reconciliation, the Olive Branch Petition, extending the hope that the issues could be peaceably resolved. Throughout these events the quandary of the indecisive colonist became increasingly acute; straddle and drift were proving less possible courses. With the King's Proclamation of Rebellion (August 23, 1775) the colonist was again confronted with the question of his paramount loyalty. To the King? Or to the constitutional rights of Englishmen which were being denied?

Many of the documents selected for the first period, October 1773–July 4, 1776, reveal the bewilderment, equivocation, and reluctance to confront these questions which characterized the attitude of many colonists. While some Loyalists, especially placemen and Anglican clergymen, took a clear stand at the outset and decried even resistance to the bills punishing Boston, the writings of others indicate a slow evolution of their position, impelled by the mounting harassment meted out to the wavering in the 2½ years before independence. A local boycott of a man's wares, ostracism, administration of the oath, threats and indignities, mob violence—these situations smoked him out. While these developments varied in time and intensity from province to province and even from one district to another, they were the early ordeals which separated the Loyalists from the rebels.

July 4, 1776, the date which opens the second group of selections from Loyalist writings, confronted the Loyalists with a more pressing crisis. The cautious colonist, foreseeing mob tyranny, denial of free speech, and even anarchy, questioned the benefits of independence and favored delaying a forthright declaration. Men who had been active in disobeying (or had at least approved of disobeying) the unjust acts of Parliament balked at this extreme measure. Among them, for example, were Joseph Galloway, a delegate to the First Continental Congress and a signer of the Association; Samuel and Joseph Shoemaker, Pennsylvania Quakers; the Reverend John J. Zubly and John Alsop, both members of the Second Continental Congress. John Zubly, pastor of the Independent Presbyterian Church in Savannah, had led the Whigs in insisting on American rights in the British Empire and was one of the Committee of Congress to draw up the petition to the King.[6] John Alsop resigned from the New York delegation when independence came, saying: "As long as a door was left open for a reconciliation with Great Britain, upon just and honorable terms, I was willing to render my country all the service in my power . . . but as you have, I presume, closed the door . . . I must beg leave to resign."[7]

[6] John Zubly was unmolested until 1777 when he refused the oath and was obliged to take refuge in the Black Swamp of South Carolina, where he died in 1781. Kenneth Coleman, *The American Revolution in Georgia, 1763-1789,* Athens: 1958, p. 176.
[7] To the New York Convention, July 16, 1776. *Journ. Provincial Congr.,* vol. I, p. 536. Alsop retired to his brother's house in Middletown, Connecticut, quietly sat out the years of the war, and at its close resumed his business in New York.

These men were not mere standpatters, obstructionists, or excessive Anglophiles; they were persuaded that certain measures were right and others wrong; they wanted changes and reforms in the relationship of the Colonies to the mother country; they loved America. Galloway called them "seekers after truth." They differed, however, as to method and extent of rebellion. They recoiled at the extremes of civil war, of mob violence, of a complete severing of long-cherished ties with Britain. The Declaration of Independence changed not only their emotional attitude but also their legal position. Treason was now defined in different terms. Now neutrality was difficult. The Loyalists found themselves in danger from the law as well as from the mob. The Declaration signaled the beginning of proscription, confiscation, and more serious and widespread persecution.

The rebels had to know how to rank the inhabitants, for every Tory became a potential informer or saboteur, a fifth columnist. The committees of safety clamped down more strictly than ever on the moderates and dissemblers who heretofore had been left alone. As emotions mounted, the milder epithets which the rebels applied to the Tories, such as "disaffected," "nonassociators," "Addressers and Protestors," changed to angry terms of "treasonable conspirators," "cursedest rascals." Washington, who in 1775 had stipulated that a person would be considered a Tory only when he had given "pregnant proof" of an "unfriendly disposition to the cause," now called them "parricides" and "unhappy wretches! Deluded mortals!" "A great many ought to have . . . long ago committed suicide."[8] Major General Charles Lee spoke of the Tories on Long Island as "dangerous banditti," adding "not to crush these serpents before their rattles are grown would be ruinous."[9] Animosities were now afire.

Selections from Loyalist writings during the years of warfare following independence to April 1783, when Congress proclaimed an end to hostilities, reflect the invidiousness and tragedy of civil war. They describe raids, fires, hideouts, imprisonments, cruelties, and executions, revealing the anguish and suffering the Loyalists experienced as they took up arms or performed services for the King, or simply tried to remain passive and avoid

[8] Peter Force, ed., *Amer. Arch:, 5th Ser.,* vol. I, pp. 98. Also Washington to Joseph Reed, April 1, 1776, and to John A. Washington, March 31, 1776, John C. Fitzpatrick, ed., *The Writings of George Washington, from the Original Manuscript Sources, 1745-1799.* 1931–1944, vol. IV, pp. 449, 455.

[9] Charles Lee to Washington, January 5, 1776. Ibid., vol. IV, p. 221 fn.

persecution. The states, following the lead of Congress,[10] drew up laws of treason, confiscation and banishment acts, and other disabling legislation until a myriad of laws penalizing the Loyalists stood on the books. The severity varied from state to state, and the implementation from one district to another was often capricious. While treason, which included joining the British forces, recruiting, and furnishing arms, carried the death penalty, Tories were executed for lesser offenses, as in the case of John Roberts and Abraham Carlisle who guided Sir William Howe and guarded the city gates as his forces occupied Philadelphia. The cases of these two unfortunate Loyalists, as well as those of Moses Dunbar in Connecticut and Jacobus Rose and Jacob Midagh in New York, became *causes célèbres,* and the victims were credited with martyrdom in Loyalist history. However, other Loyalists were executed to set an example and simply passed into oblivion. Seven Tories at one time were executed in Albany in 1778 as "a necessary example demanded by the nature of the times and the enormity of the offenses they had committed."[11] In general the death penalty was carried out only for overt acts and according to English procedures, but hostile speech and persuasion were also criminal offenses, receiving lesser punishments.[12]

In eight states Loyalists were blacklisted by name, proscribed and banished on pain of death if they returned. The other states found means of harassing them which were almost as effective in forcing them to leave. Confiscation of property was provided by law everywhere, except for a 12 percent amercement in some cases in South Carolina. Few Loyalists ever recovered either their confiscated property or their just debts, although some men left wives or patriot sons on their estates to save them and were partially successful.

Propitious developments for the Loyalists in the Southern theater are reflected in heretofore unpublished letters written by Stephen DeLancey

[10] In a resolve of June 24, 1776, Congress defined treason as levying war, adhering to the enemy, giving him aid and comfort. W. C. Ford, ed., *Journ. of the Continental Congr.,* Washington: 1904–1937, vol. V, pp. 475–476.

[11] [Simeon DeWitt Bloodgood], *The Sexagenary or Reminiscences of the American Revolution,* Albany: 1833, p. 130.

[12] Bradley Chapin says: "The record is one of substantial justice done." For his discussion of the Revolutionary experience with prosecution of Loyalists for treason see "Colonial and Revolutionary Origins of the American Law of Treason," *William & Mary Quart.,* vol. XVII (1960), pp. 8–17.

just after the fall of Savannah and by Ann DeLancey Cruger, taken prisoner en route to join her husband, John Harris Cruger, who had commanded one of the Loyalist battalions at Savannah. A few excerpts on the fall of Charleston to the British are followed by comments on the Loyalist disaster at King's Mountain and the ominous gradual losing of the Carolina backcountry. Of the many accounts of Loyalist activities on the frontiers in the Mohawk and Susquehanna Valleys and in Vermont, there are few that have not been widely utilized. These accounts have been avoided in favor of a part of Richard Cartwright's journal, which has not been published before, and two letters of Molly Brant, sister of the Mohawk chief and mother of Sir William Johnson's part-Indian children.

In addition to Molly Brant, who warned Sir John Johnson's Loyalists and Indians of the rebels' march toward Oriskany,[13] there were other notable women on the King's side: the spirited Flora MacDonald, who rallied the Scotch Highlanders to join the untimely battle at Moore's Creek Bridge; the Quaker Margaret Morris, who hid Dr. Jonathan Odell in her house; or Peggy Arnold, whose delicate beauty charmed the most notorious turncoat of the Revolution. Few of them left personal records of these dramatic incidents, a gap which reflects women's limited education and their matter-of-fact acceptance of their subordinate role. Nevertheless the women played a significant part in the destinies of their fellow Loyalists.

If a half million out of a population of two-and-a-half million (1775) is a reasonable estimate of the overall number of Loyalists, either consistent or onetime,[14] and if only eighty to one hundred thousand emigrated, the vast proportion must have been allowed to remain at home with the onset of peace. All through the war apathy had been discernible among the uneducated colonists,[15] especially among those unaffected by military operations; their opinions had been insignificant and their possessions, except perhaps for commandeered livestock, too picayune to confiscate. Kingdom or republic, they would continue harmlessly to farm a small acreage, detached from the mainstream of political events. These Loyalists, although

[13] Daniel Claus to William Knox, Oct. 11, 1777, N.Y. State Library. See Edmund O'Callaghan, *Documents Relative to the Colonial History of the State of New York,* Albany: 1853–1858, vol. VIII, pp. 718–723.
[14] Paul Smith, "The American Loyalists," *William & Mary Quart.,* vol. XXV, no. 2 (April 1968), p. 269. William H. Nelson suggests that the Loyalists were one-third of the "politically active" population. *The American Tory,* Boston: 1961, p. 92.
[15] [Bloodgood], *The Sexagenary . . . ,* p. 21.

Introduction

subjected to personal grudges and local animosities, were tolerated. Those stigmatized as actively disaffected, however, met only arrogance, vindictiveness, and continued persecution, as their accounts of events in 1783 show. Resignedly they sought to rebuild their careers, their families, their fortunes in new places within the jurisdiction of the King. Their ordeals as displaced persons, forced to evacuate their homes, to find safety in exile from a land they loved, to separate often from families, fall into a wide spectrum of readjustment ranging from true contentment to utter misery. Not all refugees in England were unhappy; some found minor positions; some of the daughters married well. For most of them, however, life in London or Bristol, without occupation, became a dull marking time; London with its exorbitant prices and closed society soon lost its luster. The struggle for the necessities added to homesickness; the prospect of compensation from government, a small antidote to nostalgia, was central to all their decisions. For most of the refugees Canada, the Bahamas, and the West Indies offered a better opportunity than England to resume their careers and make places for themselves. They became respected pioneers, the founders of Upper Canada and first settlers of many unoccupied parts of Lower Canada. In Nova Scotia, where the majority settled, they furnished an infusion of solid citizenry. These refugees to Canada were honored by the government with the designation of United Empire Loyalists. Nonetheless, in the first years of exile they encountered nigh insurmountable hardships and their buoyant expectations turned sour. Shelburne, Nova Scotia, built up rapidly by the Tory invasion and as rapidly deserted, became a symbol of Loyalist disenchantment. In the last years of the 1780s, as resentments at home softened and the disabling legislation of the states was modified or repealed, many Loyalists returned, hoping to rebuild their broken lives in a more familiar environment.

In sum, how the Loyalists dispersed to new lands, how they accepted the changes, how they responded to adversity, how they remolded their lives in new surroundings—experiences as varied as human personality and equipment for life—these were the experiences which the Loyalists themselves recount as they learned the full price of their loyalty.

Bewilderment, Equivocation, and Defiance

OCTOBER 1773–JULY 4, 1776

The Making of Some Early Loyalists

I THE TEA FRACAS

New Englanders, especially those with close ties to Boston, were the first to confront the question of their paramount loyalty. It was the Tea Act of May 10, 1773, which precipitated a stand by many merchants, marking them as enemies to America from the start. To save the British East India Company from bankruptcy, the House of Commons granted it a monopoly of the tea trade with America and allowed it to ship tea directly to American ports in its own ships to its own agents, thus avoiding British duties, bypassing colonial importers, and enabling it, even with a threepence import duty, to undersell other tea, whether honestly procured or smuggled in from Holland. The Boston radicals were determined that no tea should be landed until the invidious tax was repealed and fair treatment provided for colonial middlemen. Although committees were appointed to block the importation of dutiable tea and to urge consignees to resign, some tea consigned to Thomas and Elisha Hutchinson, sons of the Governor, was unloaded and found its way to Jolley Allen, a successful retail merchant. Jolley Allen's confrontation with a Boston committee over receiving part of the Hutchinson consignment (October 1773) highlights the immediate involvement of merchant interests in the political argument taking place with the mother country. Two months later (December 16, 1773) came the "villainous act" by the "Mob Men," hurling the tea into Boston Harbor — an event inimitably recast by Peter Oliver, Chief Justice of the Massachusetts Superior Court.

Jolley Allen Outwits the Boston Committee

❧ Some time, I think, in the month of October 177[3], I bought two chests of tea of Governor Hutchinson's two sons, Thomas and Elisha, at Boston, about eleven o'clock in the forenoon, and I thought it most prudent (for fear of being watched, as the custom of Boston is to shut up their warehouses at one o'clock and go on 'Change, and return about four o'clock in the afternoon) to leave them there until two o'clock. By agreement, Messers. Hutchinson's apprentice waited there until that time to deliver them to one William Burke, that I ordered to go with his cart to their warehouse for the said two chests of tea, which he did, and brought them with him to my shop. As he went to unload his cart of the above two chests of tea, Mr. John Hancock's (now General Hancock) head-clerk, William Palphrey,[1] happened to come by at the same time and, looking at the two chests of tea, and as he thought, took the original numbers. But he happened to be mistaken, for he took the East India marks instead of the company's house number in London. I cannot look upon him in any other light than an informer, by one of the committee, Captain Dashwood, coming to me in about half an hour afterwards and saying he had an information of two chests of tea coming in my house about half an hour before, that his business was to desire of me not to be out of the way, as the whole committee of the town of Boston was to wait on me about four o'clock that said afternoon.

I beg leave to observe that when I hired William Burke, I cautioned him, for fear of an accident, that if any inquiry should be made hereafter, that he must say he took the two chests of tea from off the Long Wharf,

---

[1] Appointed aide-de-camp to Washington and paymaster-general of the army, March–April 1776.

and that nobody was there; but, to his surprise, looking about him he saw a boat with men in it rowing towards a large ship in the stream, which he supposed had brought them two chests on shore from that ship, and was rowing to the ship again; which story he never deviated from although he was often examined by the said committee and severely threatened by them. I was likewise several different times threatened with that diabolical punishment of being tarred and feathered and under the disagreeable apprehension of the same for many days afterwards, which no mortal can tell or describe the anxiety of mind I was in. [I] expected my house to be pulled down and every thing destroyed.

The said committee came to me about half after three o'clock, thinking to catch me unprepared for their attack, but Providence had ordered it so that I was ready to receive them, for I had cut the ropes and had taken off the outside coverings, so that no person could tell from whence they came or from where I had them. The committee coming to my door, I met them and asked them their business. They told me they came to know from whence I had the two chests of tea that came into my shop at two o'clock that day. I answered, if that was their business and [if they] had nothing further to say to me, they was welcome to walk in. I then received them in my parlor. I asked them what their demand[s] were upon those two chests of tea. They told me nothing further than to be shown the two chests of tea. I then asked each of them if that would give them full satisfaction. They told me, upon a point of honor, it would and they should have nothing more to say to me at present. I answered then upon honor that I would show them the same two chests of tea that came into my house that day at two o'clock.

I accordingly went with them to my store and opened the door and showed them the two chests of tea, which they all stood amazed at, saying that was not what they meant, though they before had given their words of honor. I asked them where all their honors lay. They told me they meant to see the two outside cases, where the marks lay, that they might be able to know from whence I bought them. I told them that did not belong to that point of honor they had all given me and told them I was surprised at that whole body, which was the standing committee of the town of Boston, should want to forfeit their honors in so trifling an affair. But [they were] still aggravating the cause in wanting to see the two outside cases, which I granted by pointing to the same, saying: "There they lay, and I hope you are satisfied now." I verily believe [that in] the place where I pointed to with my finger, there lay between two and three hundred more of the same sort, and I left them to find them out, which point they soon gave up, saying that I had fairly outwitted them all, but they would watch my waters well for the time to come; which they did to the utmost of all their powers in every respect, especially in striving to hurt me in my trade, which declined from that time.

My stock in English goods at that time was very great, being well sorted; cost me a great many thousand pounds sterling, and my trade dwindling away, chiefly at last to friends of government and the army after this above tea affair. . . . But I still kept my house and continued there until, and the whole time of, the blockade of Boston. [*Jolley Allen Minute Book, Antiquarian Soc., Worcester. See Mass. Hist. Soc. Proc., February 1878, pp. 5-7.*]

The Faction Makes a "Tea Pot of the Harbor of Boston"

DECEMBER 16, 1773

❦ The Teas at last arrived, in the latter End of Autumn, & now Committee Men & Mob Men were buzzing about in Swarms, like Bees, with every one their Sting. They applied first to the Consignees, to compel them to ship the Teas back again. The Mob collected with their great Men in Front. They attacked the Stores & dwelling Houses of the Consignees, but they found them too firm to flinch from their Duty; the Mob insisted that the Teas should be sent to *England.* The Consignees would not take such a Risque upon theirselves, for had the Teas been lost, they must have been the Losers. At last, the Rage of the Mob, urged on by the Smugglers & the Heads of the Faction, was increased to such an Heighth, that the Consignees were obliged to fly for Protection to the *Castle;* as the King's Ship in the Harbor, which was ordered to give them Protection, refused it to them. There was no Authority to defend any Man from Injury.

The Faction did what was right in their own Eyes; they accordingly planned their Manoeuvre, & procured some of the Inhabitants of the neighboring Towns to assist them; this they did, in Order to diffuse the Odium of the Action among their Neighbors. The Mob had, partly, Indian Dresses procured for them, & that the Action they were about to perpetrate might be sanctified in a peculiar Manner, *Adams, Hancock* & the Leaders of the Faction, assembled the Rabble in the largest Dissenting Meeting House in the Town, where they had frequently assembled to pronounce their Annual

Orations upon their Massacre, & to perpetrate their most atrocious Acts of Treason & Rebellion—thus, literally, "turning the House of God into a Den of Thieves."

Thus assembled, on December 14th. they whiled away the Time in Speech-making, hissing & clapping, cursing & swearing untill it grew near to Darkness; & then the signal was given, to act their Deeds of Darkness. They crowded down to the Wharves where the Tea Ships lay, & began to unlade. They then burst the Chests of Tea, when many Persons filled their Bags & their Pockets with it; & made a Tea Pot of the Harbor of *Boston* with the Remainder; & it required a large Tea Pot for several hundred Chests of Tea to be poured into, at one Time. Had they have been prudent enough to have poured it into fresh Water instead of Salt Water, they & their Wives, & their Children; & their little ones, might have regaled upon it, at free Cost, for a twelve Month; but now the Fish had the whole Regale to theirselves. Whether it suited the Constitution of a Fish is not said; but it is said, that some of the Inhabitants of *Boston* would not eat of Fish caught in their Harbor, because they had drank of the *East India Tea.*

After the Affair was over, the town of *Boston,* finding that it was generally condemned, said it was done by a Crew of Mohawk Indians; but it was the Rule of Faction to make their Agents first look like the Devil, in Order to make them Act like the Devil. This villainous Act soon grew into serious Consideration. Some of the Country Towns, as well as some of the Inhabitants of *Boston,* thought that Justice demanded Indemnification to the owners of the Tea; but the Faction was great; & it prevailed; it had so repeated Success, in Impunity, from their other Disorders, that the Power of *Great Britain* did not weigh a Feather in their Consideration: but it at last shut up their Port; & deprived them of some other Priviledges, as the Sequel will relate. [*Oliver, Origin & Progress of the American Rebellion, 1781, Adair and Schutz, eds., pp. 101-103.*]

2 "THE TIDE IN HUMAN AFFAIRS": THE REVEREND HENRY CANER BELIEVES THE FLAME OF REVOLT IS KEPT ALIVE BY A HALF-DOZEN MEN OF BAD PRINCIPLES

The Reverend Henry Caner (1700-1793), rector of King's Chapel, Boston, until the British evacuation and a popular preacher, was one of the most renowned Loyalists of the Episcopal clergy. Since 1761, he had urged the establishment of a resident bishopric in America, which the Congregationalists and Presbyterians adamantly opposed; thus it was not surprising that he was among the Loyalists proscribed and banished by act of the Legislature in 1778. When he left Boston for Halifax under the protection of the British fleet, he took away the vestments, plate, and records of his church. These he refused to return in 1784 when the vestry requested them, turning them over instead to the Society for the Propagation of the Gospel. Seventy-six years old when he fled and long a widower, he took up a new residence near Bristol, England, where he passed the remaining years of his life. His long ministry in America, twenty years in Fairfield, Connecticut, and twenty-eight years in Boston, plus his keen intellect and discernment, have made his *Letterbook* an unusual source of Loyalist interpretation of the rise of dissension and its early impact.

Referring to Shakespeare's *Julius Caesar,* he wrote to Governor John Wentworth of New Hampshire on March 14, 1774: "There is a Tide . . . in human affairs which taken at its rise provides a series of Successes, but neglected till the Ebb is attended with Insignificance and Disappointment. This Observation may be applied to more Cases than one. . . ." The following excerpt from an earlier letter to Wentworth points to the rising tide which Britain was failing to take advantage of. When he reached England, he found that the tide of his own career had also ebbed. Writing to the Reverend Mather Byles at Halifax, December 26, 1776, he said: "For myself I cannot say that I am greatly disapp't because I was no Stranger to the Dissipation and self-seeking among all orders of Men which Characterize the present Times; I was beforehand sensible of this Disposition and moreover with what a jealous Eye the Clergy of this Kingdom look upon one who has served in America, esteeming him in no better light than as coming to take the Bread out of their Mouths. . . ." Again on April 22, 1778, in a letter to a friend, a Reverend Mr. Jones, he touched on the same note: "You inquire whether the Right Rev^ds have blest me with more than a Smile. I confess they have not, nor do I expect more from them [than] 'I wish, Sir, it was in my power to serve you,' etc. when God knows it is in their power every week, if it was equally in their inclination. In truth, I expect nothing from these *unsubstantial* Smiles so am not disappointed. . . ." He philosophized to Dr. Sylvester Gardiner, one of his parishioners in Boston (January 10, 1778): "If I can boast of no great matters here, at least I think my situation preferable to any prison or Dungeon in America. . . ."[1]

---

[1] Henry Caner, *Letterbook,* University of Bristol Library, England.

❏ *To Governor Wentworth*

... My friends at Boston were exercis'd wth the disagreeable entertainment of tumultuous riots, mobs, & Town Meetings w^c continued almost the whole time of my Absence & have not yet ceas'd. The pretended
ground of this disorder is the India House Tea; but every Species of rude
& indecent language of the Govr & others, whom they are pleased to look
upon in an unfriendly light, attended with threatnings of violence extending to life itself, were openly avow'd in their Town^{sp}. The Govr attempted
to call a Council, but under pretense of some necessary Avocation they
neglected to attend. So he could have no advice of Council how to proceed
in regard to the unquiet state of the people. One in the T[own] M[eeting]
publicly affirm'd in his Harangue that they had no Govr, no Courts of Justice, nor any Constitution at all. That therefore people had a right to do as
they pleased. That it was a pity they had not sunk the Commiss^{rs} at their
first arrival, & [he] intimated that it was not yet too late to do themselves
justice on them, on the G[overnor]r, & all others who wished to enslave
them. This harangue was applauded by a general clapping.

Wednesday last the people were warned to meet at [the] Liberty Tree
to hear the resignation of the Consignees of the Tea & the s^d Consignees
were summon'd & commanded to attend, but did not, it seems, think proper
to obey. 1000s, it is tho't, met at the Tree, but not finding the Gentlemen
there w^m they sought for, march'd to K. Street & surrounded Mr. Clark's
Warehouse. A riot was begun & an attempt to force themselves into the
Chamber of the Warehouse & seize the Gentlemen they wanted who were
all in the Chamber, but, being opposed by some spirited Gentlemen, were
defeated. One of the Judges of the Inferior Court being present commanded
the peace & order'd them to disperse. Him, it is said, they assaulted,
wounded, & if he had not dodged a partic[ular] blow aim'd at him with a
large stick of wood, [he] must infallibly have been killed.

Such are the Effects of popular Gov^{r}m^t, Sedition, Anarchy, &
Violence, & all this flame kindled & kept alive by about ½ doz. men of bad
principles & morals ... Bless yourself my dear Sir that, troublesome as
your affairs are, they are not, and I hope and trust never will arrive at this
pass. Tho' I have no mistrust but that all and much more than I have wrote
is strictly true, yet if your Excellency should happen to mention anything
above related among your friends, be pleased to conceal my name, who have
no inclination to expose my person to the resentment of these Sons of
Violence. [*Caner, Letterbook.*]

3 REACTIONS TO THE BOSTON PORT ACT AND TO THE SOLEMN LEAGUE AND COVENANT

The punishment meted out to Massachusetts for jettisoning the famous cargo of tea and the measures to compel her to submit to Parliament, particularly the closing of the port of Boston, created the first real confrontation with the issue of loyalty affecting the Colonies. The letters from the Boston Committee of Correspondence to the committees in other colonies, requesting support for nonintercourse, could not be ignored. Sympathy with Boston and a determination to join Massachusetts in resistance were expressed in resolutions by most of the colonial assemblies; spontaneous demonstrations broke out in many towns and villages; and collections of provisions were started to abate the physical distress of Boston.

The reaction in New York Province, however, was somewhat different and more cautious. To be sure, on May 16, four days after the receipt of the Boston Port Act, the inhabitants of New York City met at Fraunces Tavern and selected a Committee of Fifty-One to correspond with the other colonies. Isaac Low, a prominent merchant and eventual Loyalist, was made chairman. While one zealot admonished the people to rouse, like the brave Romans, and stand up for their liberties, Isaac Low addressed his fellow citizens in words of caution, appealing for reason, calm, and the abandonment of party animosity. He said: "It is but charitable to suppose we all mean the same thing, and that the only difference amongst us is, or at least ought to be, the mode of effecting it, I mean the preservation of our just rights and liberties. . . . Zeal in a good cause is laudable, but when it transports beyond the bounds of reason it often leaves room for bitter reflection. We ought, therefore, gentlemen, to banish from our hearts all little party distinctions, feuds, and animosities, for to our unanimity and virtue we must at last recur for safety; and that man will approve himself the best friend to his country whose highest emulation is to inculcate those principles both by precept and example" (May 19, 1774).[1]

Isaac Low, together with John Jay, James Duane, and Alexander MacDougall, was appointed to a subcommittee to draft a reply to the Boston Committee. The peculiar and delicate political situation in the Province influenced the committee to straddle the boycott issue and toss it to a proposed congress of all the Colonies—the First Continental Congress. Two

[1] Peter Force, ed., *Amer. Arch.:* 4th Ser., vol. I, p. 294.

factions had evolved in New York, one composed of tradesmen and mechanics dominated by the Sons of Liberty, and the other of conservatives and moderates. Although the Mechanics' Committee concurred in the nominations and the proceedings of the Committee of Fifty-One, it determined to assert a more dominant role for itself in New York's affairs and actually became progressively more powerful as its revolutionary Committee of Sixty and then of One Hundred replaced the moderate Committee of Fifty-One. The radicals embraced Boston's cause wholeheartedly, which instead of banishing party animosities became a catalyst for a deeper cleavage between the radicals and the moderates. Although Isaac Low, the chairman of the committee which drafted the reply of May 23, 1774, as well as of various other revolutionary New York committees, was chosen a delegate to the First Continental Congress, he balked at independence, was proscribed as a Loyalist, and suffered confiscation of his estate. The following letter drafted by his committee is a forceful illustration of the bewilderment and equivocation of New York moderates, such as Low, Jay, and Duane, which were evoked by the Coercive Acts. Isaac Low was the only one of the four who became a Loyalist.

In Connecticut, the Reverend Samuel Peters, a notorious and stubborn Tory, influenced Hebron and Hartford to vote adversely on supporting the Boston Relief Fund (June 1774). He describes the actions of the Sons of Liberty in Farmington on hearing of the Boston Port Act. When word of its signing reached Farmington about the middle of May, a handbill was posted urging the Sons of Liberty to attend a parade and a burning of the bill. About a thousand persons gathered around a liberty pole 45 feet high, listened to the reading of the bill, and witnessed its commitment to the flames.

In Pennsylvania, the Quakers were confronted with observing the day of fasting which had been set for all colonies to mark the date the Coercive Acts took effect (June 1, 1774). Those persons who refused to support this sympathetic outpouring were likely to be stigmatized enemies to the cause of liberty. For instance, the front page of the *Connecticut Courant* gave the names of "Persons held up to Public View as Enemies to the Country," including some whose offense had been merely to drink the forbidden tea. Notwithstanding, the Quakers in Pennsylvania made it immediately clear that no cause could evoke support of a boycott or even an expression of sympathy if it contravened their religious principles. The discipline of their church would determine their actions, whether it marked them as enemies or not.

The New York Committee Straddles the Boycott Issue and Suggests a Continental Congress

NEW YORK, MAY 23, 1774

❡ *Gentlemen:*

The alarming Measures of the British Parliament relative to your ancient and respectable Town, which has so long been the Seat of Freedom, fills the Inhabitants of this City with inexpressible Concern; as a Sister Colony suffering in Defence of the Rights of America, we consider your Injuries as a common Cause, to the Redress of which it is equally our Duty and our Interest to contribute. But what ought to be done in a Situation so truly critical, while it employs the anxious Thoughts of every generous Mind, is very hard to be determined. Our Citizens have thought it necessary to appoint a large Committee consisting of fifty-one Persons to correspond with our Sister Colonies on this and every other Matter of publick Moment: and at ten o'clock this Forenoon we were first assembled. Your Letter enclosing the Vote of the Town of Boston, and the Letter of your Committee of Correspondence were immediately taken into consideration. While we think you justly entitled to the Thanks of your Sister Colonies for asking their Advice on a Case of such extensive Consequences, we lament our Inability to relieve your Anxiety by a decisive Opinion. The Cause is general and concerns a whole Continent who are equally interested with you and us; and we foresee that no Remedy can be of avail, unless it proceeds from the joint Act and Approbation of all. From a virtuous and spirited Union much may be expected: while the feeble Efforts of a few will only be attended with Mischief and Disappointment to themselves, and Triumph to the Adversaries of our Liberty. Upon these Reasons we conclude that a Congress of Deputies from the Colonies in general is of the utmost Moment; that it ought to be assembled without Delay and some unanimous Resolutions formed in this fatal Emergency, not only respecting *your* deplorable Circumstances, but for the Security of our common Rights. Such being our Sentiments it must be premature to pronounce any Judgment on the Expedient which you have suggested. We beg however that you will do us the Justice to believe that we shall continue to act with a firm and becoming Regard to American Freedom, and to co-operate with our Sister Colonies in every Measure which shall be thought salutary and conducive to the publick Good.

We have Nothing to add, but that we sincerely condole with you in your unexampled Distress; and to request your speedy Opinion of the proposed Congress, that if it should meet with your Approbation, we may exert our utmost Endeavours to carry it into Execution.

We are with much Respect, Gentlemen

> Your most Hbl Servants
> By Order of the Committee,
> *Isaac Low, Chairman.*
> *Alexander MacDougall*
> *James Duane*
> *John Jay*
> [*Amer. Arch.: 4th Ser., vol. I, pp. 297-298.*]

The Reverend Samuel Peters Describes the Action of the Sons of Liberty in Farmington, Connecticut

MAY 19, 1774

❧ Farmington burnt the act of Parliament in great contempt by their common hangman when a thousand of her best inhabitants were convened for that glorious purpose of committing treason against their king; for which vile conduct they have not been styled a pest to Connecticut and enemies to common sense either by his Honor or any king's attorney or in any town meeting. We sincerely wish and hope a day will be set apart by his Honor very soon for fasting and prayer throughout this colony, that the sins of those haughty people may not be laid to our charge. [*Julius Gay, "Farmington in . . . Revolution," Farmington Papers, p. 82.*]

The Quakers Protest a Sympathetic Boycott

MAY 30, 1774

❧ *To the Printers of the Pennsylvania Gazette:*
Observing in the *Pennsylvania Packet* of this Day a Notification "that a Number of Persons, composed of the Members of all Societies in this City, met and unanimously agreed that it would be proper to express their Sympathy for their Brethren at Boston by suspending all Business on the first Day of the next Month," the People called Quakers, tho' tenderly

sympathizing with the Distressed, and justly sensible of the Value of our Religious and Civil Rights and that it is our Duty to assert them in a Christian Spirit, yet in order to obviate any Misapprehensions which may arise concerning us, think it necessary to declare that no Person or Persons were authorized to represent us on this Occasion, and if any of our Community have countenanced or encouraged this Proposal, they have manifested great Inattention to our religious Principles and Profession and acted contrary to the Rules of Christian Discipline established for the Preservation of Order and good Government among us.

Signed on Behalf and at the Desire of the Elders and Overseers of the several Meetings of our Religious Society in Philadelphia and other Friends met on the Occasion the 30th of the Fifth Month, 1774

> *John Reynell*
> *James Pemberton*
> *Samuel Noble*
> [*Penna. Gaz. June 1, 1774, p. 3.*]

THE REVEREND WILLIAM CLARKE SEES CIVIL WAR AHEAD:
"A SOLEMN LEAGUE AND COVENANT . . . IS SIGNING
ABOUT IN THE COUNTRY."

Even before the First Continental Congress convened, the Boston Committee of Correspondence proceeded to make the boycott of British goods effective throughout Massachusetts. It drew up a Solemn League and Covenant (June 5), binding signatories to end all commercial intercourse with Britain and to abjure consumption of British goods until the Coercive Acts were repealed. The Reverend William Clarke, rector of St. Paul's Church, Dedham, commented astutely to a friend, Joseph Patten, on the progress of the pledge and its significance: "Matters wear a Gloomy aspect and without the interposition of some hand of providence by conciliating measures from one side or the other I see nothing but the Horrors of a Civil War! The signing of a Solemn League and Covenant, which makes its way rapidly thro' the province . . . is thought will soon produce a Declaration of open rebellion. . . . People wait with Impatience for the Issue of the intended Congress the first of September. But I fear it will be by no means

Conciliating. . . ."[1] At the same time he wrote in greater length to William Fisher, another friend; an excerpt from his letter is given below.

AUGUST 6, 1774

❡ . . . An important change, you will hear, has taken place in our civil affairs in this province, by some late acts of Parliament and a New Governor, which was the *Summum Bonum* they were but lately after and now want to get rid of as much as they did Mr. H[utchinso]n and perhaps more. He is come with very extensive powers. The port of Boston is Blockaded, nothing comparatively to be seen but ships of war—the Common covered with camps, colours, red coats, and military Instruments. A later act of P[arliamen]t has repeal'd part of the charter, taking away the right of choosing councillours, Judges, Jurors, etc., forbidding all town meetings (except in March for the choice of Town officers and in May the Rep[resentati]ve), unless permitted by the Governor in writing under his hand. This takes place the 1st of August. The General Court was dissolved some short time after the Election upon the first motion they made to counterwork acts of P[arliamen]t. It would require more time than I can spare to give you the history of Publick affairs in Full. You will doubtless see the chief in the Publick papers. The town of Boston looks very melancholly, but they have brought it upon themselves. Their opposition to Good Government has in some instances been shamefully flagrant and the Destruction of the Tea was plainly by Countenance of the Leading men of the Town. His Majesty, Governor Gage says, as I am intimately inform'd, resents it to the highest Degree and says he was never treated in so ignominious a manner by his worst Enemies of other Nations. What will be the Issue of these things

---

[1] William Clarke to Joseph Patten, August 6, 1774, *William Clarke Papers,* Diocesan Library, Boston. William Clarke refused to accept the Declaration of Independence and in May 1777 gave further offense by providing refuge to two Tories. As a consequence he was assaulted, his home plundered, and he was confined on a guard ship in Boston Harbor for ten weeks. Already suffering from deafness, he further suffered during his confinement from an attack of asthma and loss of speech, regained only seven years later. He was banished and sought refuge successively in Newport, New York City, Ireland, and England. He returned to Massachusetts in 1792 and died in Quincy in 1815. (*Sibley's Harvard Graduates,* Clifford K. Shipton, ed., Boston: 1968, vol. XIV, 393–402.)

time must discover. The Day I received your Letter was kept as a Fast by the Dissenters in General thro' the province. But as the Governor did not think proper to Issue his proclamation, Episcopalians did not think themselves obliged to keep it.

M^r C-se, who was present says that even Mr. H[utchinso]n told his people the Country had been Greatly to blame and that there must be a reformation before any Good could be expected. A paper called a Solemn League and Covenant of an horrid nature and Tendency has been issued out and is signing about in the country. Above 130 merchants and Traders of Boston (some of whom have heretofore been high in Liberty Schemes) have openly protested against it. The Governor has published his proclamation against it, but the poor Deluded people of the Country go on to sign it much the faster. A Congress of certain Deputies from all the Colonies are to meet at Philadelphia the 1st of September. What measures they will take is uncertain. It is to be wished it might be something Conciliating with the Mother Country before matters come to Extreams. But of this I must have Done! . . .

> To fill a vacant page and strew a little wit
> I'll write of Governor Gage, tho' but a little Bit.

P. S. Governor Gage resides at D[anver]s about a mile from my native spot and, having met with some molestation there, has lately taken two companies from the Castle regiment to station near his house. Governor H-n, we hope, has by this time arrived safely in Great Britain. Before he sailed he received the adresses of our clergy, 123 Merchants and Traders, 33 at M. N^d., 24 Lawyers, 30 odd Justices of Middlesex, and I think some others. [*William Clarke Papers, Diocesan Library, Boston.*]

WILLIAM EDDIS OF MARYLAND REPORTS "ALL AMERICA
IS IN A FLAME"

William Eddis of Annapolis, Maryland, voiced the feeling of another section of the country. A Surveyor of Customs since 1769, he watched "the impending storm with inquietude," writing perceptively to a friend as early as October 3, 1772, when the storm seemed to be settling down: "Under pretence of supporting the sacred claims of freedom, and of justice, factions and designing men are industriously fomenting jealousy and discontent; and unless they are stopt in their progress by the immediate and determined exertions of the wise and the moderate, they will aggravate the dissention which is become but too evident and involve this now happy country in complicated misery."[1] On January 3, 1774, he again voiced alarm: "I fear . . . our statesmen have promoted measures which they will be equally embarassed to enforce or defend. . . . Should the storm burst, it must inevitably involve in the same ruin multitudes who think differently and are equally actuated by conscientious principles." By May 28 he concluded: "All America is in a Flame! . . . The colonists are ripe for any measures that will tend to the preservation of what they call their natural liberty. . . . It is the universal opinion *here* that the mother country cannot support a contention with these settlements if they abide steady to the letter and spirit of their associations. Where will these matters end? Imagination anticipates with horror the most dreadful consequences."[2] His further comments on the First Continental Congress and the Continental Association, extending the Solemn League and Covenant to all the colonies, which follow, indicate that Eddis understood the far-reaching significance of these developments better than most witnesses.

OCTOBER 26, 1774

❦ The general attention is fixed on the Congress now sitting in Philadelphia and all descriptions of people are waiting for the result of their deliberations with the utmost impatience.

The Canada Bill [Quebec Act] is as unpopular here as the Boston Port Bill and adds greatly to the universal discontent. The provinces are unanimous in the cause of their northern brethren and contribute largely in supplying their necessities. The spirit of opposition to ministerial measures appears to blaze steadily and equally in every part of British America and unless some speedy alteration takes place in the political system the consequences must inevitably be dreadful.

Every well-wisher to the interest and happiness of the mother-country and her colonies must behold this unnatural contest with inexpressible

[1] William Eddis, *Letters from America, Historical and Descriptive, Comprising Occurrences from 1769 to 1777 Inclusive*, London: 1792, p. 136.
[2] Ibid., pp. 158–161.

anxiety. There never was a period in our history more critical than the present. It is high time some methods were adopted to conciliate these growing differences. The colonies are daily gaining incredible strength. They *know,* they *feel,* their importance; and *persuasion,* not *force,* must retain them in obedience.

A general non-importation agreement will speedily take place and I have reason to believe will be resolutely adhered to. It is therefore to be feared the manufacturers and artificers in Britain will be much distressed and probably driven to great extremities. For I need not observe to a man so conversant as you are with the commercial interests of the empire how severely the mother-country must suffer by an interruption of her extensive trade with this continent. It is universal doctrine *here* that it will plunge you into violent commotions and probably be attended with fatal consequences. . . .

NOVEMBER 2, 1774

The Congress have concluded their deliberations. I have seen their resolves, the association, the petition to his Majesty, and the addresses to Great Britain, to Canada, and to the confederating American colonies.

. . . The petition is held to be a masterly performance, firm, explicit, and respectful; the Address to Great Britain is thought to be pathetic and persuasive; that to Canada to be founded on sentiments of liberty and reason; and that to the uniting provinces to be instructive and moderating. . . . It is evident the colonists are unanimous and will steadily support the proceedings of their delegates. [*Eddis, Letters from America, pp. 168–170, 186.*]

4 AUDACIOUS PROCEEDINGS: HENRY HULTON SAYS "THE PARADE THEY MAKE HERE OF RESISTANCE IS ALL A FLASK WITHOUT BOTTOM"

It was a foregone conclusion that customs officers would be a prime target for the wrath of the mob. In fact, the most famous tar and feathering case, that of John Malcom, a customs collector of Boston, was sketched and caricatured in many colonial papers. Henry Hulton, who had occupied the office of Commissioner of Customs in Boston since 1767 and who had signed the hated writs of assistance, anticipated the same abuse and moved his family from his country estate in Brookline to the security of the town. Concern for the safety of his wife and five sons, as well as for his own safety, dictated their departure with the British fleet for Halifax in March 1776. His estate was confiscated, and he was on the list of Loyalists proscribed and banished by the Massachusetts Legislature. Thanks to generous compensation for his property losses and £500 a year for loss of income during the war, he was able to buy a farm in Wells, Hampshire County, England, and settle down in comfort as a gentleman farmer.[1] Henry Hulton, as well as his sister, Ann Hulton,[2] have left many descriptive letters to friends in England on developments in America in 1775. The following letter from Boston tells of the implementation of the Association and of the actions taken by the Massachusetts Provincial Congress during the first weeks of 1775.

BOSTON, FEBRUARY 21, 1775

❡ *D*ʳ *Sir* [Robert Nicholson]

. . . I quitted my habitation in the Country, & my family have been with me in Town since the middle of Octᵇʳ, as this is the only place of security in the Province for the Servants or friends of Government. I imagine American matters are the general subject of conversation & that you are all amazed at our violent & audacious proceedings.

You will no doubt have read the resolutions of our Provincial & Continental Congresses & will have seen by the accounts published by the people themselves that they deny the authority & refuse obedience to the Acts of the British Parliament. In consequence of which we have been for some time in a state of anarchy. The Courts of Justice being suspended, the militia officers superceded & new ones appointed by the people, & a new Treasurer nominated by them to receive the Provincial Taxes in defiance of the Kings authority. The resolves of the Continental Congress are now

---

[1] Lorenzo Sabine, *Biographical Sketches,* vol. I, p. 372. *Loyalist Transcripts,* vol. IV, p. 594; vol. XI, p. 170. Hulton was awarded £1,550 on a claim of £1,820 for losses of property, far more than the one-third which other Loyalists received. He also received £500 a year for loss of income plus a pension for life. PRO, AO 12/82, 99, 109; AO 13/46, 85; AO 459/7; T 50/9.
[2] Ann Hulton, *Letters of a Loyalist Lady,* Cambridge, Mass.: 1927.

executing in the several Provinces and political inquisitors are appointed in each town to pry into the conduct of individuals that they observe the orders prescribed respecting the importation of British goods etc.

The past concessions of Great Britain have given the people confidence & their forte is in her weakness. They expect to raise a clamour amongst the manufacturers at home, that they will fight their battles for them, for the parade they here make of resistance is all a flask without bottom. They are without officers & money, military stores & places of defence; they have no sense of Order & will never submit to discipline.

It is well known that the Southern provinces had imported a supply of goods sufficient for two or three years before the resolutions of the Continental Congress took place and that none of the Colonies can keep to the resolutions of the Congress; & if the Nation shews firmness & spirit, the Americans must soon submit to the Authority of Parliament.

It were endless to relate all the instances of cruelty & oppression that have been practised for some months past in this Country on those persons who have been deemed by the people unfriendly to American liberty. Every one who did not conform in all things to the will of the people was considered as a proper object of persecution; many, to save themselves & families from destruction, signed to any articles that were imposed upon them & were compelled to make the most humiliating submission. Still this would not satisfy & he who would not take up arms, say all that they said, & justify all that they did was judged to be a Tory & an Enemy to his Country, and therefore to be expelled [from] the Society.

We have now a formidable force assembled here, waiting the Orders of Government on the resolutions of Parliament, whilst the people of the Country levying & training their Militia, keeping what they call minute men ready for action, in cases of any attack or allarm.

The Winter has passed off thus far without any material disturbances. The temper and forbearance of the General, the good conduct of the officers, the order & discipline observed by the Troops amidst repeated insults & provocations are highly to be commended. Lord Percys great condescention wins upon every one & the people must own & admire the gentle manner & good behaviour of the military general[ly].

A Provincial Congress has been sitting at Cambridge since the first ins[t] till within these few days. They have published Resolves "Strictly forbiding the People from furnishing the Army with any military Stores or supplying them with necessaries to enable them to take the field." "Urging the militia in general to perfect themselves in military discipline & the Towns & Districts to encourage the manufactory of fire Arms & Bayonets & recommended to them to cause their respective proportions of the Province Tax to be paid into the hands of Mr Hen Gardner of L[on]don, lately appointed Treasurer of the Province by the former Congress" and after appointing the 16th of March to be kept as a day of fasting & prayer they adjourned to meet at Concord the 22nd of March.

Thus after seven years of trouble & trial our situation is become still more critical and interesting. We are not subject to such frequent allarms for our own safety as here to fore, but we are concerned for the consequences which the madness of this deluded people will occasion, as it is hardly to be expected that anything less than the hand of correction can bring them back to order & obedience. [*Henry Hulton, Letterbook, Shepherd Mss. Manchester College, Oxford.*]

5 WESTCHESTER PROTESTERS DECLARE THEIR "HONEST ABHORRENCE OF ALL UNLAWFUL CONGRESSES AND COMMITTEES"

It was in Boston that the word Tory first became an epithet of ignominy. The retirement of Governor Hutchinson and his replacement by General Thomas Gage in May 1774 became another early occasion for showing one's colors. For segments of the populace, officeholders, Anglican clergy, prominent lawyers, and merchants, the choice presented no dilemma. These Tories did not equivocate. They promptly addressed Governor Hutchinson in appreciative terms, welcomed General Gage, and avowed their loyalty to the King. Similar signed addresses of sympathy, as well as protests against extralegal congresses and committees became instruments for singling out the first Tories for vilification and harassment. Groups of magistrates, merchants, and lawyers in other colonies drew up comparable addresses and protests, among them the dissenters in Westchester.

In January 1775, when the New York Assembly, dominated by open Loyalists, refused to appoint delegates to the Second Continental Congress, the radical wing determined to bypass the Assembly by presenting the issue to the freeholders of the city and, in fact, by proposing a totally new legislative body, a Provincial Convention. The maneuvers of the radicals were successful, and such a convention was called for April 20. Choosing delegates for this convention furnished an opportunity for towns and outlying counties, where Loyalism was strong, to protest the trend toward rebellion. Interested freeholders and inhabitants of Westchester County assembled on April 11 at White Plains, those opposed to electing deputies meeting at Hatfield's Tavern and those in favor gathering first at Miles Oakley's Tavern, and then surreptitiously reassembling at the courthouse. Under the chairmanship of Lewis Morris, the latter faction intended quietly to appoint the delegates and present the opposition with a *fait accompli.* The Loyalist faction having wind of these proceedings, marched to the courthouse, led by Isaac Wilkins and Frederick Philipse, and lodged a dignified protest against the unlawful proceedings of the Morris faction. Their opponents, however, went on unanimously to appoint deputies to the Convention and to pass resolutions of thanks to the Continental Congress. Both factions drew up narratives of the happenings of that eventful April 11, the Morris group claiming that many of their opponents were minors and tenants, not eligible to vote, and the protesters asserting that at least two-thirds of the inhabitants of Westchester were friends of government. The authorship of the Protest and Declaration has been ascribed to Isaac Wilkins.[1]

APRIL 11, 1775

❦ On Thursday the 11th inst., a very respectable number of freeholders and inhabitants of the county of Westchester assembled at the *White Plains* in the said county, agreeable to the notice given, that their sentiments might be known concerning the choice of a committee to meet other committees in the city of New York, for the purpose of choosing delegates to represent this Colony in the next Continental Congress.

---

[1] Three hundred and twelve protesters subscribed to the Declaration, six of whom withdrew from the action after Lexington, two saying they had not themselves signed, two that they had changed their minds, and two that they signed believing they were supporting the "liberties of the country." Jeremiah Hunter, for example, stated he was not a protester, explaining: "I never signed it but went into Capt. Hatfield's house and was asked whether I was a Whig or Tory. I made answer that I did not understand the meaning of those words, but was for liberty and peace. Upon which I immediately put down my name." Peter Force, ed., *Amer. Arch.:* 4th Ser., vol. II, pp. 321–324.

The friends of order and government met at the house of Captain Hatfield; more who were for a committee put up at another public house in the town. About 12 o'clock, word was brought to the gentlemen at Captain Hatfield's that the opposite party had already entered upon the business of the day; upon which they immediately walked down to the *court house,* although not half of their friends, who were expected had yet appeared, where they found the other company collected in a body. The numbers on each side seemed to be nearly equal, and both together might amount to two hundred, or, at most, two hundred and fifty. The friends to government then declared, that as they had been unlawfully called together, and for an unlawful purpose, they did not intend to contest the matter with them by a poll, which would be tacitly acknowledging the authority that had summoned them thither; but that they came only with a design to protest against all such disorderly proceedings, and to show their detestation of all unlawful Committees and Congresses; they then declared their determination and resolution to continue steadfast in their allegiance to their gracious and merciful sovereign, King George the Third, to submit to lawful authority, and to abide by and support the only true representatives of the people of this Colony, the General Assembly; then giving three huzzas, they returned to Captain Hatfields, singing, as they went, with loyal enthusiasm, the good and animating song of "God save great George our King," "Long live our noble King," &c., &c.

At their return, finding that many of their friends had arrived during their absence, and that many still kept coming in, they proceeded to draw up and sign the following declaration, which they seemed to do with as much patriotic zeal as ever warmed the hearts of true and faithful subjects, and afterwards dispersed to their different habitations.

"We the subscribers, freeholders and inhabitants of the county of Westchester, having assembled at the White Plains in consequence of certain advertisements, do now declare, that we met here to declare our honest

---

(fn. cont.) Henry B. Dawson comments: "one of the most important political movements in which New York has ever been engaged was carried through Westchester County in known opposition to the great body of its inhabitants and in the face of a formal *Protest* of a larger number, by only a factional minority, in the interest of an aspiring politician [Lewis Morris], and while that minority was staggering under the evil influences of the New England rum which had been freely dispensed for that particular purpose." *Westchester County during the American Revolution,* New York: 1886, p. 70.

abhorrence of all unlawful Congresses and Committees, and that we are determined at the hazard of our lives and properties to support the king and constitution, and that we acknowledge no Representatives but the General Assembly, to whose wisdom and integrity we submit the guardianship of our rights and privileges." [*Rivington's N.Y. Gaz. Apr. 20, 1775, Amer. Arch.: 4th Ser., vol. II, p. 321*]

6 READY-MADE LOYALIST: ISAAC WILKINS OF WESTCHESTER EXPLAINS THAT HE CANNOT RAISE HIS HAND AGAINST HIS KING NOR HIS SWORD AGAINST HIS COUNTRY

Isaac Wilkins (1741–1830) chose to identify himself as a Loyalist at the outset of the dissension by helping defeat the Assembly motion to appoint delegates to the Second Continental Congress and by his leadership of the Westchester protest movement. He also wrote several forthright Loyalist pamphlets, *The Congress Canvassed* and *A View of the Controversy between Great Britain and her Colonies,* copies of which were symbolically tarred and feathered and burned. He was married to a sister of Governor Morris and of Lewis Morris, the Whig whom he opposed in the Westchester encounter at White Plains.

Although he left America in 1775, he soon returned and sat out most of the war on Long Island where he rented a place to which supplies were sent from his Westchester estate. Since his name did not appear in the Act of Confiscation, he succeeded in regaining possession of his estate after the war and in securing permission to sell it, albeit at half the cost to him. In 1783, he repaired to Shelburne, Nova Scotia, and lived also for a time at Lunenburg, Canada. In 1799, now a minister, he returned to Westchester and was given the parish of Westchester which he served for thirty-one years. Here was a Tory whose competence and ingratiating personality triumphed over the bitterness evoked by his political views. When he died at age eighty-nine, he had arranged to have inscribed as his epitaph these words: "Satisfied with the pittance allowed him, rejoicing that even in that he was no burden to his parishioners."[1]

[1] Samuel Curwen, *The Journal and Letters of Samuel Curwen, 1775–1783,* G. A. Ward, ed., Boston: 1864, p. 559. Sabine, *Loyalists,* vol. II, pp. 431–434.

In 1775, two weeks after the Westchester Protesters were defeated in their efforts to prevent election of delegates to the Provincial Convention, believing he would have to leave America, he wrote his well-known address to his countrymen. It is representative of the sentiments of the conscientious Loyalist who could not take up arms against either his King or his country.

MAY 3, 1775

¶ *My Countrymen:*

Before I leave America, the land I love, and in which is contained every thing that is valuable and dear to me—my wife, my children, my friends, and property—permit me to make a short and faithful declaration, which I am induced to do neither through fear nor a consciousness of having acted wrong. An honest man, and a Christian, hath nothing to apprehend from this world. God is my judge and God is my witness that all I have done, written, or said in relation to the present unnatural dispute between Great Britain and her colonies proceeded from the honest intention of serving my country. Her welfare and prosperity were the objects towards which all my endeavours have been directed. They still are the sacred objects which I shall ever steadily and invariably keep in view; and when in England all the influence, that so inconsiderable a man as I am can have, shall be exerted in her behalf.

It has been my constant maxim through life to do my duty conscientiously and to trust the issue of my actions to the Almighty. May that God in whose hands are all events speedily restore peace and liberty to my unhappy country; may Great Britain and America be soon united in the hands of everlasting amity; and when united, may they continue a free, a virtuous, and happy nation to the end of time.

I leave America and every endearing connection because I will not raise my hand against my Sovereign, nor will I draw my sword against my Country. When I can conscientiously draw it in her favour, my life shall be cheerfully devoted to her service. [*Rivington's N.Y. Gaz., May 11, 1775.*]

7   THE SEIZURE OF SKENESBOROUGH

Philip Skene (1725–1810) was the patentee of Skenesborough, a township of 34,000 acres which extended along both sides of Wood Creek east of Lake Champlain. Here he had settled many tenant families, built a sawmill, forge, and store, put a schooner on the lake, and constructed his own stone house in full view of the Adirondack Mountains. Skene had been born into a Scottish Jacobite family and had served as a soldier in the Pretender's cause and in the French and Indian War in America. In 1775, George III had appointed him Lieutenant Governor of Forts Ticonderoga and Crown Point at £300 annual salary. His loyalism was a foregone conclusion; his prominence made him the butt of contempt. Children in Washington County called him "Old Skene" and when asked whether they preferred to meet him or the devil were taught to answer the devil.[1] His estate and person became an obvious target for the Green Mountain Boys. On May 9, 1775, John Barnes's Company seized his estate and took off his sister and daughters to Connecticut. Skene himself was en route from England to Philadelphia and was seized on shipboard as he landed in June 1775. He was taken to Hartford under a strong escort and paroled with his son to board at West Hartford. When his parole expired, he refused to renew it and was confined in a dungeon and not allowed to leave it for six months. He was exchanged in September 1776 and served with Bourgoyne's army in the 1777 campaign.

There are several accounts of the capture of Skenesborough, one by Skene himself in his memorial to the Crown for his losses during the war. His account stresses the outrages perpetrated on the women in his home. More interesting is the story collected by Dr. Asa Fitch of Salem, New York, probably from his father, Jabez Fitch, a rebel living in the vicinity of Skenesborough in 1775, included because of its revelation of the bizarre discovery of John Barnes's Company when they seized Skene's home.

---

[1] Account of Dr. Asa Fitch in H. H. Noble, "A Loyalist of the St. Lawrence," *Ontario Historical Society Proceedings,* vol. XIV, p. 8.

Philip Skene Emphasizes the Cruelty to the Women of His Family

[MAY 9, 1775]

❡ . . . [His estate] was seized upon May 9, 1775, by armed banditti to the unspeakable terror and Anxiety of a helpless aged Sister, who with his Daurs (The first example of cruelty to the Sex) were forced from their peaceful dwelling under an armed escort and obliged in this Situation to perform a Journey of near 200 miles in which, exclusive of their being prisoners to a lawless banditti, they suffered exceeding hardships from their Mode of travelling, being sometimes obliged to walk through the woods and at other times carried in a Cart drawn by Oxen with scarce a change of apparel and exposed to every insult and mortification from a licentious people by whom they were surrounded and threatened repeatedly. And by an Order from the Assembly of Connecticut, they were sent back in the same manner to Canada where unprotected and nearly unsupported they suffered a variety of distress during the Siege of Quebec. [*Memorial of 1787, Loyalist Transcripts, vol. XLV. p. 191.*]

The Barnes Company Tries to Capture "Lord Skene" and Finds a Preserved Corpse

[MAY 9, 1775]

❡ Capture of Skeenesboro: About the same time [John] Barnes's company was ordered out to proceed to Skeenesborough & capture "Lord Skeene" . . . A double sentry guarded Skeene's house, a fact which they were not aware of—a sentry was placed at the house, and another half a mile distant on the road. The party approached and when yet half a mile away, and before they were suspicious that caution in their advance was necessary, a gun was fired pointed towards the residence of Skeene. Knowing the alarm was now given, they started forward at their utmost speed but at the same instant another gun was fired at the house, satisfying them that their approach was known. They rushed on with the utmost haste, and surrounded the house on all sides. Some of their number now searched the house thoroughly, but Skeene had escaped. They supposed he had fled into the woods when the alarm was first given.

They found the corpse of his wife in a small apartment partitioned off in the cellar. It was laid in a very nice wooden coffin, superior to anything which the carpenters of the country could make. And this was inclosed in a lead coffin, which was sealed and soldered up so as to render it quite air tight. His wife had a legacy left her of a certain sum per day whilst she was above ground and Skeene had placed her here to receive this legacy. (Was not the legacy to be paid till her "burial" and thus intended in part to defray the expenses of her interment?)[1] He could not have placed a pen in her fingers to guide them to write her name without opening the lead coffin and that was soldered up tight—inasmuch that on opening it, the corpse was found but little changed. The coffins must have been purchased in Montreal or Quebec. The corpse was taken out and buried, how far or which way from the house I do not know, only the wooden coffin was buried. The lead was too much needed for bullets to be buried and it, together with the choice liquors, of which there was a considerable store found in the cellar, was delivered to the commissioners of the continental army.

There were about 40 negros of both sexes upon the premises and these were about the only occupants they found. These negros were all full blooded Africans, save one, a girl 6 or 8 years old, named Sylvia who claimed Skeene for her father. Captain Barnes brought her home with him on his return (he and most, if not all, of the company returned immediately) and when he moved from here he sold or gave her to Major Thomas Armstrong who sold her to Col. McCleary. She remained in this town, and decripid and blind with old age, died but a few years ago, 4 or 5 years since. [*Fitch, Manuscript History of Washington Co., vol. I, pp. 111-112.*]

[1] Another recollection was that of Robert Blake, who said that Skene placed his wife in the cellar in a lead coffin with all her rings and jewelry in order to take her back to Ireland or Scotland to be buried among her kindred. Dr. Asa Fitch, *Manuscript History,* vol. I, p. 118. Mrs. Doris B. Morton doubts the legacy story, claiming that Katherine Hayden Skene had been willed her uncle's estate outright. *Philip Skene of Skenesborough,* Granville, N.Y.: 1959, p. 47. If Skene's purpose in keeping his wife's body in the cellar was to take it to her ancestral burying ground, he could have taken it with him on his 1774-1775 trip.

8 OLIVE BRANCHES: WILLIAM SMITH, JR., ADVISES LEWIS
MORRIS, DELEGATE TO THE CONTINENTAL CONGRESS, ON A
CONCILIATORY ANSWER TO THE KING

A letter from William Smith, Jr., Chief Justice and council member of
New York Province, to Lewis Morris, Westchester delegate to the Continental Congress, excuses the Declaratory Act as a "Puff of Pride" and
advises him to send a conciliatory message to the King. It illustrates the
dilemma of many prominent provincials who saw justice on both sides. It
also focuses attention on some significant analogies between this letter of
June 5, 1775, taken from Smith's *Historical Memoirs* and the Olive Branch
Petition, penned by John Dickinson and signed in Philadelphia July 5,
1775. Smith was in close friendship with the leaders of both Whig and
Tory factions and, like Dickinson and Joseph Galloway, exerted every influence to avoid a rupture and to find a basis for compromise. Smith has
been called "half Whig, half Tory," as he did not make his position unequivocally clear until he refused the oath in 1777.[1] There is some jus-
tification for considering him a "weathercock," as some Whigs called him,
and for the charge of Judge Thomas Jones that he was cunning, hypocrit-
ical, and self-interested.[2] His diverse interests, such as his Vermont lands,
dictated a straddling of the issue as long as possible. Summoned before the
Provincial Congress on March 7, 1777, and asked whether he considered
himself a subject of the State of New York, he responded that he did not
feel discharged from his oath of loyalty to the Crown and that he had written to the Provincial Congress on July 4, 1776, to the same effect. Accordingly he refused the oath of allegiance and pledged his parole to abide within Livingston manor until otherwise ordered.[3] The several similarities,

---

[1] *Roy. Am. Gaz.,* July 13, 1779. See I. N. P. Stokes, *Iconography of Manhattan Island,* vol. IV, pp. 890–891. [Paul Wentworth] to William Eden, 1778, "Sketches of
Leading Persons in Each Province" in B. F. Stevens, *Facsimiles of Manuscripts in European Archives Relating to America, 1773-1783,* London: 1889–1895, vol. V, no. 487,
p. 28. Smith is described as having "the address to pass for a Loyalist . . ." but "a secret
adviser & Corresp^d to the Congress." Sabine, *Loyalists,* vol. II, p. 312.
[2] Thomas Jones, *History of New York during the Revolutionary War,* Edward F. De-
Lancey, ed., New York: 1879, vol. I, pp. 143, 167–168.
[3] Martin Delafield, "William Smith, the Historian," *Mag. Am. Hist.,* no. 13 (1881), p.
425. William Smith (1728-1793) was officially banished by the Committee for Detecting Conspiracies June 30, 1778, and was ordered to take his family under a flag

indicated below, of Smith's letter with parts of the Olive Branch Petition suggest that this letter, written two days after the appointment of the committee to draft the petition, may have influenced the tone and, at points, even the wording of Dickinson's draft.[4]

NEW YORK, JUNE 5, 1775

❡ *Dear Lewis,*

Gouverneur tells me you wish for a Line from me upon the great Subject, that now imploys the Council of an Empire upon the very Precipice of Destruction; but it is too copious for a Letter; and if it was not, I have *now* only Time for a few Words, before I set out for my Country Grotto, where my Family is, and from which I have been too long detained. . . .

Among the many Objects that probably present themselves to your Mind, I think Attention should be principally directed to the present Overture of Administration, however disinclined you may be to subscribe an Assent to it. Remember that the *last* Congress widened the Controversy unnecessarily by a Denial of the *whole Legislative* Authority of Great

---

of truce to the British lines in New York. His estate, however, was not listed among those confiscated. He was appointed Chief Justice of New York State and took the oath of office April 24, 1780, but never served because of the military occupation of the city. He sailed for England with Sir Guy Carleton December 5, 1783. In 1785, he was appointed Chief Justice of Canada. Here, joined by his wife and children, he exercised the duties of office from October 1786 until his death in December 1793. Although his attainder was canceled in 1790, he never returned to New York.

[4] William Jay claims that the Olive Branch Petition originated with his father, John Jay. Jay was a member of the committee appointed June 3 to report a petition to the Continental Congress, along with Thomas Johnson of Maryland, John Rutledge of South Carolina, Benjamin Franklin, and John Dickinson of Pennsylvania. A draft of a petition to the King in Jay's handwriting, bearing the date of 1775, appears among the John Dickinson Papers in the Pennsylvania Historical Society. See William Jay, *Life of John Jay,* New York: 1883, vol. I, pp. 36–37.

There is another occasion when William Smith tried to influence American political developments. Smith claimed that his suggestions on a stronger central government, made to Washington in 1775, appeared subsequently in Washington's Circular Letters. Sabine reports that in 1789 Smith showed Dr. Mitchell of New York a sketch of a plan of government resembling the Constitution, which he had drawn up and sent to Washington. *Loyalists,* vol. II, pp. 312–313.

Britain. There was perhaps more Prowess than Prudence in this Step. Can it then be wondered at that the Mother Country should answer, under the Influence of that Pride so natural to an Englishman, and which some may think becomes the *Old* Lady more than her Daughters? Certainly not a man in the Empire once doubted that Great Britain had the Supremacy; tho' it must be confessed at the same Time, it was as far from our Conceptions, that it would or ought to be exercised with despotic Sovereignty. It was a just Idea formed by our English Friends in the Commencement of this unhappy Quarrel that an Authority to tax us was not requisite to maintain the Legislative Supremacy of the Nation. And if the contending Parties could be brought to adopt this Principle in a reasonable Extent, all animosity would instantly cease. . . .

It was the Error of the Parent State, and a Puff of Pride, to assert a Principle that was not worth a Farthing, unless she had Power to carry it into execution; and if she had that Power needed no Declaration of it upon Paper for its Support. I call it Pride, because they who brought the Parliament to pass the Act of Supremacy in 1766 *were our Friends,* if their Repeal of the Stamp Act may pass for Evidence of their Affection. Great Britain then removed your complaint but, that you might not consider what she granted as a Favor, as an extorted Concession, she asserted that it was of her Grace and that she had Authority to take it back if she pleased. . . .

As to the Mode of answering the British Proposal, it cannot be very Material. A Petition to the King, as that of the last Congress was received, will probably be unexceptionable, especially since the Colony Assemblies will take your Tone and follow Suit. But you may declare your Sentiments in various Ways. The Nature of the Answer itself is the *great Desideratum.*

William Smith's Letter

Certainly it should in the most explicit Manner shew your Loyalty to the King, your Affection to Great Britain, and your *Abhorrence* [italics mine] of a Separation. To give the Lie to the Malignant imputation of our Enemies, and to remove the Suspicions of all Men, respecting the

Olive Branch Petition

We, your Majesty's faithful Subjects . . . Your Majesty's Ministers . . . have engaged us in a controversy so peculiarly *abhorrent* [italics mine] to the affections of your still faithful colonists . . .

The Union between our Mother Country and these colonies, and the

Charge of a Thirst for Independency, you should state your views of the *essential Benefits* of our Union and the Mischiefs inevitably consequent upon the Dissolution of it.

You will next lament the present *Calamities so destructive of both countries,* [italics mine] and (without a Word about Rights)[1] proceed to state the Line of Conduct that will calm the Stormy, troubled Sea of Discontent. Then you will in terms of the most explicit Affection, *declare your Readiness to contribute to the exigencies of the Nation,* upon Confidence that all future Aids are to be expected in the Way of Requisition, and that when Duties, as are imposed in the Regulation of Commerce, they shall pass to your Credit as part of your gifts. In further Confidence also, that your internal Police, civil and Ecclesiastical, be left to the Colonies, you engaging for such a liberal Support of Government, as shall give the Executive no just Foundation for Complaint. Adding, that if [it] shall be conceived by his Majesty to be requisite toward the Aid of the Colonies in Times of Extremity, you will cheerfully consent to send Delegates from your Assemblies towards a *General Convention,* [italics Smith's] for receiving the

energy of mild and just government produced *benefits* [italics mine] so remarkably important and afforded such an assurance of their permanancy and increase that the wonder and envy of other nations were excited . . .

We think ourselves required . . . to use all the means in our power . . . for *averting the impending Calamities that threaten the British Empire* [italics mine]. . . .

The apprehensions that now oppress our hearts with unspeakable grief, being once removed, your Majesty will find *your faithful subjects on this continent ready and willing at all times,* as they ever have been, *with their lives and fortunes, to assert and maintain the rights and interests of your Majesty and of our Mother Country* [italics mine]. . . .

. . . submitting to your Majesty's wise consideration whether it may not be expedient for facilitating those important purposes, that your Majesty be pleased to direct *some mode* [italics mine] by which the united applications of your faithful colonists to the throne,

---

[1] There is another parallel between William Smith's words *"without a Word about Rights"* and Dickinson's letter to Arthur Lee, July 7, 1775, saying: ". . . You will perhaps at first be surpriz'd, that we make no *Claim,* and *mention no Right.* But I hope, considering all Circumstances, you will be [of] opinion, that this Humility in an address [to] the Throne is at present proper. Our Rights [have] been already stated—our Claims made . . ." Edmund C. Burnett, ed. *Letters of the Members of the Continental Congress,* Washington, D.C.: 1921-1936, vol. I, p. 157.

Royal Requisition, granting Aids for all the Provinces, and ascertaining the Quotas of each; leaving to their separate consideration only the Ways and Means of raising them—Concluding with a Recommendation to every Province and Colony in the Confederacy, that whenever it shall please his Majesty and the two Houses of Parliament, to signify their Approbation of this Plan, as a Foundation of the *Restoration of the Harmony* [italics mine] of the Empire to liberate the Commerce and cultivate their ancient Affection in a firm Persuasion that every Mark of Severity, to which this unnatural Contest gave Rise, will be speedily removed, every Grievance redressed, and every Act of Violence forgotten and buried in Oblivion.

in pursuance of their common councils, may be improved into a happy and permanent *reconciliation* [italics mine]; . . .

What I mean by Duties passing to our Credit is that every Act of Parliament imposing them direct that such as are payable *in the Colonies* pass into *their* Treasuries; and that of such as are paid in England, accounts be annually rendred to the Assemblies that they may have Credit for them in their general Contributions upon Requisition and Gift.

This Course of Negotiating will feel the Pulse and try the Sincerity of the Ministry; and appears to me to be recommended by so *many* cogent Reasons that I cannot *now* enumerate them. Many of them are obvious and I leave them to your Contemplations. Remember that Time will give you every Thing which the most sanguine Zeal for your Country can desire. It will, if you can maintain Peace a few Years longer, transfer the very Power you dread. And that Consideration ought to prevent us from asking a Security which our own Posterity will not want. As every Thing but the Rocks and Soil of Great Britain must come to America, she is only concerned to prevent such a rapid Flight as will neither be for her *present* Interest *nor for our's.*

Thus, my dear Sir, you have my undisguised Sentiments. I am sorry that they happen to run in a Line not popular perhaps on either Side of the Water. I may be mistaken; and therefore commit them to your Friendship under the strictest Charge of Secrecy till we feel a calmer Sky; which I beseech the Mercy of a good God to grant us in due Time. I am, with great Truth,

> Your most affectionate humble Servant
> *W S.*
> [*William Smith, Historical Memoirs, I.*]

9 TAUNTS FROM THE MOB: JOHN WETHERHEAD IS SALUTED WITH "DAMN HIM, SEIZE HIM, AND DROWN HIM"

John Wetherhead, a native of England who had lived as an importer in easy circumstances in New York for some twelve years before 1775, was an early sufferer from mob rule and was one of the fifty-nine Loyalists proscribed and banished by the Act of Attainder, October 22, 1779. His own narrative, explaining his conduct to royal commissioners appointed to inquire into losses of the Loyalists, offers at the same time a picture of the repercussions in New York of the clash at Lexington.

[1775]

❡   In the year 1774, but principally in the year 1775, when it became evident that the designs of the Ring Leaders of the Faction throughout America were directly aimed at a Serious Revolt from the Sover^ty of Great Britain, your Memorialist was then in possession of a considerable Fortune which not only enabled him to live in Affluence and Hospitality but, together with the Character which he flatters himself he bore amongst his Fellow Citizens, naturally gave him no small degree of Influence amongst them. Which influence he constantly and very assiduously employed, not in mobbing, Riot, and Turbulence, which some persons imagined wou'd give them great Eclat in the Eyes of Government, but in the calmer methods of Reason and friendly persuasion, always endeavouring to guard the deluded people from the Horrid evils which he saw them running into with senseless violence and which must unavoidably end in the Ruin of themselves and the Country.

The Success your Memorialist had in these well meant endeavours thwarted the designs of the Faction and drew upon him their secret hatred and Resentment which they soon found opportunities of exerting too effectually ag^t him. For the affair at Lexington, having Furnished them with specious pretences, hurried the people into violences tenfold greater than ever. Men of well known loyal principles were seized by the Mob, dragged to the Liberty poles, and there insulted and beaten in a Cruel manner, if they refused to kneel down and Curse the King and his Government.

During these Commotions the last legal supreme Court of Judicature was held at New York which happened in the Month of April, 1775. It was easy to see the extreme difficulty and danger of Execut^g the Laws, when all Gov^t was nearly dissolved. Capt. Cunningham, the provost Martial of the army in America, Mr. John Hill, Inspector of Passes at Brooklyn Ferry, with some other persons, for exerting themselves with an honest bravery in support of his Majestys just Authority, were seized and Imprisoned by the populace with an Intention of having them tryed for their Lives on Accusations intirely false and without foundation. The B-h Acts of Parliament were also intended to be indicted as Nuisances and a thousand other Enormities of the like nature calculated to insult Governm^t and its friends in the most impudent and atrocious manner were committed in the open face of day.

In this very critical and dangerous Situation of Things Your Memorialist was appointed foreman of the Grand Jury, which untill then always had, and at such a time more especially ought to have, been chosen from amongst the most considerable and respectable of the Inhabitants, whose principles and Resolution were to be depended upon. Several of this descript^n were indeed Summoned to serve, but Terror at the Occasion had driven them out of Town. Your Mems^t had therefore the Mortification of finding himself obliged to go through the Business of that Office wth the only assistance of two young Gentlemen unacquaint'd with Business of that Nature and Eleven others who were openly and declaratively Enemies to Governm^t and Abettors of all the above violent measures. These Eleven Men even went so far as to Communicate to the private Caballs and Committees of the Faction whatever passed in the Grand Jury Room and personally assisted in forming Schemes to put their designs in Execution, tho in direct violation of their Oaths, but the views and dark designs of the Faction must be promoted at the Risk of their Souls; Government must be made contemptible in the Eyes of the Mob and in order to accomplish this, Law, Common Sense, and Common

Honesty must be made a Sacrifice to Sedition. It required no small degree of exertion to counteract these wicked designs and persuade 11 Men out of 13 to do right, who had been determined at all events to do wrong. A Fixt resolution and steady Firmness, however, conquered every opposition and carried the point. The above innocent persons were restored to their Liberty and for that time all the wicked and violent intentions of the Faction were happily frustrated. But what was the Consequence to Your Memorialist? He could not pass the Streets without Insult nor could he be safe in his House. His Life was daily Threatned, and still following his own determined Rule of Conduct, Viz^t to render every assistance in his power to all those who were suffering under the same Tyranny, he saw himself at last forced to seek his own safety on Board of his Majestys Ships of War, where he remained at that time an exile for two Months.

The violence of the Mob becoming somewhat more moderate or rather Several Friends to Government having been made Members of the provincial Congress as a Check upon the rest, Leave was obtained for your Mems^t to return on Shore to his Family. This however continued but for a little time. The above Gentlemen were turned out of the provincial Congress and the violences began again. Under the rediculous pretence of attacking or defending themselves against Fort George a line in the form of a half Moon was begun across the Broadway (the Street in which your Memorialist dwells) but most manifestly intended to block up the Doors of his House.

He was therefore again exposed to perpetual Insults and Menaces and was every Moment in Jeopardy of his Life and could find no other alternative but to leave New York entirely and retire with his Family to Brooklyn on Long Island. J. W. kept close in his House untill his Family and Furniture were passed over the East River. But when he ventured to go himself he was Saluted with the most insulting Taunts of the Mob, who cryed out as he passed along: "Damn him, Seize him, and drown him." And by the time he had got a few yards from the Ferry Stairs Col^l Lasher with 14 Granadiers of the Militia came down to Seize him but they did not pursue him across the River. This was not effected without Insult and great difficulty. And there also He was not suffered to stay more than Three Weeks without Molestation. The Rebel Generals [Charles] Lee and Stirling [William Alexander], having been ordered to amuse the people with Building Fortifications, began to throw up lines round the House he occupied, which made it impossible for him to stay there any longer, and besides Consultations were held by the Justices of Brooklyn in the Rebel Interest to find pretences for seizing and confining him to prison. Having procured secret Information of these Intentions, which must sooner or later be put in execution whilst he should remain within their reach, he resolved to remove his Family immediately down to the Narrows where he should always have an Oppertunity of escape from the Malicious Attempts of his prosecutors. [*Memorial of October 3, 1783, Loyalist Transcripts, vol. XLIV, p. 122 ff.*]

10 THE BRUSH ON BREED'S HILL: DOROTHEA GAMSBY
RECOUNTS THE SCENE OF JUNE 17, 1775, TO HER
GRANDDAUGHTER

Dorothea Gamsby, an eyewitness to the Battle of Breed's (Bunker's) Hill, lived in Boston with her uncle, Sir George Nutting, and his wife, ardent Loyalists, who were obliged to depart with the British fleet on the evacuation of Boston. Military activities in the countryside made it impossible for Dorothea to join her own parents in Lynn, and she sailed with the Nuttings for Halifax and thence to a new home in Quebec. Thus she grew up apart from her family, marrying in time an English saddler, Richard Jemison. After the war ended she took her small daughter to Boston to find her family, but they had moved to a remote tract in northern Coos County, New Hampshire. Despite travel difficulties, she determined to pursue their trail into the northern forest instead of returning with the same ship which had brought her to Boston. The ship foundered on the return voyage and all aboard were lost. Her husband believed she had drowned, and it was many seasons before a message to the contrary reached him via a chance traveler from the New Hampshire wilderness. Jemison sought Dorothea out only to succumb to typhoid fever shortly after their joyous reunion. Widowed at twenty-five, she lived on in Coos County for over forty years, recollecting from time to time the historic events, especially the Tea Party and the Battle of Bunker's Hill, which she had witnessed during her three years' residence in Boston. Although she was only ten in 1775, the battle left an indelible impression upon her mind. She recounted the story to her granddaughter, who wrote it down in her grandmother's own phrases and preserved it.

❡   Months passed like the dreams of childhood while the Colonys were ripening to rebelion, bloodshed, and civil war. They sent a host of troops from home. Boston was full of them and they seemed to be there only to eat and drink and enjoy themselves, but one day there was more than usual commotion. Uncle said there had been an outbreak in the country, and then came a night when there was bustle, anxiety, and watching. Aunt and her maid walked from room to room, sometimes weeping. I crept after them trying to understand the cause of their uneasiness, full of curiosity and unable to sleep when everybody seemed wide awake and the streets full of people. It was scarcely daylight when the booming of the cannon on board the ships in the harbour shook every house in the Citty. My uncle had been much abroad lately and had only sought his pillow within the hour but he came immediately to my aunt's room, saying he would go and learn the cause of the fireing and come again to inform us. He had not left the house when a servant in livery called to say that the rebels had colected in force on Breed's Hill, were getting up fortifications, and that Governor Gage requested his presence. "There must be a brush," he said, "for General Howe has ordered out the troops to dislodge them." We were by this time thoroughly frightened but uncle bade [us] keep quiet, said there was no danger, and left us.

You may depend we sought the highest window we had as soon as the light of advancing day gave us reason to hope for a sight of the expected contest. There they were, the audacious rebels! hard at work, makeing what seemed to me a monstrous fence.

"What is it they are going to do, aunt, and what are they makeing that big fence for?"

"They mean to shoot our King's soldiers, I supose," she said, "and probably the fireing is intended to drive them away."

"But, Aunt, the cannon balls will kill some of them. See, see, the soldiers and the banners! O, Aunt, they will be killed! Why can't they stay out of the way?"

The glittering host, the crashing music, all the pomp and brilliance of war moved up toward that band of rebels, but they still laboured at their entrenchment; they seemed to take no heed. The bullets from the ships, the advanceing column of British warriors were alike un-noticed. "I should think they would begin to get out of the way," said my aunt.

Every available window and roof was filled with anxious spectators, watching the advanceing regulars. Every heart, I dare say, throbed as mine did and we held our breath, or rather it seemed to stop and oppress the labouring chest of its own acord, so intensely we awaited the expected attack, but the troops drew nearer and the rebels toiled on.

At length one who stood conspicuously above the rest waved his bright weapon; the explosion came attended by the crash of music, the shrieks of the wounded, the groans of the dying. My aunt fainted. Poor Abby, [the maid], looked on like one distracted. I screamed with all my might. The roar of artilery continued, but the smoke hid the havoc of war from our view. The housekeeper attended to my aunt and beged for somebody to go for Dr. [Joseph] Warren, but everybody was to much engaged with watching the smokeing battlefield. O, how wild and terrific was that long day! Old as I am, the memory of that fearful contest will sometimes come over my spirit as if it had been but yesterday.

Men say it was not much of a fight, but to me it seems terrible. Charleston was in flames, women and children flying from their burning homes sought reffuge in the citty. Dismay and terror, wailing and distraction impressed their picture on my memory, never to be effaced.

By and by drays, carts, and every description of vehicle that could be obtained were seen nearing the scene of conflict and the roar of artillery seaced. Uncle came home and said the rebels had retreated. Dr. Warren was the first who fell that day. Then came the loads of wounded men attended by long lines of soldiers, the gay banners torn and soiled, a sight to be remembered a lifetime.

I have read many times of the glory of war but this one battle taught me, however it be painted by poet or novelist, there is nothing but wo and sorrow and shame to be found in the reality.

Want, utter destitution to many folowed and when the 12 of August came round and the British troops with the loyal citizens of Boston attempted to celebrate the birthday of their young Prince; scant and course was the cheer their stores afforded. They were temperance people then from sheer necessity.

The winter passed, I cannot tell how, but when spring came everybody went on board the shiping in the harbour, at least so it seemed to me, for the officers and soldiers went and everybody that I knew or cared for, except my Father's family, seemed huddled together in a vessel so small that no room was left for comfort. [*Dorothea Gamsby, Dorothea, written down by Belle Thorn, No. Stratford, N.H.*]

[49]

11 FLORA MACDONALD, BEAUTIFUL SCOTTISH HEROINE OF CULLODEN, INSPIRES THE LOYALIST HIGHLANDERS BEFORE THE BATTLE OF MOORE'S CREEK

In the backcountry of North Carolina, Loyalist sentiment was prematurely fanned into action. Governor Josiah Martin had been so optimistic that the inhabitants along the upper reaches of the Cape Fear River, especially the Scottish Highlanders and some former Regulators, still resentful of their defeat in 1771, would rise up in support of a British expedition coming from the coast that he urged the undertaking on General Gage. Donald MacDonald and Donald McLeod were appointed Brigadier General and Colonel, respectively, to lead a Loyalist uprising and make a rendezvous with Clinton's forces near Cape Fear in February of 1776. The Highlanders, mostly recent arrivals in America, stuck together, clinging to their own language and customs, and were loyal to their own leaders. The enterprise nonetheless was imprudent and ill-timed, for the ships were delayed and the uprising uncoordinated with the hoped-for movement of British regulars from the fleet. Although the undertaking was well equipped in Highland zeal and Scottish trappings of kilts and bagpipes, it lacked proper military materiel, adequate training, and wise tactics. It blundered into a well-entrenched enemy at Moore's Creek Bridge, and half the spirited army of some 1,700 troops were casualties; 850 were taken prisoner. Thus the first organized effort of the Loyalists to fight for the King ended in disaster.

The most colorful figure in rousing the Scotch Highlanders to rally to the King's standard was Flora MacDonald, the wife of Major Allan MacDonald, and the beauty whose rescue of Bonnie Prince Charlie after the Battle of Culloden in 1746 had made her a legendary figure among Scottish immigrants. Born in 1722 in the Outer Hebrides, she lived in Skye until 1774 when, impoverished, she emigrated with part of her family to North Carolina. In 1776, when Highlanders were being recruited to suppress the rebellion, she accompanied her husband on horseback, going from house to house to persuade fellow clansmen to join the King's standard. She wrote to a friend February 1, 1776: "Allan leaves tomorrow to join Donald's [MacDonald] standard at Cross Creek, and I shall be alone wi' my three bairns. Canna ye come and stay wi' me awhile? There are troublous times ahead I ween. God will keep the right. I hope all our ain are in the right, prays your good friend."[1]

On February 18, as the army was preparing to march from Cross Creek to Cape Fear, Flora, mounted on a snow-white horse, addressed the men in Gaelic in the public square, and then rode up and down the columns reviewing them and inspiring the troops to bravery. When the army broke camp, she returned to Killiegrey, the 550-acre estate in Anson County which her husband had bought shortly before. Nine days later the brave Highlanders were scattered, killed, or taken prisoner at the bridge. Among the captives was her husband.

Troublous times were indeed ahead for Flora MacDonald. While her husband during the next few years was confined and paroled at Halifax, North Carolina, and in Pennsylvania, she was obliged to appear before the North Carolina Committee of Safety. In November 1777, his property was confiscated. Her two daughters were mistreated; the rings were taken from their fingers and the handkerchiefs torn from around their necks. The rebels then, "putting their swords into their bosom, split down their silk dresses and, taking them out into the yard, stripped them of all their outer clothing."[2] In 1779, at her husband's insistence, she returned to Skye, selling their silverware to raise money for the passage of herself and four children.[3] Her ship was overhauled by a French privateer and again, as before the Moore's Creek Battle, she urged the sailors to vigorous resistance, risking her life and suffering a broken arm in the encounter. Excerpts from letters after her arrival in Scotland and in Skye show the same indomitable spirit in adversity as when she left Skye for North Carolina and when she sent her husband and clansmen off to a hopeless battle for the King.

DUNWEGEN, SKYE, 12th JULY, 1780

❲ *To Mrs. Alexander MacKenzie*

I have arrived here a few days ago with my young daughter, who

---

[1] J. R. McLean, *Flora MacDonald in America,* Lumberton, N.C.: 1909, p. 45.
[2] E. W. Caruthers, *Interesting Revolutionary Incidents and Sketches of Character, Chiefly in the "Old North State,"* Philadelphia: 1854, p. 391.
[3] Walter Clark, ed., *State Records of North Carolina,* Winston: 1896, vol. XIII, p. 64.

promises to be a stout Highland "Caileag," quite overgrown of her age. . . .
I hope we will soon have peace re-established to our great satisfaction,
which, as it's a thing long expected and wished for, will be for the utility
of the whole nation, especially to poor me, who has my all engaged. Fond
to hear news, and yet afraid to get it. [*McLean, Flora MacDonald, p. 81.*]

EDIN[r] MAY 17-1780

❬ *To Donald McDonald, Esq* [Glasgow merchant]
Sir—
Youl be surprised to be troubled wt a letter from one personally
unknown to you. I am Mrs. MacDonald late of Kingsborrow in Sky. I
came lately from London to this place. I crossed to there from Nova Scotia.
I have been during the winter in London & was in very bad health. . . .

It is recommended to me my Physicians to make all possible speed
to the highlands for the benefite of the goat Whey. I mean to go to Sky by
Inverness as being the most expeditious way. I propose to take up my
residence in the Longisland—I have Some things to be sent to that place.
I beg therefore that you would do me the honour to convey them to my
Cousin Boysdale first opportunity. . . . [*MacDonald, The Truth about
Flora MacDonald, p. 111.*]

12 ANDREW ELLIOT COMMENTS THAT HALF THE ACTS OF TRADE ARE IMPROPER AND KEEP THE MERCHANTS CURSING THEM

Andrew Elliot was a younger son of a noble Scottish family. Finding that
his brother, Sir Gilbert Elliot, would be the sole heir to his father's title
and estate, Andrew Elliot repaired to America in 1747 and became a
merchant. At the time of the Stamp Act controversy he held the office
of Customs Collector, continuing in that office until the Revolution. When
General Charles Lee took possession of New York in early February 1776,
Elliot's house, ideally located at the entrance of the town on a height over-
looking both rivers, was marked out for a hospital. He promptly removed
his family to Amboy, New Jersey, explaining: "As half the Town and more
had moved on Lee's coming, the destruction I saw of furniture and the

distress of the poor made me resolve to leave all mine but necessaries."
He then offered his house to a Presbyterian parson, a good friend, hoping
by this means to save it, although his garden and grounds had already been
trodden down by Connecticut troops. When the news broke that troops
from Boston were shipping to New York, he followed his family, which
he described as nineteen in all, both black and white, "packed up in four
rooms" in Amboy.[1]

Among his many letters to Sir Gilbert Elliot is the following one
describing New York as he left it and commenting on the mistakes Britain
had made in the Acts of Trade because of ignorance of the way they would
operate in America, often defeating their very purpose.

AMBOY 25 MARCH 1776

❧ *My Dear Brother*
. . . You can't form to yourself a more distressed place than NY
crowd'd with armed men, left by its Inhabitants and such a scene of misery
as that afford'd was terrible. For my part it not only oversatt my spirits but
ruin[ed] my purse. I'm still affraid that it is fated to destruction for I don't
think the hands it is now in are anxious to save the Town more than to
keep it from falling into other hands, if that can't be done. The Capts of
the Men of War, Parker and Vandeput, have great merit (They are men of
sense). Almost every step has been taken to bring on the destruction of the
Town [to keep it] from them, but they justly saw that the Inhabitants was
ans[ble] for nothing, the Town being intirely in the hands of arm'd men
from Connecticut and Jersey. So much for unfortunate NY. . . .

As to the article of internall polity, I'm convinced they [the Congress]
wou'd themselves, when they coolly considered consequences, tread back
most of their first ground. . . . Things appear in a very different light,
when you really wish to settle matters, from what they do when you are
enumerating to inflame. As to the point of taxation, Lord North's motion
seems to settle that point and, as to trade, it will make in favor of G. B.
to give up many, at least some, of the acts complained of. I coud mention
severall but only read the hatt act; it actually makes against the point it

---

[1] Andrew Elliot to Sir Gilbert Elliot, Mar. 25, 1776, *Elliot Papers,* .N.Y. Historical
Society.

means to serve, that is, stoping that manufacture in America. For legally no man in America that lives out of a Sea port Town can wear a British made hatt; so that every Township is of necessity obliged to have a hatter. This very Province of New Jersey imports no goods from England, so must make their hatts. This Act is in its effect calculated to force America[n] manufactures. G. B. continues the act and America complains of it which plainly shows that in some things they don't know their own Interests.

You must think I mean myself because I mention Custom house officers, but beleive me it will be necessary when you are settling the commerciall points to have an officer that has been in the use of executing the laws of trade to tell you how they work. Laws at home for trade are passed with a good intent but are often framed by people that neither understand trade nor know Countries. By this means they go by what they daily see so that what ans^{rs} in G. B. with ease becomes, from local Sircumstances in America, a reall Greivance never intended by Parlia^t. This is evident in the River trade. Your open boats will carry two of our Deck't boats because our bays require all boats to be Deck. But the indulgence meant to be given to inland trade boats is expressly confined to open boats. Besides after the Laws are passt Custom house Bonds and forms are to be made out and they are done in such a manner that I dare to say, there is not now above one of the Bonds taken that by law coud be recover'd, even the old enumeratd is so davided as to make it void. In short if I was with you I coud show you the impropriety of half the acts of trade and so might any fool that has been 11 years executing them. A new plan and system ought to be gon on [worked on] and a number of forms avoid'd as that is more felt here than at home. We have no Brokers, every merch^t attend[s] at the Custom house his own business so that either the multiplicity of Bonds, the delay, or Insolence of office, and often all together, always keeps the Merch^t cursing the acts of trade. Besides they are so complicated that those that want to act up to them don't know how ... [*Andrew Elliot Papers, N. Y. Historical Society.*]

Committees of Safety: Confrontations, Threats, and Rough Handling

Before adjourning in October 1774, the First Continental Congress had expanded the Massachusetts Solemn League and Covenant into the Continental Association, by which twelve colonies agreed to embargo and boycott British goods. Georgia, the thirteenth, adopted a softened form later. The Congress and the local committees set up to detect conspiracies and administer the pledge had no clear legal authority to command obedience to the boycott, only the sanction which came from extralegal assumption of power. Yet by April 1775, the machinery for administering the pledge to support the Association was in effective operation in all the colonies. Local town or county committees, often self-appointed and usually composed of the Sons of Liberty, interpreted loosely the authorization of the Continental Congress to observe the conduct of, to publicize, and to condemn those citizens who refused the pledge. The nonsigners and nonjurors were to be punished by being exposed to public scorn, by having their interests undermined and discredited, and by being ostracised. The purpose of the committees was not justice or a regard for civil rights, but rooting out Loyalists and blocking their support of the British cause. Refusal of the pledge to join the Association became the most significant early touchstone for identifying those people whose sympathies were either uncertain or out of tune with rebel purposes.

In smoking out the disloyal or the wavering, committees of safety looked into private papers, spied on people's conduct, and informed on suspects. Besides failure to join the Association, take an oath, or abide by the measures of Congress, the committees of safety examined other transgressions. These covered a wide range from passing information, guiding, recruiting for the British, or helping Loyalist refugees, to petty offenses, such as drinking tea or using abusive language about the rebels. Samuel Smith of New Britain was convicted for selling hens' eggs at 1 shilling per dozen, Samuel Scott of Farmington was accused of laboring on a fast day, and Solomon Cowles and his wife, Martha, were obliged to publish an apology in the *Connecticut Courant* for allowing two wayfarers to drink tea at their inn.[1] Neighbors reported on each other's speech, and suspected persons were ordered before their local committees to explain statements overheard, to recant and apologize, or to be labeled inimical to America.[2] The resentment aroused by the committees' activities and by the extralegal administration of oaths of loyalty was enough to turn a prospective patriot into a committed Tory. William Franklin, Governor of New Jersey, wrote that he feared his official mail would be opened by the Sons of Liberty if he did not send it under cover to a private person.[3]

The intimidation by these committees took many forms, from vilification, humiliation, and bullying to whippings, beatings, and even more serious physical violence. The committees operated capriciously, for there was no uniformity of procedure throughout the Colonies. William Davis

---

[1] Julius Gay, *Farmington in the War of the Revolution*, Hartford: 1893, pp. 13-14.
[2] Enoch Bartlett of Haverhill, N.H., acknowledged before thirty members of the Haverhill and Bradford Committees that propagating his political principles had been imprudent, that he was sorry he had kept his shop open on a fast day, and that he approved the Continental Congress. Enoch Bartlett to Nathaniel Peabody, September 23, 1774, *Nathaniel Peabody Papers*, N.H. Historical Society.
[3] William Franklin to William Strahan, May 7, 1775, Morgan Library.

of Augusta, for example, who declared his opposition to the Sons of Liberty, was mildly treated; he was ordered by the local committee to be drummed around the liberty tree three times and publicized as a "person inimical to the rights and liberties of America."[4] Daniel Leonard was forced to sit on a cake of ice to cool his loyalty.[5] The Reverend James Nichols of New Cambridge (Bristol) was dragged through a brook after being tarred and feathered.[6] Sometimes chimneys were blocked to smoke out the independent thinkers. In Virginia, one device was to handcuff a Tory to a Negro.[7] Ann Hulton, a Loyalist from Chester, Massachusetts, wrote to her friend Mrs. Lightbody about harsher treatment: "The cruelties wch are exercised on all those who are in their [the Rebels] power is shocking; by advice from Kennebec the Committee there had sentenced a Man to be buried alive for wishing success to the Kings Troops, & that the sentence had been executed upon him. At Roxbury M^r Ed. Brinleys wife whilst lying in, had a guard of Rebels always in her room, who treated her wth rudness & indecency, exposing her to the view of their banditti, as a sight 'See a tory woman' and strip^d her & her Children of all their Linnen & Cloths."[8]

Tarring and feathering, followed by a rough ride on a rail or a parade through the town amid the scorn and derision of the mob, was no mild punishment, but an effective one which the Tories seriously dreaded. Hugh Gaine's Tory paper, *Mercury,* recounted how Dr. Joseph Clarke of Reading "was seized in the Township of Hartford, Connecticut, and to the indelible disgrace of their Police, carried upon a Rail about the Parish, under which Cruelty he several Times fainted. When dismissed by his Tormentors and examined by Dr. Tidmarsh, he was found to be injured in a Manner unfit for Description in a Newspaper. The Doctor was menaced with the same

---

[4] *Georgia Gaz.,* Aug. 4, 1775. See *Historical Collections of Georgia,* Rev. George White, ed., 1854, p. 607.
[5] Frank Moore, *Diary of the American Revolution,* New York: 1860, vol. I, p. 359, Daniel Leonard called the Boston Committee of Correspondence "the foulest, subtlest and most venemous serpent that ever issued from the eggs of sedition." *Massachusetensis,* London: 1776, p. 34.
[6] E. Leroy Pond, *The Tories of Chippeny Hill, Connecticut,* New York: 1909, p. 19.
[7] Colonel Woodford to Virginia Convention, December 12, 1775. Peter Force, ed., *American Archives,* 4th Ser., p. 245. "Two gentlemen this moment brought me in a young Scotchman, named Hamilton, who confesses he has borne arms and was at this fort [Great Bridge] in Gilmore's co. I have ordered him to be coupled to one of his bro. black soldiers, with a pair of handcuffs, which is the resolution I have taken shall be the fate of all these cattle."
[8] Ann Hulton, *Letters of a Loyalist Lady,* Cambridge, Mass.: 1927, pp. 85-86.

[57]

Treatment for his Humanity to the Sufferer, whose only Crime was speaking in Terms of Respect of the King and of his Government."[9]

Peter Elting in a letter to Captain Richard Varick (June 13, 1776) commented on the rough handling of the Tories in New York: "We had some Grand Toory Rides in this City this week & in particular yesterday. Several of them were handeld verry Roughly Being Carried thrugh the streets on Rails, there Cloaths Tore from there backs and there Bodies pritty well mingled with the dust. Amongst them were C-, Capt. [Theophilus] Hardenbrook, Mr. [Rem] Rapelje, Mr. Queen the Poticary & Lessly the barber. There is hardly a toory face to be seen this morning. . . ."[10]

There follow several accounts by other Loyalists of the manner of detecting the friends of government and the rough handling meted out to suspected persons.

I   THE THREAT OF THE TAR MOP: WILLIAM AITCHISON
OF NORFOLK, VIRGINIA, WARNS JAMES PARKER TO
BE ON GUARD

William Aitchison was a prominent merchant in Norfolk. In 1758 he formed a trading company with his brother-in-law James Parker, engaging profitably and extensively in diverse branches of trade. Both Aitchison and Parker were inveterate Loyalists from the start of the Revolution, and both were imprisoned in 1776 by the rebels, during the course of which hardship Aitchison died.[1] He sent Parker the following account of events in Williamsburg which had been sparked by a tea party on the York River, an occurrence which Parker fortuitously missed.

NOVEMBER 14, 1774

❦   . . . This morning Mr. [Samuel] Inglis, [Alexander] Diach, and others returned from the City where every method has been used to [force]

---

[9] *N.Y. Gaz. and Weekly Mercury,* Feb. 27, 1775, p. 3.

[10] Richard Varick, *Papers 1775-1779,* N.Y. Historical Society. See Rapelje's *Narrative.*

[1] Memorial of James Parker to the Commissioners enquiring into the Losses and Services of the American Loyalists, March 9, 1784. 920 PAR I 19/5, Liverpool Record Office.

every one [to] sign the association. A large tar mop was erected near the Capital w^t a Bag of feathers to it and a Barl. of Tar underneath. Several people were called before the Committee and obliged to revoke any unguarded expressions they had used. Amongst the rest was Woodrich and Wallace for taking away their Tea from the Ship that lay there. Their lives were threatned but tar and feathers was thought to be the Slightest punishment they coud get of[f] w^h. However, by the interception of the Speaker, Treasurer Pendleton, Bland, and others, who employed all their oratorial powers in their favour, they got clear by promising to deliver the Tea (altho' now in Carolina) either to the Nansemond or Norf^o. Committee to be Burned. I am really glad you were not there. Mr. Diach tells me there was a complaint lodged w. the Committee against you for some words spoken here and, had you been upon the spot, there is little doubt but you would have been as roughly handled as any of 'em. I beg you to be more upon your guard for the future. There is no contending against such Numbers [920 *PAR I no. 2, Record Office, Liverpool.*]

2 A DEAD OWL: STEPHEN RESCO OF STOCKBRIDGE RECEIVES A FINAL TOUCH TO HIS COAT OF TAR AND FEATHERS

Author unknown. Sent to Mr. Printer for insertion in his paper.

[1775]

❡ One, Stephen Resco of Stockbridge, being the Summer past at work on the grants not far from Skenesborough, had the Misfortune to fall into the hands of the King's Troops; after keeping him Prisoner a few Days they set him at Liberty on his promising to remain quiet and peaceable on his Farm. Soon after he was taken Prisoner by a Company of Continental Rangers and for no other Crime but because he had once been Prisoner to the King's Troops, was for a considerable time kept under guard at Bennington and from thence sent to Great Barrington Gaol where he was a long time closely confined, till at length the Gaoler, not being able to find any observer, or prosecutor, or anyone that acknowledged themselves concerned in his Commitment, began to allow him some Liberty; he let him out to Labour and at length sent him to the Committee of Stockbridge to know whether they would do anything towards liberating him, but the Committee, professing to have nothing against him or anything to do with him, and the gaoler, finding him to be an honest, inoffensive man, suffered him to go home to his family on *Parole.* He had not, however, been at home many days before the Saints of Lenox assembled to call him to account. The pious, the humane, the godly, whining, canting *Deacon Lee,* Father-in-law to the intrepid, the valiant, and heroic *Gen*[^l] [John] *Patterson,* who acquired immortal Fame at the Evacuation of Ticonderoga, and the famous patriot *Capt*[^n] [Charles] *Dibble,* joined with one *Willard,* renowned for his Gallantry with the Copper-coloured *Females* of Stockbridge, sent forth a Herd of young Fellows and convened the said Resco before them; and after a long and godly Exhortation from the fanatical Deacon they proceeded to besmear him with Soot and Tar, which they overlaid with Feathers, *secundum Artem,* [according to the rules of the art]; they now crown him with an *Owl* which had been killed for that purpose and in that Plight they drive him before them to Stockbridge where the County Convention was then sitting, to whom they present him, expecting the universal Applause of the Board for their Patriotism, but to their great Mortification they got nothing but a severe Rebuke for their Conduct. However, the Convention, not thinking the poor Tory safe in the Neighborhood of the *godly Deacon,* the *heroic Capt*[^n], and the *gallant squaw-hunter,* recommended it to him to resign himself again to the Gaoler for his own Safety, which he patiently submited to without either Officer or Guard to conduct him.

Query: As tarring and feathering only has been found by Experience to be ineffectual in subduing that stubborn Race, whether the principal Efficacy in the present Case is not to be ascribed to the Owl? [*Pocumtuck Valley Memorial Assn., Deerfield, Mass. no. 242, 8, E-18.*]

3   JOIN OR SUFFER: JANET SCHAW DESCRIBES THE
OPERATIONS OF THE WILMINGTON COMMITTEE OF
SAFETY IN OVERCOMING THE DISINCLINATION OF THE
NORTH CAROLINIANS FOR REVOLUTION

Outstanding among the many contemporary descriptions of the methods of the committees of safety is the excerpt from the journal of Janet Schaw, a visitor from Scotland to the plantation of the Loyalist John Rutherford in Wilmington, North Carolina. She was the sister of Alexander Schaw, a customs official appointed to St. Kitts, who was on leave from his post in 1775 to look after his private affairs in North Carolina. Even though a transient in America, and thus not a Loyalist, her observations reflect Loyalist sentiments. At the same time, her parting words reveal her sympathy for her fellow countrymen on both sides of the civil war.

JULY 1775

❪ May God deliver him [the Governor] and all our distressed countrymen from the present situation. A few months ago the task would have been easy; it is still possible, but (God make me a false prophetess) it will not be long so. The inclination of this country is however far from being generally for this work [of revolution]. Indolent and inactive, they have no desire to move, even where their own immediate interest calls them. All they are promised is too distant to interest them; they suffer none of those abuses they are told of and feel their liberty invaded only by the oppressive power of the Congress and their Agents, who at this Season are pressing them from their harvest, for they know not what purpose. But tho' they show at first a great degree of reluctance to go, yet they believe there is no retreat, after they have been once under arms and are convinced that from that moment they fight for their lives and properties, which by that act are both forfeited to their blood-thirsty enemies. You may therefore be assured they will not fail to exert all the activity and courage they are able to muster up, and, once engaged themselves, are willing to draw in others.

It is a most unfortunate circumstance they have got time to inculcate this idea. Three months ago, a very small number had not any thing to apprehend; a few troops landing and a general amnesty published would have secured them all at home. . . . At present the martial law stands thus: An officer or committeeman enters a plantation with his posse. The Alternative is proposed: Agree to join us, and your persons and properties are safe; you have a shilling sterling a day; your duty is no more than once a month appearing under Arms at Wilmingtown, which will prove only a merry-making, where you will have as much grog as you can drink. But if you refuse, we are directly to cut up your corn, shoot your pigs, burn your houses, seize your Negroes and perhaps tar and feather yourself. Not to chuse the first requires more courage than they are possessed of, and I believe this method has seldom failed with the lower sort. No

sooner do they appear under arms on the stated day, than they are ha-
rangued by their officers with the implacable cruelty of the king of Great
Britain, who has resolved to murder and destroy man, wife and child,
and that he has sworn before God and his parliament that he will not spare
one of them; and this those deluded people believe more firmly than their
creed, and who is it that is bold enough to venture to undeceive them.
The King's proclamation[1] they never saw; but are told it was ordering the
tories to murder the whigs, and promising every Negro that would murder
his Master and family that he should have his Master's plantation. This
last Artifice they may pay for, as the Negroes have got it amongst them and
believe it to be true. Tis ten to one they may try the experiment, and in
that case friends and foes will be all one. . . .

[October, 1775]

Farewell, unhappy land, for which my heart bleeds in pity. Little does
it signify to you who are the conquered or who the victorious; you are
devoted to ruin, whoever succeeds. Many years will not make up [for]
these few last months of depredation and yet no enemy has landed on their
coast. Themselves have ruined themselves; but let me not indulge this
melancholy . . . [*Andrews, ed., Janet Schaw, Journal, pp. 197-199;
pp. 211-212.*]

4   RECANT OR HANG

John Hopkins was a mariner from Savannah. He was overheard to have
muttered "Damnation to America" in drinking a toast and thus offended
the Sons of Liberty, who determined to make an example of him. They
ordered him to recant or hang. His deposition and Governor Wright's
letter to Lord Dartmouth, Secretary for the Colonies, recount the incident.

---

[1] June 13, 1775, offering pardon to all persons who would lay down their arms.

John Hopkins Is Ordered to "Beg All America Pardon"

JULY 25, 1775

❡ This Deponent [John Hopkins] being duly sworn on the Holy Evangelists of Almighty God maketh Oath and saith That about nine of the Clock in the Evening of the twenty fourth Instant as this Deponent was sitting at supper with his family there came to this Deponent's House a number of Persons (some were in disguise) and opened the door. That Joseph Reynolds of Savannah Bricklayer, Capt, McCluer & Captn Bunner at Present of Savannah Mariners laid hold of this Deponent without saying anything to him. That as soon as the aforesaid People laid hold of this Deponent a great number rushed in & hurried this Deponent out of his house & led him to the out side of the Town, That they Consulted to tar & feather him but the Majority resolved to Carry him to a more public place. Accordingly they led this Deponent into the middle of the square near to the Dial in Savannah & striped this Deponent of his Jacket & Shirt and with great reluctance left the rest of his Apparel on him, And they proceeded to tar and feather this Deponent, And immediately put this Deponent into a Cart & Carted him up & down the Streets of Savannah for upwards of three Hours in the Above Condition That during the aforesaid Time they Carted this Deponent to the Liberty tree And there swore they would hang him. That the said Bunner said "he was rather fat But he would go up the tree & hang this Deponent." That the said Bunner further said "that unless he would drink 'Damnation to all Tories and Success to American Liberty'" he should be hung immediately, which request this Deponent was obliged to comply with, that they continued to abuse this Deponent, gave him a great Deal of ill Language & upbraided him with his Conduct. That some one or other said That if they Could lay hold of the Parson they would put him along side of this Deponent in the Cart. That this Deponent also heard said in the Mob that Mr. Smith [Rector of Christ Church] should be next. And that they intended to Continue on untill they had Tarred and feathered all the Tories, or Words to That Effect. . . . That between the Hours of Twelve & One of the Clock at Midnight they discharged this Deponent at the Vendue House with orders to beg "all America pardon." [*So. Car. Gazette, August 1, 1775, Ga. Hist. Soc., Collecs., vol. II, p. 200.*]

The Governor of Georgia Fills in a Few Details for Lord Dartmouth

SAVANNAH IN GEORGIA THE 29TH JULY 1775

❡ *My Lord*

On the 24th instant about 9 OClock at Night I heard a very great Huzzaing in the Streets and on Sending out found they had seized upon one Hopkins a Pilot and were Tarring and Feathering him, and Soon after they brought him in a Cart along by my House and such a Horrid Spectacle I really never Saw; they made the Man Stand up in a Cart with a Candle in his Hand and a great many Candles were Carried round the Cart and thus they went through most of the Streets in town for upwards of three Hours.

And on Inquiring what he had done, I was Informed that he had behaved disrespectfully towards the Sons of Liberty and Drank some Toasts which gave great offence. . . . I cannot believe this Conduct is Promoted or Approved of by the People in General, but only by some very Violent ones amongst them and the Mob. [*PRO Am. & W. Ind., vol. 236, Ga. Hist. Soc., Collecs., vol. III, pp. 200-203.*]

5   TEMPORARY ACCOMMODATIONS: THOMAS BROWNE OF AUGUSTA OBLIGES HIS TORMENTORS

Colonists, faced with the interrogation and pressures of the committees of safety, reacted in diverse ways, some, like the Reverend Ranna Cossitt, standing foursquare for the right of King and Parliament to legislate for the Colonies, and some accommodating the committees' demands, dissembling their true position. Two Tories, for example, who succeeded in keeping their true sentiments concealed for two years were Farquard Campbell and Thomas Rutherford of Cumberland, North Carolina. They were prominent men who served in the North Carolina Provincial Congress. They signed the Association and voted for the resolution supporting independence. All the time they were in correspondence with the enemy. Both were finally taken prisoner and their colors exposed.[1] A fair number

[1] Reverend E. W. Caruthers, *Interesting Revolutionary Incidents and Sketches of Character, Chiefly in the "Old North State,"* Philadelphia: 1854, p. 218.

of Tories recanted and joined the patriots, either from duress or a lack of dedication in the first place. Opportunism and the realities of the military situation played an important part. Occasionally a recantation did not stick, and when the opportunity was propitious, the erstwhile Tory, then penitent rebel, joined the King's cause again. These weathercocks, whether secret Loyalists or genuine neutralists, constituted a constant menace to the rebels. A large segment of the colonists, however, as in every war, merely wanted the catastrophe to pass them by; they could adjust to either victor.

One example of temporary accommodation and the most famous tarring and feathering incident in Georgia concerned the ill treatment in August 1775 of Thomas Browne, which turned him into a vindictive Tory. Some Georgia Whigs believed he was the son of Lord North and had been directed by him to subvert the dedication of the rebels to the rebellion. Browne had ridiculed the Whigs in toasts, and the committee ordered him taken. The sentence of tar and feathers was roughly executed, for the rebels burned his feet, causing the loss of several toes, and cut off his hair. They made him swear his future allegiance to America and declare his repentance of his past actions and words. Although he was not able to walk for months, he eventually recovered, repudiated his oath, and escaped, bent on vengeance. His revenge included leading the Florida Rangers in their ravaging expeditions and, as Indian Superintendent, stirring up the Cherokees, Choctaws, Chickasaws, and Upper Creeks to join the British. In 1780 his Tory regiment took Augusta, and Browne allowed them to wreak vengeance on the wounded rebels left behind, many of whom were executed in his presence.[2] James Johnson, Loyalist publisher of the *Georgia Gazette,* carried an account of the cruelty to Browne in his paper.

AUGUST 30, 1775

❡   This day a respectable body of the Sons of Liberty marched from this place to New Richmond in South Carolina in order to pay a visit to Thomas Browne and William Thompson . . . for having publicly and otherwise expressed themselves enemies to the measures now adopted for the support of American liberty and signing an association to that effect; besides their

[2] Browne denied the atrocities charged against him and vindicated his actions. Thomas Browne to Dr. David Ramsay, December 25, 1786. Ms. no. 19, Charleston Library Society. See George White, ed., *Historical Collections of Georgia,* 1854, pp. 614–619.

using their utmost endeavours to inflame the minds of the people and to persuade them to associate and be of their opinion. But upon their arrival they found the said Thompson like a traitor had run away. The said Thomas Browne, being requested in civil terms to come to Augusta to try to clear himself of such accusations, daringly repeated that he was not, nor would be, answerable to them or any other of them for his conduct, whereupon they politely escorted him into Augusta, where they presented him with a genteel and fashionable suit of tar and feathers and afterwards had him exhibited in a cart from the head of Augusta to Mr. Weatherford's, where out of humanity they had him taken proper care of for the night; and on the next morning he, the said Thomas Browne, having publicly declared upon his honour and consented voluntarily to swear that he repented for his past conduct and that he would for the future, at the hazard of his life and fortune, protect and support the rights and liberties of America and, saying that the said Thompson had misled him and that therefore he would use his utmost endeavours to have his name taken from the association he had signed as aforesaid; and further that he would do all in his power to discountenance the proceedings of a set of men in the Ninety-Six District in South Carolina, called Fletchall's Party; upon which the said Browne was then discharged and complimented with a horse and chair to ride home. But the said Thomas Browne that time, having publicly forfeited his honor and violated the oath voluntarily taken as aforesaid, is therefore not to be considered for the future in the light of a gentleman and they, the said Thomas Browne and William Thompson, are hereby published as persons inimical to the rights and liberties of America; and it is hoped all good men will treat them accordingly.

N. B. The said Thomas Browne is now a little remarkable; he wears his hair very short, and a handkerchief tied around his head in order that his intellects this cold weather may not be affected. [*Georgia Gaz., Aug. 30, 1775. See White, ed., Hist. Collecs. Ga., pp.* 606–607.]

6 DICTATES OF CONSCIENCE: ELEAZER RUSSELL, A QUAKER,
INVOKES HIS "ORIGINAL SCRUPLE" AGAINST THE SHEDDING
OF HUMAN BLOOD

New Hampshire Loyalists have been considered weak in numbers and temperate in their Loyalism, and they were only mildly punished for their choice. Called before the committees of safety, they relied for justice on the reasonableness of their positions; most of them, in short, were trying to maintain a neutral stance. After the Continental Congress, on March 14, 1776, ordered the Association Test administered to all males over twenty-one, except lunatics, idiots, and Negroes, the New Hampshire Committee of Safety, through its local committee, offered the pledge to 8,567 people. Seven hundred eighty-one refused to sign, giving various explanations.[1] For example, twelve nonjurors in Richmond stated: "We do not Believe that it is the Will of God to take away the Lives of our fellow orators, not that We Come Out Against the Congress of American Liberties, but When Ever We are Convinct to the Contory We are Redy to join our Amarican Brieathen to Defend by Arms Against the Hostile Attempts of the British fleets and Armies." The Reverend John Houston gave his reasons: "Firstly Because he did not apprehend that the Hon[ble] committee meant that ministers Should Take up arms as Being inconsistent with their Ministerial Charge. Secondly Because he was already confin'd to the County of Hillsborough, therefore he thinks he Ought to be set at liberty before he Should Sign the Sd obligation. Thirdly Because there is three men Belonging to his Family already Inlisted in the Continental army."[2]

Among the nonsigners in New Hampshire was Eleazer Russell, a Quaker of Portsmouth and Postmaster of New Hampshire. He would not commit himself to "with Arms oppose the Hostile Proceedings of the British Fleets and Armies against the United American Colonies." He explained his refusal as deriving not from "humor" but from "an original scruple." His explanation was believed and his scruples respected, for the very day after independence was declared, he received an appointment as Maritime Officer of the Port of Piscataqua.

[1] Nathaniel Bouton, ed., *State Papers, N.H. Documents and Records, 1776-1783*, Concord: 1874, vol. VIII, p. 204; pp. 317-318. Otis Waite, *History of the Town of Claremont, N.H. 1764-1894,* Manchester: 1895, p. 225.
[2] Otis G. Hammond, "The Tories of New Hampshire," N.H. Historical Society *Proc.*, vol. V, pp. 287-288.

MAY 1776

❧ *To Joshua Wentworth*

. . . Respect to public authority inclined me much to sign it; but as I am utterly unable to comply with the Letter of it; can by no means do it without restriction & reserve.

The article of Defending the country with arms is explicit and peremptory, which the total loss of health makes me incapable of . . .

There is also an original scruple in my mind—strengthened by more than 30 years' reflection on the Subject—of the Lawfulness of Shedding human blood of any nation, except for crimes condemn'd by human Laws, founded on the Divine.

A tho't never enterd my heart but what was replete with the tenderest emotions for the country in its bleeding state. My Duty is clear in Submitting to the powers now in being in the colony and my Disposition fixd to Serve the public in every view consistent with the above Discription of my health and the right of conscience, as expressed in a late resolve of the Continental Congress. [*Peirce Papers, Atheneum, Portsmouth, N.H.*]

AUGUST 17, 1776

❧ *To Meschech Weare, Chairman of the Committee of Safety*

. . . It was, and is, merely to secure the morality of my mind that I was reluctant to put my name to it. Solemnly to bind myself to the performance of what nature and necessity rendered impossible, I started at the thought of. And tho' my health is mend'd, so wreck'd are my nerves that I cou'd not do one hour' military duty to save my life. The article of shedding blood in me is not a humor, but a principle—not an evasion, but a fact. It was received in early life and has "grown with my growth and strengthened with my strength." Not a partiality for British more than Savage blood. For, all circumstances considered, I think the latter more innocent than the former. [*Bouton, ed. State Papers, N.H. vol. VIII, pp. 317-318.*]

COLONEL JOHN PETERS RECOUNTS THE CONSEQUENCES IN
1775 OF REFUSING TO ABJURE THE KING AND SIGN THE
LEAGUE AND COVENANT

Colonel John Peters, a Connecticut delegate to the First Continental Congress and brother of the Reverend Samuel Peters, was mobbed three times for refusing to join the Association and was finally seized with the Reverend Ranna Cossitt and other churchmen and placed in close confinement. After his flight to Canada in 1776, he recruited men for the Queen's Loyal Rangers and became their commanding officer with the rank of lieutenant colonel. Unable to remain in America at the close of the war, he retired to England and lived there until his death in 1788. His *Narrative* written in Quebec describes the events of 1775 in the Connecticut Valley.

JULY 20, 1778

❆ Dr. Wheelock, President of Dartmouth College in New Hampshire, in conjunction with Deacon Bayley, Mr. Morey, and Mr. Hurd, all justices of the peace, put an end to the Church of England in this State, so early as 1775. They seized me, Capt. Peters, and all judges of Cumberland and Gloucester, the Rev. Mr. Cossitt and Mr. Cole, and all the Church people for 200 miles up the river (Connecticut), and confined us in close gaols, after beating and drawing us through water and mud. Here we lay for some time and were to continue in prison until we abjured the king and signed the league and covenant. Many died, one of which was Capt. Peters' son. We were removed from the gaol and confined in private houses at our own expense. Capt. Peters and myself were guarded by twelve rebel soldiers, while sick in bed, and we paid dearly for this honor; and others fared in like manner. I soon recovered from my indisposition, and took the first opportunity and fled to Canada, leaving Cossitt, Cole, Peters, Willis, Porter, Sumner, Paptin, etc. in close confinement, where they had misery, insults, and sickness enough. My flight was in 1776, since which my family arrived at Montreal, and inform me that many prisoners died; that Capt. Peters had been tried by court-martial and ordered to be shot for refusing to lead his company against the King's troops. He was afterwards reprieved, but still in gaol, and that he was ruined both in health and property; that Cossitt and Cole were alive when they came away, but were under confinement, and had more insults than any of the loyalists, because they had been ser-

vants of the Society, which, under pretense (as the rebels say) of propagating religion, had propagated loyalty, in opposition to the liberties of
America. [*Peters Papers, N.Y. Historical Society. Also Waite, History
of Claremont, p. 97.*]

7 DECEIT: GUY JOHNSON MISLEADS THE COMMITTEE OF
SAFETY AND WARNS OF THE INDIANS' "DREADFUL REVENGE"

Separation of Loyalists and rebels in Tryon County, New York, posed
particular difficulties because of the wide influence of the Loyalist Johnson
family in the Mohawk Valley and of their popularity with the Six Nations.
The majority of the outspoken Tories lived in the lower Mohawk district
of Tryon County, while Whig sentiment predominated in the western district in the counties of Palatine, Canajoharie, German Flatts, and Kings-
land. There were also many waverers throughout Tryon County who were
awaiting military developments before hoisting their colors. Freeholders
in the Palatine District determined even before the First Continental Congress where their sympathies lay. They assembled at Adam Louck's inn
in Stone Arabia and pledged their help to the distressed citizens of Boston.
They promptly endorsed the New York delegates to the Continental Congress, appointed a standing Committee of correspondence, and secured
signatures to the Association. They went even further in drawing the line
between rebels and Tories, implementing the Association by a resolve
(May 29, 1775) that no person should have "any Dealings or other Connections in the Way of Trade with any person or persons whatsoever who
have not signed the Association;" anyone who infringed the resolution
would be "dealt with as Enemies to the District and to their Country."
Thus the Tories in Tryon County were put on the defensive early in the
war.

The Tryon County Committee of Safety focused its attention first
on the Johnson family, who were actively dissuading inhabitants of the
lower district from accepting the measures of the Continental Congress.
Sir John Johnson and Guy Johnson, Superintendent of Indian Affairs,
had fortified Johnson Hall and had armed 150 Catholic Highlanders, as
well as Indians, and their agents had been stopping and searching people on

the King's Highway. The combined threat from these activities and from the Indians led the committee on June 3 to recommend that subscribers to the Association form themselves promptly into militia companies.[1]

Guy Johnson heard rumors that he was inciting the Indians against the inhabitants of the valley and that he and his family were to be seized to counteract the threat. In his letter to the local committee of safety, quoted below, he termed these reports "idle and ridiculous" and warned the committee of the Indians' "dreadful revenge" should they find their superintendent insulted. The committee assured him that the rumors about taking him captive were not true. It requested him to keep the Indians from interfering in the dispute with England and to disperse the armed men about him. On June 25, Guy Johnson sent the committee a second letter, as misleading and mendacious as the first, saying that his intentions in calling a congress of the Indians had been misconstrued and that he was surprised that anyone would think him "capable of setting the Indians on the peaceable inhabitants of this country."[2]

GUY PARK, MAY 20, 1775

❦ *Gentlemen:* I have lately had repeated accounts that a body of New Englanders or others were to come to seise and carry away my person and attack our family under color of malicious insinuations that I intended to set the Indians upon the people. Men of sense and character know that my office is of the highest importance to promote peace amongst the Six Nations and prevent their entering into any such disputes. This I effected last year, when they were much vexed about the attack made upon the Shawanese and I last winter appointed them to meet me this month to receive the answer of the Virginians. All men must allow that, if the Indians find their Council fire disturbed and their Superintendent insulted, they will take a dreadful revenge. It is therefore the duty of all people to prevent this and to satisfy any who may have been imposed on, that their suspicions and the allegation they have collected against me are false and inconsistent with my character and office. I recommend this to you as

---

[1] The Tryon County militia was organized August 26, 1775. Samuel L. Frey, ed., *Minute Book of the Committee of Safety, Tryon County,* New York: 1905, p. 127.
[2] William L. Stone, *Life of Joseph Brant, Thayendanegea,* New York: 1838, vol I, p. 75.

highly necessary at this time, as my regard for the interest of the country and self preservation has obliged me to fortify my house and keep men armed for my defence till these idle and ridiculous reports are removed. [*Frey, ed., Minute Book, Tryon County, p. 125.*]

8 BRAVADO: "YOU D...D REBELL, . . . ONE WORD MORE, I'LL BLOW YOUR BRAINS OUT!" SHERIFF ALEXANDER WHITE, INFORMED ON BY HIS NEIGHBORS, RESPONDS

After the deceit of Guy Johnson had been exposed, the committee turned its attention to rooting out Johnson's followers. Feeling ran so high in the Mohawk Valley that the accusations acquired at times the character of a witch hunt. The Tryon County Committee of Safety was kept busy throughout 1775 listening to charges against friends and neighbors, removing some from office, jailing others, and even exonerating a few. The first sheriff of Tryon County, Alexander White, was removed from office on the complaint of his neighbors that he exercised his authority unjustly and made obnoxious statements. He had also cut down the liberty pole at German Flatts, said to be the first in the Mohawk Valley. After hearing damaging testimony at White's examination the committee allowed his commission to expire and elected John Frey sheriff. White was taken up on August 14 and sent by General Schuyler ten days later to the Provincial Congress in Albany where he was imprisoned. His wife, Elizabeth, petitioned the Provincial Congress on October 2 for his release on parole, saying the real cause of his "expressing himself unbecomingly" was the incident concerning his arrest of John Fonda, a popular resident of the Mohawk Valley. A group of some fifty Whigs had managed to release Fonda from imprisonment and had marched on to the sheriff's home, calling for his surrender. Sheriff White fired a few shots from his pistol which were answered by his opponents' muskets, and White was wounded. Just when they were about to seize White, John Johnson intervened, threatening to arouse his followers, whereupon the crowd soon dispersed. Considering the feeling evoked by this disturbance, the Provincial Congress passed the problem on to the Albany Committee of Safety, which shortly released the sheriff. But White's heated words, repeated by Major Jellis

Fonda of Caughnawaga and by William Seeber of Canajoharie, left no doubt with the Tryon committee where White's loyalty lay.[1]

One of the Indians, a supporter of Sheriff White, was William Johnson, a part-Indian son of Sir William Johnson. He had swaggered into Jacob Klock's house with pistols, gun, and sword hanging about him and made abusive remarks which were duly reported to the committee.

Jellis Fonda's testimony

AUGUST 6, 1775

❡ "He [White] would fight for his King and Country with his association and the party on the King's side like a brave man . . . they would conquer, but the party on the Country's side do fight with the halters on their Necks. . . . He Hopes to have the pleasure of hanging a good Many yet for their Resistance against the Acts of Parliament."

---

[1] Force, ed., *Am. Arch.,* 4th Ser., vol. III, pp. 86, 136, 600, 923–924. Also Sabine, *Loyalists,* vol. II, pp. 420–421.

In 1777, when passions heated up over John Butler's invasion of the Mohawk Valley, the charges against suspected persons grew more serious. Major Jellis Fonda, a judge of the Court of Common Pleas and the complainant against Sheriff White, now became the defendant and was obliged to journey to Poughkeepsie to answer accusations against himself before the Council of Appointment. He was charged with advising "Sundry Subjects of this State to forsake the Measures of Congress and submit to Taxes by authority of Parliament," and with advising a person under General Herkimer's command, three days before the Battle of Oriskany, not to fire on the Indians and to dissuade others from doing so. However, Major Fonda explained these matters so persuasively that he was exonerated and the complainants, who failed to appear, were rebuked. The Council recommended that they "forbear from any further disputes that may tend to disunite the inhabitants of Tryon County." Minutes of the Council of Appointment, April 4 and June 20, 1778, N.Y. Historical Society *Collections,* 1925, vol. II, pp. 21, 29–30.

William Seeber's Testimony As to White's Words

❧   ". . . if he [Colonel Claus] had been here this day by signing the Association, he would have shot some of 'em through their hearts and the Rest he would have carried away to the Westward to be hanged there." When Seeber's son, Jacob, answered it wasn't an easy Matter to do such a thing, the sheriff pointed his pistol to the Breast of Jacob, saying: "You d---d Rebell, if you say one Word more, I'll blow your Brains out."

Jacob Klock's Testimony,

NOVEMBER 7, 1775

❧   "I [William Johnson] am a King's Man; who dare say anything against it? I have killed so many Yankees at Fort St. John's with this Sword of my Father; they are no Soldiers at all. I kill'd and scalp'd, and kick'd their arses, and the d---d Committee here have gone too far already. I will shew them better, and will cut some of their heads off by and by; I only pity the wives and children, for I shall come with 500 Men which I have ready, to cut off the whole River and burn their houses this fall yet." [*Frey, ed., Minute Book, Tryon County, pp 55-57; p. 95.*]

"THE REBELLIOUS FOURTH PART . . . HAD THE EFFRONTREE TO PUBLISH THAT THEY WERE UNANIMOUSLY CHOSEN BY THE PEOPLE . . .": JOHN FERDINAND DALZIEL SMYTH TELLS OF HIS DEFIANCE OF THE MARYLAND COMMITTEE OF SAFETY[1]

John Ferdinand Dalziel Smyth, a Scottish immigrant to America in 1763, was a storekeeper and landholder in Charles County, Maryland, in the early part of 1775 when he successfully defied the efforts of the local committee

[1] *Narrative or Journal of Captain John Ferdinand Dalziel Smyth of the Queen's Rangers, taken Prisoner by the Rebels in 1775, lately escaped from them, and arrived here in the Daphne.* N.Y.: 1777-1778, Private collection of William Wright, Easthampton, N.Y. This account differs in phrasing from the 1784 account, reprinted in *Eye-Witness Accounts of the American Revolution,* New York *Times* and Arno Press, 1968, pp. 191-208.

of safety to seize him. Governor Dunmore commissioned him to accompany Lieutenant Colonel John Connolly and Lieutenant Allan Cameron on a secret expedition to the Ohio Valley, but all were taken prisoner November 19, 1775, before they were even out of Maryland. Smyth escaped December 30 and made a 300-mile winter trek on foot over the Alleghenies only to be retaken two weeks later. Three times he escaped from prison after suffering, as he told the British Commissioners, "a most cruel Captivity for eighteen months in Dungeons, in Irons . . . on Bread and Water." He finally reached England in 1780 and was granted a generous temporary allowance of £ 200.[2]

Twice he recorded his experiences during the years 1775-1777, writing first in the two months following his escape to a British man-of-war and thence to New York (December 25, 1777–February 25, 1778) and again in 1784, when he published in Dublin two volumes called *A Tour in the United States of America*. While the trustworthiness of his description of his exploits, sufferings, and property losses has been justly questioned,[3] his narrative of events at the start of the rebellion registers the sense of indignation and defiance felt by many early Loyalists. The following excerpt has been taken from his 1777-1778 journal.

1775

❦ It may not be amiss first to give a brief recital of my observations and what has happened to me from the beginning of this most wicked rebellion against the best of kings and the most free and mildest of governments. In the county I lived, at the first meeting of the people to consider about electing Committee, Congress, etc., I opposed it all in my power; and then three-fourths of them came over to my side on dividing; but the remaining rebellious fourth part appointed themselves Committee-men, etc., and had the *effrontree* to publish that they were unanimously chosen by the people. This was the case in general, as well as there; and it was out of such as these that the first Conventions and Congress were composed. At first I conceived this revolt was a deep laid scheme, concerted partly

[2] Sabine, *Loyalist Transcripts*, vol. III, p. 311; vol. XXV, p. 100.
[3] Harold B. Hancock, "John Ferdinand Dalziel Smyth, Loyalist," *Md. Hist. Mag.* vol. LV, pp. 346–358. Hancock says: "While the basic narrative is apparently trustworthy, his own role and hardships are greatly exaggerated. . . ."

by chance, but chiefly by design; and the event has proved that my con-
jectures were well-founded. After the first general Congress broke up,
the people began to murmur and the boldest, deepest, and most politic
stroke of all was now formed; in short, it was that on which the basis of
all their power was established. A meeting of each county on business of
great importance was desired on an appointed day. A very few only met,
and they were chiefly strollers and idle persons. The former committee
now re-chose themselves and eighty or ninety others, indeed every person
of any influence in each county, though absent and although many of them
had disapproved of their measures; any five were to act. This encreasing
the number of the Committee-men rivetted their influence and effectually
silenced those who opposed their designs. Frequent meetings were afterwards held wherein the former designers always carried their own schemes
and the nominal Committee-men were satisfied with the name and shadow
of power, for in fact they had none of the substance. Altho' I had always
openly and publicly disavowed and detested the whole of their proceedings,
yet now they nominated me in their scandalous committee, appointed me
to the command of two troops of light horse, and the chairman waited
on me with their infamous commission, (and with four papers for me to
subscribe, *viz.* one for the poor of Boston, one for a magazine, one for
the payment of the Congress, and [one for] the rebel association), thinking
thereby to corrupt my principles as they did many others; and expecting
that this ostentatious, though lawless, power would be so alluring as to
fascinate me out of my loyalty. But I positively refused the whole, gave
him for answer that I would suffer death before I would have such a stain
upon me and sent back their dirty commission which I despised. Being
then cited before them to answer for my conduct, I informed them "that
they neither represented me nor my principles, that I beheld them as an
arbitrary, petty, insolent, self-created tribunal, to which I paid no obedience;
but that I was always ready to answer in a legal and constitutional way
to any accusation against me."

This incensed them highly. And I, out of self-defence, as well as for
the support of his Majesty's government, then drew up a loyal association
and exerted my utmost influence in its favour. In two days I got 400 subscribers. We were to meet the ensuing Saturday in order to concert some
effectual measures to support constitutional government and avert the
threatened oppression of the Congress and Committees; but in the meantime they got intimation of it and in one night and day had every person

privately seized on and obliged to renounce his Majesty and his government even by oath; two Scotsmen who refused they tarred and feathered and sent a party after me. I was well provided with good arms and ammunition at my house and resolute servants, having on this account been under a necessity for some time of going constantly armed. Apprehensive of a warm reception, they returned without me.

From that time I was in continual dangers and alarms and could not sleep in my own house in safety. Several times parties of 40 men with two rounds each of powder and ball were ordered to take me and if I resisted to fire upon me; but one of the officers always privately gave me timely notice of it so that I commonly escaped in my boat over Potomack. Happening there once, before some violent rebels, to say "that instead of blaming his Excellency Lord Dunmore's conduct, I thought he had always behaved in a manner that did him infinite honour and wished that all the rest of his Majesty's governors had performed their duty with equal spirit and resolution," a Capt. Weedon from Fredericksburg (now a rebel General) came down to the riverside with his company (60 riflemen) to take me when I came over, but a lady sent her maid, who called to me when I was within 300 yards of the shore, informing me of my danger and desiring me to return immediately. Weedon and his banditti instantly ran down to the riverside, ordering me to come to the shore or they would fire upon me. Accordingly on my refusal they fired about 100 rifle balls at me; having arms with me I returned their fire 8 or 10 times, but the distance was such, there was no great danger on either side. That same day on my return I was informed that three different parties intended the next morning to beset my house on all sides to prevent my escaping. Accordingly about sunset I saw a boat with eight or nine armed men coming over; I ran down to the riverside with my fusee and ordered them not to land and if they attempted it, I would fire upon them. They persisting in it, I fired three times (under cover of the root of a tree blown up), which they also returned, but at last stood up the river and landed at Cedar-point, about two miles above. I was now beset on all sides by them, but escaped in the night by riding in Potomack on the flats up to the top of my saddle for ten miles up in the river to avoid the centinels and guards they had placed at every avenue leading to my house. Next morning they were in such rage at missing me, when they thought me quite secure, that they destroyed above 100 bushels of corn, shot two of my horses in the plow, and beat all my people. . . .

At this time I was declared inimical and could not bring any action nor recover the debts for which I had judgments in court. . . . Any person that pleased might bring actions against me, but I could bring no suits against anyone. . . .

As soon as I got home, two gentlemen, my personal friends, came begging I would pretend to comply with the measures of the Congress and join only in appearance, telling me it was madness for me alone to resist and the consequence would be that I would be sacrificed and my whole property destroyed. I answered that, as I had never countenanced them in the least, I would not now have the infamy upon me, on any account, of joining them, although in appearance only; that ever since the time I had found myself overpowered, I had made no opposition to them, that I concerned not with them and never visited them nor their meetings. But, as I did not acknowledge their authority, I was determined not to be taken by them and would sooner die than fall into their hands, that this was my final resolution from which I would never depart. They left me in sorrow saying that possibly they might never see me more. [*Smyth, Narrative, pp. 1–5.*]

9 MARY WATTS JOHNSON IS TAKEN HOSTAGE AS A CONTROL ON SIR JOHN'S ACTIONS

Although Sir John Johnson told his friends in the fall of 1775 that "sooner than lift his hand against his King or sign any association, he would suffer his head to be cut off," the Tryon County Committee of Safety did not proceed immediately against him. He stayed on at Johnson Hall under his Highlander guard until early in 1776 when he was arrested by Colonel Elias Dayton and a sizable militia force and obliged to surrender his arms. He was, however, soon released on parole and allowed to return to the Hall. Four months later (May 19), alarmed for his safety, he broke his parole and fled through the mountains to Montreal, taking with him some 175 tenants and followers.[1]

Sir John had left his wife, Mary Watts Johnson, at Johnson Hall in the hope that her advanced pregnancy would protect her from distur-

[1] F. W. Halsey, *The Old New York Frontier, 1614–1800*, New York: 1901, pp. 152–153.

bance. The delicate question of what to do with Lady Johnson was referred to General Philip Schuyler. About a week after her husband's striking out for Canada, she was arrested and taken off to Albany as a hostage, never to see her own home again. Her life, she was told, would depend upon her husband's actions. Judge Thomas Jones recounts the episode.

Judge Thomas Jones Describes the Incident

MAY 1776

❧ No sooner had the Committee of Albany intelligence that Sir John was gone to Canada than a detachment of continentals was sent up to the Hall with orders to make Lady Johnson a prisoner and bring her to Albany. This was accordingly done. The mansion was completely plundered of all its contents. The farm in Sir John's own occupation was robbed of his cattle, his negroes, his horses, hogs, sheep, and utensils of husbandry. His carriages were taken away, his papers of every kind (some of the utmost consequence) were stolen or destroyed, and all his slaves carried off. This done, Lady Johnson was escorted under a guard to Albany, a lady of great beauty, of the most amiable disposition, and composed of materials of the most soft and delicate kind. Besides this, she was more than seven months advanced in her pregnancy. She was suffered to go to Albany in her own carriage driven by a servant of her own. But in order to add insult to insult, she was obliged to take the Lieutenant who commanded the detachment into the carriage with her, who was now converted from a mender of shoes in Connecticut into an officer holding a commission under the honourable the Continental Congress. Thus was Lady Johnson conducted from Sir John's seat to Albany, guarded by a parcel of half-clothed dirty Yankees and squired by a New England officer, by trade a cobbler, as dirty as themselves, until he had decorated himself with a suit of Sir John's clothes, and a clean shirt, and a pair of stockings, stolen at the Hall. A younger sister and two children accompanied her ladyship to Albany. . . . She was permitted to reside with a venerable old Aunt, with this positive injunction *not to leave the city under pain of death.* She was, however, not in a condition to leave the town, had she been so disposed. She was also given to understand that if Sir John appeared in arms against the Americans, retaliation should be made and she should be the object, and her life depended on her husband's action. What inhuman, unfeeling conduct! And yet these were the people who during the whole war boasted of their humane, generous, behaviour and taxed the British and Loyalists as butchers, cut-throats, and barbarians. [*Jones, History of New York, vol. I, pp 76-77.*]

Mary Watts Johnson Appeals to Washington over the Head of General Schuyler

JUNE 16, 1776

❧ *Sir:*

I take the liberty of complaining to you, as it is from you I expect redress. I was compelled to leave home, much against my inclination, and am detained here by General *Schuyler,* who, I am convinced, acts more out of ill nature to Sir *John* than from any reason that either he or I have given him. As I am not allowed to return home and my situation here made as disagreeable as it can be, by repeated messages and threats from General *Schuyler,* too indelicate and cruel to be expected from a gentleman, I should wish to be with my friends at *New York* and would prefer my captivity under your Excellency's protection to being in the power of General Schuyler, who rules with more severity than could be wished by your Excellency's humble servant,

M. Johnson
[*Am. Arch. 4th Ser., vol. VI, p. 930.*]

AFTERNOTE *The Provincial Congress denied Lady Johnson permission to go to New York, but allowed her to reside at Coldenham, the home of Cadwallader Colden in Ulster County, about 12 miles west of Newburgh. With the help of one of Sir John's loyal tenants, who provided horses and sleigh at the appointed place, she and her sister, dressed as peasants, plus three small children and servants, escaped to the British post at Paulus Hook. Here her husband joined them and took them into New York and in the spring on to Canada. The youngest child died en route, and a second a few weeks later, both from the rigors of the trip.[1] However, Sir John Johnson was now free to appear in arms in the valley without fear of reprisal on his family.*

[1] Mabel G. Walker, "Sir John Johnson, Loyalist," *Mississippi Valley Historical Rev.* vol. III (December 1916), pp. 331-332.

10 A TOUGH SIXTEEN-YEAR-OLD: UNDAUNTED BY HIS TORMENTORS, WALTER BATES REFUSES TO SQUEAL ON THE TORIES

Walter Bates (1760–1842) was the son of a strong Anglican Loyalist family who lived in the present Darien area of Connecticut. His brother, William, served under Cornwallis at Yorktown, and his sister married a Loyalist, Thomas Gilbert. At the close of the war he settled in St. John, New Brunswick, where he served for many years as the sheriff of King's County. He narrates his personal adventures in 1776.

1776

❧ At length the thing I greatly feared came upon me. A small boat was discovered by the American guard, in one of these coves, by night; in which they suspected that one of my brothers, with some others, had come from the British. They supposed them concealed in the neighborhood and that I must be acquainted with it.

At this time I had just entered my sixteenth year. I was taken and confined in the Guard House; next day examined before a Committee and threatened with sundry deaths if I did not confess what I knew not of. They threatened among other things to confine me at low water and let the tide drown me if I did not expose these honest farmers. At length I was sent back to the Guard House until ten o'clock at night, when I was taken out by an armed mob, conveyed through the field gate one mile from the town to back Creek, then having been stripped my body was exposed to the mosquitoes, my hands and feet being confined to a tree near the Salt Marsh, in which situation for two hours time every drop of blood would be drawn from my body; when soon after two of the committee said that if I would tell them all I knew, they would release me, if not they would leave me to these men who, perhaps, would kill me.

I told them that I knew nothing that would save my life.

They left me, and the Guard came to me and said they were ordered to give me, if I did not confess, one hundred stripes, and if that did not kill me I would be sentenced to be hanged. Twenty stripes was then executed with severity, after which they sent me again to the Guard House. No "Tory" was allowed to speak to me, but I was insulted and abused by all.

The next day the committee proposed many means to extort a confession from me, the most terrifying was that of confining me to a log on the carriage in the Saw mill and let the saw cut me in two if I did not expose "those Torys." Finally they sentenced me to appear before Col. Davenport, in order that he should send me to head quarters, where all the Torys he sent were surely hanged. Accordingly next day I was brought before Davenport—one of the descendants of the old apostate Davenport, who fled from old England—who, after he had examined me, said with great severity of countenance, "I think you could have exposed those Tories."

I said to him "You might rather think I would have exposed my own father sooner than suffer what I have suffered." Upon which the old judge could not help acknowledging he never knew any one who had withstood more without exposing confederates, and he finally discharged me the third day. It was a grievous misfortune to be in such a situation, but the fear of God animated me not to fear man. My resolution compelled mine enemies to show their pity that I had been so causelessly afflicted, and my life was spared. I was, however, obliged to seek refuge from the malice of my persecutors in the mountains and forests until their frenzy might be somewhat abated. [*Bates, "Narrative . . ." in Raymond, Kingston and the Loyalists of 1783, p. 8.*]

11 INTREPIDITY: THE REM RAPELJE FAMILY ARE UNDAUNTED BY PERSECUTION

Rem Rapelje kept a store in the rear of his dwelling in Maiden Lane. Both he and his brother-in-law, Theophilus Hardenbrook, were marked Tories from the start, as they were Addressers to Admiral Lord Howe and Sir William Howe. They were the victims of the "Toory rides" to which Peter Elting referred. Rem Rapelje's son, George, who narrates the following account of his mother's intrepidity before the Sons of Liberty, was five years old in 1776 when the Tory rides occurred.

1776

❦ My father, when parties ran high, inclined to the old order of things; he for one, among many, was contented and happy under the British government. His property was secure, and he, no doubt, thought that many of our grievances were imaginary. My father was not of a disposition to remain still, and expressing his sentiments perhaps a little too freely, excited the indignation of some of the sons of liberty, from whom he met with rude treatment. The mob assailed my father's house in search of my brothers, who had resented the insults offered their father, but they were saved by the cool intrepidity of my mother, who invited a committee of three to come in and search the house, declaring that her sons were not there, nor did she know when they might be. They had been taken from the house disguised in female apparel and secreted for a while. They were high spirited young men; one of them was a student in medicine, and the other was preparing to be a merchant, under commissary Henry White, a man of distinction in that day.

Another circumstance happened, which was a sad grievance to our family. My maternal uncle, Theophilus Hardenbrook, chief engineer to the king in New York, was treated with every insult, and was mangled and ill used by the mob; but to their honor, be it said, that the upper classes of the whigs did everything in their power to restrain the mob. He got away from his persecutors, concealed himself on the banks of the Hudson, and at length . . . gaining a little strength, he took a small boat to go on board a man-of-war, lying in the stream, but after he had reached the ship, exhausted from the loss of blood, in attempting to get on board, was drowned. . . .

My father, for his honesty was never for a moment doubted, was allowed by the committee of safety in New York to reside in New Jersey, where he lived in great retirement until the war was over. He had pledged the word of a man of principle and honor, and he took no part in the revolutionary conflict.

While my father was in banishment, one of my mother's relations, a whig, came to her, and told her that she had better remove with her children into the country, as in the event of the city being taken by the British, it would be burnt. My mother replied, "My dear cousin, you have valuable property here and would not like to have it destroyed. What I should wish to see will not be a matter of consequence. I assure you it is the intention of General Washington to fire the city, if it fall into the hands of the British army," and it so happened that soon after they got possession of the city, a fire commenced somewhere to the east of Broad street, . . . [*Rapelje, Narrative, pp. 12–14.*]

12 ABRAHAM GARDINER OF EASTHAMPTON FINDS THAT
AMBIVALENCE IS NO PROTECTION

Following the British success in the Battle of Brooklyn the inhabitants
of eastern Long Island were in a difficult plight. They were now forced to
live under British martial law and at the same time were subject to guerilla
raids from across the Sound. The out-and-out Whigs fled to Connecticut,
but the moderate men hoped to maintain an ambivalent position, taking up
arms neither against the King nor against the Continental Congress. The
Reverend Samuel Buell, the influential pastor of Easthampton's Church of
Christ, summarized the dilemma of these moderates: "The people are as
a torch on fire at both ends, which will be speedily consumed; for the
Continental Whigs carry off their stock and produce and the British punish
them for allowing it to go. I hope the Whigs will not oppress the oppressed
but let the stock alone."[1]

Colonel Abraham Gardiner, a former member of the Easthampton
Committee of Correspondence and a signer of the Association, was one
inhabitant who learned that it was not possible to keep on good terms with
both sides. In Easthampton 248 inhabitants, supposedly all the adult males,
had signed the Association in June 1775. However, after the establishment
of British martial law the towns of Easthampton and Southampton sent
to General Howe for pardons. On September 2, 1776, Gardiner administered a counter oath to 150 persons, of whom 117 had taken the earlier
pledge. He even obliged two reluctant citizens, Colonel Jonathan Hedges
of Sagg and Colonel David Mulford of Easthampton, to sign under coer-
cion. Nonetheless, within a few days he wrote to Governor Trumbull
soliciting his help in preventing raids from Connecticut on the livestock
and possessions of the townspeople, in the naïve belief that loyalty to the
King did not exclude them from the protection of the government of
Connecticut. Henry B. Livingston, under instructions from Washington
to harass the enemy, regarded Gardiner as inimical and promptly carried
him with his family and effects to Saybrook, where he was kept prisoner
for a year.[2]

---

[1] Henry Onderdonk, Jr., *Revolutionary Incidents of Suffolk and Kings Counties,* New
York: 1849, p. 40. Frederic G. Mather, *The Refugees of 1776 from Long Island to
Connecticut,* Albany: 1913, p. 202.
[2] Henry B. Livingston to Governor Trumbull, September 10, 1776, *Trumbull Papers,*
Connecticut State Library, vol. 5, part 2, no. 181. Photostat in Easthampton Library.
See also *American Archives.,* 5th Ser. vol. II, pp. 281, 296.

Gardiner's letter from Easthampton to Governor Trumbull, September 7, 1776, written as clerk for the Trustees of Easthampton, indicates the predicament of the victims of the raids, who were considered "accessory thereto."

SEPTEMBER 7, 1776

❡ *Sir*—

In consequence of a Report prevailing in Town that the People of Connecticut are coming to take away our live Stock and Effects, the Trustees, who transact the Business of the Town, have met early this Morning and unanimusly agreed to send an Express humbly requesting your Honour's prohibition of such Measures, as [we are] apprehensive, if prosecuted, we shall be involved in Perplexities and Sufferings far beyond those we are now the Subjects of, in that it may be constructed we are some how accessory thereto, (which we are not), being Subjects of his Majesty King George, and therefore mean not to act a Part exposing of us to his Displeasure. We have therefore thought Proper to request Your Honour's interposition, as we judge, in our favour. We are your Honour's Humble Petitioners. [*Trumbull Papers, vol. V, pt. 1, no. 174, Conn. State Arch.*]

AFTERNOTE   *Although Abraham Gardiner cast his lot with the British, his eldest son, Nathaniel Gardiner, joined the Continental army, serving as surgeon to the First New Hampshire Regiment. For Abraham Gardiner, loyalty to his son transcended his loyalty to the King, and on one occasion, probably in 1780, when some British officers, including John André, were billeted in his house, he protected his son, home on leave, from arrest. Knowing his son could be seized as a spy for coming within the British lines, his father hid him in a secret compartment. André knew the son was there but did not search the house because, as he later explained, Abraham Gardiner had done so much for the Royal cause.* [1]

This compartment was well concealed in the center of the house, surrounding the main chimney which served as a flue for eight fireplaces on the first floor and four on the second floor. It was accessible only

[1] David Gardiner, *Chronicles of Easthampton*, New York: 1871, pp. 107–108. Winthrop Sargent, *Life and Career of Major John André*, William Abbat, ed., New York: 1902, p. 106 fn.

through a secret panel in a paneled room on the second floor. The panel led into a small closet to the left of the chimney. To enter the compartment it was necessary to remove the shelves and, by means of inserting a finger in a knothole, remove a board at the back of the closet, slither through the small opening, and proceed around the back of the octagon-shaped chimney. The space, made possible by the reduction of the number of fireplaces on the second floor, was adequate for several men but had no window. Ventilation was probably secured by means of cracks or well-concealed vents masked in the cornice work.[2]

[2] Descriptions of the secret room were obtained through the courtesy of Mrs. Fanny Gardiner Collins and Mr. Robert D. L. Gardiner of Easthampton. The Brown House, built in 1742, containing the secret room, was remodeled by the present owner, Mr. Lawrence Baker.

Intimidation and Abuse

of the Anglican Clergy

For the Anglican clergy, especially in New England, New York, and New Jersey, many of whom had opposed the oppressive measures of Parliament but balked at overt actions of disloyalty, the date July 20, 1775, represented a clear-cut confrontation with conscience. They had hoped the quarrel could be compromised and the spirit of rebellion would subside. However, the Continental Congress assigned that day as one of fasting and prayer and urged people to gather at their churches for services. While almost all ministers opened their churches as required, many of them, especially in New England, made the services the occasion for admonitions of the dire consequences which would result if compromise, even submission to Parliament, was not adopted. Sympathetic as many were to colonial grievances, they considered rebellion as treason as well as a contravention of the explicit vows of loyalty to the King taken at their ordination.

Thus July 20, 1775, began the identification of these Loyalist clergymen. Almost to a man the New England ministers followed the dictates of conscience, interpreting their oaths as an unequivocal commitment to the King, and were soon subjected to vilification and abuse. Several died as a consequence of imprisonment or exposure or in the course of escape.[1]

The Reverend James Nichols, a young rector at New Cambridge (Bristol) and Northbury, Connecticut, was routed out of a cellar hiding place, tarred and feathered, and dragged through a brook.[2] The Reverend Thomas Barton, rector in Lancaster, Pennsylvania, spoke for many of these clergymen when he wrote to the Society for the Propagation of the Gospel on November 25, 1776, as follows: "I have been obliged to shut up my churches to avoid the fury of the populace. . . . Every clergyman of the Church of England, who dared to act upon proper principles was marked out for infamy and insult, in consequence of which the Missionaries in particular have suffered greatly. Some of them have been dragged from their horses, assaulted with stones and dirt, ducked in water, obliged to flee for their lives, driven from their habitations and families, laid under arrest and imprisoned."[3]

The loyal Anglican clergy, especially strong in the Northern provinces, were a well-trained vocal group who exerted an extensive influence in their parishes. Long before the Revolution they had aroused antagonism and suspicion because of their urging the establishment of an American

[1] Among those who died as a consequence of abuse or imprisonment were the Rev. Luke Babcock of Philipse Manor (d. 1777), the Rev. Thomas Barton of York Co., Pennsylvania (d. 1780), the Rev. Ebenezer Kneeland of Stratford, Connecticut (d. 1777), the Rev. John Beach of Newtown and Redding, Connecticut, (d. 1782), and the Rev. Ephraim Avery of Rye, New York (d. 1776). See Wilkins Updike, *History of the Narragansett Church,* 1907, vol. II, p. 53; Franklin B. Dexter, *Biographical Sketches of the Graduates of Yale,* New York: 1896, vol. II, pp. 685–686, pp. 707–708; William B. Sprague, *Annals of the American Pulpit,* New York: 1859, vol. V, pp. 82, 168. The Reverend Henry Caner wrote that the Reverend Ebenezer Thompson of Scituate died "partly owing to bodily disorder and partly to some uncivil treatment from the rebels." To Dr. Richard Hind, January 14, 1776, Caner *Letterbook.*

[2] E. Leroy Pond, *The Tories of Chippeny Hill, Connecticut,* New York: 1909, p. 19. The Reverend James Nichols was tried for treason by the Superior Court in Hartford with Moses Dunbar but was acquitted (January 27, 1777).

[3] William B. Sprague, *Annals of the American Pulpit,* New York: 1859, vol. V, p. 169.

Episcopate.[4] About two hundred fifty Anglican ministers were serving in the colonies in 1775, most of whom were missionaries of the Society. Of this latter group 90 percent felt conscience-bound to their oath of allegiance to the King.[5] Charles Inglis, minister of Trinity Church, New York, and author of the essays *A New York Farmer,* reported: ". . . *all* the Society's Missionaries, without excepting one, in New Jersey, New York, Connecticut &, so far as I can learn, in the other New England Colonies, have proved themselves faithful, loyal Subjects in these trying Times; . . . all the other Clergy of our Church, though not in the Society's Service, have observed the same Line of Conduct."[6] In Pennsylvania, only one Anglican church remained open;[7] in New Jersey all Anglican churches were closed, and only one priest, Robert Blackwell of Gloucester County, joined the rebels, accepting a chaplaincy in the Continental army.[8] In the Southern Colonies a smaller proportion of Anglican clergymen remained loyal. In Maryland about half of forty resident ministers were Loyalists; in Virginia about two-thirds of ninety-one clergymen stood by the King.[9]

---

[4] The Rev. Henry Caner wrote to Charles Inglis (August 17, 1772): "Sure I am that it would be the best step they [the English bishops] would take towards securing the Obedience of the Colonies." Caner, *Letterbook,* University of Bristol Library, England.

[5] J. W. Lydekker, *Life and Letters of Charles Inglis,* London: 1936, p. 148.

[6] Charles Inglis to Richard Hind, Secretary of the SPG, October 31, 1776. *SPG Mss.* vol. V, B,2, no. 68. See Lydekker, *Inglis,* p. 157.

There were fourteen Anglican parishes in Massachusetts in 1775 and only four at the close of the war: Trinity and Christ churches in Boston, St. Paul's Church, Newburyport, and St. Paul's Church, Salem. Three of the fourteen were in Boston, namely, King's Chapel (Henry Caner, left 1776), Christ Church (Mather Byles, Jr., resigned April 18, 1775), and Trinity Church (William Walter replaced by Samuel Parker, the assistant rector, in 1776). Parker and Edward Bass of Newburyport remained in their parishes throughout the war by reason of omitting prayers for the King. In 1778, Stephen C. Lewis, a former chaplain to Burgoyne and a former prisoner of the rebels, assumed the pulpit of Christ Church after agreeing to comply with the orders of Congress. Edward Bass to Samuel Parker, June 21, 1784. See Daniel D. Addison, *The Life and Times of Edward Bass,* Boston: 1897, pp. 102, 138 ff., 221–222.

[7] The Church of William White, later the first bishop of Pennsylvania.

[8] Uzal Ogden, a young itinerant preacher, continued to hold services in New Jersey through the war years. See Nelson Burr, *The Anglican Church in New Jersey,* Philadelphia: 1954, pp. 406–407, 585–586, 631–633.

[9] Samuel Wilberforce, *History of the Protestant Episcopal Church in America,* New York: 1846 (1849 ed.), p. 138.

However, in South Carolina, out of twenty-three ministers only five were Loyalists.[10]

The writings of Loyalist Anglican churchmen abound. Among the most prolific and vociferous against the rebellion were Jacob Duché of Maryland and Philadelphia, who first espoused the rebel cause and switched in 1777; Thomas B. Chandler of Elizabethtown, New Jersey; Jonathan Odell of Burlington, New Jersey, the well-known Tory satirist; Myles Cooper, President of King's College; Samuel Seabury of Westchester, who became the first consecrated bishop in the United States after the war, and Charles Inglis of Trinity Church, New York, some of whose writings are excerpted in the subsequent pages.

I   THE REVEREND SAMUEL PETERS TELLS HOW THE "SOBER DISSENTERS" ABUSED THE PETERITES

One of the first Anglican ministers to be persecuted and the most odious to the rebels was the Reverend Samuel Peters, whom Governor Jonathan Trumbull blamed for the vote in Hebron and Hartford against a contribution to the beleaguered port of Boston. Already a fugitive to England in 1774, he continued to pour forth diatribes against the rebels with all his Loyalist eloquence, albeit a questionable regard for unembroidered facts. The description of the abuse of the Peterites which follows was excerpted from the *History of Connecticut,* later identified as being from the pen of Samuel Peters himself.

AUGUST 14 AND SEPTEMBER 4, 1774

❡   Among the greatest enemies to the cause of the *Sober Dissenters,* and among the greatest friends to that of the church of England, the Rev. Mr. Peters stood conspicuous. I have already represented him as so well shielded by the friendship and esteem of the inhabitants of Hebron, where he resided, as to be proof against the common weapons of fanaticism and malice. The Governor and Council, therefore, entered the lists, and, anxious at all events to get rid of so formidable a foe, accused him of being

[10] *Historical Mag. Protestant Episcopal Church,* vol. X (1941), p. 119.

a spy of Lord North's and the Bishops. This allegation was published by the Governor's order, in every republican pulpit in the colony, on Sunday August 14, 1774, which induced a mob of Patriots from Windham county to arm and surround his house the same night, in the most tumultuous manner ordering the gates and doors to be opened. Mr. Peters, from his window, asked if they had a warrant from a magistrate to enter his house. They replied, "We have Joice's warrant, which Charles the traitor submitted to, and is sufficient for you." Peters told them he had but one life to lose, and he would lose it in defence of his house and property. Finally, after some further altercation, it was agreed that a committee from the mob should search the house, and read all papers belonging to Mr. Peters. A committee was accordingly nominated, who, after inspecting his papers as much as they pleased, reported, "that they were satisfied Mr. Peters was not guilty of any crime laid to his charge."

On Sunday the 4th of September, the country was alarmed by a letter from Colonel Putnam, declaring "that Admiral Graves had burnt Boston, and that General Gage was murdering old and young." The Governor of Connecticut took the liberty to add to Mr. Putnam's letter, "except churchmen and the addressers of Governor Hutchinson." The same day 40,000 men began their march from Connecticut to Boston, and returned the next, having heard that there was no truth in Putnam's reports. Dr. Bellamy thanked God for this false alarm, as he had thereby pointed out "the inhabitants of Meroz, who went not to the help of the Lord against the mighty." No churchmen, presbyterians, or Sandemanians, were among the 40,000 insurgents; and that was judged to be sufficient proof of their disaffection to the liberties of America. The Governor seized this opportunity to set the mobs again, with redoubled fury, upon the Rev. Mr. Peters, and the loyalists, whom they then called Peterites; and the intoxicated ruffians spared neither their houses, goods, nor persons. Some had their bowels crouded out of their bodies; others were covered with filth, and marked with the sign of the cross by a mop filled with excrements, in token of their loyalty to a king who designed to crucify all the good people of America. Even women were hung by the heels, tarred, and feathered. Mr. Peters, with his gown and cloaths torn off, was treated in the most insulting manner: his mother, daughter, two brothers, and servants, were wounded; one of his brothers so badly, that he died soon after. Mr. Peters was then obliged to abscond and fly to the royal army in Boston, from whence he went to England, by which means he has hitherto preserved his life, though not his property, from the rapacious and bloody hands of his countrymen. — The Rev. Messieurs Mansfield and Viets were cast into jail, and afterwards tried for high treason against America. Their real offence was charitably giving victuals and blankets to loyalists flying from the rage of drunken mobs. They were not indeed convicted in so high a degree as the court intended; but were fined and imprisoned, to the ruin of themselves and families. — The Rev. Messieurs Graves, Scovil, Dibblee, Nichols, Leaming, Beach,[1] and divers others, were cruelly dragged through mire and dirt. In short, all the clergy of the church were infamously insulted, abused, and obliged to seek refuge in the mountains, till the popular phrenzy was somewhat abated. [[*Peters,*] *History of Connecticut, London: 1781, pp. 414-419.*]

2   THE PLIGHT OF THE CLERGY IN BOSTON

The Reverend Henry Caner describes the plight of the clergy in besieged Boston.

AUGUST 16, 1775

❬ *To the Right Reverend Richard, Lord Bishop of London*
My Lord
    . . . The distress of this Town occasions his [Robert Auchmuty] embarking with his family for England. As the Rebellion is general thro' the provinces, the friends of Government have no certain place to fly to for safety but to England. It is impossible to tarry here, for if the rebels should not storm the town, which is hourly expected, and in which, if they succeed as probably they will, and put every man in it to the Sword, yet, should this event not take place and we should escape the Sword, we must perish by famine as some of the poorer sort within my knowledge have already done. The town is so closely besieg'd and all means of subsistence witheld from us that it is hardly possible any of us should subsist thro' the approaching winter; besides the food we have been reduc'd to, which is

---

[1] Matthew Graves (New London), James Scovil (Waterbury), Ebenezer Dibblee (Stamford), James Nichols (Bristol), Jeremiah Leaming (Stratford), John Beach (Newtown).

chiefly fish and salt pork, hath contributed to improve the sickness which has taken place among us, yet it is not uncommon to bury 20 to 30 a week among the troops and Inhabitants. I have myself suffer'd in common with others, both in the Sickness and Scarcity of provisions, nor have I any prospect but that things will be still worse. Out of 115 proprietary Heads of familys belonging to my Church, about 50, and those of the wealthier sort, have left me and retired to England, Halifax, etc. for safety, so that I can expect little support from my Congregation. My money, even all I was worth, is fallen into the hands of the Rebels. If I tarry here I am almost certain to perish by famine or the Sword. If I could muster money enough to pay my passage to England and follow my flock, who are chiefly gone before, I must starve when I come there.

We have a strong Fleet here which might have done much, but in truth, for what reason I know not, have done nothing, or if they have done anything it has been to distress the Inhabitants and such as are friends to Government but very little to annoy the Enemy. If our lives must pay for our loyalty, God's will be done. . . . [*Caner, Letterbook*]

3 WITNESSES TESTIFY TO THE COMMITTEE OF SAFETY CONCERNING THE CONTEMPTUOUS UTTERANCES OF THE REVEREND JOHN RUTGERS MARSHALL OF WOODBURY, CONNECTICUT

Among the "younger consciences," as Peters called the young clergymen, but not necessarily the more flexible ones, was the Reverend John Rutgers Marshall, a graduate of King's College in 1770, and a newly ordained missionary of the Society. He resided with his family in the Glebe House in Woodbury, Connecticut, throughout the Revolution. He was so outspoken and obnoxious that twice he was beaten and once even left for dead by the roadside. Cruel treatment undermined his health and led to an early death in 1789. He dared leave his house openly only on Sunday when Puritan practice precluded arrest. On Mondays, when the Committee of Safety periodically sought him out at Glebe House, he was nowhere to be found. A tunnel had been opened up from the cellar to a place across the road, with access through a hinged flap behind the firewood in the wood closet next to the fireplace or through a panel which could be pried loose from the molding under the hall stairs. This hidden escape route enabled him to survive the war and to become one of the ten clergymen present at the secret meeting at the Glebe House on March 23, 1783, when Samuel Seabury was selected to go to England to seek consecration as the first American bishop.

Marshall was cited to appear before the Connecticut Assembly of October 1775, after the Committee of Safety had reported him for contemptuous and derisive utterances against the actions of the Assembly. He was charged with showing an "inimical temper and unfriendly disposition against the measures, modes, and plans . . . adopted for the defence of the American cause."[1] Nine witnesses gave information to the Committee of Safety on conversations held at his house or at the tavern and on offensive references used in his sermons. Marshall's heated words in response to the events of 1775, as reported by these witnesses, caused the committee to put him on limits and subjected him to the usual restrictions applied to suspected persons.

APRIL 4, 1776

❆ Isaac Brownson of Waterbury of Lawful Age Testifies & says that some time the latter part of November or the Beginning of December 1774, I went into my Son Eli^g, who keeps the Tavern, and Mr. Clark of New Milford and Mr. Marshall of Woodbury and Mr. Backus, the Goldsmith, was there, and said Clark and Marshall were talking in a very high Strain of the horrible Abuse that the Revnd Mr. Peters had received from the Mob. I told them I did not like that way of treating Men, but he deserved much worse, tho' in a different way. Mr. Marshall replied, "why so? He is a distracted Man." I replied, "no more than ever he was." Said Marshall asked me what I ever knew of him before. I told him he was one of the Convention that met at Mr. Marshall's to agree not to keep the Fast before any Proclamation came out, only they knew there was to be one when the Governor and Council thought fit. He asked me how I knew that. I told him I took it for Truth by Information and I had often been told that they did agree not to keep it, and I made no Doubt that they agreed upon Mr. Peters going to England at the same time, notwithstanding the Apology a

---

[1] Charles Hoadly, ed., *Colonial Records of Connecticut, 1775-6*, Hartford: 1890, vol. XV, p. 158.

Number of the Episcopal Clergy made at New Haven; for in that they never disapproved of, or resented it, that their Names were made free with by Mr. Peters, only that they knew nothing of his going. One of them, s^d Marshall or Clark, said that they had no Right to keep a Fast before they had petitioned the King. I mentioned the Case of Nehemiah & Esther. Mr. Marshall said that was nothing to the Case, for they were Captives; but our Governor and Authority aimed at being at the head of all Mobs, Fasts, and Riots. And further the Deponent saith not. [*Conn. State Archives, Revolution, vol. V, doc. 450.*]

APRIL 15, 1776

❡ Amos Hinman of Stratford in Fairfield County of Lawful Age who Testifies and Says: that Some time in the fore part of April [1775] last past he, the Deponant, was at Woodbury at the House of Ebenez^r Hinman where Mr. Marshal, a Missionary of the Church of England, was preaching a Lecture and the Deponant saith the s^d Mr. Marshal was a-justifying the proceedings of King and Parliament against America and from thence came to the Blockading of the Town of Boston, which Blockade, he says, made a great outcry or Noise; but (says he) if I can bring something similar from that old Book (the word of God I mean), it will wipe off the Reproach from the King & Parliament. Says he, we Read in the 20th of Judges of the Children of Israel's Destroying the Tribe of Benjamin respecting the Levite's Concubine. And the Deponant further saith that when the s^d Mr. Marshal came towards the close of the Sermon he used these words: "My Dearly beloved, it is time (or high time) to Crush this Dam'd Rebellion" or words to the same purport, according to the best of his remembrance. And further the Deponent saith not. [*Conn. State Arch., Revolution, vol. V, doc. 451.*]

❡ *John Baker testified that he had been at John Marshall's house in October, 1775 and had asked Marshall if the King had not committed unconstitutional acts in the Boston Port Bill and the Quebec Bill.* Marshall answered: "No, the King had a right to do as he did." Baker rejoined that the Law of Nature never gave the King that power. Marshall said it did. [*Ibid., vol. V, doc. 452.*]

❧   *Henry Tomlinson testified that he remarked in front of Marshall that he hoped the Boston Port Bill and other Parliament Acts would soon be repealed.* Marshall's answer was that he hoped that Parliament never would repeal them. But if they should repeal them and thereupon the Colonies should appoint a day of Thanksgiving, he, s^d Marshall, would not pay any regard to it . . . that if he, s^d Marshall, was at the head of affairs, he would subject the Colonies & bring them at his feet or he would kill every blood of them. *[Ibid., vol. V, doc. 453.]*

APRIL 4, 1776

❧   *David Bosworth of New Milford testified that in the latter part of February or the beginning of March, 1775, he went to Judea to hear Mr. Marshall preach and between meetings he heard Mr. Marshall say that* the Distress among the People run so high that nothing but Bleeding would cure it, and that, had General Gage taken five or six of the Members of the Congress and hanged them, the rest would have submitted; and that, had they enforced the Stamp Act in the time of it, the Americans would have been peaceable Subjects now . . . I told him that if General Gage had taken that Method he would have been cut off and all his Troops. S^d Marshall asked: "Who would oppose the King's Troops? Would you? If you set out upon that Errand, you are a dead Man, for if you are not shot, you'le be hanged. . . ." *[Ibid., vol. V, doc. 449.]*

MAY 7, 1776

❧   *Joseph Woodruff of Woodbury said that he was at Marshall's house a few days after Lexington and that Enos Beach remarked on some bloodshed at Boston.* "Don't be concerned," says Mr. Marshall, "for I know our Men began first," and said, "the Assembly is about some Devilish Act for they are going to inlist Men to go to Boston and I wish they would inlist me. I would go till I came in Sight of the regular Army and then push my Boat to them soon." "But," says Beach, "they can't inlist under King George for they Rebel against him." Mr. Marshall says: "these Saints pretend to inlist under King Jesus, but it is more like King Devil." *[Ibid., vol. V, doc. 454.]*

4 THE REVEREND JOHN WISWALL OF MAINE DESCRIBES THE OUTBREAK OF DISORDER IN FALMOUTH AND THE TRAGEDIES ACCOMPANYING HIS ESCAPE FROM THE REBELS

Within a week of the fracas at Lexington and Concord, harassment of the Anglican clergy started as far as one hundred miles from Boston. The Reverend John Wiswall, rector of St. Paul's Church in Falmouth (Portland), was among the early Anglican ministers to confront the issue of allegiance. As the political storm was gathering, Wiswall had endeavored to avoid its impact by neutrality or silence, but neither he nor his church could long escape the crisis. His confrontation, like that experienced by Peters, Marshall, and Seabury, was precipitated by the Massachusetts Assembly's recommendation that the churches name a day of fasting and prayer in support of resistance to the Coercive Acts and take up a collection for those who would suffer from the closing of the port of Boston. He refused both requests. His journal carries a stark recording of the tragic personal impact of events: "On the 21 [June] my Family left Fal. & arrived 3 July at Boston. On the 19th Daughter Elizabeth taken down with the Flux. 21st My Wife with same Disorder. My daughter died the 23^{d} and my Wife the 26th—buried in Family Tomb the 28th. October 18: Falmouth canonaded and burnt by order of Admiral Graves."[1] His letter from Boston to the Reverend Richard Hind, Secretary of the Society for the Propagation of the Gospel, gives details of the outbreak of the rebellion in Falmouth and of his escape the previous month.

BOSTON, MAY 30, 1775

❡ *Revd Sir*

Since my last, the Disorders of the *eastern country* have grown to so great a pitch, that I have been obliged to flee to this Town for Protection. On Tuesday, 9th May, walking with Mr. Mowat, commander of one of his Majesty's Ships then in the Harbour, on a Hill contiguous to the Town, apprehensive of no danger, we were on a sudden surrounded by a Body of men armed with Muskets and Bayonets, who commanded us to surrender ourselves Prosoners. We were with this company of Banditti (which con-

---

[1] *Wiswall Papers,* Acadia University, Wolfville, Nova Scotia.

sisted of 67 men commanded by one Thompson, their Colonel) three hours and a half before the People of Falmouth were made acquainted with our Situation; during which time we were greatly insulted and abused, and in great danger of being shot to death. They had lain there in ambush from Sunday; their Intention was (as their Colenol informed us) to have surprised us in Church, but contrary Winds prevented their arrival in Season. By 1 o'Clock the Towns-people and the Country folks in the neighbouring Towns were informed of our Situation, and a large Body of men appeared upon the Hills where we were, most of them with an intention to carry us into the Country and confine us there; but some of the Towns-men [tried] to interceed for our liberty; being induced thereto by the spirited Conduct of Cap Mowat's Lieutenant. He upon information of the danger we were in, sent out his Boats and, among others, had apprehended J. Prebble Esq. of Falmouth, appointed by the Provincial Congress General of the Eastern Forces. And by letter had assured the Select-men of his resolution to fire from the Ships upon the Town, unless we were immediately dismissed.

After much altercation it was agreed to carry us to a Tavern at the entrance of the Town; where we were guarded by a body of near 300 men. And the officers of this Militia after some debate agreed to dismiss us for this night, E. Freeman, Select man of the Town, and I. Prebble Esq^rs being bound for us forth coming in the morning. As we were retireing (tho guarded by the Cadet company of the Town) one of the mob fired at us, but providentially we escaped unhurt. The next morning the officers sent for Cap. Mowat, who (as was his duty) refused to go from his Majesty's Ship. By this time they were joined by several other companys from the Country and made up a body of 500 armed men. They possessed themselves of a large House in the centre of the Town belonging to one of my Parishioners, and converted it into a Barrak—Turned out the Family—His Wife, tho sick in bead, they forced out of doors and pillaged the House of almost everything that was valuable. They forced me in the afternoon to appear before them. I was strictly examined and questioned by their leaders, and it gave me pleasure that I could assure them that I had never in my Sermons so much as glanced at their political disputes, tho I declared that [not] the sever[es]t punishment, not the fear of Death, should tempt me to violate the oath of Allegiance and Supremacy to K. George, of Canonical Obedience to my Diocesan, or, in conformity to the provincial Congress, to deviate from the Rules of the C[hurch] of England or the Instructions I had received from the venerable Society for the Propagation of the Gospel in foreign parts, whose servant I was. And that I was resolved by God's help, that no temptation should prevail with me to do, or even *promise* any thing unworthy [of] my ministerial character. I was then allowed to retire to my House. The next day they placed a guard at another of my Parishioner's houses and carried away all his Plate. They permitted me upon my parole to walk about town unguarded. And on Saturday I made my escape on board the King's ship, having good reason to believe that they intended to carry me away with them & confine me close prisoner in the Country. Sunday I read prayers and preached on board the Ship. Monday, we put to Sea, and the next Sunday I arrived at this place where I am without money and without Cloathing—my Family at more than 100 miles distance from me—a Wife and three Children, destitute of bread, among enemies, who bear the greatest malice to the Church of England—my little Flock persecuted and many of them obliged to flee from their Dwellings. I have not been able to hear from Falmouth since I have been at Boston—no letters are suffered to pass by Land, nor has there been any communication by Water. In one word, Rev. Sir, I am stripped of every thing. . . . [*Wiswall Papers, Acadia Univ.*]

5 THE REVEREND SAMUEL SEABURY OF WESTCHESTER
PROTESTS HIS ARREST: MEMORIAL TO THE CONNECTICUT
ASSEMBLY

Some members of the clergy who were singled out at the outset for persecution appealed to reason and law for protection, underestimating the extent to which the colonial protest had passed into the hands of an unreasoning mob. Samuel Seabury's memorial to the Connecticut Assembly, recounting the circumstances of his seizure in Westchester and subsequent detention, is illustrative of the mistaken faith that civil rights would be legally protected. He pointed out to the Assembly that it was inconsistent for those who protested against the act of Parliament directing certain persons to be carried from America to England for trial to carry him from Westchester to Connecticut for trial.

❡   That on Wednesday, the 22d day of November last, your memorialist was seized at a house in West Chester where he taught a grammar school, by a company of armed men, to the number, as he supposes, of about forty; that after being carried to his own house and being allowed time to send for his horse, he was forced away on the road to Kingsbridge, but soon meeting another company of armed men, they joined and proceeded to East Chester.

That a person styled Captain Lothrop ordered your memorialist to be seized. That after the two companies joined, the command appeared to your memorialist to be in Captain Isaac Sears, and the whole number of men to be about one hundred. That from East Chester your memorialist, in company with Jonathan Fowler, Esq., of East Chester, and Nathl. Underhill, Esq., of West Chester, was sent under a guard of about twenty armed men to Horseneck, and on the Monday following was brought to this town and carried in triumph through a great part of it, accompanied by a large number of men on horseback and in carriages, chiefly armed. That the whole company arranged themselves before the house of Captain Sears. That after firing two cannon and huzzaing, your memorialist was sent under a guard of four or five men to the house of Mrs. Lyman, where he has ever since been kept under guard. That during this time your memorialist hath been prevented from enjoying a free intercourse with his friends; forbidden to visit some of them, though in company with his guard; prohibited from reading prayers in the church, and in performing any part of divine service, though invited by the Rev. Mr. [Bela] Hubbard so to do; interdicted the use of pen, ink, and paper, except for the purpose of writing to his family, and then it was required that his letters should be examined and licensed before they were sent off; though on Friday last, Captain Sears condescended that your memorialist should be indulged in writing a memorial to this Hon. Assembly. That your memorialist hath received but one letter from his family since he has been under confinement, and that was delivered to him open, though brought by the post.

Your memorialist begs leave further to represent, that he hath heard a verbal account that one of his daughters was abused and insulted by some of the people when at his house on the 22d of November. That a bayonet was thrust through her cap, and her cap thereby tore from [her] head. That the handkerchief about her neck was pierced by a bayonet, both before and behind. That a quilt in the frame on which the daughters of your memorialist were at work was so cut and pierced with bayonets as to be rendered useless. That while your memorialist was waiting for his horse, on the said 22d day of November, the people obliged the wife of your memorialist to open his desk, where they examined his papers, part of the time in presence of your memorialist . . . That your memorialist then asked an explicit declaration of the charges against him, and was told that the charges against him were:—

That he, your memorialist, had entered into a combination with six or seven others to seize Captain Sears as he was passing through the county of West Chester, and convey him on board a man-of-war.

That your memorialist had signed a protest at the White Plains, in the county of West Chester, against the proceedings of the Continental Congress.

That your memorialist had neglected to open his church on the day of the Continental Fast.

And that he had written pamphlets and newspapers against the liberties of America.

To the first and last of these charges your memorialist pleads not guilty, and will be ready to vindicate his innocence, as soon as he shall be restored to his liberty in that province to which only he conceives himself to be amenable. He considers it a high infringement of the liberty for which the virtuous sons of America are now nobly struggling, to be carried by force out of one colony into another, for the sake either of trial or imprisonment. Must he be judged by the laws of Connecticut, to which as an inhabitant of New York he owed no obedience? or by the laws of that colony in which he has been near twenty years a resident? or, if the regulations of Congress be attended to, must he be dragged from the committee of his own county, and from the Congress of his own province, cut off from the intercourse of his friends, deprived of the benefit of those evidences which may be necessary for the vindication of his innocence, and judged by strangers to him, to his character, and to the circumstances of his general conduct in life?

One great grievance justly complained of by the people of America, and which they are now struggling against, is the Act of Parliament directing persons to be carried from America to England for a trial. And your memorialist is confident that the supreme legislative authority in this colony will not permit him to be treated in a manner so destructive to that liberty for which they are now contending. If your memorialist is to be dealt with according to law, he conceives that the laws of Connecticut,

as well as of New York, forbid the imprisonment of his person any otherwise than according to law. If he is to be judged according to the regulations
of the Congress, *they* have ordained the Provincial Congress of New York,
or the committee of the county of West Chester, to be his judges. Neither
the laws of either colony nor the regulations of the Congress give any
countenance to the mode of treatment which he has met with. But considered in either light, he conceives it must appear *unjust, cruel, arbitrary,*
and *tyrannical.*

With regard to the second charge, viz.: That your memorialist signed
a protest against the proceedings of the Congress, he begs leave to state the
fact as it really is. The General Assembly of the province of New York,
in their sessions last winter, determined to send a petition to the king,
a memorial to the House of Lords, and a remonstrance to the House of
Commons, upon the subject of American grievances; and the members of
the house, at least many of them, as your memorialist was informed, recommended it to their constituents to be quiet till the issue of those applications should be known. Sometime in the beginning of April, as your memorialist thinks, the people were invited to meet at the White Plains to choose
delegates for a Provincial Congress. Many people there assembled were
averse from the measure. They, however, gave no other opposition to the
choice of delegates than signing a protest. This protest your memorialist
signed in company with two members of the assembly, and above three hundred other people. Your memorialist had not a thought of acting against
the liberties of America. He did not conceive it to be a crime to support
the measures of the representatives of the people, measures which he then
hoped, and expected, would have had a good effect by inducing a change
of conduct in regard to America. More than eight months have now passed
since your memorialist signed the protest. If his crime was of so atrocious
a kind, why was he suffered to remain so long unpunished? or why should
he be now singled out from more than three hundred, to endure the unexampled punishment of captivity and unlimited confinement?

The other crime alleged against your memorialist is, that he neglected
to open his church on the day of the Continental Fast. To this he begs leave
to answer: That he had no notice of the day appointed but from common
report. That he received no order relative to said day either from any
Congress or committee. That he cannot think himself guilty of neglecting
or disobeying an order of Congress, which order was never signified to him
in any way. That a complaint was exhibited against your memorialist to the

Provincial Congress of New York, by Captain Sears, soon after the neglect with which he is charged, and that after the matter was fully debated, the complaint was dismissed. That he conceives it to be *cruel, abitrary,* and in the highest degree *unjust,* after his supposed offense has been examined before the proper tribunal, to be dragged like a felon seventy miles from home, and again impeached of the same crime. [*Beardsley, Life of Seabury, pp. 36-41.*]

6 THE REVEREND RICHARD MANSFIELD OF DERBY AND OXFORD, CONNECTICUT, SAYS THAT "NO PAINS HAVE BEEN SPARED TO VILIFY AND DEGRADE THE CLERGY"

The Reverend Richard Mansfield, before the close of 1775, was forced to abandon a family of thirteen children and his parish in Derby and Oxford, Connecticut, and flee to Hempstead, Long Island. Like the Reverend Mr. Marshall, he found that speaking disrespectfully of the Continental Congress was a punishable offense, but labeling King and Parliament as tyrants and butchers was commendable. *"O Tempora, O Mores!"* were the words with which he expressed his incredulity at such a turnabout. He analyzed the rancor of the people in New England against the British government by pointing to the efforts of their leaders to inflame them, not because those leaders genuinely feared the loss of liberty but because they were ambitious for power for themselves.

JANUARY 12, 1776

❦ *Revd Sir* [Samuel Peters]

After I saw you last at the Commencement in New Haven in September, 1774, that violent Spirit in the Whigs of harrassing and oppressing the loyal Tories, which then prevailed most in the Eastern parts of Connecticut, spread itself by Degrees into the Western Parts, where during the last Summer and Autumn it raged with as much, and I believe more, unbridled Fury than ever it had done at the Eastward. And I have been obliged a little more than a Month since to leave my Parishes, my Family and Friends, and to fly into Exile in order to escape Violence and Imprisonment, if not immediate Death, . . . I shall be glad to return back again to my Family and Parishes so soon as I can do it in Safety, but this, however, I do not expect unless the Colony shall be reduced to Subjection to the King and the supreme Authority of the Empire. The King's Speech to the two Houses of Parliament in Octr and the Address of the Lords which have been lately published here in the NewsPapers give the Friends to Government here some Hopes that such vigorous and effectual Measures will be pursued next Summer as will crush the Opposition and restore desired Peace and Tranquility before the Expiration of the Year now newly begun, but this, it may be, is a Thing rather to be desired and wished for than expected, for at present the Combinations in the Colonies against the Parent State and their Efforts for Independancy seem not a little formidable and have been but too successful. The same People in our Colony which at the Beginning of the present Disputes were loyal and averse to take up Arms against the King do generally, and I believe I may say universally, retain their Loyalty and Duty still; those Methods which the other party hath made Use of to gain them over to their Side, such as Minute Men and Mobs, dragging them before ignorant, dirty, domineering Committees of Inspection, imprisoning some and tarring and feathering others, and the like, have had no other Effect than to confirm them the more as well in their Attachment to the British Government as in the Abhorrence of the Tyranny of their new-made Masters.

Professors of the Church of England have sustained the chief Load of Insult and Abuse, it being known that they are firmly loyal and no Pains have been spared to vilify and degrade the Clergy for no other Crime but merely that of inculcating upon their Hearers the Duties of Peaceableness and quiet Subjection to the Parent State. A great Deal of the Rancor and Bitterness which is fixed in the Minds of the New England People against British Government is manifestly owing to the great Pains which their Teachers have taken to inflame them. The main Drift of their Prayers, Sermons, and Harangues at Town Meetings for twelve Months past hath been to make People believe that his Majesty, his Ministry, and the Majority in the two Houses of Parliament have a fixed Design against the Protestant Religion and English Liberties and to introduce Popery and Slavery in England, America, and throughout the whole Empire. But those who are best acquainted with them and have had the nearest view of their Conduct and Practices for a Number of Years past are well satisfied that their Clamours have proceeded not from a Fear of the Loss of Liberty, but from a Lust of Power, and that they have sought the civil Independence of the Colonies in order to gain a State Establishment of their Church on the Ruins of the Church of England and of all other Churches. But it is needless, perhaps impertinent to me, to mention this to you who are so well acquainted with the ambitions, Views, and dark Practices of these People. . . .

Mr. Marshall was summoned to appear and answer before the Assembly in Octr. last on a Charge of speaking disrespectfully against them (the Assembly) and even saying that they were devising (he supposed) some Devilish Acts. But they, perceiving that the Charge could not be proved (for it was not true), they deferred his Appearing to a late special Session, and then again deferred it till the next, to keep him (as is supposed) uneasy in a State of Perplexity and anxious Fear. I am credibly informed they have made a Law with a very severe Penalty for only speaking disrespectfully of the Continental Congress while at the same time, it is thought, not only allowable but commendable, and even meritorious, to bestow upon the King and the two Houses of Parliament the Epithets of Tyrant and Ministerial Butchers. O Tempora, O Mores! and that they have made another Law forbidding any Person either to correspond with any of the King's Governors or Commanders or to put or continue himself under the Protection of his Majesties Troops on Pain of incurring a Confiscation of his Estate.

My present Situation, my dear Friend, is not a little uneasy and uncomfortable; at a somewhat advanced Stage of Life, being fifty-two Years old, I am forced to leave my Parishes, my Wife and numerous Family. . . . I see no Prospect that I can soon, if ever, return. . . . Perhaps I might return in law [if] I should make a base, servile Submission to the violent Party, acknowledge that I had committed a heinous Crime by giving a true account to Governor Tryon of their Proceedings, beg their Forgiveness, and then Join with them in scurilous and treasonable Invectives against the King and Parliament, and to crown all do my Utmost to spirit up the People to Arms. But as I cannot do this without violating the plainest Duty and going contrary to the Dictates of my own Reason and Conscience, I am determined never to do it as it would be giving too great a Price for the Purchase only of temporary Tranquility. I am too far advanced in Years and in too poor a State of Health to think of coming over to England where I suppose there are as many Clergymen already as can ever be provided for. I determine therefore to continue under the Protection of the King's Troops either at New York or Boston till such Time as this horrid and unnatural

War shall be concluded. And as I have Reason to fear that my small paternal Inheritance (the only Means of Support for my numerous Family) will be confiscated and as I have now nothing left me for my own personal Support but my Salary from the Society, I hope they will continue to me at least my usual Salary; and as I am suffering for my Loyalty and doing my Duty, I cannot entertain any Thoughts that they will refuse it and thereby render me compleatly abandoned and wretched. [*Peters Papers, Church Historical Soc., Austin, Texas.*]

7 THE REVEREND JOHN BEACH DOGGEDLY ADHERES TO
HIS ORDINATION OATH

The Reverend John Beach of Newtown and Reading, Connecticut, courageously refused either to cease praying for the King, as the Continental Congress ordered, or to close his churches. He continued to conduct services as before and was seized by the rebels in July 1776, dragged out of his church, and threatened with a bloody means of silencing, namely the cutting out of his tongue. An excerpt from the *Narrative of Walter Bates,* a prominent Loyalist of Stamford, depicts this dramatic incident. Six months later John Beach died, defiant and unflinching to the end.

[JULY 1776]

❡ In July, 1776, Congress declared Independency and ordered the Commonwealth to be prayed for instead of the King and Royal family. All the loyal churches were thereupon shut up, except one at Newtown, Connecticut, of which the Reverend John Beach was rector. His gray hairs adorned with loyal and Christian virtues overcame the madness of his enemies. This faithful disciple entered his church saying: "If I am to credit the surmises kindly whispered to me that unless I forbear from praying for the King I shall never pray or preach more, I can only say, whilst no intimation could well be more distressing, it admits not one moment's delay; with all due respect for my ordination oaths, I am firm in my resolution while I pray at all to conform with the unmutilated liturgy of the church and pray for the King and all in authority under him."

Upon this the rebels seized him, resolved to cut out his tongue. He

said: "If my blood must be shed, let it not be done in the house of God."
The pious mob then dragged him out of the church. "Now, you old devil,"
said they, "say your last prayer!" Whereupon he devoutly kneeled down,
saying: "O Lord and Father of mercies, look upon these mine enemies and
forgive them. They know not what they do; they are blindly misled. O God,
in mercy open their eyes."

By the Providence of God, the council of his enemies was brought
to naught and his life spared. [*Raymond, ed., Kingston and the Loyalists,
p. 7.*]

8 THE REVEREND EBENEZER DIBBLEE OF STAMFORD REVIEWS THE WARTIME TRAGEDIES TO HIS FAMILY, BEGINNING IN 1775

The Reverend Ebenezer Dibblee, a graduate of Yale, was a Puritan minister who changed to the Church of England and served as rector of St.
John's Church, Stamford, for fifty-one years. He was one of the few
Connecticut clergymen who remained at their posts throughout the war
even though his support from the Society for the Propagation of the Gospel
and from his congregation was cut off. In the spring of 1775, when he saw
the approaching dangers to his country and to the well-being of the church,
he wrote: "Our duty as ministers of religion is now attended with peculiar
difficulty: faithfully to discharge the duties of our office, and yet carefully
to avoid taking any part in these political disputes, as I trust my brethren in
this colony have done as much as possible . . ."[1] His letter to Samuel Peters
in London details the personal dangers and tragic cost of his determination
"to ride out the storm or perish in the Ruins of the Church and Country."[2]

STAMFORD, MAY 3, 1785

❧ *My Dear Rev*ᵈ *Sir* [The Reverend Samuel Peters]
You know the former Laws & Constitutions of this State, not a
Rate was made up and Collected for me among my people from the year

---

[1] *Historical Mag. Protestant Episcopal Church,* vol. II, no. 2, p. 57. Original in the
Archives of the Diocese of Connecticut.
[2] September 10, 1784. Ibid., p. 60.

1775 to 1783. Every man did what was right in his own eyes for the support of religion. Fences on the Glebe Lands . . . all destroyed, . . . like a common, which cost me better than £10 Sterling to repair. Add to this the flight of my Eldest Son (unhappy man—would to God I had died for him) about Christmas 1776, his house plundered, a Wife and 5 children turned out and myself obliged to take them in until Spring, then Sent off to him. Destitute of necessary bedding and Cloathing; not a grandson, whom I would have kept, permitted to stay, the Cloathing given him taken from him.

The Banishment of my Son Frederick in Novr 1776 till Spring, then lately graduated at Kings College, New York, to Lebanon (with about 20 of my Parishoners, chiefly heads of families) supported at my cost. Myself Obliged to flee in March 1777 to my Dauter at Sharon to be inoculated for smal Pox. The town then a Hospital Town, and the smal Pox brought in by ye return of Soldiers, prisoners at Fort Washington. The flight of Frederick (left to take care of the family in my Absence) to save his life (Occasioned by ye alarm of his Excellencies Genl Tryons Excursion to Danbury) to his brothers on Long Island. My Sons looking to me for Assistance, not daring to enter into Service wh they might have done to advantage, in regard to my safety; cost me better than 150 sterling in Bills Drawn and privately conveyed; wanted for my own Support. Add to this the diminution of my Parish by the flight of numbers, reputable families and (best) support of the Chh. The Dangers attending my person. One bold attempt on my life being Shot at as I was going to attend a funeral. Waylaid, and not presuming to return the same way but seldom, when I went to attend the private Duties of my Cure. The billeting and Quartering of Soldiers upon me, sometimes a Company of a Troop of Horse, or a Militia Company, Officers and Men. Terrors by night and Day for fear of the Violence of Lawless Mobs & ungoverned Soldiery. The Ruin of one of my Daughters by frights, for a long time wholly Insane; and to this Day not wholly recovered her former composure & tranquility. Add to this the Burden of Publick Duty since our Churches were opened (wh mine was Christmas, 1779) wh I never neglected within or without our Lines, when permission could be obtained to pass & repass; and for one or two years before the peace I met with less Interruption.

I have given you some general hints, my Dear Sir, before of those past occurrences; and my preservation, I can ascribe to nothing but the providential care of Almighty God. [*Hist. Mag. PEC, vol. II, no 2 (1932), pp. 65-66.*]

9 THE REVEREND EDWARD BASS OF NEWBURYPORT AVOWS
HIS UNSHAKEN LOYALTY TO THE KING DESPITE HIS MIDDLE
COURSE DURING THE REVOLUTION

"If many of the other ministers in Massachusetts · had done the same
thing [as Edward Bass] and placed their religious duties above the political
ones, the scattered missions and churches would not have dwindled
away. . . ."[1] Such was the comment of Daniel Addison, the biographer of
Edward Bass, about the conduct during the Revolution of various prominent missionaries of the SPG. While the Society's missionaries, such as
Samuel Peters, Henry Caner, and John Troutbeck, took a clear-cut stand
for King and Parliament from the outset, Edward Bass compromised by
complying with fast days set by Congress and by omitting prayers for the
King. He was thus able to keep his church open throughout the Revolution.
He was charged by the rebels with taking the side of the King and by some
Loyalists, as well as by the Society, with assisting the rebel cause. Trying
not to antagonize either side during the war, he managed to straddle the
main issue and circumvent the confrontations, but at the close, when his
support was withdrawn, he found it necessary to assert to the Society that
his loyalty had ever been "firm and unshaken." Bass, a Harvard graduate
in 1744, was rector of St. Paul's Church, Newburyport, when the troubles
began. While the charges against him discussed in the following letter
were serious enough to destroy his career, they were not sustained and he
continued to occupy his pulpit, completing fifty-one years as rector of St.
Paul's Church and serving as well as Bishop of Massachusetts from 1797
until his death in 1803.

JANUARY 9, 1784

❧   *Rev ᵈ D ʳ* [William Morice]

I am sorry to trouble you with any more of my Letters but cannot
help observing to you the Singularity of my fate in being a Sufferer on
both Sides, here for my Loyalty, with you for the contrary, without being a
Trimmer.

When the late Rebellion commenced I preserved as firm and unshaken a Loyalty to his Majesty and attachment to the British Government

[1] Daniel D. Addison, *The Life and Times of Edward Bass,* Boston and New York,
Houghton Mifflin: 1897, pp. 153-154.

as was consistent with my remaining here in the Country, whereof I have given to the Society all the proof that I thought to be requisite, having exhibited ample Testimonials in my favor not only from my Wardens but also from some of the most respectable Characters and noted Loyalists in the Capital of New Hampshire, who, without my Seeking, made me a voluntary tender of their Services, not to mention the testimony of Sundry refugee Loyalists now in London who resided in this Town and perfectly knew my Character and conduct. Nothwithstanding which the Society has thought proper to distinguish me by uncommon marks of neglect and displeasure. When they were pleased to strike me off their list of Missionaries they left me to vindicate myself against I knew not what and to pick up the articles I was charged with here and there by accident and from common report; and I took much pains to exculpate myself before I was accused, which I flatter myself, was the only Sign of guilt I had. The articles against me which have come to my knowledge in the abovementioned way are that, being a chaplain in one of his Majesty's Regiments I endeavoured to seduce the Soldiers from their Allegiance, that I have said I did not care whether I pleased or displeased the Society for that my Parishioners were able and willing to support me, that I read the Declaration of Independence in my Church, that I preached a Sermon exhorting my Hearers to contribute liberally towards cloathing the rebel Army, and that I observed the Fasts appointed by the Congress. All these charges against me are absolutely false, except the last. I did indeed, for I do not deny it, generally open my Church on those Fasts, tho' not in consequence of the orders or commands of any rebel power whatever, none of whose papers or proclamations I ever read in publick, but of the application and earnest Desire of my Congregation who represented it as necessary in order to preserve the Church from Destruction. Such was the spirit or Frenzy of people in general at that time. It was, I certainly say, with reluctance that I complied, nor was I Singular in this practice. Several Missionaries who remained in the Country and who stand well with the Society, having, if I am not much misinformed, done the same. Some of the Missionaries and others who quitted the Country were extreamly prejudiced against us who staid behind and kept our churches open and were, I doubt, too ready to hearken to any reports against us. You must allow me, Sir, to express my feelings of the Society's neglect of me.

Had there been no means of correspondence during the war, I should not have tho't much of it, but I had the Mortification of knowing that others were noticed and particularly of hearing a letter from the Society to the Rev^d Mr. [Samuel] Parker of Boston, who is no Missionary, read thanking him for looking after some Interest of theirs in his neighbourhood. If there be any merit in this I can lay claim to the same, being able to show the Society's letter of thanks to me for my attention to their landed interest in N. Hampshire. I have had two protested Bills lately returned to me of 50 pounds each, the one drawn upon Messrs Hoare & Co., the other upon the Society's Treasurer. The Disappointment [was] great, not to mention the charges of the protest to one who has nothing to pay.

I am not ignorant that the Society has power to relinquish any Mission whenever they judge proper, but that they should discard a Missionary upon an allegation of misdemeanor, a Missionary of long standing, depending upon their Salary and daily incurring expences upon a full expectation of continuing to receive it, without giving him any notice or chance of vindicating himself, is, to say the least of it, an unexampled method of proceeding and such as must imply some very atrocious crime fully proved. I must beg it of the Society either to let me know what proof of my innocence will be sufficient, or that no proof whatever will avail me, or, if they refuse me this, at least to do me the common act of justice to let me know who are my accusers and what the nature of my crime or crimes. For whatever becomes of my living, I am determined to clear up my character in point of Loyalty to my late Sovereign. [*Bass Papers, Diocesan Lib., Boston.*]

Some First Expatriates

The Tories in and around Boston were confident that the ten well-equipped British battalions under General Gage would make short shrift of the mobbish colonial forces when a showdown came. This confidence is reflected in the remark of Cortlandt Skinner, Attorney General of New Jersey: "A few Regiments and fleets . . . will sett us Right." Thus the reality of March 17, 1776, was hard to believe, and even harder to accept. General Howe was evacuating Boston on orders from home. The rebels had occupied and erected formidable fortifications on Dorchester Heights. Reinforced by cannon from Ticonderoga and by fresh militiamen, and providentially aided by a storm which prevented a British attack, they controlled the heights which commanded both the harbor and the town. Howe's position was untenable. This disastrous turn of events had come about so suddenly—almost in one night—that the remaining Tories were flabbergasted and unprepared for the personal upheaval involved in an evacuation order.

Although many people had already left Boston, over eleven hundred Loyalist refugees departed with General Howe. Seventy-eight vessels carried them, along with some eight thousand five hundred British soldiers, to Halifax.[1] A few ships, such as that of Jolley Allen, foundered on the way. The voyage, however, was only the beginning of the Loyalists' misfortunes. Washington wrote about their distress to General Charles Lee: "It seems, upon their arrival at Halifax, that many . . . were obliged to encamp, although the ground was covered deep with snow; and . . . to pay six dollars a week for sorry upper rooms and stow in them men, women, and children, as thick comparatively as the hair upon their heads. . . ."[2]

Many of these expatriates who went to Halifax in the Boston exodus eventually sailed on to England, where they met a chilly reception of a different sort. London was already crowded with unwelcome refugees wrestling with the problems of finding a livelihood in an extravagant milieu and a place in a hierarchical society, of securing government bounty, and of combating homesickness. The following selections furnish a sampling of Loyalist reactions to the sudden evacuation of Boston, of their experiences in flight, and of the adversities they had to contend with as first expatriates.

While Phila DeLancey (Mrs. Oliver DeLancey), one of whose letters is also quoted, did not become an exile until somewhat later, her social chitchat about ignoring the sacred rules of hospitality was as characteristic of the London life of a prominent Loyalist family in 1776 as in 1778 and has therefore been included here.

I   PEGGY HUTCHINSON FEELS THE WRENCH OF PARTING
FROM FAMILY AND FRIENDS

Peggy Hutchinson was only seventeen when she left Boston for London with her illustrious father, whose ineptitude as Governor had led to his replacement by General Thomas Gage shortly after the Boston Tea Party. One of the Governor's sons, Elisha, accompanied him and Peggy, while Thomas Jr. and Elisha's wife, Polly, remained in Massachusetts. It is to the latter that Peggy pours out her distress and homesickness on leaving her native shores.

[1] General Howe to Lord George Germain, April 25, 1776. Fitzpatrick, ed., *Writings,* vol. IV, p. 418 fn.
[2] Force, ed., *Am. Arch., 5th Ser.,* vol. I, p. 98.

AUGUST 2, 1774

❡ *My Dear Polly,*

. . . You wish for an account of what has passed since we saw each other; it seems a little age since the chariot drove from the door and conveyed me from so many dear friends, to suffer more than I should have thought possible for me to have borne. I had not left you many hours before I was the most miserable creature on earth: it is impossible for me to describe or give you any idea of what I endured the first fortnight; the second was bad enough, and I am not yet what I used to be. Your beloved [Elisha Hutchinson] has I suppose given you an account of our passage, though I recollect nothing material except the death of poor Mark, which happened when we were about half way over. London my dear is a world in itself: you ask me how I like it? very well for a little while: it will do to see once in ones life, and to talk of ever after; but I would not wish to fix my abode here. In the country methinks, had I my friends with me, I could not but be happy: for seventy miles round it is a perfect garden, and exceeds all that the most romantic fancy could paint. I cannot say much in favour of the climate; the weather has been as cold as our Novembers, and excessively damp, except two or three days, and I have not been free from a cold since I came.

I must not forget to tell you I have been presented to their Majesties, and met with a most gracious reception, but must leave the particulars for the next ship, being very much hurried at present. . . . The Watchmen are just telling me 'tis past ten o'clock, which is but the beginning of our evenings; but as I have another letter to write to go tomorrow, I must bid you good night. . . .

Accept the best wishes of your very affectionate sister, [*Hutchinson, ed., Diary and Letters, pp. 200-201.*]

2 "A FEW REGIMENTS AND FLEETS . . . WILL SETT US RIGHT": CORTLANDT SKINNER INDULGES IN WISHFUL THINKING

Attorney General Cortlandt Skinner, a cousin of Oliver DeLancey and a large New Jersey landowner, was expatriated from New Jersey in March 1776 only as far as the *Asia* in New York Harbor. He left his wife and thirteen children in Perth Amboy. His activities in support of the Royal cause led to his capture, but he was exchanged in September 1776, along with Montfort Browne, Governor of New Providence (Nassau), for General William Alexander. He tried to buttress the optimism expressed in the letter of December 1775 to his brother in England by organizing the New Jersey Volunteers, the largest of the Loyalist regiments. Despite the ravages of Skinner's Cowboys on rebel centers, neither his regiment nor the formidable British fleet succeeded in setting the Empire right.

DECEMBER 1775

❧ *Dear Brother* [Lt. Col. William Skinner],

. . . I have always fondly, I may say foolishly, hoped that the unnatural dispute now Subsisting w^d have an amicable Conclusion. I find myself sadly disappointed. The Tea duty began the Controversy; it has branch'd out into divers others and now the contest is for dominion; for the Rise of the dispute we are indebted to Smuglers, for the present State of it to the Pride, Ambition, and Interest of those who, Enemies to the Ecclesiastical Establishment of their Country, have long ploted and to others who have become of Consequence in the Struggle. They who began [it] had their Interest in View and feared the Ruin of their Smugling here. They, I believe, were willing to leave the dispute; the others with deeper Views took it up and, building on the foundation, are attempting a Superstructure, a Republic that will deluge this Country in blood. This is not new; all history, as well as our own, shews great Convulsions, Rebellions, & Revolutions from mad enthusiasm and designing Men. . . . We are now upon the Eve, I May say, have actually begun a Revolution. The Congress are our King, Lords, and commons. They have taken Canada with the Consent of its gratefull Inhabitants; they block up the Royall Army in Boston. They say they have Secured the Indians, have appointed an Admiral, are fitting out a fleet and are universally obeyed. Is this, or is it not Independency? They say it is not and We must believe even against our own Senses. An Edict, Manifesto, or what you please to call it, has been issued from the Congress in which they say we have taken into Consideration a proclamation issued by the Court of St. James, meaning the late Royall Proclamation. You will soon see it. I fear bad Consequences will attend the mistaken people who are so obstinately Loyall as to favour the Royall Cause; when or what will be the end I know not. The Mistakes of Genl^s and Adm^s and the Strange Security in Sending Succors, Ammunition, etc. to the Country last year, while [there was] Success here in every mad measure, vexes me. The S[ain]ts say Heaven won their Side. I rather think the old saying more applicable: the Devil is blind to Young Beginers. We must have in every War a Campaign at Least of Blunders. This [one] may be called so from the ill-timed March to Lexington to the Loosing of Canada. Another Year may sett us Right but not five. Only Succor Boston. A few Regiments and fleets to different provinces will sett us Right, at least bring us to our Senses and support the friends of Gover^t. [*Joseph Reed Papers, vol. III, 1774-1775.*]

3 FRANKLIN THE ARCHTRAITOR: HENRY HULTON[1] APPLIES A HARSH EPITHET TO FRANKLIN

BOSTON, JANUARY 22, 1776

❡ [To Robert Nicholson]
... I imagine every one now is convinced of the intentions of the Americans of which we on this side the water had long been persuaded & [we] could not but lament to see a man in the confidence of Government deceiving Administration, working himself into the favor of Men of Science by his Philosophy and deluding well disposed people at home whilst he was fomenting the flames of rebellion in America.

This arch-traitor! this most atrocious of men is Dr Franklin! The only question now seems to be whether it is more advisable to transport the Scepter of Empire to the Delawar than to retain it on the Thames! and I hope there is no old Briton can hesitate at the question.

The intention of these people are no less than to establish one or more independent Republicks.

This town [Boston] is now deserted by most of its inhabitants, friends as well as Rebels; however we have plays acted by the officers & assemblies & Concerts are just set a going—but I imagine our Winter Quarter amusements will not be of long continuance; for we expect an early vigorous, extensive, & decisive Campaign. The winter began very boisterously, but it seems to soften away & is likely to go off soon without a severe frost.

The only cheap thing here is house-rent & the dwellers therein are

---

[1] See pp. 28-29.

frequently changing. Many people are glad to get a family into their houses with the furniture standing whilst they flee from fear or to join the Rebels. [*Hulton, Letterbook.*]

4 AHOY FOR HALIFAX: JOLLEY ALLEN AND THE *SALLY*
FOUNDER ON CAPE COD

Jolley Allen, the merchant who had hoodwinked the Boston Committee about a consignment of tea, relates a harrowing adventure at sea as he and his family join the evacuees. His account of the foundering of the *Sally* under a "fresh-water captain" affords a day-by-day glimpse of the mounting distress of the Boston Loyalists. Allen, a West Londoner by birth, had repaired to Boston in 1755, where as a merchant he had accumulated many thousand pounds sterling before the evacuation.[1] He had married an Irish girl, Eleanor Warren, and, as he records in his *Minute Book,* "had seventeen children by her plus five miscarriages in thirty-seven years of marriage." Following the events of March 1776 described below, Allen was confined for nearly a year in Boston, but succeeded in making his escape to England. He was obliged to leave his six remaining children behind, parceled out evenly in the homes of their uncles, Lewis Allen of Shrewsbury and Thomas Allen of New London. The only letter Jolley Allen ever received from his children after his escape was from his daughter Eleanor, written from New London October 23, 1778, in which she commented: "It was very Disagreeable to be parted from the other three of us. But my uncle's [Lewis Allen] ingratitude and unhappy Disposition made it Necessary it sho'd be so." A friend wrote her father the following fall that this daughter was going to marry the man who helped him escape: "I hear from New London Nelly is going to marry Pardon Taber. He lay in *Gaol* Eight Months on your account so he is going to take your Daughter for Damages. A very good Match."[2]

Jolley Allen reached England in March 1777 and died in 1782, before he could be reunited with his children, deeply troubled over the suffering his loyalty had caused to his "poor Fatherless, Motherless, and Friendless

---

[1] The property on the *Sally* lost through shipwreck was valued at £ 3,000 sterling. *Loyalist Transcripts,* vol. III, p. 102.

[2] *Minute Book,* Nov. 18, 1779, pp. 13-14. Antiquarian Society, Worcester, Massachusetts. See Mass. Historical Society *Proc.,* February 1878, for parts of the *Minute Book.*

Six Children now Suffering in America. . . . Their great Affliction has been wholly on the Account of my Loyalty to my most gracious King and Country. . . . Without your kind goodness . . . to look on them after my Death . . . I [will] have brought all my Children to Poverty and they must beg their daily Bread. But if this should be the case, I do not repent that I have lost my all for the sake of my good King and Native Country, who, I pray God, may Conquer all her Enemies both by Sea or by Land. This is my Daily Prayer."[3]

❡ The 11th March, 1776, I hired a vessel for my effects and family of one Captain Robert Campbell (as he styled himself); he . . . offered me his vessel . . . and told me it was entirely at my service . . . and if I had a mind to have part or the whole of the vessel it was for me to say. I asked him who was to command the vessel. He said the vessel belonged to him and he was the captain. I then asked him if he was used to go to sea; he answered he had, for above twenty years and upwards he had gone captain of his own vessel. Upon that, I showed him my shop and two warehouses all full of goods, and likewise I showed him the furniture of my house, which . . . alone cost me above one thousand pounds sterling. I then asked this villain (for I cannot look upon him in any other light) how much of his vessel he thought I should want, being myself not acquainted therewith. He told me he thought three-quarters of the vessel would hold all my effects. I answered, if that was the case, I had rather hire the whole of the vessel, that I might have room enough, which I accordingly did, and agreed with him for fifteen guineas sterling to carry me, my family, and effects to where the fleet and army went; and paid him down half the money and took his receipt for the same—for at that time we did not know where we was going.

Accordingly, I began to take my goods down and pack them up immediately and was obliged to put my goods in the street, as I packed them up; and myself and family was obliged to watch them two days and two nights before I could get any carts to carry them down to the vessel, which was about a quarter of an English mile from my house to where the vessel lay, which cost me upwards of forty-two pounds sterling, all ready cash from me, to carry my goods to the said vessel.

[3] To George Irwin [November 22, 1779], *Minute Book,* pp. 26-27.

The 14th of March myself and family lay on board the said vessel. The 17th towed down below the castle by strange sailors. 19th towed down to Nantasket Road by other strange sailors and there lay till the 27th of March. At three o'clock in the afternoon sailed under the convoy of Admiral Gratton. I believe the fleet . . . made about eighty sail . . . at that time. . . . When we came to weigh anchor and got it three-quarters up, a large ship of about five hundred ton came foul . . . of our bowsprit with bitter oaths that they would sink us if we did not let go our anchor immediately. . . . We had carried away all their side rails and a carriage that was hung over, with our bowsprit. When they got clear of us, we fell to work to get our anchor up again, and another vessel of near seven hundred ton fell foul of our bowsprit, which carried away their quarter gallery and did them abundance more mischief, which obliged us to let our anchor down again. Accordingly we weighed our anchor a third time and got it up so high that the vessel moved.

I then seemly was glad to think we should get out of Nantasket Road and get up to the fleet which hove to for us, but I was soon disappointed of my hopes; the stern of our vessel got aground. I turned to the captain and asked him what he thought would become of us. He told me he could not tell. I then desired him to look over the stern of the vessel where we was aground, which he did. I asked him whether the tide was a coming in or a going out. He said he could not tell without an almanac. . . . I told him to go to the stern of the vessel and look at it again and let me know his opinion, which he did, in these words, after looking some time: if the tide was going out, our vessel would grow faster in the sand and we should be more aground, but if the tide was coming in, the vessel would rise and we should get away, which I thank God we did.

Now we are going to sea without either captain, master, or sailor, or even a boy that had been a week at sea. He put a young man at the helm that never saw salt water before and gave him directions in the following manner, . . . pointing to a vessel before him . . .: "Follow that vessel and wherever it goes do you keep it in view." . . . I called the captain once more aside and asked him what that man at the helm must do when night came on and he could not see that object. "Oh," said he to me, "Mr. Allen, I am surprised at you; all the men-of-war will throw out lights and then we shall be as light as day." This was easy enough to believe of him, but I soon found a fatal reverse for before the day closed in the whole fleet was out of sight and we was left by ourselves in this melancholy situation.

I went down to the cabin to see my dear wife and children. Soon after I heard something of a bustle upon deck. I went up and was told by the captain that the clew at the mainsail had given way, and to my great surprise found it had blown off the other side the shrouds and was in danger, as I thought, of oversetting the vessel. I then called the captain to me and said . . .: "You are the man that has brought me into all these difficulties . . . and I do insist upon your doing your duty on board this vessel as long as I am in it, both by night and day; and I command you that you get the clew of the mainsail in immediately and I will give you all the assistance in my power, with all the other help on board." There being room in the vessel, I gave him liberty to take in more passengers in order to put more money in his pocket, and in all we were . . . twenty-nine souls on board. All endeavored . . . to get the mainsail in again. With all the help we were able, the captain tied it to one of the pumps, and, for want of knowing how to tie a sailor's knot, it gave way in less than a quarter of a minute. I told him that he must now renew his strength again and we would likewise all do the same, for I feared the vessel would overset. Accordingly, we got it in again and he then tied it to both the pumps (in such a manner as not to be able to untie it again and, when we came to Cape Cod, it was obliged to be cut with an axe.)

I likewise asked him a little while after this accident . . . if he had no such thing as a compass in our binnacle. He said he had two but he had no occasion for them and they was both under his bed; and if I went down with him he would show me them, which he did and said he was going directly after the fleet. Then he made an apology to me that he had broke open my box and took out my candles, as he had forgot to bring any on board.

At this time we went about five knots an hour, but had shifted several seas in the interim. . . . All the water we had on board the vessel that could be drank, which was on deck, was about three-quarters of a barrel. We shifted a heavy sea about eight o'clock that same evening, which loosed the cask and the bung started; we lost all the water we had, there not being one drop left in the whole vessel to wet the mouths of the twenty-nine souls on board. In about half an hour after we shifted a much heavier sea, which carried away the whole of our caboose off the deck, which was the place we had to dress our victuals in, and we had no place in the vessel to dress a bit of victuals after this.

I then turned to the captain and said . . . "I fear we shall all perish before half an hour's at an end; had you not better try your pumps to see if the hold of the vessel is filling with water to know if we was not sinking?" "Oh, dear sir," says the captain, "I am glad you thought of it for I had forgot it." He tried the pump, which was choked, and he could not get any water out of it, and the hold was at least a quarter full of water. I told him then to try the other pump. He then went to look for the tackling to rig the other pump, but could not find anything to do it with, and if he had, I am convinced he did not know what to do with it.

In this disagreeable situation we continued, shifting seas often. I walked the deck till near twelve o'clock at night until I was not able any longer, for the seas breaking in upon us so often and from the intense cold, for it froze to solid ice, so that it was dangerous to move a foot on deck. In this deplorable state I went down into the cabin to my wife and seven children, thinking every minute would be the last I had to live in this world. . . . I took my wife by the hand as she lay in bed in the cabin; . . . I thought myself a happy man to think I should die in her arms along with her. . . . But I did not let her know the imminent danger we was in.

About two o'clock in the morning those passengers that lay in the hold of the vessel came running to the cabin and begged for God's sake we would permit them to come in, that a plank in the side of the vessel had given way, and the sea was pouring in, and the vessel was sinking. They begged that they might be permitted to stay in the cabin till we all went to the bottom together. . . . I then insisted on the captain to go . . . to see where the plank had given way in the vessel. I myself went along with him and found it not quite so bad. We had a great deal of water in the hold that had got between the ceiling and the vessel and had broke its way through, and made as much noise as if a plank had given way every time the vessel moved. I then desired the captain to come upon deck with me. . . . I asked him whereabout he thought we was at sea . . . what distance we was from land. He said that was impossible for him to tell, for he had not kept any reckoning, and the reason he gave . . . was that he had forgot to bring pens, ink, and paper. I told him, if he had applied to me, I had all these things. He then made me answer he had never learned navigation and that he never was on salt water before, but he knew how to row a boat in a river. . . . I was sorry we had not a boat that we might save our lives at the sinking of the vessel. . . . If we had a boat with oars it was my opinion he knew as little of it as he did of navigation. . . . I then turned my back to him, almost froze[n] to death, and looked out for daybreak. . . . Every rope on board was, with the breaking in of the sea, froze almost as thick as my thigh, and no person on board able to walk on deck. In this manner we lay at the mercy of the waves, with our sails and rigging torn in ten hundred thousand pieces, that we could neither get them up or down.

The joy it gave me when I saw daybreak I am not able to express. About seven o'clock . . . the captain said he saw a vessel. I entreated him if he knew how to steer for that vessel, he would with all speed. He made me answer that he did not understand steering the vessel. . . . Some time after, he said he thought he never saw so large a ship before and desired me to look at it. . . . I turned round from him and thought to myself how kind good Providence had been to me during the night past to live to see that happy hour. Of the vessel he had been so much surprised at, I soon perceived it was the main land. . . . He was fully convinced it was Nantucket. I told him if that was the case, we must all perish very soon, for the amazing rocks and shoals that lay off Nantucket I could remember very well, as I saw them above twenty-two years ago . . . when I came from London.

. . . This captain of ours was at the greatest loss to know what to do in this situation. . . . Providentially for us, the day turned out very fine and warm. We got clear of all the ice upon deck soon after. I then desired the captain to order every one upon deck that was on board the vessel, which was twenty-nine souls. . . . I told them that we now appeared in coming up to land and I was of opinion that no soul on board knew what land it was, and we came up with it very fast. We all advised on this matter together; . . . some was for scuttling the vessel . . . sooner than fall into the hands of the Americans again. . . . I was for running the vessel on shore in the most convenient place . . . which we all agreed to except the captain; he was for going to sea again. . . . Accordingly we endeavored to set in for the land as fast as we could. Thank God, there was a strong current . . . with a full tide in our favor, which brought us in quick. We struck upon the bar of Cape Cod most violently either seven, eight, or nine times which made her shake in such a manner that at every stroke we thought she would have gone to pieces. . . . But luckily for us, we got off the bar. . . . Soon after we got into twenty-four fathom water (as the fishermen told me), where the captain let go his anchor. . . . This was about two o'clock in the afternoon after we left Nantasket Road, the 28th of March.

The captain says to me, by way of advising with me, seeing no boat come off to us, whether or no we had not better hoist a signal of white sheet or table-cloth, to let them know we was in distress for want of a boat. The answer I made him was that . . . there was upwards of nine hundred thousand signals more than there need to be . . . After waiting some time in this distress we espied a man on shore; we made motions to him, as we could not hear each other speak, for the conduct of our captain was all of a piece; he had no speaking trumpet on board. . . .

At last, to our great joy, we saw a cart with a boat (or canoe) in it drawn by ten oxen, and six men more which came down to our assistance. They soon got the boat into the sea and two men in it to know from whence we came. We told them we was from Boston with the fleet. They answered they was surprised, for they thought we was from a foreign country and durst not come near us for fear we had the plague on board. . . . These two men did not come on board, as we had a Mrs. Wezzle on board with us that had the small-pox, just then on the turn, of which she died. . . . They returned with two more men that had had the small-pox a number of years before and they came on board of us. This was about seven o'clock in the evening, the 28th of March, 1776.

In this canoe, I and my family, eleven in number, came on shore . . . and then we had three miles to go through the woods before we came to the town of Cape Cod, which I walked and the rest of my family rode in that dung-cart that brought the boat to our assistance, drawn by ten oxen. We arrived in the town about ten o'clock that same evening, and to my great surprise was ordered into a small cottage, not fit to put a hog in, where we remained. . . . The vessel they seized and all the effects that they could find therein and I was never allowed to see the vessel more. . . .

But the people, as incensed as they was against government and their friends, when they heard my case, how I had been used by the captain that brought my family and effects from Boston to Cape Cod, they was ready to tear him to pieces. They called him a fresh-water captain; that they should not choose to hang a salt-water captain, but a fresh-water captain it would give them the greatest pleasure imaginable; and it was with great difficulty I could prevail on them not to hang him, as they declared he did not deserve to have time to say: Lord, have mercy upon him, to bring such distress as he had done to twenty-nine unfortunate souls. [*Allen, Minute Book, Nov. 18, 1779.*]

5 "THE CURSED REBELLION": DR. SYLVESTER GARDINER
IS DRIVEN FROM A STATE OF AFFLUENCE TO A STATE
OF INDIGENCY

The letter from Dr. Sylvester Gardiner, written after his arrival in Halifax, is in accord with Washington's description, with a few personal details added about the "wretched place." Dr. Gardiner had amassed considerable wealth not only from an extensive medical practice but also from a store and warehouse for the importation and sale of medicines. His stock of drugs was confiscated and used to supply the Continental army. He followed the British army from Halifax to New York, where he continued for 2½ years until, as he said, "I had spent every farthing I brought from Boston, even my Plate and the little household furniture I brought with me, which obliged me to come to England . . . and throw myself on Government." He settled down on the southeast coast of Dorset, supported by a pension of £150 annually from the British government. Most of his property in Massachusetts was confiscated, but his Maine property was spared because of an error in the proceedings. In 1785, he returned to the United States and continued his practice in Newport, Rhode Island, until his death the following year.[1] The following letter from Halifax was written to one of his sons-in-law.

HALIFAX, MAY 9, 1776

❆ *Dear Sir*

I wrote you in Jan^r last wherein I mentioned my fears of the Troops leaving the Town of Boston, which they did on the 17th day of March in such a precipitate manner as gave the friends of Government only four or five days' notice, which put them under necessity of leaving almost every thing they had, as no Vessel or Seaman were to be found so suddenly to transport themselves with their effects; which threw them into the utmost distress. Indeed, the General gave them all the assistance he could by assigning them some places in the Transports but then there was not room to carry off any of their effects and but very little of their Household furniture; and what they did was chiefly distroy'd or stolen by the Soldiers or Saylors on their arrival at this miserable place. It was with the greatest

[1] Henry S. Webster, "Dr. Sylvester Gardiner," *Historical Series,* no. 2, Gardiner, Me.

difficulty they could get Houses to screen themselves from the weather. Houses did I say? They scarcely deserve that name. The wretched inhabitants took every advantage of our Misfortune and made us pay at the rate of 50 £ pr Ann. for Houses that would not before rent for five Pounds and had the conscience to make us pay 50 s. a cord for cord Wood that would not fetch Ten Shillings pr cord before our arrival. The stated price of Beef, Mutton, and Veal is at 12d a pound, butter at 1/6, and everything else in proportion, except fresh fish which is always cheap enough.

I found I could not stay in Boston and trust my person with a set of lawless rebels whose actions have disgraced human nature and who have treated all the King's Loyal Subjects that have fallen into their hands with great cruelty and for no other crime than for their Loyalty to the best of Kings and a peaceable Submission to the best constituted Government on Earth. I don't believe there ever was a people in any age or part of the World that enjoy'd so much liberty as the people of America did under the mild indulgent Government (God bless it) of England and never was a people under a worser state of tyranny than they are at present. I find there are people among you that have imprudence enough to abet this horrid rebellion and even in the Senate House to give the highest incomiums to a wretch [Sam Adams] that had nothing else to recommend him but perjury and rebellion and, had he taken the side of Government, never would have been heard of. But I would advise those trumpetors to Sedition and rebellion to remember that some men's praise and panegericks are like the pillory, infamy, and disgrace.

We have heard nothing from Quebec for a long time but have reason to hope and believe it is still in the hands of the King. Genl Howe detach'd the 47 Reg^t for that place 21 Days ago and by a Vessel that arrived here yesterday we learn that 22 Days ago 12 Sail of Ships from England were seen to the westward of Newfoundland bound to Quebec and by the winds we have had both fleets must have arrived there before now, which is sooner, I am sure, than the rebel reinforcements can pass the lakes and get before that place. The 19th April cut me of[f] from all my Estate in the Country both in Lands, Mortgage bond and book Debts and now, being drove from Boston, have lost all the rest [of] my estate there, both Stock in trade and the income of my Houses that I have nothing more left I can call my own but about £ 400 in Cash which I happen'd to have by me. By this cursed rebellion I am drove to this miserable place and from a state of Affluence (could truly say I did not know a want) to a mere state of indegency; that is to say, when this poor £400 is gone God only knows what I shall do. For the present I purpose staying here during this summer's campaign to see if it will give the King's Troops a footing in some point of America. If it should not, I purpose going to some part of the West Indies or in some Town in England or Ireland, for the severity and length of the Winter in this place and badness of the houses will render it impossible for me to stay here during the Winter Season. [*Gardiner Papers, vol. II, p. 7, Mass. Historical Society.*]

6 THE REVEREND HENRY CANER DEPARTS FROM THE COLONIES AND ARRIVES IN LONDON

The Reverend Henry Caner wanted to stay at King's Chapel as long as possible. Even though he had heard from British officers that the troops would evacuate Boston and burn it in March or April, he was unprepared for the speediness of the movement. Before his ship left for Halifax he heard that his house had been plundered, £500 sterling worth of household goods thrown into the street or carried off, and his library, worth some £200, destroyed. After a crowded and uncomfortable trip he arrived at Halifax April 1 and reached London finally in June. He wrote the Reverend John Breynton, who had befriended him in Halifax, that his reception in London had been cool and his prospects of receiving support were slight. The "great ones" repeatedly put him off. He told Governor John Wentworth he had received "many good Morrows . . . but that is all, except a share of the Benefactions collected for the suffering Clergy" (July 1, 1776). To Mrs. Elizabeth Wentworth, a former parishioner at King's Chapel, he wrote: "Pleasure, Dissipation occupy everyone here, which produces much Insensibility in regard to the Sufferings of others" (July 10, 1776). He commented further to the Reverend Mather Byles: "with what a jealous Eye the Clergy of this Kingdom look upon one who has served in America, esteeming him in no better light than as coming to take the Bread out of their Mouths" (December 26, 1776). He soon joined critics of the conduct of the war, commenting to Dr. Sylvester Gardiner: "Lord North lately fell from his Horse and broke his arm; many people here wish it had been his Neck" (September 30, 1776). He concluded that he had a good prospect of starving and planned to perish with as much decency as possible.

"To get rich is the grand desire of every busy individual." (London, Sepr 1776). *From the diary of Edward Wyer of Massachusetts (1751–1788) who went to London early in 1776 to pursue medical studies. He practiced medicine in Halifax, returning after the war to Massachusetts, where he died.* (Courtesy of Mrs. Donald Sealy, Scarsdale, New York.)

The Reverend Henry Caner Says He Had Only Six Hours' Notice to Prepare for Embarkation and the Abandonment of His Parish

HALIFAX, MAY 10, 1776

❡ *Revd Sir* [Richard Hind]

. . . As to the Clergy of Boston, indeed they have for eleven months past been expos'd to difficulty and distress in every shape. And as to myself, having determined to maintain my post as long as possible, I continued to officiate to the small remains of my parishioners, tho' without a support, till the 10th of March, when I suddenly and unexpectedly rec^d Notice that the King's Troops would immediately evacuate the Town. It is not easy to paint the distress and confusion of the inhabitants on this occasion. I had but six hours to prepare for the Measure and was obliged to embark the same day for Halifax where we arriv'd the 1st of April. This sudden Movement prevented me from saving my Household goods, Books, or any part

[127]

of my Interests except Bedding, Wearing Apparel, and a little provision for the passage of myself and little family. I am now at Halifax with my Daughter and Servant but without any means of support but what I receive from the Compassion and Benevolence of the worthy D^r [John] Breynton. I have greatly suffer'd in my health by the cold weather and other uncomfortable Circumstances of a passage to this place, but, having by the good providence of God survived the past Distress, I am in hopes some charitable hand will assist me in my purpose of proceeding to England where the Compassion of the well dispos'd will, I hope, preserve me from perishing from want of the necessaries of life. If otherwise, God's will be done. [*Caner Letterbook. See Sprague, Annals of the American Pulpit, vol. V, p. 62.*]

His Reception in London Was Characterized by "Many Good Morrows" But Little Support, He Writes His Friends

LONDON, JULY 1, 1776

❦   *Rev^d and Dear Sir* [John Breynton]

Since my last to you I have seen the B^p of Lond. and Arch B^p of Cant. Many compassionable expressions were the chief result of our meeting— "I am glad to see you but sorry for the occasion." "Be ye warmed and filled," without providing the means of either, is but cold comfort. At present I have obtained nothing except a share of the Donations for the Suffering Clergy nor have I even the promise of any stated provision. When I offer my Service to enter upon any duty here the answer is: "We can't think of your residing here. We want such men as you in America." "Favor me then with some temporary provision till a return is become practicable." "We hope the force that is gone from here will soon bring that about." (Such is my present State w^c I leave to your own reflection.) This Day Week the B^p of London went to Tunbridge to reside for 5 Weeks and Dr Hind was out of Town at my Arrival nor likely to return for some time and so no meeting of the Soci. for two Months. Such is etc. Lord George, who is said to be the active Minister, is now out of Town. I purpose to attend his Levee at his return, but have no expectation, as he declared before his going out of Town that no further pension should be granted to any one American Claim nor any Notice taken of them till the Dispute is settled in America. In my opinion that is not likely to happen in my time, so I may rest contented as I can. I wish I could give you a more promising account of my Affairs, because I am persuaded it would give you pleasure. I am led to this Conclusion from the many singular testimonies of Civility and Benevolence I have met with from you and yours and for which I have at present no other return to make but Love and gratitude. [*Caner, Letterbook.*]

7   PHILA DELANCEY FINDS "THERE IS NOT SUCH A THING AS DISINTERESTED FRIENDSHIP" IN LONDON

Shortly after the raid on Bloomingdale, the home of.General Oliver De-Lancey, his wife, Phila Franks DeLancey, who had hidden in the doghouse under the stoop on that grim night of November 1777, removed to London with Charlotte, an unmarried daughter. Several letters from Phila De-Lancey to her husband offer a glimpse of the social life and social expectations of one of New York's most prominent families. Several DeLancey daughters had already married into titled English families, Susanna (d. 1777) to General Sir William Draper, and Phila into the Payne-Galwey family. Charlotte subsequently became the wife of Sir David Dundas. Even with an *entrée* to high social circles through these connections and through her husband's position in America, Phila Franks was disappointed in her reception. Society seemed callous and friendships insincere. On May 23, 1780, she wrote to her husband: "People have no Idea of hospitality; it is banish'd this World; there are only a few individuals who support its sacred Rules; among the Number is the Earl of Huntingdon; he sends his Carriage for my Daughters & me, to his Villa in Leisestershire to Stay a Month this Summer." She barely mentions the events shaking the nation, commenting merely: "There is not the least occurence to write of; the debates are warm as usual." Her children and grandchildren, her support, and the important people who showed her kindness—these concerns absorbed her interest.

NOVEMBER 23, 1778

❡   *My Dear Mr. DeLancey*
        . . . The Letters to you are often intercepted. Believe me, My Dear Mr. DeLancey, I never omit writing to you when I do to my Children and am concerned I was so unhappy to displease you when I mentioned last Spring that I had not heard from you. Believe me that your friendship is

my principal comfort. I was very secure that you would recieve from Nancy's Conduct all the satisfaction you express; her understanding & heart are superior in goodness to most women; her Sisters have great Merit; Mrs. Gallwey [Phila DeLancey] a Patren of Prudence. She is very happy in a Husband, as I am in his Friendship to me & Charlotte; he is as attentive to us as possible, a very hospitable Man & a fond Father to two fine children. Yr other Granchildren are well, the Friendship I recieve from my Friends are not only Complimentary as you imagine. I wrote to you that the best of Brothers, Moses [Franks], allowd me £ 150 str per year; after this year his bounty will, I presume, cease. I wrote to you not to remit me more Money this Year, being pleasd with the oppertunity you have of realising all you Pay to your own use. House Rent & every other concuring circumstance is exorbitantly high. I am a perfect oeconomist.

I have not seen Gen[l] Howe [again]; he and his Lady visited me and asked me to a card Party; they are parties I do not engage in. I shall visit Lady Howe this Week & hope to find an oppertunity of mentioning the account which tis shameful not to discharge. I expected Sir H. Clinton would pay the greatest regard to every requisition of yours. I am rather old to be taught, but I learn every day that there is not such a thing as disinterested Friendship here.

I believe Gen[l] FitzRoy[1] well temper'd but I am never admitted in his House. . . . Lord Abingdon & Col Skinner are very Civil; Gen[l] & Mrs. Gage show more kindness to Charlotte & me than we have a right to expect. We were ask[d] to dine there the day after Robertsons arrival with him & Family. Coll. Sherrif is very fat, & G[l] Robertson exceedingly emaciated; his time is so entirely engrossd by Ministers that he has scarely a moment for himself. I hope you may depend on his Friendship. Mrs. Tryon is extreamly Civil to me. Mr. [John] Watts & [James] DeLancey are ever wishing themselves in America and I can't discover what detains them, this only a world for Men of Affluence to live in. Its a comfort to know the Markets at New York are so plentifuly provided. My anxiety for you & my Children are beyond expressing & I hope your next favor will tell me that you are restord to some degree of tranquility. The Ministry & the few loyal Subjects place great dependance on S[r] H. Clinton. May it be well founded, with honor to his Army & benefit to the publick wellfare. I have no other prevention to going to Court but my hearing being so imperfect. Many think

---

[1] Lord Southampton, Lord Chamberlain in 1780.

it proper but I dread the confusion. Charlotte will go soon to return thanks for both of us, with Mrs. Galwey & Lady Payne, who is a modest, wellbred pleasing Lady & a favorite at Court.

. . . Your account of expenses for us in yr letter by Gen[1] Robertson distrest me. I hope Bloomingdale is not an added expence to you and that the servants occasion you no trouble. I wish them to live comfortable. London is filld with free Negro's from America. . . .

Sir Wil[m] [Draper] is greatly embarrassd at present by his immence Debt, for since your Dear Daughters Death [Susanna DeLancey Draper] his Uncle will not assist him, except that his Government of Yarmouth was made over to the old Man for Money Lent & he has now given it back to S[r] W[m], but that is only a drop of Water in the occean. But you and I have no more concerns with him & his affairs can only affect himself; its best that he has had nothing from you. He is extream Civil to us & I return it, tho I often feel a Repugnance in exerting my Civility to one who has my entire disaprobation in a most essential Point. There is Lord Amherst with not half his sence and talents [who] is now the most Conspicious Man in the kingdom. I had a flattering Letter from him but did not experience the exertion of his interest. I hope in the course of the Winter I shall have the satisfaction of conveying some acceptable intelligence respecting your affairs. I have a few acquaintance, & they are among the most respectable, by whom I am treated with great politness.

I have not any Political news. This ill advis'd Government does not permit their state affairs to transpire; indeed they engage so much in lighter occupations that the weighty Business of the Nation must needs suffer. . . .

Farwell my Dear Mr. DeLancey & be assurd I shall ever wish to prove myself your Sincere Friend & affectionate Wife

P DeLancey
[Courtesy of Mrs. Norman Duffield, Buffalo.]

Animosities Afire

JULY 4, 1776–DECEMBER 1782

The Rubicon: Independence

Makes the Difference

Acceptance of independence as the goal of the political strife was a gradual development. Many Tories in 1774–1775 approved of resistance to British acts and defended the steps taken by the First Continental Congress. On the other hand, many Whigs, Jefferson and John Jay among them,[1] were reluctant to see an irrevocable break with England and hoped throughout most of 1775 for a reconciliation. The reconciliation became less and less possible as events following Bunker Hill (June 17) continued to harden the division, especially the King's August 23 Proclamation of Rebellion, the burning of Falmouth in October, and the King's December 23 move closing colonial ports to all commerce, effective March 1. Paine's *Common Sense* early in 1776 crystallized for many the notion of independence. Others who tended toward Loyalism continued to regard a reconciliation

---

[1] Jefferson to John Randolph, Aug. 25, 1775. See Richard B. Morris, *John Jay: The Nation and the Court,* Boston: 1967, p. 7. See Jefferson, *Writings,* A. A. Liscomb and A. L. Bergh, eds. Washington: 1903, vol. IV, pp. 28–30.

as possible even after the British had opened hostilities in the South and attacked Charleston. Jacob Duché, chaplain to Congress for a short time, even thought it was possible to reverse course and rescind the Declaration fifteen months after its adoption. Neutrals, as well as avowed Tories, hoped the peace mission in June 1776 of Sir William Howe and his brother, Admiral Richard Howe, would produce a friendly dénouement of the quarrel, but the announcement of their purpose, issued a week after the Declaration, was untimely, and their instructions were so restricted and out of date as to be ineffectual.

Thus the Declaration presented the neutralists and straddlers with the second crisis of allegiance. Now more than an oath to abide by the Association was involved. Now the states would form governments of their own, and laws of treason, attainder, and confiscation would be forthcoming. It was necessary to make a choice. If a man did not support the Continental Congress, he was ipso facto considered against the rebel cause. Committees of safety would administer oaths of allegiance as a test. To the Loyalists the converse was true; if they sided with Congress which had usurped government, they were traitors to Britain.

I   JOSEPH GALLOWAY REFLECTS ON THE VOTE FOR INDEPENDENCE

Joseph Galloway, a prominent Philadelphia lawyer and author of Galloway's Plan of Union, wrote extensively on the possibility of reconciliation and on the political events with which he was intimately acquainted. An excerpt from his *Reflections on the American Rebellion* offers his interpretation of the vote for independence.

1780

❦   The necessity of their affairs now compelled them to throw off the mask. That design which they had disguised under the most solemn professions of loyalty, and of the most ardent desire to be united with Great Britain on constitutional principles . . . was now to be openly, and as solemnly avowed. To effect this in Congress much cabal and intrigue was necessary. Many of the members, recollecting their instructions, knew the sentiments of the people in general, and besides saw the ruin and horrors of a measure so bold and dangerous. Their cabals continued near a month; the republican faction met with much opposition, and for a time despaired of success; at length, however, having made some proselytes to their opinion, they resolved to risque the vote of Independence. And yet after all the arts of intrigue had been so long essayed, the question was put and the Colonies were equally divided. But upon the next day, the question being again resumed, contrary to their own rules, Mr. Dickinson, a gentleman naturally timid and variable in his principles, retracted his opinion and gave the casting vote. Thus did this great event, which was to support a dangerous and seditious faction in the heart of the Mother Country, and to involve it in a war with two powerful nations, depend on the vote of an individual member of its own community.

The vote of Independence was soon followed by another, recommending to the people to abolish the old and to institute new forms of Government. This measure was eagerly adopted by their adherents, who had now all power in their own hands. They were combined in Congresses, Conventions, and Committees. They were arrayed in arms by voluntary associations, and there was moreover a regular armed force under the Congress to support them; while the loyalists, and friends to the British constitution, were without a head, and without weapons. These had been long since disarmed. The Governors of all the royal Colonies had been driven from their governments, while those of Pennsylvania, Rhode Island, and Connecticut, were permitted to remain unmolested and in office. The King's Governors had given opposition to their measures, while the others (excepting the Governor of Maryland) either had not disapproved of, or had openly abetted them. The Proprietary Governor of Pennsylvania, if he did not abet, did not, from the beginning of the sedition, discover the least disapprobation of their conduct. His friends, his magistrates, and all the officers of his own appointment, not ten in the whole Colony excepted, were leaders in the opposition. In the two Charter Governments of Rhode Island and Connecticut, the Governors were the creatures of the faction, and at the head of their measures. All obstacles being thus removed, they were not long in establishing their new States, in which they excluded every trace of the powers of royalty and aristocracy.

The time was now come when the independent faction, having obtained by their arts sufficient power, were not afraid to acknowledge that they had deceived the people from the beginning of their opposition to

Government; and that notwithstanding all their solemn professions to the contrary, they ever had independence in their view. *[Galloway, Reflections on the American Rebellion, 1780 ed., pp. 107-108.]*

2 THE LOYALIST DECLARATION OF DEPENDENCE: LOYALISTS OF NEW YORK CITY GIVE A LASTING TESTIMONY OF THEIR FERVOR FOR BRITISH CONSTITUTIONAL SUPREMACY

While Massachusetts had its "Addressers" and "Protesters" in 1775, identifying some of the obdurate Loyalists, New York City had a hard-core group known as "Signers." After the Declaration of Independence they first affixed their names to a petition to the Howe brothers (October 16, 1776) asking for a restoration of civil law,[1] and, when martial law was continued, to a second memorial, dated November 28, 1776, known as the Loyalist Declaration of Dependence. It expressed the wish of the Signers for some way to attest their loyal conduct and their dedication to the preservation of British constitutional supremacy over the Colonies.[2]

NOVEMBER 28, 1776

❦   To The Right Honorable Richard Viscount Howe, of the Kingdom of Ireland, and His Excellency The Honorable William Howe, Esquire, General of His Majesty's Forces in America, the King's Commissioners for restoring Peace in His Majesty's Colonies and Plantations in North America, &c. &c. &.

May it please your Excellencies.

Impressed with the most grateful sense of the Royal Clemency, manifested in your Proclamation of the 14th. of July last, whereby His Majesty hath been graciously pleased to declare, "That he is desirous to deliver His American subjects from the calamities of War, and other oppressions, which they now undergo:" and equally affected with sentiments of grati-

---

[1] Mercantile Library Association of New York City, *New York City during the Revolution*, 1861, pp. 117-119. This petition carried 948 names.
[2] Seven hundred and four names affixed to the Declaration are extant. Original in N.Y. Historical Society. See R. W. G. Vail, "The Loyalist Declaration of Dependence of November 28, 1776," N.Y. Historical Society *Quarterly*, vol. XXXI, no. 2, pp. 68-71.

Loyalist Declaration of Dependence. See New York Historical Society Quarterly, vol. 31, no. 2. (Courtesy of the New York Historical Society, New York City.)

tude for that generous and humane attention to the happiness of these Colonies, which distinguishes your Excellencies subsequent Declaration, evincing your disposition "to confer with His Majesty's well affected subjects, upon the means of restoring the public Tranquility, and establishing a permanent union with every Colony as a part of the British Empire."

We whose names are hereunto subscribed, Inhabitants of the City and County of New-York, beg leave to inform your Excellencies: that altho most of us have subscribed a general Representation with many others of the Inhabitants; yet we wish that our conduct, in maintaining inviolate our loyalty to our Sovereign, against the strong tide of oppression and tyranny, which had almost overwhelmed this Land, may be marked by some line of distinction, which cannot well be drawn from the mode of Representation that has been adopted for the Inhabitants in general.

Influenced by this Principle, and from a regard to our peculiar Situation, we have humbly presumed to trouble your Excellencies with the second application; in which, we flatter ourselves, none participate but those who have ever, with unshaken fidelity, borne true Allegiance to His Majesty, and the most warm and affectionate attachment to his Person and Government. That, notwithstanding the tumult of the times, and the extreme difficulties and losses to which many of us have been exposed, we have always expressed, and do now give this Testimony of our Zeal to preserve and support the Constitutional Supremacy of Great Britain over the Colonies; and do most ardently wish for a speedy restoration of that union between them, which, while it subsisted, proved the unfailing source of their mutual happiness and prosperity.

We cannot help lamenting that the number of Subscribers to this Address is necessarily lessened, by the unhappy circumstance that many of our Fellow-Citizens, who have firmly adhered to their loyalty, have been driven from their Habitations, and others sent Prisoners into some of the neighbouring Colonies: and tho' it would have afforded us the highest satisfaction, could they have been present upon this occasion: yet we conceive it to be a duty we owe to ourselves and our posterity, whilst this testimony of our Allegiance can be supported by known and recent facts, to declare to your Excellencies; that so far from having given the least countenance or encouragement, to the most unnatural, unprovoked Rebellion, that ever disgraced the annals of Time; we have on the contrary, steadily and uniformly opposed it, in every stage of its rise and progress, at the risque of our Lives and Fortunes. [*N. Y. Historical Society Quart. vol. XXXI, no. 2, pp.* 70-71.]

3 "[LONDON] IS ALONE A MATCH FOR TEN AMERICAS" HENRY HULTON EXULTS AT HIS RETURN TO ENGLAND

Shortly after the Declaration of Independence was signed, Henry Hulton, former Commissioner of Customs in Boston,[1] sailed for England from Nova Scotia, satisfied that England offered all the benefits, if not more, that the rebels sought in proclaiming their independence.

BERKELEY SQUARE, AUGUST 22, 1776

❦ *Dear Sir* [Robert Nicholson]

We sailed from Halifax the 18[t] of July and had rather a rough passage, but thank God I landed with my family safe at Dover the 13[t] inst. and we feel ourselves very happy in being once more in our native land, of which blessing no one can be sufficiently sensible who has not lived out of it, and I would wish all murmurers to make the experiment especially if they are sons of liberty, that they may enjoy the sweets of it for a while under the Boston Demagogues. I am persuaded that in no Country in no period of time there ever was a state of society in which the people were so improved, so generally comfortable and happy as in the present one of Great Britain. In other Countrys where you see the magnificence and splendor of the great they are counterballanced by the poverty and misery of the peasantry; they are oppressed, whilst the other live in luxury, but in England there is an air of ease, an appearance of general opulence, and everyone seems to enjoy their property in security and to speak and act with freedom. Such a view must strike every Stranger and make him wish to enjoy life in this blessed land where he can live without dread of oppression from the great, without fear of offending a popular Demagogue, and having his house pulled down by the Rabble. . . .

The many severe circumstances we have of late experienced, the frequent scenes of mortality and distress that have been around us made us in a manner almost resigned to any events and little anxious about life, but when we came to see the happiness of this land, we were almost tempted to say, "it is good for us to be here." Indeed several of the Americans I have conversed with in town say they had no idea of the opulence and grandure of this place, that it is not a City, but an empire of itself, and is alone a match for ten Americas. [*Hulton's Letterbook.*]

[1] See pp. 18-19.

4 "IF THIS BE THE LIBERTY WE ARE CONTENDING FOR . . ."
FREDERICK PHILIPSE III IS TAKEN FROM HIS FAMILY INTO
CONNECTICUT

Frederick Philipse III, proprietor of the largest estate in Westchester,[1] a colonel of the militia, and for twenty-five years a member of the New York Assembly, was inclined to favor the Whigs at first. However, when he attended the meeting in White Plains on April 13, 1775, to elect representatives to the Continental Congress, he refused to join the rebel group in the courthouse and protested against their unconstitutional proceedings. His memorial to the Crown reported that when the tumults in America "tended to weaken and destroy his Majesty's Authority over it, . . . he exerted his influence to prevent it. . . . In the Spring of 1776, he conveined a large Number of the Freeholders and Inhabitants of the Town of Westchester and prevailed on them to enter into an Association to preserve the Peace and to support the legal Government, but that his laudable Intentions were frustrated by the Superior force of several Parties which were after formed in the County and others which came from Connecticut. And at length the Person of your Memorialist was seized on by a party of American Volunteers from New York and carried from his Family a Prisoner into Connecticut where he was confined for the space of six Months—that, being released from his confinement by a Parole granted by Governor Trumbull, he made his Escape with his Family, consisting at that time of a Wife and nine Children, and Sought for Refuge within the British Lines at New York."[2]

While Philipse was being escorted through Westchester and Connecticut to Governor Trumbull's residence at Lebanon, he wrote several letters to his wife, Elizabeth Williams Philipse, indicating that the treatment he received, other than the loss of his liberty and some inconvenience, was not harsh, but polite and reasonable.

[1] Philipse's estate consisted of 3,000 acres and extended for 24 miles up the Hudson. The Commissioners Enquiring into the Losses of the American Loyalists made Philipse an annual allowance of £200 in 1782 and a compensation for losses of £62,075 sterling. *Loyalist Transcripts,* vol. XLI, p. 575.
[2] Ibid., copy in *Philipse Papers,* Sleepy Hollow Restorations, Irvington, N.Y. Paroled December 23, 1770. See *Trumbull Papers,* Connecticut State Library. Sabine, *Loyalists,* vol. II, pp. 537–539.

NEW ROCHELLE, AUGUST 14, 1776

❧ *My Dearest Life*

I am really tired & sick of this Filthy place. The house is Crowded from Morning to night with four Company's of Militia that are parading here for what purpose I cannot learn but are verry Noisy Companions . . . If any news should come to your knowledge write it on the Inside of the Cover of your Letters not with Ink but the Juice of a Lemon and I shall do the same . . .

AUGUST 16 or 17, 1776

❧ Our Departure is now determined. We are to go by Land upon our parole only one officer to attend us which is a great Indulgance. Considering all things Shall not be a Spectacle to the mobbs thro which we shall pass as if we had Guards to attend us. I therefore send Diamond back and beg you'll send to morrow my horse & Chair.[1] . . . Adieu my Dearest Love and may the Great and Good God take you, my Children & all my Friends into his holy protection and believe me to be with the greatest tenderness & affection your most Affec^t

Husband *F. P.*

[In margin] A few Good Lemons would be verry acceptable by Diamond.

AUGUST 17 or 18, 1776

❧ *My Dearest Life*

. . . Am heartily sick of this vile place. I should therefore be greatly Oblidged to you if you could get Abram Odell to hire Jacob Post Waggon with his own horses to Carry up my baggage as far as New haven where I can procure another and send this back. Abram must set of[f] by day break as we promised to meet the Officer who is to Conduct us to Governor Trumbull, one Cap^n Prentice who is known to Mr Babcock. He is of New haven and behaves with remarkable politeness and Civillity. He shewed us his orders from Gen Washington which are remarkable kind and favourable to us. We are to travel at our Leasure and not to hurry us in the least and to provide for us the best Accommodations on the road & to keep an

---

[1] Diamond was Philipse's slave. Philipse was said to be so large a man that his wife seldom rode in the same carriage with him. See Sabine, *Loyalists,* vol. II, pp. 537–539.

Acc^t of all the Expence on the road. In short, I could not have wish'd for better orders and am verry positive will keep up to them but loose no time in sending Abram up by daybreak to morrow. . . . The General has given us the Strongest Assurance that as soon as the Battle is over, let who will get the Victory, we shall be Imediately released —

God of his Infinite Goodness take you and our Children Into his protection and am my Dearest Love

Your Affection^t hus^d
F. P.

HORSENECK, AUGUST 20, 1776

❡ *My Dearest Life*

We arrived here yesterday evening and in Company . . . I am (thank God) In good Spirits and am in no Anxciety but for you & the Children. . . . Our Company are all hearty & well and are just going of[f]. Sam Bush was taken into Custody last night for speaking too freely. . . . Caution our boy's not to open their lips to any Friends or foes . . .

NEW HAVEN, AUGUST 22, 1776

❡ *My Dearest*

I am Just Arrived at this Place after a verry hot & disagreable Journey tho (thank God) am in Good health and Spirits Considering all things and Should be more so was I assured that our Separation did not Affect you so much as I am confident it must do, tho' you Pretend to say to the Contrary. But I intreat you not to be dejected on my Acc^t as I am Conscious that I have done nothing (upon the Strictest Examination) Inimical to the Liberty's of my Country or ever would, let the Consequences be what it will. Nothing Affects more than to be taken up in such an hostile manner without any Crime for it to my Charge and without a hearing. If this be the Liberty we are Contending for — but I have done and shall say no more on that Subject. Tomorrow we shall set out for Lebanon, the Residence of Governor Trumbull, by the way of Middletown, Weathersfield & Hartford. . . .

We have been verry Lucky in meeting with Good Entertainment

Particularly good & Clean Lodging to this place. Our Company is very
Social and Agreeable . . .

Adieu my Dearest
Sincerely your Affec^t Husband
F. P.

[Frederick Philipse Papers, Sleepy Hollow Restorations, Irvington, N.Y.]

5 ROELOF ELTING OF NEW PALTZ, NEW YORK, REFUSES CONGRESS MONEY AS GOOD FOR NOTHING

About 241 million dollars of unsupported Continental currency was issued
by the Continental Congress during the Revolution. Refusing to accept
this paper money as legal tender was tantamount to refusing to take the
oath to the Association; it was another means of singling out the Tories.
Congress money, as it was often called, circulated at par for only about
a year and a half from mid-1775, when the first issue was voted by the
Continental Congress. There were many subsequent emissions, but from
January 1777, they all depreciated rapidly until in March 1780 they were
worth one-fortieth of their face value. The states were uncooperative in
levying taxes to redeem them. Holders of these bills suffered losses, except
for speculators who bought confiscated Loyalist property with Continentals,
and debtors who used depreciated money to discharge debts. Tradesmen
and creditors were loath to accept money which was depreciating, even
though a refusal was generally interpreted as inimical to the rebel cause.[1]

Roelof J. Elting was one of the tradesmen who objected to receiving

---

[1] Congress resolved that persons refusing Continental bills or discouraging their circulation should, on conviction, be published, treated as enemies to the country, and precluded from all trade with inhabitants of the Colonies. Thomas and Samuel Fisher, sons of Joshua Fisher, Philadelphia merchants and disaffected Quakers, were charged before the Committee of Safety with refusing Continental money. They acknowledged the fact, were censured in the press, and were among the twenty-two Quakers sent to Winchester, Virginia, for nine months as dangerous men. William Duane, ed., *Extracts from the Diary of Christopher Marshall . . . during the American Revolution, 1774-1781*, Albany: 1877, p. 59.

Congress money and suffered for his caution. He lived in New Paltz and ran a store in the Elting house on Huguenot Street. Although he signed the Association in 1775, he was suspected of Toryism and was brought before the Committee of Safety to explain his refusal to accept payment in Continentals. As a consequence, he was sent to Exeter, New Hampshire, under arrest and was eventually proscribed and banished under an act of the New York Legislature. In August 1778 he was permitted to remove within the British lines. After five years of banishment, he and his brother Solomon, who suffered similarly, petitioned the Legislature for permission to return on the grounds that they had not taken an active part in the war and that they had been absolved from their allegiance to Britain by the treaty of peace. Both brothers were allowed to return to their homes.[2] Roelof's deposition explains the tradesman's quandary.

1776

❡   Mr. Roelof Eltinge, being summoned by the Sub Committee, appeared accordingly and says in his Defence, on the first Emmitting the Continental Money there was Sundry Disputes about the Money. Some said it was Good, others said it was Good for Nothing. However, when he found he Could pass it readily he received it in payment, but to tell the truth of the matter, for it was a Folly to Lie about it, I Never liked it for I always thought if the King Got the better of the Country the money would be Good for Nothing. Farther, that a certain Mrs. Wirtz, wife of Doctor Wirtz, Came to my house in Order to purchase Some Goods out of my store, when I told Mrs. Wirtz that I did not like to take Congress money for my Goods, as I supposed She intended to pay me in that money, and that I would rather Trust her for the Goods. Unless She would run the risk of the money Passing from me again, for I would be no Looser by it, on which Mrs. Wirtz had the Goods Cut of[f], after which She offered me for part of the S^d Goods which She purchased for her mother in Continental Currency. I told her I would not Take that money without She would

---

[2] Roelof Elting was the son of Magdalen DuBois and Josiah Elting, the wealthiest man in Ulster County, according to the 1765 tax list. *New Paltz Independent,* Sept. 14, 1888; Aug. 9, 1889. See also William and Ruth Heidgerd, *New Paltz,* 1955, pp. 6, 9–10, and Clarence J. Elting, "Lineage of the Elting Family," *Olde Ulster,* vol. III, Kingston: 1907, p. 156.

do as I told her Before, but would Trust her for the Goods, on which She took the Goods away without paying anything for them and after returning home Some Time, the Goods was Brought home to me again and I received them. After this, our Troops Retreating from Long Island, there was a General rumour amongst the people of my Neighborhood that in a Little time Congress money would be Good for Nothing, as the King was likely to overcome, and at this Time numbers of People came to pay me money who, I do believe, would not have thought of doing it, had they not been afraid the money would be Good for Nothing, on which I told them I would not receive the money only on the Conditions Mentioned above to Mrs. Wirtz. [*Elting Papers, Courtesy of the Huguenot Historical Society, New Paltz, N.Y., Inc.*]

6 BEVERLY ROBINSON TELLS THE COMMITTEE OF SAFETY "IT IS NATURAL WHEN A MAN IS HURT TO KICK"

With the Declaration of Independence committees of safety became more active in rooting out the disaffected and in forcing them to leave rebel country. Beverly Robinson, a prominent resident of the Hudson Valley, occupied a fine estate opposite West Point. He had married Susanna, a daughter of Frederick Philipse, and through his marriage had become the owner of a choice piece of Philipse land. He would have liked to remain neutral in the controversy, living quietly on his estate, but independence forced him to a commitment and he chose to remain loyal to Britain, accepting an assignment to form the Loyal American Regiment and become its colonel. Once the choice was made, Robinson became a serious trouble-maker. He carried on the negotiations with Arnold for the delivery of West Point to the British, and he tried to bring Ethan Allen to the British side. Robinson went to England at the peace and lived near Bath until his death in 1792 at age seventy. John Jay, chairman of the Committee of Safety, on examining residents of New York in 1777, made it clear to Robinson that he could not equivocate indefinitely.

❦ Beverly Robinson appeared before the Committee appointed by the Convention of the State of New York for inquireing into Detecting and defeating all conspiracies that may be formed against the Liberties of the Same and the Board of Commissioners appointed By the Convention for the Same purpose.

John Jay Esqr Chairman ⎫ Members
Judge Graham ⎬ of
Nathl Sackett ⎭ Committee

Colonel Swartwout ⎫
Egbert Benson ⎬ Commissioners
Melancton Smith ⎭

He was interigated in the following manner Viz^t

M^r JAY: Sir, you having observed an Equivocal neutrality thro' the Course of your conduct the Committee is at a Loss to know how to Rank you.

Mr ROBINSON: Sir, it is True, at first I offered my Servis to the publick but they did not think proper to Chuse me Since which Time I have made my Self Prisoner on my farm in order to keep myself from a necessity of Expressing my Sentiments.

M^r JAY: Sir, your son has gone to New York to the enemy.

Mr ROBINSON: No Sir, he is gone to Long Island.

M^r JAY: Sir, this Committee is informed that when your Son was about Taking a Commission you was much Displeased at it.

Mr ROBINSON: I was not, Sir, but I believe that committees thro' their severity have made a Great many Tories, for it is natural when a man is hurt to kick.

M^r JAY: Sir, we have passed the Rubicon and it is now necessary every man Take his part, Cast of all alliegiance to the King of Great Britain and take an oath of Aliegiance to the States of America or Go over to the Enemy for we have Declared outselves Independent.

Mr ROBINSON: Sir, I cannot take the Oath but should be exceeding Glad to Stay in the Country, to Inable me to Stay in the Country, and Expecting that there wold be a great Deal of Trouble about the forts in the Spring have already Sent Some of my Goods farther Back in the Country to Patersons and I should be extreemly unhappy in being obliged to go over to the enemy, for I have no way to maintain my family there, but I have here. If I go to the enemy, can I carry with me any of my effects? It is very uncertain who will Rule yet, for the matter is not Determined.

M^r JAY: Yes, Sir, undoubtedly you can carry your effects but we don't Desire you, Sir, to give your answer now. We would Chuse that you Should take Time to Consider of the matter before you give your answer for I can assure you, Sir, without flattery we Should be exceeding happy to have you with us.

Mr Benson then Laboured much to Show Mr Robinson the propriety of the measures and the great pleasur it would give us to have him with us.

Mr ROBINSON: How long before I must give my answer, a Day or Two?

M^r JAY: No, Sir, you need not hurry your Self. You can take a Month or Six weeks.

Mr ROBINSON: You Gentlemen are not ingaged on Sundays, will you come and see me one Sunday?

M^r JAY: I am obliged to you, Sir, but I don't Expect to be Long here.

Mr BENSON: I am much obliged to you, Sir, and will Do myself the Pleasure of Coming to See you one Sunday.

Mr. Robinson then retired.

[Examination of Beverly Robinson,
Washington's Headquarters, Newburgh]

7 BEVERLY ROBINSON, JR., EQUATES FREEDOM TO SUBSERVIENCE TO HIS BELOVED'S HAPPINESS

Five sons of Beverly Robinson also served the British during the war, four in their father's regiment. Beverly Robinson the younger, who was a law student in James Duane's law office when the troubles began, helped his father form the Loyal American Regiment, serving first as its captain and eventually as lieutenant colonel. He was with Sir Henry Clinton in October

1777 when Forts Clinton and Montgomery were captured. This Beverly Robinson, in 1783, retired to a farm opposite Fredericton, New Brunswick, and became in time a member of the Legislative Council.

In 1777, however, when he was a subordinate officer under his father and in love, he chafed at the military discipline which kept him from his girl and wrote that it almost made him hate his father.[1]

1777

❧ *My dearest Girl*

Once more I am arrived at Harleam on the way to Morrissania. We met with a great Deal of difficulty in crossing & as I dont expect to see you this two days I could not be easy till I acquaintd you with my safe Arrival; I never felt dependence so severely as at present, when I am dying to see my beloved to be prevented by the calls of duty; when shall I be so free as to be only subservient to your Happiness; at any time restraint is disagreeable to my disposition, at present insupportable, I almost Hate my Father (if it was any one Else I should certainly mutiny) for depriving me of my Nancey's Company; he has certainly forgot his feelings at my age & in my situation or he would in some degree relax the rigid discipline of the Army. God Bless you. The more I write the more impatient I grow and if I don't conclud you will perhaps see a Lunatic instead of

Bev Robinson

P S your Brother goes tomorrow to see susan d. I verily Beleive 24 Hours more would kill him as he is married. I shall wait till next Day.   [*Beverly Robinson Papers, Box 1, shelf 128, New Brunswick Museum.*]

8   SAMUEL TOWNSEND TELLS THE NEW YORK COMMITTEE OF SAFETY HIS TORYISM IS JUST A DRUNKEN JOKE

Many suspected persons were penalized as Loyalists, even forced into the British camp, when their actual leaning was toward the rebel side. It was difficult to eradicate suspicion, although taking the oath was sometimes

---

[1] Anna Dorothea Barclay, daughter of the Reverend Barclay, former rector of Trinity Church, married Beverly Robinson, Jr., at Flushing in January 1778. *N.Y. Gaz.,* Jan. 26, 1778. See also Sabine, *Loyalists,* vol. VII, p. 225.

sufficient to remove the charge. Samuel Townsend, an indigent farmer from Ulster County, found himself in the Kingston jail for loose, Tory-sided talk while drunk and was hard pressed to prove it merely a joke. When the Crown was trying to recruit Tories for service, the Committee of Safety ordered the townspeople of New Marlborough to block this action. Townsend refused, saying he did not care for the committee's orders, that it was "damned nonsense" to run after Tories who had gone off to the British, and that five hundred men would not be able to take them. He suggested instead that twenty-five of the best Whigs should meet twenty-five Tories on the plain at Lattin Town and fight it out. Such offensive language brought him to jail and to trial, where he pleaded intoxication. The Committee of Safety accepted the explanation and released him on hearing his oath.[1]

KINGSTON JAIL, APRIL 30, 1777

❡ *To the Honorable the Representatives of the State of New York in Convention assembled:*[1]

The petition of Samuel Townsend humbly sheweth

That ye petitioner is at present confined in the common jail of Kingston for being thought unfriendly to the American States. That ye petitioner some few days ago went from home upon some business and happened to get a little intoxicated in liquor, and upon his return home inadvertantly fell in company upon the road with a person unknown to yr petitioner and discoursing and joking about the Tories passing through there and escaping, this person says to yr petitioner that if he had been with the Wigs, [they] should not have escaped so. . . . To which your petitioner, being merry in liquor, wantonly and in a bantering manner told him that in the lane through which they were then riding five and twenty Whigs would not beat five and twenty Tories and, joking together, they parted, and yr petitioner thought no more of it. Since, he has been taken up and confined and he supposes on the above joke.

Being conscious to himself of his not committing any crime or of being unfriendly to the American cause worthy of punishment . . . That yr petitioner is extremely sorry for what he may have said and hopes his intoxi-

---

[1] G. M. Woolsey, *Marlborough in the Revolution.* No. 4,541, Senate House Museum, Kingston. The Council of Safety acted as the provisional government from April 22, 1777, when the state constitution was proclaimed, until Clinton's inauguration on July 30.

cation and looseness of tongue will be forgiven by this honorable convention as it would not have been expressed by him in his sober hours. That yr
petitioner has a wife and two children and a helpless mother all which must
be supported by his labor and should he be kept confined in this time his
family must unavoidably suffer through want, as yr petitioner is but of
indigent circumstances and fully conceives it is extremely hard to keep him
confined to the great distress of his family as well as grief of yr petitioner.
Yr petitioner therefore humbly prays that this honorable convention be
favorably pleased to take the premises under their serious consideration so
as that yr petitioner may be relieved and discharged from his confinement
or [granted] such relief as to the honorable house shall seem meet and ye
petitioner shall ever pray

Samuel Townsned
[Minutes of the Council of Safety Journ. of the Provincial
Cong., vol. I, p. 937.]

9 "WHAT PHRENZY POSSESSED YOUR MIND?" ABEL CURTISS
WRITES TO HIS DARTMOUTH CLASSMATE, LEVI WILLARD, ON
THE LATTER'S JOINING THE BRITISH FORCES

Levi Willard was Abel Curtiss's close friend and classmate in the class of
1776 at Dartmouth. When Willard, the top scholar of his class, made his
choice of loyalty to the British standard, serving in the commissary department, Abel Curtiss was both startled and grieved. He implored him to
return, to acknowledge his error, and to submit to justice. The letter,
written at Dartmouth College, addressed to "Mr. Levi Willard, Supposed
to be with the British Forces at the Northward, unless Taken—To the Care
of any Patriot," was never received. Nonetheless, it serves to show how
two men of similar background, both born in the New Hampshire Grants
and exposed to the same educational influences, viewed the colonial quarrel
from two opposing angles.

After a postwar employment among trappers and Indians in the
service of a fur trading company in Canada, Levi Willard returned to
Sheldon, Vermont, to round out in obscurity almost eighty years in the
country he had repudiated. The two friends evidently never met again,
as Abel Curtiss died of consumption in 1783, although not before he had

served Vermont in several official capacities, as an assemblyman, as an agent to the Congress in Philadelphia, as a county judge, and as a member of the Vermont "board of war."[1]

SEPTEMBER 22, 1777

❦ *My dear Willard,*
    You can hardly guess my surprize and grief when first I heard the melancholy news that you had forsaken a Fathers house, Friends, and Acquaintance and had gone;—Gracious Heavens—where? To join yourself with (let me use as favorable terms as possible) those savage and unnatural destroyers of Our Country! What phrenzy possessed your Mind? or rather what evil genius directed you and in an unguarded hour persuaded you, in spite of your wonted steadiness, reason, and other dictates of your Conscience, to sacrifice your peace, good name, and reputation to procure the favor and friendship of those whose footsteps spread horror and desolation and whose conduct evidences that their minds are void of every tender feeling of humanity? Why else do we often hear, and many see, helpless victims whom the Fortune of War has thrown into their power, some perishing with hunger, others mangled in the most cruel manner, their hands cut off, their bodies pierced with Bayonets; nor does their insatiate Fury stop with Breath, but relentless and deaf to the voice of humanity, they stab the lifeless Corpse?—Why else do they let loose a bloodthirsty Savage indiscriminately to scalp and torture Friends and Foes, and why else in Virgin Innocence betrayed to satiate their Brutal Lust?— O Britain how art thou fallen! Is thy pristine glory reduced to this! . . .
    Permit me to ask what would be the reason of your so abrupt departure? Why might not a friend once have the opportunity to advise you, or, at least bid you farewell? Was you convinced that the American cause is unjust? Or did you join the Enemy from a prospect of gain or Honor? Or (which I am ready to think was the case) was you seduced by the persuasions of others?—If you think our cause unjust, I shall not at present multiply words, only ask you to look into the natural and equal right every man has to freedom and then see if one may in justice assume power over another so as to "bind him in all cases whatsoever?" If so, then the notion

---

[1] George T. Chapman, *Sketches of Dartmouth College,* Cambridge: 1867, pp. 19-20.

[153]

of freedom is a mere *chimera,* a creature of the brain. It is this arbitrary power these States are opposing and indeed I am so convinced of the justice of our cause that, should every man in the United States of America, even to his Excellency Genl Washington, willingly submit to the power of Britain (which I am confident is far otherwise), I should by no means be persuaded to think that we are not fighting in the cause of Heaven and all mankind.

> Without a sign his sword the good man draws
> And ask no omen but his country's cause—

If you had honor or wealth in view permit me to ask have you attained your end? If you have not, then too late you find your disappointment; but if you have, I ask, Can it sufficiently compensate the resentment of an injured People, or make amends for that peace of mind you must unavoidably lose thereby? But if you was seduced, I heartily join with you in Cursing the man who was so criminally guilty, to persuade a young Gentleman possessed of every admirable qualification, in the prime of life, and capable of extensive usefulness to forsake Friends and Relations—to incur the revenge of an affronted Country—to entail upon himself the execrations of thousands—and, (shocking to relate,) to join himself to worse than savage Foes, the destroyers of the rights of Mankind. Such conduct, I say, is the most impious, inhuman, and ungenerous that can be conceived or committed by mortal. . . .

Having lately heard that Ticonderoga is taken by our Troops, I hope to hear that you are falling into our hands. If not, I but very little expect that you will receive this. If you should, take for once the advice of a Friend—Return to your Duty and deliver yourself up to Justice—if you have not taken arms, follow my advice and do not appear in arms. . . . It is more honorable, when a person has once taken a wrong step, to go back than persist in it. As your abrupt departure was the grief and amazement of Friends, so your returning and delivering yourself into the hands of justice, I presume, cannot fail to excite their pity and endeavours for your pardon. . . .

That you may be thoroughly convinced of your error—return to your allegiance to the American States—be a faithful and true Subject of the same—and experience the happy, happy effects of a pardon from God and your injured Country, is,

Once dear Sir
the hearty desire and Prayer of your real
well wisher and my Country's devoted Servant
A. Curtiss
                    [*Vt. Historical Society, Montpelier.*]

10 JACOB DUCHÉ WRITES WASHINGTON TO URGE CONGRESS TO RESCIND "THE HASTY AND ILL-ADVISED DECLARATION OF INDEPENDENCY"

Two days after the Declaration was issued, Jacob Duché, the prominent rector of Christ Church and St. Peter's Church in Philadelphia, was made chaplain to the Continental Congress. He accepted the appointment "rashly," he later explained in a fourteen-page letter to Washington, because he thought the churches were in danger and as chaplain he could prevent harm from coming to them. Also he felt independence had been adopted as an expedient to secure better terms from the British when the Committee of Congress met with General Howe. He said that as soon as he realized that independence was a measure which Congress intended to uphold, he determined to resign and actually did so less than three months after taking office. He took another year, however, before he unburdened his uneasy conscience in the well-known letter, quoted below, to Washington, saying: "I could not Enjoy a moment's peace 'till this Letter was written." In this letter he not only urged a reversal of the Declaration,[1]

---

[1] John Randolph, Loyalist Attorney General of Virginia and father of the patriot Edmund Randolph, also urged rescinding the Declaration. He wrote to Thomas Jefferson, October 25, 1779: "Wou'd it not be prudent to rescind your Declaration of Independence, be happily reunited to your ancient & natural Friend, & enjoy a Peace which I most religiously think w'd pass all Understanding? I can venture to assure you that your Independence will never be acknowledg'd by the Legislative Authority of this Kingdom. . . . Every immunity, which you can reasonably ask for, will be granted to you; the rapacious Hand of Taxation will never reach you, Your Laws & Regulations will be establish'd on the solid Basis of the british Constitution; & your Happiness will be attended to with all the Solicitude which belongs to an affectionate Parent. . . ." The letter was probably never sent. Leonard L. Mackall, ed. Amer. Antiq. Soc. *Proc.*, new series, vol. XXX (April 1920), p. 30.

but also attacked the leadership of Congress, belittled the army and navy, and warned how vain was the hope that France would help the Revolutionary cause. This letter proved to be a grave mistake. Washington turned it over to Congress and soon it circulated widely throughout the Colonies, arousing scorn among the rebels and embarrassment among the British. Duché was obliged to sail for England in December 1777, where he was relegated to a minor chaplaincy of a girls' orphan asylum. In 1792, he returned to America, a semi-invalid, and remained until his death in 1798.

OCTOBER 8, 1777

❡ *Sir* [Washington]

. . . What have been the consequences of this rash & violent measure? A degeneracy of representation—Confusion of Counsels—Blunders without number. The most respectable Characters have withdrawn themselves & are succeeded by a great majority of illiberal & violent men.

Take an impartial view of the present Congress & what can you expect from them? Your feelings must be greatly hurt by the representation from your native province. You have no longer a Randolph, a Bland or a Braxton, men whose names will ever be revered, whose demands never rose above the first ground on which they set out & whose truly generous & virtuous Sentiments I have frequently heard with rapture from their own Lips. O my Dear Sir! What a sad Contrast? Characters now present themselves whose minds can never mingle with your own. Your [Benjamin] Harrison alone remains & he disgusted with his unworthy associates.

As to those of my own province, some of them are so obscure that their very names never met my Ears before, & others have only been distinguished for the weakness of their understandings & the violence of their tempers. . . .

From the New England Provinces can you find one that, as a Gentleman, you could wish to associate with? Unless the soft & mild address of Mr. Hancock can attone for his want of every other qualification necessary for the Station he fills. —Bankrupts, Attornies & men of desperate fortunes are his Colleagues. . . .

Are the dregs of a Congress then still to influence a mind like yours? These are not the men you engaged to serve. These are not the men that America has chosen to represent her. Most of them were elected by a little lone faction & the few Gentlemen that are among them, now well known to be upon the Ballance & looking up to your hand alone to move the Beam. 'Tis you Sir, & you only that support the present Congress. Of this you must be fully sensible. Long before they left Philad^a their dignity & consequence was gone. What must it be now since their precipitate retreat? . . .

After this view of Congress turn to the Army. The whole world knows that its very existence depends upon you, that your Death or Captivity disperses it in a moment, & that there is not a man on that side the Question in America capable of succeeding you. As to the Army itself what have you to expect from them? Have they not frequently abandoned even yourself in the hour of extremity? Have you, can you have the least confidence in a set of undisciplined men & Officers, many of whom have been taken from the lowest of the people, without principle, without courage. —Take away those that surround your person, how very few are there that you can ask to sit at your Table?

Turn to your little Navy. Of that little what is left? Of that Delaware Fleet part are taken, the rest must soon surrender. Of those in the other Provinces some taken, one or two at sea, & others lying unmanned & unrigged in their Harbours.

And now where are your resourses? O my Dear Sir! How sadly have you been abused by a faction void of Truth & void of tenderness to you & your Country? They have amused you with hopes of a Declaration of War on the part of France. Believe me from the best authority 'twas a fiction from the first. . . .

From your friends in England you have nothing to expect. Their numbers are diminished to a Cypher. The spirit of the whole nation is in full activity against you. . . . All orders & ranks of men in Great Britain are now unanimous & determined to risque their all in the Contest. . . . In a word your Harbours are blocked up, your Cities fall one after another, fortress after fortress, battle after battle is lost. A British army after having passed almost unmolested thro' a vast extent of Country have possessed themselves with ease of the Capital of America. How unique the contest now! How fruitless the expence of Blood!

Under so many discouraging circumstances can virtue, can honour, can the love of your country prompt you to persevere. Humanity itself (and sure I am humanity is no stranger to your breast) calls upon you to desist. . . . 'tis to you & you alone your bleeding Country looks . . .

Your penetrating Eye needs not more explicit Language to discern my meaning. With that prudence & delicacy therefore of which I know you to be possessed represent to Congress the indispensable necessity of rescinding the hasty & ill advised Declaration of Independency. Recommend, & you have an undoubted right to recommend, an immediate cessation of hostilities. Let the controversy be taken up where that declaration left it & where Lord Howe certainly expected to find it. Let men of clear & impartial characters in or out of Congress, liberal in their Sentiments, heretofore independent in their fortunes . . . be appointed to confer with his Majesty's Commissioners. Let them prepare some well digested constitutional plan to lay before them at the Commencement of the negociation . . .

Your interposition and advice I am confident would meet with a favourable reception from the Authority under which you Act. If it should not, you have one infallible resource still left, NEGOTIATE FOR AMERICA AT THE HEAD OF YOUR ARMY. [*Washington Papers, Lib. Congress Van Doren, Secret History, pp. 39–42.*]

11 GOLDSBROW BANYAR SEEKS A COMPROMISE TO THE
OATH AND PERSUADES THE NEW YORK COMMISSION TO
ACCEPT COMPURGATORS

New York allowed two years to elapse following the signing of the Declaration of Independence before it confronted persons of "conscientious doubts and scruples" with the necessity of taking an oath of allegiance if they wished to remain inhabitants of the state. The Act of June 29, 1778, "to prevent the Mischiefs arising from the Influence and Example of Persons of equivocal and suspected Characters," directed the Commissioners to Detect Conspiracies to examine such persons and administer the oath. Goldsbrow Banyar, former Deputy Secretary of the Province and Judge of Probate, was promptly called up. He had managed judiciously to follow a middle course between his pro-British views and conscience and his material interests; now under a new act, directed specifically at neutrals, he needed to find a new expedient to permit him to stay. In principle he was a Loyalist, but he took no part in the war, retired to Rhinebeck, and in the end saved some of his valuable lands from confiscation and himself from banishment. Gorham A. Worth has described him as "the most perfect type of the *Anglo-American* then living. He was the last of a race, or class of men, now totally extinct—a race, born in England, grown rich in America, proud of their birth, and prouder of their fortune."[1] Banyar postponed his appearance before the commissioners several times, pleading ill health, and finally requested the expedient used in a few other cases of finding twelve reputable "compurgators" (character witnesses) who would sign a certificate to the general effect that the suspected person was not a dangerous character, a perpetrator of mischief. Banyar obtained the certificate from the commission and, although worded too strictly, he felt it was not sufficiently objectionable to keep his friends from signing. In the following letter to James Duane, a good friend and at the time a delegate to the Continental Congress, he tries to square the oath with his conscience by adding his own interpretation of the word "State" and indicates his willingness to take it.

RED HOOK, SEPTEMBER 16, 1778

❦ *My dear Sir* [James Duane]

. . . My Views are yet what you always suppos'd them to be, but I never expected to be driven to the present Alternative of sacrificing them or violating my Conscience. I suppose you have seen the Oath, lest you might not, I subjoin a Copy—The Chancellor's Construction is that the *State* there means the People tho he acknowledges in the penal Clause (declaring it Misprission of Treason if found afterwards in any part of the State) the State means the Territory—My Opinion is, where the Sense will admit, it means both—There is some Diversity of Sentiment whether the State extends beyond or within the Lines of the Enemy and indeed it appears more consistent with Common Sense and the common Acceptation of the Term to confine it to those Limits, however the other seems the Construction adopted by the Legislature. You know in constructing Acts, the Construction must be uniform, and if you admit a Word or Expression in any Signification in a particular Part, it shall receive the same Exposition throughout the Law, if the Sense will admit of it. You know also that Oaths are to be understood in the Sense of the Authority that imposes, not in that of the Person who takes them. It must appear I think to anyone a Matter of great Difficulty to swear a Country of *Right Independent,* while the Contest exists, the Event of which can only determine whether it shall be so or not.

[1] Gorham A. Worth, *Recollections of Albany, 1800–1808,* Albany: 1866, p. 112.

But if he can even digest this, must not his Conscience revolt, when he is call'd to swear also, that the State or Country comprehends Places never in their Possession, and that no Authority can be exercised of Right in those Places, but what is derived from the People of the State, when the Fact is that there is an Authority exercised there not by them, and whether of Right cannot be doubted, as it might be the same that existed there before the State was formed, on an authority exerted in Right of Conquest. Can you deny the Legality of either, under an opinion which the Chancellor seems to have adopted, that all Right is vested in the people in all Governments? Suppose even this a just Position in Theory, what ought it to avail if counteracted in 19 Instances out of 20. I pay great Deference to his Judgment, and the long Conversation we had on the Subject confirm'd me in the opinion you know I ever entertain'd of that Gentleman.

He suggested an Expedient which as it was a Proof of his Friendship I am highly oblig'd to him for, An Explanation of the Sense in which I understand the Act, but this if admitted is a Medicine in my present Opinion inadequate to the Disease. I hear the Commissioners have in the Cases of Mr. [Parker] Wickham and Mr. Gabriel Ludlow delivered their Certificates to be signed by at least 12 reputable Persons, which if produced is to excuse the Party from taking the Oath. I hear also the same Course has been taken with others. If so I should hope I might too be delivered over to Compurgators.

I wish much to see you but am still so much indisposed as to render it imprudent to travel so far. As soon as I go abroad, Expect a visit, I long for that Satisfaction. My distress has been great beyond what I ever felt before, or could have had any apprehension of, at least from this Quarter, for who could have expected such a Law in such a Country even tho under the most extreme Circumstances of Distress. I am my Dear Sir with kindest Respects from all this Family to yours and all under the same Roof.

Most affectionately yours
G. Banyar

P.S. Sept. 25th. I returned last Evening from Pokeepsing & finding your Letter still here I sat down to acquaint you that I obtained the same Certificate that had been granted to others. It is too strict to suit the Case of one Whig in three but as I have paid a ready obedience where the Laws have required Taxes Horses Carriages or Money in lieu of personal Service and have ever been ready to give the Government the Pledge of my Fidelity contain'd in an Oath of Allegiance, I think I am not a dangerous Person and that if this Law & the Certificate requires more it ought to be no Objection to any reasonable Person not at Enmity with me of whom I believe there are few. Adieu, I shall see you when this disagreeable Business is finished. G B.

I AB do solemnly and without any mental Reservation or Equivocation whatever swear and call God to witness (or if of the people called Quakers affirm) that I do believe and acknowlege the State of New York to be of Right a free and independant State And that no Authority or Power can of Right be exercised in or over the said State but what is or shall be granted by or derived from the People thereof. And further that as a good Subject of the said free and Independant State of New York I will to the best of my knowlege & Ability faithfully do my Duty And as I shall keep or disregard this Oath so help and deal with me Almighty God. [*Duane Papers, Box 5, N.Y. Historical Society.*]

12 ORB AND SCEPTER: JOEL STONE DETERMINES "SOONER
TO PERISH IN THE GENERAL CALAMITY THAN ABET . . .
THE ENEMIES OF THE BRITISH CONSTITUTION"

Opposite the church on the village green at Washington, Connecticut, stands a colonial house which conceals a little-known story of divided loyalties during the Revolution, a house built about 1774 and owned jointly by two brothers, Joel and Leman Stone, one Loyalist and one rebel. Each occupied a front bedroom opposite the other and each decorated his own walls according to his own inclination. Joel's room displayed British warships and other symbols of his British fealty, while Leman's was papered with alternate panels of deer and spread eagles, with fauns and other figures from ancient mythology surrounding the room below a dark wainscoting. The oval-shaped panels with the eagles showed some variations; a few of the eagles were depicted with an olive branch in one talon and a bunch of arrows in the other; a few had thirteen stars surrounding the head; one eagle's beak held a scroll carrying the words "Federal Union." The eagle in the most prominent panel between the two front windows, however, was the most arresting one, for it symbolized the split allegiance and poignant strife of the two brothers; the objects in its claws had been carefully altered from arrows and olive branch to orb and scepter while the crown of George III had been placed on its head.[1]

The Stone brothers were rivals in other ways. Both had sought the hand of Mary Belden of Judea (Washington, Connecticut) and had agreed to comply with her choice. Both were engaged in trade, sharing an interest in a nearby store until Joel's property, including half of the house, was confiscated in 1777.

The crises of the spring of 1775 brought a parting of their ways. Despite the distresses meted out to Joel, the Loyalist, during the war, he married happily and after the war located on 500 acres on the Gananoque River, becoming the prosperous and beloved founder of Gananoque in Upper Canada. Leman's trade, however, diminished after his brother's flight, and he was even unable to secure his unconfiscated half of their joint property. He then set up an export-import business in New Haven, venturing his vessels in the West Indies trade, but his ships fell prey to the French. Unable to recoup his losses, he died impoverished. Moreover, Mary Belden turned him down for a Philadelphia sea captain.[2]

Joel Stone returned three times to Connecticut, once in 1778 as a prisoner charged with high treason, again in August 1783 to try to collect monies owed him and procure vouchers for his losses, and finally in 1791, when he returned to place two children, William and Mary, in a Hartford school. It may have been on his visit in 1783 that he altered the emblems in the eagle's claws and set the crown firmly on its head to taunt his rebel brother.

His *Narrative,* composed in England in 1784 as part of his memorial to the commissioners on Loyalist claims, begins with the auspicious prospects he faced in 1774, namely, a partnership with Jabez Bacon, a substantial local merchant, and the enjoyment of the confidence and esteem of his neighbors. How suddenly their attitude changed; how stern the price of loyalty—such reflections are the substance of the excerpt from Joel's *Narrative* below.

---

[1] The wallpaper has been reproduced on the end papers of this book through the courtesy of the present owners, Dr. and Mrs. Henry D. Fearon, Washington, Connecticut.
[2] Mary M. Smith, "The Story of the Old Red Hurse," *Town Historical Papers,* Washington, Conn.: 1905. Sabine, *Loyalist Transcripts,* vol. VI, p. 10; vol. XII, pp. 414, 633.

The Rubicon

❡ By dint of an unwearied diligence and a close application to trade I found the number of my friends and customers daily increasing and a fair prospect of long happiness arose to my sanguine mind in one of the most desirable situations beneath the best of laws and the most excellent government in the Universe. But, alas, the dreadful commotion that commenced about this period quickly involved that once happy country in all the dreadful horrors of an unnatural War and filling the pleasant land with desolation and blood removed all my fair prospects of future blessings. Yet amidst all this anarchy and rage I was fixed in my resolves rather to forego all I could call my property in the world than flinch from my duty as a subject to the best of Sovereigns, sooner to perish in the general Calamity than abet in the least degree the enemies of the British Constitution.

In the year 1775 I was violent[ly] suspected of being inimical to the Provincial party and treated with much malevolence. Being cited to appear before the committee, I was accused as with a crime the most enormous of supplying the people whom they called Tories with sundry articles of provisions and charged with having supported and assisted the British prisoners confined in Connecticut. It was with the utmost difficulty that I at that time escaped a very severe prosecution from the Emissaries of Congress. . . .

In the year 1776 I discovered that it was perfectly impracticable any longer to conceal my sentiments from the violent public. The agents of Congress acted with all the Cunning and cruelty of Inquisitors and peremptorily urged me to declare without further hesitation whether I would immediately take up arms myself against the British Government or procure a substitute to serve in the General insurrection. . . .

Thus perpetually perplexed and harrassed, I determined in my own mind to withdraw as soon as possible to the City of New York and there by joining his Majesty's forces cast what weight I was able into the opposite scale, but before I could carry my design into execution a warrant was issued out in order to seize my person. . . . I had the good fortune to get away on horseback and being in a dark night happily eluded their search, but my sister, as I was afterwards given to understand, met the resentment of the mob who from language the most approbrious proceeded to actual violence, breaking open every lock in the house and seizing all the property they could discover. . . .

I soon found that my person was one principal object of their aim. Being informed to what place I had fled, a party of about twelve armed men with a constable came up and, seizing my horse, were proceeding into the house when I found an opportunity to slip from their hands. It was full fourteen days before I was perfectly secure during which time several parties were detached after me whom they were taught to consider as a traitor to the United States and unworthy to live. An invincible frenzy appeared to prevade the minds of the country people and those very men who so recently had held one in the highest esteem became the most implacable enemies. . . .

However, I had the unspeakable happiness to escape the utmost vigilance of my pursuers and at length reached Long Island. There I soon joined the King's Army as a Volunteer. . . . I remained thus until the 15th April, 1778, when finding my money just expended . . . I accepted a warrant to raise a company. . . .

On the night of the 12th of May, 1778, as I was lying at Huntingdon on Long Island in order to carry my purpose of Recruiting further into execution, I was surprised whilst asleep by a company of whale boat men who took me prisoner and carried [me] over to Norwalk in Connecticut.

The Magistrate before whom I was taken refused to consider me as a prisoner of war which I claimed as a right but, charging me with the enormous crime of high treason against the States, I was committed a close prisoner to Fairfield Jail. I was there indicted, threatened with the vengeance of the law and warned solemnly to prepare for that death which most certainly would be inflicted upon me. . . . I petitioned the Governor of Connecticut that I might, agreeable to justice, be deemed a prisoner of war, treated as such, and be permitted to appear before himself and Council in person. . . .

The result turned out quite contrary to my wish. My petition was rejected with the utmost disdain and I was reminded to prepare for that approaching fate which was irrevocably fixed, as I was afterwards informed, by a decree which could not be thwarted. . . .

The dungeon was truly dismal, the walls strong and the place perpetually guarded, yet, being in the prime of life, my spirits were warm and my passions violent. I therefore firmly determined to effect an escape if I even should be obliged to sink the last shilling and go out naked into the world. . . . By the generous aid of my friends and a judicious application of almost all the money I could raise we [Stone and a fellow prisoner] happily emerged from that place of horror July 23, 1778, and with quick despatch pursued our way into the Wilderness of that Country to wait the further assistance of our friends. . . . We lived upon a fruit which grows spontaneously in those parts called Nurtle berries. When the alarm was somewhat subsided we met the help which we expected from our friends. . . . I found my strength much impaired by the close confinement and so sudden a transition from a warm prison to be exposed to the dews and damps of the wood had like to have been attended with the most fatal consequences to my health. Amidst this sudden sickness we travelled every night, rested sometimes in caves of the rocks and sometimes on the cold ground in wild marshes; at the same time the heart of my companion failed him and the dread of falling into the hands of the enemy struck him with an unmanly panic. . . .

Discovering opportunely a small boat concealed amongst the reeds in a marsh a considerable distance from the sound, we carried it by turns on our shoulders to the waterside and so on the night of the 29th July, 1778, all got in, rowed from shore, and proceeded without sail or compass. The north pole awhile proved our friendly guide but the darkness of the night soon eclipsed it also from our sight. We found our little craft begin to leak before we were half over and the wind not serving, Mr. H——, my late fellow prisoner urged to return with every argument his fear could frame. Indeed the danger was great as the boat leaked faster and faster every moment, yet we treated his dastardly demeanour with dastardly disdain. Still he insisted upon our instant return and refused to row or any way to assist in the voyage. This enkindled the latent fire in my breast and that of our newly acquired companion and made us breathe the air that Liberty alone inspires. We resolved rather to perish in the attempt to secure our freedom than return to meet death in a more dreadful form. We positively told our trembling companion that, if he would not sit still and bail the boat with his hat whilst we rowed, we would without the least hesitation throw him overboard. . . . About day break next morning arrived safe at Satocket in Long Island, worn out with fatique and ready to expire for want of sustenance. Fortunately, we found a friend (viz. Colonel Benjamin Floid), who supplied us with food and lent me a horse to carry me directly to Huntingdon where a part of the King's Army then lay. . . . [*Stone, Narrative, Canniff Papers, Public Archives, Ontario. Talman, Loyalist Narratives, pp. 323-326.*]

Raids, Retaliation,

and Refuge

I   THE NEW YORK FIRE, SEPTEMBER 21, 1776

Eight weeks after the Declaration of
Independence established independence
as the clear-cut objective of the rebellion, the New York campaign opened
up. The British triumph on Long Island and
Washington's decision (September 12) to withdraw
his forces from New York City warmed the spirits of the Loyalists. A few
weeks of inactivity followed the skirmish on Harlem Heights (September
16) while the British cemented their possession of the city and Howe
dillydallied over his next move. The struggle for the occupation of New
York, however, was not quite finished; it ended in one final strike, a departing attempt by the rebels, according to Loyalist accounts, to deprive
the British by fire of the prize they had won. In the early hours of September 21, aided by a high wind, an awesome conflagration consumed from
one-fourth to one-third of the city. Charles Stedman, a Philadelphia Loy-

alist who served as commissary to Howe's troops, provides the essential facts in his 1792 *History of the . . . War,* while the Reverend Charles Inglis, one of the fire fighters himself, describes to Dr. Richard Hind, the Secretary of the SPG, the destruction of Trinity Church, giving his own conclusion as to the perpetrators of the dastardly act.

The Rebels Cheer As the Trinity Church Steeple Falls

SEPTEMBER 21, 1776

❦ Several persons having purposely secreted themselves in the deserted houses, contrived to set fire to the town, . . . One-third of the town was thus destroyed; and had not the military exerted themselves in a most extraordinary manner, the whole would have been levelled with the ground. The flames first broke out at some wooden store-houses, at the southern-most or windward part of New York, near the Whitehall-stairs, just by the battery, and soon became general up the Broadway, &c. by the violence of the wind blowing burnt shingles from the houses on fire to others, and setting them on fire in rapid succession. The wind was so strong, that it was almost impossible to face it, for smoke and flakes of fire. The next day (Saturday) a great many cart-loads of bundles of pine sticks, dipped at each end for five or six inches in brimstone and other combustible matters, were found concealed in cellars of houses to which the incendiaries had not had time to set fire. Between one and two hundred men and old women were taken up during the night, and sent to gaol on suspicion, and three or four men detected with matches and combustibles were killed by the enraged soldiers. Most, if not all the men and women put into gaol, were released in a few days, after having their names taken and examined by a committee. The old English church, [Trinity Church] and a German church, near it, with about eleven hundred houses,[1] were burnt. The rebels at Paulus Hook gave three cheers when the steeple of the old English church fell down, which, when burning, looked awfully grand. [*Stedman, History of the . . . War, vol. I, p. 209.*]

[1] This figure varies from 500 to 1,500. See Stokes, *Icon,* vol. V, pp. 1020–1024.

Charles Inglis Acquaints the Secretary of the SPG with the Origin of the Fire

OCTOBER 31, 1776

❑   Alas! the Enemies of Peace were secretly lurking among us.

Several Rebels secreted themselves in the House to execute the diabolical Purpose of destroying the City. On the Saturday following an Opportunity presented itself; for the Weather being very dry, & the Wind blowing fresh, they set Fire to the City in several places at the same Time, between 12 & 1 o'clock in the Morning. The Fire raged with the utmost Fury, & in its destructive Progress consumed about one thousand Houses, Or a fourth part of the whole City. To the vigorous Efforts of the Officers of the Army & Navy, & of the Soldiers & Seamen, it is owing under Providence, that the whole City was not destroyed. We had three Churches, of which Trinity Church was the oldest & largest. It was a venerable Edifice, had an excellent Organ which cost £850 Sterl. & was otherwise ornamented. This Church, with the Rector's House & the Charity School, the two latter large expensive Buildings, were burned. St. Paul's Church & King's College had shared the same Fate, being directly in the Line of Fire, had I not been providentially on the Spot, & sent a Number of People with Water on the Roof of each. Our Houses are all covered with Cedar Shingles, which makes Fire very dangerous. The Church Corporation has suffered prodigiously, as was evidently intended. Besides the Buildings already mentioned, about two hundred Houses which stood on the Church Ground were consumed; so that the Loss cannot be estimated at less than £25,000 Sterl. This melancholly Accident, the principal Scene of War being here will occasion the Clergy of this City to be the greatest Sufferers of any on the Continent by the present Rebellion.   [*SPG Mss., B. 2, no. 68. Lydekker, Life and Letters of Charles Inglis, p. 168.*]

Sir Guy Carleton's Commission Endeavors to Fix the Blame

Other Loyalists too believed that the fire had been deliberately set by the rebels to handicap the British occupiers and that the scheme had been concocted in Massachusetts. One eyewitness, Ambrose Serle, Secretary to Admiral Howe, wrote in his journal that "the New England people are maintained to be at the bottom of this plot which they have long since threatened to put into execution."[1] John Wetherhead, who lost five houses in the conflagration, agreed with Inglis that strangers in the city, who he believed were rebel spies, were the culprits.[2] On October 18, 1783, seven years later, Sir Guy Carleton authorized an investigation by a commission of three "to ascertain whether the cause was accidental or the effect of design, and if of design, to whom generally or individually the same is imputable." The commission was to report "with all convenient speed."[3] Dr. Mervin Nooth, Superintendent General of His Majesty's Hospitals, was one of the witnesses interviewed. He had been on the hospital ship *Pigot,* anchored between Manhattan and Staten Island at the time of the fire, and what he saw led him to believe that the fire was deliberately set. Even assistance in fighting the fire appeared deliberately handicapped as the alarm bells had been carried away and the fire engines were out of order.[4]

Charles Inglis was at his home opposite St. Paul's Church when he heard the alarm, dressed, and went toward White Hall where the fire was. He recalled that although a fresh wind from the southeast carried sparks across the Battery, Pearl Street, and Fort George, fire broke out in several houses which were out of the line of the sparks, that the essential bolt on the water pump was missing, that an important cistern was empty, and that matches and combustibles had been found in many houses. He not only concluded that the fire was purposely set, but he also had reason to believe that some Massachusetts seamen were the actual incendiaries.

---

[1] Edward H. Tatum, Jr., ed., *The American Journal of Ambrose Serle, Secretary to Lord Howe, 1776-1778,* San Marino: 1940, p. 111.

[2] "An almost unpardonable want of Caution in the Officer then commanding in New York admitted without examination a promiscuous Number of Strangers into the City, many of whom were spies. This encouraged them to try to burn the City, and the whole Fleet of Transports then along the Docks. This dreadful Scheme they found a favorable opportunity of executing too effectually by means of Incendiaries they had sent into the City for that infernal purpose. And it was your Memorialist's Misfortune to lose nearly the whole of his Estate in Houses in that tremendous Conflagration." Memorial of John Wetherhead, *Loyalist Transcripts,* vol. XLIV, pp. 134ff.

[3] Minutes of the Commission, October 18, 1783, to investigate the cause of the fire in New York City, September, 1776. *Misc. Mss.* Box XII (1776), N.Y. Historical Society.

[4] Diary of the Reverend Mr. Shewkirk, Pastor of the Moravian Church. See H. P. Johnston, *The Campaign of 1776 around New York and Brooklyn,* Brooklyn: 1876, pt. II, p. 119.

Dr. Mervin Nooth Testifies That the Fire Was a Deliberate Act

OCTOBER 20, 1783

❦ [He] soon after plainly discovered with a glass a man upon the top of Trinity Church with a fire-brand or torch in his hand, going backward and forward upon the roof with great rapidity. . . . He, the Deponent, soon after saw the fire break out in several parts of the roof of the same Church. . . . He then did and still does believe that the Person he so saw, set fire to the Church; he does not think the fire could have been communicated to the Church from the houses he first saw on fire, as the distance was considerable and the wind blew a different way. . . . Some time after the fire [in October] an official report was made to him that the Vaux-hall hospital was discovered to have combustibles concealed in one of the chimneys, that upon a fire being made, there was an explosion from them which forced the wood off the hearth below into the room with some violence. [*Minutes of the Commission. Misc. Mss. Box XII, (1776), N.Y. Historical Society.*]

Charles Inglis Presents His Evidence to the Commission

OCTOBER 1783

❦ [He concluded] that the City was set on Fire on Purpose; & he was the more inclined to that Opinion as he recollected that the Rebels . . . had frequently thrown out Threats that they would burn the City, if compelled to abandon it. . . . The Deponent was informed that Persons had been repeatedly detected in the Act of setting Fire to Houses, & that some of the Persons so setting Fire to Houses were instantly put to Death; & he was moreover informed that Bundles of Matches & other Combustibles were found in many Houses & in different Parts of the City, with Design, as was supposed, to promote & increase the Conflagration.

And this Deponent further saith that he received the following Narrative from James Devereux, formerly an Inhabitant of this City but now of the City of London, a man of veracity & good Character, to whose Testimony . . . the utmost Credit is due. . . . That the said James Devereux, Master and partly Owner of a Brig, on his Voyage from London to New York, was taken by a Rebel Privateer from Boston some time in the latter End of Autumn . . . 1776 . . . was put on Board the Privateer which proceeded on her way for Boston. That one Day, when walking the Deck, three Sailers belonging to the Privateer came to him & one of them asked him whether he was not from New York and whether he had heard that the City was burnt? . . . One of the sailers asked him . . . whether he knew such & such Places in the City, to which the said Devereux answered in the Affirmative, that he knew them well. The Sailer then replied that those were the places to which he & his Companions had set Fire; & one of the Sailers declared further to said Devereux that he, the Sailer, & the other two sailers then present were part of forty Seamen from Boston & Marble-Head who had been left in the City . . . when it was evacuated by the Continental Army for the purpose of setting it on Fire. [*Minutes of the Commission. Misc. Mss. Box XII (1776), N.Y. Historical Society.*]

2 THE BURNING OF WHITE PLAINS: A TORY WOMAN HELPS AN AMERICAN COURT-MARTIAL CONVICT A REBEL

Hardly had the embers of New York's disastrous fire been extinguished than the same scorched-earth technique was applied to White Plains, then a village of about seventy houses, two churches, and two taverns.[1] The battle of Chatterton Hill had left the British in possession of both the hill and the village, although the cost in casualties suggested a Pyrrhic victory. Moreover, Howe had been checked in his objective of either destroying Washington's army or cutting his communications. Howe was retiring to Dobbs Ferry and Washington to Newcastle. As the rebel troops withdrew from White Plains, Major Jonathan Austin of the Sixteenth Massachusetts Regiment on his own initiative ordered the burning of the village. The courthouse and thirteen or fourteen houses went up in flames with reckless disregard for their military or sanctuary value. The rebel command was so angered at the wanton destruction and the inhuman treatment of women and children that a court-martial of Austin was ordered. Austin

---

[1] Otto Hufeland says there were twelve buildings in the village proper, seventy, including the environs. In 1790, the population of White Plains was still only 505, of which 49 were slaves. *Westchester County during the Revolution 1775-1783*, White Plains: 1926, p. 6.

was charged with conduct "not only unworthy the character of an officer, but of a human creature." Although he pleaded not guilty, he admitted he had received no order from a general officer to burn the village, and he was promptly discharged. One of the witnesses against Austin was Mrs. Nathaniel Adams, the wife of a Tory blacksmith who later joined De-Lancey's Refugees. Her testimony, that is, the testimony of a woman identified as a Tory, was not only sought after and listened to by a panel of fourteen high-ranking rebel officers, but also helpful in their conviction of a fellow officer.[2]

NOVEMBER 12, 1776

❦ Mrs. Adams being sworn, says, that on the night of the 5th instant, there came a party of men into her house on White Plains, and immediately set the house on fire. When she went out of the house, some of the men began to carry things out of the house, when she asked them why they took those things. Then Major Austin spake, and told her he should carry them to the General's and alleged General Sullivan's orders for it. That her sister took Major Austin by the arm crying, and he said to her, What the devil do you take me by the arm for? Because, said she, you are an officer, and can prevent such treatment. Then her mother told Major Austin she hoped he would not burn her house too; on which he told her there was another house above that she might go into; after which Major Austin told his men to go and set the other houses on fire as quick as they could. Mrs. Adams further says, that when they first came to the house, they told her to get things out of the house as quick as possible; that she attempted to take some things out of a bedroom, when some of the men told her to be gone or they would blow her through; that the party would not suffer her to dress her children, but drove them out of doors naked; that she asked Major Austin why he could not save her house, and burn others; he replied, Because you are all damned Tories, and there was a damned Tory taken out of your house this night. That after some of her things were carried out of doors, some of the men insulted her with ill

[2] Force, ed., *Am. Arch.*, 5th ser., vol. III, pp. 654–655. Hufeland, *Westchester*, pp. 157–158. On November 2 Washington had expressly forbidden anyone belonging to the American army from setting fire to any house or barn without a special order from a general officer. Ibid., p. 163.

language (in the presence of Major Austin), such as damned Tories, &c., threatening to blow her through. [*Force, ed., Am. Arch., 5th Ser., vol. III, pp. 654-655.*]

3 COWBOYS AND SKINNERS

As Washington's army was retreating from New York toward White Plains, James DeLancey, a spirited young nephew of Oliver DeLancey and the former sheriff of Westchester, gave his parole to the rebels that he would stay at his home at West Farms in the Bronx. Despite his parole, a week later he boarded a British man-of-war in the East River and joined the enemy. As the British gained control of the Bronx, he returned to West Farms and made it a base from which he could plunder Westchester farmers, rounding up their horses and cattle and raiding their produce to supply the British. He was so successful that early in 1777 Governor Tryon granted him a colonel's commission to form a corps of Westchester militia. He raised a volunteer troop of Light Horse to continue guerilla-like operations in the Neutral Ground of the county[1] and keep open the supply route to New York. His hit-and-run raids were so effective that his troop became the scourge of the area and the elusive DeLancey himself the principal quarry of the Westchester rebels. At one point he took refuge in an old pine tree for two weeks, securing food through his sweetheart, Martha Tippett, who made her way secretly to the tree at night and eventually helped him escape.[2] In late November 1777 a rebel scouting party caught up with him. They found him in his home under the bed hiding behind a barricade of baskets. He was dragged out and carried to Connecticut, mounted in front of his captor on one of his own prize horses.[3] Despite the pleas of the Committee of Safety that he be put in irons, he was again

[1] The Neutral Ground was an area 20 miles wide, extending from Kingsbridge and Morrisania on the south up the county for 30 miles to the mouth of the Croton River and across to the Sound. The Americans, needing their troops elsewhere, were never able to wipe out the guerillas in this area. It became a no-man's land between the two armies.

[2] D. A. Story, *The DeLanceys: A Romance of a Great Family,* London: 1931, p. 51. See also Stephen Jenkins, *The Story of the Bronx,* p. 392.

[3] *The Remembrancer,* Dec. 4, 1777, London, vol. VI, p. 97.

put on his parole, this time at Hartford, and eventually exchanged. He was free once more to recruit Tory volunteers, equipped at their own or De-Lancey's expense. In effect, he built up a young, mounted, elite corps of about sixty men. They plundered homes and stole horses and cattle from Westchester farmers until the DeLancey name became anathema and his Light Horse earned the epithet of "Damned Cowboys."[4]

The rebel counterpart of the Cowboys were the "Skinners," so-called because they robbed and often murdered their victims. They were banditti, some of whom sought a just retaliation for the miseries inflicted by the Cowboys, and some of whom were simply bent on depredation and gainful plunder under the sinister guise of patriotism. They sometimes failed to discriminate between friends and enemies of the rebel cause, committing inhuman acts of banditry on hapless Westchester farmers wherever convenient.

Rivington's *Gazette* of December 16, 1780, carried an account, offered below, of one of the Cowboys' effective blows against rebel outposts, while DeLancey's memorial to the Crown of February 20, 1784, summarized the achievements of his guerillas.

DeLancey's Guerillas Effect a Coup against Rebel Outposts near North Street

DECEMBER 10, 1780

❡   In the night of the ninth instant a detachment of Colonel James DeLancey's Refugees under the command of Major Hugerford penetrated Connecticut as far as North Street & on the morning of the 10th before

---

[4] The corps was later called the Westchester Refugees and expanded to 490 men. Colonel James DeLancey of Westchester (1747–1804), son of Peter DeLancey and Elizabeth Colden, is often confused with his cousin James DeLancey (1732–1800), wealthy landowner and Loyalist leader in New York and son of the Chief Justice and Lt. Gov. James DeLancey and Anne Heathcote.

John W. Barber and Henry Howe, *Historical Collections of the State of New York*, New York: 1841, p. 592; Otto Hufeland, *Westchester County during the American Revolution, 1775-1783*, New York: 1926, pp. 250–251; Robert Bolton, *History of Several Towns, Manors, and Patents of the County of Westchester*, New York: 1905, vol. I, p. 306.

day made a successful attack on the rebels posted there. From the situation of the enemy it was necessary to make an attack on three different posts at the same instant; the divisions for that purpose were led on by Captain Simons and Lieutenant Totten and Kipp in a manner that does them great credit. The loss of the rebels was fifteen killed and twenty-five prisoners, amongst which were Colonel Wells, one Brigade Major, one Captain, two Lieutenants, and two Ensigns.

Colonel Wells expressed his astonishment at the bravery of the conquerors and acknowledged the humanity and great civility of Lieutenant James Kipp who commanded the attack against him and to whom he surrendered himself. The West Chester detachment consisted of 25 mounted & 25 dismounted Loyalists. Their march was sixty miles out and home, which after effecting the above *Coup,* was performed within the space of twenty-four hours. [*Roy. Gaz., Dec. 16, 1780, p. 3.*]

Colonel James DeLancey, the Scourge of Westchester, Keeps King's Bridge "Free from the Insults of the Enemy"[1]

1777-1781

❧ Colonel James DeLancey Sheweth that
. . . In January, 1780, he was appointed Colonel of the Westchester Refugees, a Corps wch at the Close of the War Consisted of 490 Men all fit for duty which were raised by himself and Officers under his Command without any expence to Government.

That by means of their exertions the important post at King's Bridge was kept free from the insults of the enemy and the communication with the Country so perfectly open as to enable the Inhabitants to supply the Magazines and Market in New York with provisions and Forage in such quantities that one-third of the Provisions sent to New York Market were from that part of the Country.

That in the many Engagements he had with the Enemy, he Captured such a number of Prisoners as enabled him to exchange not only his own

---

[1] James DeLancey was attainted October 22, 1779. The British government allowed him a pension of £200 a year, starting July 5, 1783.

Men that were taken by the Enemy, but to furnish upwards of 500 Men for the release of British Prisoners and at the Close of the War he had the Paroles of 200 Prisoners more.

That he was at great expence in keeping his Corps togeth[r] and paid large Sums of Money to Surgeons for attending the Wounded Men that were not able to pay for themselves and in procuring intelligence of the situation, strength & Movements of the Enemy in his Front. [*Loyalist Transcripts, vol. XLI, pp. 253-255.*]

THE SKINNERS PLUNDER AND BURN THE SEAT OF GENERAL OLIVER DELANCEY AND TREAT THE LADIES OF HIS FAMILY BARBAROUSLY

Brigadier General Oliver DeLancey (1718-85) occupied one of the choicest estates and mansions in New York in the section called Bloomingdale, between the present Central Park and the Hudson River. It was a special target of the guerilla rebels operating out of Westchester. Not only did Oliver DeLancey enjoy a prominent position as senior Loyalist officer in the British army, but also, as he wrote to his brother-in-law John Watts, "our family are particularly pointed at" owing to wealth and long political power in the Province.[1] Under Abraham Martling of Tarrytown about twenty of the rebel waterguard slid quietly down the Hudson River, past the anchored British men-of-war, to Bloomingdale, plundered DeLancey's house, and set fire to it. The New York Council of Safety was not pleased with the raid, fearing that the destruction of such a well-known place would invite retaliation on prominent rebel homes.[2]

The raid, however, was already a retaliation for one of November 17, 1777, perpetrated by the Loyalist captains Andreas Emmerick and Barnes on the homes of Cornelius and Peter Van Tassel near the Elmsford Church

---

[1] Oliver DeLancey to John Watts, October 3, 1775. Private collection of Mrs. Norman Duffield, Buffalo, New York. His fortune ranked with those of John Johnson and Frederick Philipse III, who were the two other wealthiest claimants of New York Province.
[2] Council of Safety to Governor Clinton, December 16, 1777. See Thomas Jones, *New York during the Revolutionary War,* vol. I, p. 671.

in the Saw Mill River Valley.[3] These plunderers burned the Van Tassel houses, "stripping the women and children of the necessary apparel to cover them from the severity of a cold night," and carried off Cornelius and Peter as prisoners, tying their hands ignominiously to their horses' tails. When General Samuel Parsons, the commander of the rebel forces in Westchester, protested to Tryon about such inhuman treatment, the latter answered: " . . . I should, were I in more authority, burn every committeeman's house within my reach, as I deem those agents the wicked instruments of the continued calamities of this country. . . . The ruins from the conflagration of New York by the emissaries of your party last year remain a memorial of their tender regards for their fellow beings exposed to the severity of a cold night. . . ."[4] The practice of plunder for plunder and fire for fire was well under way.

Thomas Jones, a nephew-in-law of Oliver DeLancey, whose Loyalist *History of New York during the Revolutionary War* teems with outrage, has left a dramatic account of the destruction of DeLancey's house, embellished by some details added in 1835 by one of the young victims, Miss Charlotte DeLancey.[5]

November 26, 1777

❲ In November, a parcel of rebels in the dead of night passed the North River from the Jersey shore, landed at Bloomingdale, the seat of General DeLancey, about seven miles from the city of New York, surprised, and made prisoners a guard at the landing place, broke into the house and plundered it, abused and insulted the General's lady in a most infamous manner, struck Miss Charlotte DeLancey, a young lady of about sixteen, several times with a musket, set fire to the house, and one of the wretches attempted to wrap up Miss Elizabeth Floyd (an intimate acquaintance of

[3] Cornelius and Peter Van Tassel were tenants of Frederick Philipse and occupied adjacent farms along the Saw Mill River just south of present Elmsford. They were released October 17, 1778. John L. Romer, *Historic Sketches of the Neutral Ground,* Buffalo: 1917, pp. 43–44.
[4] General Samuel Parsons to William Tryon, November 21, 1777. Romer, *Sketches,* pp. 48–49.
[5] Charlotte DeLancey married Sir David Dundas who became a Field Marshall and had a distinguished military career. *Dictionary of National Biography.*

Miss DeLancey's about the same age, and the daughter of Colonel Richard Floyd of Suffolk County . . .) in a sheet all in flames, and, as she ran down the stairs to avoid the fire, the brute threw it after her. One of the party below, of more humanity than the rest, advised the young ladies to make their escape. Mrs. DeLancey had . . . concealed herself under the stoop, where she continued until the rebels left the house and recrossed the river. Miss DeLancey and Miss Floyd made their flight through several fields until they reached a swamp into which they entered and there continued until eight o'clock the next morning without either shoes or stockings and nothing upon them except such thin clothes as ladies use to sleep in, when they were discovered and carried to the house of Charles Ward Apthorpe, Esq., a gentleman who lived in the neighborhood and an intimate acquaintance of General DeLancey. . . . This was in the middle of the night in the month of November when the weather is very cold in this part of America. Miss DeLancey took with her in her flight her brother's child, an infant in arms, and held it safely in her lap the whole time. Miss Floyd's feet and legs were so torn and lacerated by the briars, brambles, and hedges that she passed, as to render her unable to walk for three weeks. . . . The house was totally destroyed with all its effects, which they could not carry away.

[Miss Charlotte DeLancey adds some details:] She and Miss Floyd were sleeping together and were roused by the sound of voices in the grounds. Thinking it was some of the negroes, who ought at that hour to have been in the house, they went to the window, and, throwing it open, exclaimed, "Who is there?" "Put in your heads, you bitches," was the reply, and instantly the house was broken into, front and rear, and the robbery began. They were told "to get out quick," as the house was to be burnt. Some of the party began to strike them with their muskets, and were also inclined to keep them from escaping, but one of them ordered the others to stop, and bid the ladies "be off as fast as you can." Miss Floyd started down stairs first, both being in their night-dresses merely, and as she did so, one of the men threw a lighted window curtain directly upon her. Luckily she dashed it off as she ran and escaped the horrid fate intended. Miss DeLancey rushed for the baby of her brother and followed Miss Floyd instantly, with the child in her arms, its mother being absent at the time. Mrs. DeLancey was an elderly lady and unable to run, she therefore crept into a dog-kennel under the stoop, which fortunately was of stone. The other ladies fled into the woods and swamps, in what is now Central Park, and passed the night in the thickest bushes they could find, sitting upon their feet to keep a little warmth in them until they were found and taken to Mr. Apthorpe's in the morning. Mrs. [Ann DeLancey] Cruger got out and off by herself, and walked about all night, instead of hiding in one place and so wandered far and got lost. . . . No attempt was made to insult them . . . "as the rebels were too eager to plunder, burn the house, and get off safe." [*Jones, History of New York during the Revolutionary War, vol. I, pp. 185–187; 669–70.*]

NATHANIEL UNDERHILL EVENS THE SCORE WITH ISAAC MARTLING

The burning of General DeLancey's house was only one score for the Cowboys to even out. There were personal vendettas as well, such as the Underhill-Martling feud. Just before the Battle of White Plains in late October 1776, the stock and horses of Nathaniel Underhill were taken by the American troops from his farm in Philipse Manor near the Bronx River, about 4½ miles from White Plains. This Nathaniel Underhill, born 1751, son of John Underhill, of Yonkers, was an unwavering Loyalist. He wrote in his memorial to the Crown in 1788 that he was "a native of America, lived in West Chester County, joined the British in 1777, went into New York, joined Colonel DeLancey, served with him one year, then was in Carleton's Legion three or four years." One of his witnesses, George Hauger, certified that "he had behaved with Spirit and also had been of Service to Governor Tryon as a Guide."[1] His spirited behavior referred in part to his run-in with the Skinners and his revenge. Early in the war he was captured by a

---

[1] *Loyalist Transcripts,* vol. XIX, p. 189ff. Nathaniel Underhill was discharged in October 1781. He remained on Long Island until the evacuation when he went to Maugerville, New Brunswick, to live. He should not be confused with several other Nathaniel Underhills. Nathaniel Underhill, Jr., born 1723, the son of Nathaniel and Mary Hunt Underhill, was a judge of the court of common pleas and in 1775 Mayor of Westchester. Isaac Sears's gang, on returning from their raid on Rivington's press, stopped in Westchester, took the mayor prisoner, and carried him to Connecticut, along with Samuel Seabury and Jonathan Fowler. At New Haven the prisoners were carried triumphantly through the town, insulted by the mob at every corner. Thomas Jones, *History,* vol. I, pp. 66–67. *Am. Arch.* 5th Sec., vol. III, p. 708.

band of Skinners led by Isaac Martling, taken to a barn, strung up by the feet, and made to eat oats from the barn floor. He vowed to get even with Martling if he ever had a chance. The opportunity came on May 26, 1776, when Underhill, accompanying a marauding party, saw Martling defenseless in front of his house in Tarrytown, carrying water from the well, and shot him. To immortalize the dastardliness of this act Martling's family had inscribed on his tombstone the words "inhuminely slan."[2]

VIVE LE COQ'S TAIL! A TORY ROOSTER POPULARIZES THE
DRINK AT ELIZABETH FLANAGAN'S TAVERN, JULY 1781

In the Neutral Ground, somewhere in the vicinity of the Four Corners (Elmsford), where the road from Sleepy Hollow to White Plains intersects the Saw Mill River Road, there used to hang a battered tavern sign, carrying the notice "Elizabeth Flanagan—Her Hotel." Here the Skinners supposedly found a rendezvous, and here some of Washington's men from the barracks at Joseph Young's place nearby would congregate for refreshment and song. Betty Flanagan is said to have mixed a rousing drink of rum, rye, and fruit juice and, on one occasion, to have decorated it with a feather which she had wrenched from the tail of her Tory neighbor's rooster. A French officer, exuberant over the unusual concoction, lifted his glass and exclaimed "Vive le Coq's Tail!" This origin of the cocktail may have derived from James Fenimore Cooper's *The Spy,* in which his unsurpassed description has immortalized the tavern, the drink and Mother Flanagan herself.[1]

---

[2] Robert Bolton, *History of the Several Towns of Westchester,* vol. II, p. 412; J. L. Romer, *Historical Sketches and Tales of the Neutral Ground,* p. 61; Frederick Shonnard and W. W. Spooner, *History of Westchester,* p. 459.

[1] J. F. Cooper, *The Spy: A Tale of the Neutral Ground,* New York: 1821, ch. XVI, p. 237. "A cluster of some half-dozen small and dilapidated buildings formed what, from the circumstance of two roads intersecting each other at right angles, was called the village of the Four Corners. As usual, one of the most imposing of these edifices had been termed, in the language of the day, 'a house of entertainment for man and beast.' On a rough board suspended from the gallows-looking post that had supported the ancient sign, was, however, written in chalk, 'Elizabeth Flanagan, her hotel,' an ebullition of the wit of some of the idle wags of the corps. The matron, whose name had thus been exalted

Although Cooper used the scene for the capture of his fictitious spy Harvey Birch, the tavern and its colorful matron were nonetheless a reality.[2]

4 THE PHONY TORY: ENOCH CROSBY INFILTRATES THE TORY RANKS

Another controversy, one concerning the identification in real life of Cooper's spy, Harvey Birch, does not die down.[1] Whether Cooper modeled him after Enoch Crosby or not, Crosby was a genuine secret agent for the Committee for Detecting and Defeating Conspiracies under the chairmanship of John Jay. Crosby left an account in his own words of infiltrating the Tory ranks and gathering information for nine months by parading as a dedicated Tory. In 1832, when he applied for a government pension, he

---

to an office of such unexpected dignity, was the widow of a soldier who had been killed in the service. Betty was well known to every trooper in the corps, could call each by his Christian or nickname, as best suited her fancy; and, although intolerable to all whom habit had not made familiar with her virtues, was a general favorite with these partisan warriors. Her faults were a trifling love of liquor, excessive filthiness, and a total disregard of all the decencies of language; her virtues, an unbounded love for her adopted country, perfect honesty when dealing on certain known principles with the soldiery, and great good-nature. Added to these, Betty had the merit of being the inventor of that beverage which is so well known at the present hour . . . which is distinguished by the name of 'cock-tail.' Elizabeth Flanagan was peculiarly well qualified, by education and circumstance to perfect this improvement in liquors, having been literally brought up on its principal ingredient. . . ."

[2]Chauncey K. Buchanan, writing in the Tarrytown *Argus,* Feb. 10,1900, says that Betty Flanagan and her inn were not just a product of Cooper's imagination, but actually existed. He located the inn as a log house near the pond on the Bonner Farm. His verification, however, came only by word of mouth, passed on by George W. Campbell from Abram Coles. Coles had heard it from his grandfather, William Yerks, who was a contemporary of Betty Flanagan.

[1]The controversy began with H. L. Barnum, *The Spy Unmasked,* 1829, identifying Cooper's character with Enoch Crosby. More recently Warren S. Walker found Harvey Birch's prototype in a combination of Abraham Woodhull and Robert Townsend (alias Samuel Culper, Sr. and Samuel Culper, Jr.). "The Prototype of Harvey Birch," *New York History,* vol. 37, no. 4 (Oct., 1956), p. 399ff.

gave the details of his espionage services for Jay's committee.[2] His declaration tells about the curious way in which he accidentally became a pseudo Tory when he was actually employed in the rebel secret service. He enlisted in late August 1776 in Colonel Jacobus Swarthout's regiment of Dutchess County, but found that his company had already left Carmel for Kingsbridge and that he had to catch up with them. His declaration continues in the third person.

SEPTEMBER 1776–MAY 1777

❡   He started alone after his said enlistment & on his way at a place in Westchester County about two miles from Pines bridge he fell in company with a stranger, who accosted the deponent & asked him if he was going *down,* declarant replied he was: the stranger then asked if declarant was not afraid to venture alone, & said there were many rebels *below* & he would meet with difficulty in *getting down.* The declarant perceived from the observations of the stranger that he supposed the declarant intended to go to the British & willing to encourage that misapprehension & turn it to the best advantage, he asked if there was any mode which he the stranger could point out by which the declarant could *get through* safely. The stranger after being satisfied that declarant was wishing to join the British army, told him that there was a company raising in that vicinity to join the British army, that it was nearly complete & in a few days would be ready to go *down* & that declarant had better join that company & *go down* with them. The stranger finally gave to the declarant his name, it was Bunker, & told the declarant where & showed the house in which he lived and also told him that Jonathan Fowler was to be the captain of the company then raising and James Kipp Lieutenant.

After having learned this much from Bunker the declarant told him that he was unwilling to wait until the company could be ready to march & would try to get *through alone* & parted from him on his way down & continued until night when he stopped at the house of a man, who was called Esquire [Joseph] Young, & put up there for the night. In the course

---

[2] John Bakeless investigated Enoch Crosby's pension claim of 1832 and pointed out the firsthand narrative of espionage which Crosby gave. *Turncoats, Traitors, and Heroes,* Philadelphia and New York: 1959, pp. 136-137; 381. The full text of Crosby's deposition appears in James H. Pickering, "Enoch Crosby, Secret Agent of the Neutral Ground: His Own Story," *New York History,* vol. 47, no. 1, (Jan. 1966) pp. 61-71.

of conversation with Esquire Young in the evening declarent learned that he was a member of the committee of safety for the county of Westchester & then communicated to him the information he had obtained from Mr. Bunker. . . . The next morning the declarent in company with Esqr. Young went to the White plains & found the Committee there sitting. . . . It was by all thought best, that he should not join the regiment, but should act in a different character as he could thus be more useful to his country.

He was accordingly announced to Capt. Micah Townsend who then was at the White plains commanding a company of rangers as a prisoner, & the Captain was directed to keep him until further orders. In the evening after he was placed as a prisoner under Capt. Townsend, he made an excuse to go out & was accompanied by a soldier. His excuse led him over a fence into a field of corn then nearly or quite full grown. As soon as he was out of sight of the soldier he made the best of his way . . . & when the soldier hailed him to return he was allmost beyond hearing. An alarm gun was fired but declarent was far from danger.

In the course of the night the declarent reached the house of said Bunker, who got up & let him in. Declarent then related to Bunker the circumstance of his having been taken prisoner, of his going before the committee at the Court house, of being put under the charge of Capt. Townsend & of his escape, that he had concluded to avail himself of the protection of the company raising in his neighborhood to get down. The next morning Bunker went with declarent & introduced him as a good loyalist to several of the company. Declarent remained some days with different individuals of the company & until it was about to go down, when declarent went one night to the house of Esqr. Young to give information of the state & progress of the company. . . . At the house of Esqr. Young declarent found Capt. Townsend with a great part of his company & after giving the information he returned to the neighborhood of Bunkers & that night declarent with a great part of the company which was preparing to go down were made prisoners. The next day all of them about thirty in number were marched to the White plains, and remained there several days, a part of the time locked up in jail with the other prisoners, the residue of the time he was with the committee.

The prisoners were finally ordered to Fishkill in the County of Dutchess where the State Convention was then sitting. The declarent went as a prisoner to Fishkill. Capt. Townsend with his company of rangers took charge of the company. At Fishkill a committee for detecting conspiracies was sitting composed of John Jay, afterwards Governor of N York, Zepeniah Platt afterwards first judge of Dutchess County, Colonel [William] Duer of the County of Albany, & a Mr. [Nathaniel] Sackett. The declarent was called before that committee, who understood the character of declarent & the nature of his services, this the committee must have learned either from Capt. Townsend or from the Committee at White plains. The declarent was examined under oath & his examination reduced to writing. The prisoners with the declarent were kept whilst declarent remained at Fishkill in a building which had been occupied as a Hatters shop & they were guarded by a company of rangers commanded by Capt. [William] Clark. The declarent remained about a week at Fishkill when he was bailed by Jonathan Hopkins; this was done to cover the character in which declarent acted. *[National Arch, S/10/505. Pickering, "Enoch Crosby, Secret Agent of the Neutral Ground: His Own Story," New York History, vol. 47, no. 1, pp. 63-65.]*

AFTERNOTE *The information which Crosby confided to Jay's committee led not only to the capture of Fowler's and Kipp's Loyalist company, but also to the breaking up of another company of about thirty men recruited in Ulster County by Captain Robinson, son of Beverly Robinson. Crosby recounts that "Capt. Robinson occupied a cave in the mountains. . . . They slept together nearly a week in the cave." He learned where the company would stop the first night after mustering and conveyed the information to the committee at Fishkill, leading to the capture and imprisonment of the whole company. His next mission was in the area of the Walloomsac River and from there south to Pawling in Dutchess County. Here, during the months of February and March 1777, he learned that still another company was forming under Captain Joseph Sheldon and a Lieutenant Chase and that it would soon march to join the British. They, too, were surrounded at the critical moment and captured, giving rise to the suspicion that there was a traitor among them. Thus three times the intelligence which Crosby transmitted to Jay was responsible for blocking the effective formation of Loyalist companies bent on joining the British forces. In May 1777, Crosby concluded "that a longer continuance in that employment would be dangerous," and he quit the secret service for an undisguised enlistment in a rebel unit.*

The possibility that Crosby was the prototype for Cooper's Harvey Birch is not the only aspect of his declaration which attracts attention.

Other points of interest are the use of the cave in the Highlands, the meet-ing with Joseph Young near Betty Flanagan's tavern, the knowledge which Jay had of the unfriendly activities of Robinson's son when the father was brought before the committee, [1] *and finally the information Crosby gave concerning the confiscation of Loyalist property. In this connection, he reported to the committee "that the confiscation of the personal property of the Tories & leasing of their lands had a great tendency to discourage them from joining the British army." The legal measures of confiscation and proscription taken against the Tories were thus as much a deterrent and a war measure as a punishment. New York was encouraged by Crosby's report to enact more severe legislation, namely the Act of Attainder of October 22, 1779.*

5   TORY HIDEOUTS: MARGARET MORRIS CONCEALS DR. JONA-THAN ODELL IN HER BURLINGTON HOUSE AND DECEIVES THE GONDOLA MEN

Margaret Morris was the widow of William Morris, a Philadelphia mer-chant who died in 1766 leaving her with four small children. In 1776, when she wrote her *Journal,* she had established a residence in Burlington, New Jersey. As a Quaker, she was opposed to the war. While her sympa-thies wavered somewhat, she disavowed any rapport with the rebels and assisted Loyalist friends in trouble. She tried at first to steer a middle course, and was evidently successful, as in the instance described in her *Journal,* in making the rebel gondola men believe she was on the rebel side.

DECEMBER 1776

❡   (the 13th): This day we began to look a little like ourselves again. The troops were removed some miles from Town. . . . Our friends began to shew themselves abroad; several calld to see us, amongst the Number was one (Dr. Odell,) *esteemed* by the *whole family & very intimate* in it, but the spirit of the Divil still continud to rove thro the Town in the shape of Tory Hunters. A Message was deliverd to our intimate fr [Dr.

[1] *Supra* p. 148.

Jonathan Odell] informing him a party of Armd Men were on the search for him, his horse was brought, & he *retired* to *a place of safety.* . . . Parties of Armd Men rudely enterd the Houses in Town & diligent search made for Tories. . . .

(the 16th): A very terrible account of thousands coming into Town & now actually to be seen on Gallows Hill. My incautious Son catchd up the Spy Glass & was running to the Mill to look at them. I told him it w^d be liable to misconstruction, but he prevaild on me to let him gratify his curiosity & he went, but returnd much dissatisfyd, for no troops could he see; as he came back poor Dick took the glass & resting it against a tree took a view of the fleet. Both of these was observd by the people on board, who suspected it was an Enemy that was watching thier Motions. They Mannd a boat & sent her on Shore. A loud knocking at my door brought me to it. I was a little flutterd & kept locking and unlocking that I might get my ruffled face a little composd. At last I opend it & half a dozen Men all Armd demanded the keys of the empty House. I asked what they wanted there. They said to Search for a D-d tory who had been spy^g at them from the Mill. The Name of a Tory so near my *own door* seriously alarmd me, for a poor *refugee* [Dr. Jonathan Odell], dignifyd by that Name, had claimd the shelter of my Roof & was at that very time conceald, like a thief in an Auger hole. I rung the bell violently, the Signal agreed on, if they came to Search, and when I thought he had crept into the hole, I put on a very simple look & cryd out, Bless me, I hope you are not Hessians—say, good Men, are you the Hessians? Do we look like Hessians? asked one of them rudely. Indeed I dont know. Did you never see a Hessian? No never in my life but they are Men & you are Men & may be Hessians for anything I know, but Ill go with you into Col Co [xe] house, tho indeed it was my Son at the Mill. He is but a Boy & meant no harm. He wanted to see the Troops. So I marchd at the head of them, opend the door, & searchd every place but we coud not find the tory—strange where he could be—we returnd; they greatly disappointed, I pleasd to think *my house* was not Suspected. The Capt, a smart little fellow Named Shippen, said he wishd he coud see the Spy glass. S D [Sarah Dillwyn] produced it & very civilly desird his acceptance of it, which I was soory for, as I often amusd myself in looking thro it. They left us & Searchd J V^s [James Verree] & the two next houses, but no tory coud they find. This transaction reachd the Town & Col Cox was very angry & orderd them on board. In the Evening I went to Town with my refugee [Dr. Jonathan Odell] & placed him in other lodgeings. I was told today of a design to seize on the person of a Young Man in town, as he was deemd a tory. I thought a hint w^d be kindly rec^d & as I came back called on a fr^d of his & told him. Next day he was out of the reach of the Gondolas. [*Morris, Journal, pp. 47-49.*]

SEVENTEEN FARMINGTON TORIES, PREFERRING TO "SIGN AND EAT" RATHER THAN "FLY TO STARVE ON LOYALTY," PETITION THE ASSEMBLY FOR RELEASE[1]

Factional disputes in the church at New Cambridge (Bristol) led to a split between Calvinist adherents and communicants who preferred to worship under the Church of England. In 1773, the latter group invited the Reverend James Nichols, a graduate of Yale in 1771 and just ordained, to assume the joint pulpit of two parishes, Northbury and New Cambridge. He served the seventy-eight families of his parish only a short time before the troubles erupted and services were suspended, but he continued meetings in the homes of his parishioners. He instilled in them a staunch devotion to England; in fact, his influence was so strong that the rebels yanked him from a cellar hiding place, tarred and feathered him, and dragged him through a brook. Tried for treason with Moses Dunbar in Hartford in 1777, he was acquitted, while Dunbar was convicted and executed.

The minister's influence was a prime factor in the use of the Tory Den, a well-concealed cave in which the Tories, many from Nichols's church, hid out from time to time. The cliff shielding the den is the highest point of wooded area, called "The Ledges" because of the rocky outcroppings studding the hill. While there is no authentic list of refugees,

---

[1] The Pausing American Loyalist

Who would bend to fools,
And Truckle thus to mad, mob-chosen upstarts,
But that the dread of something after flight
(In that blest country, where, yet, no moneyless
Poor wight can live) puzzles the will,
And makes ten thousands rather sign—and eat
Than fly—to starve on loyalty—
Thus dread of want makes rebels of us all.
Quoted in E. LeRoy Pond, *The Tories of Chippeny Hill*, New York: 1909, p. 72.

some of the seventeen Tories from New Cambridge, whose memorial to the Assembly appears below, presumably hid out there. Joel Tuttle and Stephen Graves, both of whom were scourged by the rebels, sought refuge in the Den. Graves's wife, Ruth Jerome Graves, who lived about a mile from the cave, brought food to the hidden men and warned them of trespassers by blowing on a conch shell.

These seventeen Tories were jailed in Danbury in 1777 on suspicion of adhering to the enemy. The names of fifteen were found among the baptismal records of the First Episcopal Society of New Cambridge, of which Nichols was pastor. All were released on taking an oath to the state and the blame for their temporary defection was placed on the Reverend Nichols.[2]

MAY 16,1777

¶ *To the Honorable the General Assembly of the State of Connecticut Convened at Hartford on the 2nd Thursday of May 1777*
The Memorial of Nathanael Jones, Simon Tuttle, Joel Tuttle, Nathan[l] Mathews, John Mathews, Riverus Carrington, Lemuel Carrington, Zerababel Jerom Jn[r], Chauncey Jerom, Ezra Dorman, Nemiah Rice, Abel Rice, George Beckwith, Abel Frisbey, Levi Frisbey, Jared Peck, & Abram Waters, All of Farmington humbly Sheweth—That the Memorialists are now Confined in the Common Goal in the County of Hartford by virtue of a Mittimus from some of the Civil Authority, Selectmen & Com[tee] of the Town of Farmington for certain supposed unfriendlyness to this & the other united States of America—whereupon the memorialists beg leave to observe to your Honors, That the only Crime they can possibly conceive themselves to have Commited is because they did not hastily & without proper Order run for the Relief of Danbury in the late Alarm, without

---

[2] The Act of the Legislature freeing the group read: ". . . it appeared that they had been much under the influence of one Nichols, a designing clergyman who has instilled into them principles opposite to the good of the States; . . . that they were indeed grossly ignorant of the true grounds of the present war with Great Britain; that they . . . professed themselves convinced since the Danbury alarm that there was no such thing as remaining neuters; . . . that since their imprisonment upon serious reflection they are convinced that the States are right in their claim and that it is their duty to submit to authority . . ." Bill Informing on the Committee Report, Farmington Tories, May 1777, Conn. State Arch., ser. I, *Rev. War,* vol. VIII, p. 154.

Arms or Ammunition, of which some of the Mem^{lts} had been deprived, as well as confined to their Farms & Certain Limits, by Order of s^d Com^{tee} upon mere suspicion only that they were not in favor of American Measures. They further observe to your Honors that tho they have not altogether concured in Sentiment heretofore with every Step taken for the preservation of the Liberties of their Country, yet they never have in any respect interfered therein, but have done and are still ready to Contribute everything with their Estates & properties in Defense of the same; and many of us, not so far advanced in years, are ready to take up Arms & Step forth for its Relief, being now Convinced of the Justice of the American Cause. We therefore most humbly & earnestly beg your Honors Consideration in our behalf that we may not be left in Confinment and our Farms & Familys in the meantime lying waste & Suffering—& pray that a Com^{tee} may be appointed to Examine & Enquire what we have done and are willing to do, that some proper measures may be taken for our Inlargment or otherwise grant them Relief, and we as in Duty bound shall Ever pray [*Conn. State Arch., Rev. War, Ser. I, vol. VII, p. 152 a.*]

HECTOR ST. JOHN DE CRÈVECOEUR DESCRIBES "THE GROTTO ... THE REFUGE OF THREE WORTHY MEN"

Hector St. John de Crèvecoeur, the author of the famous question, "What then is the American, this new Man," was in fact a British colonial, naturalized in New York in 1765-1766, and a Loyalist.[1] He left his native France in 1754 at age nineteen, served with Montcalm in Canada during the French and Indian War, and afterwards lived for a few years in Philadelphia and Shippensburg. His marriage in 1769 to Mehitabel Tippett, daughter of a Loyalist merchant of Yonkers and sister of Martha, Colonel James De Lancey's wife, and his purchase of 120 acres in Orange County the same year brought him to the Hudson Valley. Here, on the road from Chester to Blooming Grove, he settled down for the next ten years, developing his farm, "Pine Hill," and raising his three children. Here he composed his twelve "Letters from an American Farmer," romanticizing American rustic

---

[1] H. L. Bourdin, R. H. Gabriel, and S. T. Williams, eds., *Sketches of Eighteenth Century America,* by Hector St. John de Crèvecoeur, New Haven: 1925, pp. 8-9.

life.[2] In 1779, unable to sit out the civil war at Pine Hill undisturbed, as he had hoped, he secured a safe conduct and went to New York with his seven-year-old son, intending to sail for Europe.[3] Accused in an anonymous charge of stealing a plan of New York Harbor and corresponding with Washington, he was arrested by the British and his departure delayed until 1780. Eventually he reached his native home in Caen, Normandy. Appointed French consul in New York in 1783, he returned to America to find his home burned, his wife dead, and his children's whereabouts unknown.[4]

Some time after independence was declared, but before persecution dictated the necessity for his own flight, Crèvecoeur found the refuge of three worthy Loyalist friends who had disappeared and composed the sketch of their "Grotto." This essay, like the "Letters," shows the qualities of the idyllist and naturalist in Crèvecoeur and points up the love of freedom, the self-reliance, and the ingeniousness in the American character which contributed to "the American, this new man."

1776-1777

❡   The spirit which animates the breast of our new people is a spirit of rancor which often becomes blind to its own future interest. 'Tis so with most passions given us for the most salutary purposes; they often transport us beyond the bonds intended. An old friend of mine suddenly disappeared at the same time that two of his neighbours were missing; this caused a great alarm among their connections and much greater ones among those who could have wished to have apprehended them, for they had been long suspicious. I made all the inquiries I possibly could but the universal distrust which possesses all minds was so great that nothing could be discovered. Different parties were sent to search the woods, to explore every place; the search proved vain.

This elopement so sudden and so private filled the country with sur-

---

[2] London: 1782. All, except the last letter, were written before the Revolution.

[3] F. B. Sanborn, "The Conversion of a Loyalist to a Patriot," Mass. Historical Society *Proc.*, vol. L, p. 90.

[4] By assisting in the repatriation of Captain Gustavus Fellowes of Boston, a rebel naval officer who had escaped from an English prison, Crèvecoeur had gained his goodwill. In return Fellowes had located the two children and taken them into his own family until they could be reunited with their father. Robert de Crèvecoeur, *St. John de Crèvecoeur: Sa Vie et Ses Ouvrages,* Paris: 1883, p. 57.

prise. Some were glad to see innocence escape the hands of tyranny, and the Rulers reproached themselves with their too tardy indulgence. But how cou'd they remain long concealed? They had left wives, children, great property, and these are ponderous chains which fasten men to their blocks. By repeated guesses and hints, by sollicitations, I was at last admitted into the secret: They were safe and at no great distance from their former habitations. It was not only the pleasure of seeing them I coveted as that of viewing the singular scituation of a retreat which had baffled the inimical ingenuity of the Times.

I was at last conducted to the spott, the most romantick I had ever seen. It was gloomy but not frightfull, entirely sequestred from common paths yet accessible, but only to the experienced foot. It might be called a pleasant habitation when compared to putrid gaols and narrower confinement. This was the azilum of security and silence, and who wou'd not have preferred this retreat to the vexations to which they might have been exposed. . . . I was led through the woods for a considerable distance, then ascended a pretty high ledge of rocks, not laid stratum super stratum but lying at various angles, then we descended into a valley which was so filled with fragments that we cou'd hardly pass along. We climbed over old decayed trees whose strong roots had once reached at a considerable distance among the crevices of the surface in quest of early subsistence, now laid prostrate. We passed under others which tho' living yet were so inclined and distorted as to make us afraid least they shou'd crush us in their fall. Quitting at last this valley, we passed by two large perpendicular rocks like a couple of huge pillars. I observed how a late thunderstorm had wasted its fury on a lofty spruce tree whose roots had reached at a great distance, the trunk was split in shivers, it had been stript of all its limbs and branches. Soon after this we suddenly turned to the south towards a spott almost devoid of vegetables but exceeding full of rattle snakes. Hard by was a morass incompassed all around with very craggy grounds which we were obliged to pass. It was a trembling surface, how formed? I cannot tell, supported by water which was not about 2½ feet distance under our feet as we experienced it by thrusting our poles down. On this doubtful surface there grew some bogs and great quantities of aquaticks: water elder, angelica, and some bushes of alder. We at last arrived on the opposite shore. As we were obliged to follow the shores where bushes grew thicker, we often pulled off our hats and stoop'd and scrambled to get through. Just as I was looking down and searching for a sure foothold, we felt a sudden agitation of the air and an uncommon noyse which startled us the more so as we apprehended being discovered or being the cause of the discovery of our friends. But, behold, it was a great heron we had disturbed from its nest. The great impediment he met with in the distention of his wings had caused both the strange noyse and uncommon agitation of air we had felt. Sometime after we agreed to rest a while, being extremely weary. The sun was scarcely an hour high. "How much farther is it?" asked ——— "About ¼ of a mile," answered our guide. — "What a horrid part of the creation," observed another, "nothing is to be seen but useless morasses, broken rocks, thunder struck trees." — "Had it been created," said another, "for no other purpose than to save these gentlemen from popular fury, it seems to me that it wou'd be sufficient to extort from us some simbols of gratitude." — "We join you in the pleasing offering" said 3 unseen and unknown voices which appeared to be quite contiguous to us. We arose and looked at each other with astonishment, but perceiving our guide to smile, fear vanished from our wonder. We searched and examined every spott around us, but in vain. Just as we were returning to the stone on which we had set down, a moving green surface seem'd to open with difficulty and the 3 well known heads of our friends thrusting out, beckoned us to come in. No sooner had we entered than the door was immediately shutt. — "How can it be," said I, "that we have been a full ½ hour so close to the entrance of this grotto without having perceived it, and not even been able to discover the least traces of any aperture after we were convinced that the voices we had heard were not inimical? I was so near the pretended door that it struck my feet when it was open, yet with all my attention, was not able to trace the least representation of any such thing." — "So much the better," said a third, "if the eyes of friends overlook these mysteries of iniquity, it is to be hoped that the more hurried and less composed sight of enemies will search in vain as well as we."

This is really a most astonishing natural contrivance taken and view'd together. When we entered, a small fire covered with embers at about 30 feet distance was just perceivable. In the middle there hung a large lamp, the still light of which afforded us no other means of conducting ourselves through this gloomy habitation than as a distant landmark. It was a b[e]acon to lead us towards the fire. Contiguous to what might be called a chimney there sat a small table, a book or two, a pair of spectacles, and a candle which was lighted soon after we came in. Its light was greatly dimm'd by a kind of rainbow proceeding I suppose from the dampness of the air. The

first appearance of all these objects put me in mind of a sepulchral monu-
ment inhabited by some happy spirit permitted to revisit this peacable mansion in order to attone by new prayers for sins not yet expiated. This Grotto
was the refuge of 3 worthy men who had preferred it to the more splendid
ones of Court Houses and Publick Gaols.

—"Pray how long have you lived here gentlemen?"

—"3 months"

—"Nature seems to have done everything here for you, but sure I
am that she did not condescend to make a door to this retreat."

—"No, it was sufficient for her to have built these impenetrable walls
and to have laid on this huge roof, so we might well do the rest." I observed
with pleasure the chairs they had contrived with crooked bows of trees
fasten'd together with withes. A flatt smooth stone properly supported,
served them for a table. They had enlarged a natural aperture on the west
side so as to make it receive a casement of 4 paines of glass. At the north
end, a passage was left, near where the roof stone joined the perpendicular
wall; this they had converted into a chimney, thus what little vapor their
coal fire exhaled was carried up, and the smoke of any other fewell might
have betrayed them. In every other respect this Antre was hermetick and
yet had no disagreeable smell, its floor partly of earth, partly sand was levell
with the ground on which we rested before we came in, all the rest was
composed of flatt slate stones which in some antient percution had accidently left the void in which we now stand. I perceived with surprise a small
shelve full of books, one was a Critical Review of State tryals, another,
Clarendon's History of his own time; those were used for implements of
leisure and improvement. On the opposite side there hanged few fowls
and gammons. After I had been there an hour I began to think that it
was not so dreadful a hole as I had represented it to myself. . . . Their
door was the most ingenious as well as the most awfull of their con-
trivances; in the interval which had been left by the antient fall of the roof
stone, there was accidently left an aperture large enough to enter. To this
opening they had fixed a wooden door made of thin boards the outside of
which they had lined with a coarse blanket on which they sow'd large moss
which being often watered allways appeared fresh and presented to the eyes
nothing but the deceiving surface of a smooth mossy rock perfectly similar
to the rest. On the left hand side there grew and flourished a large wild
vine such as you often see in our forests; its limbs and branches extended a
great way and covered great part of the south front as well as the roof. This

appeared to have been planted on purpose, they luckily improved the fortunate hint and made a most excellent use of that which nature intended only for the food of birds and foxes. . . .

Warmed by the new kindled fire, animated by a few glasses of good wine, rejoiced at the safe scituation of our friends, we spent the most cheerful evening at which nothing was wanted. [*Bourdin & Williams, "Crèvecoeur the Loyalist . . . ," The Nation, vol. 121, pp. 328-330.*]

THE CLAUDIUS SMITH GANG

The Claudius Smith gang was another independent group of marauders who operated in guerilla-like fashion in the Highlands, using caves for bases and for refuge. They too were Loyalists; some had been with the British in New York and had taken part in the attack on Fort Montgomery above Peekskill (October 6, 1777). Their principal enterprise was robbery—taking horses, cattle, silverware, and other valuables from rebel families near the Clove, a ravine in the Ramapo Mountains. Some of the loot they turned over to the British, some they kept for themselves. They were also reputed on occasion to have acted in the tradition of Robin Hood, extracting money from a victim and giving it to the poor. Although Claudius Smith was tried and hanged on robbery charges, his pack of ruffians did not draw the line at larceny; they were also guilty of brutish treatment of their victims, of incendiarism, and even of murder. When Governor Clinton proclaimed Smith an outlaw and put a price of $500 on his capture, he fled to a safer sanctuary on Long Island. The reward, however, was enough to induce an alert rebel, venturing a visit to Smithtown, to uncover Smith's hideout, organize a posse from Connecticut, and slip over by whaleboat to seize him. He was carried back to Fishkill and then taken to Goshen for trial. Following Smith's execution (January 22, 1779), his band, which included his sons, sought revenge by murdering an innocent Whig, John Clark, whom they dragged from his home and shot. On the victim's coat they pinned a warning to the rebels not to hang or mistreat any more friends of government.

William Cole, one of Smith's associates who had been apprehended, made a confession revealing both the names of his companions and the location of secret caves in the rocky Highlands used for their refuge and rendezvous. Not only have these two documents survived, but also the "Claudius Smith" cave near Monroe, which still may be visited by the persistent climber.[1]

Claudius Smith's Avengers Pin A Warning to the Rebels on the Murdered Body of John Clark

MARCH 26, 1779

❡ A WARNING TO THE REBELS—You are hereby warned at your peril to desist from hanging any more friends to government as you did Claudius Smith. You are warned likewise to use James Smith, James Flewwelling, and William Cole well, and ease them of their Irons, for we are determined to hang six for one, for the blood of the innocent cries aloud for vengeance. Your noted friend Capt. Williams and his crew of robbers and murderers we have got in our power, and the blood of Claudius Smith shall be repaid. There are particular companies of us who belong to Col. Butler's army, Indians as well as white men, and particularly numbers from New York that are resolved to be avenged on you for your cruelty and murder. We are to remind you, that you are the beginners and aggressors, for by your cruel oppressions and bloody actions, you drive us to it. This is the first, and we are determined to pursue it on your heads and leaders to the last—till the whole of you are murdered. [*Fishkill Packet, Apr. 28, 1779, Ruttenberger & Clark, Orange County, p. 72 fn.*]

[1] Samuel W. Eager describes the cave which was east of the Augusta Works in the southern part of Monroe. "This place of retreat was on the side of the mountain and shaped like a shed, some ten feet high, with the front partly built up to protect from winds and storms, the stones of which are still to be seen there. The entrance was upon a level, and a large flat rock came out an covered it. From the rear of this room which was about one hundred feet deep, there was a way of escape to the outside, by a difficult and winding passage and clambering up the rocks. . . ." *History of Orange County,* Newburgh: 1846-1847, p. 500.

William Cole Reveals the Whereabouts of the Hideouts of the Claudius Smith Gang

MARCH 29, 1779

❡ Confession of William Cole, taken at New Barbadoes, March 29, 1779.

. . . That the persons who harbor these gangs are Benjamin Demarest, Tunis Helme, John Harring, John Johnson under Kakiate mountain; William Concklin, Elisha Babcock, Elisha Babcock Jr., John Dobbs near Kakiate; Edward Roblins in the Clove; Ezekiel Eumans and John Winter in Kakiate; Peter Acker in Paskack; and Jacobus Peak. That there is a Cave dug under ground by the sons of Isaac Maybee and on the said Maybee's land, about half a mile from John Horrings, and another at about a quarter of a mile distant from the former, dug by the same persons, and a third about three miles from the House of Joseph Wessels in the Clove, and well known by Roblins in the Clove, each of which may contain about eight persons, where these Robbers generally resort; and that John King, Jacob Acker, and John Staat are now in the Clove at Paskack, or in the houses around it. That Harding, Everitt, etc., as soon as the wheather grows warm, intend to plunder Coll Malcom at Walkill, to burn Col. Nicols' House, the Gaol, and some other Houses in and near Goshen, and to remain in the County for that purpose. That there is a Gang of the same kind on the East side of Hudson's River, whose names are Mandeville Lennerbeck, Peter Wood, William Heiliker, William Danford, Aaron Williams, James Houston, and Others, who plundered and brought some Cattle and Horses from Tarrytown to New York the day before Cole left it. [*Washington's Headquarters, Newburgh.*]

6 CONNECTICUT WHALEBOATERS RAID LONG ISLAND WITH HIT-AND-RUN TACTICS AND MURDER ISAAC HART OF RHODE ISLAND

Rivington's *Royal Gazette* had the reputation throughout the war as the mouthpiece in New York for the King's cause and Rivington himself as the arch-Tory, a notability which served as a cloak for his services as a double agent.[1] Typical of the Loyalist tone of his paper is the article

[1] See pp. 327-332.

about the murder of Isaac Hart, drawing attention to the "savageness and degeneracy" of the rebel whaleboaters in carrying out a raid on Long Island.

[NOVEMBER 23, 1780]

C A party of rebels about eighty in number headed, it is said, by a rebel Major [Benjamin] Talmadge, assisted by a certain Heathcot Muirson, Benajah Strong, Thomas Jackson, and Caleb Brewster, officers belonging to the said party, formerly all of Long Island, came across in eight whaleboats from somewhere about Newhaven on the Connecticut shore and landed between the Wading River and the Old Man's, and are supposed to have been concealed two or three days on the island by their old friends the rebels. On Thursday morning the 23d inst. about 50 of them marched across the island, the remainder being left to guard the boats; just after daylight arrived at Smith's Point, St. George's Manor, south-side Long Island, where they surprized a body of respectable loyal Refugees belonging to Rhode Island, and the vicinity thereabout, who were establishing a post in order to get a present subsistence for themselves and their distressed families. The sentry upon observing them fired, which they returned and mortally wounded him and rushed into a house. Mr. Isaac Hart of Newport in Rhode Island, formerly an eminent merchant and ever a loyal subject, was inhumanly fired upon and bayoneted, wounded in fifteen different parts of his body, and beat with their muskets in the most shocking manner in the very act of imploring quarter, and died of his wounds in a few hours after, universally regretted by every true lover of his King and country. Four more Refugees were wounded also, but in a fair way of recovery. A poor woman was also fired upon at another house and barbarously wounded through both breasts, of which wound she now lingers a specimen of rebel savageness and degeneracy.

The rebels carried off about 40 prisoners. On their return at Coram they burnt a magazine of hay, about 100 tons, and the same day embarked for the Connecticut shore. [*Roy. Gaz., Dec. 2, 1780.*]

7 "OH THOU GREAT RULER": AARON DOANE, LOYALIST
OUTLAW, PETITIONS GOVERNOR JOHN DICKINSON AND THE
PENNSYLVANIA COUNCIL FOR PARDON

Another band of notorious banditti were the Doanes of Plumstead, Bucks
County, Pennsylvania. Five of the desperadoes were brothers: Moses, the
leader; Aaron; Levi; Joseph, Jr.; and Mahlon; and one, Abraham, was a
cousin. Still another, Israel Doane, Abraham's father and uncle of the
others, was the most daring and influential of the gang. The careers of
three of these men ended in violent death; the others were captured but
managed to escape, and one, Aaron, was pardoned. The Doane brothers,
sons of Hester Vickers and Joseph Doane, Sr., a carpenter and upright
Quaker, possessed large athletic physiques; were said to be expert horse-
men, superior wrestlers, and marksmen; and were all under twenty-one at
the close of the Revolution. Two were under seventeen when their depredations started in 1776. Not willing to serve in the rebel army, nor pay taxes
to the Continental Congress, they were taunted by their neighbors and soon
became branded as Tories. Ill treatment of their fathers by the Committee
of Safety and confiscation of Doane property rankled in their hearts, and
they sought reprisals, robbing tax collectors, but avoiding the plunder of
private property, except for horses. They were not interested so much in
personal gain as in revenge or just retribution from public monies. Operating between the Delaware River and Virginia, they terrorized the countryside, eluding both sheriffs' posses and militia, traveling at times in disguise,
and hiding out in caves and cellars. Although horse and cattle stealing was
their particular bent, they also spread counterfeit notes, passed information, and did errands for the British until their daring deeds led to their outlawry. Moses Doane is reported to have guided Cornwallis's division to the
Jamaica heights where it trapped John Sullivan's forces in the Battle of
Long Island. He also served as an aide in Major André's intelligence net-
work and is supposed to have been the "farmer" who delivered to Colonel
Johann Rall on Christmas Day 1776 a note warning of the rebel movement
across the Delaware River toward Trenton—a note later found unopened in
Rall's pocket reading: "Washington is coming on you down the river, he
will be here afore long."[1]

[1] George McReynolds, ed., *The New Doane Book,* Doylestown, Pa.: 1952. This is the
2nd edition of John P. Rogers, *The Doane Outlaws* or *Bucks County's Cowboys in the
Revolution,* Doylestown: 1897, written from verbal reminiscences of Bucks County
residents, pp. 54–55; 58–62; 59 fn; 43.

The Doanes' most brazen act was the robbery, October 22, 1781, of the Bucks County Treasury. The gang pilfered over £ 1300 in specie and paper money from the Newtown house of John Hart, the Treasurer, and from a nearby office, and then escaped into New Jersey. For the next seven years the outlaws were hunted down. John Tomlinson, one of the co-plotters, was caught, convicted, and hanged in Newtown about a year after the robbery; Robert Johnson Steele, another participant, was hanged in Philadelphia in 1785 for the same offense. As for the Doanes, Moses was captured by a posse on Gallows Run in Plumstead, bound, and shot, September 1, 1783; Levi and Abraham were captured five years after the close of the war, tied to the tail of a cart, carried out Market Street, and publicly executed on the Philadelphia commons, September 24, 1788. Among the unruly crowd which followed the cart was the sad figure of Levi's fiancée, who bade him farewell at the gallows.[2] Of the remaining Doane brothers who were all captured at one time or another, Joseph, Jr., who had been in Newtown jail for six months and had been sentenced to death, escaped in 1784 to New Jersey where he taught school under an assumed name, and when discovered, took refuge in Ontario. Mahlon escaped from the Bedford jail, releasing almost all his co-prisoners, fled to New York, and sailed in 1783 in the general evacuation. Israel Doane, the uncle, was convicted in 1782 of the lesser offense of harboring refugees and served a year's term.

Aaron's case, however, followed a strange and different course. In August 1784, he too was caught, convicted, and sentenced to hanging for complicity in the robbery of the Bucks County Treasury. He appealed to the Governor and Council of Pennsylvania, pleading innocence and no knowledge of the proclamation calling on him to surrender following the robbery. The Council granted him a pardon in March 1785, contending that he could not be put to death as an outlaw because certain technicalities of an act of 1718 had not been strictly observed and because Pennsylvania had no precedent for an execution for outlawry based exclusively on judicial proceedings. The sheriff's proclamation contained several errors, referring only to the writ of capias and not mentioning the day and year; it told Doane to appear at the Supreme Court, when the words "Said Justices" of the act referred to the Courts of Quarter Sessions. In a case of life and death these details had to be observed with exactness. Moreover, the Council worried about establishing a precedent which would "weaken that security which the Constitution of the State appears to have intended for its citizens."[3]

[2] Ibid., pp. 305, 422, 351, and 24 fn.
[3] Ibid., pp. 442–447.

Aaron Doane had been condemned for outlawry but had not been tried by jury for the specific offense of being an accomplice in the robbery. His petition stresses this injustice.

OCTOBER 17, 1784

❡ The humble Petition of Aaron Doane, a poor unhappy Man, now under Sentence of Death in the Gaol of Philadelphia. Most humbly Sheweth,

That your unfortunate Petitioner, deeply Impressed with a full Sense of your merciful Generosity for the Extension of a few days Life, most humbly throws himself at thy Mercy Seat praying thy Compassion, Humanity, and Mercy.

Innocent of the Crime laid to his Charge, Outlawed and being absent from the State, which hinder'd his knowledge thereof, He is now Condemned to Suffer an Ignominous death, unheard or even Tried, to know if he was guilty of the Crime or not.

Oh thou Great Ruler, to whom the Laws have given the Power of being the Dispensor of Life and death—Seal not my Death—Have mercy on an innocent Man—Shed not my Blood unheard or Tried—If by the Outlawry I am to Suffer—Consider thou great Governor,—my innocence, my not being Tried, not being heard and the Power vested in thee, to Extend it to Objects of Mercy—Save then my Life oh gracious Judge—Let thy Government be Crowned by Lenity, Moderation, and Mercy, not Rigor or Resentment—Pardon thy Suppliant Petitioner, Extend thy mercy towards him,—Give thy distressed Servant another Sentence—Bannish to other Territories thy unfortunate Suppliant—But Let not thy humane hand Seal my Death, Unheard or Untried, but Shew thy Mercy; and may the Almighty Dispensor of Life and Death take thee in his Charge will be ever the prayer of the wretched unfortunate

Aaron Doane

[1st *Penna. Arch., vol. X, p. 348.*]

Cruelties, Imprisonments,

and Executions

Neither side in the war was prepared to handle prisoners. Cruelties and mistreatment were the inevitable consequence. Stories of suffering for both rebel and British prisoners abound. The Loyalists, however, were subjected to more brutal abuse than ordinary prisoners of war because they were regarded as criminals—as a despicable fifth column in the rebel midst. Retaliation was the most effective restraint on the cruelties which the rebels felt the Loyalists deserved. The lack of prison facilities meant that every device would be utilized for handling captives—paroles, exchange of prisoners, leg and wrist irons, and improvised strongholds such as church and sugarhouse cellars and unseaworthy vessels. If the rotting *Jersey* in Wallabout Bay was an example of British inhumanity, the Simsbury mines furnished a rebel equivalent. The mortality from scurvy, dysentery, untreated wounds, and disease was notoriously high and the torments so great that death in an attempted escape was often preferable to acquiescence. Escapes from ramshackle local jails, even from the stronger provosts, were frequent enough to give a monotonous repetition to the accounts of captures, escapes, and recaptures. However, cruelties, imprisonment, and the extreme penalty are a significant part of the Loyalists' experience and need sampling.

I BRYAN LEFFERTY SKETCHES CONDITIONS IN THE
KINGSTON JAIL

The crowded and filthy conditions in the Kingston jail, located under the courthouse where the Provincial Convention was sitting, have been dramatized by Gouverneur Morris's motion that members be allowed to smoke in the interest of their health to counteract the "nauseous and disagreeable effluvia" arising from below.[1] Bryan Lefferty, former clerk of the Inferior Court of Tryon County, a prisoner confined amidst the stench and squalor, sketches below the inmates' wretchedness for Captain Richard Varick, secretary to General Schuyler, hoping the message will reach Schuyler and appeal to his humanity.

APRIL 14, 1776

❦ *Dear Sir*

I Embrace this Opportunity of writing you & giving a short sketch of this Place. We arrived here on the ninth Instant and from the Character you gave me of it I Expected to Spend my time as agreeable as a Person in my Situation cou'd do, but to my great Surprise, as well as that of Captain Dundee & Mr. Falknes, we were Immediately sent to the Publick Goal and close confin'd in a Room which the Moment before had been Occupied by a Person who was Imprisoned for Murder.

There is not anything provided for us to lay on Except two Bundles of Straw. Neither had we any Provisions till some Days after our Arrival, and what we now get is cut in Small pieces and handed thro a Small peeping hole. The Room is about fourteen foot Square and Decorated with the one half of an Elegant Necessary House; the other Half is made use of by nine Persons who are confined in the Room Adjoining to ours, without any

---

[1] *Journ. Prov. Congr.,* vol. I, p. 842.

Partition lower than the floor. The Disagreeable Smell that the Place I have just Described must Occasion you will be better able to judge of than I am Describing. The Surgeon of the twenty-sixth Reg^t and the Doctor living in this Town have given it as their Opinion that the consequence of confining so many Persons in this Horrid Place will be attended with a Goal fever, the Effects of that Disorder, from History and General Report, you cannot be unacquainted with. I cannot (neither can the other Gentlemen who are with me) be Persuaded to believe that Genl. Schuyler had the least Idea of this Place being such as it really is, otherwise his feelings as a Gentleman Possessed of the least Spark of Humanity wou'd be Sufficient to have pointed out some other mode of confinement to Persons who have ever been unaccustomed to treatment of this kind. It wou'd swell to a Small Volume to give you a Particular Account of our Lodging & living. We have lice & fleas in abundance which are the only Companions our habitation affords. No Servants being admitted into us nor any Human Specie unless the Doctor who with Difficulty got Admittance this Morning on Account of my Illness. I am scarce able to hold my pen to write this. I was bled this Morning and have been lying on the Straw the whole day Notwithstanding that Mrs. Lefferty is not Permitted to see me unless for the few Moments I am able to stand up & look thro the grate, a Circumstance which I sincerely wish you, nor no other friend of mine, may ever Experience. [*Richard Varick Papers, Misc., N.Y. Historical Society.*]

2 CADWALLADER COLDEN, JR., A PRISONER ON THE
FLEET AT ESOPUS, RECORDS HIS PRIVATE THOUGHTS ABOUT
TAKING THE OATH

Cadwallader Colden, Jr., son of the former Lieutenant Governor, was one of the first suspected persons of Ulster County called before the local Committee of Safety. Although he had signed the Association, he was charged with being an enemy to the American cause (July 4, 1776). His answers were unsatisfactory, and two days later he was placed in the county jail at his own expense.[1] Although the county committee permitted him to post security and return to his own farm at Coldenham, the confrontation

---

[1] *Journ. Prov. Congr.,* vol. II, p. 245.

was the beginning of a series of arrests, imprisonments, and paroles. The New York Committee on Conspiracies was not satisfied to have Colden at liberty, even restricted to his own farm. They considered him "from his disposition and influence, as well as from his vicinity to the enemy, . . . too dangerous; . . . he hath countenanced and abetted measures prejudicial to the rights of America."[2] His house was searched, his papers seized, and in the spring of 1777 he was confined to the Kingston jail under the courthouse.

Colden did not allow the Convention to forget his close presence, for he had ample time to bombard the members with complaints and requests. When a change of keeper threatened, he requested transfer to the Fleet Prison as preferable to the Kingston jail under a mean keeper. The Fleet Prison was composed of two or three ships plus some guard ships anchored in Rondout Creek at Esopus.[3] When a British force of thirty ships under General John Vaughn moved up the Hudson threatening Kingston (burned October 16, 1777), the rebels maneuvered one or more ships, including the *Lady Washington,* into shallow water up the Creek and burned them. According to Thomas Jones, not all the prisoners were released before the scuttling.[4] British sailors boarded the remaining ships of the Fleet Prison and set fire to them even as flames were wrecking havoc with Kingston itself. Other Loyalist prisoners on the ships had been moved to Hartford, many escaping on the way.

Colden spent four months on the Fleet Prison, but was paroled to Hurley six weeks before the burning of the prison ships. His continued evasive answers when tendered the oath kept him under restriction until September 1778, when he was finally permitted to move to New York with his family. He left his oldest son, Cadwallader III, at Coldenham. The latter sympathized with the rebels and was thus able to preserve the estate

---

[2] *Calendar of Historical Manuscripts in Albany, Revolutionary Papers,* vol. I, p. 660.
[3] The Convention authorized the preparation of two or more vessels as a prison on May 2, 1777, and by May 19 they harbored 175 Loyalist prisoners, according to Egbert Dumond, Sheriff. On July 22, thirteen prisoners under the Loyalist Andries TenEyck escaped from one ship, for which TenEyck was put in irons. *Journ. Prov. Congr.* vol. I, pp. 907, 937, 1010. See "Olde Ulster," *Historical & Genealogical Mag.,* Kingston: 1906, vol. II, pp. 40–45; *New York in the Revolution,* Suppl. Albany: 1904, pp. 235–237.
[4] *Jour. Prov. Congr.,* vol. I, p. 1063; vol. II, p. 487. Thomas Jones, *History,* vol. I, pp. 220, 702.

from confiscation, making possible the return of the family in 1783 and of Colden himself in 1784 when the banishing act was repealed. Colden never left the country nor did he suffer permanent injury. In fact, he wrote to his brother, David, that he was kindly received by his neighbors when he returned home.[5]

AUGUST 7, 1777

❰ . . . I have Ever Look'd upon the Inhabitants of these American Collonies as Enjoying the Greatest share of Blessings and Liberty both Civill & Religeous of any People in the known World. And this I have heard Confessed by the Most judicious. Notwithstanding . . . , as Long as I Can Remember, I have known and heard of Evill and Discontented Spiritts among us who by their writings and other Practices have been Endeavouring to overthrow this happy Constitution both in Church and State and to fill the Minds of People with groundless jealousys and Uneasyness. Therefore I Conclude that our Troubles & Unhappy Disputes with the Mother Country Proceed more from the aspiring and ambitious Views of Some of her Sons together with a Rooted inveterosy against the Church then from a Design in Great Britain to Inslave a Brave and free People. . . . Therefore I have ever been opposed to any such measures as I thought were brought about with no other View but to advance this Grand Scheem of Independency or Republick Govern[t] which (if Confirm'd), however it may gratify the Ambitions and Malignant Views of Some men, will never Leave the Country at Large so happy a People as they were and might for Ages have Remain'd, . . . For professing these Sentements I have been abused, Insulted, threatened with distruction of Body & Estate, Imprisoned and Condemned to Banishment unless I would take the oath of Alegence to this Imaginary State. This I have Refused to do in as Modest, but as positive Terms as I could, at the same time willing to give any Security for my Remaining Nuture [Neutral] during the present Disputes. Yet still the Oath is now urged upon me Tho' I have Declared that, should I be vile enough to take it, I should not think myself bound by it.—And notwithstanding this Declaration I am Yet now Promised that if I will but take the Oath I shall Remain with my family Quiet and Undisturbed. *Temptations* great indeed. (But that I may not be Led into Temptations is my Daily

[5] July 7, 1784, uncalendared Ms., N.Y. Historical Society.

Prayer.) Shall I now to Avoid a Little temperary Uneasyness and Inconveniency, Give the Lye to all my former Conduct and even appeal to the Majesty of Heaven to confirm this Lye?—God forbid!—Shokeing thought that one Christian Can Expect this from another!—No, the Idea of being torn from my family, Distressing as it was to me, never suggested such a thought. And now that the Temptation is Less and that it has Pleased God to put it into their Hearts to Let me Remove with my Family, Resolved In the Name of God Let Me Go. *[Colden Journ., (microfilm) N.Y. Historical Society.]*

3 "LET HIM STARVE AND BE DAMNED!"; NATHANIEL GARDINER OF RHODE ISLAND EXPERIENCES BARBARITIES EN ROUTE TO JAIL IN FALMOUTH

Nathaniel Gardiner, a relative of Dr. Sylvester Gardiner, and a former Rhode Island justice, demonstrated a steadfast loyalty to the Crown. He was a resident of Pownalboro, Maine, when he fled rebel harassment in 1780. Once in New York, he received the command of a privateer, the *Golden Pippin,* intended to prey on rebel ships off the New England coast. Even before his first cruise he had the hard luck to be taken captive on the Penobscot River and to be inhumanly treated en route to and at the Falmouth jail. After four months of bullying, torture, and confinement he escaped to Penobscot and was among the Loyalists who retired to Shelburne at the end of the war. The story entitled "An Account of Nathaniel Gardiner Esq." appears among the *Samuel Peters Papers.*

1780

❧ Mr. Nathaniel Gardiner was formerly a justice in the colony of Rhode Island but lately an inhabitant of Pownalboro on Kennebeck river. By his attachment to British Government and inflexible loyalty, from the commencement of the American rebellion, he quickly became obnoxious to the leaders of sedition and drew upon himself their fervent resentment. After being cruelly harrassed and plundered he escaped from the Dominions of revolt and thro various obstructions arrived in safety at New York. He, appearing to be a man of ability and enterprize, some gentlemen of distinction fitted out a privateer and entrusted him with the command. In this character Mr. Gardiner sailed from New York in May, 1780, with his family and after a short passage came to anchor in Penobscot road. Before he could collect a sufficient number of hands for a cruise, at the instance of Comodore Mowat, he ventured up the river and while he was employed in this department he had the misfortune to be surprized by a detachment of rebel soldiers from general [Peleg] Wadsworth. He was immediately conveyed by water to Brunswick and there delivered into the custody of John Wood and John Robby, formerly travelling Taylors by occupation, but now men of eminent consequence and authority, exalted and dignified for their distinguished zeal and indefatigable malice against loyalists and churchmen. These gentlemen with some of their obsequious adherents carried him to the house of one Benjamin Lemon who, under the pretense of moderation, had ensnared many of his N^w Y^k neighbours to their ruin. Here he was secured under a strong guard during the night and when the morning appeared was hurried along amidst the insulting acclamations of the rabble about seven miles to be examined by Dummer Sewal, who, tho a petty farmer, acted in the double capacity of muster master and inspector of prisoners. This man was allowed to be the most sanctified character in the whole eastern country and since his wonderful conversion had excluded every denomination except the rigid independant Calvinist from all possibility of future happiness—this holy patron of liberty, without condescending to ask Mr. Gardiner a single question, commanded him with a pious solemnity of countenance to be loaded with irons and committed to Falmouth prison at the distance of near 50 miles, notwithstanding Pownalboro jail was in the neighbourhood. His next removal was to the blacksmith's shop and, while Vulcan was forging his fetters, an abandoned set of villains assaulted him with outrageous violence and after abusing and buffiting him in the most indecent manner threatened to tear him instantly in pieces. His limbs being sufficently secured in rugged irons, the procession began to move towards Falmouth. The same evening they arrived at a public house kept by Capt Stone, a notorious money-gitting rebel. In order to prevent Mr. Gardiner from effecting his escape (for these wretches always conduct [themselves] as if they imagined the friends of Britain endowed with supernatural influence) they conducted him into a chamber, secured the door with a strong lock, and placed four men, compleatly armed, on the inside; but least this powerful precaution should be insufficient, they compelled him to wear his irons in Bed. The next day, tho Mr. Gardiner was ready to expire with fatigue and vexation they reached Falmouth. But, previous to their entering the town, they dragged him to the gallows and with that meaness and inhumanity peculiar to American rebels repeated with insolent vociferation—"this will be the place of your final destination." He was that evening delivered into the custody of Jo Prime, the commanding officer, who after stripping the unfortunate offender of his commission, papers, Money, and even his cloathing, thrust him with brutal violence into prison. In this lodgment he was not allowed a bed, blanket, a bundle of straw, or any kind of refreshment, but shackled, spiritless, exhausted, and ready to perish with hunger and thirst, was compelled to throw himself down on the floor closely beset with iron spikes. In this deplorable situation he continued for four or five days and when some persons who had more sensibility than their companions ventured to represent his starving condition to authority, they received this very polite and human reply "let him starve and be damned." At length his son arrived from Kennebeck and brought him some relief.

The next week he was indicted before the superior court for high treason when Mr. Bradbury and Lowel generously undertook to be his counsel. But as the rebel judicature would not permit any indulgence of this nature and were afraid openly to oppose such a claim of liberty least it should alarm the people, they had recourse to their usual finess. A number of wretches, who are always ready upon such occasions and who are represented as the voice of the people, instantly convened, insulted these gentlemen as they were entering the court, and threatened them with immediate destruction for presuming to appear in defence of a Tory. After much altercation the trial of Mr. Gardiner was defered till the next year. He continued four months in close confinement and then by some fortunate accident escaped to Penobscot where he remains with his family in circumstances which demand both pity and assistance. [*Peters Papers, Church Historical Society, Austin.*]

4   IRON FETTERS TORMENT JAMES MOODY OF NEW JERSEY IN THE WEST POINT PRISON

Lieutenant James Moody (1746–1809) of New Jersey describes himself in his *Narrative* as "a plain contented farmer, settled on a large fertile, pleasant, and well-improved farm of his own, in the best climate and happiest country in the world." He says he had no other wish than "making happy and being happy with a beloved wife and three promising children." Nonetheless, convinced that "rebellion was the foulest of crimes," he determined to support Britain and not join the Association, ignoring the popular slogan *Join or Die,* borrowed from Franklin's warning to the colonies in 1754. Moody was given command of an independent company which made incursions behind the rebel lines recruiting, picking up information, and twice making a successful raid on rebel mail. He was finally captured by Anthony Wayne and confined at West Point. After his escape and further service he left for London, where his *Narrative* was published in 1782. Eventually he became a colonel of the militia and a resident of Nova Scotia, never returning to New Jersey.

Moody's experience with imprisonment in West Point is told partly by a fellow prisoner, William Buirtis of Westchester. Buirtis had gained release from prison in White Plains in 1779 by offering information to the rebels. However, in August 1780, he was in the West Point prison under sentence of death for communicating with the British general Edward Matthew. His deposition concerning Moody's treatment in August 1780 was given at the Judge Advocate's Office in New York May 11, 1782. Moody includes it as part of his *Narrative,* adding some details of his own. His *Narrative* continues with his account of his escape from the provost in Washington's camp.

William Buirtis Describes the Ordeal

MAY 11, 1782

❡   "That some time in the month of August 1780, he (the deponent) was confined in a dungeon at West Point Fort, under sentence of death, having been charged with giving certain intelligence and information to General Mathew, one of his Britannic Majesty's Generals serving at that time in America; that, about the middle of the month of August aforesaid, Lieutenant *James Moody,* of Brigidier General Skinner's first batallion, was brought under guard, and confined in the same dungeon with him (the deponent); that, the day following, he (Lieutenant Moody) was put in irons and hand-cuffed; that the hand-cuffs were of a particular sort and construction, *ragged on the inside* next the wrist, which raggedness caused his wrists to be much cut and scarified; that soon after he (Lieutenant Moody) was ironed and hand-cuffed, an officer came and demanded his money, saying, *he was ordered to take what money he had, and should obey his orders punctually;"* that the money was not delivered, as he (Lieutenant Moody) was resolute in refusing, and determined not to give it up. He (Lieutenant Moody) then petitioned General Benedict Arnold, at that time in the Rebel service, and Commanding Officer at West Point, to grant him relief; in which petition he set forth the miserable situation he was in, as also the torment he suffered, occasioned by the hand-cuffs; to which petition he received no answer, though he was told, by two officers in the Rebel service, his petition had been delivered to General Arnold.

That about a week after his first petition had been sent, he petitioned a second time for relief from his suffering, requesting moreover to be brought to a trial, observing, that if he should be found guilty of death he should desire to suffer, as death was much preferable to torment, and being murdered by inches. Some little time after the delivery of the second petition, one of General Arnold's Aids de Camps, whose name he (the deponent) cannot recollect, came to the dungeon; and, on seeing him (Lieutenand Moody), asked, if that was the *Moody* whose name was a terror to every good man? On his replying that his name was Moody, he (the Aid de Camp) replied in a scoffing manner, *"You have got yourself into a pretty situation;"* on his (Lieutenant Moody's) saying the situation was disagreeable, but he hoped it would not be of long continuance; he answered, he believed not, as he would soon meet with justice (pointing at the same time to a gallows that was erected in the sight and view of the dungeon); and also added, *there* is the gallows ready erected, which he (meaning Moody) had long merited. Lieutenant Moody answered, he made no doubt he (the Aid de Camp) wished to see every Loyal Subject hanged, but he thanked God, the power was not in *him;* but if he (Lieutenant Moody) was hanged, it could be for no other reason than being a Loyal Subject to one of the best of Kings, and under one of the best of Governments; and added, if he had *ten* lives to lose, he would sooner forfeit the ten as a Loyal Subject, than *one* as a Rebel; and also said, he hoped to live to see him (the Aid de Camp), and a thousand such other villains, hanged for being Rebels. The officer then said he was sent to examine his irons, as he (Lieutenant Moody) had been frequently troubling General Arnold with his petitions. On examining the irons, he said *they were too bad;* and asked, who put them on? —saying, *Irons were intended for security, not for torment; but if any one merited such irons, he* (Lieutenant Moody) *did in his opinion.* Lieutenant Moody, however, was not relieved at that time from his irons; but, about a week or ten days afterwards, an officer came from General Washington, ordered the irons to be taken off, and Lieutenant Moody to be better treated. In consequence of General Washington's order, he was better used: that he (the deponent) knows nothing farther that happened, as he (Lieutenant Moody), in a few days afterwards, was removed from that place.

Moody's Description of the West Point Prison

❡ The above-mentioned dungeon was dug out of a rock, and covered with a platform of planks badly jointed, without any roof to it; and all the rain which fell upon it immediately passed through, and lodged in the bottom of this dismal mansion. It had no floor but the natural rock; and the water, with the mud and filth collected, was commonly ankle-deep in every part of it. Mr. Moody's bed was an old door, supported by four stones, so as just to raise it above the surface of the water. Here he continued near four weeks; and, during most of the time, while he was tormented with irons in the manner mentioned above, no food was allowed him but stinking beef, and rotten flour, made up into balls or dumplins, which were thrown into a kettle and boiled with the meat, and then brought to him in a wooden bowl which was never washed, and which contracted a thick crust of dough, grease, and dirt. It is a wonder that such air, and such food, to say nothing of the wounds upon his legs and wrists, were not fatal to him, especially as the clothes on his back were seldom dry, and at one time were continually wet for more than a week together. After Mr. Washington interfered he was served with wholesome provisons, and he was allowed to purchase for himself some milk and vegetables.

"Moody Is Escaped from the Provost!"

SEPTEMBER 17, 1780

❡ Every precaution had been taken to secure the place in which he was confined. It was nearly in the centre of the rebel camp. A sentinel was placed within the door of his prison, and another without, besides four others close round, and within a few yards of the place. The time now came on when he must either make his attempt, or lose the opportunity for ever.

On the night, therefore, of the 17th of September, busy in ruminating on his project, he had, on the pretence of being cold, got a watch-coat thrown across his shoulders, that he might better conceal, from his unpleasant companion, the operations which he meditated against his hand-cuffs. While he was racking his invention, to find some possible means of extricating himself from his fetters, he providentially cast his eye on a post flattened in the ground, through which an hole had been bored with an auger; and it occured to him that it might be possible, with the aid of this hole, to break the bolt of his hand-cuffs. Watching the opportunity, therefore, from time to time, of the sentinel's looking another way, he thrust the point of the bolt into the above-mentioned hole, and by cautiously exerting his strength, and gradually bending the iron backwards and forwards, he at length broke it. Let the reader imagine what his sensations were, when he found the manacles drop from his hands! He sprung instantly past the interior sentinel, and rushing on the next, with one hand he seized his musquet, and with the other struck him to the ground. The sentinel within, and the four others who were placed by the fence surrounding the place of his confinement, immediately gave the alarm; and, in a moment, the cry was general—"*Moody* is escaped from the Provost." It is impossible to describe the uproar which now took place throughout the whole camp. In a few minutes every man was in a bustle; every man was looking for Moody, and multitudes passed him on all sides—little suspecting, that a man whom they saw deliberately marching along, with a musket on his shoulder, could be the fugitive they were in quest of. The darkness of the night, which was also blustering and drizzly, prevented any discrimination of his person, and was indeed the great circumstance that rendered his escape possible.

But no small difficulty still remained to be surmounted. To prevent desertion, which at that time, was very frequent, Washington had surrounded his camp with a chain of sentinels, posted at about forty or fifty yards distance from each other; he was unacquainted with their stations; to pass them undiscovered was next to impossible; and to be discovered would certainly be fatal. In this dilemma Providence again befriended him. He had gained their station without knowing it, when luckily he heard the watch-word passed from one to another—"Look sharp to the chain—Moody is escaped from the Provost." From the sound of the voices he ascertained the respective situations of these sentinels; and, throwing himself on his hands and knees, he was happy enough to crawl through the vacant space between two of them, unseen by either. Judging that their line of pursuit would naturally be towards the British army, he made a detour into the woods on the opposite side. Through these woods he made as much speed as the darkness of the night would permit, steering his course, after the Indian manner, by occasionally groping and feeling the *white-oak.* On the south side the bark of this tree is rough and unpleasant to the touch, but on the north side it is smooth; hence it serves the sagacious traverser of the desart, by night as well as by day, for his compass. Through the most dismal woods and swamps he continued to wander till the night of the 21st, a space of more than fifty-six hours during which time, he had no other sustenance than a few *beach* leaves (which, of all that the woods afforded, were the least unpleasant to the taste, and least pernicious to health), which he chewed and swallowed, to abate the intolerable cravings of his hunger.

In every inhabited district he knew there were friends of Government; and he had now learned also where and how to find them out, without endangering *their* safety, which was always the first object of his concern. From some of these good men he received minute information how the pursuit after him was directed, and where every guard was posted. Thus assisted, he eluded their keenest vigilance; and, at length, by God's blessing, to his unspeakable joy, he arrived safe at *Paulus-Hook.* [*Moody, Narrative, pp. 24-27. Bushnell, Crumbs for Antiquarians, vol. II, pp. 31-34.*]

5 ELIJAH AND JOHN WILLIAMS OF DEERFIELD CAST THEIR LOT WITH THE KING: JOHN WILLIAMS AND TWO OTHER DEERFIELD TORIES PETITION THE COUNCIL FOR RELEASE FROM PRISON

Elijah and John Williams, two grandsons of the Reverend John Williams (1664-1729), the first minister at Deerfield and author of *The Redeemed Captive,* were Tories, as were in fact many, if not a majority, of Deerfield inhabitants.[1] Elijah (1745-1793) was a lawyer settled at Keene, New Hampshire, when the war broke out. He tried to stop his neighbors from

---

[1] Inhabitants of Deerfield to the General Court of Massachusetts, Read March 9, 1781. Force, *Misc.,* January–May 1781, Library of Congress.

signing the Association and was so persecuted by the mob that he had to leave home following the Battle of Lexington. For a time he lived in Deerfield, fleeing from there to New York in June 1777. He joined Governor Wentworth's Volunteers as a lieutenant. At the close of the war, proscribed, with his estate confiscated, he emigrated to St. John.[2] When he tried to return to New Hampshire in 1784 to collect debts, a mob attacked him and carried him before a justice of the peace. Then, fearing he would be freed or escape, they took him to Ash Swamp near Deerfield with the intention of forcing him to run the gauntlet between men armed with rods to beat him. Some friends intervened and he made a getaway.[3]

John Williams (1751–1816), who helped found Deerfield Academy, practiced law for a time in Salem, but soon opened a business in Deerfield, exporting masts, staves, and horses to the West Indies. Like his brother, he was outspoken against the Whigs. Arrested as a dangerous person in 1781, he was sent to jail in Boston along with two other Deerfield inhabitants, Seth Catlin and the Reverend Jonathan Ashley, both prominent in town affairs. These three fellow townsmen petitioned the Massachusetts Council for release on the plea of tragic hardship to their young families, if deprived of their support. Their first petition of March 23, 1781, was rejected by the Council. They tried again a month later and were this time released on bail, plus two sureties, on condition of good behavior toward their fellow citizens and of not speaking against the independence of the United States.

MARCH 23, 1781

❡ [He] "hath left a wife and Small children without supplies of some necessary articles even to this time, without means to procure these supplies & without a male person in the family more than 8 years old. He hath likewise a slender constitution & small share of health at ye Best, now much impaired & attacked in a Degree & manner alarming to his Fears without a possibility of using ye proper means for his recovery in his present Situation. . . .

[2] His confiscated property included acreage in Conway, N.H., 24 acres in Deerfield, 12 in Greenfield, and 5 in Ash Swamp. *Loyalist Transcripts,* vol. XIV, pp. 559–61.
[3] George Sheldon, *History of Deerfield,* Deerfield: 1895, vol. II, p. 381.

APRIL 24, 1781

❊ [We] humbly sheweth that in Addition to the Reasons offered—March 23—and to the obvious Personal Motives, which again prompt us to address you—are urged by the irresistable impulses of sympathy for our unoffending wives and children, whose circumstances, when we left them, being peculiarly inconvenient, we fear have now become almost intolerable.

We beg leave further to observe, as we each of us depend upon Agriculture for the support of ourselves and families, we cannot revolve in our minds that it is now seed time & think of our wives & children & immediate dependants, without being stung with the most anxious Apprehensions of the Consequences of our longer Confinement to them—which besides prostrating the expectations of our harvest—will we fear, overburthen that charity & Humanity of their Friends to which we know they must be indebted for a large share of the Comforts they enjoy—

Induced by these and Many other Reasons, and ever willing & wishing that the Laws of the Commonwealth may be made the criterion of our Conduct—We pray that it may consist with these and the safety of our community we may be restored to our Liberty & families again & that your Excellency & Honors will prescribe a mode whereby we may obtain this privilidge

And as in Duty bound will ever pray

John Williams
Seth Catlin
Jona Ashley
[*Sheldon, Deerfield, vol. II, pp. 743-745.*]

AFTERNOTE   *Unlike his brother, John Williams stayed on in Deerfield at the close of the war, even standing successfully for election as Deerfield's representative to the General Court in 1783. The court, however, twice excluded him as "incapable of being a Representative" because of his Loyalist leanings and wartime imprisonment. He was then indicted for sedition and arraigned in May 1784 before the Superior Court at Northampton. His plea was that Article VI of the peace treaty barred prosecution or future loss against any person for his part in the war. The court agreed, freeing him from the complaint. He was then selected a third time by his neighbors to represent them in the General Court, and this time was seated.* [1]

[1] May 1784. Sheldon, *Deerfield,* vol. II, pp. 747-748.

6 THE BLACK HOLE OF CONNECTICUT

The ultimate of man's inhumanity to man for the Loyalists was Connecticut's Newgate, formed from the abandoned copper mines at Simsbury. Connecticut prisons at Hartford, Litchfield, and Sharon furnished convenient places of confinement for prisoners from nearby colonies, especially New York. David Mathews, former mayor of New York, and Governor Franklin of New Jersey were both imprisoned in August 1776 in Litchfield without even pen or ink. While prison facilities in general during the Revolution were cruelly inadequate, the horrendous conditions to which the Loyalists were subjected in the Simsbury copper mines can still unnerve even the callous visitor. These caverns were utilized from 1773 until the destructive fire of 1782, and again from 1786 until 1827,[1] and were so uniformly dreaded as a place of confinement that they were called every damning epithet from Bastille, Inferno, and prison of the Inquisition to sepulchre, living tomb, and catacomb. The prisoners were brought up from the hole at daybreak, three at a time, conducted to their place of work, and often chained to the block or fettered by foot or neck. Hunks of meat or bread were thrown at their feet to be grabbed, cleaned, and perhaps held for cooking. These rations were supplied from a tavern across the road, built in 1763, and used for the next 164 years as an eating place for transients. Here lived the keeper, Captain John Viets.

The use of the dank abandoned mines as a prison was repeatedly endorsed by those in authority. The Connecticut Assembly endorsed it when it accepted the proposal of the committee which explored the mines and recommended the expenditure of £ 37 to make them escape-proof. The Superior Court at Hartford approved use of the mines when, on March 8, 1776, it remanded a counterfeiter to hard labor at Newgate. Washington endorsed it when he asked the Connecticut Committee of Safety to confine some "atrocious villains" sentenced by court-martial to the mines, "so that they cannot possibly make their escape. The charges of their imprisonment will be at the Continental expence."[2]

Several contemporary descriptions of the prison survive, written by witnesses to its atrocities, one by the famous Connecticut Tory, the Rever-

---

[1] Richard H. Phelps, *History of Newgate of Connecticut,* Hartford: 1844 (2d ed., 1860), pp. 26, 114.
[2] December 11, 1775. Fitzpatrick, *Writings,* vol. IV, pp. 155–156.

end Samuel Peters, and another by Ebenezer Hathaway and Thomas Smith, prisoners who made a spectacular escape on May 18, 1781. This escape was the third break effected by setting fire to the blockhouse over the shaft of the subterranean dungeon. In the spring of 1776 the prisoners had set fire to the heavy wooden door of the blockhouse, killing one inmate by smoke and nearly suffocating the rest. In 1777, another such fire razed the wooden structure to the ground and permitted nearly all the prisoners to escape. In the bloody break of 1781, described below by Hathaway and Smith, all the prisoners slipped away, although many, handicapped by wounds, were retaken in their flight. Still a fourth fire, on November 6, 1782, destroyed the wooden buildings.

The Catacomb of Connecticut

❧ Symsbury, with its meadows and surrounding hills, forms a beautiful landskip, much like Maidstone in Kent. The township is 20 miles square, and consists of nine parishes, four of which are episcopal. Here are copper mines. In working one many years ago, the miners bored half a mile through a mountain, making large cells 40 yards below the surface, which now serve as a prison, by order of the General Assembly, for such offenders as they chuse not to hang. The prisoners are let down on a windlass into this dismal cavern, through an hole, which answers the triple purpose of conveying them food, air, and—I was going to say light, but it scarcely reaches them. In a few months the prisoners are released by death and the colony rejoices in her great *humanity,* and the *mildness* of her laws. This conclave of spirits imprisoned may be called, with great propriety, the catacomb of Connecticut. The light of the Sun and the light of the Gospel are alike shut out from the martyrs, whose resurrection-state will eclipse the wonder of that of Lazarus. [[*Peters*] *Gen. Hist. Conn., pp.* 175-176.]

Account of the Escape of Ebenezer Hathaway and Thomas Smith, Captain and Member of the Crew of the Privateer Adventure, *from the Simsbury Mines on May 18, 1781*

JUNE 6, 1781

❡ This day arrived here Ebenezer Hathaway and Thomas Smith, who on the 18th of May last made their escape from Simsbury Mines after a most gallant struggle for their liberty. These men declare that they were two of eight belonging to the Privateer Boat Adventure duly commissioned, &c; that they were taken in Huntington Bay off Long Island on the 7th of April, by seven rebel whaleboats manned by 73 men, and that night carried across the Sound to Stamford in Connecticut; that the next day they were carried to what they called headquarters before General Waterbury, who with the air of a demagogue ordered them to Hartford gaol, and told the guard they had liberty to strip them of their cloaths remaining on their backs, but the captors had already stripped them; there they lay on the 27th following, when their trial came on before the Superior Court; that they were brought before the court and directed to plead not guilty; but aware of their knavish tricks, they declared themselves British subjects, and refused to plead either 'guilty' or 'not guilty', therefore they were ordered to New-gate gaol, or rather to that inquisition Simsbury Mines, which from the following description, exceeds anything among their allies in France or Spain.

These poor unfortunate victims relate that they were taken from Hartford gaol, and marched under a strong guard to Simsbury, distant about 14 miles. In approaching that horrid dungeon they were first conducted through the apartments of the guard, then through a trapdoor down stairs into a room half underground, from thence into another on the same floor called the kitchen, which was divided by a very strong partition door. In the corner of this outer room and near the foot of the stair, opened another large trap-door covered with bars and bolts of iron, which they called Hell; they there descended by means of a ladder about six feet more, which led to a large iron grate or hatchway locked down over a shaft of about three feet diameter sunk through the solid rock, and which they were told led to the bottomless pit. Finding it not possible to evade this hard fate, they bid adieu to the world and descended the ladder about 38 feet more, when they came to what is called the landing; then descending about 30 or 40 feet more they came to a platform of boards laid under foot. Here, they say, we found the inhabitants of this woeful mansion, who were exceedingly anxious to know what was going on above. We told them Lord Cornwallis had beat the rebel army, with which they seemed satisfied, and rejoiced at the good news.

They were obliged to make use of pots of charcoal to dispel the foul air, which in some degree is drawn off by a ventilator or auger hole, which is bored from the surface through at this spot, said to be 70 feet perpendicular. Here they continued 20 days and nights, resolved however to avail themselves of the first opportunity to get out, although they should lose their lives in the attempt. Accordingly on the 18th aforesaid, 18 of them being let up into the kitchen to cook, they found means to break the lock of the door which kept them from the foot of the ladder leading up to the guard room; they now doubly resolved to make a push should the door be opened, which fortunately was the case about ten o'clock at night to let down a prisoner's wife who had come there and was permitted to see him. Immediately they seized the fortunate moment and rushed up, but before any one [else] had got out, the door was closed down on the rest, and he, the brave Captain Hathaway, scuffled with the whole of them for a few minutes and was wounded in three different places, when he was nobly seconded by his friend Thomas Smith, and afterward by the others. They then advanced upon the guard consisting of 24 in number and took the whole prisoners, which was no sooner accomplished than they brought their companions out of the bottomless pit and put the guard down in their room; then marched off with their arms and ammunition but were soon afterwards obliged to disperse.

This we the subscribers declare to be the way the King's loyal subjects, vulgarly called Tories, are treated in Connecticut.

Ebenezer Hathaway
Thomas Smith
[*Rivington, Roy. Gaz., June 9, 1781. Moore, Diary, vol. II, p. 434.*]

AFTERNOTE *A committee of investigation, appointed by the Connecticut Assembly, reported on the break:*[1]
"Jacob Southwell was awakened by the tumult, took a gun and run out of the guard-house, and durst not go back for fear they would hurt him.

[1] Phelps, *Newgate,* (1860 ed.), pp. 43–44.

N. B. A young man more fit to carry fish to market *than to keep guard at Newgate. Nathan Phelps was also asleep—wak'd but could do nothing, the prisoners having possession of the guard-house (a small lad just fit to drive Plow with a very gentle Team.) He went to Mr. Viets and stayed till morning (poor boy)! Abagail, the wife of John Young, alias Mattick, says that the first night she came to the prison, she gave to her husband 52* silver dollars. *Her husband told her after he came out that he had given Sergt. Lilly 50 of them in order that he may suffer the prisoners to escape. That he told her the Sergt. purposely left the door of the south jail unlocked, that Sergt. Lilly was not hurt; that she borrowed the money of a pedlar; that she heard Lilly say it was a great pity that such likely men should live and die in such a place."*

THE REVEREND SIMEON BAXTER PREACHES A SERMON IN THE SIMSBURY MINES ON "TYRANNICIDE PROVED LAWFUL"

Despite the fire and the break, the mines continued to be used for political prisoners. On September 19, 1781, the Reverend Simeon Baxter gave his fellow Tories, confined in a brutal section called *Orcus,* a sermon to contemplate, admonishing them that their Christian duty was to assassinate Washington and the members of the Continental Congress. The Reverend Baxter, whom Richard Phelps called "the choicest specimen of black hearted treason under the cloak of priestly sanctity,"[1] accompanied his *Discourse,* when it was later published in London, by two letters, one to Washington and the Continental Congress and the other to the Protestant rebel ministers of the Thirteen Colonies. The two letters and excerpts from the vituperative sermon preached in the subterranean *Orcus* follow.

[1] Phelps, *Newgate,* p. 47.

*To General Washington, and the Congress, Styling Them-
selves Governors and Protectors of Thirteen Colonies,
Belonging to the Crown of England.*

❡ Gentlemen,

That you have have the honour of dying for the people, instead
of their dying for you and your allies, was the design I had in preaching and publishing this discourse; and, should it produce the desired effect,
I shall think myself paid for all my trouble and expence. If you can bestow
one generous deed on your ruined country, adopt the act of Suicide, to
balance the evils of your lives, and save the virtuous citizens of America
the glorious trouble of doing justice on you.

Remember Judas was not a patriot till he hanged himself for betraying
his Saviour and his God—*Go and do thou likewise;* and you will prove
yourselves real Saviours of America, and, like him, hold a place in the
temple of everlasting Fame. Should your courage or your virtue fail in so
meritorious a deed, sacred Religion stands on tiptoe to inspire all her children, by some hidden thunder, or some burnished weapon, to do it for you,
and to save themselves from Nimrod's paradise.

When you are dead, your grateful countrymen will not let your Honours lie in dust, but will raise you to some airy tombs between the drooping
clouds and parching sands: then your exaltation will make islands glad;
Peace with her new-fledged wings shall fly through every state, and echo
happiness to weeping willows; nay, the mourning doves shall forsake the
wilderness to chant your praises; and the mope-eyed owls, in open day,
shall view with wonder your patriotic virtues.

*To the Protestant Rebel Ministers of the Gospel, in the
Thirteen Confederated Colonies in America.*

❡ Gentlemen,

The bloody part you have acted, in obedience to your creditors,
the merchant smugglers, both in the pulpit and the field,—with your
spiritual and temporal swords,—intitles you to the second class of patriots, who disgrace religion with hypocrisy, and humanity with barbarity.—Spectators, with great justice, have decided, that you are the suc-

cessors of him who *went to and fro seeking whom he might devour,* and not of him who *went about doing good. —*

Inasmuch as you began rebellion, because your King would not persecute, but tolerate his faithful Catholic subjects in Canada, and, to support your rebellion, you have since joined yourselves unto idols, and made alliance with the Papists of France, to root up the protestant religion, for which our fathers bled and died;—inasmuch as you have out-acted the Pope, discarded and abjured your rightful King, neglected to visit those in prison, and forbid the exercise of that charity to the miserable which *hides a multitude of sins;*—I must take leave of you in the words spoken to your predecessors by the Saviour of all penitent sinners,—"Go your way, for I know "you not!"—

Tyrannicide Proved Lawful by Reverend Simeon Baxter

SEPTEMBER 19, 1781

❡ ... Nothing is more absurd than to kill thieves, vipers, and bears, to prevent their cruel designs, and at the same time preserve Congress for acting much worse than the others intended. No one can any longer doubt of the lawfulness of destroying public robbers, whenever prudence points out the way, since the laws of God and men make it lawful to extirpate private robbers. Let us live in constant faith that heaven will soon sanctify some patriotic hand, armed with some sacred weapon, to bring down that bloody and deceitful house, which holds its existence, not only to the misery, but to the everlasting infamy of Protestant America. The action is not only lawful, but glorious in idea, and immortal in its reward. ...

Some people pretend to believe Congress are not usurpers and tyrants, because traffic and appeals are carried on under their dominion, which argues a tacit consent of the public. To prove those men are mistaken, I need only say, that commerce and pleading were carried on in Rome under Caligula and Nero, yet those who conspired against them were not deemed rebels, but eternized for their virtue.

Having pointed out the marks and practices of tyrants and usurpers, and shewn the lawfulness and glory of killing them; I shall now, in the third and last place, hint the benefits and necessity of doing it.

What is our present condition? Are we not slaves and living instruments of Congress, Washington, the Protestant Ministers, and their Romish allies? Poor wretches indeed are we! cozened out of peace, religion, liberty, and property; robbed of the blessings of Judah; and cursed with the spirit and burdens of Issachar, by a set of men without virtue, or the generous vices attending greatness! . . . Liberty and bondage are now before us; those who chuse bondage are to murder Brutus; and those who chuse liberty are to kill the uncircumcised Congress. Yet I find some men scruple to kill their oppressors with a dagger in the dark, although they allow it lawful to destroy a thief that comes unarmed to rob; those men seem to forget the law of self-preservation, the danger of open force, and that tyrants are such devils as rend the body in the act of exorcism. How can it be lawful to kill oppressors in an open field prepared to rob the men they mean to murder, and unlawful to kill such villains in the dark, without hazard to the patriot or the commonwealth? If it is expedient to lance an imposthume to save a life, it is lawful to lance the Congress to save the liberties of our country;—for those boars of the wilderness have broken down the walls of the vineyard, and destroyed the vintage with unlimited power, which always subverts civil society, and turns a Cicero into a Caligula. Our religion, and all we can call valuable, are in danger. Despotism is now predominant. . . . Are we so far degenerated as to bow down to tyrants and usurpers? Our fathers resisted lions and killed tyrants, without committing murder, and shall we submit to wolves and beasts of prey to let usurpers live? No! . . . Therefore, let safety rouse us into action—let Fame reward the sacred hand of him that gives the fatal blow— let his name live for ever with Cato and with Brutus. O how I long to save my country by one *heroic, immortal* action! but alas! my chains and dreary mansion, where the light of conscience reigns, without the light of the sun, of the moon, or stars! To you, my virtuous countrymen, who are free of the chains with which I am loaded, I conclude my address. It is now in your power to circumcise, put down, those uncircumcised tyrants, and to restore yourselves to your social rights. You know the action that will do the business, and which shall register your names among the Gods and bravest men. . . . Make haste! . . . *Let death and destruction fall upon Congress, because they have oppressed and forsaken the poor; let a fire not blown consume them; if they escape the iron weapons, strike them through with a bow of steel—for knowest thou not this of old, since man was placed upon earth, that the triumphing of the wicked is short, and*

*the joy of the hypocrite but for a moment. . . . The vipers tongue shall
pierce them through, and their greatness shall be chased away as a vision
of the night. This is the portion of the wicked.*

Finis

[*Simeon Baxter, Tyrannicide Proved Lawful.*]

7   THE EXTREME PENALTY

In almost every colony Tories were deliberately put to death, whether killed
by a pitiless mob, murdered by a marauding party, hanged by a council of
safety or assembly order, or executed after court-martial proceedings.[1]
Some were executed without trial or with only a sham trial; some soldiers
were tried according to the common law, some citizens by court-martial.
Guerilla activities in a civil war made the distinction between a soldier's
rights and a citizen's rights a nebulous one. For example, David Redding,
a soldier in the Queen's Rangers, was hanged at Bennington, convicted
by a six-man jury in a civilian trial on a charge of horse stealing in Dutchess
County.[2] Trials of Loyalists for treasonable activities which resulted in
carrying out the death penalty were not frequent. Activities considered
treasonable included recruiting for the British, accepting a commission,
giving information or other aid to the enemy, or even simply adhering to
the King, although the severity of the application varied from province to
province or according to the need for reprisal or example. The New York
Provincial Congress provided the death penalty for anyone residing in the
state or owing it allegiance who was convicted of levying war against the
state or merely of adhering to the King or other enemies of the state or

[1] Wallace Brown's study of Loyalist claims mentions fifteen executions in New York,
four in Connecticut, two in Massachusetts, four in Maryland, six in New Jersey, four
in Pennsylvania, four in Virginia, one in Delaware, five in North Carolina, twenty in
South Carolina, none in Georgia or in New Hampshire, although two New Hampshire
counterfeiters were executed in Connecticut, and two Loyalists were murdered in Rhode
Island. *The King's Friends,* Providence: 1966, pp. 79, 65, 47, 34, 115, 134, 183, 158,
169, 198, and 215.
[2] John Spargo calls David Redding's trial and execution, June 11, 1778, "a discreditable
travesty of justice." *David Redding, Queen's Ranger,* Bennington: 1945, p. 53.

giving them comfort.[3] Gouverneur Morris wrote Alexander Hamilton in 1777 that there was a need for more executions.[4] Washington, however, at about the same time, reprimanded General De Borre for executing a Tory citizen.[5]

Many Tories were sentenced to die but were rescued in time or secured a reprieve in return for taking the oath or enlisting in the rebel army. For example, Lieutenant James Moody tells in his *Narrative* that sixty of his Loyalist party en route to join the British in June 1777 were taken prisoner near Perth Amboy, and that "these prisoners, after being confined in Morristown jail, were tried for what was called high treason; and above one-half were sentenced to die. Two, whose names were Iliff and Mee, were actually executed, the rest having been reprieved on condition of their serving in the rebel army. The love of life prevailed. They enlisted; but so strong was their love of loyalty at the same time that, except for three or four who died under the hands of their captors, they all very soon made their escape to the British army."[6]

There were numerous executions in New York. Simeon Bloodgood recounts the indelible impression made on him in 1778 when, as a lad of thirteen, he watched with his father the execution of seven "disaffected men, who, to bad political principles, had added crimes against society which even a state of war would not justify." These men had escaped once; as prisoners once again, they had taken bricks from the fireplace, had barricaded the door of the Albany prison against the sheriff, and had laid a

---

[3] *Journ. Prov. Cong.,* vol. I, July 16, 1776.

[4] "The spirit of the Tories, we have reason to believe, is entirely broken in this State. If it is not, it will soon be so; for they shall have a few more executions than which nothing can be more efficacious. I speak from experience; but then it is necessary to disperse the victims for public justice throughout different parts of the several states; for nothing but ocular demonstration can convince these incredulous beings that we do really hang them. I wish the several States would follow our example; Pennsylvania in particular would experience many good effects from a vigorous manly Executive. Adieu!" See J. C. Hamilton, ed., *The Works of Alexander Hamilton,* N.Y.: 1850–1851, vol. I, p. 28.

[5] Washington to General Preudhomme De Borre, August 3, 1777. "With respect to the Tory, who was tried and executed by your order, though his crime was heinous enough to deserve the fate he met with, and though I am convinced you acted in the affair with a good intention, yet I cannot but wish it had not happened. . . . There is none in our articles of war that will justify your inflicting a *capital* punishment even on a soldier, much less on a citizen." Ford, *Writings,* vol. VI.

[6] Bushnell, *Crumbs for Antiquarians,* vol. II, pp. 8–9.

line of stolen gunpowder so as to blow up their adversaries along with themselves, should the door be battered in. Guards cut a hole through the ceiling and introduced a fire hose which quickly inundated the powder. A brave Irishman jumped in with a cudgel and, followed by other intrepid citizens, subdued the captives. The gloomy prisoners, dressed in white, were then led slowly up the State Street hill by an unmerciful mob to a rudely constructed gallows northeast of the Academy and there executed "as a necessary example demanded by the nature of the times and the enormity of the offenses they had committed."[7]

Albany was the scene of another Tory execution in 1780, namely of Lovelass, the leader of a small marauding party of Tories in the Saratoga-Albany area. He was tried by court-martial. Although he claimed the right to be treated as a military prisoner, and not to be punished as a spy, since he was taken with arms in his hands, "he was considered too dangerous a man to be permitted to escape. . . . He was brought out upon the hill, on the south side of General Schuyler's house and suffered death upon the gallows. . . . Public policy seemed to require an unbending sterness on the part of the court and his punishment certainly put an end for that time to all marauding expeditions by the tories."[8]

JACOBUS ROSE AND JACOB MIDAGH ARE EXECUTED AT
KINGSTON AS AN EXAMPLE

The most notorious execution in New York was that of Jacobus Rose and Jacob Midagh by order of the Provincial Convention. They were accused of acting under the direction of the British military authority to secure recruits in Ulster County; they were tried by court-martial at Fort Montgomery (April 30, 1777) and were condemned to death along with several others. Rose's trial revealed that, as a lieutenant in Captain Hasbrouck's company in Colonel Pawling's rebel regiment, he had been tried earlier for insubordination, fined £ 30, dismissed from service, and rendered incapable of again wearing a commission in New York. He had been accused on that occasion of being "rather unfriendly to the States . . . and com-

[7][Bloodgood], *The Sexagenary,* Albany: 1833, pp. 127–130.
[8] Ibid., pp. 185–186.

monly associated himself with those People that is Disaffected."[1] Now the charges were more serious. In transmitting the proceedings of this second trial to the president of the Convention sitting at Kingston, George Clinton wrote (May 2, 1777): "The Conduct of many of these Traitors was so daring and Insolent that a sudden & severe Example to me seems absolutely necessary to deter others from the Commission of like Crimes and I am perswaded to suffer these to pass with Impunity woud be Cruelty in the End."[2] Many others were also condemned to death at Fort Montgomery at the same time and sent to Kingston with Rose and Midagh. The subsequent story of these two victims after their arrival at Kingston jail is told in a letter to John Jay from their fellow prisoner, Cadwallader Colden, Jr., as well as in their own futile petition to the Convention for a few days stay of execution.

Cadwallader Colden, Jr., Helps Rose Prepare for Martrydom

MAY 12, 1777

❦ On Monday the 12th [May] Poor Rose and all the condemned Prisoners who came up in the Boat with Me Was put into the adjoyning Room which was Separated from ours only by an Iron grate and in which Room was now no less than 26 Mostly all in Irons. Here for the first time I got acquainted with Rose, (for I had scarcely spoke to him on board the boat), and learning that the Sentence against him and one Midaugh was to be put in Execution the Next Day and observing Rose not to be affected as I expected, I fear that he was not Properly toutch with the Thoughts of his approaching End or that he did not believe he should Die. I therefore took upon me to talk with him on the Subject and found him to Reason in a Manner I Little Expected. He told me that it was true he hardly thought they would be so Mad as to put him to Death, yet, should that be the Case, he Should Die with an Easy Conscience with Respect to what he was to Suffer for, for that he had not taken the Part he did from any Lucrative Motive, or the Sake of gaining any Preferement, but that he thought his Country would never be happy again till Reduced to a Proper Obedience to its former State of Government, and that the sooner this be brought

---

[1] *Public Papers of George Clinton,* vol. I, p. 613.
[2] Ibid., p. 783.

about the better. And to this he was Willing to Lend a helping hand which Enduced him to prevail upon as Many of his neighbors to joyn the Kings forces as he Could, and then added, if he must Suffer for this, that he hoped Vengeance would overtake and fall on the heads of his Persecutors — . . . Here I interrupted and told him that as a dying Person, (for so he ought to Look upon himself), he should forgive all men as he hoped to be forgiven, that God had said Vengeance was his and that he Would Repay and therefore we ought to Leave that to him and even to Pray that, however they might suffer in the World as he was now going to do, Yet in the World to Come that they might be forgiven as he hoped for forgiveness. And I had the Satisfaction to find this admonition to have Weight with him, for I heard him Repeatedly forgive and Pray for all his Enemies.

There happened to be in our Room a verry Pious and good Book, the Worke of Phila Kempe by Bishop Stanhop, out of which I Selected very Useful and Seasonable Pieces and Meditations for the occaison — which I and some other of the Company Read in turns and in this Manner We Spent the Day and a Good Part of the Night. And while some others of the Company was Reading I wrote the following Letter to Mr. Jay:

Colden Writes John Jay That Hanging Rose and Midagh Will Not Make One Man Change His Sentiments

KINGSTON JAIL MAY 22, 1777

❡ *Sir* [John Jay]

You are not Unacquainted with my Sentements in Regard to this Unhappy affair that has already Cost so Much Blood and treasure and Likely Yet to Cost a Vast Deal more, and that notwithstanding my Determined Resolution to keep a Clear Concience by Takeing no active Part on Either Side of the Controversy, yet it Seems I have a full Share of Punishments.

But it is not on My Own Account that I am goeing to trouble you at this time. — No! — it is on a Matter that gives Me Much More Concern, Both on Your Account and that of a Number of fellow Prisoners I hear You have Condemned to Die. Oh! My dear Sir, Consider the Consequences that must Attend Such a Scene both in this World and the Next. Cooly and Deliberately to take the Life of our fellow Creatures must add much to the Account of those, who have been Instrumental in bringing Publick affairs to this Pass. But I fear this Arguement will have but Little Weight.

I would therefore Endeavour to Persuade you upon the Principles of good Pollicy to Delay putting in Execution this Sentence of Death, at Least for Some Days; for, Depend upon it, the Hanging of them will not make one Man Change his Sentements in Your favour, But the Very Reverse. And tho' it may Prevent some from Exposing themselves as foolishly as these Poor men did, Yet the time May be Drawing near when they will not have that Risque to Run and when Many a One who is forced to Pretend to be fighting Your Cause will prove not to be so honnest as these Poor Men You are Now going to Hang.—Besides the President [Precedent] may have awfull Effects should the other Party take the Exeample.

I found myself Constrain'd to say this much to you as an old friend and acquaintance for whom I have had a Particular Regard. God Grant that it may have the Desired Effect. [*Cadwallader Colden Journal, N. Y. Historical Society.*]

Petition of Jacobus Rose and Jacob Midagh for a Stay of Execution

MAY 13, 1777

❦ *To the Honourable the Convention of the State of New York.*

The Humble Petition of Jacobus Rose and Jacob Midagh, two un-happy Prisoners, now by order of your House under sentence to be Hanged this Day, Most Humbly Showeth,

That, altho their Conscience doth not in the least accuse them of being Guilty of any sin against God or their Country, by doing what they are condemned to suffer Death for, yet your Petitioners are heartily sorry for having incurr'd the Displeasure of your House in so sensible a manner. That as sinfull men it is an awfull and Dreadfull thought to be so suddenly sent to Eternity without any time to Repent of the Sins of our past Lives and to make our peace with that God who must finally judge us all for the Deeds done in the flesh, that therefore to prepare for this great and awfull trial your Petitioners most Humbly beg they may have a Respite of a few Days, and your Petitioners as in duty bound shall in the mean while earnestly pray—

JACOBUS ROSE

his

JACOB   X   MIDAGH

mark

[Petition rejected]   [*Rev. Papers, New York, vol. III, p. 160.*]
AFTERNOTE   *Colden wrote in his* Journal *that he helped Rose and Midagh write their petition for a reprieve or a respite of a few days and continued: "He [Rose] had great need of some longer time offered him to Repent and prepare to meet that judge who would judge all men. . . . About this time his Sister and Children Came to take their leave of him. This was as Mellancholy a Scene as Ever I met with, yet I must say I was greatly Pleased with his Manner of Parting with them, . . . telling them that he hoped it would not be a Reproach to them that their father was Hanged in this Cause. . . . After this he beg'd me to Pray for him. I told him I had. But get your Book, said he, and we will pray together. . . . About one o'clock he was taken out of the Room to be Carry'd to the Place of Execution, and they say he behaved with the greatest Composure and Resolution—Dying a true Maryter to the Cause he had Espoused. . . ."*[1]

8   THE INFLUENCE OF THE CLERGY BRINGS MOSES DUNBAR TO THE GALLOWS IN HARTFORD

The rebels in Connecticut found it necessary to convince the Tories that their activities amounted to treason against the state and would not be allowed to pass unpunished. Although the Tories in Connecticut were numerically weak,[1] they made up in ardor what they lacked in numbers. Where the Anglican Church had strong leadership, as in Hebron, Fairfield, Norwalk, Stamford, and Redding, pockets of Loyalists could be found. There were many other scattered instances where the clergy influenced young men toward Loyalism, to their ultimate disaster. One of the young

---

[1] J. W. Barber and Henry Howe, *Historical Collections of the State of New York* New York: 1841, p. 558.

    Judge Hasbrouck, a lad in 1777, was deeply impressed by the event and reported that the men expected to be reprieved at the last minute. When they saw the gallows, they were overwhelmed and exclaimed: "O heer! Vergeeven onze zonde!" (O Lord! Forgive our sins!)

[1] W. H. Siebert estimates there were about 2,000 male Tories in Connecticut at the start of the Revolution. "*Refugee Loyalists of Connecticut,*" Royal Society Ottawa, *Trans.,* Ser. X. Wallace Brown figures the Connecticut Tories were about 5 percent of the population. *The King's Friends,* p. 355 fn 2.

men, who had been persuaded by the Reverend James Scovil of Waterbury to leave the Puritan Church for the Church of England, and whose conscience led him subsequently to serve the King, was Moses Dunbar of the same town. He was arrested in January 1777, and a captain's commission in Colonel Fanning's regiment was found in his pocket. The petit jury appointed by the Superior Court in Hartford found him guilty of treason for joining the British army, enlisting others, and giving intelligence to the enemy.[2]

Knowing that he faced the gallows, Dunbar, with the aid of a knife smuggled to him by a friend, broke his fetters and tried, unsuccessfully, to escape from the Hartford jail. It was his last chance for life. He was executed on March 19 on a hill on the present site of Trinity College—a scene witnessed, according to the *Connecticut Courant* (March 24), by "a prodigious Concourse of People." He left for posterity two significant documents, one a letter to his children, and the other his "Last Speech and Dying Wordes," both written the day before his execution and both revealing his deep religious commitment. The letter to his children was brief:

> "My Children: Remember your creator in the days of your youth. Learn your Creed, the Lord's Prayer, and the Ten Commandments and catechism, and go to church as often as you can, and prepare yourselves as soon as you are of a proper age to worthily partake of the Lord's supper. I charge you all, never to leave the church. Read the Bible. Love the Saviour wherever you may be.
>
> I am now in Hartford jail, condemned to death for high treason against the state of Connecticut. I was thirty years last June, the 14th. God bless you. Remember your Father and Mother and be dutiful to your present mother."[3]

---

[2] January 23, 1777, *Superior Court Records,* Conn. State Archives, Hartford.

[3] Judge Epaphroditus Peck, "Loyal to the Crown," *Conn. Mag.,* vol. VIII (1903), no. 1 and 2.

The Last Speech & Dying Wordes of Moses Dunbar Who Was Executed at Hartford on Wednesday the 19th of March, 1777, for High Treason against the State of Conecticut

MARCH 19, 1777

❡ I was born at Wallingford in Conecticut 3ᵈ of June A.D. 1746, being the second of sixteen Children, all born to my Father of one Wife.

My Father, John Dunbar, was born also in Wallingford & Married Temperance Hall of the same place about the Year 1743. I was Educated in the business of Husbandry. About 1760 my Father remov'd Himself & his Family to Waterbury, where May the 30th 1764, I was Married with Phebe Jearom of Farmington, by whom I have had Seven Children, five of whom are Now living. The 1st Year of our Marriage, my wife & I (upon what we thought Sufficient & rational Motives) declar'd our Conformity to the Church of England. The Revᵈ Mr. Scovil being a Missionary at Waterbury.

May 26th 1770 My honored Mother departed this Life. She was a Woman of much Virtue & good Reputation, whom I rememb̄ʳ with the most filial Honour & Gratitude for the Greatest Care and Affection which she Continually Shew'd me.

My Joining myself to the Church Occasion'd a sorrowfull breach between my Father & me, which was the Cause that he never Assisted me but very little in gaining a Livelihood; as Likewise it caused him to treat me very harshly in many Instances, which I heartily forgive him as well as my Brothers, as I hope for Pardon from my God & Saviour for my own Offences. I Likewise Pray God to forgive them thro' Christ.

From the time that the unhappy Misunderstanding between Great Britain & the Colonies began (I freely Confess) I never could reconcile my Opinion to the necessity or Lawfulness of takeing up Arms against Great Britain, & having Spoken somewhat freely on the Subject, I was attacked by a Mob of about 40 Men, very much abused, my Life threaten'd and nearly taken away, by which I was Compell'd to sign a Paper Containing many Falsehoods.

May 26th A.D. 1776, my Wife died in full hope of future Happiness of which I doubt not in the least she is now in Possession. The Winter preceding had been a Time of Great tryal and Distress with Us. I, my Wife & 1 Child Sick all Winter, another of my Children had a broken Leg, with many other Afflictions, which I omit relating.

I had now determined, if Possible, to live peaceably & give no Offence by word or deed. I made some proposals of that Kind to the Committee, Offering to Enter into a Voluntary Confinement, within the Limits of a Farm, instead of which I was Carried to Newhaven Gaol. But the Sheriff and Gaoler both refused to receive me. A few days Afterwards I was taken again, Carried before the Committee, & by them Ordered to Suffer imprisonment during their Pleasure, not exceeding 5 Months. But when I had remained there about 14 days, the Authority of Newhaven Dismissed me.

Finding my life uneasy, & as I had reason to Apprehend in great Danger, I thought it my safest method to fly to Long Island, which I accordingly did. But having a desire to see my Friends & Children, & being under Engagements of Marriage with her who is now my Wife & the Banns of Marriage having before been published, I Return'd & was Married.

Having an Inclination to remove myself & Family to Long Island, as a Place of Greater safety, I went there a Second time to prepare Matters accordingly, when I accepted a Capt^{ns} Warrant for the King's Service in Col^l Fanning's Reg^t. I Return'd to Connecticut, where I was betrayed by Jos^h Smith, was taken, Carried before the Authority of Waterbury. They refusing to have any Concern in the Affair, I was Carried to Farmington before Justice Strong & Justice Whitman and by them Committed to Hartford, where the Superior Court was then sitting, where I was tried on Thursday 23^d Jany 1777 for High Treason against the State of Connecticut, by an Act Passed in Octr Last, being Accused of Inlisting Men for Genl Howe, & having a Capt^{ns} Commission for that Purpose. I was adjudged Guilty & the Saturday foll^g was brought to the Bar of the Court & rec^d Sentence of Death. The Time of my Suffering was afterward fixed to the 19th Day of March 1777 which Tremendous & awfull Day now draws near, when I must Appear before the Searcher of all Hearts to give an Acc^t of all the things done in my body whether they be good or Evil.

I shall soon be dilivered from all the Pains & Troubles of this Mortal State, & shall be Answerable to None but the allseeing God, who is infinitely Just & who knoweth all things. As I am fully persuaded that I depart in a State of peace with God & my own Consience, I can have but little doubt of my future Happiness thro' the Mercy of God & Merits of Jesus Christ. I have sincerely repented of my sins, Examined my Heart, prayed Ernestly to God for Mercy for the Gracious pardon of my Manifold & henious Sins, & now resign myself wholly to the disposal of my heavenly Father, submiting my will to his.

From the very Bottom of my heart I forgive all my Enemies, and Earnestly pray God to forgive them all. Some part of J[osep]h S[mit]h's Evidence was false, but I heartily forgive him. I Likewise sincerely beg forgiveniss of all Persons whom I have injured or Offended. . . .

I die in the Possession and Communion of the Church of England. Of my Political Sentiments I leave the Readers of these lines to Judge. Perhaps it is neither Necessary nor proper that I should declare them in my Present situation.

I Cannot take my last farewell of my Countrymen without desiring them to shew Kindness to my poor Widow & Children, not reflecting upon them Concerning the Method of my Death.

Now I have given you a Narrative of all things Material Concerning my Life, with that Veracity which you are to Expect from a Man going immediately to Appear before the God of Truth. My last Advice to you is that you, above all other Concerns, prepare yourselves (with God's Assistance) for y^r future, Eternal State. You will all shortly be as near Eternity as I *now* am & will then view both worldly and Spiritual things in the same Light in which I do *now* view them. You will then see all worldly Things to be but Shadows, but Vapours, but Vanity of Vanities; and the Things of the Spiritual World to be of importance beyond all Discription. You will then be sensible that the Pleasures of a Good Consience & the Happiness of a near Prospect of Heaven infinitely outway all the Riches, Pleasure & Honor of this Mean, sinfull World.

God the Father, God the Son, God the Holy Ghost, have Mercy upon me & recieve my Spirit Amen! Amen! [*Morgan Lib. Anderson, History of Waterbury, vol. I, pp. 134–136.*]

9   JOHN HOWE'S *NEWPORT GAZETTE* RECOUNTS
THE EXECUTION OF JOHN HART OF NEW YORK AFTER
A SHAM TRIAL

The *Newport Gazette* was a product of the British occupation of the town (December 8, 1776–October 25, 1779). It was an out-and-out Loyalist paper, edited throughout its existence by the Loyalist John Howe. During the British occupation of Boston, Howe had assisted Margaret Draper, widow of the proprietor, in editing and printing the *Massachusetts Gazette and Boston Newsletter,* the only newspaper published during the siege of Boston. At the British evacuation he retired to Newport, married a sixteen-year-old town beauty, Martha Minns, and on January 16, 1777, started the *Newport Gazette.* When Newport in turn was evacuated Howe accompanied the troops to New York and thence to Halifax. Once again Howe started a newspaper, the *Halifax Journal,* and was soon designated King's Printer.[1]

MAY 17, 1777

❧ The sufferings of his Majesty's liege Subjects who are in the Power of those imperious Demagogues are beyond Description. . . .

We hear that one [General James M.] Varnum has put himself at the Head of about 40 Villains, who make it their Business to go from Town to Town upon the Narraganset Shore distressing the peaceable Inhabitants and taking up all Persons who are suspected of being friendly to Government. This Villain apprehended Mr. John Hart, belonging to New York Government and carried him to Providence, where he underwent a sham Trial for certain supposed Offences against their impious Government. They declared him guilty, carried him immediately from the Place of Trial to the Place of Execution, and there hung him. Such is the Impudence of those Candidates for Tyburn. *It is well known who were concerned in the Death of this unfortunate Man and it will be as well remembered.*

We hear that Mr. Hart made a short but very pathetic Speech to the persons concerned in his Execution, told them that their Conduct was owing to an Insensibility of their real Situation, warned them of those Consequences which would in a few Months ensue, and then with the greatest Serenity of Mind submitted himself to his Fate. He has left a Widow with several Children to join that Train of disconsolate Mourners, whose Cries have already extended to the remotest Corners of this unhappy Continent. . . .

Desertions and Deserters "ad infinitum!" Shou'd they apprehend all that advertised, it would require a new Emission of Paper to pay the Rewards, though the Price of an American military Patriot is very reasonable; many they only offer two Dollars for; the highest Price Six; Ten and Twelve for Negroes deserted from Private Masters. In this Land of Liberty the overflow of Patriots is such that they offer twice the Price for a Slave

[1] James H. Stark, *The Loyalists of Massachusetts,* Boston: 1910, pp. 361–363.

that they would chuse to give for the Defenders of that Privilege handed down to them by their theocratic Lawgivers. [*Newport Gaz., May 29, 1777.*]

10 THE EXECUTION OF ABRAHAM CARLISLE AND JOHN ROBERTS

In Pennsylvania, following the British withdrawal in 1778, the deliberate execution of Abraham Carlisle, a Philadelphia carpenter, and John Roberts, a miller from Lower Merion, created an intense stir and apprehension of further widespread and ruthless persecution. The men were tried by the Court of Oyer and Terminer with Judge Thomas McKeon presiding. Carlisle's offense was keeping one of the gates during the occupation of Philadelphia, and Robert's was enlisting with the British and urging others to do the same. Although the juries found them guilty, twelve of the grand jurors and ten of the petit jurors petitioned for mercy for Roberts, and all the jurors requested a reprieve for Carlisle. Five members of the clergy and 387 Philadelphians, several of high military rank and others leading Whigs, interceded by petition in their behalf. Nonetheless, the Executive Council was unmoved and the hanging was carried out on November 4, 1778, because Whig authorities considered it necessary to terrorize the Quakers and appease the popular demand to balance the score with the occupying forces of the enemy.[1] Every newspaper of account carried the story. Tories and Whigs alike wrote to faraway friends about the "injustice," among them two of Joseph Galloway's Tory friends, Isaac Ogden, a lawyer from Newark, New Jersey, and Joseph Humphreys, the owner of *The Pennsylvania Ledger,*[2] from whose letters to Galloway the following excerpts have been taken.

[1] J. Thomas Scharf and Thompson Westcott, *History of Philadelphia,* 1884 vol. I, p. 394.
[2] *The Pennsylvania Gazette* had closed in November 1776 but reopened as *The Pennsylvania Ledger* during Howe's occupation. Humphreys wrote Galloway: "In January, 1775, while parties were very high, I opened a paper in favor of government—the only one in Pennsylvania, and in my very first number published a piece against taking up of arms—in consequence of which was sent for by some leading men, orators of those times, and offered any sum I would rate the profit of my paper at, not exceeding £2500, to drop my paper. . . ." Nov. 23, 1778, James Riker, *Memoria,* vol. 15, N.Y. Public Library.

John Roberts and Abraham Carlisle Are Executed in Pennsylvania to Appease the Extremists

22ND NOV'R 1778

❡ . . . You may not possibly have heard of the Fate of Poor Roberts & Carlisle in Philadelphia, They were condemned, I believe, before You left this [city]. Great Interest was made to save their lives. Roberts's Wife with ten Children went to Congress, threw themselves on their knees & supplicated Mercy—but in vain. His Behavior at the Gallows did Honor to human Nature. He told his Audience that his Conscience acquitted him of Guilt; That he suffered for doing his Duty to his Sovereign; That his Blood would one day be demanded at their hands—and then, turning to his Children, charged & exhorted them to remember his Principles, for which he died and to adhere to them while they had Breath. This is the Substence of his Speech, after which he suffered with the Resolution of a Roman. . . .

Isaac Ogden

James Humphreys Describes the Tragic Scene for Joseph Galloway

NEW YORK, NOV. 23 [1778]

❡ . . . By the enclosed papers you will find that poor Roberts and Carlisle have been cruelly and wantonly sacrificed. They were walked to the gallows behind the cart with halters round their necks attended with all the other apparatus that make such scenes truly horrible—and by a guard of militia, but with hardly any spectators. Poor Carlisle, having been very ill during his confinement, was too weak to say anything; but Mr. Roberts, with the greatest coolness imaginable, spoke for some time—and, however the mind shrinks back and startles at the reflection of so tragical a scene, it is with pleasure that I can inform you they both behaved with the utmost fortitude and composure. After their execution their bodies were suffered to be carried away by their friends—and Mr. Carlisle's body buried in the Friend's Buying Ground, attended by above four thousand people in procession. . . .

James Humphreys, Jun.
[Riker, Memoria, vol. XV, pp. 2, 6, N.Y. Public Library.]

11 ANTHONY ALLAIRE DESCRIBES THE MOCK TRIAL AND
EXECUTION OF NINE TORY SOLDIERS AT BICKERSTAFF'S,
NORTH CAROLINA

Although there were few instances of civilian Loyalists executed for treason, there were many instances of execution of Loyalist prisoners of war.
When 700 Scottish Loyalists under Colonel John Boyd of South Carolina
were defeated at Kettle Creek (February 14, 1779), 70 of them were condemned to death as traitors (although under civil law) and 5 were actually
hanged.[1] After the British had hanged some captured rebels at Camden,
Ninety-Six, and Augusta, and had incited the Cherokees to attack trans-
Allegheny settlements, the rebel mountain men were bent on retaliation
against captives taken at King's Mountain (October 7, 1780). Nine prisoners from Major Patrick Ferguson's troops were summarily hanged on
"Gallows Oak" at Bickerstaff's (Forest City) after a drumhead trial. In this
instance civil and military law became confused. Many of the rebel officers
at the court-martial were also civil magistrates and applied a North Carolina
law of 1776 which provided capital punishment for Loyalists who took up
arms or knowingly aided the enemy.[2]

The account of the trial and execution given below, which appeared
in Rivington's *Royal Gazette,* has been attributed to Lieutenant Anthony
Allaire, an officer of Ferguson's Sharpshooters and adjutant to Captain
Abraham DePeyster on whom the command devolved at Ferguson's death.[3]
Allaire participated in the siege of Charleston and the destruction of the
rebel post at Monck's Corner, keeping a diary of the Carolina campaign
from March 5 to November 25, 1780.

OCTOBER 14, 1780

❅ The morning after the action [King's Mountain, October 7] we were
marched sixteen miles, previous to which orders were given by the Rebel
Col. [William] Campbell (whom the command devolved on) *that should*

[1] Charles Stedman, *The History of the Origin, Progress, & Termination of the American War,* London: 1794, vol. II, pp. 107–108.
[2] J. B. O. Landrum, *Colonial and Revolutionary History of South Carolina,* Greenville:
1897, p. 217.
[3] The wording of Allaire's letter of January 30, 1781, follows closely his diary entry for
October 14, 1780. See L. C. Draper, *King's Mountain and Its Heroes,* Cincinnati: 1881,
pp. 510–511.

they be attacked on their march, they were to fire on and destroy their prisoners. The party was kept marching two days without any provisions. The officers' baggage, on the third day's march, was all divided among the Rebel officers.

Shortly after we were marched to Bickerstaff's settlement, where we arrived on the thirteenth. On the fourteenth, a court martial composed of twelve field officers was held for the trial of the militia prisoners; when, after a short hearing, they condemned thirty of the most principal and respectable characters, whom they considered to be the most inimical to them, to be executed; and at six o'clock in the evening of the same day executed Col. [Ambrose] Mills, Capt. [James] Chitwood, Capt. Wilson, and six privates, obliging every one of their officers to attend at the death of those brave, but unfortunate Loyalists, who all, with their last breath and blood, held the Rebels and their cause as infamous and base, and as they were turning off extolled their King and the British Government.

On the morning of the fifteenth, Col. Campbell had intelligence that Col. Tarleton was approaching him, when he gave orders to his men that should Col. Tarleton come up with them, they were immideately to fire on Capt. [Abraham] DePeyster and his officers, who were in the front, and then a second volley on the men. During this day's march the men were obliged to give thirty-five Continental dollars for a single ear of Indian corn and forty for a drink of water, they not being allowed to drink when fording a river; in short, the whole of the Rebels' conduct from the surrender of the party into their hands is incredible to relate. Several of the militia that were worn out with fatigue, and not being able to keep up, were cut down and trodden to death in the mire. . . . Dr. [Uzal] Johnson was . . . knocked down and treated in the basest manner for endeavoring to dress a man whom they had cut on the march. The Rebel officers would often go in amongst the prisoners, draw their swords, cut down and wound those whom their wicked and savage minds prompted.

This is a specimen of Rebel lenity—you may report it without the least equivocation, for upon the word and honor of a gentleman, this description is not equal to their barbarity. [*Allaire*] *to Roy. Gaz., Jan. 30, 1781. Draper, King's Mountain, pp. 518-519.*]

Loyalists on the

New York, Pennsylvania,

and Vermont Frontiers

The Mohawk Valley in Tryon County was a frontier area where civil warfare was perfidious and bloody. Here was a strong pocket of Tories—independent farmers who were stubborn when it came to principle. The strong influence of the Johnsons, the most prominent and wealthiest family in the valley, was one reason for widespread Loyalism. Although Sir William had died in July 1774, his son, Sir John Johnson, and his sons-in-law, Guy Johnson and Daniel Claus, were ardent Loyalists. So was Molly Brant, his Indian housekeeper and paramour (a sister of Joseph, Chief of the Mohawks). Kinsmen and followers of the Johnsons, friends like John Butler and his son Walter, the Mohawk Indians, as well as Sir William's natural children, were so numerous that two Tory regiments were readily recruited from the settlements in the valley, Sir John Johnson's Royal Greens and John

Butler's Tory Rangers. Families were irreconcilably divided; the brother of rebel General Nicholas Herkimer, Lieutenant Colonel George Herkimer, was a Loyalist, as was Colonel Henry Frey, the brother of Major John Frey, Chairman of the Tryon County Committee of Safety. The Hooples of Cherry Valley were another split family; two brothers, Jurgen and John, joined the rebels, while another brother, Francis, chose the King. When Brant marked the Hoople house as Tory during the Cherry Valley massacre and the Indians spared it, John switched to the Loyalist side and joined Johnson's Royal Greens in Canada.[1] Another divided family in the Mohawk valley was that of Lucas Vetter, husband of Maria Eva Serviss, a family attached to the Johnsons through Sir William Johnson's wife. Lucas cast his lot with Sir John Johnson and removed to Montreal. His two sons, Wilhelm and Lucas Jr., disagreed about allegiance; Lucas, a playmate of the Johnson boys at Johnson Hall, fought with the Royal Greens and settled in Canada; Wilhelm, who had spent his boyhood on a Stone Arabia farm among the sturdy Palatines who abhorred the Johnson arrogance, joined the rebels. These divided families were not exceptional, for the dilemma of allegiance was particularly acute in the valley.

1 DANIEL CLAUS LAYS THE FAILURE TO REDUCE FORT STANWIX TO A "WANT OF TIMELY AND GOOD INTELLIGENCE"

For the residents of Tryon County the most significant battle of the Revolution was Oriskany, where Herkimer's troops, moving to the support of Fort Stanwix (Fort Schuyler), were ambushed August 6, 1777, some six miles from the fort. Although the British won the field at Oriskany, they were unable to reduce the fort which guarded the portage between the Mohawk River and Wood Creek, a tributary to Oneida Lake. The failure to dislodge the rebels from the fort blocked St. Leger from joining Burgoyne's forces above Albany. Colonel Daniel Claus, son-in-law of Sir William Johnson, ascribed the failure to faulty intelligence on the location, unavailability of equipment for the Indians, and on the strength of the garrison at the fort. When the Indians became restless over the deficiency in every

[1] Elizabeth L. Hoople, *The Hooples of Hoople's Cree,* Toronto: 1967, p. 3.

necessary item of equipment, St. Leger's way of quieting their disgust was to order a quart of rum apiece and get them drunk. As for the Stanwix garrison, Colonel Butler reported its strength as 60 men, whereas Claus's reconnoitering party learned that it was 600, entrenched in a well-repaired fort, alert to the route and size of the British force. St. Leger brushed aside this intelligence, failed to send for more adequate artillery, and pushed on for a surprise attack with small arms on the fort. Here the official intelligence was faulty, but not so the information transmitted by Molly Brant, nicknamed "The Rip." The famous ambuscade at Oriskany was, in fact, made possible by the intelligence she gleaned concerning Herkimer's militia from watching the signals at Herkimer's home, visible from her house across the river. Daniel Claus's account of the Battle of Oriskany sent from Montreal October 11, 1777, to William Knox, British Undersecretary of State, confirmed the fact.

OCTOBER 11, 1777

℘ *Sir*

    . . . The 26th of July left Oswego, and 2 of August arrived with the Brigadier [Barry St. Leger] and the greatest part of the Troops before Fort Stanwix, which was invested the same Evening. The Enemy, having stopd up a narrow River called Wood Creek by cutting of Trees across it for abt 20 Miles, along which our Artillery, Provisions & Baggage was to pass, which passage to cut open required a number of Men, as well as cutting a Road thro the Woods for 25 Miles to bring up the Artillery, Stores &c. that were immediately wanted, which weakend our small Army greatly. The 3d, 4th. & 5th the Indns. surrounded the Fort and fired from behind Loggs & rising grounds at the Garrison whenever they had an Object, which prevented them from working at the Fortifications in the day. The 5th in the Afternoon Accot. was brought by [an] Indian sent by Josephs Sister [Molly Brant] from Canajoharee, that a Body of Rebels were on their March, and would be within 10 or 12 Miles of our Camp that Night. . . . The Rebels having an imperfect Accot. of the Number of Indians that joind us, (being upwards of 800:) not thinking them by ¼ as many, and being sure as to our Strength & Artillery, (wch. we learnd by prisoners), that they knew it from their Emissaries before we left Canada; They therefore on the 6th marched on, to the Number of upwards 800, with security & Carelessness, when within 6 Miles of the Fort they were waylaid by our party, surprised, briskly attacked, and after a little Resistance repulsed & defeated, leaving upwards of 500 killed on the Spot among which were their principal Officers & Ringleaders. Their General was shot thro the Knee and a few days after died of an Amputation.

During the Action when the Garrison found the Indians Camp . . . empty, they boldly sallyd out with 300 Men & 2 field pieces, & took away the Indians packs with their Cloaths, Wampum & Silverwork, they having gone in their Shirts or naked to Action; and when they found a party advancing from our Camp they returnd with their Spoil, taking with them Lieut Singleton & a private of Sr. Johns Regt. who lay wounded in the Indn. Camp. The Disappointment was rather greater to the Indians than their Loss for they had nothing to cover themselves at Night or agst. the weather, & nothing in our Camp to supply them till I got to Oswego. After this Defeat [Oriskany] . . . a Flag was sent with the [acco^t of] the Disaster of their intended Relief, and the Fort was summond. . . . The Rebels knowing their Strength in Garrison as well as Fortification and the Insufficiency of our Field pieces to hurt them, and apprehensive of being masacred by the Indians for the Loss they sustained in the Action, they rejected the Summons sd that they were determined to hold out to the last Extremity. The Siege then was carried on with as much Vigor as possible for 19 days, but to no purpose. . . .

The Indians finding that our besieging the Fort was of no Effect, our Troops but few, a Reinforcement, as was reported, of 1500 or 2000 Men with Field pieces, by the way, began to be dispirited & file off by Degrees. The Chiefs advised the Brigr. to retreat to Oswego and get better Artillery from Niagara & more Men and return & renew the Siege, to which the Brigr. agreed and accordingly retreated wch. was on the 22 of Augt. . . .

Thus has an Expedition miscarried merely for want of timely & good Intelligence. [*Orig. in N.Y. State Lib. See O'Callaghan, Documents, vol. VIII, pp. 718-723.*]

2 HON YOST SCHUYLER, THE TORY HALF-WIT, EXAGGERATES "HEAP FIGHTING CHIEF'S" (BENEDICT ARNOLD'S) FORCES AND PANICS THE INDIANS

A second incident connected with the siege of Fort Stanwix focused on the Tory Hon Yost Schuyler, the simple-witted son of Pieter Schuyler and Elizabeth Herkimer. A nephew of General Herkimer and a relative of General Philip Schuyler, he had nonetheless grown up among the Mohawks and Oneidas, learned their language, and understood their superstitions and psychology. During the siege of the fort he was taken prisoner along with Walter Butler and others, was court-martialed, and was sentenced to death as a traitor and spy. His life was spared by General Arnold in return for his carrying a false report to the Indians which would induce them to quit the siege. Hon Yost's brother was kept as a hostage. The story of his part in precipitating the flight of the Indians and in making St. Leger's retreat inevitable, thus affecting the outcome at Saratoga, has been frequently told by historians.[1] Although the Arnold *Memoirs,* which present the story here, were written by F. J. Stimson as if Arnold were recording them, the facts have been validated in other contemporary accounts. Moses Younglove, who was taken captive at Oriskany by the Indians, gave substantially the same account to his father and brother immediately on his escape.[2] St. Leger also confirmed the facts in his letter to Burgoyne of August 27, 1777. He wrote that as his men were sapping close to the fort, scouts brought word of a thousand rebels marching toward them; then "the first number was swelled to two thousand; immediately after, a third [scout] reported that General Burgoyne's army was cut to pieces and that Arnold was advancing by rapid and forced marches with three thousand men. It was at this moment I began to suspect cowardice in some, and treason in others. . . . This [to retire at night] did not fall in with their

[1] Christopher Ward, *The War of the Revolution,* New York: 1952, vol. II, p. 490. B. J. Lossing, *Field Book of the American Revolution,* New York: 1850-1852, vol. II, pp. 251-252. Timothy Dwight, *Travels in New England and New York,* New Haven: 1821-1822, vol. III, pp. 196-197. William L. Stone, *The Campaign of Lt. General John Burgoyne and the Expedition of Lt. Colonel Barry St. Leger,* Albany: 1877, pp. 212-216.
[2] Samuel Younglove, "Record of the Narrative of Dr. Moses Younglove," December 1777, *Herkimer Family Portfolio,* N.Y. State Library, *The Remembrancer,* vol. V, pp. 444, 447-448 fn.

[the Indians] views, which were no less than treacherously committing ravage upon their friends, as they had lost the opportunity of doing it upon their enemies. To accomplish this, they artfully caused messengers to come in, one after the other, with accounts of the nearer approaches of the rebels, one, and the last affirmed that they were within two miles of Captain Lernoult's post. . . . They [the Indians] grew furious and abandoned; seized upon the officers' liquor and clothes . . . and became more formidable than the enemy we had to expect. . . . On my arrival at the Onondaga Falls, I received an answer to my letter from your Excellency, which showed in the clearest light the scenes of treachery that had been practised on me. The messenger had heard, indeed, on his way, that they were collecting the same kind of rabble as before but that there was not an enemy within forty miles of Fort Stanwix. . . ."[3] Hon Yost's cooperation with the rebels, which proved so effective, was merely a temporary expedient to save his brother's life. As soon as the latter was released, Hon Yost joined the Loyalist forces again and returned to Canada.

AUGUST 22, 1777

❡   It was a case for artifice if there ever was one. Now, at Dutch Flats, my scouts had brought in a certain half-witted Dutchman named Hon Yost Schuyler or Cuyler, who, with Lieutenant Butler, had been caught at a public meeting in our lines urging the people to join the British cause. Both were promptly tried by court martial, and sentenced to be hanged as spies, but the mother of Hon Yost came to me to intercede for his life. Now I never despise information about men, I try to know a little of all men; and it was within my knowledge that this Hon Yost was regarded by the Mohawks with superstitious awe, as one stricken by Manitou. I was really quite unable to cope with St. Leger's regular force, to say nothing of the hostile Indian. The thing to do was to frighten them away before they overwhelmed the fort. It was a chance; and I told the old mother that I would spare her son if he would proceed to St. Leger's camp and spread the news that I was approaching with overwhelming numbers. She gladly accepted,

---

[3] St. Leger to General Burgoyne, August 27, 1777, John Burgoyne, *A State of the Expedition from Canada as Laid before House of Commons,* London: 1780.

   Henry B. Dawson, *Battles of the United States,* vol. I, pp. 252–253. Dawson is skeptical of the truth of the story. Ibid., p. 247.

and proposed that she remain with me as a hostage for his good faith. This I declined, but took her other son Nicholas instead, and Hon Yost started on his curious mission,—which indeed reminds one more of the Iliad than of Anglo-Saxon warfare! As one never knows whether spies may not be present in one's own camp, I had several bullets shot through Hon Yost's coat, and urging him to run for his life, had a discharge of musketry at his heels to give the proper color to his story of escape. Moreover, after he had gone, I despatched an Oneida Indian in whom I had confidence, who was to go to St. Leger's camp on a separate line and corroborate the Dutchman's story.

It was a thing to laugh at. It was true that St. Leger's Indians had become restless and discontented. They had been promised plenty of scalps and of plunder, and had only got plenty of fighting instead. They also had had rumors of my approach, and they knew me of old. As I heard the story, they were actually holding a council when Hon Yost, the Manitou-stricken one, burst in, showing his garments riddled with bullets, and declaring that he had barely escaped death in his effort to warn them and tell them of their coming danger. The General inquired the number of our troops; and Hon Yost pointed to the leaves of the trees! He was taken to St. Leger's tent, where he gave a perfectly true account of his capture and of his escape, so far as the staging went; and indeed, St. Leger had already heard the same story. And just at this time the Oneida Indian arrived, bringing a belt and saying that the Americans were approaching in great numbers under their war chief Arnold; that they did not wish to fight the Indians, but were determined to destroy every British soldier and every tory in the valley, as well as the rangers and the Greens, (which was the name we gave to the tory royalists). The terrible Bostonians, they declared, led by their "Heap Fighting Chief," were at their doors in numbers like the leaves of the forest! Apparently my name was enough. The Indians were all seized with wild panic and scattered in the forest depths, the Canadians following them, and after them the so called regulars, all in disorderly flight, throwing away arms, knapsacks, and blankets. Thus it may fairly be said that the siege of Fort Stanwix was raised by a half-witted Dutchman and the name of Arnold.

Hon Yost himself pretended to fly with them for a short time, but soon made a détour in the forest, fell behind, returned to Fort Schuyler, and gave Gansevoort the news of my advance, and how he and my name had put St. Leger to flight. Then he hastened back to me with a letter from

Gansevoort, in which he told me that his scouts reported St. Leger's army retreating with the utmost precipitation, their camp deserted, and that he had heard of my advance with 2,000 men. This was considerably more than my number, but I had thought it as well to let even our friends have an exaggerated notion of our strength. [*Stimson, My Story, pp. 281-283.*]

3 MOLLY BRANT IS HARASSED BY THE ONEIDAS AND OBLIGED TO FLEE FOLLOWING ORISKANY

The allegiance of the Six Nations was divided, with the Mohawks, Senecas, Cayugas, and Onondagas siding with the British and the Oneidas and some of the Tuscaroras joining the rebels. The loyal tribes at Oriskany had lost heavily—thirty-two killed, including some of the principal Seneca chiefs, thirty-three wounded, and baggage plundered. Dispirited and bitter, they turned on the Oneidas, burning their houses, crops, and killing or carrying off their cattle. The Oneidas in return took revenge on Molly Brant and her family, robbing them and forcing them to flee to Niagara, and in time to Carleton Island, Upper Canada. The Six Nations now vowed to give her satisfaction by further retaliation on the Oneida tribe which had perpetrated the abuse.[1] Two rare letters sent by Molly Brant to Daniel Claus after her flight follow.[2]

NIAGARA, 23 JUNE 1778

℄ *Dear Sir*
I have been favor'd with Yours and the Trunk & parcels by Mr. Street. Everything mentioned in the invoice you sent me has come safe, except the pair of gold Earrings which I have not been able to find.

We have a report of Joseph having had a brush with the Rebels, but do not know at what place. A Cayuga Chief is said to be Wounded, one

---

[1] Daniel Claus to Secretary William Knox, Montreal, November 6, 1777. O'Callaghan, *Documents,* vol. VIII, p. 725.
[2] These letters are not in Molly Brant's handwriting, as she could only make her mark, MARI. *Claus Papers,* MS. Group 19, F 1, II, pp. 29, 32, 135-136, Public Archives Canada.

Schohary Indian (Jacob) killed, & one missing since when it's reported that Col Butler & Joseph have Joined; Every hour we look for a confirmation of this news.

I am much obliged to you for the care & attention in sending me up those very necessary articles & should be very glad if you have any accounts from New York that you would let me know them, as well as of the health of George & Peggy whom I hope are agreably settled. My Children are all in good health, & desire their loves to You, Mrs. Claus, Lady & Sir John Johnson. I hope the time is very near, when we shall all return to the Mohawk River.

> I am Dr Sir ever
> Affectionately Your
> *Mary Brandt*
> [*MSS 1 - 443a, PAC. Copy in Johnson Hall, Amsterdam.*]

CARLETON ISLAND, 5TH OCTOBER 1779

❦ *Sir*

We arraived here the 29th last month after Tedaous and dissagreable voyage; where we remain and by all Appearance may for the winter. I have rote to Col° Butler and my brother acquainting them of my Situation, desireing there advice, as I was left no Directions Concerning my self or family. Only when a Vessel Arraived, I could get a passage to Niagara—I have been promised [by] Col° Johnson at Montreal that I should hear from the Genl [Haldimand] and have his directions and order to be provided at whatever place my little services should be wanted which you know I am always ready to do. Should you think proper to speak to the Genl on that head will be much Oblidged to you. The Indians are a good deele dissatisfied on acct of the Col°.s hasty temper which I hope he will soon drop. Otherwise it may be Dissadvantageous. I need not tell you whatever is promised or told them it ought to be perform'd.

Those from Canada are much Dissatisfied on Account of his taking more Notice of those that are suspected than them that are known to be Loyal, I tell this only to you that you may advise him on that head. Meantime beg leave to be remembred to all your family. . . .

> Your wellwisher
> *Mary Brant*
> MSS 1 - 443b, PAC.

4 SARAH CASS McGINN OF TRYON COUNTY "TAMPERS" WITH THE INDIANS IN FAVOR OF THE BRITISH

Sarah Cass McGinn was another Loyalist lady of Tryon County who understood the language of the Six Nations and was useful to the British as an interpreter and intermediary. She and her children, all Loyalists, lived on her father's estate in Tryon County after the death of her husband. She was jailed by the Committee of Safety just before the siege of Fort Stanwix in order to serve as an interpreter for the rebels. She was released, and when the committee attempted to pick her up again eight days later, she escaped to the British army. After the Indians deserted the siege and took flight, Sir John Johnson sent her to the country of the Six Nations to mollify them and assuage the loss of their men and chiefs at Oriskany. Her memorial to the Crown for compensation for her losses, dated July 14, 1787, tells of one signal service to the British which she performed shortly after Burgoyne's defeat at Saratoga.

OCTOBER 1777

❡ . . . The Rebels have destroyed, plundered and taken almost all her Property, because they alledged and not without reason that she was tampering with the Indians in favour of Government. . . .

She made her escape to it [British army before Fort Stanwix] with her Family except a Son who she was obliged to leave to their Mercy, who was out of his Sences and bound in Chains, as he had been for several Years, and sometime afterwards was burn'd alive in said Situation.

That if your Petitioner had not got away, the Rebels would certainly have obliged her to act for them with the Indians. The Rebels by way of inducement to come over to their Side offered her 12/ York Currency per day and a Guard of 30 Men to protect her against any harm from the King's troops, which offer she refused with Contempt.

That after our Forces returned from Fort Stanwix to Oswego your Petitioner was sent . . . to Quayonga (Cayuga) Castle to be of every Service in her Power to Government among the Indians during her stay there. It happen'd that an Indian was going with a Belt of Wampam to the different Indians from General Schuyler acquainting the Six Nations that all the King's Troops had been defeated and taken Prisoners at Saratoga by the American Army, and if the Six Nations would not come immediately and make their Peace with the Congress they would find means to compell them; which Belt your Petitioner stopt and prevailed upon the Indian to carry an Account of a different Nature favourable to Government and encouraged the Six Nations, who soon after went to War against the Rebels on the Frontiers. [*Loyalist Transcripts,* XXI, *pp. 399–401.*]

5 "OH, VIRTUE, THOU, THEN REALLY EXISTEST!"
CRÈVECOEUR DEPICTS A FRONTIER HANGING IN THE
SUSQUEHANNA VALLEY

War on the frontier was so uncontrolled and so inhuman that even eye-witness accounts of the barbarities are hard to believe. Each inhuman act invited a retaliatory one which in turn had to be avenged. Each side believed it had a righteous score to even out. In July 1778, Butler's Rangers and Mohawk allies ravaged the Wyoming Valley, destroying crops, maiming cattle, burning, and butchering. Women and children were victims as often as were the Continentals assigned to frontier defense. After the massacre along the Susquehanna River, the embittered frontiersmen turned their vengeance on innocent neighbors, whether neutral or Loyalist, blaming them for the tragic disaster. One such victim was Joseph Wilson, who was accused of harboring some Tories and was hung by his thumbs and toes to wring a confession from him. Crèvecoeur, himself a Loyalist who was forced to flee from his home in 1778, has sketched the tragic scene in "The Man of Sorrows." Wilson protested his innocence, was untied temporarily, and then in the heat of demagoguery was condemned to hanging by the neck.

[1778]

❧ On hearing of his doom he flung himself at the feet of the first man. He solemnly appealed to God, the searcher of hearts, for the truth of his assertions. He frankly owned that he was attached to the King's cause from ancient respect and by the force of custom; that he had no idea of any other government, but that at the same time he had never forcibly opposed the measures of the country. . . . He earnestly begged and entreated them that they would give him an opportunity of proving his innocence: "Will none of you hear me with patience? I am no stranger, no unknown person; you well know that I am a home-staying man, laborious and peaceable. Would you destroy me on a hearsay? For the sake of that God which knows and sees and judges all men, permit me to have a judicial hearing." . . . Their hearts were hardened and their minds prepossessed; they refused his request and justified the sentence of death they had passed. . . . Seeing that it was all in vain, he peaceably submitted to his fate, and gave himself up to those who were preparing the fatal cord. It was soon tied round the limb of a tree to which they hanged him. . . . The shades of patibulary death began to spread on his face; the hands, no longer trying to relieve the body, hung loose on each side.

Fortunately at this instant some remains of humanity sprung up in the breasts of a few. They solicited that he might be taken down. It was agreed and done. They next threw cold water on him, and to the surprise of some and the mortification of others he showed some signs of life. He gradually recovered. . . .

Again he was commanded to confess the crime he was accused of, and again he solemnly denied it. They then consulted together, and, callous to the different impressions occasioned by so complicated a distress, unwilling to acquit him, though incapable of convicting him, they concluded him guilty and swore that he should die. . . . On hearing his second final doom, he tenderly and pathetically reproached them with making him pass through every stage of death so slowly, when malefactors have but one moment to suffer. "Why, then, won't you confess that you have harboured our enemies? We have full and sufficient proofs." "Why should I confess in the sight of God that which is not true? I am an innocent man. Aren't you afraid of God and His vengeance? . . . I have nothing but words to make use of. I repeat it again for the last time: I am innocent of the accusation."

"What say you, men, guilty or not guilty?" "Guilty he is and deserving of death."

"Must I then die a second time? Had you left me hanging, now I should be no more. Oh, God, must I be hanged again? Thou knowest my innocence, lend, oh, lend me a miracle to prove it." He shed a flood of tears, and looking once more toward his children and wife, who remained stupid and motionless. . . . "If I must die, then God's will be done." And kneeling down close by his wife, who kneeled also, he pronounced the following prayer: . . . : Gracious God, in this hour of tribulation and of mind and bodily distress, I ask Thee forgiveness for the sins I have committed.

. . . Receive the repentance of a minute as an atonement for years of sin.
. . . Allowed but ten minutes to live, I seize my last to recommend to Thy
paternal goodness my wife and children. . . . This is, thou knowest, the
strongest chain which binds me to thy earth, and makes the sacrifice of this
day so bitter. . . . I here before Thee pardon all my persecutors and those
by whose hands I am now going to be deprived of life. . ."

"You have prayed so well and so generously forgiven us that we must
think at last that you are not so guilty as the majority of us had imagined.
We will do you no further injury for the present, but it is our duty to send
you to ———where, according to law, you may have a fair trial. . . ."

With a feeble voice he thanked them and begged a few minutes with
his wife. [To his children he said:] "Kiss me, my dear little ones, your
daddy thought he would see you no more, but God's Providence has spoken
to the heart of these people." . . .

Oh, Virtue, thou, then really existest! [*Crèvecoeur, Sketches,
pp. 185–188.*]

6 RICHARD CARTWRIGHT, JR., CONFIRMS THE ATROCITIES CHARGED AGAINST THE INDIANS, CALLING THEM "LURKING ASSASSINS"

Both sides used the Indians in their warfare, but on the New York–Pennsylvania frontier where the Iroquois lived and hunted the British were
better able to exploit these allies and thus were charged more regularly with
condoning barbarities. The Mohawks, Cayugas, Senecas, and Onondagas
sided with the British, partly from the influence of Sir William Johnson's
family and partly from habit. They seemed to associate the invasion of their
lands and the conflict it engendered with white Americans, not white British, although their quarrel was with the white man in general. The Oneidas
and about half of the Tuscororas joined the rebels, as did the Delawares of
the Wyoming Valley, the traditional enemy of the Iroquois. Fort Niagara
was the principal base from which Butler's Rangers, under Colonel John
Butler and his son Captain Walter, and the Indians, led by the renowned
Mohawk chief, Joseph Brant, pushed out to attack frontier settlements.
The two bloodiest raids, which rankled for generations after the war, were

those of Wyoming in July and of Cherry Valley in November 1778, but other towns, such as German Flats and Minisink, did not escape. [1] Demands from other Western settlements led to the appointment of Major General John Sullivan and Brigadier General James Clinton to the command of an all-out expedition in 1779 against the Iroquois settlements in the Finger Lakes in order to cripple their power. Sullivan was to apply a scorched-earth technique to the Indians' buildings, orchards, and fields, which had become a significant source of food supply for the British. He was, in addition, to take hostages as surety for the good conduct of the Indians in the future. If possible, the expedition was to invest Forts Oswego and Niagara. Sullivan's division, one of the three prongs of the expedition, reached Tioga on the New York border on August 22, burning thirty to forty Indian villages and the council house at Chemung on the way. Joining Clinton's forces, they traveled up the Chemung River to Newtown, near Elmira. Here on August 29 they had an encounter with Butler's Rangers and 500 of Brant's Indians. This short conflict and the retreat of Butler and Brant opened the way for the burning of Indian crops and towns from Newtown to Canandaigua and Honeoye. Turning back after destroying Genesee Castle, Sullivan's troops burned many other small settlements around Cayuga Lake before returning to Wyoming.

The retreating Indians in turn took many prisoners and turned their vengeance on these hapless men and women for the destruction of their towns, scalping and butchering in a wanton orgy of sadism. Many victims were forced to run the gauntlet, subjected to barbaric beatings, which Richard Cartwright, Jr., a captain in the Rangers, said in his *Journal* (quoted below) he could not force himself to behold.

Richard Cartwright's residence in Albany was raided in August 1776, yielding to the rebels not only Cartwright, but also Abraham C. Cuyler, the former mayor, and Stephen DeLancey. All were accused of being "with a number of the lower sort of people, carousing and singing God Save the King" and were committed to the Tory jail. Cuyler and DeLancey were soon taken to Connecticut. Cartwright, with permission of the Committee of Safety, left Albany October 27, 1777, for Montreal, eventually joining Butler's Rangers and acting as Butler's secretary. [2] After the war he entered

[1] September 12, 1778, and July 19, 1779, respectively.
[2] *American Archives,* 5th ser, vol. I, p. 890. *Loyalist Transcripts,* vol. XXX, p. 227.

into partnership with Robert Hamilton in Kingston, serving also as a Judge and on the Council of Upper Canada.

The following section of Cartwright's *Journal* was written at Canadesaga (Seneca Castle), the chief town of the Senecas, and one of those burned on the marauding trek of Sullivan's men. Cartwright's comments confirm the barbarities of the Iroquois to their prisoners and indicate, on the part of at least some British officers, revulsion from, not condonation of, this mode of warfare.

1779

❡ June 30: . . . We have been now two Months in the Indian Country, a Time too long to spend among the Savages in the Woods, where we are wasting too many of our liveliest and most cheerful Days, the Days of our Youth, in Idleness and Disipation. . . .

July 13: The Indians for these two or three Nights past have stolen several Things both from Men and Officers. . . .

July 24: What he [Captain McDonell] says of the Indians he is among may Serve as the General Character of the Whole . . . "they don't know their own Minds an Hour; the most trivial occurrence alarms them and carrys off their Attention from the Object they had an Hour before in View; such another Set of credulous, whimsical, capricious Devils the World cannot produce. They attribute their Delays to a Multitude of superstitious Reasons which would be too tedious to insert here."

July 25: . . . I can consider these small Parties of [Mohawk] Indians, going out on the Frontiers, only as so many Bands of lurking Assassins seeking an opportunity to destroy the peaceful and industrious Inhabitants and ready to Glut their Cruelty alike with the Blood of Friend and Foe without distinction of Sex or Age. There are but too many Instances which would be shocking to repeat which evince this to be a just Estimation of them. Tho' much Pain has been taken, it is impossible to bring them to leave Women and Children unmolested and as for the Rest it must be expected that they will regard all White People alike, and if they can but bring off a Prisoner or a Scalp 'tis all one to them.

August 5: [J. McDonell to Richard Cartwright] "I did everyThing in my Power to prevail upon the Indians to pursue their Success but they were so glutted with Plunder, Prisoners and Scalps that my utmost Efforts could not persuade them from retreating to Fort Wallace that Night."

August 14: Some Prisoners that had been taken by Mr. Brant's Party were brought thro' this Village to Day; they were cruelly beaten, as I am informed, for I could not bring myself to behold so inhuman a Sight.

August 29: The Behaviour of the Indians on this Occasion [defeat of the forces under Walter Butler and Joseph Brant by General John Sullivan at Newton near Elmira] has fully convinced me that tho they may exert themselves against defenceless People or an Enemy taken at Surprise with great Fury, they will soon give Way when taken at equal Terms in the Field. [*Cartwright, Continuation of a Journal, June 25 to Aug. 29, 1779. Courtesy of Richard L. Cartwright, Port Hope, Ontario.*]

7 COLONEL CRAWFORD IS TORTURED BY THE DELAWARES IN REVENGE FOR A MASSACRE HE DIDN'T COMMAND OR COUNTENANCE

The Ohio Valley was another scene of savage warfare and barbarity. Raids and retaliation here continued long after Yorktown had ended the fighting elsewhere. The British held the forts at Niagara, Sandusky, Michilimackinac, and Detroit all through the war, and their influence spread out effectively among the Shawnee, Wyandot, and Delaware tribes living in the area between the Upper Ohio and the Great Lakes. In the Illinois country, however, George Rogers Clark's capture of Vincennes in July 1778, and then again in February 1779, after it had been retaken by General Henry Hamilton's men, gave Clark control in the Wabash Valley. Although Clark intended an attempt against Detroit, he never had sufficient men and supplies to mount the attack.

Despite the news of Yorktown, frontiersmen were still bent on killing Indians and securing their lands. The death of the Delaware chief White Eyes, who had been favorable to the rebels, and the succession of the pro-British faction under the Delaware chief Captain Pipe gave some rebel Pennsylvanians an excuse to attack the Moravian Christians at Gnadenhütten (Muskingum) [(March 7 to 8, 1782)]. An unprovoked massacre of ninety-six hymn-singing Delawares ensued. The massacre touched off the single most barbarous murder of the war on the frontier, the torture and burning at the stake of Colonel William Crawford, an experienced Continental officer, who, ironically, was not responsible, but was blamed by the Indians, for the Gnadenhütten affair. The hideous incident is described by Captain William Caldwell in a letter to Major Arent S. De-Peyster, Loyalist Commandant at Detroit. Caldwell commanded the Loyalist Rangers and the Indians at the encounter with Crawford's troops on the Upper Sandusky River. Major DePeyster in turn sent an account, also included below, to Thomas Brown, Superintendent of Indian Affairs, expressing apprehension that the old custom of putting prisoners to death had been revived. A further excerpt from Major DePeyster's correspondence, this time to Alexander McKee, a Loyalist Indian agent,[1] expresses outrage over Indian cruelty, indicative of the general anger among British officers involved in Indian warfare. Contrary to the belief that the British encouraged the Indians in terror tactics on the frontier, most attempted to stop the Indian practice of torture and killing of prisoners, threatening even to withdraw their troops if the Indians persisted.

Simon Girty's Report of Colonel Crawford's Torture

JUNE 12, 1782

❡ Simon Girty[1] arrived last night from the upper village (Half King's town) who informed me that the Delawares had burnt Colonel Crawford and two captains at Pipes-Town after torturing them a long time. Crawford died like a hero; never changed his countenance tho' they scalped him alive

---

[1] Alexander McKee had served as lieutenant in the French and Indian War and had acted as agent between Indians and the troops in Pontiac's Rebellion, for which services he was awarded 1,400 acres at McKee's Rocks near Fort Pitt. Knowing the Delaware and Wyandot languages, he enjoyed considerable influence among these tribes and worked with Captain John Connolly to retain their loyalty as well as that of the Six Nations. When the Revolutionary War broke out he gave his parole to the Committee of Safety, but violated it in February 1778, when he learned he would be taken up and imprisoned. With Simon Girty and Matthew Elliot, another Indian trader, he trekked across Indian territory to Detroit. Walter R. Hoberg, "Early History of Colonel Alexander McKee," *Penn. Magazine History & Biography*, vol. LVIII, pp. 26–36.

[1] Simon Girty was an infamous frontier fighter who had lived among the Senecas, learned their language, and could act as interpreter. In 1778 he abandoned the rebels for the British and took part in many of the battles in the Old Northwest, including Crawford's defeat on the Sandusky River. When the latter, during his torture, begged Girty to shoot him, Girty answered that he had no gun. He married a white captive and at the close of the war went to live in Canada. C. W. Butterfield, *History of the Girtys, passim.*

and then laid hot ashes upon his head; after which they roasted him by a slow fire. He told Girty if his life could be spared, he would communicate something of consequence, but nothing else could induce him to do it. He said some great blows would be struck against the country. Crawford and four captains belonged to the Continental forces. He [Girty] said fourteen captains were killed. The rebel doctor [Knight] and General Irvine's aid-de-camp [Rosenthal] are taken by the Shawanese; they came out on a party of pleasure. [*Haldimand Papers, Public Archives Canada. Butterfield, History of the Girtys, p. 183.*]

Arent DePeyster Deplores the Savage Custom of Killing Prisoners

JULY 18, 1782

❦ *Sir* [Thomas Brown]—
I am happy to inform you that the Indians from this quarter have gained a complete victory over six hundred of the enemy who had penetrated as far as Sandusky, with a view of destroying the Wyandots, men, women, and children, as they had done with ninety-six of the Christian Indians at Muskingum (Tuscarawas) a few weeks before.

The affair of Sandusky happened on the 4th of June when the enemy left two hundred and fifty in the field; and it is believed that few of the remainder escaped to Wheeling.

Their major [John] McClelland, and most of the officers were killed in the action. Colonel Crawford, who commanded, was taken in the pursuit and put to death by the Delawares, notwithstanding every means had been tried by an Indian officer [Matthew Elliott] present to save his life. This the Delawares declare they did in retaliation for the affair of Muskengum [the Gnadenhütten affffair].

I am sorry that the imprudence of the enemy has been the means of reviving the old savage custom of putting their prisoners to death, which with much pains and expense we had weaned the Indians from in this neighborhood. [*Butterfield, Washington-Irvine Correspondence, p. 372 fn.*]

Arent DePeyster Admonishes the Indians against Barbarities to Their Prisoners

AUGUST 6, 1782

❦ *Sir* [Alexander McKee]

It having been reported to me by Isaac Zeans that the Shawneese and the Delawares push their retaliation to great lengths by putting all their prisoners to death, whereby if not prevented they will throw an odium upon their friends the English, as well as prevent their Father [DePeyster] from receiving the Necessary intelligence of the enemy's motions, so essential to carry on the service for their mutual interests; I must therefore reiterate my injunctions to you of representing to the Chiefs that such a mode of War will by no means be countenanced by their English father, who is ever ready to assist them against the common Enemy, provided they avoid Cruelties. Tell them I shall be under the Necessity of recalling the Troops (who must be tired of such scenes of Cruelty) provided they persist, and assure them that the Lake Indians complain much of their late treatment to the three prisoners taken near the Falls.

I am confident, Sir, that you and the Officers do all in your power to instill humane principles into the Indians; it is however a duty incumbent on me to beg of you once more to speak to the Chiefs and assure them that Brigad^r General Powell was greatly shock'd at hearing the reports spread by Zeans and strongly recommends that it may be stopp'd. He is, however, still in hopes that Zeans must have greatly exaggerated Matters. [*Claus Papers, M.G. 19, F 1, III, Public Archives of Canada.*]

8 ETHAN ALLEN DEFIES CONGRESS OVER THE ISSUE OF VERMONT'S SEPARATE INDEPENDENCE: CHARLES INGLIS WRITES GALLOWAY ABOUT THE INTERNAL DISSENSION

The role in the Revolution of the more active of the six Allen brothers, Ethan, Ira, and Levi, has long confronted historians with a problem in interpretation, and the adjectives applied to them, such as "quixotic," "notorious," or "impetuous," are indicative of the quandary the Allens' actions have presented.[1] Before the Revolution they promoted a reign of terror against farmers who settled in the New Hampshire Grants under New York titles. They fought against the British in 1775 at Ticonderoga, at Crown Point, and in Canada, but worked to unite Vermont with British Canada in 1778-1781 in order to secure the New Hampshire titles. In 1777 Vermont declared its independence, but, as the Reverend Charles Inglis reports, Congress refused to receive its delegates. Ethan Allen was leading a rebellion within a rebellion which the British might exploit.

DECEMBER 12, 1778

❏ Ethan Allen is now Governor of the newly erected State Vermont. That State had sent Delegates to Congress, but were refused admittance— nay, Congress was so ungracious as to deny their Right to Independence, which was taken in high Dudgeon by that *potent* State. It consists of about 30 Millions of acres, west of Connecticut River, formerly claimed by New Hampshire, but lately annexed to this Province [New York] by the Crown. Allen has lately published a Manifesto, declaring he will maintain the Independence of his State to the last Extremity; and the Assembly of this Province, [N.Y.], in their address to Governor Clinton, have not long since threatened Vengeance against these *Rebellious Subjects;* so that if the Matter is not compromised this Winter, there will be an internal War, and an Expedition will go against Vermont next Spring. It would not be difficult to bring over Allen; and this might be a matter of great consequence in case any Diversion were made on the side of Canada next Summer. [*Riker, Memoria, vol. XV, pp. 4-5, N.Y. Public Library.*]

---

[1] Hugh F. Rankin, *The American Revolution,* New York: 1964, p. 54; Jack M. Sosin, *The Revolutionary Frontier, 1763-1783,* New York: 1967, p. 26; Henry S. Commager and Richard B. Morris, *The Spirit of Seventy-Six,* Indianapolis: 1958, vol. I, p. 186. "No one has ever succeeded in unraveling the tangled strands of patriotism, state pride, self-seeking, war, speculation and diplomacy, which the Allen brothers of Vermont wove during these years." Ibid., vol. I, p. 326.

9   JUSTUS SHERWOOD'S *JOURNAL* SHOWS ETHAN AND IRA
ALLEN READY TO DETACH VERMONT AND ABANDON THE
REVOLUTIONARY CAUSE

The British were not slow to exploit the disaffection in the New Hampshire
Grants and started negotiations with Ethan Allen. Sir Henry Clinton wrote
to the Commander of the British forces in Canada, General Frederick
Haldimand, September 9, 1779, that he had sent a trusted emissary to
Allen to propose separate provincial status for Vermont if he would join
the British and that Allen had agreed, indicating he would bring at least
four thousand men to the British side.[1] Colonel Beverly Robinson also
made an overture to Allen in a letter of March 30, 1780, one of the several
Robinson letters which Allen turned over to Congress in March 1781. In
late October 1780, Justus Sherwood was sent to carry on the negotiations
with Allen under the guise of transacting a prisoner exchange which would
be accompanied by a cease-fire along the Vermont and New York borders.
Vermont historians, denying Allen's defection, explain his motive as a
move to protect Vermont from invasion or to induce Congress to accept
Vermont as a state.

Justus Sherwood, like the Allens, was a grantee in the New Hampshire Grants but one who early and actively demonstrated his loyalty to
Britain. A native of Connecticut, he moved to New Haven, Vermont, in
1774, intending to settle down to farming. Under harassment from the
Bennington Committee of Safety in 1776 he fled to Canada. Accepting a
captain's commission, he recruited a company for the Queen's Loyal Rangers under Lieutenant Colonel John Peters and joined in the Battle of Saratoga. Sherwood was then twenty-five and only at the start of his usefulness
to Britain. He fought at Bennington as well as at Saratoga; he served as a
British agent; he built the Loyal Blockhouse on Hero's Island in Lake
Champlain. His most important mission, however, was the conduct of
negotiations with Ethan Allen which are detailed in the extract from his
Journal. At the close of the war he received a grant of a thousand acres in
Ontario, retiring permanently to Canada, a noted figure among the Loyal-
ists on the Upper St. Lawrence.

[1] H. S. Wardner, ed., "The Journal of a Loyalist Spy," *The Vermonter,* vol. 28, pp.
61–62. Also Vermont Historical Society *Collections,* vol. II, p. 70 ff.

❐ Miller's Bay, 26th Octo., 1780: Rec^d His Excellency's Instructions for a negociation with the State of Vermont and Major Carleton's order to proceed to that State with a Flag. Sett off at 7 o'clock in the evening with a Drum, Fife and five privates. . .

28th: . . . proceeded to the head of East Bay. Landed at 4 afternoon. Sett off Immediately with the Drum, Fife and two men, leaving a flag and three men with the Cutter. Arriv^d at 7 o'c at Co. [Samuel] Herrick's Camp, a frontier post of 300 men at the Mills about 4 miles west of the Block house in Castleton. Was blindfolded & led to Co. Herrick's room. He demanded my Business. I inform^d him I was sent by Maj^r Carleton to Negotiate A Cartel for Exchange of Prisoners; that I had Dispatches from his Excellency Genl Haldiman and from Maj^r Carleton to Govr Chidenton and Genl Allen. Co. Herrick said Genl Allen Commanded at Castleton and that my Dispatches should be forwarded without delay. . . .

29th: Had an Interview with Genl Allen. After breakfast remov^d to Major [Isaac] Clark's house. Genl Allen summons^d a Council of ten field officers & inform^d them that I was sent to negociate a Cartel for Exchange of prisoners but as he found my instructions was somewhat Discresionary he desir^d (previous to Entering on business) to have a short Conference with me by himself that he might Clearly Understand my ideas & assist me in Explaining my Business to them. To this they Consented. I walk^d out with him and after Much Conversation inform^d him that I had Some Business of importance with him, but before I communicated it must request his honour as a gentleman that, should it not please him, he would take no Advantage of me nor Ever mention it while I remain^d in the Country. He said he would, if it was no Damn^d Arnold Plan to Sell his Country and his own honour by Betraying the trust repos^d in him. I reply^d my Business with him was in my opinion of a very honourable nature but, as I did not know how far his opinion & mine would differ, Should insist on his most Sacred promise that in whatever Light he might view it he would not expose me. To this after some Consideration he consented.

I then proceeded to tell him that Genl Haldiman was no stranger to their disputes with the other states respecting Jurisdiction and that His excellency was perfectly well informed of all that had lately pass^d between Congress and Vermont and of the fix^d intentions of Congress never to their being a Separate State; that from Genl Allen's Common Character

His Excellency Genl Haldiman Conceiv^d he was a man of too much Good Sense and solid reason; that Congress was only duping them and waited for a favourable opportunity to Crush them and that this was a proper time for them to Cast off the Congress yoke and resume their former Allegience to the King of Great Britain, by doing which they would secure to themselves those Privileges they had so long Contended for with Newyork. I then made known to him the Genl's proposals, then expressed my own anxious desire that they would accept of them. Assuring him that it was not from any selfish motives of my own but the tender sentiments of regard and friendship which I felt for the people of Vermont that induc^d me to wish them to accept of those proposals and to save themselves from that General Calamity that seem^d to threaten the other states.

Genl Allen observ^d that the proposals so far as they respected his personal promotion had not the weight of a straw with him, that he was not to be purchas^d at any rate, that he had been offer^d a L^t. Col's Commission on Condition of Changing sides while in Captivity which he refus^d, as he ever meant to be govern^d by the strictest rule of honour and Justice; but that, since the proposals seem^d Materially to Concern the whole people of Vermont whose Lybertys & propertys for a number of years past was much dearer to him than his own life, he should take them into very Serious Consideration.

He then said we must go in as we had already been too long togeather, that I might rest assur^d our present conference should remain a secret. He advis^d me to tell the Council that I had Explain^d my business Respecting the Cartel to him and desire him to Assist me in Communicating it to them.

We then went in and he laid Genl Haldiman's and Maj^r Carleton's letters before the Council. . . . They appeared well satisfyd with the contents of them except that part . . . respecting the Limits of the truce. Some of them suspected a design on the frontiers of Newyork while the negociation was on foot with Vermont. To this I became a pledge on the part of Gov^t that no movement would be made on the offencive by Maj^r Carleton. . . . After this Genl Allen wrote Circular letters to all his officers commanding Frontier Posts, informing them of the truce and Cesation of hostilitys, Commanding them to call in all their scouts and not to suffer any more to be sent out during the present truce. . . .

I had another short conference with Genl Allen this evening.

30th: Conversed with him till 2 o'Clock free from any restraint. Inform^d him I had brou^t written proposals and had secreted them but could procure them if he thought proper. He advis[d] me to let them rest. Said he would send me Co. Ira Allen and Maj[r] Fay; that he would open the Business to them so far that I might venture to shew them the proposals but said I must not communicate to them the whole of our Conversation; must be very cautious not to Exhibit the smallest Idea to them of anything than Neutrality nor Even that to take place Except Congress force them to it by their Tyranny and obstinate refusal to grant Vermont her just and lawful Claims.

The Result of our Several Conferences is as follows: Gen[l] Allen says he finds himself surrounded with enemys on Every side, the most inveterate is Newyork; that he is heartily weary of war and wishes once more to enjoy the sweets of peace and devote himself to his Philosophical studys; that he is sincerely attach[d] to the Lybertys of America and cannot cherish the remotest thought of bearing arms against his country while Virtuously contending for Lyberty and that nothing (short of the same Tyrannical proceedings from Congress towards Vermont which Congress at first complain[d] of suffering from Great Britain and the manifest appearance of the total subversion of the Lyberties & propertys of many thousands of honest people now inhabitants of Vermont), should Ever induce him to harbour the most distant Idea of deviating from the cause he has been so long engaged in and for which he has been so great a sufferer; and was he ever so much inclin[d] to take part with Britain, it is not in his power to do it at present, for in the first place, should he now make a declaration of that nature, his own people would cutt off his head; but, allowing he could reconcile them to such a plan, they are by no means able to defend themselves nor is Gen[l] Haldiman at present able to send a force sufficient to protect them; that he is positive the Neighboring provinces would on such an occasion pour in upon them thirty thousand men in thirty days time.

That being fully persuaded Congress never intends to acknowledge the Jurisdiction of Vermont but on the contrary has predetermined to support the Claims of Newyork, he intends shortly with the assistance of the Gov[r] and council to publish manifestos setting forth the Tyrannical proceedings of Congress and the necessity Vermont is under of declaring herself a neutral state; that after these have had time to circulate, should Congress continue obstinate, Vermont will Declare herself a neutral power free and independent of any other power on Earth and will invite all people to a free trade with her. He expects this will draw on him the resentment and force of Congress. He shall closely watch their motions and as soon as he finds they are raising a force against him he will march with his own Brigade and take possession of Albany and invite all friends to the Lybertys of America to join him. He is confident he shall soon be reinforced by some thousands from the Frontiers of the Neighboring Provinces already well attach^d to the State of Vermont. Especially the County Berkshire, which is the Northern frontier of Massachussetts, has a well regulated Militia of near 4000 men and from their vicinity and likeness of manners are very anxious to join and make part of Vermont State. If he should be obliged to retreat from Albany he will make a stand at Ticonderoga; then, rather than be ruin^d by Congress will ask help from Canada and thinks it will be much for the Interest of Gov^t that Genl Haldiman then has a force not only sufficient to support him but to establish a post at Albany and another at No. 4 [Charlestown, N.H.] or Bennington which he thinks will require at least 20,000 men. This, he thinks, will be the readiest method of bringing the whole contest to a speedy decision in case Great Britain is able to command the seas and prevent a French invasion by the way of St. Lawrence. But if Britain is not able to do this he has no dependence on any protection Genl Haldiman can offer. Hopes, therefore, that he will consider how far he is able to support Vermont.

. . . He will expect to command his own forces, Vermont must be a Gov^t separate from and Independent of any other Province in America, must choose their own Civil Officers and Representatives, be entitl^d to all the Privileges offer^d to the other states by the King's Commissioners; the Newhampshire Grants as charter^d by Benning Wentworth Govr of Newhampshire must be confirm^d free from any Patents or Claims from Newyork or any other Province.

He desires me to inform His Excellency that a revolution of this nature must be a work of time, that it is impossible to bring so many different minds into one channel on a sudden, hopes he will not be anxious to hurry matters on too fast as that will certainly ruin the whole. . . .

If Congress should grant Vermont a seat in that Assembly as a Separate State, this negociation to be at an end & kept secret on both sides. [*Wardner, ed., "Journal of a Loyalist Spy," Vermonter, vol. XXVIII, pp. 76–80.*]

10 "WHY DO I CALL THE LADY FORTUNE BY HARD NAMES?":
LEVI ALLEN'S LETTER SUGGESTS AN ANSWER TO HIS
REPEATED MISFORTUNES AND TO HIS QUESTIONABLE
LOYALTY

Levi Allen's conduct during the Revolution and immediately thereafter has
been especially puzzling. Was he just a renegade Whig, as indicated by
Ethan Allen's public condemnation of him, January 9, 1779, when Levi
joined the British cause?[1] Was he thereafter consistently a Loyalist, as his
wife claimed, or was his conduct too quixotic to put his loyalty above suspicion? His character offers eccentricities, his life some perplexing developments. After Ethan Allen's capture in 1775, Levi made every effort to
rescue him from prison; then quarreled with him, challenging him to pistols; then quickly effected reconciliation.[2] His business endeavors repeatedly turned sour. Several land ventures proved impractical. He lost £1,500
in Florida land speculation by the treaty of peace. In 1786 he settled in St.
Johns, proposing to start a factory for beaver hats, which he conceived of
as a world center, without considering customs regulations. At the same
time he had grandiose plans to settle over two thousand families in the Eastern Townships of Quebec. He naïvely submitted six different lists of names,
rather than signatures, with his petitions. The Canadian council refused
his request, observing that five of the lists appeared to have been written by
the same hand and the sixth was deficient in addresses. In 1792, he petitioned for a grant of Barford Township only to be rebuffed again.[3] He was
always the injured party, plagued by hard luck. In the spring of 1789, he
was in London promoting again the scheme of joining Vermont to the British Empire. The secrecy of his mission suited his temperament, and he
liked to write under various aliases, such as Lewis Alden, Dr. Alonzo, and

[1] Mary G. Nye, ed., *State Papers of Vermont*, vol. VI (1941), p. 21. Ethan Allen asked
the Court to confiscate his brother's Vermont property and the court complied.
[2] Ethan Allen excused his brother for avoiding the confrontation, explaining that friends
"put in their arguments that Levi was only mad through long confinement." Levi had
been jailed for six months for Loyalist activities around New York. Zadoc Thompson,
"Ethan Allen and his Family," Vermont *Historical Gaz.,* A. M. Hemenway, ed., vol. I,
p. 562. Thompson describes him as an "obstinate and wayward youth." Ibid.
[3] Minutes of the Executive Council, March 20, 1788, *Public Records and Archives of
Ontario,* 1928. Levi Allen's *Statement,* no date, *Wilbur Collection,* University of Vermont, Burlington, Vermont.

Bumper B.[4] Toward the end of his life he became "more dissipated than usual" and died in a final debauch in Burlington's debtors' prison.[5]

After his death in 1801, when his wife petitioned for a grant in Barford Township, she offered an explanation for the suspicions leveled against his loyalty. She stated that from the time of her marriage in 1779 he had "uniformly and unequivocally expressed a partiality for the British government, and at all times, when in the exercise of reason, given it a decided preference." The suspicions against him arose, she wrote, from "a mental derangement. . . ." He had "at times and more especially within a few years . . . exhibited evident marks of a deranged mind and at such times had said and done things which he never would have said or done in the full possession of reason. . ."[6] Certain irregularities of expression, incoherence, and queer reactions shown in the following letter from Levi to his wife suggest the possibility that Nancy Allen's statement that Levi suffered from mental illness was not farfetched and offers the explanation of his bizarre behavior.

SAVANNAH, MARCH 28TH 1795

❡ *Dear Girl.*

As the Post will not go out (to the northward) till tuesday next, I wish to have a little more confab with you tho' at a distance. Tho' Matters of course must appear extremely odd to you, yet Please to consider I have been absent much longer and returned with the Affection I carried away. . . .

The matter or thing that has kept too good Friends so long apart

---

[4] Series S., CXXV Barford; Series Q, XIC, *Canadian State Papers*, pp. 78–79. See Ben Cockerhan, "Levi Allen," Master's Thesis, Vermont University, Burlington. William C. Harrington, a friend of the Allens, said that Levi had always been "exantrick" in some things, although he contended that his mind failed only three or four months before his death. Ibid., ser. S, vol. XLIX, p. 79.

[5] Samuel Hitchcock to Lucy Hitchcock, December 16, 1801, Missouri Historical Society, St. Louis, Mo.

[6] Nancy Allen to Lt. Governor Robert S. Milnes, February 10, 1802, *Lower Canada Land Papers*, R. G. 1, L3, vol. 30, 15,933–15,934. It was recommended that she be paid £30 for the survey and given 1,200 acres in any of the townships set apart for Loyalists (August 14, 1802). *CO Records*, Q Series, M. G. 11, vol. 91, p. 79. Chilton Williamson says Levi's mind gave way "under the impact of successive disappointments." *Vermont in Quandry*, p. 240. The reverse could be true, that the illness brought about the frustrations, and jeopardized his family relationships.

grew out of Misfortune and had its Origin in disappointment. If matters had succeeded which was all but done in the year 1789, there had been no Seperation between us more than those Short turns of business for a week or so, which rather nurrishes & Cherrishes love, like too Fond lovers, for I know no difference between a good agreeable Weded pair and two true constant lovers; (except in one respect).

I Flatter myself you will agree with me that I am no Part of a miser and have enough now in Vermont (exclusive of the large scattered Sums due me in different Parts of America.) If I only thought so, and there is no other way or means given whereby one can come to the knowledge of enough, or a competancy of Property (which by the bie is a very uncertain word) and if I had not one shilling, and only had a good rich faithful *Friend* to give motion and activity to my Plans, I beg leave to say a man as well acquainted with the world as I am, and would industerously attend, with calling to his aid and assistance two Sisters, Temperance & Frugality, a Fortune might Soon be Obtained, especially if one has, as thank God I have, my health in the South of the States, Provided no extra Misfortune Interfeared.

But my ambition and Success in the bloom & career of the early Part of life, badly Prepaired my mind to Brook misfortunes and my education so far from being Scholastic or Scientific, it was a Proper wild Gander education Obtained flying.

My loosing £1500 Stg. in Florida, not by Harrycanes, or other convulsions in *nature,* but by an outright robery of those then in Power, would never materially [have] disturbed my happiness, If I could have divested my mind of the ungodly and shameful Injury.

But the impression was two deeply made to be easily eradicated. Together with Some ungenerous reflections touching Patriotism, and unrighteous Attempts, made in my absence, of Confiscation; at the time I was spending my money & time to Save the lives of the *defenders* of our *Country,* and actually suffered imprisonment for such an heinous *Crime.* Together with many concomitant matters too prolix for a letter, all coming at once or in immediate Succession one after the Other in true Order of *Damnation,* as devised by *Belzebub,* the prince of *Devils,* and *Chairman of the Hell-fired* Committee assembled to devise what to do with honest *Job,* who had unfortunately fell into their power.

This was too much for one to beare whose heart was not callast, but too sensibly felt the misfortune of Others to be indiferent to Such Extra ones of his *own.*

And the leers & flirts of the favourites of that Fickle inconstant Jade *Fortune* was Particularly distresing, and the more so having so recently been one of the Court Party and attended the M (illegible) levies.——— Why do I call the Lady *Fortune* by hard names? No no, I will again assume the character of *a man* and do honor to human Nature & learn to bear with Fortitude the Ills I cannot avoid—and march in the Rout[e] of Nature Till I come to the first Cause (God) and look not back on the Past, but regard the two Sisters, Fortune & Misfortune, both alike, Firmly believing the former often comes as a Curse and the latter as a Blessing. The latter I say has done many good things; she has made Philosophers, Poets, and what is more, fools Wise, and pray what has her Sister done? why Just ye reverse; She has Set the World mad, and Debauched half mankind, and laughed at them when she had done. Curse on her impudence.

Hark, here deare Nancy, I cannot at Present write a good letter Because I am low Spirited, & no one can force nature.

Dear Nancy Yours Sincearly
LEVI ALLEN.
[*Allen Papers, Bailey Library, Univ. Vt.*]

The Southern Theater

I GEORGIA LOYALISTS TAKE HEART

In the early years of the war British reversals in the South, especially the defeat of the Loyalist Highlanders at Moore's Creek Bridge in North Carolina (February 29, 1776) and the failure of British naval forces to reduce Fort Moultrie on Sullivan's Island and to push an attack on Charleston (June 1776), had kept the South in rebel hands. The friends of government had sought to lie low, moving quietly to country places, keeping their Toryism under the surface. Yet the Carolinas and Georgia continued to be vulnerable to British invasion. Their principal towns, Savannah and Charleston, were accessible by sea; St. Augustine, Florida, furnished a convenient staging area for British troops; and the region, especially the backcountry, was thought to be the promised land of Tories. As the Lieutenant Governor of Georgia, John Graham, noted: "The best friends of Great Britain are in the back parts of Carolina and Georgia."[1]

[1] To General James Grant, 1775. See Hugh McCall, *The History of Georgia*, Savannah: 1812–1816, vol. II, p. 57.

When Sir Henry Clinton took command from General Howe (May 8, 1778), he was under orders to take advantage of those assets and to plan a Southern campaign. Before 1778 closed and for the next two years, events in the far South gave new heart to the Southern Tories. Christmastime 1778 marked the seeming turn in British fortune.

Britain's move against the South culminated in two of her most startling successes of the war, the easy taking of Savannah (December 29, 1778) and the siege and occupation of Charleston two years later (May 12, 1780). As to Savannah, Lieutenant Colonel Archibald Campbell, recently exchanged as a prisoner of war for Ethan Allen, commanded a British fleet which was to coordinate its attack on the city from the water with the move of General Augustine Prevost, pressing from the south toward Sunbury on the Savannah River. Campbell's forces arrived at Tybee Island at the mouth of the river two days before Christmas, and six days later Savannah fell to the British. Sir James Wright resumed his post as Royal Governor. Although D'Estaing's fleet, in cooperation with General Benjamin Lincoln's rebel troops, laid siege to Savannah nine months later, it was not returned to rebel hands. Georgia remained under British control for 3½ years, until the evacuation of July 11, 1782, at the conclusion of the war.

STEPHEN DeLANCEY WRITES HIS WIFE THAT THE NEGROES IN SAVANNAH ARE INHUMANLY TREATED

Among the troops on Campbell's transports was the battalion of Lieutenant Colonel Stephen DeLancey, the thirty-one-year-old son of Brigadier General Oliver DeLancey.[1] Its function, after the first landing of troops at Gerridoe's Plantation, was to cover the landing place while other troops moved on Savannah. Two weeks after the capture of Savannah, DeLancey wrote a description of the engagement to his wife, Cornelia Barclay Delancey, in

[1] Stephen DeLancey (1748–1798) was educated in Europe and practiced law in New York until the outbreak of the Revolution. In 1783, he took his family to Annapolis Royal, Nova Scotia, where he served as a member of the Assembly. He resigned this office in 1789 in order to accept appointment as Chief Justice of the Bahamas. Two years before his death he became Governor of Tobago. He died at Portsmouth, New Hampshire, en route to England to visit his relatives.

New York, commenting freely both on the faulty American generalship and on the cruel treatment of the Negroes to which, he said, he could not become "habituated."

SAVANNAH JAN^Y 14TH 1779

❡ Long have I wish'd my dearest Cornelia for the Departure of a Vessel from this Place that I might communicate to you the glad Tidings of my Health and Safety but much more for the Arrival of one from N York that I might hear from you. How anxious every Hour passes that cannot indulge us with the Knowledge of the Situation of those we love, I flatter myself you have experienced. Tho' my dearest wife I wish you all the Happiness that you deserve or any Being is capable of experiencing, yet I cannot help owning (from the Frailty of Human Nature) that I should not be pleased at the Idea of your enjoying perfect Satisfaction in my Absence. Your Affection is the great Object of my Heart and while I possess that it will always furnish those Sentiments which will render my Presence necessary to you. Never since I was yours have I met with so great a Trial of Philosophy. What pleasure the external Objects here might afford me were you present with me, I will not pretend to say, but a mere military Life is for me a very dull Scene. I may say with a favorite Author of Yours, the inimitable Thompson,

"All my Labour is to kill the Time,
"And Labour dire it is, & weary woe

Our Passage was long and Tempestuous, seldom fair for twenty four Hours together and the slow Mode of sailing necessary to keep a fleet from separation renderd it very disagreably tedious. (I was agreably disapointed in not being in the least Sea Sick). After we had been at Sea more than a Month we arrived at the Light House at the Entrance of the River Savannah, from whence we proceeded to a Place near the Town in flat Boats and landed on a Causeway in a Rice Plantation which was form'd out of a Swamp on the Banks of the River. This narrow Passage led up to a House situated on an Eminence very steep. Had the Rebels been there in Force with Cannon, it would in my opinion have been impracticable to have made good the Landing. In Consequence of the very strong Ground, we should have been obliged to ascend in Opposition to the Rebels and [by] the narrow Passage thro' the Swamp in approaching the Eminence. But from great want of Generalship they had but thirty men at this strong Post. We had a Captain and three Men of the Light Infantry of the 71st Reg^t killed at this Place when the Rebels immediately retreated. The main Body of our Army then advanced towards the Town, on this Side of which the Rebels appear'd with a good Front, and we expected they would have behaved better than usual but were deceived. By a quick and well conducted March of the Light Infantry of the 71st and the New Corps, under the Command of Sir James Beard, round a Swamp, the Rebels were so intimidated that they fled with the utmost Consternation, leaving us in quick Possession of the Town. Forty Officers and upwards of Five hundred Men were killed or taken in a Space of Time almost incredible. We took Possession of the Town with the trifling Loss I first mention'd.

The Town of Savannah is situated on the Banks of the River of that Name on a Sand Bank of which your Shoes are full in crossing a Street. The Inhabitants have been extremely wealthy, as appears from the great Profusion of Elegant Furniture we found in the Town and the great Quantity of Cattle, Hogs, Poultry etc. with which their Plantations are stock'd. Almost all the People had deserted their Habitations but are daily coming in and receiving Protections for their Persons and Property. The Government here established is to the greatest Degree lenient, so that I conclude it is imagined they will be sooth'd into a Change of Sentiments and receive Money and Property as Greater Goods than Rebellion and Poverty. Our Troops are extended in different Ports upwards of thirty Miles from the Town along the River. My quarters are Eight Miles from the Town—a very bad House but Plenty of Provisions. Colonel [George] Brewerton is from the Regiment with a separate Command. At present not any Rebels are in arms in this Province. They have collected a small Force in South Carolina I suppose to prevent a Passage over the River. A Movement will soon take Place when we shall be sent, in Consequence of our Weakness to do Garrison Duty in the Town. General [Augustine] Provost with all the Troops from St. Augustine is but twelve Miles from this Place and expected before Night. Colonel Innes is Commandant of the Town here, for which Station he appears well adapted and gives universal Satisfaction. His Behavior is easy and affable and he dispatches Business in a very expeditious Manner. Captain Moore is Barrack Master, very usefull and also well adapted to it. I can at present communicate nothing of what is intended in the Military Line but by every Opportunity I shall inform you of all things within my Knowledge. I am now sitting with the Windows open without any Fire, although the Inhabitants have complain'd of the Severity of the Weather and I suppose you are ordering more Wood to the Fire.

The People here are sallow and in general disgusting. Pale faces and large swolen Bellies proceeding from the Fever and Ague seem to be the Characteristics of the Georgia Ladies and their Speech is so Negroish that I cannot help imagining that some of them cannot boast of a Number of Ancestors thoroughly White. This is not the Case with all; I am told they have fine Women tho I have seen very few. The Negro's and Negro Women are inhumanly treated, are two-thirds naked, and are very disgusting to the Eye and another Sense, Tho I begin to be more habituated to the Sight, yet I cannot be to the great Cruelty made Use of to the poor ignorant Wretches. Indeed the Title of the Overseer is a sufficient Explanation of the Whole. He is stiled a Negro Driver. These circumstances of Cruelty to these People render the Persons who exercise it disagreable, nay odious to me. When a Set of People can sit down enjoying all the Luxuries of Life without feeling the least Sensation or Compunction for the Sufferings of those poor Wretches whose Lives are render'd Miserable and Constitutions destroyed for those Purposes, I must conclude them Obdurate, Selfish, and Unfeeling to the greatest Degree imaginable. At what an Expence of Life and Happiness do we eat Rice and Sugar! One thing more I must add, that their Diet is almost entirely on Rice and sweet Potatoes as they are allowed Meat but once a Year.

I am ever wishing, my dearest wife, to be able to send to you for your Use some of the Good things that we have in the greatest Profusion here and which I am much afraid you will want. Indeed it gives me great Pain to think that you want anything which I enjoy, for tho I am a great advocate for the Principle of Selfishness as the prime Motive to Action in every Body, yet I can so far wrest the argument as to wish you to enjoy every thing to satisfy my feelings. By the next opportunity I shall transmit a Bill for Money, as my Expences here are very limited, and happy I shall be to be able to furnish you with any thing for your Ease and Happiness which the Narrowness of my Circumstances has too frequently prevented.

Present my Compliments to your Mother and my best Love to Nancy and Tom. Inform him that I depend on him to oversee everything for you, tho' I know his Love for you and Friendship for me will dictate the Utmost Assiduity for us; desire him to present my Love to Susan and tell her to prepare to romp with me when I come back. Remember me to Heathcote Johnston and all freinds. If Jacob behaves well, tell him I mention'd him.

God grant you my ever dear Wife uninterrupted Health and may you and my family be his peculiar Care and if it should be his Will to take any of our Children to himself may you be endued with Resolution to bear it as on you all my Happiness depends. I mean to write to Mrs. Cruger; if I do not, tell her nothing but something unavoidable could have prevented what my great Attachment and her Goodness would always dictate.

> I am My most dear Wife
> Yours
> *Sfn DeLancey*
> [*Courtesy of Mrs. Norman Duffield, Buffalo, N.Y.*]

ANN DeLANCEY CRUGER, EN ROUTE TO SAVANNAH, IS TAKEN PRISONER BY ONE OF D'ESTAING'S SHIPS

After Georgia seemed secure in British hands, Ann DeLancey Cruger, a sister of Stephen DeLancey, sailed from New York to join her husband, John Harris Cruger, lieutenant colonel of one of Oliver DeLancey's Loyalist battalions stationed in Savannah. When Colonel Cruger was subsequently moved to the difficult post at Ninety-Six, she followed him there. During the rebel siege of that post (May 22 to June 19, 1781), General Greene placed a guard at her residence to protect her, a Loyalist lady. She returned the favor by directing a rebel scouting party to the correct route to their own army.[1] In the following letter to her father, Brigadier General Oliver DeLancey, she told of her misfortunes en route, at the same time making some brusque comments on D'Estaing, the Marquis de Chabert, and on their British opponents, Generals Tryon and Leslie.

FEBRUARY 18, 1780

❆ *My Dear Sir*

. . . I gave you a description of my sufferings at sea. I shall not repeat the account till we meet as it is too disagreeable. I will only say I was very Ill, was for some time in expectation of being drown'd, and was, being

---

[1] Sabine, *Loyalists,* vol. I, p. 345.

near our Port, taken by the French and kept on board a Man of War four weeks, where I was treated with the utmost attention & politeness. The Marquis de Chabert was Captain, a sensible agreeable old Gentleman, — behaved to me like a father. Count de Estaing was not so civil. I sent him many messages but could not obtain his permission to go on shore an hour sooner than the other prisoners. His disappointment and his being badly wounded, I suppose, was the cause of his inhumanity. I agree with you, my dear sir, in thinking my escape from Sir James Wallaces ship a most fortunate event; they suffer'd more in the Storm than we did and had an engagement, which we had not.

I am sorry General Tryon is troublesome to you, his vanity always made him intolerable. The most friendly easy great man I have seen is General [Alexander] Leslie. I am much pleased with him. He seldom neglected visiting me once a day while he remained here.

Believe me Dear Sir your most affectionate

Obedient Daughter
Ann Cruger
[*Courtesy of Mrs. Norman Duffield, Buffalo.*]

2 CHARLESTON LOYALISTS ARE "CLAMOROUS FOR RETRIBUTIVE JUSTICE"

The occupation of Georgia led to new British moves to return South Carolina also to British allegiance. Twice before the British had threatened Charleston, first in June 1776, when Sir Henry Clinton and Admiral Sir Peter Parker had been repulsed by Colonel William Moultrie's garrison on Sullivan's Island, and secondly, in May 1779, when General Augustine Prevost had demanded the surrender of the city but had been obliged to withdraw at the approach of General Benjamin Lincoln's rebel troops. Now, however, nearly a year later (April 1780), the situation was reversed. It was General Lincoln's troops which were caught between Admiral Marriott Arbuthnot's cannon and Banastre Tarleton's Loyalist troops on shore, their escape corridor cut off. D'Estaing's fleet could no longer help, as it had left the American coast. The week of May 7 to May 12 saw the successive surrender of Fort Moultrie, of Lincoln's 5,000 troops and supplies, and finally of the city of Charleston—a British triumph of the first order. Although British and rebel successes and failures in other parts of the Carolinas seesawed for the next sixteen months, Charleston, as well as Savannah and St. Augustine, remained in British hands for the remainder of the war.

With the fall of Charleston it was now the Tories' turn to emerge from the obscurity of country retreats and boast their loyalty. A surprising number of outright rebels suddenly changed their colors and took the oath to the King, in the same way that many Tories had turned Whig when the rebels were in control. A Hessian officer, Captain Johann Hinrichs, commented in his diary: "The back-country people, saying they were tired of fighting have come in parties to surrender their arms voluntarily to different corps."[1] John Mathews, attending the Congress at Philadelphia, wrote of his discouragement over the disaffection to Thomas Bee, Lieutenant Governor of South Carolina: "It is distressing beyond expression to hear the accounts I do from all quarters of the disaffection (I can call their late conduct nothing else) of our back country people. Good God! is there nothing to be done that will tend either to perswaid or coerce them to do their duty? Indeed, my Dear Friend, the day is not to come it does not depend on our Militia's not turning out to repel your *present* danger, which may subject us to the imputation of a want of vigour. The brand is already fixed on us."[2] In Charleston itself, 110 prominent residents sent an address to Clinton and Arbuthnot of "warmest Congratulations on the Restoration of this Capital and Province to Great Britain."[3]

Some of the consistent Loyalists, those who during the rebel ascendancy had fled to country retreats rather than knuckle under or pretend a false espousal of the rebel cause, had suffered persecution and now demanded retribution. One of the royal placemen, former Attorney General James Simpson, was sent along with Clinton's army to feel the temper of the populace and report to Clinton on the prospects of Loyalist assistance and of reconciling the rebels to Britain. Simpson's report to Clinton three days after the surrender of Charleston indicates the extent of Loyalist resentment and forecasts the malevolent civil strife to follow.

[1] "Diary of Captain Hinrichs," May 28, 1780. See Bernhard Uhlendorf, ed., *The Siege of Charleston,* Ann Arbor: 1938, p. 303.
[2] January 1780, Ms. no. 52, The Library Society, Charleston.
[3] The list of Addressers appears in Barnet A. Elzas, *Leaves from my Historical Scrapbook,* Charleston: 1907–1908, p. 5. Also *Royal S. C. Gaz.,* Sept. 21, 1780.

The Southern Theater

James Simpson Reports to Sir Henry Clinton on the Disposition of the Charleston Inhabitants toward the Crown

MAY 15, 1780

❡ I have conversed with some of the people of the first fortunes in the province whose dispositions are as favourable as could be wished, from a conviction of their Error, and feeling too late the miseries their fatal Politiks have produced, with the necessity there is to head back the Paths by which they have been led to their destruction. I have seen others, who without reasoning upon the subject, or perhaps being incapable of it, but by being Tools to a faction, have been of great weight in keeping up the Flames of Rebellion, that now declare their inevitable Ruin will ensue unless that Government which they all acknowledge was preferable to any they can ever hope to establish is restored. There are others who still assert that their Cause was founded in Virtue, but that it is impossible to maintain it any longer. And some there are who say it ought never to be relinquished but by the general Consent of America. The Sentiments of the last two Classes I have only from report, for I have thought it proper to avoid a Conversation or Intercourse with any of them, unless it hath been sought for—and of the whole of them, I beg to be understood that I do not mean the Bulk of the People, but Individuals whose Influence would formerly have preponderated in turning the scale whatever way they inclined; and in drawing a comparison between the four Classes, the number and consequence of the two first by far exceed the last.

The Loyalists who have always adhered to the King's Government are not so numerous as I expected; besides those who have been drove from the Province there are many who left the Town and settled in the Country, where they found themselves less liable to persecution. Elated with their present Triumph, and resentful for their past Injuries, they are clamourous for retributive Justice, and affirm that the Province will never be settled in Peace until those People whose persecuting spirit hath caused such calamities to their fellow subjects shall receive the punishment their Iniquities deserve. Indeed, I am convinced there are some who are deservedly so obnoxious that whatever measures may be adopted by Government, it will be impossible for them to escape the Effects of private Resentment.

With respect to the lower Class of people (which with those I have above mentioned) will comprehend all the Inhabitants, I am convinced they will without trouble submit quietly to the Government that supports itself.

I am pretty confident that I am near the Truth in the above description, and that matters are not painted in more flattering terms than they deserve. The obvious consequences which appear to me are that it will be very practicable to re-establish the King's Government in S. Carolina. Altho' it will require both Time and address, whilst conviction operates upon those I first mentioned, Interest upon the second, and despair upon the third. Those whose madness would still prompt them to oppose it will sink of course, especially if that severe vengence which is so justly their due should be denounced & executed upon all those who under colour of their Tyrannical Laws, under which the blood of so many of H. M. faithfull subjects hath already been shed, in future should attempt to drag out the unwilling People to oppose the King's Government. If the terror they have excited was once removed, a few months would restore this country to its former good Government. [*Clinton Papers, Clements Library, Brown, "Simpson's Report. . . ," Journ. Southern Hist., vol. XXI, pp. 518-519.*]

WHIGS AND TORIES IN SOUTH CAROLINA HOPE THE FALL OF CHARLESTON WILL BRING "RESPITE FROM THE CALAMITIES OF WAR"; ROBERT GRAY'S OBSERVATIONS

The fall of Charleston was such a disaster to the Southern rebels that most of them believed their cause was lost as far as the Southern colonies were concerned. Robert Gray, former Justice of the Peace for Cheraws District and a colonel in the Provincials, described the mood of the people and the calm which followed as Whigs and Tories alike accepted the inevitable, hoping to return to their prewar situation. However, when the affable Brigadier General James Patterson was replaced as commandant of Charleston by the despotic Lieutenant Colonel Nisbet Balfour and British abuses became the order of the day, the rebels resumed their active disaffection. A few even chose the Provost dungeon in the cellar of the Exchange or a prison ship to taking the oath to Great Britain.

MARCH 1782

❡ The conquest of Charlestown was attended with the conquest of the back country because all the Continental troops in the Southern department were taken in that place except the party under Col Beaufort[1] [Abraham Buford] which was soon after cut to pieces at the Wexaws by Col. Tarlton. The people at that time not much accustomed to arms & finding no troops to support them submitted when they saw the Kings troops in possession of the back country. Posts were established at Augusta, Ninety-Six, Camden, [withdrawn] Cheraw Hill & Georgetown. The conquest of the Province was complete. The loyal part of the inhabitants being in a number about one third of the whole & these by no means the wealthest, readily took up arms to maintain the British government, the others also enrolled themselves in the Militia party because they believed the war to be at an end in the Southern provinces & partly to ingratiate themselves with the conquerors. They also fondly hoped that they would enjoy a respite from the Calamities of war—and that the restoration of the Kings Government would restore to them the happiness they enjoyed before the war began. With these views on both sides, the Whigs & Tories seemed to vie with each other in giving proof of the sincerity of their submission & a most profound calm succeeded. This was not confined only to the Country within the new established posts. The panic of the Whigs & the exultation of the Tories produced the same consequences in the back Country beyond the reach of the posts, the people in many places coming in from the distance of fifty miles to take the Oath of Allegiance or to surrender themselves prisoners on parole. All the inhabitants seemed intent upon cultivating their farms & making money. Great quantities of produce were sent to Charlestown & great numbers of wagons even from the mountains crowded the roads travelling in every direction.

This tranquility was of short duration. The abuses of the Army in taking the peoples Horses, Cattle & provisions in many cases without paying for them, abuses perhaps inseperable from a Military Government, disgusted the inhabitants, but this was by no means the principal cause of the disorders which followed. They flowed from another source, the disaffection of the Whigs. The establishment of the King's government naturally & unavoidably occasioned an entire change of Civil & Military officers throughout the province. A new set of men were elevated into power & place, whilst their predecessors in office were stripped of their consequence & sent to cultivate their plantations. The pangs of disappointed ambition

---

[1] Alexander R. Stoesen, "The British Occupation of Charleston, 1780-1782," *So. Car. Historical Mag.*, vol. LXIII, p. 74.

soon made these men view all our transactions with jaundiced eyes, and, as Gen[1] Gates' approach [July 1780] put an end to the hopes of tranquility they had at first expected to enjoy, they were in general, especially the Militia officers, determined to avail themselves of that opportunity to re-establish themselves in power, never doubting of Gen[1] Gates being able to effect it, as, like other men they easily believed what they eagerly wished for. Lord Cornwallis with great sagacity foresaw what followed. He instantly ordered all the leading Whigs who had been paroled to their plantations, to repair to Johns & James Island. [*Gray, "Observations . . ." So. Car. Hist. & Gen. Mag., vol. XI, pp. 140-141.*]

RIVINGTON'S *GAZETTE* PUBLICIZES THE "ELECTRICAL STROKE" WHICH THE FALL OF CHARLESTON SPARKED IN EUROPE

About six weeks after the occupation of Charleston the news of this British feat crossed the Atlantic and warmed the spirits of the Loyalist refugees in England. An unidentified gentleman in London reported to a friend in New York (July 4, 1780) the "electrical" impact of the victory, the implications of which the Loyalists in their rejoicing exaggerated. Rivington's *Gazette* lent itself readily to purveying the letter, thus continuing the Loyalist tone of his paper at the very time when he was serving Washington as a double agent, passing on information gleaned at his coffeehouse.[1]

SEPTEMBER 6, 1780

℄   Never was there a thicker gloom settled upon the minds of men than that which had overspread your friends during the interval Sir Henry remained before Charleston; our late glorious accounts from that quarter have had a contrary effect proportionably strong. Europe has felt the electrical stroke; the different powers have already fallen from the high and contemptuous tone they had assumed. France, so far from meditating to send any more troops or ships to cooperate with the Congress, would now most heartily rejoice at having those she *has* sent safe in her own camps and ports. God grant that their policies may be well founded. For their speculation was certainly this: Charleston was an object of the first magni-

[1] See pp. 327-332 for the Rivington story.

tude to the Congress, taken in the light of an issue, through which not only the most valuable products of the country were to pass, but of a channel of the most important communication; this the Congress stretched every nerve to defend; . . . but, notwithstanding their countenance and high-sounding menaces, they have been covered with disgrace and ruin, the credit of their money must in consequence be utterly annihilated, no new levies will go on, and their internal enemies will take courage from their embarrassments, and thicken round them. To commit herself therefore any further would be to promote her own destruction and dishonour. [*Royal Gaz., Sept. 6, 1780.*]

3 THE CAROLINA BACKCOUNTRY: THE PROMISED LAND OF TORIES

The Carolina backcountry may have been thought the promised land of Tories, but these independent farmers proved difficult to organize. Twice during the war Tory leaders called upon backcountry settlers to assemble for a fight, only to be soundly trounced. The first was at the beginning of the war, February 27, 1776, when Governor Josiah Martin thought former Regulators and Scotch Highlanders would rally to the King's colors and suppress the rebels. They failed to appear in the expected numbers, and were lacking in arms, equipment, and organization. As a result, the premature encounter at Moore's Creek Bridge turned into a prime military fiasco. The second truly Loyalist battle came toward the end of the fighting, October 7, 1780, and was an even more far-reaching disaster for the King's cause.

KING'S MOUNTAIN: "HAD IT NOT BEEN COVERED WITH WOODS . . . ": ALEXANDER CHESNEY EXPLAINS HOW THE TREES GAVE THE REBELS AN ADVANTAGE

Despite the fall of Charleston and the subsequent establishment of British posts in the backcountry, at Ninety-Six, Cheraw, Camden, and Georgetown, there was no respite from the calamities of war. Within a month rebel militia crushed a Loyalist uprising of 1,300 men at Ramseur's Mills (June

20); then the British forces scored a success at Camden (August 16). More significant was the encounter of Loyalist militia under the British officer, Major Patrick Ferguson with rebel militia at King's Mountain (October 7). Ferguson, boastful and intrepid, compounded his mistakes and allowed his army, stationed on an elevation of the Blue Ridge Mountains, to be encircled and annihilated. He himself fell under a rain of rifle shot. The disaster marked the turning point of the war in the Southern theater, for Cornwallis was now obliged to postpone his push northward and withdraw into South Carolina instead. It was a portent, ominous for the Loyalists, of the final dénouement of the war. Alexander Chesney, Ferguson's Loyalist Adjutant General, in his *Memoirs* ascribes the catastrophe to the disadvantage of rocky terrain and heavy woods, good for guerilla tactics and rifles of the enemy, but not for the bayonet charges of the Loyalists. However, far more was at fault than terrain—poor judgment of Cornwallis in approving an expedition with less than a thousand troops, and the incompetence and carelessness of Major Ferguson, who failed to withdraw before superior forces when he had the chance. Thus a non-Loyalist commander brought discredit to the military capacity of an all-Loyalist force, engaged in an all-American battle, Loyalists against their countrymen.

1780

❆ Octr. 4th. Our spies from Holsteen as well as some left at the Gap of the mountains brought us word that the Rebel force amounted to 3,000 men; on which we retreated along the north side of Broad river, and sent the waggons along the south side as far as Cherokeeford, where they joined us. We marched to King's Mountain and there camped with a view of approaching Lord Cornwallis' army and receiving support. By Coll. Ferguson's orders I sent expresses to the Militia Officers to join us here, but we were attacked (Octr. 7th) before any support arrived by 1500 picked men from Gilbert's-town under the command of Colls. Cleveland, Selby and Campbell, all of whom were armed with Rifles, well mounted, and of course could move with the utmost celerity. So rapid was the attack that I was in the act of dismounting to report that all was quiet and the pickets on the alert when we heard their firing about a half mile off. I immediately paraded the men and posted the officers. During this short interval I received a wound which however did not prevent my doing duty; and on going towards my horse I found he had been killed by the first discharge.

King's Mountain from its height would have enabled us to oppose a superior force with advantage had it not been covered with wood which sheltered the Americans and enabled them to fight in their favourite manner. In fact after driving in our piquets they were able to advance in three divisions under separate leaders to the crest of the hill in perfect safety untill they took post and opened an irregular but destructive fire from behind trees and other cover. Coll. Cleveland's was first perceived and repulsed by a charge made by Coll. Ferguson. Coll. Selby's next and met a similar fate, being driven down the hill; last the detachment under Col. Campbell and by desire of Coll. Ferguson I presented a different front which opposed it with success. By this time the Americans who had been repulsed regained their former stations and, sheltered behind trees, poured in an irregular, destructive fire. In this manner the engagement was maintained an hour, the mountainiers flying whenever there was danger of being charged by the Bayonet, and returning again so soon as the British detachment had faced about to repel another of their parties. Col. Ferguson was at last recognized by his gallantry, although wearing a hunting shirt and fell pierced by seven balls at the moment he had killed the American Coll. Williams with his left hand (the right being useless.)

I had just rallied the troops a second time by Ferguson's orders when Capt. [Abraham] De Peyster succeeded to the command and after gave up and sent out a flag of truce, but as the Americans resumed their fire afterwards ours was also renewed under the supposition that they would give no quarter. And a dreadful havoc took place until the flag was sent out a second time, then the work of destruction closed. The Americans surrounded us with double lines, and we grounded arms with the loss of one-third our numbers. I had been wounded by the first fire but was so much occupied that I scarcely felt it until the action was over. We passed the night on the spot where we surrendered amidst the dead and groans of the dying who had not either surgical aid or water to quench their thirst. Early next morning we marched at a rapid pace towards Gilbert's-town between double lines of mounted Americans, the officers in the rear and obliged to carry two muskets each, which was my fate although wounded and stripped of my shoes and silver buckles in an inclement season without a cover or provisions until Monday night when an ear of Indian corn was served to each. At Gilbert's-town a mock tryal was held and 24 sentenced to death, 10 of whom suffered before the approach of Tarleton's force obliged them to move towards the Yadkin cutting and striking us by the road in a savage manner. Coll. Cleaveland then (Octr. 11th) offered to enlarge me on condition that I would teach his regiment for one month the exercise practised by Coll. Ferguson which I refused, although he swore I should suffer death for it at the Morovian town. Luckily his threat was not put to the test as I had the good fortune to make my escape one evening when close to that place. In the hurry to get off I took the wrong road and did not discover my error until I found I was close to the Morovian town. I then retraced my steps until close to the pickets I had left and taking a fresh departure I crossed the Yadkin river before morning, and proceeded through the woods towards home. John Weedyman, one of my company, had supplied me with a pair of shoes, which were of great use on this occasion, but as he remained a prisoner I never had the opportunity of making him a return.

The first night I slept in the woods. The next day I was supported by haws, grapes, &c., as I could find them in the woods.

The second and third days in pushing through the woods to get to a ford, I heard a noise of some people (whom I knew to be Americans by white paper in their hats) on which I lay down and was so close to them that I could have touched one of their horses in passing. Fortunately I was not observed, and soon after crossed the creek after them. I then made for the mountains in order to be guided by the Apalachian range and get over the rivers with greater facility. After crossing Broad river I met one Heron who had been with me in King's Mountain and who had with some others taken flight early in the action, putting white papers in their hats, by which disgraceful strategem they got through the American lines. I passed the night at Heron's house and once before at another man's on whom I could depend. From both I took some provisions; the other nights I slept out; I do not remember the number exactly but must have been nearly a fortnight.

Octr. 31st I reached home on the 31st October. I found that the Americans had left me little. My wife had a son on the 20th whom I named William which was all the christening he had. [*Williams, ed., "Memoirs . . . Alexander Chesney," Tenn. Hist. Mag., vol. VII, pp. 58-59.*]

LEVI SMITH NARROWLY ESCAPES HANGING ON REBECCA MOTTE'S GATE

The internecine warfare in South Carolina continued its inhuman course, with both sides committing brutalities and excusing them as retribution for some outrage committed by their opponents. When the rebels controlled South Carolina it was the Loyalists who suffered from harsh laws and persecution. After the British conquest of Charleston (May 12, 1780) and the backcountry, it was the rebels who were the victims of Loyalist revenge. Plunder, imprisonment, sequestration of their estates, and execution were measures used to retaliate. When the rebels retook the outposts in South Carolina (May–September 1781) and finally entered Charleston (December 14, 1782), the Loyalists once again experienced retribution.

It was extremely difficult in the backcountry of South Carolina to identify Tories with any certainty, but it was commonly known that they were numerous. A man could be a Loyalist one day and a rebel the next, depending upon the expediency of the situation. Fear, as much as principle, created Tories. So also did greed and ambition among those who believed the rebel cause could never succeed. The wavering Tory, the cowards, and the grabbers—all part of the unsophisticated backcountry folk—were easily fooled and subjected to taunting. As the British posts across South Carolina were reoccupied without civil government's being restored, the Whigs made sport of these Tories, baiting them, deceiving them, and even ruthlessly murdering them. Ninety Tories, part of a group led by Dr. John Pyle trying to reach Cornwallis in Hillsborough, North Carolina, mistook the green jackets of Colonel Henry Lee's legion for the green uniforms of Tarleton's men and were treacherously massacred (February 1781).[1] The chance to get even with Tarleton's butcheries turned Lee and his men into unreasoning barbarians.

At Fort Motte, a British post on the Congaree River recovered by the rebels on May 12, Colonel Lee continued his bloodthirsty sport by hanging a few Tories on Rebecca Motte's fence. Levi Smith, a Tory who miraculously escaped the fate of the rest, tells his own story, carried in the Charleston Tory paper, the *Royal Gazette*.

[1] Hugh F. Rankin, *The American Revolution*, New York: 1964, pp. 278–279.

❡ *Gentlemen,*

By one of your late papers, I perceive that Colonel Hayne's unhappy case[1] has made some noise in England. This confirms the truth of an assertion I have often heard made that nothing is less understood there than the true state of affairs in this country, which is certainly not at all surprising, when we consider that our enemies are indefatigable in propagating and spreading accounts of every circumstance by which they think themselves aggrieved or improperly treated by our Government, while a uniform silence prevails on our side, under the harshest usage, and although we have had by far the greatest reason to complain.

The gentle and humane treatment which the Rebel prisoners in our hands receive from us is well known; but it is by no means equally well known that our militia, when prisoners to them, are in general treated in the most cruel manner. I beg leave, through the channel of your paper, to make known to the world the usage which I and many other prisoners received from General Greene's army last summer. . . .

I was born in Bedford county in Virginia and settled as a merchant in this province in 1774, near Col. Thompson's in Amelia Township. After the reduction of this country by British arms in 1780, I took an active part in favour of Government and on the 12th of October I received a commission to act as a Justice of Peace from Col. Balfour, the commandant of this place. In February, 1781, after Lord Cornwallis had marched into North Carolina, Lord Rawdon, who commanded on the frontiers of this province, applied to me to procure him intelligence of the movements of Sumpter and the other Rebel partizans on the western frontier. From this time I gave his Lordship, whose headquarters were at Camden, all the information I could procure and, to prevent accident from my letters being lost, I kept copies of those I sent to Camden and also preserved such as I received from thence. About this time a plundering party of the enemy, having robbed my

---

[1] Isaac Hayne was taken in arms at the head of a rebel regiment of militia. When Charleston surrendered to the British he was paroled on taking the oath of allegiance to the King. He was told he would not be required to bear arms against the United States, but was later ordered into the British army. He felt that this was a violation of the terms of his taking the oath, releasing him from it. Thereupon he rejoined the American militia. Consequently, the British, on retaking him, executed him as a traitor (August 8, 1781). The patriots were bent on reprisals for this execution, as he was a young, popular figure. *Royal Gaz.,* Aug. 8, 1781, Apr. 10, 17, 1782.

store, which was on the north side of the Congaree River, near M'Cord's Ferry, and finding neither my life nor my property secure in that situation, I removed my effects to a house within two hundred yards of Fort Motte on the opposite side of the river. The fort was commanded by Captain M'Pherson of DeLancey's corps and had a garrison of British troops and militia. That gentleman appointed me to take command of the militia in the fort until a commission in the proper form could be procured from Lord Rawdon. Shortly after, General Greene, having marched to Camden, detached Col. Lee with his legion to join Gen. Marion with his brigade of Rebel militia from the country betwixt Santee and Pedee, with orders to Gen. Marion to invest Fort Watson on Wright's Bluff on the north side of Santee. Having reduced that post Marion crossed Santee on the night of the 8th of May and invested Fort Motte next morning about 10 o'clock.

Having no suspicion of any enemy being then near me, I had walked down from the fort to my own house to breakfast, when a party of Lee's cavalry under the command of Capt. Rodolph rode up suddenly and made me a prisoner. I told him I hoped to be treated as an officer and a gentleman. He assured me I had nothing to fear on that score and then rode off, leaving me in charge with a Cadet called Lee, generally known among them by the name of Little Lee. This gentleman immediately ordered the dragoons to strip me, which they soon did, leaving me nothing but my shirt. Then they set out for Col. Thompson's where Gen. Marion lay, which was about a mile distant, and rode at a hard trot, making me run before them. As my breath and feet soon began to fail, they wounded me with their swords in three places in the head to make me keep up. It was in vain to beg for mercy and interest them to moderate their speed. It only served to increase their rage and redouble their blows. As I grew weaker I fell several times, but they continued to beat me until I got up again. When I reached General Marion's camp I fainted, being quite spent with fatigue. I was then given in charge to the Quarter Guard and had a supply of decent cloaths from Mrs. Thompson. Next morning I was accused by one William Cooper from Peedee. . . .

During the siege of the fort I was treated with humanity and indulgence being suffered to walk about during the day with only Lieut. Cooper as a guard. Sometimes we went a fishing in a canoe . . . and every day I dined in my own house. . . . Except that my house was plundered and my property destroyed, I was treated in all other respects as a gentleman and had no suspicion of the dreadful doom that was allotted for me.

On the 14th in the afternoon, the house in the fort being set on fire by the enemy, the garrison was compelled to surrender at discretion. The regulars and militia were instantly plundered of their cloaths and some of the latter were even stripped of their shirts. They were all, except the regular officers, confined at Col. Thompson's mill-house at the foot of the hill on which the fort stood. These last remained with Col. Lee and the other continental officers.

A little after sunset Colonel Lee sent Little Lee to the mill-house for Lieut. Fulker of the militia, with orders to carry him to the fort and hang him on the gate of Mrs. Motte's fence. This unfortunate young man, who did not exceed nineteen years of age, was accused of being the cause of the death of a Mrs. Tate on Poplar Creek, who was turned out of her house when in the small-pox, by which she catched cold and died. Her husband, after having taken protection from us, joined General Marion along with several others. . . . As they often crossed Santee in small parties and committed depredations and murders, for which purpose they received intelligence from their families who often concealed them, Capt. M'Pherson had sent Lieut. Fulker to their place, ordering them to remove twenty miles from the river before a certain day. . . . Fulker utterly denied his being the cause of her death and begged he might be brought to trial to make his innocence appear, but that was refused him and Little Lee told him it was in vain to expect mercy. . . . He was accordingly carried to the gate where he was stripped naked and hanged without a trial or even a hearing in his own defense. When he was dead and cut down, Col. Lee sent the same messenger for John Jackson, a private militia man and ordered him to prepare for death, accusing him of having carried expresses for the King's troops and having killed in action one of Gen. Sumpter's men. . . . The poor man begged to be brought to trial . . . but to no purpose. He was hurried off, stripped, and tied up about dark, and left hanging all night on the gate. . . . As soon as Jackson was cut down, Hugh Maskelly . . . was sent for and ordered to prepare for death. . . . Maskelly was immidiately stripped of his cloaths, and had an old dirty shirt tied round him, and was then turned off, as the others had been, without the slightest trial or hearing.

All this while I had no suspicion that I was doomed to the same fate. As I had been treated with so much indulgence, I expected to be sent to Charlestown along with the regular officers on parole, there to remain until exchanged. . . . These agreeable ideas did not last long. A serjeant and two privates of the Continentals came to the quarterguard and asked if one Levi

Smith was among the prisoners. I immediately came forward and avowed myself; but I leave your readers to guess the horror and astonishment with which I was seized when they told me they had orders from Col. Lee to carry me to Mrs. Motte's gate and hang me. I replied it was impossible; it could not be; but the serjeant answered he would shew me his authority, and produced a written order in these words: . . .

"Bring Levi Smith from the quarter guard and hang him."

I now found that I had not a moment to spare. I therefore begged one of the quarter guard to run to my house and desire my wife and children to meet me at the gallows and take their last farewell. The fellow instantly went off and I was delivered to the serjeant. When we began to ascend the hill on which the fort stood, my new guard desired me to strip, declaring they would have my cloaths. I very readily pulled off the coat from Mrs. Thompson but this did not satisfy them; they declared they would have my shirt also. I begged them not to treat me with so much indignity but wait till I was dead, but they swore they would have it then and wounded me slightly in two places with a bayonet upon which I pulled it off and delivered it to them. I now walked to the gallows, having no other cloaths on but a pair of trousers Mrs. Thompson had also given me. . . . Being arrived, I found Maskelly had just been turned off and my wife and children coming up. They were instantly ordered away by a captain Smith of the Continentals who desired them not to come within a hundred yards of the spot. An officer now rode up whom I took to be Col. Lee. . . . I asked him if it was lawful to hang a man without a trial and received for answer that I had got all the trial I need expect to get; that I had acted as a Justice of Peace and Militia Officer under the Crown, that I was an enemy to the United States, and that I had been the cause of Mrs. M'Cord's house at the ferry being burnt, . . . a transaction of which I knew nothing until two hours after the house was burned. I found that all protestations of my innocence were vain and that no appeal could be made to the Laws of Nations. . . . I heard one of the Continental Officers say to another, . . . "It is a shame to take the life of any man without a trial. This man, let him be the devil or what he will, ought to have had a trial."

I was now made ready for execution. The old dirty shirt was taken from Maskelly's body and wrapped round mine and my arms were pinioned. A number of indecent jokes were passed on Maskelly's naked body, and as he did not appear to be quite dead, some of the soldiers pulled down his feet to dispatch him quickly, the reason of which was that no rope could be got to hang me by and they were obliged to wait for Maskelly's being dead to get his halter for that purpose. In the mean time, as they did not use a cart and the gate was pretty low, . . . enquiry was made for a tall horse to mount me on. . . . Maskelly was now ordered to be cut down and I had nearly taken farewel of the world, when a sudden noise turned my attention to the outside of the crowd, where I perceived Gen. Marion on horseback with his sword drawn. He asked in a passion what they were doing there. The soldiers answered, "We are hanging them people, Sir." He then asked them who ordered them to hang any person. They replied, "Col. Lee." "I will let you know, damn you," replied Marion, "that I command here and not Col. Lee. Do you know that if you hang this man Lord Rawdon will hang a good man in his place, that he will hang Sam Cooper who is to be exchanged for him?" The General then ordered me to be returned to the quarter guard and I found that I was indebted for my life to Lieut. Cooper, who, . . . being apprehensive of what the consequences might be to Samuel Cooper, instantly went in quest of Gen. Marion, who arrived barely in time to save my life; but his interjection must have been too late if a spare rope could have been found for me when I came to the gallows.

I was now put in irons. . . . I continued at Mr. Colcock's until the 2d of June when I received a note from Mr. Williams, the Adjutant-General, commanding me to appear in the trenches next morning with a spade. I had now no choice left but either to submit to every species of indignity and perhaps to an ignominious death or else to endeavour to get out of their hands. I chose the latter. Strictly speaking, it was a breach of parole, although I never had received one. But when the treatment I suffered is considered, I fancy few will blame me for making my escape which I did that night. When I got into Orangeburgh district, I kept the road, . . . very much disguised by my dress, which consisted of Maskelly's hunting shirt and the old trousers I had on when brought to the gallows. At Dorchester I met Lord Rawdon . . . and returned with him.

Levi Smith
[*Royal Gaz., Apr. 17, 1782.*]

JOHN CRUDEN OF SOUTH CAROLINA OFFERS TO TRY GUERILLA TACTICS ON UPRIVER HAVENS FOR REBEL PRIVATEERS

All through the war American privateers harassed British shipping trading with the West Indies. They clung to the coast, hovered in the shallow inlets of South Carolina and Georgia, and pounced on British vessels which had the temerity to sail without a convoy. The captured ships were then burned or sent north as prize. The shallow water of these inlets prevented British armed ships from routing out these stealthy privateers. Meanwhile the British West Indies suffered from the interception of necessary supplies while the French West Indies benefited.[1] There were several attempts on the part of the Loyalists to counteract this plundering by securing letters of marque for Loyalist privateers, including some of shallow draft, but the British did not take full advantage of their help. Admiral Howe's dampening reaction was recorded by a disgusted Loyalist in a letter of February 7, 1778, to a friend in London:

"The Admiral was some months ago applied to for Letters of Marque and Commissions for Privateers, to ferret out a numerous nest of small craft, which go between the *Carolinas* and the *French West India-Islands,* and supply the whole Rebel continent. With great heat and emotion he exclaimed, 'Good God! will you never have done teazing me? will you leave no room for a Reconciliation?' Such are the Principles he acts upon; the Consequences speak aloud to every man for themselves."[2]

Toward the close of 1780 Clinton was told to employ "the zeal of his [the King's] faithful refugee subjects within the British lines in annoying the seacoasts of the revolted provinces and distressing their trade."[3] He accordingly set up a Board of Associated Loyalists (January 1781) to organize raids along the coast. The Board's overzealous activities proved an embarrassment to Clinton, and he rebuffed further Loyalist offers of help. John Cruden,[4] the Commissioner for Sequestered Estates in South Caroli-

---

[1] Hugh McCall, *History of Georgia,* Savannah: 1812-1816, vol. II, p. 388.

[2] *Historical Anecdotes, Civil and Military in a Series of Letters Written from America in the Years 1777 and 1778 to Different Persons in England.* By a Loyalist. London: 1779, p. 69.

[3] Germain to Clinton, April 21, 1780. *Historical Manuscripts Commission, Report on American Manuscripts in Britain.* London: 1904-1909, vol. II, p. 237.

[4] John Cruden, merchant, refused in March 1775 to sign the Association and was pronounced by the Committee of Safety unworthy of the rights of freemen, and was boy-

na, was one who endeavored to help by wresting control of the upper rivers and inlets from the rebels. After the rebel reconquest of the Carolina back-country,[5] and especially after Yorktown, Cruden's task of protecting up-river estates was a frustrating one.[6] Nonetheless he offered again to raise a guerilla corps of marines to suppress rebel privateers by hit-and-run tactics on their secluded havens. The excerpt from his letter to Sir Henry Clinton, February, 19, 1782, shows his surprise at British failure to exploit such Loyalist goodwill and competence.

FEBRUARY 19, 1782

❦ . . . As I have the honor of adressing your Excell^y permit me to mention a Circumstance that I presume you are not acquainted with. —Anxious to do my utmost for the good of my Country, I offered some time ago to raise a Corps to Consist of 700 *men* at my own expence but Col^l Balfour did not think himself Authorized to accept of the Offer without your Excell^ys previous Sanction —

I meant to raise them from Amongest the people that were employed by me in various parts of the Province, & who escap'd from the Barbarous Bendittie that Overrun the Country, and from the North and South Carolina Refugees, and by joining a few Companys of determined Negroes, and to employ them as a Corps of Independent Marriner. On board of Vessells properly Calculated for entering the Inlets on the Coast, and the men occasionally to land and take Post for such a time as might be necessary to distroy those *places* and Harbours that have become a Recepticle for Privateers and Trading Vessels. I have no earthly motive but my Country's good in this offer. I neither ask rank or pay untill your Excell^y thinks I am entitled to them. The knowledge I have of the people in the South^n Provinces leaves me no room to doubt that I should If your Excell^y approves of my *plan* make many good and Loyal men very usefull.

---

cotted. He was made Commissioner of Sequestered Estates September 16, 1780, carrying out Cornwallis's proclamation to sequester rebel estates. See McCrady, *South Carolina in the Revolution,* pp. 727–729 and Tarleton, *Campaigns,* p. 186.

[5] The British evacuated Ninety-Six, their last post in the South Carolina backcountry, in July 1781.

[6] "Narrative of John Cruden," *South Carolina Loyalists, Ford Collection,* N.Y. Public Library.

My Brother will have the honour of delivering this Letter. And I beg your Excell^y may be pleased to Signify to him whether I have the good fortune to propose what may be agreeable to you. [*Crary, Misc. Papers.*]

4 THE EDITORS OF THE ROYAL GAZETTE SIGN OFF

With the British evacuation of Charleston in view, the editors of *The Royal Gazette* sign off.

SEPTEMBER 7, 1782

❡ The Editors of the *Royal Gazette,* in order to apply themselves to the Settlement of their private Affairs, are under the Necessity of discontinuing their periodical Labours for the Entertainment and Information of the Publick. Should any Intelligence, however, that reflects Honour on the British Name be received before the Day arrives on which that direful Event shall happen, the Dread of which now fills every loyal Breast with Terror and Dismay, they trust that many will be found in this Garrison patriotick enough to hear with Pleasure whatever shall promote the GENERAL GOOD, while they, though a part of the same Whole, are labouring under every Species of Distress. In such Case the Editors of this Paper shall not be found deficient in the Performance of what can be required of them as a Duty, and which Gratitude will demand of them in return, for the many Favours they have received from a generous and indulgent Publick. [*Charleston Library Society, Microfilm for 1781-1782, Reel 12. N.Y. Historical Society.*]

Loyalists' Reactions to

Events of the War

Loyalists' reactions in general to the ups and downs of the war were mercurial, swinging from high optimism to extreme despondency. With their personal destinies on the line, they responded to events with more passion than reason. The Battle of Long Island made them overconfident that the war would be short; Burgoyne's capitulation precipitated an acute dejection. Their optimistic mood a few months before Saratoga was reflected in the opinion of the Reverend Thomas B. Chandler, eminent New Jersey rector, that "the Force of the Rebellion is nearly spent . . . a Submission of the Colonies to legal Authority may soon be expected. Such an Event must give Transport to Millions and to no one greater than to me, who am hourly experiencing the cruel Effects of this unrighteous Banishment from my Family and Country. . . ."[1]

[1] To John Moore at New York, June 14, 1777, *John Moore Collection, 1755-1785.* Courtesy Chicago Historical Society.

[294]

No event of the war evoked such apprehension as the French Alliance and the widening of civil conflict into a European war. The steady fall of stocks on the London Exchange for a fortnight was hardly an adequate barometer of the gloomy spirits of the Loyalists, who now saw reconciliation improbable and victory postponed. Some Loyalists never lost hope for British arms or at least for a peace which would keep the Colonies within the Empire and restore their homes, careers, and fortunes. Colonel John Hamilton's remark six months after Yorktown, when peace negotiations were already under way, that the loss of Cornwallis's army was no reason to mourn forecast the blow which the terms of peace would mean to the Loyalists. The full realization of the sacrifice which would be exacted for their constancy to the Crown came slowly.

I "OH MY POOR HEART!": EDWARD OXNARD AGONIZES OVER THE BURNING OF FALMOUTH AND SUBSEQUENT REVERSES OF A DESTRUCTIVE WAR

Shortly after the rebellion broke out in Falmouth (Portland), Edward Oxnard left the town and sought refuge in London. He arrived August 17, 1775, making it his home in exile until April 30, 1785. The following year he returned and opened a business with his brother, Thomas, a former collector of customs in Falmouth. Both brothers had been proscribed by the Massachusetts Act of 1778 and had lost their property by the Absentee Act of 1782. By returning from banishment in 1784 Thomas had violated Massachusetts law. He was tried, convicted, and jailed. He secured a writ of habeas corpus on the ground that the treaty of peace had superseded and annulled a state law which conflicted with it. His successful challenge of Massachusetts law brought his freedom and enabled the brothers to pursue their business in Falmouth, despite animosities.

Edward Oxnard, like Samuel Curwen, kept a journal during his exile, revealing the diversions used to pass the wearisome years and the typical reactions of a Loyalist in London to the distant events of the war.

❡ Dec. 18, 1775—Mr. [Daniel] Silsbee called on me & informed me of the disagreeable news of the burning of the town of Falmouth. Oh my poor heart, how can I support the tidings; my tenderest connections driven to the extremes of poverty & distress by the acts of designing villains. I spent a most melancholy day. . . .

May 2, 1776—Received the disagreeable intelligence that General Howe had been obliged to evacuate Boston. My feelings on this occasion are such that I lack words to express them. To divert our melancholy we strolled to Cashaltin, one of the pleasantest villages in England. . . .

Aug. 22, 1776—This day the news came of Gen. Clinton⁵ ill success in South Carolina, the loss of two hundred killed & wounded & the burning of the ship Actaeon & another vessel. . . . I wish my own spirits were good, but they have been much depressed for ten days past. . . .

Oct. 23, 1776—At home till 12. Then to Mr. [Jonathan] Sewall⁵ & there heard that Gen. Howe had landed at York on the 15 Sepᵗ. & the provincials endeavoring to retreat, meet with great slaughter. It is further stated that he had taken post half a mile from their strong works. . . . There was great joy thereat. . . .

Oct. 29, 1776—The rumors of a war with France gain ground. The citizens are much alarmed & stocks are falling fast from the great fears of a French War. . . .

Nov. 3, 1776—Received advices from Boston that the inhabitants were in a very melancholy condition and that paper money was refused to be taken. Returned home to dine. Spent the evening at the club. . . .

Nov. 7, 1776—Went to the New England Coffee house to read the papers. Am much surprised to see how the NE papers misrepresent matters of fact, as for instance the battle of Long Island. The Club at Col. Murrays. Won 1 s. . . .

—This day is set apart by government as a day of fasting and prayer for the sins of the people, & that it would please Heaven to prosper his majesty⁵ arms against his subjects in America. The day has been kept more sacredly than I have ever known the observance of Sunday. . . .

Feb. 11, 1777—Spent the day at home. An extract said to be from a New York paper has much alarmed the people. It is as follows: "Wednesday morning last, one of the Hessian brigades, stationed at Trenton, was surprised by a large body of rebels, and after an engagement which lasted for a little time, between three and four hundred made good their retreat. The whole loss is computed to be about nine hundred men." . . .

March 17, 1777—St. Patrick's day, multitudes of Irishmen in the streets with green in their hats. Went into the city & called at the NE Coffee house, where I heard that the states had elected Genˡ Washington *Lord Protector.* . . .

July 30, 1777—This day I complete my thirtieth year of age. May Heaven grant me the happy sight of my native land before the return of another birth day. Driven by the unhappy situation of my country to seek that peace in a foreign clime which was denied me in my own—my anxiety, since I left it, words cannot express. Oh God! Whatever afflictions thou shalt see fit to lay upon me—grant me the resolution & fortitude to support them manfully. . . .

Nov. 20, 1777—Went to the House of Commons to hear the debates upon the king^s speech. . . . It was 3 o'clk before the usher of the Black rod came to acquaint the House that his Majesty waited for them. The Speaker preceeded by the Mace bearer & followed by a number of the members attended, & after being gone about twenty minutes returned, and having commanded silence, read to the House the King Speech, which being finished, a short pause succeeded.

Lord Hyde then rose & after a short speech moved the address, which was Seconded by Sir Gilbert Elliot. They represented the necessity of prosecuting the war & that the nation had nothing to fear from the other powers of Europe; that the manufacturers were fully employed, and that Commerce had been but little injured so that the people were abundantly able and could well afford to carry it on. On the part of the opposition, Lord Granby rose and after shewing the inexpediency of continuing the war & observing how little had been accomplished by the most able commanders in the service during the course of three campaigns, moved an amendment to the usual address, praying his majesty to order an immediate cessation of hostilities to be continued until some plan for a perpetual union between the mother country & its colonies could be definitely arranged.

His motion was seconded by Geo. Johnson. Mr. Butler & Honble Charles Fox joined in the discussion. The former, a very rapid speaker, deals too much in tropes and figures; the latter is by far the most formidable. He is strong & nervous in his language, but too apt to be scurrilous.

Lord North was the last speaker & convinced me that he was a good statesman & an able minister. Lord Germaine is clear & distinct in his expressions, but is far from being the eloquent speaker I have heard him described. [*Oxnard, "Diary of a Loyalist," N.E. Hist. & Gen. Reg, vol. XXVI, p. 5ff.*]

2 "HELTER SKELTER OUT OF TOWN": PETER DUBOIS INFORMS
CADWALLADER COLDEN ABOUT THE REBEL RETREAT FROM
NEW YORK

Peter DuBois, a New York City Loyalist whose estate was confiscated
in 1779, was active in land deals in the previous decade and saw service
as a colonel of a corps of Loyalists from New York under Sir John Johnson.
He was a good friend of Cadwallader Colden, writing him often of rebel
activities and denouncing the proceedings of the Committee of Safety.
Here he reports to him on the Battle of Long Island and the retreat of
Washington's forces.

SEPTEMBER 16, 1776

❡   . . . It becomes a business of a very hazardous Nature here to Speak
or Write with any degree of Freedom of Public Occurances. And I assure
you it is Exceedingly difficult To Arrive at the truth, Such a Number of
People, and of the better Sort too, being Engaged in the Suppression of
It. However, this I believe May be depended on: That the Provincials lost
between 1500 and 2000 Men in the Action on Long Island, about 7 or
800 of which were kill'd and wounded—That the [rebel] Maryland and
Pensilvania Batal^{ns} behav'd with distinguish'd bravery as did one of the
Jersey Battalions and Coll^{o} Lasher's—but the N. England Troops Most
Shamefully—That Lord Stirling [William Alexander] outshone all the
General Officers in Calmness and Intrepedity and exhibited a pattern of
Gallantry to his Successors, But is a prisoner on board The Eagle Man of
War—That the Retreat from Long Island was a Wise, Necessary and Prudent Measure, as the Provincial Engineers had not take the Precaution to
secure any of the Commanding heighths. The Possessions acquired of them
by the Regulars gave them the full and absolute Command of the Provincial Lines and the Island battery which would have Enabled them to Cut
off all Supplies as well as their Retreat in a very Short time—That the
Retreat was well Conducted, as they brought off all the Men and Some
pieces of their Artillery. . . .

You will undoubtedly have heard that Lord Howe and the General
have had an Interview with a Committee of Delegates from Congress. As
yet Nothing is known with certainty of what passed between them—A
Gentleman who was at Princetown the day the delegates went thro'it on

their Return, told me, he was Informed there that the Delegates had said to one of their particular friends that, having been very politely Received By his Lordship and dined with him, The General, and the Hessian General, the latter after having drank one glass of Wine after dinner Retired. Shortly after, his Lordship open'd the Business by asking the Gent^m Whether it was the Unalterable Determination of Congress to Adhere To the System of Independency They had Lately Adopt'd. And being Answer'd in the affirmative His Lordship then Said there was an End then to all Negotiation and of Consequence of all Hopes of an Amicable Accomodation for the present. . . .

The British Troops took possession of This City yesterday afternoon, Struck The Continental Flag on the Fort, and hoisted British Colours. It appears also that a Landing was Effected near Kip's Bay under Cover of the fire of Two Men of War. But what Number are Kill'd or prisoners it is Impossible any body sho^d know. One of The Committee who is Just Return'd from a Ride towards Powles Hook in Quest of Truth says Those who have Escaped came off in Such a Cursed fright that he believes from the incoherence of most of their Tales they must have been out of their Senses; that from the Representations of the Most Calm and Composed among them he Learned a General Order has been Issued on Saturday Late in the Evening for all Troops in N.Y. to Parade by 5 o'clock in the Morning with their Baggage and proceed to Fort Washington. That as those Troops consisted of Genl Putnam's Brigade, That Genl came down to Town at Midnight to See the orders Executed, that the Assembling the Troops with their Baggage and *Plunder* passed away the Time till near Eight oClock, when the Yankees told Their General They were Desperately hungry and Must Cer-tain-ly Eat before they Could March—whereupon the kind Goodnatured Genl Indulged his Neighbours' Children to go and get their Breakfast with the Rest of the Troops by which Means they all became Scatter'd thro'ut the Town. And in the Meantime the fireing Commenced at Kips's Bay when the Drums Beat to Arms and the Troops came Rushing together from all Quarters, took up their Arms and Helter Skelter out of Town as fast as foot cou'd carry them. And what's become of them Since, whether they Reach'd fort Washington All or in part or whether the Regulars made few or many prisoners was not to be Learnt with Certainty. [*McKesson Papers, vol. II, no. 26, N.Y. Historical Society.*]

3 "O CURSED AMBITION!" WASHINGTON IS MADE TO EX-
CLAIM IN THE LOYALISTS' FARCE ON THE BATTLE OF LONG
ISLAND

Following the British success on Long Island, a two-act farce called *The
Battle of Brooklyn,* presumably of Loyalist origin, was presented in New
York ridiculing the military incompetence of the rebel leadership. In the
play the rebel generals are denigrated, especially William Alexander (Lord
Stirling), who is represented as a heavy drinker, a liar, a counterfeiter, and
a pompous talker, and Washington, who is portrayed as being interested
in Lady Gates's servant. A shoemaker and rum retailer, elevated in the
play to colonels, are portrayed as ruffians plotting to secure the captured
horses and cattle and as being ready to cheat each other of the spoils. The
regular rebel troops are made out as cowards on the run, and colonels of
some New England regiments are portrayed as being on the point of mutiny
if boats were not ready for a safe retreat. Lady Gates exclaims: "O, Horatio!
that you should sully your laurels in the abominable cause of republican
Tyrants and Smugglers in power! To be a runnagate for such miscreants
almost distracts me."

When Stirling is asked for his military opinion on how to handle
Howe's troops on Long Island, he says he is for surrounding them and
hemming them in. Both Sullivan and Washington recognize the advice as
nonsense and continue with the following conversation in scene 4 as
Stirling leaves.

The farce also suggests that jealousy on the part of the Puritan
Church of the growing influence of Anglicanism, as well as covetousness
of Loyalists' estates, were the real motives behind the rebel movement.
Scene 5 between General Putnam and his chaplain, a New England parson,
attempts to propagandize these beliefs.

❮ *Act I, Scene 4: Brooklyn Church*
WASHINGTON: . . . After this fustian [Lord Stirling], a little sober reasoning, General Sullivan, may fit the mind for the doubtful events of war.
My apprehensions from the King's troops, believe me, are trifling, compared with the risque we run from the people of America at large. The
tyranny that our accursed usurpation has made necessary, which they now
feel and feeling, I fear, will soon make them see thro' the disguise. Their

rage, no doubt, will be heightened by the slaughter that will probably ensue; and we, as members of the Congress, fall the first victims of it. O Sullivan! My heart never consented to this ruin of my native country!

SULLIVAN: My dear General, the moments for reflection are elapsed and irrecoverable. Our safety is first in conquest; if that is denied to our endeavours, I am sure we can obtain better terms from our much injured Sovereign than from our more injured country. But wear a less rueful countenance; it is a proverb among the troops that their General is much melted down since the fleet arrived.

WASHINGTON: Our soldiers are a standing miracle to me; they desine sensibly upon matters that are unimportant to them and resign their powers of thinking to us in a case where their all is at stake and do not yet discover that we make them the engines of our power at the expence of all that is dear and sacred to them as men! Our hope, my dear Sullivan, is in you. . . .

Act I, Scene 5: A Room in a House in Brooklyn
THE REVEREND EBENEZER SNUFFLE: My dear General, the great, the important day advances; big with the fate of empire in the United States of America.

GENERAL PUTNAM: True, good Sir, and I laugh to think that, when we have established our power and driven these Red-coats into the sea, what ripping reformation you gentlemen will make in church affairs. Down goes Episcopacy and Quakerism; at least I hope you won't leave one broad-brim on the continent.

SNUFFLE: Why, really General, we shall be very apt to make free with those Gentlemen. We have long beheld with a jealous eye, the growing power of the Episcopal Clergy and considered them as the only obstacle to our becoming the heads of the Church in America, a dignity that so properly belongs to the Elect, and for which they have had the assurance to contend with the Lord's own people. As for the Quakers, who in general have joined the Tories against us, we shall not fail to produce "an ancient testimony" in their behalf; I mean the testimony of our forefathers, till with fines, whipping, imprisonment, and the gallows we have extirpated them from the face of the earth.

PUTNAM: In the meantime we shall not be behind-hand with the Tories, for as the best estates in America belong to them, it is but cooking up some new-fangled oath, which their squeamish consciences won't let them swallow; then whip go their estates, like a juggler's ninepence, and themselves to prison, to be hanged as traitors to the commonwealth . . .

SULLIVAN: . . . I shall aim to infuse such sentiments into the troops that our next meeting may be ushered in with greetings of congratulations. Till then, my dear General, farewel.
   Exit Sullivan.

WASHINGTON: Greetings of congratulation!—oh! could I congratulate myself on finding my lost peace of mind!—on the restoration of my honour! O! cursed ambition! What have I sacrificed to thee? An ambition too of foreign growth, obtruded upon me by the most artful, insinuating villains that ever enslaved a once free and happy country. To behold myself, against my principle and better judgment, made the tool of their diabolical determinations, to entail a war upon my fellow-subjects of America.—Heigh ho! (looking at his watch) Bless me, so late, and my engagements to a lady not complied with.
   Exit.

   [Battle of Brooklyn, A Farce . . . 1776,   Boston Atheneum,
   Copy N. Y. Pub. Lib.]

4   THE UNLUCKY HESSIAN AFFAIR

Andrew Elliot[1] believed that New Jersey would have submitted had it not been for the Unlucky Hessian Affair at Trenton.

SANDY HOOK   13 FEBY 1777

❈   *Dr Brother* [Sir Gilbert Elliot]
   . . . The unfortunate Affair at Trenton has thrown things for the present much back, but the Spring is coming on and things will take a proper turn again. Even now the Rebells are repulsed and lose many Men every week in the attacks they make upon our people that are obliged to go out for forage. Harrassing the troops in winter quarters and on such

[1] Andrew Elliot was Collector of Customs at New York.

occasions is just the trade of War in which the Rebells can act with any degree of seeming spirit, as it is just firing and retyring into the Woods and, as the Country is theirs and well known to them, they are sure of lodgings. These are advantages so wanting to our Army as to make every movement attend'd with danger. I dont like to mention what every Body hangs on but the spirit of Plundering that has broke out too Generally has been unfortunate, as it has in short hurt, dispirited, and disappointed many and descouraged numbers from leaving the Rebells and encouraged and determined others to do anything to keep at a distance certain ruin which plundering brings on those it falls on. I dare say this will be prevented as soon as Genl How takes the field as I hear he disapproves much of it. Had not that unlucky Hessian Affair happend at Trenton I'm persuad'd the Province of New Jersey, seeing themselves abandond by Washington and his Army, wou'd have befor this time revolted from the American connection and made a regular submission to the Commissioners who in that case coud have given them the terms which Great Br. intends for her Colonies, and I'm persuad'd from what has already been offerd that they are such terms as all America will jump at when once they can with propriety be made known, and the total submission of one province is, I think, the only event that will give an opening for that propriety and Jersey, as a small province and a pass to others, is, I think, the one that will of course be first brought to a sense of her duty. Our fleet are very Successfull and send in many prizes. This delay and seeming unlucky turn at Trenton, I believe, will turn out all for the best. It brings indeed distress and ruin on many of us but it teaches more plainly the Americans the lesson they ought to be masters of, that without the Friendship of G. B they can neither have trade nor necessaries of life. They are now all in rages [rags] and Dying for want of Salt, and the life of the Common people, rum, is now at Phila. 22/ pr Gallon in place of 3/2. [*Andrew Elliot Papers, N.Y. Historical Society.*]

5 MRS. JOHN PETERS IS READY TO SEND SIX MORE SONS AGAINST THE REBELS DESPITE THE BENNINGTON DEFEAT

John Peters was a nephew of the Reverend Samuel Peters, the Connecticut arch-Tory and early victim of the Sons of Liberty. John Peters, thirty-five years old at the outbreak of the Revolution, lived with his wife and seven children in Moortown in the disputed New York Grants. As a militia officer, Justice of the Peace, Judge of Common Pleas, Judge of Probates, and owner of several parcels of land with house and mills, he was in comfortable circumstances. In 1774, he was appointed to the First Continental Congress. While en route to Philadelphia he stopped to visit his uncle in Hebron, only to share with him the abuse meted out by the Sons of Liberty. His *Narrative* relates that he and Samuel Peters then and there "agreed in Opinion that the Bankrupt, dissenting Teachers and Smuglers meant to have a serious Rebellion and a Civil and Religious seperation from the Mother Country."

Peters refused to sign the covenant opposing the King's forces. Denounced by his own father as a Loyalist, he was mobbed and confined, and his house was searched several times. Worn down by these vexations, he decided to escape by the subterfuge of joining the rebel expedition to Montreal. He was thus in a position to pass information to the British, especially a timely warning that General Arnold had issued private orders to plunder and burn Montreal. As the expedition was returning to Crown Point during the last days of June 1776, Peters escaped and joined Carleton's forces, serving with them throughout the rest of the war.

Like his uncle, he has left a detailed narrative of his revolutionary experiences including the story of his family's flight to Lower Canada.

1777

❧ March 1777. Two deserters from the Rebel Country arrived at Montreal and informed that my property had been seiz'd, Confiscated, and myself outlawed, and that Mrs. Peters and the Children had been turned out of my House in the Month of January, 1777, that she and her Children had been sent of[f] in a Slay with one Bed by *Deacon* Bailey to Ticonderago 140 Miles thro' the Woods, Snow, Storm, and bad Roads. That Mrs. Peters, a small and delicate Woman, had been compelled to travel with her young Children in her Arms in deep Snow and Rain and were almost dead when they arrived at Ticonderago, where the Rebel General Wayne received them with humanity and used them kindly till April, when he sent her and her Children thirty Miles on their way to Canada and left them with three Weeks provisions in a deserted House near fifty Miles from any Inhabitants between them and Canada. Here she stayed Eighteen Days with her Children only (the oldest but fourteen Years), her Servant having been detained by Deacon Bailey (for which General Wayne said he ought to be damn'd). At length a British Boat discovered and carried them to a Vessel and thence to Saint Johns [St. Jean on the Richelieu River], where they all arrived on the 4th of May, 1777, well but naked and dirty.

May 6th, 1777, I met my Wife and Children at Saint Johns . . . with Cloathing and other necessarys and I carried them to Montreal by Water, over the Rapids at Chamblee. I had a French pilot and four Men (Sailors) in a Batteaux . . . Descending these Rapids we struck a Rock and the Stern of the Batteaux broke and open'd. We was near the trough of a Mill; the Sailors were in the water in a moment. It was lucky we was so nigh shore. I was but up to my middle in water to take Mrs. Peters on my Shoulders and landed her safe. In the meantime the Sailors had haul'd the broken boat so near shore as my eldest Son John (he was fourteen Years old) took the Youngest, my Seventh, in his Arms, and the sailors the rest. The French Pilot ran of[f] very fast. The sailors were for following and beating him, but I stopped them. They said he told them he knew every Rock. I told them it was true, for we had struck every one above where we were wreck'd. I put them in good humour & give them some Grogg. We lost a loaf of Sugar in the Water. Got another Batteaux from the Commanding Officer at Chamblee and went down the River Sorrel 40 Miles . . . Mr. McCummings . . . provided Lodgings and in the morning gave us a breakfast and we went up the River to Montreal. The reason we went by water was the roads were so bad. We could not by land get from St. Johns to Montreal . . .

August 16th, 1777, I commanded the Loyalists at Bennington, where I had 291 Men of my Regiment with me, and I lost above half of them in that Engagement. The action commenced about nine o'Clock in the Morning and continued till near four o'Clock afternoon, when we retired in much confusion. A little before the Royalists gave way, the Rebels pushed with a Strong party on the Front of the Loyalists where I commanded. As they were coming up I observed a Man fire at me, which I returned. He loaded again as he came up and discharged again at me, and, crying out: "Peters, you Damned Tory, I have got you," he rushed on me with his Bayonet, which entered just below my left Breast, but was turned by the Bone. By this time I was loaded and I saw that it was a Rebel Captain, and old School-fellow & Playmate, and a Couzin of my Wife's. Tho' his Bayonet was in my Body, I felt regret at being obliged to destroy him. . . .

The report of the defeat of the Royal Troops at Bennington reaching Montreal, Gen¹ McLean, Colonel of the 84th Regiment, went to Mrs. Peters and told her bad news had come from General Burgoynes Camp and that she must expect to hear of many being killed and wounded, but if Colonel Peters or her son were among them she must hold up with good courage and not despond, as he would see to care being taken of her and her Family that they should never want.

After some conversation in like manner, Gen¹ McLean thought proper to let her know that there was a report that Col¹ Peters and his Son were both wounded and since Dead. Mrs. Peters said "my calamaties are very great, but, thank God, they died doing their duty to their King and Country. I have Six Sons left who, as soon as they shall be able to bear Arms, I will send against the Rebels, while I and my Daughter will mourn for the Dead and pray for the living." [*"A Narrative of John Peters . . . ," Misc. Mss. P, N.Y. Historical Society.*]

6 LIEUTENANT COLONEL JOHN PETERS DEFENDS THE PROVINCIALS AND INDIANS AGAINST BURGOYNE'S CHARGES OF COWARDICE

The report of Burgoyne's capitulation produced a general gloom among the Loyalists, who now intensified their search for a scapegoat for British reverses. One Loyalist, John McAlpine, a Scottish farmer at Crown Point, admitted he had none too sanguine expectations for success at Saratoga because of the disaffected countryside and the faulty leadership, especially the arrogance of Burgoyne and his scorn for provincials. He had served in Canada under Carleton, Burgoyne, and others, and had already had an unpleasant encounter with Burgoyne's unreasonable anger. He was afraid, he wrote in his *Narrative,* that "over much trust was put in men who misled or betrayed our people, while our commanders distrusted and despised their loyal adherents and substantial friends."[1] Criticism of Bur-

---

[1] John M'Alpine, *Genuine Narratives and Concise Memoirs . . . Adventures of J. M'Alpine, a Native Highlander, 1773-1779.* Greenock: 1780 (reprinted 1883), p. 36, N.Y. Historical Society.

goyne, however, tended to be lost in the sharper and wider criticism of the Howes, on whom the Loyalists' bitterness exploded. Not so for those whom Burgoyne blamed. In addition to Germain and Howe, Burgoyne laid the defeat at Saratoga to the "ill conduct of the Indians, Canadians, and Provincials." The charge had to be answered. Among the John Peters papers is a defense of the provincials and the Indians, dated December 9, 1779, ascribed to John Peters, Lieutenant Colonel of the Queens Loyal Rangers, and a commander of the men who suffered severe casualties at Bennington.

DECEMBER 9, 1779

¶   Sir[1]

As much has been said about Gen[l] Burgoine & as he has wrote Letters to Canada & England "that his Defeat or Convention at Saratoga in 1777 was brought on him by the ill Conduct of the Indians, Canadians & Provincials on whom he found too late was no Dependence." I have presumed to (again) trouble you with what is said by the Provincials in Vindication of themselves & Indians which has been conveyed to me by various Letters from Canada. The substance of all is—that

Gen[l] Burgoine while at Quebec encouraged the Indians to join him under their own Captains and to fight the Enimy in their own way, the only Argument that could have prevailed with the Indians to join him. The General also encouraged the Canadians & Provincials (Refugees from other Provinces) to inlist & be under their own officers. Many Colonels with their Regiments composed of many Gentlemen went with the royal Army over the Lakes & landed at South bay when and where the Generals Humanity overcame his Engagement to the Indians (tho Indians were employed by the Enimy against him) and he told the indian Chief that he & his Men Should be hanged if they carried on the War in their own way—at which he cryed—Maw—Maw—that is, Death in the Pat[ois] whereupon they Set up their Howl, fled & left him. The General next told the Provincial Officers that, as they knew not the Art of War, his sa[r]jeants & officers should take the Command of their Men (& kept back their Commissions which had been promised them at Quebec when they should be on the Lake)—at which a Mutany sprung up among the Americans, and they resolved to follow the Indians Sooner than submit to the Order.

---

[1] Addressee unknown.

N.B. The Americans had no Boats, nor Provisions, and must obey the Order, or return to Canada through the Woods, or join the Rebels. In this Situation they obstinately chose to follow the Indians—whereupon an Order came that they should proceed with their Men as usual, (but their Commissions were not given). However the Americans (not the Indians) rejoin'd the royal Army and marched to Fort Miller about 40 Miles (on the Bank of Hudson's River where centred or met the three Roads from the three new England Colonies with that from New York & New Jersey and become one Road to the Lake Champlain or Southbay, by which Single Road the royal Army must have Supplies from Canada). Here (at Fort Miller) the General ordered a Party to proceed to Albany on Connecticut Road through Bennington only 60 miles out of the way in a wilderness where nothing could be obtained if they met with Success (and a hundred to one against Success). This Order was refused by several Provincial Colonels because they knew the certain Danger & the Mountains between which they must pass. General Fraiser gave Countenance to the Provincial Colonels, for which Gen¹ Burgoine told Gen¹ Fraizer, "when I want your Advice I shall ask for it." The General added that the Americans were Cowards and disobedient. At this Colonel Peters told the General that he was ready to obey his Orders but "we shall not return."

Peters was the guide to Bennington, but between the Mountains the Rebels, secreted behind Rocks & Trees, killed in half an Hour above one thousand Men. Peters returned to the royal Army at Saratoga with only 117 of his Regiment which contained 603. But a few Rebels were seen that Day.

The royal Army having left Fort Miller & passed the River to Saratoga, the rebels soon seized upon & kept Fort Miller which cut off all Intercourse between Canada & the royal Army. The General received Peters and those who had escaped Death at Bennington with great Goodness & Commendations. The Night before the Convention was signed the General gave Leave to Peters & others to return to Canada according to their Petition. 700 went off to Canada without Loss. After all these things the loyal Provincials were traduced by General Burgoine as the Cause of his Misfortunes—and he has Settled with Government but neglected Payment (contrary to his Promise) which was due, and *is due,* to the Canadians & provincials under his Command.

The Provincials further say that if Gen¹ Burgoine had condescended to the Advice of those who knew the Country and stayed at Fort Miller until he could hear from New York, all America could not have tarnished his Glory, nor hurt or Starved his Army. The Provincials think themselves ill treated, as their Characters are wounded by the General for whom they went to die, and offered to die, to save him if he would retreat from Saratoga to Fort Miller—a thing no way impossible in their Opinion.

They wish that Gen[l] Burgoine would consider this Question as he calls the rebel Americans *bold & brave*—how it comes to pass that loyal Americans are Cowards, when he (the General) knew that they had had Courage to leave their Wives & Children, their Friends & Property and turn Soldiers and go in the forefront of all his Army to receive the first Blows of the Enimy and be Guardians to each Wing & Rear—when in fact the loyal Provincials under his Command were killed ten to one of the royal Army. If anyone can consider us as Cowards for what we did under General Burgoine the General cannot prove it from our Obedience to his Command at Southbay which was called a Mutany.

N.B. Neglect is a Persecution that may be attended with equal bad Consequences to Insult or Reproach— [*John Peters Papers, Misc. Mss. P., N.Y. Historical Society.*]

7 "THE *COUP DE GRACE* IS GIVEN TO BRITISH GLORY!": SAMUEL CURWEN VIEWS THE FRENCH TREATY WITH FOREBODING

Of the many Loyalist writings, the *Journal and Letters of Samuel Curwen* is one of the most revealing and literate records of life in exile, a source of reliable information which has been thoroughly mined by scholars. Curwen, age sixty at the start of the war, was a judge of the Vice-Admiralty Court at Boston and a supporter of Governor Hutchinson. In May 1775, he left the country for London rather than recant his beliefs, thus, he was one of the earliest Loyalist refugees. As his unhappy exile wore on, he found life tedious and insipid, and he wrote Jonathan Sewall that he preferred insults and reproaches, even tar and feathers, to the anguish he suffered at separation from his home, his country, and his friends, which he had left "for what now appears to me a chimera."[1] His wife remained in Salem, calling her husband a renegade, a charge which created a breach between

[1] January 19, 1777, George A. Ward, ed., *The Journal and Letters of Samuel Curwen, 1775-1783,* Boston: 1864, p. 96.

them which was never fully healed. Curwen returned to Massachusetts in 1784 after nine years of exile and remained at Salem until his death in 1802. His wife's securing a substitute for him in the army and her continued residence in their Salem home saved him from attainder and the property from confiscation. Thus Curwen escaped the serious penalties imposed on other outspoken Loyalists. Nonetheless he felt he had been completely ruined and wrote Sewall that he would retreat to Nova Scotia as soon as he could settle his "deranged affairs."

Curwen was prone to look at the dark side of events, not just for himself but also for Britain and America. He viewed independence as folly and British failures as disasters for both America and Britain. News of the French Alliance produced exceptional gloom, but he correctly interpreted its significance as decisive in the contest, writing to his friend, Dr. George Russell, in Birmingham, July 13, 1778: "The prophetic falling off of the best jewel from our king's crown . . . is now accomplished by the loss of America, which I consider irrevocably gone."[2] To the Reverend Isaac Smith he referred to it as the *coup de grace.*

1778

❡ February 25. *To the Reverend Isaac Smith,* SIDMOUTH

This fatal treaty is at length executed; the *coup de grace* is given to British glory—its sun is set—alas, how fallen! How short-sighted is human wisdom, how weak is human power at best! The roar of the British lion will no more be heard; the French cock may now crow and strut undisturbed.

Americans that lately were humble supplicants to Great Britain for aid against a few French troops and Indian savages, disturbing her frontier settlements, have dared—what have they dared?—to renounce her authority; have set her power at defiance; reduced her commerce; defeated her armies; sunk her national credit, nay, insulted her coasts, established their independence in spite of all efforts, and, tell it not in Gath, allied itself to her natural, professed, and most dangerous enemy.

March 8. Yesterday the French Ambassador declared to Lord Weymouth that France had signed a treaty of amity and alliance, or of friendship and commerce, with the United States of America, who, said he, are in full possession of independence, as pronounced by them on the Fourth of July,

[2] Ibid., p. 197.

1776, without stipulating any exclusive advantages in favor of the French nation, and that the United States have reserved to themselves liberty of treating with every nation whatever, upon the same footing of especiality and reciprocity.

Being in the country, our advices from London are that a war with France is dreaded; there is fear of a general bankruptcy. It is further said the present Administration is almost universally reprobated—'tis in my mind a doubt whether in the dregs of the State less interested ministers can be found, though perhaps of more salutary politics; but the problem time only can solve. All men here love money and power too ardently to sacrifice either to interest or peace of State. 'Tis therefore, I fancy, equally indifferent who are or shall be our political cooks; the pottage, I fear, will be spoiled. Stocks have fallen to 59½, which has produced an almost universal panic. . . .

March 20. Heard the dreaded sound, war declared against France! It is reported the House of Lords is almost in a tumult, and that they implore the King to drive from his service his ministers, and take Lords Chatham, Camden, and Shelburne. [*Journal & Letters of Curwen, 4th ed., 1970, pp. 192-193, 196-197.*]

8   MISS REBECCA FRANKS ENJOYS THE GAIETY OF OCCUPIED
PHILADELPHIA. SHE COMPARES UNFAVORABLY THE LADIES OF
NEW YORK WITH THOSE OF HER OWN TOWN

One of the belles of Philadelphia, popular with British officers during the occupation, was Miss Rebecca Franks, the daughter of David Franks, a prominent merchant. About eighteen in 1778, she had the qualities needed for livening up social life for Howe's officers—wit, beauty, Loyalist sympathy, and no attachments—and thus was surfeited with beaux, as the first excerpt from her correspondence shows. This letter, written February 26, 1778, from Philadelphia, was directed to a friend, Mrs. Anne Harrison Paca, in Maryland, the wife of William Paca, a delegate to Congress. Although this family had chosen the opposite side in the conflict, Rebecca writes to her friend as freely as if there were no disagreement between them. She eventually married one of the British officers, Colonel Henry Johnson, who commanded at Stony Point when it was taken by Anthony

Wayne, and at the close of the war she went to live in England, where her husband in time inherited a baronetcy and a substantial estate.

The second excerpt is taken from a letter to her sister, Abigail, the wife of Andrew Hamilton III, the son of a member of the Pennsylvania Council bearing the same name. It was written from the VanHorn home in Flatbush in 1781, after her family sought refuge behind the British lines, and contains some frank comments and unfavorable comparisons of ladies in New York with those in her own town. It was intercepted and never reached Mrs. Hamilton. Both letters not only reveal social customs and styles of the day, but more particularly are representative of the superficial interests which occupied cultivated young ladies who had been educated primarily to be pleasing to men.

FEBRUARY 26, 1778

❡ *Dear Nancy*
. . . You can have no idea of the life of continued amusement I live in. I can scarce have a moment to myself. I have stole this while everybody is retired to dress for dinner. I am but just come from under Mr. J. Black's hands and most elegantly am I dressed for a ball this evening at Smith's where we have one every Thursday. You would not Know the room 'tis so much improv'd.

I wish to Heaven you were going with us this evening to judge for yourself. I spent Tuesday evening at Sir Wm Howes where we had a concert and Dance. I asked his leave to send you a Handkerchief to show the fashions. He very politely gave me permission to send anything you wanted, tho' I told him you were a Delegate's Lady. I want to get a pair of Buckles for your Brother Joe.

If I can't, tell him to be in the fashion he must get a pair of Harness ones. The Dress is more ridiculous and pretty than anything that ever I saw—great quantity of different coloured feathers on the head at a time besides a thousand other things. The Hair dress'd very high in the shape, Miss Vining's was the night we returned from Smiths—the Hat we found in your Mother's Closet wou'd be of a proper size. I have an afternoon cap with one wing—tho' I assure you I go less in the fashion than most of the Ladies—no being dress'd without a hoop. B. Bond makes her first appearance tonight at the rooms.

No loss for partners, even I am engaged to seven different gentlemen for you must know 'tis a fix'd rule never to dance but two dances at a time with the same person. Oh how I wish Mr. P. wou'd let you come in for a week or two—tell him I'll answer for your being let to return. I know you are as fond of a gay life as myself—you'd have an opportunity of rakeing as much as you choose either at Plays, Balls Concerts or Assemblys. I've been but 3 evenings alone since we mov'd to town. I begin now to be almost tired. Tell Mrs. Harrison she has got a gentleman in her house, who promises me not to let a single thing in it be hurt and I'm sure he'll keep his word—the family she left in it still remain. I had a long conversation about you the other evening with John Saunders. He is just the same as when you knew him—two or three more of your old acquaintances are in town such as Prideaux & Jock DeLancy they often ask after you. Is Mrs. White with you. I long to hear all that concerns you. Do pray try to get an opportunity. The clock is now striking four, and Moses is just going out to dinner— quite the Congress hours. Moses wrote to your Mother about her house six weeks ago. Did she get the letter. All your Philadelphia friends well and desire their loves—Mine to all in Maryland. . . .

FLATBUSH, SATURDAY 10 O'CLK. AUGUST 10th 1781

❡   *My Dear Abby,*

. . . You will think I have taken up my abode for the Summer at M[rs] V[an] Horn's, but this day I return to the disagreeable hot town— much against my will, and the inclinations of this family,—but I cannot bear Papa's being so much alone—nor will he be persuaded to quit it—tho' I am sure he can have no business to keep him. Two nights he staid with us, which is all I've seen of him since I left home. I am quite angry with him. . . .

You ask a description of the Miss V[an] Horn that was with me— Cornelia—she is in disposition as fine a girl as ever you saw—a great deal of good humour and good sense. Her person is too large for a beauty, in my opinion, and yet I am not partial to a little woman; her complection, eyes and teeth are very good, and a great quantity of light brown hair. (Entre nous, the girls of New York excell us Philadelphians in that particular and in their forms.) A sweet countenance and agreeable smile. Her feet, as you desire, I'll say nothing about—they are V[an] Horn's and what you'd call Willings. But her sister Kitty is the belle of the family I think, tho' some give the preference to Betsy. You'll ask how many thousand there are, only five. Kitty's form is much in the stile of our admir'd Mrs Galloway, but rather taller and larger—her complection very fine, and the finest hair I ever saw. Her teeth are beginning to decay, which is the case of most N[ew] Y[ork] girls after eighteen: and a great deal of elegance of manner. By the by, few New York ladies know how to entertain company in their own houses unless they introduce the card tables, except this family, (who are remarkable for their good sense and ease.) I don't know a woman or girl that can chat above half an hour, and that on the form of a cap, the colour of a ribbon or the set of a hoop-stay or jupon. I will do our ladies, that is Philadelphians, the justice to say they have more cleverness in the turn of an eye than the N[ew] Y[ork] girls have in their whole composition. With what ease, have I seen a Chew, a Penn, Oswald, Allen, and a thousand others entertain a large circle of both sexes, and the conversation without the aid of cards not flag or seem the least strain'd or stupid. Here, or more properly speaking in N[ew] Y[ork], you enter the room with a formal set curtsey and after the how do's, 'tis a fine, or a bad day, and those trifling nothings are finish'd, all's a dead calm 'till the cards are introduced, when you see pleasure dancing in the eyes of all the matrons and they seem to gain new life. The misses, if they have a favourite swain, frequently decline playing for the pleasure of making love—for to all appearances 'tis the ladies and not the gentlemen, that shew a preference nowadays. 'Tis here, I fancy, always leap year. For my part that am used to quite another mode of behaviour, I cannot help shewing my surprise, perhaps they call it ignorance, when I see a lady single out her pet to lean almost in his arms at an Assembly or play-house, (which I give my honour I have too often seen both in married and single), and to hear a lady confess a partiality for a man who perhaps she has not seen three times. Well, I declare such a gentleman is a delightful creature, and I could love him for my husband,—or I could marry such or such a person; and scandal says most who have been married, the advances have first come from the ladie's side, or she has got a male friend to introduce him and puff her off. 'Tis really the case, and with me they lose half their charms,—and I fancy there wou'd be more marriage was another mode adopted; but they've made the men so saucy that I sincerely believe the lowest Ensign thinks 'tis but ask, and have,—a red coat and smart epaulette is sufficient to secure a female heart. [*Penna. Mag. Hist. Biog., vol. XXIII, pp. 303-305.*]

9 "HAD ... THIS BEEN THE FEAST OF PEACE IT WOULD
HAVE BEEN VERY PROPER": JAMES PARKER OF VIRGINIA
RECOUNTS THE JOUSTING OF THE KNIGHTS AT
THE MISCHIANZA

A month before Howe's evacuation of Philadelphia an elaborate tribute
called the Mischianza was staged in honor of the General. Newspapers and
onlookers have left descriptions of this extravagant pageantry, the most
extensive of which is that of John André, a participant in the spectacle.[1]
James Parker, a Norfolk merchant, has contributed in his *Journal* a fresh
account which highlights the synthetic chivalry of the exhibition and points
up the impropriety of complimenting the Commander in Chief at an inaus-
picious time when Philadelphia was being evacuated and the French Alliance had just become a reality.

James Parker had joined Lord Dunmore's forces as a captain and
engineer early in the war. Sailing from Gwynn's Island on the *Vulcan* in
July 1776, he was shipwrecked on the Accomack shore, taken prisoner,
and confined in one of his own warehouses in Northampton County. While
on parole, awaiting trial by the local Committee of Safety, he lived undisturbed but shunned by former friends. He commented: "In this county I
formerly lived five years in the greatest harmony with all ranks, male and
famel, young, old. They were greatly altered; very few would speak with
me."[2] He was tried as a traitor, condemned to prison, and all his real and
personal property confiscated. In April 1777, along with eight others, he
managed to escape, traveling some five hundred miles, mostly by night,
and finally reaching Sir Andrew Hamond's fleet in Delaware Bay. He was
in the action of Brandywine and Germantown and thus was with Howe's
troops when they spent the gay winter of 1777-1778 in Philadelphia, the
climax of which Parker describes for his friend Charles Steuart in London.

1778

❡ May 6th Great works are erecting at the large house of Mr. Wharton
near the south end of the Town for a fête champêtre. A Space 180 feet by

[1] André, to a friend, May 23, 1778. See Winthrop Sargent, *Major John André,* New
York: 1861, pp. 186-197 in 1902 edition. *The Remembrancer,* London: 1778, vol.
VI, pp. 208-210.
[2] *James Parker Journal,* June 26, 1776, p. 5. Record Office, Liverpool.

30 is building with an arched roof covered with canvas & floored with plank. A Reggatta and Tournament are also talk'd of as part of this great intertainment. . . .

17 Sunday . . . The preparations are going on briskly for compleating the four Capital branches of the Great intertainment, Viz. Reggatta, Fireworks, Tournament, and Champêtre. The tournament carries us back to the pueril stories in the twopenny books of Argus & Parthenia, Parismus & Pariaminus, Valentine & Orson, & [illegible], Princess of Babylon. Here we have Knights of the blended rose, [knights] of the burning mountain with their Squires, heralds, armor bearers, who are to combat for peerless princesses attended by damsels, etc. On the front towards the Delaware the fireworks are erected and the lawn is smoothly laid off down to the river about a half mile. Sir Henry Clinton has been constantly employed since his arrival. I do not understand he has enjoyed yet any of the entertainments common in this City.

18th . . . At four this day Lord & Gen[l] Howe with the Officers concerned in the Machianza embarked at the upper part of the Town in Galleys, Barges, & flat boats, finely decorated. They row'd slowly down the River. The *Vigilant,* the highest Ship in the River, was dressed & man'd. The *Fanny* transport in the Middle opposite Market Street was dressed & the *Roebuck* below was man'd. The Ships at the wharfs, being very numerous along the whole bank of the River, with Colours, exhibited a very fine appearance, filled with people, as were also the tops of the houses. The Regimental bands played going down in the line; they Landed in front of Duke Wharton's house and were saluted by the *Roebuck.* Then moved up in front of the firework, an arch supported by pillars. On the front above was Neptune driving his Marine Chariot. On the top of the Angle a Triton mounted on a fish. Motto: *Laus illi debetur et a me gratia Major.* On each side in front were Thrones for the Peerless Princesses and the attendent damsels, they being Seated. The Herald for the Knights of the Blended rose, preceded by two trumpeters, proclaimed in three different parts of a very large Sq[r] formed by the people that the Ladies of the Order of the Blended Rose were superior in Wit and beauty to any Ladies in the World, immaculate and spotless, and that the Knights of that order, (if any could be found who did not consent to the truth of this declaration) [would] combat it with arms according to the ancient laws of Chivalry. This part of the ceremony being ended, the Herald, preceded by two Trumpeters, pranced [firm]ly on, followed by two pages, then a Squire bearing the

Halmet of his particular Knight with a fine device. The Knight, mounted, followed him and so followed the Six Sq^{rs} & Knights of that order. After a short silence forth pranced a Herald & advanced near the Thrones and with an audible voice denyed that the Blended rose Ladies were near equal to those of the Burning Mountain. They all paraded round the Square, as the others had done, & both Partys met in the Center where the Glove was exchanged. The order of Combat settled, all retirnd to the outline of the Square. Each Knight [faced] his antagonist. After a short silence the trumpets sounded and all charged. The first Charge was with lances which were all shiver'd and thrown away; the second and third they discharged pistols, the fourth and fifth were with Swords. After this a Knight of each order was selected to determine the whole, [illegible] of the Blended Rose and Capt. Watson of the Guards, of the Burning Mountain, who engaged some little time, when the peerless princesses, by the Master of Ceremonies, Maj. Guyn of the Light dragoons, ordered that no more blood should be spilt. There that farce ended.

The Girles, with Turbans, in white silk fancy dresses rather loose, with blended Roses, and knots of black and yellow Ribbons looked very well. The Knights, Sq^{rs}, heralds, Horses etc. were all in the same stile. The Regatta and Tournament being over, they all marched through the Arches up to the house, and additional appointments [were] provided, painted, and decorated for the purpose, and dined about Seven. The upper Arch had a frame on top, on the front a Group of Military implements—the Motto: *I, bone, quo te tua Virtus tua te vocat; I pede fausto.* The fireworks were played off at Ten, but indifferent. [The] head is too fat. The whole with eating, drinking, dancing, etc. was concluded about Seven the next morning. Had the Rebels got such a correction as they deserved, restored to their senses, and this been the feast of peace, it would have been very proper. But there are [those] who think it ill-timed, our Country by procrastination being involved in a french War. On the tickets of invitation to the Machianza a sun [was] setting behind a Mountain. The feathers of the 2nd. Reg^{t}. or crest, Motto: *Luces discedens aucto Splendore Resurgam. . . .* It was altogether a Compliment of some officers to the General [and] his departure. And hereafter we go upon a new account. [*Parker Journal, 920 PAR I 19/5, pp. 65-68, Record Office, Liverpool.*]

10 JAMES PARKER AND ABRAHAM WAGG REACT TO THE CARLISLE PEACE COMMISSION

To forestall the ratification of the French Alliance in 1778, Britain appointed the Carlisle Peace Commission and empowered it to negotiate peace on the basis of suspension of all measures passed since 1763 which were objectionable to the Colonies. The Commission reached Philadelphia June 6, a month after the ratification by Congress of the French treaties and just as preparations were under way for the evacuation of Philadelphia. Congress answered the request for a meeting by saying that the only basis for the restoration of peace was the acknowledgment of independence and the withdrawal of the British armed forces.

The Loyalists' various reactions to the instructions of the Commissioners ranged from criticizing the concessions to urging full acquiescence in the terms set forth by Congress. For the most part Loyalists were bitter, believing that the concessions would end their chances of recovering their property. The writings excerpted below of two voluble Loyalists, James Parker, the prosperous trader of Norfolk and British army captain who described the Mischianza, and Abraham Wagg, a wholesale grocer of New York City, represent the two extremes. Parker felt that the concessions which the Commission was prepared to make were unreasonably compromising, while Wagg believed that the concessions did not go far enough. Calling himself a friend to both Great Britain and America, Wagg suggested that the Commission should agree to a withdrawal of the British armed forces. Britain should then acknowledge independence and negotiate an alliance with the thirteen states. He believed that Anglo-American friendship was the most natural relationship and that an alliance with France was not in the best interests of America. His suggestions did not alter the Commissioners' instructions nor the unfavorable developments that condemned the mission before it arrived. Wagg left America in July 1779 with his wife and three children, a victim, like other Loyalists, of confiscation and impoverishment.[1]

---

[1] Cecil Roth, "A Jewish Voice for Peace in the War of American Independence," *American Jewish Historical Society Publications,* vol. XXXI (1928), p. 33ff.

"Low is the Dignity of Great Britain Fallen!": James Parker Views the Carlisle Peace Commission as Humiliating

JULY 8, 1778

❦ . . . In last week's Gazettes we have the Act of Parliament passed last session respecting America, the Commissions & the Com^rs to the President of the Congress. It is humilliating, shewing an ardent desire to Settle all differences & give up more than the most unreasonable of them all [the rebels] ever expected (it is not the reasonable men, whose intent is peace, we have to deal with); it concludes "If after the time that may be necessary to consider this communication & transmit your answer, the horrors and devastation of War should continue, We call God & the World to Witness that the evils which must follow are not to be imputed to G. Britain & we cannot without the most real sorrow anticipate the prospect of Calamities which we feel the most ardent desire to prevent." Their answer was much as might have been expected, nor could his Grace of R-h-nd[1] [have] made it better. Nothing but the earnest desire to stop the further effusion of human blood would have induced them to read a paper containing expressions so disrespectfull to their good & great ally.[2] Every idea of dependence on G. Britain is inadmissible, and the only solid proof his B. Majesty can give of his sincere disposition to enter into a treaty is to Acknowledge the Independence of these States or withdraw his fleets & armys. By Cruelty Cowardice falsehood & Unanimity have a Set of the worst men on Earth become important. Whilst one of the most powerfull Nations on it, her councils thwarted by her factions no less & her force misapplied either by ignorance or design, hath these three years contended to little purpose. Low is the dignity of G. B. fallen indeed—Solliciting audience from her Rebellious subjects, the [British force fighting] at the same time on the spot to destroy the most [promising trade] and most Valuable of the Colonies. Govr Johnson[3] has [written to Henry] Laurence,

---

[1] On April 7, 1778, the Duke of Richmond moved in the House of Lords for an evacuation of America and recognition of independence.

[2] The Commissioners' letter to Congress, June 9, tactlessly referred to "the insidious interpositions of France."

[3] Former Governor of West Florida and a member of the Carlisle Peace Commission. He was tactless, insubordinate, and hot-tempered. *Dictionary of National Biography.* He tried to bribe Joseph Reed and Robert Morris to help restore peace, and when his approach became public, he resigned and left for England.

[319]

precident of the Congress, solliciting an im[mediate meeting, professing] an ardent desire to see that Country & those Heroes who stand [bravely] up for the libertys of mankind, desiring that they may not [scorning Bri]tain in the hour of her Insolence, refuse her request. Laurence answered that he had but one Vote, but if the whole were centered in him he would nigative that request even to Govr Johnston. Next day the following advertisement appeared: "To be sold, The British rights in America consisting, amongst other articles, [of] the 13 provinces now in Rebellion which Britain *In the hour of her insolence* attempted to subdue, the reversion of the Govm^t of Quebeck, Novascotia, Newfoundland, East & W. florida, the territories of the Hudsons bay Company, a respectfull body of Troops, a Considerable part of the Royal Navy, & all the loyal subjects in America; the British W Indies will be included in the sale if agreeable. Apply to George Johnston Esqr who is desirous to Conclude a private bargain. Conditions of the sale to be seen in the hands of Henry Laurence Esqr President of the Congress. To make it easie to the Purchaser a seat in the Congress will be taken in part payment, the rest in Continental Curr^y.

No discount will be made for all the loyalists murdered since ye 1st April 1775. This appeared at Rivingstons shop door. The author is not known.

The Governor's conduct has been very Extr^a since his arrival; he has been remarkably complasant to suspected people; to one revered Rebel lady he presented a Snuffbox having on it a picture of Washington crowned with laurels. To a friend of mine he was boasting the advantageous terms he had obtained from Govm^t for America and all at once burst out in exclamation "God damn my blood, after all we shall not be able to turn out Germaine."[4] Some think his conduct is to ingratiate himself so as to bring on a meeting with the Congress. We expect no good from the Negotiations of the Commissioners. [The point] to which they have held out, agreed to, will in a very short [time make the dignity] of G. B. of as little importance in America as [has] become his Majestys title to that Crown. Viz., To agree that [Britain must give the] Right up, in the different *States* of N° America, [of legislation to the] General Congress or particular assemblys [made up of persons] formed like me with the pollitical designs of yrs, . . . if she gives up this point, What does she contend for? Or [why]

---

[4] He had insulted Germaine and been obliged to fight a duel with him in December 1770. See M. M. Boatner, *Encyclopedia of the American Revolution*, p. 563.

does not France oblige the Congress to close with those terms by which, without the los of a man or a liver [livre], she will get the Kernel and we the Shell? [*Parker Journal, 920 PAR I 19/5, pp 87-89. Liverpool Record Office.*]

Abraham Wagg of New York Suggests to the Commission a Way to Restore Peace

AUGUST 22, 1778

❦ *May it Please your Excellencies* [Carlisle Peace Commissioners] Congress letter to your Excellencies dated 17th June, 1778, concludes thus "the only solid proof of this disposition will be an explicit acknowledgment of the independence of these States or withdraw his fleets and Armies." Your Excellencies complying to their last request opens a great field for success. The Congress have candidly pointed out a method to settle with great Britain. . . .

The fleets and armies leaving America admits of the independency of the colonies and must distress the loyal friends to Government. In answer to such objections, it is obvious to the World what conquest Great Britain has made or can make in America. It is not the burning of Cities and Towns or laying waste to Sea coast &c—[this] cannot be said is subdueing an enemy. It is to disarm an enemy or rebellious subjects &c; it is to keep up standing armies to quell the spirit of Revolution. On a modrate computation, could America be conquered, it would require to keep thirteen colonies in due subjection, on an average at nine thousand men to each colony, will amount to One hundred seventeen thousand men. This is but a modrate calculation founded on a letter of Dr. Franklyn shewing the naterual strengt of America, published in the London Chronicle of the 8th february, 1766. . . .

By all circumstances it plainly appears that America will certainly be lost to Great Britain. Why does not Great Britain revenge her wrongs on France and Spain as abettors to America, which will sound better in the annals of England? That in the years 1778 and 1779 Great Britain possessed themselves of the French West India Islands and took from Spain several of their shiping and the Spanish floata to the amount of several millions for the profidousness of these two Nations in abetting and incouraging the subjects of Great Britain to revolt and declare themselves free and independent and as an example for one sovereign not to interfer with the subjects of another Sovereign or power contrary to the laws of Nations. . . .

If the King's armies and fleets are to continue at New York and Rhode Island at such enormous and extravagant expences, Great Britain will be baffled by America, triumpht over by France, insulted by Spain, and laught at by all Europe. . . .

The object [independence] is great and important. The Americans say that the Colonies can never be enslaved whilst they are determined to be free. . . . They have raised independence upon the pillars of freedom. They have purchased it at so high a price as the loss of one hundred and three thousand lives, who have bled in the cause of freedom, a Virtue known to but few British subjects. Their towns have been burnt, their seacoast have been ravaged. They [have] been oppressed and distressed to evry degree that human nature can suggest.

The voice of the people now in Arms in America and the Congress are for a perpetual alliance with Great Britain. They acknowledge that an alliance with France is only to obtain independence. Witness the late disturbance between some of the men from De. Estaing fleet and the inhabitance of Boston. . . . The majority of the inhabitance of North America are for independence, but wish and would prefer an alliance with Great Britain rather than with any other power in Europe. . . .

Great Britain will derive more extencive and more durable advantages from such a Natural Alliance than from their former Conexions when self interest Governors and placemen had in their power to cause feuds and animosities, as have been the case between Great Britain and her collonies &c.

If such a Natural treaty of Alliance should take place, the Americans will then through of the mask and tell France and Spain that the law of Nature and Natures God intitles America to enter into treaties and be perpetualy allied with Great Britain by the nearest ties of consanguinity, being of the same religion, speaking the same language, and remembering the former intercourse of good offices &c. . . .

Your Excellencies may be assured what suggestions or informations humbly offered altho synonymise is from a

Friend to Great Britain

[*A. O. 13/79, PRO. Roth, "A Jewish Voice for Peace . . . ," PAJHS, vol. XXI, pp. 60–67 passim.*]

11 GRACE GALLOWAY STAGES A SIT-DOWN PROTEST AND CHARLES WILLSON PEALE EVICTS HER BY FORCE

"Grace Galloway turned out of her House this forenoon and Spanish officers put in," ran the entry of Elizabeth Drinker's *Journal* for August 20, 1778.[1] The sentence was a terse summary of a petulant sit-down protest by the wife of Joseph Galloway, the civil governor of Philadelphia during the British occupation. For eight months through the winter of 1777–1778 the Philadelphia Loyalists had enjoyed the protection of Howe's forces, while Washington's army shivered and starved at Valley Forge. The spring, however, brought several ominous developments, the news of the French Alliance and the rejection by Congress of the Carlisle Peace Commission unless independence was first acknowledged. Sir Henry Clinton, who succeeded Howe in May, was alert to the possibility that the French fleet might bottle up his ships in Philadelphia and the rebel army effect a squeeze on his troops. He ordered a prompt evacuation of the city. Rather than leave the Loyalists to the vindictiveness of the rebels, he arranged for some three thousand to accompany him. Galloway knew that it was unsafe for him to remain and sailed with his daughter, Betsy, for New York. Not so Grace Galloway, who remained behind, believing that her presence would be the means of saving her house on Market Street and her family property, if not the possessions of her husband.[2] How mistaken she was is revealed through two months of daily entries in her diary. Her indignation mounts progressively as her legal moves meet with frustration and the help of friends evaporates.

1778

❧   This day Thursday ye 18th [June] ye American Troops came into Town

Friday ye 19th was warn'd by peal [Charles Willson Peale, the artist, an agent for confiscated estates in Philadelphia] that he must take possession of my house for ye state

---

[1] *Journal of Elizabeth Drinker*, N.Y. Historical Society.

[2] Grace Growden's family had large land holdings, including control of the Durham iron furnaces. Galloway's property was confiscated and lost and he was never allowed to return to Pennsylvania. Her inheritance was sequestered during the life of her husband. However she died in 1789 and her husband in 1803 and thus it never returned to her. Ernest H. Baldwin, *Joseph Galloway, The Loyalist Politician*, Philadelphia: 1902, p. 88.

Tuesday ye 21st . . . about 2 o'clock they came—one smith a hatter & Col Will & one Shriner & a Dutch Man I know not his Name—they took an inventory of everything even to broken China & empty bottles . . . they told Me they must advertise the house I told them they must do as they pleased but till it was decided by a Court I wou'd not go out Unless by ye force of a bayonet but when I knew who had a right to it I should know how to act; . . .

Wednesday ye 22 . . . Sent for Mr. Dickison last Night & he told Me he wou'd look over ye law to see if I cou'd recover My own estate & this evening he came & told Me I cou'd Not recover dower & he fear'd my income in My estate was forfeited likewise & y^t no tryal wou'd be of service: but advised Me to draw up a Peti'on to ye Chief Justice Mccean [Thomas McKean] for the recovery of my estate . . . so I find I am a beggar indeed. I expect every hour to be turn'd out of doors & where to go I know not no one will take me in & all ye Men keeps from Me . . .

[August] Saturday ye 8th . . . Peal & Will came to let Me know that I must go out a Monday Morn: for they wou'd give the spaniard Possession . . .

Monday ye 10th . . . Lewis sent Me word smith had gave his honour not to Molest Me till the Opinion of ye executive council was known but in a short time after came Peel Will & shriner with a spanish Merchant & his attendants & took Possession of My house I was taken very ill & obliged to Lay down & sent them word I cou'd not see them; they went every Where below stairs & ye spaniard off'd to let Me chuse My own bed chamber; but I sent them no Message but was very ill Up stairs but between 2 & 3 o'clock the last went away . . . they took the Key out of ye front parlor door & locked Me out . . .

Wednesday ye 12th . . . just after dinner Peal came & asked Me what rooms I intended to let the spanish Gentleman have I told him None Nor wou'd I give Up possession of my house & that I had been very ill Used in haveing my parlour shut Up & the Key taken away . . . he told me if I intended to dispute with ye executive council of ye State he had nothing more to say: I told him not to mistake me for I wou'd not contend with ye executive council but I contend with you Sir & this Spanish Gentle Man & will not go out of My house till I know the opinion of ye council he told me I must I reply'd I wou'd not and if I did go they must Turn me out he reply'd then we Must Turn you out I said very well . . . Mr. Buddenot came . . . & he told me to Keep in My house & if they made a forcible Entry he wou'd bring an Action Against them . . .

Thursday ye 20th Lewise sent me word that I must shut my doors & windows & if they wou'd come to let them Make a forcible Entry Accordingly I did so & a little after 10 oclock they Knocked Violently at the door three times the Third time I sent Nurse & call'd out myself to tell them I was in possession of my own House & wou'd keep so & they shou'd gain No admittance Hereupon which they went round in ye yard & Try'd every door but cou'd None Open then they went to the Kitchen door & with a scrubbing brush which they broke to pieces they forced that open [—] we Women standing in ye Entry in ye Dark they made repreated strokes at ye door & I think was 8 or 10 Minuets before they got it open when they came in I had ye windows open'd they look'd very Mad their [sic] was Peel [,] smith [,] ye Hatter [,] & a Col Will [,] a pewterer in second street [.] I spoke first & told them I was Used ill: & show'd them the Opinion of ye Lawyers Peel read it: but they all despised it & peel said he had stud[i]ed ye Law & knew they did right I told them Nothing but force shou'd get me out of My house Smith said they knew how to Manage that & that they wou'd throw my cloaths in ye street: & told Me that Mrs. Sympson & forty othere ware put out of ye lines in one day: I said they had their furniture to take with them he said that was owing to ye Generosity of ye british officers but ye Police would let no favour be shewn I told him I knew that was not True he told me he knew better & hinted that Mr G had treated people Cruely. I found the Villan [sic] wou'd say anything so I stop'd after hearing several insulting things: . . . In ye Mean While Peel & Will went over ye House to see Nothing was Embassell'd [sic] & Locking Up the things at last Smith went away: . . . Peel went to the generals & asked for his Chariot & then returned & told me ye General was so kind as to let me have it & he [,] Mr Peel [,] was willing to Accomodate Me as well as he cou'd I told him he Need not give himself the Trouble for if I wanted ye Charriot I cou'd send to ye General myself Just after ye General sent in his Housekeeper with His compliments & to let me know that I was wellcome to His Chariot & he wou'd have it ready any hour I pleased I then Accepted of it & told her I wou'd send [for it for] after every Mortifying treatment was tiard & wanted to be turn'd out Peel went Upstairs & brought down My Work bag & 2 bonnets & put them on the side table at last we went in the Entry to sit & I asked ye two Grays if they wou'd witness for me but they both went away two of ye Men went out & after staying some time return'd & said they had been with the council & that they had done right & must proceed I did not hear this myself but ye rest of ye Women did Mrs Craig asked for My Bed but they wou'd let Me Have Nothing & as I told them acted entirely from

Malice: after we had been in yᵉ Entry some time Smith & Will went away & Peel said yᵉ Chariot was ready but he would not hasten me I told him I was at home & in My own House & nothing but force shou'd drive me out of it he said it was not yᵉ first time he had taken a Lady by the Hand an insolent wretch this speech was made some time in the room; at last he becon'd for yᵉ Chariot for yᵉ General wou'd not let it come till I wanted it & as the Chariot drew up Peel fetched My Bonnets & gave one to me yᵉ other to Mrs Craig: then with greates[t] air said come Mʳ[ˢ] Galloway give me your hand I answer'd indeed I will not nor will I go out of my house but by force. he then took hold of my arm & I rose & he took me to the door I then Took hold on on[e] side & Look[ed] round & said pray take Notice I do not leave my house of My own accord or with my own inclination but by force & Nothing but force shou'd have Made Me give up possession Peel said with a sneer very well Madam & when he led me down yᵉ step I said now Mr Peel let go My Arm I want not your Assistance he said he cou'd help me to yᵉ Carriage I told him I cou'd go without & you Mr Peel are the last Man on earth I wou'd wish to be Obliged to Mrs Craig then step'd into yᵉ Carriage & we drove to her house where we din'd. [*"Diary of Grace . . . Galloway," Werner, ed., Penna. Mag. Hist. Biog., vol. LV, pp. 40–53 passim.*]

12 JOHN POTTS WRITES GALLOWAY OF THE DESPONDENCY GENERATED BY THE BRITISH EVACUATION OF PENNSYLVANIA

At the outbreak of revolutionary activities in 1775 John Potts, a judge of the Court of Common Pleas in Philadelphia, retired with his wife and three children to his 270-acre farm in Pottsgrove, thirty-nine miles from the city, and remained there for the first two years of the war. On Howe's arrival in the environs, September 1777, Potts joined the British army and gave intelligence to Howe. During the occupation of Philadelphia from September 26, 1777, to June 18, 1778, he served as police magistrate. Along with Galloway, the Allen brothers, Jacob Duché, Samuel Shoemaker, and others, he was one of the thirteen attainted in the first Pennsylvania Act of Attainder and was obliged to flee to New York with Howe's troops and eventually to London. His estate was confiscated in 1779, but he was given a generous allowance of £ 200 by the British soon after his arrival in New York. Despite his early attainder, he received a pardon from the Pennsylvania Council May 26, 1786, which enabled him to return to his former province.[1]

❡ It appears to me that the greater part of our Countrymen depressed by the evacuation of Pennsylvania and their confidence in Government destroyed by that measure, have abandoned themselves to a lethargy very nearly bordering on despair. They will not even exert themselves sufficiently to cultivate their own ground. They say they cannot be certain of possessing the fruits of their labor and they publickly declare that they would rather suffer their ground to remain uncultivated by which it will gather strength, than have their property taken from them by Commissioners or Quarter Masters who will pay them in Paper which depreciates so fast that no man knows what value to affix to it. [*Balch Papers, 1775-1782, N.Y. Pub. Lib.*]

13 JAMES RIVINGTON, THE TORY PRINTER, PROVES A DOUBLE AGENT

The excerpts from the writings of James Rivington, the King's Printer, reputedly the arch-Tory, are of double interest, first in Rivington's comment on the waning of the Revolution in 1778, despite the British evacuation of Philadelphia and the fiasco of the Carlisle peace mission in June, and secondly, in the change of tone apparent in his apology to the public four years later. In the first instance he appears a genuine Tory; in the second he expects public understanding.

Why would Rivington expect his readers to overlook his past errors; in fact, why was he allowed to stay on in New York after the Revolution, when other less obnoxious Loyalists were forced to leave? Why did Wash-

---

[1] *Loyalist Transcripts*, pp. 49, 173-198; Sabine, *Loyalists*, vol. II, p. 199; *Colonial Records Pennsylvania*, vol. XV, p. 26; W. H. Siebert, *Loyalists of Pennsylvania*, Columbus: 1894, p. 57.

ington honor him with a call as he entered New York in 1783? Why was he protected against the exuberant American troops? The explanation lies in his role as double agent and his switch of allegiance to the rebel side probably some time in late 1779 or 1780. His service to Washington, sending him information gleaned from British officers who frequented his coffee house and bookstore, was long suspected and finally confirmed by Allan McLane's clear statement in his journal: "After I returned in the fall [1781] was imployed by the board of war to repair to Long Island to watch the motion of the Brittish fleet and if possible obtain their Signals which I did threw the assistance of the noteed Rivington. Joined the fleet Under the Count D Grass with the Signals . . ."[1]

When the troubles first started, *Rivington's New York Gazetteer* fulfilled its claim to be "Open and Uninfluenced," but by November 1774 it carried the royal arms on its masthead and became Tory in tone. Following the events at Lexington and Concord Rivington issued to the public an apology and pledge "to conduct my Press upon such Principles as shall not give Offense to the Inhabitants of the Colonies. . . ."[2] Arrested in May, he signed the Association. He also wrote a protest to Congress in which he again declared his resolve not to give further affront, saying, ". . . he is desirous of devoting his life, in the business of his own profession, to the service of the country he has adopted for his own."[3] Nonetheless, as rebellion and emotions mounted throughout 1775, his paper became so obnoxious that he was hung in effigy and his press destroyed by Isaac Sears's mob. He spent a year in England, returning to New York in 1777 to reopen his press and start a coffeehouse. His attacks on the rebel cause continued throughout the war, furnishing a consummate cover-up for his double role.

Seven years passed between the time of the above pledge to the public and to Congress and his later apology of July 10, 1782. Events had moved

[1] Recollections of Allan McLane, *McLane Papers,* vol. II, p. 56. Other statements of Rivington's secret service to the rebel cause appear in George Washington Parke Custis, *Recollections and Private Memoirs of Washington,* Benson J. Lossing, ed., pp. 293–299; Lossing to Canopy Jenifer, Apr. 2, 1856, and Custis to Jenifer, Aug. 15, 1857, N.Y. Historical Society; William Hooper to James Iredell, January 4, 1784 in Griffith J. McRee, *Life and Correspondence of James Iredell,* vol. II, p. 84. See Catherine S. Crary, "The Tory and the Spy: the Double Life of James Rivington," *William & Mary Quart.,* vol. XVI, pp. 61ff.

[2] *N.Y. Gaz.,* Apr. 27, 1775.

[3] Rivington to Congress, May 20, 1775, Charles R. Hildeburn, *Sketches of Printers and Printing in Colonial New York,* p. 123.

James Rivington: Loyalist Turncoat (above). Author unknown. Document indicating Rivington as Allan McLane's contact in New York. (Courtesy of the New York Historical Society, New York City.)

James Rivington: Loyalist Turncoat (two following pages). Recollections of Allan McLane naming Rivington as his informant (McLane Papers). (Courtesy of the New York Historical Society, New York City.)

was at the ... Stony
Point, and ... ...
... was in the year
1781 elected by Baron
Steuben and Marquis
Lafayette to command a
body of ... in
the lines near Portsmouth
... in the month
of May ... ...
made a ... in the
ship Congress Capt.
... fought the
ship Savage of 20 Guns
of Charles Town Capt.
Stirling for 5 glasses
... ...
the morning

After I returned in
the ball was ... ...
by the board I went to
repair to Long Island
to watch the motion
of the British fleet and
if possible obtain their
Signals which I did
throu the assistance of the
... during two I and
the fleet Under the
Count D grof with
the Signals. During the
siege was at the ——
Surrender of ... ...
and was after this
employed six months

rapidly to alter a Loyalist printer's outlook, not only independence and military developments, but also personal happenings. Rivington's salary of £ 100 a year was in arrears, his press in financial straits, and his family expanded to six children. Perhaps self-interest took the upper hand; perhaps he was the detestable, chameleon-like character or Judas he was labeled;[4] or perhaps his Loyalism all along had been only skin-deep and his words to Congress in 1775 a genuine resolution.

James Rivington Gives His Opinion to Richard Cumberland, Secretary of the Board of Trade, That the Revolution is on the Wane

NOVEMBER 23, 1778

❆ The Royal Commissioners will apprize his Majesty's Ministers of the state of the rebellion, which, without any force exerted against the enemy, is now in its wane; and, when followed up by military operations next spring, will be soon suppressed. Had my humble suggestions, communicated to you immediately after that shabby affair at Saratoga, been adopted, a single insurgent would not at this day have been found in arms against the mother country. However, things may yet terminate happily and much more honorably for Great Britain than if the Congress had treated with his Majesty's Commissioners. An augmentation of the army in this country, serving to replace the troops lately departed under General Grant for the West Indies, and orders unlimitted allowing the Commander in Chief to act with the utmost spirit, in concert with Colonel Butler & Captain Brant who head large bodies of Refugees and Indians and occasion tremendous alarms in the back settlements of N York, Jersey, Pennsylv^a, and Maryland, I presume Sir, to assert that such an application of our force by Land, with a vigilant attention to the annoyance of the Rebels' Commerce at Sea, will tend most directly to bring about an humiliating submission. . . .

The *march* of Sir Henry Clinton thro Jersey (and thereby securing the whole army from Mons. D'Estaing's squadron, which would have intercepted them on shipboard in Delaware had not the General preferred the former method of returning to New York) proves downright wormwood whenever it is mentioned in the presence of any of Sir Wm. Howe's

---

[4] *Massachusetts Spy,* Dec. 29, 1774, N.Y. State Library.

creatures & partisans in this city. . . . My press shall never exist under the influence of any individual of that faction which has, ever since the arrival of the army from Halifax, in many instances betrayed the King and his Ministers and aggrandized the military abilities of Mr. Washington, who had none to boast of before S^r W H. landed on Long Island. . . .

We want here very much such a Gentleman as Mr. [John] Lind[1] to defende the measures of the British Government, which are daily insulted in terms most illiberal by publications in the Rebel Gazettes. Had I abilities for the purpose they should ever be called forth to confront and counteract them. An Englishman named Paine, the author of Common Sense, is now publishing a Series of papers, entitled the Crisis. This man has every capacity to serve Congressional purposes. All the King's friends here regret that there is not a person of temper & proper abilities sent hither with a respectable appointment to be constantly employed in this very necessary department. My Gazette goes weekly and universally over the continent, for the Rebels *will read it* tho it militates against all their favourite objects. This would prove a ready channel of conveying to the people at large all the publications addressed to them from a proper Champion in the Royal Cause. I hope I shall be pardoned for taking the liberty to point out any plan to my superiours; whatever I propose is the emanation of an heart fervently devoted to the service in which I have the honour to be embarked. [*CO 5/155, PRO.*]

James Rivington Asks His Readers to be Generous and Overlook Past Errors

JULY 10, 1782

❡ To the Public

The publisher of this Paper, sensible that his zeal for the success of his Majesty's arms, his sanguine wishes for the good of his country, and his friendship for individuals, have at times led him to credit and circulate paragraphs, without investigating the facts so closely as his duty to the Public demanded; trusting to their feelings, and depending on their generosity, he begs them to look over past errors and depend on future correctness; for henceforth he will neither expect nor solicit their favours longer

[1] Author of "An Answer to the Declaration of Independence."

than his endeavours shall stamp the same degree of authenticity and credit on the *Royal Gazette* (of New York) as all Europe allow to the *Royal Gazette* of London. [*Royal Gaz., July 10, 1782.*]

14   ROBERT AUCHMUTY TELLS HIS SISTER THAT THE FRENCH ALLIANCE HAS WEANED AWAY AMERICA'S BRITISH FRIENDS

Robert Auchmuty, a brother of the Reverend Samuel Auchmuty of Trinity Church, New York, was an eminent lawyer and a judge of the Vice Admiralty Court in Boston at the outset of the Revolution. He also had acted as counsel, along with John Adams and Josiah Quincy, for Captain Thomas Preston following the Boston Massacre. His house in Roxbury, built in 1761, was a rendezvous for Crown officials and army officers during the siege of Boston and was a part of his property that was confiscated. He joined the 1776 exiles in England and never returned to America.

In the following letter from England to his sister Caty, in Massachusetts, he indicates that the Act of Attainder and the French Alliance were boomerangs to America, the first helping the Loyalists gain support from the British government, and the second turning American sympathizers in England against the American cause. The French Alliance had turned the struggle into a European war, with a vengeful France Britain's enemy once again.

MARCH 13, 1779

❧   *Dear Caty*
. . . The Assembly of Massachusetts were rather too officious in solemnly passing an Act [of Attainder] to prohibit my return thither, as I had not the least idea of it. The treatment wich every man, differing in opinion from the popular gentlemen in that country, meets with, is, by every one of common sense, deemed more than sufficient to have answered all the purposes of the above mentioned act. And though the same was unquestionably intended to injure me and others, I am sure it has had a direct contrary effect. It is complete evidence to the british government of the malice of our enemies, of our loyalty to our King, and consequently the justice & necessity of protection & support. Than which, as we are situ-

ated, nothing better for our interest could have been devised, except an act for the confiscation of our property, which I flatter myself I shall very soon hear of. Perhaps such a law will not be enacted in positive terms, but will be introduced under some false colour of justice, such as subjecting our property to illegal and monstruous taxes to prosecute a war against ourselves. This will answer my purpose as well as the other. But whether the criminality of the proceedure will not thereby be greatly enhanced, I submit to the sensible and honest man to determine.

Whatever ideas of the justice and humanity of the british government and people may prevail in America, I am so absolutely confident of both, as to feel myself perfectly easy and secure under their protection. Nor would I exchange this anchor of hope for all the promises, attended with the most pressing invitations to return, which are in the power of the crude and unsettled states of America to make. I am now in a country where no set of men dare maliciously or wontonly injure the innocent, which happy situation I never will part with for one directly contrary to it. Nothing is obligatory here but the known laws of the land, but with you an act innocent, nay meritorious, when committed, may, by an after law, be worked up to the highest degree of criminality, and be punished accordingly. Such a community will ever be shun'd by every true Lover of liberty, by every man of sense and virtue. . . .

The laws of justice and humanity are immutable. Neither time, circumstances, or excuses will ever be able to bend or alter the same. Therefore all pretenses of necessity, and all heats of resentment, finally will prove ineffectual for that purpose. As my present situation is far removed from riot and tumult, from arbitrary mandates, from distress and penury, to all which my deluded countrymen, I fear, are subject, a few excepted, and those not the most deserving, I feel myself happy, except in our separation. . . .

I am no stranger to the complicated sufferings of the poor Americans in general, though you prudently avoid saying any thing about them; nor am I yet so revengefull as not to pity them, though they use none towards me. . . .

In this happy country you may live just as you please. If your taste leads to gaiety & high life, and your fortune will admit of it, you may satiate yourself with both, if to quietude and rational pleasure, in those you also may indulge, and on easy terms. And so far am I from wishing my self or friends in America, that I am really concerned that all such had not left it when I did. I confess I knew America a very happy country. But I am con-

[335]

vinced that it is now, and for many years to come must be, exactly the reverse. The enormous debt therein contracted, and the detestable alliance with France, are evils, which will not easily subside. But by slow though sure degrees will sink the unhappy people in general into extreme poverty, will debauch their morals, and rob them of all true happiness. I really pity my unfortunate country when I seriously contemplate the complicated miseries which in my opinion, await it. As to your french connexion, it has weaned [away] the few friends you had in this country, irritated your enemies, and made all cool and indifferent persons join the latter. It has greatly strengthened the hands of Government, & probably in the end will produce a severity against you, which will terminate extremely to your disadvantage. For the Americans to connect themselves with a people whose faith and promises are no more to be relied on than the most glaring and notorious falsities, whose manners & customs are immoral, irrational, and destructive, whose government is most unjust, arbitrary, and wicked, and whose religion is nothing more than an audacious mockery of Heaven is a political manoeuvre, which astonishes every true lover of civil and religious rights. I fear I have tired you on this subject. And therefore an apology is due, which I will make by assuring you, that the within sentiments flow from my heart, and are produced from a source of pity towards many innocent and deluded people. [*Naval Hist. Soc. Collection, N.Y. Historical Society.*]

15   SYLVESTER GARDINER ATTRIBUTES REBEL·SUCCESS TO
THE "SHAMEFUL AND SCANDALOUS CONDUCT" OF THE TWO
HOWES

Many Loyalists were cynical onlookers of the Mischianza, honoring Sir William Howe, for they were bitterly critical of the Howes' conduct of the war, even suggesting that the Howes courted failure to discredit the ministry to which they were opposed. James Parker's comment to his friend, Charles Steuart, that "the Howes would have rather lost America than subdued it under the present administration," was typical.[1] Other Loyalists, such as Jonathan Boucher, Peter Van Schaack, Edward Winslow, Isaac

[1] January 9, 1779, *James Parker Journal*, p. 116, Parker Papers, Liverpool Record Office.

Wilkins, Thomas Jones, and Galloway were particularly scathing about the Howes' mismanagement of the war. There was considerable criticism in England, too, which led to a parliamentary investigation in 1779 with inconclusive results. One unidentified Loyalist, a prolific letter writer, gave a devastating expose of repeated blunders, commenting: "As to the military maneuvers, there has been such a concatenation of blunders as no drill Serjeant would have been guilty of. . . . Rebellion which a twelve-month ago was really a contemptible Pigmy is now in appearance become a Giant."[2] Sylvester Gardiner's letter from England to his daughter represents the opinion commonly held by the Loyalists.[3]

1780

❡ *My Dear Mrs. Browne*
. . . I never have entertained that Gloomy despondency relative to the reducing of America as you have. The People in general of these kingdoms know very little of the [feeble] Force and [low] Strength of the Rebels, no more than the officers that have return'd from there, whose attention (I am sorry to say) have been more taken up with a life of Dissipation than attention to the knowledge of their country and the duty of their office, witness the most scandalous affair of Stony Point and Paulus Hook last year. No history can be produced of a war being carried on in the manner this has been since the world was made. It was in the Power of the infamous Howe to have finished this rebellion more than four times to my own knowledge. In short, Government has done everything but appointing proper officers and it is not owing to the Prowess of the Rebels that they have not been [beaten] but to the most shameful and Scandalous conduct and behaviour of the two Howes. Since their time this Poor Nation has not only the Americans to contend with but France and Spain, the blackest and [most] daring Enemy of the whole [world]. As for Ireland, I hope better things than you fear and you will find that I am not mistaken when I tell you they will find them a Loyal, well disposed People. From these unhappy

---

[2] *Historical Anecdotes Civil and Military in a Series of Letters Written from America in the Years 1777-1778 to Different Persons in England,* London: 1779.
[3] Troyer Anderson, after reviewing the military strategy of the war, concluded the Howes' conduct accorded with the military practices of the time. *The Command of the Howe Brothers during the American Revolution,* New York: 1936, p. 148.

times I have lost *everything* but a good Conscience, but what comforts me in my distress is that God Governs the world, sees and suffers these things no Doubt for some good and wise ends. His holy will be done is the daily Prayer of your aff[ectionate] F[ather]. [*Gardiner Papers, vol. II, p. 7, Mass. Historical Society.*]

16 BENEDICT ARNOLD FEELS THE RECTITUDE OF HIS CONDUCT IN REVEALING THE STATE OF THE AMERICAN FORCES AND FINANCES

Benedict Arnold's treason might have been anticipated, had his earlier transgressions been viewed more seriously. His profiteering as military commandant of Philadelphia after the British evacuation was recognized by the Loyalist, Charles Steuart, who wrote to Galloway in London: "Arnold, it is said, will be discharged, being generally thought a pert Tory. Certain it is that he associates with these people and is to be married to Miss Shippen, daughter of Edward Shippen."[1] His callous exploitation of his office led to an executive order, February 3, 1779, for his court-martial on four charges: he gave permission for a private vessel, the *Nancy*, to go to sea and to enter other American ports without proper authorization; he closed the shops of the city to prevent army officers from making purchases while he bought at will for his own benefit; he imposed menial tasks on Sons of Liberty when Congress drafted them for military duty; and he secured wagons from the quartermaster general to transport private property at public expense. He was acquitted of the second and third charges, but was convicted on the first and last counts and received a reprimand from the Commander in Chief. Congress confirmed the sentence in a formal resolution February 12, 1780.[2] Nonetheless Washington acceded to his request to be given the command of West Point. The court-martial, his association with the Loyalist Shippen family, his unfavorable reputation in Connecticut, which led to that state's refusal to endorse him when Congress made him a general, should have been a forewarning of his defection.

[1] December 1, 1778. *James Riker Memoria,* vol. XV, p. 3, N.Y. Public Library.
[2] Jesse Smith Orderly Book, Headquarters Morristown, Feb. 21–May 17, 1780. Entry for Apr. 6, 1780, N.Y. Historical Society.

However, his state of mind was best revealed in his self-righteous letter to Lord Germain written just after he fled from West Point to New York (September 26).[3] He sought to justify his conduct, at the same time enclosing information on the military and financial state of Washington's forces.

OCTOBER 7, 1780

❡ *My Lord* [George Germain],
 Conscious of the rectitude of my Intentions (whatever Constructions may have been put on my Conduct,) and convinced of the benevolence and goodness of your Lordship, I am emboldened to request Your Interest and Intercession, that I may be restored to the favor of my most gracious Sovereign; In the fullest Confidence of his Clemency, I most cheerfully cast myself at his Feet, imploring his Royal Grace and Protection.

I have that Confidence in the Goodness of Sir Henry Clinton, That His Majesty will not remain long, uninformed that some considerable time has elapsed, since I resolved to devote my Life and Fortune to his Majesty's Service, and that I was intent to have Demonstrated my Zeal by an Act, which had it succeeded as intended, must have immediately terminated the unnatural Convulsions that have so long distracted the Empire.

Your Lordship will perceive by the enclosed address to the Public, by what principles I have been and am now actuated, to which I shall at present only add my most sacred Assurance that no endeavors of mine shall be wanting to confirm the Profession I make of an unalterable Attachment to the Person, Family and Interests of my Sovereign, and the Glory of his Reign. . . .

I have the honor to be with the greatest Respect My Lord Your Lordships Most Obedient and most humble servant

B. Arnold.

---

[3] Arnold also wrote an Address to the American People (Oct. 7, 1780) and an Address to the Officers and Soldiers of the Continental Army Oct. 20, 1780. See Edward Dean Sullivan, *Benedict Arnold: Military Racketeer,* New York: 1932, and *The Royal Gaz.,* Oct. 25, 1780.

*The Present State of the American Rebel Army, Navy, and Finances, with
some Remarks.*

The present operating Force under the immediate Command of
general Washington as stated by himself to a Council of general Officers
the 6th ult° amounts to. . . .   10,400 men
One Battalion of Contin^l troops at Rhode Island   500
Two State Regiments of Contin^l Militia at
North Castle.   500
                                                                    11,400

About one half of these Troops are Militia, whose time of service
expires on the first day of January next, which will reduce the Army
engaged for the war to less than Six Thousand men, exclusive of the Troops
in the Southern Department under General Gates, who may amount to
eight hundred or a thousand regular troops, besides Militia; about 350
Light Horse are included in the above Calculation. All these troops are illy
clad, badly fed, and worse paid having in general two or three years pay due
to them. Many of the best officers of the Army have resigned, and others
are daily following their Example, through Disgust, necessity, and a Conviction that the Provinces will not be able to Establish there Independence.

There has long subsisted a Jealousy between Congress and the Army.
The former have been Jealous of the Power of the latter, and the latter
have thought themselves neglected, and ill treated by the former, who have
excluded the Army from every Appointment of honor, or profit in the Civil
Line. The Common Soldiers are exceedingly disgusted with the Service,
and every effort to recruit the Army (except by Temporary Draughts of
Militia) has hitherto proved ineffectual. Congress and General Washington
last Spring made the most pressing Demands on the Colonies to furnish a
Body of Troops to complete the Army to 35,000 men, every Argument was
urged to enforce the Demand, among others that it would enable General
Washington (in conjunction with the French Troops) to oblige Sir Henry
Clinton to evacuate New York—and thereby put a Period to the War: The
Colonies promised to Comply with the Requisition, every effort was used,
but without Success. The Body of the People heartily tired of the war refused to Inlist Voluntarily, and not more than one-third of the men ordered
to be Draughted, appeared in the Field. The Distress and Discontents of
the People are daily increasing, and the difficulty of Recruiting the Army
another year will undoubtedly be greater than ever.

The Navy is reduced to three Frigates, and a few small vessels, who
are generally in Port, for want of hands to man them.

The Treasury is entirely empty and the finances are at the lowest Ebb. The Public Debt inclusive of Paper emitted by Congress, and the Colonies, Loan Office Certificates, and Arrears due to the Army, Commissaries and Quarter Masters amounts to upwards of Four hundred Million of Paper Dollars. Congress have lost all Confidence and Credit with the People, who have been too often deceived and duped by them to pay any regard to their promises in future, the different Provinces have very little more Credit with the People than Congress. Their late Emissions of Paper for the payment of which they have given every possible Security, can hardly be said to have any Currency, and is Depreciating Rapidly.

As the result of their Distresses the Eyes of the People are in general opened, they Feel their Error and look back with Remorse to their once happy Condition, and most ardently wish for a reconciliation on Terms safe and honorable to both countries. Many would Return to it with implicit Confidence. Some doubt the Sufficiency of the Powers of the present Commissioners [John Adams and John Jay] to Offer or Accept Terms for an Established accomodation. It would serve very good uses if the commissioners have Authority for it, to Signify that the Colonies upon returning to their obedience, shall be restored to their Antient Condition with Respect to their Charter, Rights, and Privileges, Civil and Religious, free from British Taxation, and to Invite to Negociation for General Regulations. It will increase the number of Advocates for the reunion.

But the best step is to Vest Commissioners with Decisive Powers on such Settlement as Great Britain may be willing to Establish. There will always be Jealousies seen while a Power is Reserved to Great Britain to approve or disapprove what Her Commissioners have done. With power in a Sett of Commissioners to bind the Nation as firmly as she would bind herself, by Future Acts of Parliament, I am of opinion that a Pacification would immediately take place.

But should the Artful and Designing who have assumed the Reins of government, continue to have sufficient Influence to mislead the Minds of the People, and continue the Opposition to Government, I am Clearly of Opinion that an addition of Ten thousand Troops to the American army (including those who may be on their way to America) will be a sufficient Force under the Direction of an Officer of the Experience and abilities of Sir Henry Clinton to put a period to the Contest in the Course of the next Campaign.

I have forgot to mention that the want of Provision in the Army is not owing to the Scarcity of Provision in the country, But to the weakness of the Usurpation in every Colony; without Money or Credit Supplies must be Collected by Force and Terror; wherever the Army are they take without opposition. But this force acts against Itself by Creating internal Enemies, and by making Friends to Great Britain. It is One of the Principal Saps hourly undermining the Strength of the Rebellion.

N. B. In the foregoing Estimate the French Troops at Rhode Island who amount to about 5000 Effectives are not Included.

B. Arnold.

[Ford, Ed., Winnowings, no. 5.]

"THE SCOUNDREL IS OF GREAT USE!": JAMES PARKER DESCRIBES THE ARNOLD-ANDRÉ AFFAIR

As for the Loyalists' reaction to Arnold's treason, James Parker probably expressed the feelings of his fellow refugees when he described him as infamous, as a scoundrel, as enriched by peculations, but as of great use all the same. His letter to Alexander Elmsley covers the daily events in the affair from September 20 to October 10.

1780

❮   *Dear Sir* [Alexander Elmsley]

. . . The World says a negotiation has been sometime on foot with the Rebel General Arnold for the surrender of West point, the strongest post on Hudsons river and key to the back Country, all their best artillery lys there, and it covers all the boats which enables them to cross and recross at pleasure.

Wednesday the 20th [September]. Washington with the Marquis Fayette crossed the North river with one hundred horse to visit the Comte de Rochambault at Hartford. About the same time Major André, our first Aid de Camp, went up the North river in the *Vulture* Sloop of War. Colonel Beverly Robinson, whoes estate is up there, went privately up before that and was in the secret. Washington was not expected to return in less than eight days. Major André landed friday morning—

Monday about 10 in the morning two of Washingtons aides arrived at Col Robinsons house which was Arnolds Quarters, told him that Washington was returning, and intended to dine with him that day. Business of importance obliged them to go on, and off went they.

They were hardly mounted when Arnold met at the door a person who slipt a note into his hand and went off. "Your friend is taken with your passport in his pocket" was the Contents. He went instantly down to the landing where lay a baye of his man'd. They were just put off when another appeared round a point a mile distant in chace; the wind was fair and he had a sail which give him the advantage, and after being fired on, got safe on board the *Vulture,* from whence he wrote to Washington, requesting that Major André, who he heared was taken, might be used with proper respect, adding, remember that I know all the Incendiarys in New York. Arnold arrived here the 26th and is very much attended to.

His private Character is infamous, like 99 in the 100 of all the rebel chiefs, but in the meantime the Scoundrel is of great use. By his peculations he had realized a very considerable estate about Philad^a; very probably the present state of their affairs made him flexible, as the Authority of the Lords of Congress is daily declining; In and about Paxton in pensylvania two thousand people have publickly associated to pay no more taxes and will resist the Collectors with force of Arms.

There is no doubt with me but the rebels have some very fast friends in this place, and higher up than they should be, tho' it is probable Arnold may not know Washingtons most confidential favourites, for notwithstanding A—was the favourite General of the Congress, W was allways jealous of him, suspecting, money being his God, that he would leave them. Had Washington staid his time, that fort, artillery, ammunition, boats, and a great part of his army would have been delivered up. The intelligence that occasioned his return certainly went from this place. Whilst an expedition to Rhode island or to Virginia was only talk'd of, West point never was thought of, tho' it appears now it was to have been the first object. One of the others will probably soon take place.

. . . Arnold is promoted to the rank of Brigadier General in the provincial line, and is to raise a regiment out of the rebel army. . . .

30th Major André with a Mr. Smith who was his guide part of the way are both under sentence of death. Genl [Archibald] Robertson, Mr. Elliot and Wm Smith, brother to the Other, go up to Morrow to try if they can make any terms to save them. . . .

[October] 2^d Govr Robertson etc. returned. They did not see Washington. Green carried some messages between them to very little purpose.

5th Major André was executed at the very time Green was carrying the Messages. His servant is returned with his Cloaths. He beg'd to be shot, they would not indulge him. Washington signed his death warrant. Few here expected this would have been his fate. The Congress left the whole to Washington, who, regardless of what was said of retalliation, would not harken to any terms to save him.

10th . . . Arnold has been burnt in effigy at Phil[a]. They seized his papers there whereby some discoverys are made that greatly distress the Congress. D. Franks, Wm. Hamilton and Bell the printer are put in jail and many are absconded. [*Parker Papers,* 920 PAR I, no. 13/1.]

17 "THAT MEMORABLE NIGHT": ANNA RAWLE EXPLAINS
THE NECESSITY OF ILLUMINATING THE TORIES' HOUSES ON
THE RECEPTION OF THE NEWS OF CORNWALLIS'S SURRENDER

When the news of Cornwallis's surrender was officially confirmed, Philadelphia broke out in wild celebration, while the Loyalists nursed their melancholy and condoled with each other over the bleakness of their future. The immediate problem for them, however, was to protect their homes through the night of jubilation, which they accomplished, as Anna Rawle portrays it, by illuminating their own windows as if they too were celebrants. Anna Rawle, a stepdaughter of Samuel Shoemaker, a prominent Pennsylvania Loyalist, had remained in Philadelphia after her parents had taken refuge in New York. She recorded the details of the memorable night of October 24 in diary form for her mother's interest.

1781

❧ October 24—. . . It is too true that Cornwallis is taken. [Colonel Tench] Tiligman is just arrived with dispatches from Washington which confirm it. B[enjamin] S[hoemaker] came here and shewed us some papers; long conversations we often have together on the melancholy situation of things.

October 25—. . . I suppose, dear Mammy, thee would not have imagined this house to be illuminated last night, but it was. A mob surrounded it, broke the shutters and the glass of the windows, and were coming in; none but forlorn women here. We for a time listened for their attacks in fear and trembling till, finding them grow more loud and violent, not knowing what to do, we ran into the yard. Warm Whigs of one side, and [James] Hartley's of the other (who were treated even worse than we), rendered it impossible for us to escape that way. We had not been there many minutes before we were drove back by the sight of two men climbing the fence. We thought the mob were coming in thro' there, but it proved to be Coburn and Bob Shewell, who called to us not to be frightened, and fixed lights up at the windows, which pacified the mob, and after three huzzas they moved off. A number of men came in afterwards to see us. French and J. B. nailed boards up at the broken pannels, or it would not have been safe to have gone to bed. Coburn and Shewell were really very kind; had it not been for them I really believe the house would have been pulled down. Even the firm Uncle [William] Fisher was obliged to submit to have his windows illuminated, for they had pickaxes and iron bars with which they had done considerable injury to his house. . . . In short it was the most alarming scene I ever remember. For two hours we had the disagreeable noise of stones banging about, glass crashing, and the tumultuous voices of a large body of men, as they were a long time at the different houses in the neighbourhood. At last they were victorious, and it was one general illumination throughout the town. As we had not the pleasure of seeing any of the gentlemen in the house, nor the furniture cut up, and goods stolen, nor been beat, nor pistols pointed at our breasts, we may count our sufferings slight compared to many others. Mr. Gibbs was obliged to make his escape over a fence, and while his wife was endeavouring to shield him from the rage of one of the men, she received a violent bruise in the breast and a blow in the face which made her nose bleed. Ben Shoemaker was here this morning; tho' exceedingly threatened he says he came off with the loss of four panes of glass. Some Whig friends put candles in the windows which made his peace with the mob, and they retired. John Drinker has lost half the goods out of his shop and been beat by them; in short the sufferings of those they pleased to style Tories would fill a volume and shake the credulity of those who were not here on that memorable night, and today Philadelphia makes an uncommon appearance, which ought to cover the Whigs with eternal confusion. . . .

October 26—. . . It seems universally agreed that Philadelphia will no longer be that happy asylum for the Quakers that it once was. Those joyful days when all was prosperity and peace are gone, never to return; and perhaps it is as necessary for our society to ask for terms as it was for Cornwallis. [*Rawle Diary, Penna. Mag. Biog. Gen., vol. XVI, pp. 104–107.*]

18 "THE LOSS OF CORNWALLIS AND 6000 MEN IS NOT AN OBJECT FOR GREAT BRITAIN TO MOURN FOR," JOHN HAMILTON TELLS A FRIEND

Even as the peace negotiations were under way in France a Charleston Loyalist, John Hamilton, was writing to a London friend that Yorktown was not the final determinant of the struggle and that Britain should expend her last man and shilling before acquiescing in American independence.

John Hamilton was part of the flow of Scotch-Irish immigrants who came to America during the pre-Revolutionary decade. A native of northern Ireland, he reached New York in 1767, and a few years later settled in Charleston as a merchant. After the Loyalist Highlanders were defeated at Moore's Creek (February 29, 1776) and the British had failed to push an attack on Charleston, Hamilton was among the friends of Britain who sought a quiet retirement in the backcountry, hoping to avoid service and sit out the disturbances. He settled on his frontier plantation and continued to trade there until called up by the rebels in 1778. Expediency dictated that he should take their oath to avoid dispossession and persecution; he joined their forces, but was confined to his tent for refusing to cooperate. With the resumption of a Southern campaign, he reverted to the King's side and soon held the commission of lieutenant colonel of militia. His company was garrisoned at Savannah during the siege by the rebel forces; he was taken prisoner during the siege of Charleston, but exchanged; he served under John Harris Cruger at Ninety-Six until the frontier posts were abandoned in June 1781.[1] A generous-hearted man, he was popular with his troops and respected by the rebels.[2] Eight months after he wrote the following letter to a friend in England urging that America was not yet lost, he joined the Loyalist trek to Nova Scotia.

[1] *Loyalist Transcripts*, vol. XLIII, p. 133 ff.
[2] Edward McCrady, *The History of South Carolina, 1775–1780*, New York: 1901, p. 337.

❡ I was in a State of Despondence for some time untill his Majesty's speech arrived when it revived my Spirits, but what was my astonishment when I Read Lord George G[ermai]n's and Lord North's speech in parliament; surely they can never be so weak as to give up this Country.

Our Country is lost in dissipation, luxury and faction. There is no publick Spirit or virtue left either to reward merrit or punish offences. Remove all Such wretches from power and leave the Execution of affairs to the brave, zealous Loyalists, who have lost their fortunes and Risk'd their lives in defence of their King and Country; such are the men who will save their Country from Ruin and distruction.

This Country is not yet lost; it's to be gain'd still and easier than ever, but the Ministers seem to give all over at a time when they ought most to Exert themselves and Convince their Enemies that the loss of Lord Cornwallis and 6000 men is not an object for Britain to mourn for.

Great Britain has more to fear from her internall Enemies than her externall ones; it's the Villainy of your great people at home that has Ruin'd the Nation, not your open Foes.

Notwithstanding all our Misfortunes, Great Britain can never, must never relinquish America. The last man and shilling must be expended before she gives America her independence; if she looses America, she looses all her West Indies and must Revert again to her insular Situation, which hardly made her visible on the face of the Earth.

Some examples must be made. A General, an Admiral and others must pay for our Misfortunes; a Spirited minister must take place and an honest man who will reward merit and punish the offenders. Then we may Expect to become ourselves again, but not before a very great change is made.

I still flatter myself the war will be carried on with vigour in North Carolina and Virginia and a large reinforcement sent out this season. The inhabitants are tired of their French Connections and with the Tyranny of their Leaders which is more conspicuous than ever. It behooves the nation at large to interfere and prevent the Ministry from giving America her independence. Your Salvation depends on Spirited Exertions at present, if not and America is given up, Britain must become a Province of France and America. [*PRO H.O. 42-1.*]

19 FREDERICK SMYTH OF NEW JERSEY FEELS IT IS HIGH
TIME TO TERMINATE THE WAR

Lawyers in New Jersey were among the first residents to be complained against and maltreated by the rebels. Frederick Smyth, who had occupied the office of Chief Justice of New Jersey since 1764, knowing that he was marked a Tory, retired to New York City in 1776. Feeling that his advice and assistance on New Jersey matters would be useful, the British government requested him to stay rather than sail for England and continued to pay him a generous salary of £400 through 1783. On the evacuation of New York he removed to Philadelphia where he married a woman of fortune and found employment in helping in the recovery of debts. Although he retained his allegiance to Great Britain, he was allowed to settle down unmolested. In fact, he made no effort to dissimulate, saying: "It has been said, I believe, that I am become a sworn Citizen of the States. God forbid! I live in Philadelphia at present, but if I could be assured that Government wou'd provide for me in any manner worth a Voyage at my time of Life, I certainly wou'd come to England."[1]

Following the surrender at Yorktown he saw clearly that British interests lay in ending a conflict which was draining the Treasury and wrote accordingly to Sir Charles Blagden in London.

DECEMBER 5, 1781

❡ . . . As I have seen our affairs year after year growing from bad to worse and little prospect of any amendment, I think it high time to terminate the war in this Country, for, in truth, the war in this Country is now little more than a war upon the Treasury, and we have a list of Generals in this place under the denomination of Quartermaster, Barrackmaster, etc., who have shown vast intrepedity, great generalship and by no means, like some other Generals, any signs of fainting in the chase. . . .

MAY 10, 1782

❡ Sir Guy Carleton arrived here a few days past and our revolution in offices is as extraordinary as yours in England; his language of the Ameri-

---

[1] *Loyalist Transcripts,* vol. XL, p. 67.

cans is all gentleness, good will, and forbearance. . . . A Letter to General Washington, I am told, is sent to announce his arrival and taking the command of the Army with instructions of his wishes that the war may be carried on with as much attention to humanity, justice, and civility as possible; this seems to have been necessary as a cursed spirit of revenge called retaliation has of late been very prevalent. What effect the change of Ministry or the very submissive (prudent shall I call it) Act of Parliament may have on the minds of Congress I know not, but I have neither heard of or discover^d any symptoms of an inclination to relinquish independence. Tis said in the country the general report is independence is agreed on by the present ministry, that the Congress has no doubt reconciliation, even on that condition, will be agreed to, but you know how fond we are in this Town of catching at reports. [*Blagden Letters, Royal Society, London.*]

Casting Accounts

DECEMBER 1782–1800

The Onset of Peace

The terms of the preliminary treaty of peace, signed in Paris November 30, 1782, were known in New York shortly after the start of the new year and an armistice was declared January 20, 1783. The definitive treaty, however, was not signed until September 3, more than nine months later. Meanwhile confusion and uncertainties about some of the articles penalized the Loyalists. While Articles V and VI supposedly provided protection of their persons and their interests, there was no assurance that local committees would observe them or that the states would follow the recommendation of Congress to restore estates of Loyalists who had not borne arms against the victors. Article V provided that all persons, whether they had borne arms or not, "shall have free Liberty to go to any Part or Parts of the thirteen United States and therein to remain twelve Months unmolested in their Endeavors to obtain the Restitution of such of their Estates Rights & Properties as may have been confiscated." Also, they were to "meet with no lawful Impediment in the Prosecution of their just Rights." According to Article IV, these rights included "the recovery of the full value in Sterling Money of all bona fide Debts heretofore contracted." Article VI was stated in unequivocal words:

"There shall be no future Confiscations made nor any Prosecutions commenc'd against any Person or Persons for or by Reason of the Part which he or they may have taken in the present War, and that no Person shall on that Account suffer any future Loss or Damage, either in his Person Liberty or Property. . . ."

This chapter deals primarily with the wanton disregard of these terms by individuals and local committees and the fateful consequences to trusting Loyalists who ventured home. A spirit of retaliation and bravado dominated the victors, bringing to the losers the realization of the full price which they would pay for their loyalty to the Crown.

I   A MILITARY STRATAGEM: ANDREW DEVEAUX, UNAWARE OF THE PEACE, SECURES NEW PROVIDENCE (NASSAU) FROM THE SPANISH BY INGENUITY

One final military episode in the events of the war occurred nine days after Britain and Spain had signed a peace treaty which restored the Bahamas to Britain. It concerned a spirited officer of the South Carolina militia, Lieutenant Colonel Andrew Deveaux, Jr. He was only seventeen when the war began and already enjoyed a reputation for expert horsemanship and for chicanery. Edward Rutledge referred to him as "that young rascal Deveaux."[1] Typical of his rascality was the trick perpetrated on his rebel cousin, Robert Barnwell of Beaufort, who had taken him prisoner and been hoodwinked into permitting his escape through violation of parole. Shortly thereafter Deveaux returned to Beaufort to plague his cousin again. Taking advantage of Barnwell's poor eyesight, Deveaux seized a spyglass as he entered the house, pointed it at Barnwell, and demanded his surrender and parole. Thinking the glass was a blunderbuss, Barnwell capitulated and gave his parole as a prisoner.[2]

Deveaux's best-known prank was one which helped capture the Span-

---

[1] Edward Rutledge to Arthur Middleton, Mar. 16, 1782. *So. Car. Hist. Gen. Mag.*, vol. XXVII, p. 10.

[2] Joseph Johnson, *Traditions and Reminiscences of the American Revolution*, Charleston: 1851, p. 177. After the war Deveaux returned to New York, married Anna Verplanck, and settled along the Hudson, ibid., p. 181.

ish-held island of New Providence (now Nassau) in the Bahamas in April 1783. The island had been occupied by seven hundred Spanish troops for almost a year and now Deveaux planned to retake it by means of an ingenious stratagem which would deceive the Spanish commander as to the size of his forces. In St. Augustine he gathered arms, British uniforms, provisions, six small vessels, and some sixty-five men, including some Cherokees, Choctaws, and Seminoles. The expedition sailed from St. Augustine March 30, convoyed by some privateers, the *Perseverance* with twenty-six guns and the *Whitby Warrior* with sixteen guns, and two smaller vessels. At Harbour Island another 170 men were recruited and equipped with uniforms and arms brought along from Florida. Fifty fishing boats were added to the expedition to be used in deceiving the enemy as to the numbers landing. The first objective was Fort Montagu at the eastern entrance of New Providence Harbor. Captain Roderick Mackenzie has vividly described Deveaux's ruse—making a misleading display of fishing boats, Indians, fascines, and scaling ladders—and its success in securing a bloodless surrender of the fort. Boats, overflowing with troops, Indians, and even men of straw, were ferried to land and returned to the ships seemingly empty, but actually with the men crouched in the bottom, ready to be used again in the next ferrying. The Spaniards, counting boats and trips, seeing the prominent ladders and siege equipment and hearing the Indians' war whoops, spiked their cannon and withdrew to Fort Nassau, the larger fortress back on the hill. The Spanish Governor, Don Antonio Claraco Sanz, and the entire garrison, overawed by Deveaux's supposedly formidable numbers, capitulated three days later.[3]

Deveaux's own account to Sir Guy Carleton of the expedition against New Providence plays down the artful techniques of his military genius, but the loyal inhabitants of the island, in a grateful address to Deveaux, readily attributed their deliverance to his Military Stratagem. The commissioners examining Loyalist claims granted Deveaux an annual allowance of £ 100, commenting that his ruse was "an act of Spirit which we admire and which we think ought not to go without Reward."[4]

---

[3] Roderick Mackenzie, *Strictures on Lt. Col. Carleton's History of the Campaigns of 1780 and 1781 in the Southern Provinces of North America. . . . To Which is added a Detail of the Siege of Ninety-Six and the Recapture of the Island of New Providence,* London: 1787, pp. 176–178, 181; 185–186.
[4] *Loyalist Transcripts,* vol. VI, p. 517.

❦ *Sir* [Sir Guy Carleton]

I have the pleasure to inform Y^r Excellency that on the first of April last, not hearing of the confirmation of Peace at St. Augustine, formed from thence an expedition against New Providence to restore the Inhabitants of it, with those of the adjacent Ilands, to the blessings of a free government. I undertook this expedition at my own expence and embarked my men, which did not exceed 65, and Sailed for Harbour Iland where I recruited for four or five days. From thence I set Sail for my object, which was the Eastern fort on the Iland of Providence, which I carried about daylight, with three of their formidable Gallies, on the 14th of the Month. I immediately Summoned the grand fortress [Fort Nassau] to a Surrender, which was about a Mile from the fort I had taken [Fort Montague]. His Excely the Governor avaded the purport of my Flag by giving me some trifeling informations which I took in its true light. On the 16th took pocession of two commanding hills and erected a Battry on each of them of 12 pounders. At daylight on the 18th, my Bat.^{s} being compleat, the English colours were hoisted on each of them which were within musketshot of their Grand fortress. His Excellency, finding his shot & shells of no effect, thought proper to capitulate. . . . My force never at [any] time consisted of more than two hundred & twenty men and not above one hundred & fifty of them had muskets, I not having it in my power to procure them at St. Augustine.

I took on this occasion one Fort consisting of thirteen pieces of cannon, three formidable Gallies with 24 pounders & about 50 Men. His Excellency surrendered four formidable Batteries with about 70 pieces cannon & 4 large Gallies (Brigs & Snows,) which have sent to the Havanna with the Troops as Flags. I therefore stand in need of Y^r Excellencys advice & directions in my present Situation & will be exceedingly happy to receive them as Shortly as possible. . . .

On inquiry you will find that I^m an American, a loyalist who have sacrafised a considerable fortune in S^o. Caralina for my attatchment to the crown, & have been just able to save as much from the wreck of my lost fortune [to have] supported this expedition, which have unfortunately prooved too late. I therefore humbly Request Y^r Excellencys attention & recommendation to His Majesty. I have been particularly known by every commanding officer in the Southern district during the war & have acted for the three last years of this unhappy war with a Commission from Lord

Cornwallis for a provincial Regiment raised by me, which was afterwards cut up & disolved.

I have the Hon^r to be Y^r Excel^{ys} most obed. & very humble Servt

> A. *Deveaux,* Col^o & Command^g Royal
> Forresters New Providence
> [*Headquarters Papers, PRO 305, vol. LXX, no. 7906.*]

2 THE SPIRIT OF VINDICTIVENESS: THOMAS JONES RECORDS THE MERCILESS TREATMENT OF LOYALISTS ON THE BRITISH EVACUATION OF CHARLESTON

One of the first moves of Sir Guy Carleton, the new Commander in Chief, on his arrival in New York (May 5, 1782) was to evacuate the Southern ports—"a deplorable necessity," he said, "in consequence of an unsuccessful war."[1] The British garrisons left Savannah July 11 and Charleston five months later, delivering the ports to the victorious rebels. Some five thousand Loyalists, some of whom were former rebels, who had sought protection in Charleston in response to British proclamations offering them pardons and security chose to flee with the British troops rather than brave the rancor of their enemies.[2] The British military occupation for 2½ years had engendered so much bitterness against collaborators that the distinction between those who cooperated with the British out of necessity and those who were genuine or self-interested Loyalists broke down. The victors believed that Tories of all degrees were responsible for the prolongation of the war and punished them fairly indiscriminately. The civil conflict was too personal, the tyranny of military occupation too real for forgiveness or justice. For the time being safety for most Tories lay in flight. Thomas Jones relates the distress of the Loyalists fleeing from Charleston and the way the rebels took vengeance on those who opted to remain, some of whom were promptly hanged.

[1] Sir Guy Carleton to Lt. General Alexander Leslie, July 15, 1782. Carleton Papers, no. 5071. See *Report on American Manuscripts in the Royal Institute of Great Britain,* Hereford: 1907, vol. III, p. 19.
[2] *The Charleston Year Book, 1883,* gives 9,127 as the number who left with the British, p. 416. See also Robert Barnwell, "The Migration of Loyalists from South Carolina," *So. Car. Historical Soc. Proc.* (1937), pp. 40–42.

❧ To provide in some measure for these poor wretches, the commanders of the garrisons (though contrary to their orders) protracted the evacuations as long as they possibly could, without offending the Ministry. Transports were procured, and several hundreds with their personal property went to St. Augustine, in Florida, the Governor of which granted each family a tract of land, upon which they sat down and began the world anew. Numbers went to the Bahama Islands, others to the Summer Islands, to Jamaica, to Nova Scotia, to Newfoundland, and to Canada. But such a number were still left behind, that properly to describe their situation upon the evacuations is scarcely possible. There were old grey-headed men and women, husbands and wives with large families of little children, women with infants at their breasts, poor widows whose husbands had lost their lives in the service of their King and country, with half a dozen half starved bantlings taggling at their skirts, taking leave of their friends. Here, you saw people who had lived all their days in affluence, (though not in luxury) leaving their real estates, their houses, stores, ships, and improvements, and hurrying on board the transports with what little household goods they had been able to save. In every street were to be seen men, women, and children wringing their hands, lamenting the situation of those who were about leaving the country, and the more dreadful situation of such who were either unable to leave, or were determined, rather than run the risk of starving in distant lands, to throw themselves upon, and trust to, the mercy of their persecutors, their inveterate enemies, the rebels of America.

Their fears and apprehensions were soon realized. No sooner had the evacuation taken place at Charleston than the rebels, like so many furies, or rather devils, entered the town, and a scene ensued, the very repetition of which is shocking to the ears of humanity. The Loyalists were seized, hove into dungeons, prisons and provosts. Some were tied up and whipped, others were tarred and feathered; some were dragged to horse-ponds and drenched till near dead, others were carried about the town in carts with labels upon their breasts and backs with the word "Tory" in capitals written thereon. All the Loyalists were turned out of their houses and obliged to sleep in the streets and fields, their covering the canopy of heaven. A universal plunder of the friends to government took place and, to complete the scene, a gallows was erected upon the quay facing the harbour, and twenty-four reputable Loyalists hanged in sight of the British fleet, with the army and refugees on board. This account of the evacuation of Charleston I had from a British officer who was upon the spot, ashore at the time and an eye-witness to the whole. [*Jones, History New York, vol II, pp. 235-236.*]

3 "THE MOB NOW REIGNS": A LOYALIST IN NEW YORK
APPRAISES THE DIRE SITUATION OF REFUGEES BOTH BLACK
AND WHITE

In other states the picture was not far different from that in South Carolina. Instead of justice, equity, and a spirit of conciliation which the peace treaty said "on the Return of the Blessings of Peace should universally prevail," a spirit of rancor, vengeance, and injustice reigned. While legislation injurious to the Loyalists appeared in all the states, it was particularly severe in New York where Loyalists had been concentrated and active. Instead of the promised end to confiscations, instead of protection against further suffering in person or property for any part taken during the war, there was ostracism, persecution, barbarity, and new miseries.[1] During the months from April to November 1783, when the British evacuation of New York was in progress and state government was still ineffective, committees in various districts assumed control and meted out punishment to the Loyalists in a reckless, inhuman way. As William Smith wrote about Dutchess County: "There is undoubtedly a particular Set in the County (and tis likely in every other within the State) that are promoting Measures to intimidate as many Loyalists as they can to force them to leave this Country. . . . [The Bill of Attainder] found against several persons last week is directly contrary to one of the articles of the Treaty, vizt., that no future Confiscation or Prosecution shall take place against any Person for the Part they may have taken *in the War.* I am informed that the greatest Part of the Jurors summoned to this Court were Persons that have incouraged and been concerned in the late Committee Businesses in this County."[2] A Loyalist in New York,

---

[1] See Article VI, pp. 353-354.
[2] Extract from a letter from [William Smith] to [Sir Guy Carleton], Poughkeepsie, July 25, 1783, Carleton Papers, PRO 30/55, vol. 76, no. 8,523.

appraising the ruinous situation of the refugees in that city, wrote Lord Hardwicke about the confusion which permeated the city and in fact the whole countryside.[3]

[1783]

❡ The Rebels breathe the most rancorous and malignant Spirit everywhere. Committees and Associations are formed in every Colony and Resolves passed that no Refugees shall return nor have their Estates restored. The Congress and Assemblies look on tamely and want either the Will or the Power to check those Proceedings. In short, the Mob now reigns as fully and uncontrolled as in the Beginning of our Troubles and America is as hostile to Great Britain at this Hour as she was at any Period during the War. From all this many people conclude that the Army will not be withdrawn from hence this Year, that the British Troops at least will keep Possession of New York, as it will be very difficult, if possible, to send off any more than the Foreign Troops, and as it would be highly imprudent to abandon this Place in the present Posture of Affairs. Certain it is that, if the whole Army goes away this Year, very few Refugees or Inhabitants within the British Lines will be able to stay behind. Besides those gone to Europe and Canada, upwards of eleven thousand persons have already removed to Nova Scotia and twelve thousand more have given in their Names to be carried to Nova Scotia and other Places. Almost all the principal people here are gone or going; not the tenth part of the Inhabitants will be able to remain if the Army goes this year.

Without the Lines every thing is equally gloomy. Confusion and Discontent prevail. The Load of Taxes is intolerable. Farms in general pay a Tax which is greater than the Rents they paid formerly. Every other Species of Property is proportionably taxed. This, joined to the Insolence of the new

---

[3] Captain Gideon White, a former Portsmouth merchant and one of the founders of Shelburne, Nova Scotia, wrote to Lt. Henry Paget on April 14, 1783: "The uncommon close of this War has distracted every Good man—you can have no Idea of the confusion here. There are now in this Garrison about fifteen Hundred of the Subject of Congress, come in to take possession and Speculate in Trade—any man comes in as he pleases. . . . The Rebells are determined not to allow the Loyalists to returne to take possession of their Estates, a Circumstance many of us hope will be the Cause of damning them Yet. I think we may have a little amusement ere long with them. God direct it may be so. . . ." *White Collection of Manuscripts,* no. 191, vol. 3, Public Archives Nova Scotia.

Rulers, the unsettled State of Government, and the want of Security for the Persons and Property of Individuals induce Multitudes to wish for a removal and accordingly have applied to Sir G. Carleton for the purpose. I am told that upwards of One hundred thousand people without the Lines have already applied to be transported to Nova Scotia and Canada. At the same time the cool and dispassionate Adherents to Congress are of Opinion that their present System of Government cannot hold long and that the Powers of Congress are utterly inadequate to the Government of this Country. A very sensible Man from without the Lines told me lately that the judicious people among them did not expect their present Form of Government could last longer than four or five Years, if so long; and, on asking him what Form would be adopted in its Place, he answered, Monarchy.

In the several Assemblies there are some liberal Persons who are for recalling all the Loyalists, or for excluding none but a few that are most obnoxious hitherto. However, there has been a Majority against such Motions in each Assembly and the Leaders of the Mob will not listen to anything of that Kind. The purchasers of confiscated Estates and all who have risen from Obscurity to Power and Eminence are violent against the Loyalists and the Return of Refugees, the former least they should lose the Estates which they purchased for a Trifle, the latter least they should again sink into their Original Obscurity; and it unfortunately happens that those two Descriptions are not only numerous, but also include many of the most active Men and such as have most Influence.

The Congress have disbanded most of their Army—all that were enlisted during the War. None remain but those that were enlisted for three Years and amount, as I am told, to about 4000. Congress have also stated their public Debt, the whole of which, Foreign and Domestic, as far as it could be ascertained, amounts, according to their Statement, to forty-two million of Spanish Dollars. It is supposed that it must be much more, as many Domestic Debts could not be ascertained and the Debts of particular Colonies which cannot be less than a fourth part of this Sum are not included. But supposing the Debt to be no more, it is absolutely impossible for America in its present exhausted State to pay either the Interest or Principal; and indeed many declare without Hesitation that the Americans neither can nor will pay either. Moral Principles, I do assure you, are at a very [low] Ebb in America at present, and I should not be surprized to hear of an explicit Refusal to pay any part of this Money.

The only good Tidings I have to send you is that Sir G. Carleton is not leaving us. While he stays I think myself safe; and were he left intirely to himself to manage Affairs as he pleased, with the Army he has, I have not the least Doubt but he would yet bring everything in America to a happy Conclusion. He sees Things in a just Light, has Judgment and Penetration to manage Affairs properly, and will neither be frightened, cajoled, nor diverted by Congress or their Adherents in any Measure he undertakes. He has an Altercation with those People at present about Negroes. An Article of the *wise* provisional Treaty obliges us to give up all Negroes and, accordingly, the Rebels have claimed all that came within the Lines. But many Negroes came in Consequence of Royal Proclamations promising them Protection and Liberty. Sir G. thinks that no minister can by a Treaty disannull those Proclamations; and indeed it would be inhuman to the last Degree and a base Violation of Public Faith to send those Negroes back to their Masters who would beat them with the utmost Cruelty. Accordingly, such Negroes as came in by Virtue of those Proclamations are permitted to go wherever they please. If they chuse to go to their Masters, it is well; if not, they are transported to Nova Scotia or else where as they desire. Sir Guy Carleton in this, as in every thing else, has acted with Openness and Candor. Before any Negroes went off, he desired M^r. Washington to appoint Commissioners to inspect all Embarkations. The Commissioners accordingly came and take Account of all Negroes that go away. The Rebels bluster about this Matter and declare it a Violation of the Provisional Treaty, but Sir Guy goes on deliberately and steadily and refers the Business to future Discussion, that Compensation may be made to the Masters of the Negroes if judged necessary. No Man can be a warmer Friend to the Loyalists than Sir Guy and perhaps no Man has it so much in his Power to serve them. [*"Extract of a Letter from an American at N.Y."* British Museum, *Add. Mss, 35,621, pp. 364-366.*]

4 "THE POWER IS IN THE HANDS OF THE LOWEST OF THE PEOPLE": STEPHEN SKINNER EVALUATES THE COUNTRY'S PLIGHT

Stephen Skinner, a brother of Cortlandt Skinner, the last royal Attorney General of New Jersey, was also a distinguished New Jersey resident, a member of the Council and a judge of the Court of Common Pleas of Middlesex County. In 1768, when he was Treasurer of the Colony, a shortage of £ 6,000 in the Treasury's iron chest was discovered. The culprit was never found and thus Skinner was never cleared.[1] After his brother fled, he too was strongly advised to leave Amboy. In March 1776, he took refuge on a British brigantine, taking with him his wife, his sister, ten children, and a few friends.

Taken prisoner in July 1776, he was allowed to return to the vicinity of his home only after he agreed to post a £ 10,000 bond. The following spring his home, storehouses, wharf, and other houses in Amboy which he owned were burned and he was forced to remove to New York. During the remainder of the war he served as major of a Loyalist battalion, losing in the end all the rest of his real and personal property through confiscation. Before leaving for England to push his claim for compensation, he wrote his friend Effingham Lawrence that the "giddy multitude" was dictating to a "tottering" Congress, producing anarchy and confusion in the land.

JUNE 11, 1783

❦ *Sir*

. . . This Country is all confusion. The very Government, said to be established, is tottering, Committees forming in every state and declarations of Resolves from those Committees that no restoration [to the Loyalists] shall be made. The present Government will comply with what the Giddy multitude please to dictate; in short, all at present Anarchy and confusion and must be so for some years to Come.

The letters from your side the water congratulate their friends here on the Harmony and good understanding that prevails in this Country but believe me, my dear sir, when I tell you it is the reverse and that no good can happen till the reasonable and thinking part of the Community step forth, men of Character and moderation, for their Rulers, for at present the power is in the Hands of the lowest of the people and they will not easily part with it. This City is crowded with people from without and every indulgence Granted them that is possible, but Change the scene, and if a Loyalist makes his appearance amongst them, he is sure to be insulted. My resolution is fixed to remain and not stir a Peg, for I think it is time enough to take leave of my Estate when there is no prospect left.

. . . No doubt there will be a great run of Business from Europe to this Country. Goods will be low here and from the Scarcity of Cash and the

---

[1] Sabine, *Loyalists,* vol. II, pp. 307–38.

little produce of this Country that is saleable in Europe many adventurers will be ruined in the article of Dry goods. I wish my friends not to enter too largely in the Credit of this Country. If they do, the chance is ten to one they will suffer. [*Skinner, Letterbook, N.Y. Historical Society.*]

5 "TAKE YOUR ALL ... AND FOLLOW YOUR FRIENDS": JOHN COOK OF DUTCHESS COUNTY GIVES HIS INFORMATION ABOUT THE COMMITTEEMEN BEFORE WILLIAM SMITH

One of the Loyalists successfully intimidated by local committeemen was John Cook of Nine Partners, Dutchess County. When he tried to return home he was greeted abruptly with the words: "You are hereby notified to Depart this County by the first day of September, as you are considered an Enemy to your Country—therefore take your all, and your Family, and follow your Friends to that Country that the King, your Master, has provided for those of your Character; or Else you may expect the Blood of your injured Country will fall on your Head."[1] Although John Cook was taking care of a wife and 11 children on his 260-acre farm in Dutchess County, he left his estate and sought refuge in Livingston Manor. His deposition given before William Smith a month later describes the usurpation of power by the committeemen. Congress could recommend to the states fair treatment of the Loyalists, as provided in Article V of the peace treaty, but the state assemblies and local committeemen would act as they saw fit.

SEPTEMBER 16, 1783

❡   It appeared to him to be dangerous to abide any longer within the limits of their power, and he is in great apprehension for his safety in the Manor; nor indeed knows any Quarter in the Colony where any loyal Subject may hope for Protection, or the Benefit of the Provisional Articles. The Country in general is under the Dominion of Committees, and there can be no Confidence even in the new created Government, which the Committees despise. Mr. Clinton indeed talks favorably to those who are

[1] Rufus Herrick, Chairman of the District Committee, to John Cook, Aug. 19, 1783. *Carleton Papers*, PRO 30/55, vol. 81, no. 9143.

oppressed and against the usurped Power of Committeemen, but they find no Relief. The Language of the Committees is that none shall rule but the Majority of the People, and that the Committees represent the Majority; that the Acts and Agreements of the Congress, the Legislatures, Governors and Rulers are all to be subject to the will of the People expressed by the Committees, as the Representatives of the Majority of the People.

The Informant is credibly informed that very lately an Exchange was made of a farm in Dutchess County for another upon Long Island with Governor Clinton's Privity and Approbation, and yet after the removal of the Proprietor of the latter from Long Island to Dutchess County he was abused by the Committee of Rombout Precinct, whipped 39 lashes, and a Resolution made to repeat the whipping if he remained 24 hours in the Precinct, and to give the same Punishment to such as harboured or assisted him. The Informant had his Information from a Mr. Wyley of Rombout Precinct, who added that the Transaction had been represented to Governor Clinton, but it was followed with no Remedy, and it is a recent Event of within five or six Months. [*Carleton Papers, PRO 30/55, vol. 81, no. 9143.*]

6 DAVID COLDEN WRITES HIS NIECE OF THE PERSECUTION PREVAILING AS COMMITTEES REASSUME EXTRALEGAL POWERS

There was no consistency in the rebels' treatment of the Loyalists. Even the two sons of Lieutenant Governor Colden fared quite differently at the close of the war. Cadwallader II, who had first been imprisoned and then, in September 1778, obliged to move with his family from Coldenham (near Newburgh) to his brother's Flushing home, was able to return to his farm in 1784, when the Banishment Act was repealed. He had saved his estate by having his oldest son, Cadwallader III, a rebel sympathizer, stay on at Coldenham. David Colden, however, was not permitted to stay on at his home but was banished as a felon on pain of death by a special act of the Legislature, November 24, 1783. He wrote to Governor Clinton that if those in power would restore his estate and let him go home, he would be "a Faithful Citizen and give them as little Trouble as possible."[1] Neverthe-

---

[1] *Colden Papers,* Box XI, N.Y. Historical Society.

less, taking only his fifteen-year-old-son, Cad, with him, he was obliged to leave his home, wife, and six other children, for Aquahannock, New Jersey, and from there to flee to London, where he died shortly after arrival. The irony was that David never bore arms nor took an active part with the British, although he held the civil office of superintendent of police on Long Island, while his brother had actively aided the British by housing a messenger and having him safely conducted to the British lines.

The following extract from a letter, September 15, 1783, to Mrs. Richard Nicholls Colden, David Colden's niece living in Scotland, presents another glimpse of the confusion and persecution under which the Loyalists suffered when local committees assumed the right to punish the Loyalists in defiance of the terms of the peace.

SEPTEMBER 15, 1783

❦ . . . Some hundred Freeholders, Merchants and Inhabitants of Long Island, New York and Staaten Island have been indited under this Act [of Attainder, October 22, 1779] since the cessation of hostilities. So little effect have the preliminary articles yet had! I do not know that they have proceeded against any person not in full life, altho' they might under this very extraordinary act, declared by the preamble to be made in order to work a confiscation of estates for the use of the State. Tyrannical Law! made to take a man's life for the express purpose of getting his estate. Be not surprised at the warmth of my expressions; it affects me to the quick. . . . It is too severe to be continued. Hitherto it has lain unnoticed. It must now be annimadverted upon and stigmatised with such censure by the world that for the credit of a national character it must be blotted out. . . .

We have pass'd a twelve month in the most perplexing state of uncertainty that ever a people did. Long waiting for the [preliminary] articles, expecting they would certainly provide some security for the unfortunate loyalists, they have only increased our distress and cause of anxiety and to this hour we do not know that they will have the smallest effect in our favour. No measures have yet been taken by Congress, except the release of prisoners, or by any of the states, that we know of, in consequence of the treaty. Even the recommendation of Congress, to which the English Ministry have devoted the lives and fortunes of thousands, whose virtuous attachment to Government shall render their characters immortal, while that of the ministers shall be execrated, I say, even this recommendation has not yet come forth. The spirit of persecution and violence against the unhappy loyalists does not appear to abate in any degree since the cessation of hostilities. They are not suffered to go into the country even to take a last farewell of their relations. Committees are formd throughout the country who publish the most violent resolves against the loyalists and give instructions to the legislative bodies directly repugnant to the treaty. We are told that these committees have allarmd the people in power who wish to suppress them but know not how. The people have been taught a dangerous truth, that *all power is derived from them.* Nothing can now render the country tolerably happy but the strength and firmness of the Governors [and] the Legislative Bodies, those in whom the Constitution have placed the Power of Governing. The most dreadful anarchy must ensue, should the new Government prove unequal to the Task. An event most devoutly to be deprecated by every good Man! . . .

General Charlton [Carleton] has informed Congress by letter of the 17th of last month that he has received the Kings orders for the final evacuati[on] of New York, but that the infractions of the Treaty and violences committed in the country upon the loyalists has driven such multitudes of them to apply to him to be removed to some place of security that he cannot say when he shall be able to leave the place, being determind not to leave any loyalist behind who choses to go away. Above 30,000 men women and children have already been transported to Nova Scotia, etc. and a very large number are still waiting for ships to carry them. Many substantial farmers of Long Island and inhabitants of New York are gone and going, freightend away by inditements, and menaces, the fear of taxes, and an abhorrence of a republican government. . . .

Now for myself, here am I, condemnd to suffer death, if ever I am found in the State of New York; and yet my determination is to put them to the test. They have condemnd me while living at my usual place of residence, without calling on me to appear and take a tryal. I am not guilty of the treason alledged against me. My going or staying will not I conceive affect the recovery of my estate. If they are determined to have it, they surely will let me off with my life at any time. My family will be . . . in certain distress if I leave them, which they may escape if I stay with them. This, and a consciousness of innocence, determines my present resolution to keep possession of that part of my estate where I lived before and during the war. [*PRO, A. O. 13, 97. Amer. Hist. Rev., October 1919, pp. 82–86.*]

7 LOYALISTS INFORM SIR GUY CARLETON OF MEETING WITH
RANCOR AND RETRIBUTION WHEN THEY ATTEMPT TO
RETURN HOME

The Loyalists had no better friend than Sir Guy Carleton who, like William
Smith, saw "associations for the exclusion of the Loyalists daily extending
and with circumstances of additional rage." He wrote Lord North on
June 2, 1783: "The violence of interested men in the new States, more
particularly in that of New York, and of their popular assemblies had driven
so many Loyalists to the necessity of seeking new habitation from considerations of personal safety that the quantity of tonnage is wholly inadequate to
the various demands for it. . . . It is utterly impossible to leave exposed to
the rage and violence of these people men of character whose only offense
has been their attachment to the King's Government."[1]

The *Carleton Papers* are replete with information and petitions from
Loyalists in many other states telling of the abuse and suffering they met
with when they tried to return to their homes. The individual testimonies
which follow are indicative of the barbarities perpetrated on the Loyalists
which led Carleton in the interest of humanity to exert his utmost efforts
to help them leave.

Prosper Brown, asking for assistance to go to Nova Scotia with his
wife and two children, tells of the savage treatment he met with in Connecticut. He had been taken in 1781 by a privateer and kept in chains for over a
year and a half because of his efforts to promote the King's cause. He was
released by the Assembly's order and, trusting the terms of the peace treaty,
returned to New London to look after his property. George Beckwith, aide-
de-camp to Carleton, tells of mob activity around Simsbury, commenting
that "the Country in general is forming into Mobs, Committees, and Town
Meetings, which, if persevered in, will sap the foundations of any Government whatever."[2]

Thomas Hassard, a sea captain, trying to visit his family in Rhode
Island, tells how he was plundered and abused in Rhode Island. The resentment in New York was particularly bitter. A Loyalist refugee, returning to
the Walkill Valley to see his parents in October 1783, was tarred and feathered, head and eyebrows shaved, a hogyoke with cowbell put on his neck,

[1] *Carleton Papers,* PRO 30/55, vol. LXXI, no. 7902 and 7868.
[2] PRO 30/55, vol. LXXVII, no. 8671.

and a sheet of paper attached bearing a picture of a double-faced man representing Arnold and the Devil's imps. [3]

The guerilla conflict between DeLancey's Cowboys and the rebel Skinners under Israel Honeywell continued in Westchester long after hostilities ended. Rebel sufferers from this vendetta during the war, seeing a chance in the spring of 1783 to get even, took out grudges against Loyalists who had dared to remain in the area. Passive, sick, or elderly Loyalists suffered along with members of DeLancey's Cowboys. There are many accounts of Loyalists who were mistreated, whipped, and driven from their farms and homes, their horses, money, and clothes stolen. The memorials to Sir Guy Carleton of several victims of this ruthless feud show how implacable was the Skinners' revenge. For example, the brutalities to William Foshay, living on a farm near Tarrytown, described by his son, Isaac Foshay, is representative of the mistreatment of many Westchester farmers. Robert Hunt said his sister tried to intervene and she too was beaten. She gave the assailants £10 but they still took her brother outside and beat him until he lay motionless on the ground.

Considering the active part Oliver DeLancey took in the war as a brigadier general in the British forces, his deposition shows that he got off lightly with the Honeywell gang. About fifty armed men came to his home in Westchester; a number of them struck him with a club, bullied, insulted, and robbed him, and told him to run to "his damned King."

John Segee, one-armed, a soldier's son from Long Island, tried to visit a friend in Bedford. He was told to return or have his head cut off. Charles Ward and three men, he reported, "flogged him the whole way from North Castle to the White Plains. That at the White Plains they cut his hair . . . gave him between twenty and thirty strokes with his cane and told him to go about his Business and let his Friends on Long Island know that every Rascal of them that attempted to come among them would meet with the like treatment." John Mitchel of Cow Neck, Long Island, said that some armed men from New Rochelle forced the door of his home about 10 P.M., fired pistols, rushed the room, and knocked the deponent and his son down. The son fired and both escaped to collect some neighbors. When Mitchel returned he found his seventeen-year-old grandson dying at the door with two shots in him. The murderers were gone. [4]

[3] John Hardy, ed., *Valentine's Manual of the Corporation of the City of New York,* New York: 1870, p. 815.
[4] PRO 30/55, vol. LXVIII, no. 7623 (4); vol. LXIX, no. 7740.

Finally, Adam and John Graves and Nicholas Andrews of Maryland, imprisoned for recruiting, tell Sir Guy Carleton they prefer instant death to being again confined on the *Romulus* from which they had escaped. In all these instances and many more Carleton felt he could not force these Loyalists to return to the vengeful brutalities of their neighbors and did everything in his power to help them resettle under the more benign British rule.

Memorial of Prosper Brown of New London, Connecticut, to Sir Guy Carleton

JUNE 4, 1783

❡ The said Petitioner did in a civil and honest manner repair to his native place, namely New London, but was immediately secured and dragged by a licentious and bloodthirsty mob and hung up by the neck with his hands tied on board of a vessel laying alongside of the wharf and continued in that posture, the cruelty of which your Excellency can better conceive than his pen can dictate, after which he was taken down, stript, and whipt with a Cat and nine tails in a most inhuman manner and then tarred and feathered and again hung up at the yard arm as a public spectacle where he continued naked about a quarter of an hour exposed to the shame and huzzas of the most diabolic crew that ever existed on earth from whence they released him and put him on board of a boat and sent to this City on condition of never returning again to the Continent on pain of death. To conclude and crown his misery they robbed him of the sum of twenty-five Guineas in Gold and your Petitioner has arrived here in a most distressed situation about eight days since. [*Carleton Papers, PRO 30/55, Vol. 1, no. 7878.*]

George Beckwith [to Sir Guy Carleton]

AUGUST 9, 1783

❡ An Excise Master, the son of a Colonel in that Neighborhood [near Simsbury] being employed in the duties of his Office, the People rose in a mob and beat him cruelly, put him in a coal Basket, placed the Basket in a wheelbarrow, and wheeled him round the Town; they made him promise to resign his Office and never more to undertake such dirty business, which he did in the most solemn terms. His Father, hearing how roughly the Son had been treated, rode to Town the succeeding day to reprimand the People; they put him into the same Basket, turned his wig round, and placing the Basket in a Wheel Barrow, wheeled him round the Town till they forced him to promise never to come there on such a business again; they afterwards obliged him to ride home, with his wig turned Tail foremost. [*Carleton Papers, PRO 30/55, vol. LXXVII, no. 8671.*]

Thomas Hassard of Rhode Island to Sir Guy Carleton

JULY 25, 1783

❦ This is to inform your Excellency that I went Down to Martins Vineyards in a Vessel by a Permition from His Excellency Admiral Digby to Settle with some People their and Git my Property so as I might go to Noviscosie and a Coming Back from their I put into Rhod-island for a Harbour and went on Shore to see my family and was seased upon and was put to Prison and kep five Days in Prison and my Vesel seased upon and broke open and plundered and abused Threatned to take my Life and made me pay them the most Extravagant Carges for it and then Sent me there by a warent from the Governer Never to Return upon Pane of Death. And I Thout it was Proper to Inform your Excelencey of it and if the friends to Government is to be Treated in This Manner and no notis taken of it I should be Glad to Know How to Conduct myself for the futer. [*Carleton Papers, PRO 30/55, vol. LXXVI, no. 8522.*]

Deposition of Isaac Foshay of Philippsburg, New York

❦ ... His father ... was very sick, not able to ride or walk; the party then got a common wood Slide and put his father on it and carried him down to Tarrytown; said Honeywell then ordered his father out of the Slide and to walk and threatened to whip him if he did not and did drive him a few yards, but ye old man was so very weak and low that he could not walk and beged they would spare him. Honeywell then ordered him into the Slide again and ordered his said son William to drive him down to Morrissania, shaking his Sword over s^d Williams head to make him drive faster, telling him to drive his Corpes to Nova Scotia.

That his Brother William drove on and got about eight miles that night, when his father began to spit Blood and grew worse. The next day he proceeded to Morrissania, that his father died in three days after he got there always complaining of the hurts and bruises he received from Honeywell and his party by puting him on ye Slide and using him in the rough manner they did. [*Carleton Papers, PRO 30/55, vol. LXVIII, no. 7623 (1).*]

Deposition of Oliver DeLancey to David Mathews, Mayor of New York

MAY 16, 1783

❡ [About fifty armed men under Israel Honeywell came to his house in Westchester and struck him] in a most violent manner, calling out to this deponent . . . to run to Halifax or to his damned King, for that neither he nor one of his breed should be suffered to remain in the Country, that the Deponent apprehending his life in danger leapt out of the window . . . but was pursued by one of the Gang who informed the deponent that if he would deliver up the money he had in his pockets he would not beat him any more . . . [He] gave him all the money he had in his pockets, that the deponent was then carried back to his house where he received the most opprobrious Language from the said Honeywell and was again struck by one of the said Gang, that shortly after this they quitted the deponent's house. . . . Seven or eight of the said party . . . returned to his said house and carried away his most valuable Effects. [*Carleton Papers, PRO 30/55, vol. LXIX, no. 7727.*]

Memorial of Adam Graves, John Georg Graves, and Nicholas Andrews of Maryland, to Carleton

JULY 25, 1783

❡ . . . That they were tried and condemned to suffer death and that during a great part of the time they were confined at Frederick Town their coffins were kept in the place of confinement with them, that their situation might be render'd more distressing by all the terrors of approaching death. That your Memorialists were repreived the morning appointed for their execution on condition to be transported to France during life. . . .

That they were accordingly removed on board the *Romulus* in York river and confined in the hold for seven weeks with nothing but the ships ballast to lye on and when they had . . . obtained permission to walk the Deck they were obliged to perform the most menial offices and subjected to every species of insult, indignity, and abuse that human nature is capable of sustaining. That your Memorialists prefering instant death to a situation so insupportable had the good furtune to effect their escape. [*Carleton Papers, PRO 30/55, vol. LXXVI, no. 8521.*]

8 SIR GUY CARLETON RECEIVES PETITIONS FOR FREEDOM

Many blacks came within the British lines in answer to a royal proclamation that they would obtain their freedom and receive protection. Sir Guy Carleton believed this pledge was a solemn obligation of the British government which could not be altered by the treaty of peace, and he refused to return them unless they wished to go. Representative of the attitude of those people who had sought sanctuary and freedom under the proclamation are the petitions of Towers Bell and Judith Jackson.

Towers Bell, Stolen in England, Indentured in Maryland, Asks Carleton to Help Him Go Home

JUNE 7, 1783

❡ *Honnoured Sir*
It was my Misfortune to be Stole in England and Brought to Baltimore and Sold for four years as a Slave which I Suffered with the Greatest Barbarity in this Rebelious Cuntry. I have been Six years what they Call Free in this Cuntry and Never Had the Opportunity to Go Home to Old England as I am without Money or Friends. I hope you will assist me in Going Home I cant Get two Days work in one week. I was brought up at the Plough.

I thought it the Best Honnoured Sir to Acquaint you of these my Misfortunes So I Remain

True Brittan
Towers Bell
[*Carleton Papers, PRO 30/55, vol. LXXI, no. 7915.*]

Judith Jackson, Former Slave, Refuses to Go Back to Virginia

SEPTEMBER 18, 1783

❦ *Please your Excellency*

I came from Virginia with General Ashley When I came from there I was quite Naked. I was in Service a year and a half with Mr Savage the remaining Part I was with Lord Dunmore. Washing and ironing in his Service I came with him from Charlestown to New York and was in Service with him till he went away My Master came for me I told him I would not go with him One Mr. Yelback wanted to steal me back to Virginia and was not my Master he took all my Cloaths which his Majesty gave me, he said he would hang Major Williams for giving me a Pass he took my Money from me and stole my Child from me and Sent it to Virginia

And as in Duty Bound Your Petitioner Shall Ever Pray

Judith Jackson

[Carleton Papers, PRO 30/55, vol. LXXXI, no. 9158 (1).]

9 JUSTUS SHERWOOD IS CONVINCED OF THE ARROGANT SPIRIT OF THE WHIGS

Justus Sherwood, whose farm was located at New Haven in the New Hampshire Grants (Vermont), took an early part against the rebels, refusing the oath and passing information to the British. In August 1776, he was imprisoned by the local Committee of Safety and a month later condemned by the "Grand Committee" to life imprisonment in the Simsbury mines. He managed to break away from his guards and reach the mountains where some forty other harassed Loyalists joined him. Together they made their way to Carleton's forces at Crown Point. Sherwood's knowledge of the Champlain area made him valuable to the British secret service during Burgoyne's campaign and subsequently to various commanding officers. He was named on the list of Tories proscribed by the Vermont Act of Banishment of 1779. His most important confidential mission was to conduct negotiations with the Allens in 1780 to detach Vermont and return that area to its former allegiance.[1] A further service

[1] See *Supra,* part II, p. 260.

rendered to the British was the building of the Loyal Blockhouse on Hero's Island at the northern end of Lake Champlain, from which post, in the spring of 1783, he wrote to General Haldimand's secretary, Robert Mathews, about the blustering behavior of the victors.

APRIL 27, 1783

❡ . . . I find the present duty of this post [Loyal Blockhouse] too intricate & complicated to be left with either of my Subaltern officers. I never was at any time so much Embarressed as I have been Since the declaration of peace. Not a day passes but the Country people are coming in. Some of them are Loyalists who come to ask advice & seek a safe Settlement and others a[re] Rebels, who come (under pretence of trading or to procure the discharge of their brothers in our Army or prisons, &c.) but appearently to insult us, for many of them are so very Naughty & provoking that my soldiers would certainly cut them in pieces if I did not keep a Cautious look out. They Naughtily boast that they are Independent, that this is their Ground & that they shall have possession of it by the middle of May &c. And when I refuse to let them proceed to trade in Canada, they reply that it will not be a month before they will trade, and no thanks to me, and that they will take good care that no Dam'd tory shall have the Lyberty of trading from the Country here, or from Canada into the Country, and that they will soon have a Marchent of their own in this Block House &c. I Consider'd those expressions as the mad sallies of Vulgar fools, which would soon subside, untill I saw the Act Against the Loyalists in the Inclos'd paper. But that fully convinces me that it is the General Spirit of the Whigs throughout America. I constantly send them immediately back; but are informed that one Canoe containing three infamous Rascals, in defiance to my orders, proceeded round the Isle à Moth by night to Isle aux Noix, where they sold their Tobacco & other Articles and purchesed what they thought proper. But notwithstanding this, I am determined to Act with my former caution until I have His Excellency's further Commands. [*Haldimand Papers, Ser. B, vol. 178, pp. 187-190, PAC.*]

10 STEPHEN JARVIS DEFIES THE MOB TO MARRY THE GIRL
FOR WHOM HE WAITED SEVEN YEARS

Stephen Jarvis of Danbury, Connecticut, and his fiancée, Amelia Glover,
waited through seven years of war for an opportunity to marry, never even
having a chance to see each other during that time. Although both Britain
and Congress had proclaimed the cessation of the war when the incident
described below occurred and although a permit to visit Connecticut had
been granted to Jarvis, the mob was nonetheless bent on vengeance.[1]
Equally determined to marry the girl before seeking asylum in Canada,
Jarvis returned to Connecticut for his bride. He attempted to cajole the
hostile posse which soon appeared by inviting them to share in his wedding
and drink to the bride's health.

The Jarvises took up their residence in 1784 at Frederickton, New
Brunswick, starting out on a half-guinea and one year's half pay to draw
on. In 1809 they moved to York, Upper Canada (Toronto). As Jarvis records in his *Journal,* he found economic success and happiness in his new
country. "I commenced building and opened a small Store of Goods and
in October [1784] got into our new Dwelling [Fredericton] and thought
ourselves as Happy as Princes. . . . Although I made a good deal of money
and acquired some considerable property, I left the Province . . . and only
brought to Upper Canada a little upwards of £700 with a family of a wife
& six children."[2]

MAY 1783

❦ . . . In April, 1783, peace was proclaimed. . . . On the 21st May,
1783, I reached my father's house, to the great joy of my aged parents and

---

[1] On the conduct of the people of Danbury toward Loyalists Jarvis wrote to Carleton,
June 15, 1783: "Several other people have been punished very severely, carried on a rail
and then mounted on horseback without a saddle with their face to the horse's tail; their
coat turned, and a wooden sword by their side; then drove back and forth, to the great
joy and satisfaction of the spectators." PRO 30/55, vol. 72, no. 8036.
[2] *Journal of Stephen Jarvis Esquire, . . . during his Service in the British Army in the
American Rebellion, his Residence in the Province of New Brunswick and in the Province of Upper Canada.* Written at age 74. Typescript, N.Y. Historical Society, pp. 99–
100. Wording varies in Talman, *Loyalist Narratives.* "Having not yet sold my property
in New Brunswick, I had left there with £300," pp. 228, 247.

the rest of my family. Their meeting with me can be better imagined than described. I had been absent for seven years without having the least communication with my home. And here I met the Young Lady to whom I was engaged and whom I the next day married. [Miss Amelia Glover] . . .

There was then in Danbury a regiment of Dragoons belonging to the American Army and commanded by a Colonel Jeamison. One of his Dragoons requested to speak with the British officer. I went down to the kitchen where he was and he apologised for the liberty he had taken: "For although you see me in this uniform I have a brother in the British Army and for his sake, sir, have come to warn you of the danger to which you are exposed." This gave me no small uneasiness and I began to consider how I should best defend myself. My father in the meantime walked out and went to where the Militia were embodied and in a few moments returned much agitated and said: "For God's sake, son, what will you do? They are certainly coming. What will be the consequence, God only knows!"

My intended was also in the house as the mob arrived. I embraced her and desired her with the family to leave the room. I said: "I'll despatch as many of them as my two pistols and my sword will assist me in doing." I then closed the door and in a few moments the house was filled, and for a short time great confusion—all the females imploring for mercy. The noise ceased and for a few moments a profound silence. In the meantime my brother mounted his horse and rode after Colonel Jeamison who was celebrating a wedding some distance off. My father went for the magistrates and other persons of influence who had signed my passport. During their absence the mob became more tranquil and at least declared they would not injure me if I would come down and let them see and converse with me.

This was communicated to me by my sister and after a few moments' hesitation I consented and went downstairs. I saw many whom I knew, went up to them and offered them my hand. Some shook hands with me. Others again damned me for a damned Tory. Others charged me with cutting out prisoners' tongues. This scene lasted for some time. At last one of them who seemed to be their leader addressed me in these words: "Jarvis, you must leave this town immediately. We won't hurt you now, but if you are seen within thirty miles of this by sundown you must abide the consequences."

I replied that it was impossible. From Danbury I would not go until my marriage with the lady in the next room "on whose account and for her only have I put myself in your power. I now warn you against injuring a hair of my head. Here is my permit from the authority of your Government; here is my leave of absence from my Commander-in-Chief. I am now in your power and you may destroy me, but not unrevenged, if not by myself my friends in New York will avenge my death an hundredfold on your near and dear friends. If I cannot remain in peace, give me a suitable time to make that lady my lawful wife and then I will leave you; for, be assured, I have no wish to become an inhabitant of the States and of this place in particular."

By this time Captain Jeamison had arrived, looked into the house, went to his regiment and sent a sergeant and twelve Dragoons for my protection. Many other of our friends also arrived with the magistrates, and some of the mob began to disperse; others again were very hostile in their manners and swore vengeance. I now began to feel quite safe and began conversation with the respectable part of those who had assembled, quite at my ease, and I found I was gaining friends even of some of the mob themselves. They, however, were not disposed to depart.

At last it was by some of our friends proposed to my father that the best mode to be adopted to tranquillise the mob was that I should be that evening married. On this my father sent the brother of my intended to propose the matter to me and he undertook to prevail on the lady and, as they found no great objections from either of us, a parson was sent for, we retired to a room, and were that evening married. The mob and all others, except my guard of soldiers who remained all night, retired and we were left to our repose. At daylight the soldiers went to their barracks. Soon, however, my father knocked at my door and told me that Hunt had obtained a warrant for me and that the sheriff was coming to arrest me and to be on guard.

As my door was fastened I felt secure, but I was mistaken, the door soon opened and the sheriff entered. My pistols were in my mother's room and I was unarmed. I however sprang from my bed and ordered him to retire or I would blow out his brains. He was so alarmed that in quitting the room he fell from the top to the bottom of the staircase. I then fastened the door more securely and returned to my bed.

In the meantime the sheriff raised a posse and surrounded the house. The Dragoons had again taken their station in the house and sent me notice that they were ready to protect me if I chose to leave my chamber. The morning was fair. I rose, dressed myself, raised one of the windows, and bade the posse "good morning." They looked sulky and made me no answer. I threw them a dollar and desired they would spend it drinking the bride's health. Their countenances now began to brighten and when they sent for a bottle of bitters they said I must drink their health first. But how to get the bottle up to me was a question. However, by tying together pocket handkerchiefs, that difficulty was got over and I received the bottle with a glass in a bucket. Nothing would do but the bride must make her appearance at the window also, which she at last did and touched her lips to the glass as we drank their health and then conveyed the bottle in the same way to them; and before they had emptied the bottle they swore I was a damned honest fellow, I had married the finest woman in the country, that my conduct had deserved her, and that they would protect me with their lives.

The sheriff, finding it useless to remain any longer, retired. After breakfast I left my father's house by the back door and proceeded through his fields to a road in the rear of the house, when my brother met me with a horse, which I mounted and rode from the town. I went to Newtown, to a Mr. Hawley, whose wife was sister to my own. This was the place where we took leave of each other seven years before. . . . The next day my wife joined me and we remained here for a short time, when I again left her and returned to New York. [*Jarvis, "Reminiscenses. . ." Canadian Mag., vol XXVI, pp. 366–369. Talman, Narratives, p. 217ff.*]

11 "OLD MATCHIOAVELL . . . MIGHT GO TO SCHOOL TO THE AMERICANS," ARENT S. DePEYSTER COMMENTS TO GENERAL MACLEAN

Trouble with the Indians continued long after the peace, and Congress made several efforts to bring them to terms. In the summer of 1783 Ephraim Douglas was sent as a deputy from Congress to treat with the Indians around Detroit, whom the British regarded as their Indians. Douglas assembled the Indians without consulting either Brigadier General Allan MacLean or Major Arent S. DePeyster, commandant at Detroit. DePeyster gives vent to his resentment in the following letter to General MacLean, indicating the prevailing British attitude about continuing their control of the region south of the Great Lakes.

PHOTOS BY SALLY ELLYSON

JULY 8, 1783

❦   Ephraim [Douglas] is a suspicious name. I therefore am glad you have sent to bring him to Detroit, for we really cannot be too much on our guard against these designing Knaves, for I do not believe the world ever produced a more deceitful or dangerous set of men than the Americans. And now they are become such Arch-Politicians by eight years' practice that, were old Matchioavell alive, he might go to school to the Americans to learn Politics more crooked than his own. We therefore cannot be too cautious . . .

The Americans being now Independent, States will say they have a right to send Ambassadors or Emissaries to whom they please without our consent . . . but in the present case, with respect to our Indians, I am of a different opinion, it being clearly an exception to the Rule. The Indians . . . are not only our allies, but they are a part of our Family, and the Americans might as well attempt to reduce our children & servants from their duty and allegiance as to convene and assemble all the Indian Nations without first communicating their intentions to His Majesty's Representatives in Canada. [*Mag. Hist., vol. III, no. 10 (extra), pp. 70-71.*]

Mock Money: A Weapon of War. Genuine $4 note (facing page, top). (Courtesy of the American Numismatic Society, New York City.) *Counterfeit $4 note* (facing page, bottom). (Courtesy of the Money Museum, Chase Manhattan Bank, New York City.) *The counterfeit bill is crudely engraved. Notice in particular that the "R" touches the "S" in "MORS," and the letter "h" in "Spanish" is oversized. See Eric P. Newman, The Early Paper Money of America, Racine, Wis., 1967, p. 354.*

12 MOCK MONEY: THE COUNTERFEITERS CONFESS BUT CLAIM THEY PERFORMED A SERVICE FOR THE KING

Counterfeiting during the Revolution was as much a weapon of war as in the twentieth century.[1] The British encouraged and practiced this means of economic subversion from the beginning. As early as January 1776, a counterfeiting operation was being sheltered by the *H.M.S. Phoenix* in New York Harbor from which spurious notes were supplied to Tories in nearby provinces.[2] A counterfeiting ring was also found operating from the house of Isaac Youngs at Huntington, Long Island. Searchers of the house in May 1776 detected a crack in the wall, concealed behind a bed, which they pried open. The aperture led to a narrow stairs to the attic where a rolling press, ink, paper, tools, and a copperplated engraving of a Connecticut bill were uncovered. The owner, Isaac Youngs, and a frequent boarder, Henry Dawkins, were promptly apprehended.[3]

To stop the flow of counterfeit bills the provincial assemblies took drastic measures. A Connecticut law of July 1776 imposed imprisonment in the Simsbury mines for up to ten years;[4] the New Hampshire Assembly the same month provided a penalty of "being set on the gallows for the space of one hour, with a rope around the neck, and pay a fine . . . suffer six months imprisonment and be publickly whipped, not exceeding 39 stripes . . . and treble damages to the person defrauded."[5] Counterfeiting in New Jersey and New York had carried the death penalty since 1746 and their bills of credit carried the warning, "Tis death to counterfeit."[6] South

---

[1] In 1967, five million pounds of counterfeit money was discovered in a church organ in Merano, Italy, and identified as part of the money which the Nazis printed during World War II, intended for use in subverting Britain's financial system. *Wall St. Journ.,* Aug. 14, 1967.

[2] George and John Folliett of Ridgefield were charged in Superior Court, Fairfield, Conn., with going on the *Phoenix* to receive the bills. Kenneth Scott, "A British Counterfeiting Press in New York Harbor," N.Y. Historical Society Quart., 1955, pp. 117–120.

[3] J. Smits, ed., "Long Island's Counterfeiting Plot," *Journ. of L.I. Hist.,* vol. II (1962), no. 1, pp. 22–23. Dawkins repented and became an official engraver doing the New York coat of arms as well as currency for the Continental Congress.

[4] *Amer. Arch.,* 5th Ser., vol. I, p. 43. Jonas Mace, Jr., was committed to Newgate for counterfeiting March 8, 1776. Original warrant at Newgate Prison, E. Granby, Connecticut.

[5] *Amer. Arch.,* 5th Ser., vol. I, p. 89.

[6] Ibid., p. 1,504. *Journ. Prov. Cong. N.Y.,* vol. I, p. 571.

Carolina in 1777 had "Death to Counterfeit" printed twice on the back of each note. In Pennsylvania also counterfeiting was punishable by death, but altering the denomination of a bill of credit was to be punished with pillory, cutting off ears, and a public whipping "on his or her back with 31 lashes, well laid on," plus forfeiture of £100 and payment of double damages, or if too poor, the offender was to be sold for a term not exceeding seven years.[7]

Dealing in bogus currency continued nonetheless. Whigs in New Hampshire complained that the wives and families of persons gone off to the British were serving as an outlet for forged notes passed to them by "miscreants, sapping the foundations of Publick Credit."[8] Some of these miscreants were caught red-handed; others, when taken up, claimed ignorance of the spurious character of the bills they had passed. Other counterfeiters confessed, with pride, believing any advantage gained over the enemy was fair in wartime.

One ring, uncovered in July 1783, from whom the following confessions are taken, found benefit in continuing their operations after the preliminary treaty of peace was known, much to the embarrassment of Sir Guy Carleton, who was trying to end hostilities and to evacuate the British forces. Disclosure came about when William May passed some fraudulent notes to George Fisher, a baker who had furnished bread to the Continental army. John Fisher of Fishkill, brother of the baker and late assistant quartermaster of that army, witnessed the passing of the notes and told the American commissioners who had been appointed to settle matters of debt. These facts came out: John Power (Poor), a native of Ireland and a man trained in copperplate printing, had turned his skill to counterfeiting as a service to the King. George Fisher, with a guard of Hessians, arrested Power, demanded his keys, and opened up two or three chests of clothes under which he found plates and types wrapped in a sheet as well as paper money tied in a handkerchief. He took the bundles to Fraunces Tavern, stopping on the way to lock up Power and Daniel Forward, a confederate, in the main guardhouse. One of the witnesses of Power's arrest, Benjamin Lewis, testified that the types were taken to Black Sam's (Fraunces), and opened before six gentlemen, some of whom were American commission-

---

[7] *Amer. Arch.,* 5th Ser., vol. I, p. 710.
[8] Petition to the Council, October 20, 1779. Ms. Papers of the House of Representatives of New Hampshire, N.H. Historical Society, no. 17, C, 10.

ers. One of them, pointing to the types, exclaimed: "these are the things that have killed our money!" Another of the men, bitter against Power, declared he would have him hanged.[9]

Power, however, regarded the matter in a different light. Admitting freely that he had printed the bills, he claimed it was a service to the King to undermine the currency of the enemy. Moreover, he was acting under official permission. In fact, a gentleman in disguise promptly visited Power in prison and offered him £ 200 to 300 to keep secret the names of the principals for whom he had acted.[10] His memorial to Sir Guy Carleton and his deposition on examination a few days later confirm the extent of the counterfeiting and implicate some commissary officials.

Memorial of John Power, a Loyalist from Massachusetts

17th JULY, 1783

❡ . . . Your Memorialist since the commencement of the Rebellion rendered all the services in his power to the Royal cause by counterfeiting the several emissions of paper money in circulation throughout the Rebel Provinces, some millions of which he bestowed on distressed loyalists with views to help them in their necessities and bringing the paper currency of the Enemy into contempt. That a few weeks ago a certain James May came to your memorialist and requested of him to make a few blank notes of Mess[rs] [Robert] Morris and Hillegas's for him in order, as he expressed it, to take in some Rebels in the Country that injured him much. That your Memorialist, not considering it a crime, as he was not nor ever will be under a Rebel constitution, after long solicitations from said May, complied, May himself assisting in picking out the Types. That your Memorialist struck him off 75 blanks of Morris's Notes and gave him 1200 £ of what the Rebels term Specie money, for which he received two coarse pieces of linnen and an old watch.

That your Memorialist afterwards discovered that said May and his Confederates passed to several luke warm loyalists in this City said money and notes for goods, etc., for which transaction your Memorialist refused

[9] *Carleton Papers,* PRO 30/55, vol. 76, no. 8584.
[10] Daniel Forward said he thought the person in disguise was Smith, one of the American commissioners. PRO 30/55, vol. 76, no. 8584.

furnishing him with any more of Morris's [notes] . . . notwithstanding the Types for the purpose was already set. *[Carleton Papers, PRO 30/55 vol. 76 no. 8574.]*

John Power's Deposition

JULY 23, 1783

❡   He had printed some Millions of Paper money Bills for the purpose of depreciating the Continental Currency during the War. He thought he did the Crown a good service by that Work. He was generally employed at the instance of persons residing on the other side of the lines. Some at whose instances he worked in this Business were in Office and particularly in the place of Commissaries, but he will lose his life before he will disclose their names. He has had paper brought to him for the purpose of the very forms used for Emission of Paper Money on the other side of the lines. *[Carleton Papers, PRO 30/55, vol. LXXVI, no. 851.]*

WILLIAM MAY'S CONFESSION

John Power's confession had implicated William May of Woodstock, Connecticut, a graduate of Dartmouth and a man who had served as a substitute chaplain in a rebel regiment. He had purchased a farm at Woodstock from confiscated estates. However, May said he had never taken an oath to the United States and he had always been a Britisher. May confessed to taking and trying to pass some of the bills, although he denied he was a member of the ring. His confession tells what he knew about the counterfeit operation. Carleton determined to send him outside the British lines, which May considered equivalent to the death penalty. He petitioned Carleton, saying: "If this intention is carried into Execution, certain death will await him immediately after he is apprehended by the People of the Country, which cannot but soon happen. If he must be deprived of his Choice in respect to the place he is to reside in in future, he humbly supplicates Your Excellency that he may be banished to some Province or Place which remains still in allegiance to His Majesty, He being a Britisher and Loyal Subject of His Majesty. . . ."[1]

[1] *Carleton Papers,* PRO 30/55, vol. XCIII, no. 10169.

[385]

❡ Mr. Poor [Power] was a man that had made large sums of paper money and sent without the Lines, whereby some had made a fortune . . . and that he could and would at any time make any kind with such exactness that they could not be distinguished. I had the curiosity to become acquainted with him, he telling me he had permission from authority to do it. I frequented his House and see numbers of people at it every day—their names I do not know, many of them from the Jersey and almost every state—purchasing money to carry out with them—and some in town put it away to people of the Country, and purchased many things, also sold it for money. I asked him if he had made any of Robert Morris's Bills; he told me he never had, but that he intended [to] make them soon, for he had a pattern and wanted nothing but paper. . . . I told him it was dangerous for anyone to carry them into the Country, to put them away for good; their lives would be exposed by it. He said he supposed it to be so but anyone might pass them in town here and get what they could for them and the Author[it]y wou'd take no notice of it. I told him if that was the case I would take some of them. . . . I received some of Mr. Poor—about twenty, some of which I offered for a pair of Oxen.

Those who have been concerned in this matter and have passed the Counterfeit money are 1st Dan'l Forward from Connecticut, who tells me he has been within and out the line and passed above twenty thousand pounds for three years past; he has also passed considerable States money, viz. of Connecticut. [*Carleton Papers, PRO 30/55, vol. LXXVI, no. 8573.*]

Displaced Persons: Evacuation, Flight, and Dispersal

Probing and testing the effectiveness of the peace treaty had shown that the safety and best interests of Loyalists who had been active and outspoken lay in emigrating with the departing British troops. Each one nonetheless debated the wisdom of upheaval and resettlement. The number of Loyalists who chose to leave has been variously estimated between eighty and one hundred thousand persons, while the number who stayed, ready to adjust to new circumstances, is even higher. The outcome of the war, so contrary to Loyalist expectations, evoked for many Loyalists reflections on their earlier choice of allegiance. As John Williams commented: "Exiles now see Objects in a very different light."[1] Many exiles would have preferred to stay

[1] To Francis Bailey, Philadelphia Printer, April 20, 1783, Clements Library. Copy N.Y. Public Library.

but were forced to emigrate by local enmities; by mob violence; or by laws punishing and incapacitating them through confiscation, through blocking their careers, and through denial of citizenship and of recourse to the courts. Those banished on pain of death if they returned had no choice but to leave, for cases of treason that had already come to trial pointed to conviction and punishment. Many Loyalist regiments were disbanded in Canada partly to avoid the victors' revenge; however, ex-soldiers from the regular British army and deserters from the Hessian corps were able to remain in the States.

Representative of the attitude of Loyalist troops is the statement of Captain William Potts of Butler's Rangers to General Haldimand, August 14, 1783: "The late views of great part of the Corps was to return to their former Home as soon as a reduction should take place, but . . . the late Publication of the Colonists, and the disposition they seem to have avowed to abide by it, has much abated the ardor & anxiety of the men on the purpose to return home, & the promises & hope of Coll. Butler to obtain some general settlement for them upon the neighboring Lands of this Lake & River seems to have taken up & engaged very much both their consideration, hope, wishes, and expectation that they may succeed in Grants of land to that end, which I believe most of them at present are disposed to settle upon. . . ."[2]

Despite the handicaps, a few prominent Loyalists never left America and were permitted by the victors to stay on. In general they were men who had held Loyalist views but who had been inactive in the war, kept their own counsel, and had a reputation of being neutral. In New York John Alsop and Goldsbrow Banyar sat out the war and stayed on at its close. Peter Kemble, father-in-law of General Gage and a council member in 1775, not only remained unmolested during the war but also retained his lands near Morristown. Edward Shippen, father of Peggy Arnold, and Robert Proud, classics teacher at the Friends Academy, never tasted exile; William Samuel Johnson, although arrested in Connecticut for Toryism in 1779, was not prevented from staying on at Stratford at the war's end. His obscure position during the war did not interfere with his serving in the Continental Congress or becoming President of Columbia College in 1787. William Byrd III, Richard Corbin, Sr., and Ralph Wormley in Virginia and

[2] E. A. Cruikshank, ed., *Records of Niagara,* Niagara Historical Society, 1927, no. 38, pp. 63–64.

Daniel Dulany in Maryland, where Toryism had been unobtrusive and weak, were allowed to remain on their estates, although they suffered some confiscations. In fact, Virginia, as early as the fall of 1783, permitted the return of all exiles from the state who had not borne arms for Britain and ended further punishment for Loyalists.

As laws against Loyalists in other states were gradually mitigated or repealed in subsequent years and as persecution ceased, many well-known Loyalists returned despite disabilities and unpleasantness.[3] Some were surprised at finding a friendly reception, even enough support in time to occupy political office. On the other hand, other Loyalist exiles shared the feeling of the Reverend James Scovil, formerly of Waterbury, who remarked after sixty years in New Brunswick that no temptation on earth would ever induce him to set foot on soil where he had received such unprovoked and cruel wrongs.[4]

While the exodus had started even before the evacuation of Boston in 1776, the real flood of refugees from the States came as the British garrisons were withdrawn from Savannah (July 1782), Charleston (December 1782), and New York (April–November 1783), engulfing refugee towns ill prepared to shelter them. The exiles who reached England early in the war found a better reception—some even a minor professional niche—than those who came when London, Bristol, and other towns were swarming with emigrés. Their poverty, rendered bleaker by contrast with the luxurious and pleasure-prone life of Londoners, increased their homesickness. Whether early or late refugees to Britain, they were soon absorbed with the pressing issue of obtaining support and compensation for losses from the government. Drawing up memorials to the commissioners, securing papers and evidence of sale of American properties, garnering witnesses—these tasks occupied their interest until the commissioners closed their books in 1788. Of the 5,072 persons who filed claims for losses, 4,118 received some compensation. Of the 8 to 9 million pounds requested by claimants about £ 3,300,000 was paid out, plus annual pensions to public servants entitled to them.

---

[3] Returnees included Isaac Wilkins, Samuel Seabury, Peter VanSchaack of New York; Samuel Curwen, Ward Chipman, Dr. William Paine of Massachusetts; Edward Oxnard of Maine; Jacob Duché, James Humphreys, Chirstopher Sauer, Benjamin Chew, Samuel Shoemaker, John Penn of Pennsylvania; Robert Eden of Maryland; Frederick Smyth of New Jersey.

[4] James Shepard, "The Tories of Connecticut," *Conn. Mag., vol. IV, p. 262.*

Besides Great Britain, the exiles found new homes in many areas. They fanned out to Nova Scotia, the Lower and Upper St. Lawrence region and along the northern shore of Lake Ontario, to British posts at Niagara and Detroit, and southward to the Bahamas and the West Indies. Some went first to Florida, and when Florida fell to Spain by the peace treaty, they moved again to the Bahamas, Caribbean Islands, and elsewhere. While Nova Scotia furnished the prime refuge, Loyalists from provinces adjacent to Canada made their way via Lake Champlain to the Lower St. Lawrence. Machiche near Three Rivers had been the hub of the traffic after the Saratoga defeat in 1777; Sorel, Chambly, and Montreal attracted the refugees in 1783–1784. From these points, as well as from Niagara and Oswego, they penetrated further west to Upper Canada; to Cataraqui (Kingston), the Bay of Quinte, Prince Edward Island; and to the western side of the Niagara River. The British government promised land, tools, seed, and provisions, but the land grants bogged down in bureaucracy and favoritism, the short-handled axes were useless in clearing a pristine wilderness, and the promised supply of food and seed was unreliable and inadequate. The accretion of troubles brought on the "Hungry Year" in 1787–1788.

Although a vast majority of Loyalists emigrated to Canada, eighteen thousand or more preferred the more benign climate of the British West Indies, Bahamas, and Bermuda.[5] Not only were the islands underdeveloped, but also they offered a better opportunity for slave-owning Loyalists whose slaves left with them.

A royal proclamation of September 1783, granting forty acres in the islands to every head of family, plus twenty additional for every white or black in the family, encouraged a choice of refuge in the Bahamas. Lieutenant John Wilson, sent in 1783 to scout the islands and assess prospects for settlement, reported reassuringly, as did Oswell Eve about Cat Island. Despite these favorable judgments, the Loyalists met serious setbacks: hurricanes, tropical disease, lack of provisions, inflation, restrictions on trade, and conflict with the older inhabitants. Political bickering with officials was so constant that Governor John Maxwell left his post in disgust in February 1785. One main point of conflict was the Bahamian Slave

---

[5] An estimate for the Bahamas is 8,000, three-fourths blacks. Michael Craton, *History of the Bahamas,* London: 1962, pp. 162, 164, 166. For Jamaica, over 11,000. W. H. Siebert, *The Legacy of the American Revolution to the British West Indies and the Bahamas,* Columbus: 1913, pp. 14–16.

Code, put through in 1784 by ruling whites fearful of the augmented proportion of blacks to whites. While cotton growing thrived in certain parts of the islands, reaching a peak of production in 1786–1787, two years later the chenille bug had undermined the crop. The appointment of the boorish Lord Dunmore as Governor in 1789 produced further quarrels, for the refugees were essentially a disturbing and complaining group, discontented with their forced migration. Nonetheless most of them stayed on, becoming the planters, merchants, and officeholders from whom notable island families of today trace their descent.

The following accounts of the refugees themselves dramatize the vicissitudes of evacuation and flight and illuminate the overoptimistic expectations of many Loyalists for their asylum from persecution and mob tyranny.

I   THE TORY'S SOLILOQUY

"To go or not to go"—to face disabilities and ostracism in a familiar land or to start life anew in an unfamiliar, possibly wilderness, environment— was a diliemma which each one worked out according to his own experiences and his life situation.

1783

    ❦   To go—or not to go—is that the question?
Whether 'tis best to trust the inclement sky
That scowls indignant oe'r the dreary Bay
Of Fundy and Cape Sable's rock and shoals,
And seek our new domains in Scotia wilds,
Barren and bare; or stay among the rebels,
And by our stay, rouse up their keenest rage
That, bursting oe'r our *now* defenceless heads,
Will crush us for the countless wrongs we've done them?
Hard choice! Stay, let me think,—To explore our way,
Thro' raging seas, to Scotia's rocky coast,

At this dire season of this direful year.
Where scarce the sun affords the cheerful ray;

Or stay and cringe to the rude surly whigs,
Whose wounds, yet fresh, may urge their desperate hand
To spurn us while we sue—perhaps consign us
To the *kind care* of some *outrageous* mob,
Who for their sport our persons may adorn
In all the majesty of *tar and feathers;*
Perhaps our necks, to keep their humour warm,
May grace a Rebel halter!—There's the sting!
This people's, the bleak clime, for who can brook
A Rebel's frown—or bear his children's stare
When in the streets they point and lisp *"A Tory?"*
The open insult, the heart-piercing stab
Of satire's pointed pen, or worse,—far worse—
Committee's rage—or jury's grave debate
On the grand question: "shall their lives forsooth
Or property—or both—atone their crimes?
Who'd bear all these calamities, and more
We justly may expect, while Shelburne's shore
Invites us to decide the case ourselves. . . .

Then let us fly, nor trust a war of words
Where British arms and Tory arts have failed
T'effect our purpose. On bleak Roseway's shores
Let's lose our fears, for no bold Whig will dare
With sword or law to persecute us there. [*The New York Morning
Post, Nov. 7, 1783, Copy in St. John Pub. Arch. Author unknown.*]

2 JOHN PIPER WANTS TO RETURN TO RHODE ISLAND AND BE
A GOOD CITIZEN

Typical of the inquiries on the reception the Loyalists would meet, should
they return home, was the letter of John Piper, a Rhode Island merchant,
to a friend in London who could ascertain for him not only the climate of
opinion in Rhode Island in 1783 but also the goods which might be most
readily marketable in that new state.

JULY 19, 1783

❧ . . . Our only reasons for retiring at such a distance from the capital and into Wales was to wait and Sojourn in hopes of better times and untill we heard from our valuable friends in R^d Island that the coast and every other [area] was quite clear, that we might return again and be received with open arms and as good citizens. I can safely say that I wish for nothing so much as to be a good Subject, in all things to comport myself to the laws of that land I live in and if I am found usefull to take a part either in civil or Military Matters and in all things to act for the good of the State. . . .

My dear Vilett, I am to request of you as a Sincere good friend that you will see Messrs. Ayrault, Bours & Cranston and tell them that I wish and long for their Opinions and advices and that they will give me them fully and explicitly whether or not it would be an advisable measure in Me and family to come out soon, with Invoices of every kind and sort of goods which they may think will best answer the Market and be the most saleable.

As the Season is now so far advanced and its' being dangerous to get upon the American Coast in the Winter, we have one and all made up our Minds to remain here untill next March and then if we have that pleasing encouragement which we expect, we will go up to London or Bristol for to find a good Ship to convey us to Old Rhode Island. *[John Piper at Saugharin near Carmarthen to John Vilett in London, July 19, 1783, Box 45, Folder 5, Newport Historical Society.]*

3 COLONEL JAMES DELANCEY, "THE OUTLAW OF THE BRONX," BIDS THEOPHILUS HUNT GOOD-BYE

The story of James DeLancey's poignant good-bye to his neighbor is taken from the reminiscences of a contemporary of the war years who was interviewed by John M. McDonald. McDonald (1790–1863) was a lawyer and local judge and long a resident of White Plains. Suffering from a paralytic stroke for twenty-eight years and unable to continue his profession, he steeped himself in Revolutionary history. He gleaned Westchester stories from 1844–1850 from interviews with some 240 participants or witnesses of the incidents he recorded.[1] The incident of DeLancey's farewell is in-

[1] William S. Hadaway, ed., *The McDonald Papers*, White Plains: Westchester County Historical Society, 1927, chaps. 8 and 9 *passim*. For James DeLancey, see p. 173.

cluded as illuminating not only the painful separation of a Loyalist from his native spot but also the sternness with which attainder was carried out against the most obnoxious Tories in Westchester.

1783

❧ . . . Among the most reluctant of the exiles was the celebrated commander of the "Westchester Refugees." The Commonwealth of New York had withdrawn from him her protection (by a formal act of her Legislature), had declared his estate, real and personal, to be forfeited to the people, had banished him forever, and in case of his return to the State at any future time declared him thereby guilty of felony, and sentenced him to death without benefit of clergy. Yet, notwithstanding his attainder and the approaching relinquishment of royal authority, he had clung to his early home with all the fondness of an infant for the bosom of its mother and that too, long after a further stay had become dangerous. Of all the Tories he was the most obnoxious to the violent Whigs; and when, by common consent, a cessation of hostilities took place, individual enterprise had made more than one effort to carry him off. From some of these attempts he had narrowly escaped, but the British outposts in Westchester were now about to be withdrawn and personal safety compelled him to seek another abode.

It was on a brilliant morning in one of the last days of April [1783] that Colonel James DeLancey took his final departure from West Farms. A bright vernal sun gilded hill and plain, birds sang their matin hymns, and early flowers were beginning to bloom. Nature seemed to revel in the freshness and beauty of infancy. Under such circumstances the youthful heart beats high. Even the weary pilgrim of life while approaching his journey's end can sometimes pause to look upon a scene like this and for a moment fancy himself rejuvenated. But the welcome sounds and cheerful sights that move in the pageant of spring awakened no responsive feelings in the Outlaw of the Bronx, who with a heavy heart mounted his horse and, riding to the dwellings of his neighbors, bade them a sad farewell. The last upon whom he called, though much his senior in years, had been a friend and associate from early life and was just returned to the farm which civil dissention had compelled him for a while to abandon. "Hunt," said the Colonel, "I have called to bid you goodbye. I hope you may prosper." "I do not know how that will be," answered the husbandman. "Peace, it is true, has come at last; but I am now a poor man with a large family to provide for. My cattle have all been stolen, my negroes have run away, my fences are burnt up, and my house and barns in ruin. Of all my property nothing now remains but naked fields. I don't know *how* I shall get along."

"Say no more," replied DeLancey. "Look at *me. You* can remain here and cultivate your lands in quiet, while *I* must leave my native country, never to return." As he spake these prophetic words he turned in the saddle and gazed once more over Bronxdale, which in all its beauty lay full before him. His paternal fields and every object presented to his view were associated with the joyful recollections of early life. The consciousness that he beheld them all for the last time and the uncertainties to be encountered in the strange country to which banishment was consigning him conspired to awaken emotions, such as the sternest bosom is sometimes compelled to entertain. It was in vain that he struggled to suppress feelings which shook his iron heart. Nature soon obtained the mastery and he burst into tears. After weeping with uncontrollable bitterness for a few moments, he shook his ancient friend by the hand; ejaculated with difficulty the words of benediction: "God bless you, Theophilus," and, spurring forward, turned his back forever upon his native valley. [*Hadaway ed., McDonald Papers, vol. VII, pp. 50-52.*]

4 "THIS IS TO BE THE CITY, THEY SAY": SARAH FROST'S ANTICIPATION TURNS TO DISMAY

Among Connecticut Loyalists who had made themselves obnoxious to the rebels and had found a refuge on Long Island during the war was William Frost of Stamford. Frost had particularly incurred their wrath for leading an armed raid (July 21 to 22, 1781) across the Sound to Stamford and capturing the Reverend Mather and his entire congregation. The minister and forty-eight of his parishioners were carried off as prisoners to Lloyd's Neck. The Frost family, not daring to return to Stamford in 1783 and brave the resentment of their neighbors after this exploit, embarked for Nova Scotia on the *Two Sisters.* Sarah Frost, the wife of William Frost, recorded their daily progress from Lloyd's Neck to the St. John's River, from May 25 to June 29, in a felicitous diary, from which a few excerpts have been taken.

❧ May 25. I left Lloyd's Neck with my family and went on board the *Two Sisters,* commanded by Capt. Brown, for a voyage to Nova Scotia with the rest of the Loyalist sufferers. This evening the captain drank tea with us. He appears to be a very clever gentleman. We expect to sail as soon as the wind shall favor. We have very fair accommodation in the cabin, although it contains six families, besides our own. There are two hundred and fifty passengers on board. . . .

Wednesday, May 28. We weighed anchor at Harlem Creek at a quarter after six in the morning, with a fair breeze, but the tide being low we struck a rock. We soon got off, but in a few minutes struck again. At half past seven we got off and went clear, and at ten we anchored at the lower end of the City of New York, the tide not serving to go round into the North River as we had intended. . . .

Sunday, June 8. We are still lying at anchor in the North River. We expected to sail tomorrow for Nova Scotia, but I believe we shall remain at Staten Island or Sandy Hook for some days or until our fleet is all got together.

Monday, June 9. Our women with their children all came on board today and there is great confusion in the cabin. We bear with it pretty well through the day, but as it grows towards night one child cries in one place and one in another, whilst we are getting them to bed. I think sometimes I shall be crazy. There are so many of them, if they were as still as common, they would be a great noise amongst them. I stay on deck tonight till nigh eleven o'clock and now I think I will go down and retire for the night if I can find a place to sleep. . . .

Monday, June 16. *Off at last!* We weighed anchor about half after five in the morning with the wind north-nor'west, and it blows very fresh. We passed the lighthouse about half after seven. . . . We have now got all our fleet together. We have thirteen ships, two brigs, one frigate. The frigate is our commodore's. The wind dies away. It is now three o'clock and the men are fishing for mackerel. . . .

Tuesday, June 24. The sun appears very pleasant this morning. Ten ships are in sight. The fog comes on and they all disappear. We have been nearly becalmed for three days. A light breeze enables us to sail this evening two miles and a half an hour.

Wednesday, June 25. Still foggy; the wind is fair, but we are obliged to lie to for the rest of the fleet. The commodore fires once an hour. The frigate is near us and judging by the bells we are not far from some of the other ships, but we can't see ten rods for the fog. We have *measles* very bad on board our ship.

Thursday, June 26. . . . We are now nigh the banks of Cape Sable. At nine o'clock we begin to see land, at which we all rejoice. We have been nine days out of sight of land. At half after six we have twelve ships in sight. Our captain told me just now we should be in the Bay of Fundy before morning. He says it is about one day's sail after we get into the bay to Saint John's River. Oh, how I long to see that place, though a strange land. . . .

Saturday, June 28. . . . At a quarter after one our ship anchored off against Fort Howe in St. John's River. Our people went on shore and brought on board spruce and gooseberries and grass and pea vines with the blossoms on them, all of which grow wild here. They say this is to be our city. Our land is five and twenty miles up the river. . . .

Sunday, June 29. . . . It is now afternoon and I have been ashore. It is, I think, the roughest land I ever saw. It beats Short Rocks, indeed, I think, that is nothing in comparison; but this is to be *the city,* they say! We are to settle here, but are to have our land sixty miles farther up the river. We are all ordered to land tomorrow, and not a shelter to go under. [*Sarah Frost Diary in Bates, Kingston and the Loyalists. . . pp. 27-30.*]

5 LIEUTENANT MICHAEL LAFFIN TELLS HIS BROTHER
OF HIS BEING SHIPWRECKED ON THE *MARTHA* OFF THE
COAST OF ST. JOHN

The Loyalists who embarked in the fall fleet were not as fortunate as Sarah Frost's family. These ships carried troops from Oliver DeLancey's Brigade, men who had served faithfully throughout the war. Not only did they meet inclement weather, but also they found no shelter, no surveyed land, no preparations for them. One of the vessels, the *Martha,* carrying 174 persons, part of Colonel Richard Hewlett's battalion, struck a rock when the topsail went to pieces, and 99 passengers perished. The captain, with disregard for the lives of his passengers, jumped into the jolly boat, reached a small cutter, and made for shore, setting the empty jolly boat adrift. Michael Laffan, a Maryland Loyalist from Colonel Hewlett's troops, tells how he and three companions saved themselves by clinging to some wreckage.

OCTOBER 11, 1783

❡ Yesterday evening I had the good fortune to arrive at this place. On the 25th of September, about 4 o'clock in the morning the "Martha" struck against a rock off the Tusket River and was in the course of a few hours wrecked in a thousand pieces. I had the good fortune to get upon a piece of the wreck with three more officers, viz., Lieut. Henley, Lieut. Sterling, Dr. Stafford, and two soldiers (all of the Maryland Loyalists) and floated on it two days and two nights up to near our waists in water, during which time Lieut. Sterling and one of the soldiers died. On the third day we drifted to an island where we lived without fire, water, victuals or clothing, except the remnants of what we had on, about one quart of water per man (which we sipped from the cavities in the rocks) and a few raspberries and snails. On the seventh day we were espied and taken up by a Frenchman, that was out a fowling, who took us to his house and treated us with every kindness. We staid with him six days and then proceeded to a place called Cape Pursue, where we met with Captain Kennedy and about fifty of both regiments, who were saved at sea by some fishing boats, about 36 hours from the time the vessel was wrecked. Capt. Doughty, Lieut. McFarlane, Mrs. McFarlane and Ensign Montgomery perished. [*Raymond, River St. John, pp. 542-543.*]

6 GREGORY TOWNSEND OF BOSTON SENDS THE DANIEL
HUBBARDS GLOWING REPORTS OF CONDITIONS AT HALIFAX

Gregory Townsend, an Addresser of Governor Hutchinson and a Loyalist named in the Banishment Act of September 1778, served the King's forces during hostilities as Assistant Commissary General at New York. Sent to Halifax with the British forces, he wrote to his brother-in-law, Daniel Hubbard, and his wife, Mary, in Boston, about the plentiful life he found there on his arrival and the violent political bickering he witnessed ten months later.

JULY 8, 1783

❡ We abound in the finest Strawberries, Sallad, Cucumber, Green Peas etc. and are not wanting in Meat, Fish for almost nothing, the finest Mackeril at ½ penny apiece. The Roads for 11 Mile as good as the Massachusetts [ones]. . . . Were your Family and three or four more here, I could bid adieu to Boston without any great reluctance, although it far exceeds this or any other place I know of. . . .

APRIL 20, 1784

❡ The State of the British Nation is Such as must be very pleasing to her Enemies and distressing to those who wish her prosperity. Of this number I most sincerely count myself and greatly lament the distracted State of a Country which 25 Years ago was at the Pinicle of Glory. Nothing going forward but ins & outs of Violent Contests between the two Houses of Parliamint and their unhappy Sovereign.

In the mean time Trade is as flourishing as Ever. The busy part of the World disturb their minds very little with Politics and the gay fashionable part think of nothing but their own amusement. The late inverted Aerial Machine called a Balloon furnishes Conversations for the Curious Part of Europe. Nothing is heard but Balloon Hats, Balloon Caps, and Even Colours. Some surprising Experiments have really been made at Paris; two Gentlemen ventured themselves 9000 feet in the Air and sat down quietly to diner; had a Sail of above two hours. . . .

The News that Concerns this Country Most is the Division of the Government which is certain to take Place. The Western Part of the Province is to be formed into a Seperate Government and will make a very respectable one. The Bay of Fundy makes the communication with Halifax so uncertain as to make that seperation necessary. Most of the Emigrants from the late Provinces will take Refuge there as the Climate and Soil is more Similar to what they have left than the Eastern Parts, but they will be long mindful of that Country from whence they came out and retain a desire to return. As that is not to be permitted, they must reconcile themselves to this till they take their leave of this troublesome World and remove to a better [one] where, God grant, we may all meet. [*Misc. Townsend, G., N.Y. Historical Society.*]

J. TOMLINSON, JR., FINDS NOVA SCOTIA AN ASYLUM OF FREEDOM AND SAFETY

J. Tomlinson, Jr., probably one of the King's American Dragoons who were disbanded at Camp Manawagonish on the St. John River, also expressed a philosophy of contentment to his friend Joel Stone, finding satisfaction in the prospects for a new life which Nova Scotia offered.

AUGUST 18, 1783

❡ *To Joel Stone*
    . . . Here is an asylum of freedom and safety not only for you but for all our loyal American friends and well worthy their acceptance; and were the prospects here a thousand times less than they are, who among the noble sons of honest loyalty would not sooner accept them than deign to ask or condescend to reserve protection (longer than entitled to demand it . . .) from the hands of men who have so cruelly and unjustly robbed them of their just rights and drove them from all their connexions? I presume no one will ever have cause to envy the boasted freedom of the American States with all their ill gotten possessions . . .

To convince you we are not deprived of society or all its gay amusements, I must tell you that three evenings ago we had a most agreeable ball at this place. Our music appeared to have the same influence which it used to inspire in our native walk, and the lady appeared as gaily decorated. Why should we attribute as misfortune to leave New York or Connecticut for Nova Scotia or any other country while we still enjoy and carry along with us the only valuable blessing of life, the society of our friends, the necessary comforts of life, and the blessings of a happy government. For my part I conceive no difference (so the climate is healthy and my friends are with me), whether I were to live in the Antipodes or where I am.   [*McDonald, "Memoir of Colonel Joel Stone, . . ." Ont. Historical Society Papers, vol. XVIII, pp. 71-72.*]

7 HANNAH INGRAHAM RECALLS THE SNOWY RECEPTION AT FREDERICTON

Hannah Ingraham was the daughter of a farmer at New Concord near Albany who was a sergeant in the King's American Volunteers. Her father served in the British army for seven years and was once taken prisoner but escaped. For four of these years his wife and family heard nothing from him and did not know whether he was alive or dead. When he joined the army, his farm and implements were confiscated, but the family was allowed to remain on a rental basis. Hannah Ingraham was only eleven when her father returned home and announced that they were to prepare for immediate emigration to Nova Scotia. Her recollections of the trip and the inhospitable reception they met at St. Anne's Point (Fredericton), which then consisted of two houses, were told in her later years to Mrs. Henry Tippet, wife of the rector of Queensbury, who wrote them down and preserved them.

SEPTEMBER–NOVEMBER, 1783

❧ . . . [Father] said we were to go to Nova Scotia, that a ship was ready to take us there, so we made all haste to get ready, killed the cow, sold the beef and a neighbour took home the tallow and made us a good parcel of candles and put plenty of beeswax in them to make them hard and good. Uncle came down and threshed our wheat, twenty bushels, and grandmother came and made bags for the wheat, and we packed up a tub of butter, a tub of pickles, and a good store of potatoes.

Then on Tuesday, suddenly the house was surrounded by rebels and father was taken prisoner and carried away. Uncle went forward and promised those who had taken him that if he might come home he would answer for his being forthcoming the next morning. But no, and I cried and cried that night. When morning came, they said he was free to go.

We had five wagon loads carried down the Hudson in a sloop and then we went on board the transport that was to bring us to Saint John. I was just eleven years old when we left our farm to come here. It was the last transport of the season and had on board all those who could not come sooner. The first transports had come in May so the people had all the summer before them to get settled. This was the last of September. We had a bad storm in the Bay of Fundy but some Frenchmen came off in a canoe and helped us (piloted us I suppose).

There were no deaths on board, but several babies were born. It was a sad sick time after we landed in Saint John. We had to live in tents. The government gave them to us and rations too. It was just at the first snow then and the melting snow and the rain would soak up into our beds as we lay. Mother got so chilled and developed rheumatism and was never well afterwards.

We came up the river at last in a schooner and were nine days getting to St. Annes. . . . We were brought as far as Maugerville in a schooner but we had to get the rest of the way, twelve miles, walking or any way we could because the schooner could not get past the Oromocto shoals. . . .

We lived in a tent at St. Annes until father got a house ready. He went up through our lot till he found a nice fresh spring of water. He stooped down and pulled away the fallen leaves that were thick over it and tasted it. It was very good so there he built his house. We all had rations given us by the government, flour, butter, and pork. Tools were given to the men also.

One morning when we awoke we found the snow lying deep on the ground all round us and then father came wading through it and told us the house was ready and not to stop to light a fire and not to mind the weather, but follow his tracks through the trees, for the trees were so many we soon lost sight of him going up the hill. It was snowing fast and oh, so cold. Father carried a chest and we all took something and followed him up the hill through the trees to see our gable end.

There was no floor laid, no windows, no chimney, no door, but we had a roof at least. A good fire was blazing and mother had a big loaf of bread and she boiled a kettle of water and put a good piece of butter in a pewter bowl. We toasted the bread and all sat around the bowl and ate our breakfast that morning and mother said: "Thank God we are no longer in dread of having shots fired through our house. This is the sweetest meal I ever tasted for many a day."

It was not long before father got a good floor down of split logs, a floor overhead to make a bedroom and a chimney built. Who built the chimney? There were no mills then, no bricks, nothing but wood. Our chimney was made of stones for the back and a kind of mud mortar. The front and sides were just sticks and mud. They took care to plaster mud all up the inside of the chimney. Captain Clements came in one day to see father and he said: "Why, Ingraham, you've got a chimney up before me!" . . .

We soon got things planted the first spring. They would grow so easy. The bushel of wheat yielded thirty, the ground was all so new, you see. We had brought wheat and beans and seeds with us and we could sell anything we had for money down. Many people wanted the things we had and father was always getting jobs of work to do for the gentry that soon followed the Loyalists. . . .

I went to school the first winter up at St. Annes on snowshoes. The next winter I hauled my brother on a hand sled. . . . My brother John had chopped his toe off when cutting wood with father. He was a big boy then. . . . Father said if I would haul John to school he would give me another quarters schooling and I did it, but it was hard work through the deep snow and once it was so cold that the poor boy got his toe frozen before he reached school and that put back the healing. Mother had to poultice it and it was a bad piece of work for him. . . .

There were plenty of Indians coming to sell furs in those days. I've counted forty canoes going up the river all at one time. They used to come ashore to sell their furs to Peter Fraser and folks say he used to cheat them. He would put his fist on the scale and say it weighed a pound. One day when I was all alone in the house except the baby, I saw a big Indian coming up the hill to the door. I was terribly afraid at first for I knew he would perhaps stay all day and eat up everything in the house, so I ran to the cradle and catched up the baby and wrapped him in a quilt and went to the door just as the Indian got there. So I said: "Have you had the smallpox," hushing the baby all the while. And he darted away as if he had been shot and we had no Indians all that summer. [*Gorham, ed., Narrative of Hannah Ingraham, PAC.*]

8 "THIRTY-SEVEN THOUSAND PEOPLE CRYING FOR PROVISIONS": EDWARD WINSLOW DESCRIBES THE ARRIVAL OF THE LOYALISTS AT HALIFAX

Although letters, such as those from Gregory Townsend and J. Tomlinson in the summer of 1783, encouraged the Loyalists to seek refuge in Nova Scotia, it was soon apparent that the provisions offered by the British government were woefully inadequate to meet even the basic needs of the flood of immigrants. The person to whom the Loyalists' distress was most poignant was Edward Winslow, Jr., whose unpleasant assignment it was to handle the daily complaints of the refugees and their applications for relief.

During the war Winslow had filled several important posts, especially that of Muster Master General of Loyalist troops. In 1783, Sir Guy Carleton had appointed him, then a lieutenant colonel, Secretary to the Commander in Chief in Nova Scotia and assigned him the task of settling the troops aand other Loyalist refugees as they disembarked. To his wife and to Ward Chipman, his former deputy in the office of Muster Master General, he poured out his impatience with the inefficiency of the government and with the delay in setting up a separate provincial government for New Brunswick, a step which would have alleviated communication problems across the Bay of Fundy. Chipman answered: "Everything is at a stand here. . . . So undecided and indeterminate the conduct of ministers that you can depend upon nothing."[1]

MAY 12, 1784

❧ *To Ward Chipman*

What in the world are you about?—Not a packet arrived—a General without Commission or Instructions—37,000 people crying for provisions —Magazines empty—& no provisions at Market. That's the situation of the Country at present. Add to this a Governor without abilities—a Council of Republicans—combating with every weapon in their reach the whole corps of Loyalists, & embarrassing them by every possible impediment.

This is a pretty picture, but alas it is a true one. . . .

SEPTEMBER 25, 1784

❧ *To Mary Winslow, his Wife*

It is not possible for any pen or tongue to describe the variety of wretchedness that is at this time exhibited in the streets of this place, and God knows I am obliged to hear a large proportion of it. This is what we call a board day, & the yard in front of my House has been crowded since eight o'clock with the most miserable objects that ever were beheld.

As if there was not a sufficiency of such distress'd objects already in this country the good people of England have collected a whole ship load of

[1] W. O. Raymond, ed., *Winslow Papers,* p. 208.

all kinds of vagrants from the streets of London and sent them out to Nova Scotia. Great numbers died on the passage of various disorders—the miserable remnant are landed here and have now no cover but tents. Such as are able to crawl are begging for a proportion of provisions at my door. Two other ships were loading with the same kind of cargoes. Heaven only knows what will become of 'em. As soon as we get rid of such a sett as these, another little multitude appears of old crippled Refugees, men and women who have seen better days. Some of 'em tell me they formerly knew me, they have no other friend to depend upon and they solicit in language so emphatical and pathetic that 'tis impossible for any man whose heart is not callous to every tender feeling to refuse their requests.

Next to them perhaps comes an unfortunate set of Blackies begging for Christ's sake that Masser would give 'em a little provision if it's only for one week. "He wife sick; He children sick: and He will die if He have not some." I am illy calculated for this services. These applications make an impression on my mind which is vastly disagreeable. I cannot forget them. It is not possible to relieve all their distresses. I long to retreat from such scenes. My views are humble, I ask no more than a competency to support myself, my wife, and children decently and to live and enjoy them I care not where. This has hitherto been out of my power but I flatter myself that the time is not far distant when I shall be gratify'd in this first wish of my heart.

. . . By the way, since I am on the subject of Rations, you have heard that by the late orders the Loyalists are to receive only two thirds allowance of provisions from the first of last May, but the disbanded officers and soldiers are to receive a full allowance to the 24th of October. [*Raymond, ed., Winslow Papers, pp. 205, 208, 233-234.*]

9   SETTLERS ON THE BAY OF QUINTE

Beyond the division line between Upper and Lower Canada, forty miles above Montreal, there was only wilderness in 1783. That year the refugee families started coming, and the following year some ten thousand settlers hacked out farms in the forests of Upper Canada. They penetrated the area by batteaux and canoes up the St. Lawrence and along the Bay of Quinte in Lake Ontario or via the Mohawk River, Lake Oneida, and the Oswego

River to the first of the Great Lakes. The first land surveyed was meted out to disbanded Loyalist troops of John Johnson's, Edward Jessup's, and John Butler's corps. To lead the first group of Loyalists to the Bay of Quinte Sir Guy Carleton selected Captain Michael Grass, a German immigrant to Tryon County in 1752, a saddler and farmer, and one already acquainted with the region through imprisonment at Fort Frontenac during the Seven Years War. Grass's party, said to number about three thousand and composed of all ages, spent the winter of 1783–1784 at Sorel and reached Cataraqui (Kingston) only in June 1784. Although he found "scarce the vestige of a human habitation," according to his recollections in 1811, a military post had already been established at Cataraqui under the command of Major John Ross, together with a sawmill, gristmill, barracks, and a storehouse.[1] Grass's reminiscences are among the scarce accounts of an actual participant in the struggle to clear the primeval forest of Upper Canada.

Those of Catherine Chrysler (Crysdale) White, from which an excerpt also appears below, are taken from her recollections at age seventy-nine (1860) about her family's settlement. While Michael Grass was the first recipient of land at Cataraqui, the Chrysler family, former residents of St. Lawrence County, New York, were among the earliest settlers to receive a grant—800 acres farther along the Bay of Quinte.

A third selection describing the "Hungry year" comes from an account set down in 1860 by James Dittrick telling of the ingenuity of his parents in meeting the scarcities of that dire winter. His father, Jacob Dittrick, formerly a Mohawk Valley farmer, had served in Butler's Rangers and at the close of the war had sought refuge in the vicinity of Niagara.

Jacob Lindley, a Quaker traveling along the Ontario shore, recorded that the scarcity was so great that each person was allowed one spoonful of meal per day and that they "eat strawberry leaves, birch leaves, flaxseed dried and ground in a coffee mill—catched the blood of little pigs—bled the almost famished cow and oxen—walked twelve miles for one shive of bread. . . . The children leaped for joy at one robin being caught, out of which a whole pot of broth was made. . . ."[2] These were the conditions

---

[1] Richard A. Preston, ed., *Kingston before the War of 1812,* Toronto: 1959, Introduction, xliv, 1, lii.

[2] Jacob Lindley's Narrative, quoted in E. A. Cruikshank, ed., *Records of Niagara, 1784–1789,* Niagara Historical Society, no. 40, p. 92.

faced also by Brant's Mohawks as the Hungry Year stretched into a second winter and caused Brant to write Robert Mathews about the critical times for the Indians.

Wigwams and Tents on the Bay of Quinte. Captain Michael Grass Recalls the Scene in 1784

DECEMBER 7, 1811

❦ Seven and twenty years, Mr. Printer, have rolled away since my eyes, for the second time, beheld the shores of Cataraqui [Kingston]. In that space of time, how many changes have taken place in the little circle in which fate has destined me to move! How many of the seats of my old associates are now vacant! How few of these alas! to mourn with me the loss of the companions of our sufferings, or to rejoice with me at the prosperous condition of this our land of refuge! Yet will I not repine. . . . Yes, seven and twenty years ago, scarce the vestige of a human habitation could be found in the whole extent of the Bay of Quinte. Not a settler had dared to penetrate the vast forests that skirted its shores. Even on this spot, now covered with stately edifices, were to be seen only the bark-thatched wigwam of the savage or the newly erected tent of the hardy loyalists. Then, when the ear heard me, it blessed me for being strong in my attachment to my sovereign and high in the confidence of my fellow-subjects. I led the loyal band, I pointed out to them the site of their future metropolis, and gained for persecuted principles a sanctuary—for myself and followers a home. [*Kingston Gaz., Dec. 10, 1811. Caniff, Upper Canada, p. 523.*]

Catherine White Remembers Her Family's Contentment Living in the Isolated Wilds along the Bay of Quinte

(RECORDED 1860)

❦ The Country at that time was a complete wilderness but by energy and perseverance and a long time we got on very happily. . . .

Mother used to help to chop down the Trees, attended the household duties, and, as the children grew up, they were trained to Industrious habits. We were very useful to her, attended the cattle, churned the butter, making cheese, dressing the flax, spinning, (in those days the spinning-wheel looked cheerful), made our own cloth and stockings. . . . We had no neighbours but an old Englishman who lived at some distance off who was an occasional visitor. Before our crops came round, having brought seed with us, supplied by Government, we had rations from the Military posts; also, when these were nearly exhausted, father collected our Butter, Cheese, and spinning, taking them in a Batteaux to Kingston, which he traded off for salt, Tea, and flour. We had no Grist Mill at that time nearer than Kingston. The first Mill was put up at Napanee afterwards.

The Bay of Quinte was covered with Ducks of which we could obtain any quantity from the Indians. As to fish, they could be had by fishing with a scoup. I have often speared large Salmon with a pitchfork. Now and then provisions ran very scant, but there being plenty of Bull frogs we fared sumptuously. This was the time of the famine, I think in 1788; we were obliged [to] dig up our potatoes after planting them to eat.

We never thought of these privations but were always happy and cheerful. No unsettled minds, no political strife, about Church Government, or squabbling Municipal Councils. We left everything to our faithful Governor. I have often heard My father and Mother say that they had no cause of complaint in any shape and were always thankful to the Government for their kind assistance in the hour of need. Of an evening My father would make shoes of deer skins for the Children and Mother homespun dresses.

We had no Doctors, no Lawyers, No stated Clergy. We had prayers at home and put our trust in Providence. An old woman in the next clearing was the Chief Phys[i]cian to the surrounding Country as it gradually settled. [*Coventry Papers, Lib. of Parl., Ottawa.* Talman, *Narratives, pp. 354-355.*]

Captain James Dittrick Describes His Parents' Ways of Surviving the Hungry Winter of 1787-1788

(RECORDED FEBRUARY 7, 1860)

❡ No one can tell the privations we all underwent on our first moving into the Bush.

The whole country was a forrest [*sic*], a wilderness which had to be subdued by the axe and toil.

For a time we led a regular Robinson Cruso[e] life and with a few poles and brushwood, formed our tents on the Indian plan.

As the clearances enlarged, we were supplied with some agricultural implements, for we brought nothing with us but a few seeds prepared by the careful forethought of the women.

My father who had naturally a mechanical turn, amused himself of an evening in making spinning wheels, a loom, and a variety of useful things for farming purposes. Time passed and having grown some flax and obtained some sheep, my mother set to work to prepare the same for some cloathes in which we were greatly in need of.

She had not any thread, so my father which doubtless he learned from the Indians, stripped off the Bass Wood Bark, saturated it in water like Flax, and obtained a fine strong and useful thread. Necessity has no law. Consequently it was immaterial to us how the cloathes were made, as long as the material kept together. We none of us had any shoes or stockings, winter or summer, as those we brought with us were soon worn out. At length my father tanned some leather, and I recollect the first pair of shoes he made which fell to my lot, I greased and putting them too near the fire, on returning to my grief found that my shoes were all shrivelled up, so that I could never wear them. It was twelve months before I obtained another pair, so many daily occurrences of life having to be attended to. . . .

The most trying period of our lives, was the year 1788 called the year of scarcity—everything at that period seemed to conspire against the hardy and industrious settlers.

All the crops failed, as the earth had temporarily ceased to yield its increase, either for man or beast—for several days we were without food, except the various roots that we procured and boiled down to nourish us. We noticed what roots the pigs eat; and by that means avoided anything that had any poisonous qualities. The officers in command at the military stations did all in their power to mitigate the general distress, but the supplies were very limited, consequently only a small pittance was dealt out to each petitioner.

We obtained something and were on allowance until affairs assumed a more favorable aspect. Our poor dog was killed to allay the pangs of hunger, the very idea brought on sickness to some, but others devoured the flesh quite ravenous. Dogs are very common food around the Rocky Mountains, but the people became in time habituated to the taste. We next killed a horse which lasted us a long time and proved very profitable eating; those poor animals were a serious loss to our farming appendages, but there was no help for it. People shipwrecked on desert islands or lost in the Woods will take hold of anything almost to satisfy the cravings of hunger and to keep life together.

The mills of rude workmanship were thinly scattered about the country, so that we had to content ourselves with a hollow stump to pound our grain in, which was done with a cannon ball fastened to a cord or bark of a tree, and affixed to a long pole which served as a lever. The bread or cakes thus made were not particularly white, but were eaten with a good appetite and proved wholesome.

We none of us experienced much sickness, but whenever any illness occurred we had recourse to medical roots found in the woods, the virtues of which we acquired by our intercourse with the Indians. [*Talman, Narratives, pp.* 65-70.]

Joseph Brant Complains of Critical Times for the Indians

SEPTEMBER 23, 1789

❦ *Dear Friend* [Major Robert Mathews]
 . . . I am in hopes that you will write me at this time and tell me all your Civiliz'd good news and as well as bad ones—whether our friends the English has determined at last to keep the posts for good & all not let the Yankys have them, and whether they mean to keep the Indian Department with the same footing & the same care as they did before or not. . . .

Dear friend, it is a critical times for us here I mean we the Indians. I felt very unhappy oftentimes of late. The most difficult Part for me is of having a many children which concerns me about them very much. Particularly when our Indian affairs and situation stands so unsettled the civilized cruelties I mean the Yankys are taking advantage all the while and our friends the English seems getting tired of us. If I have not got so many children I would soon do some thing to drown my unhappiness & Leave more marks behind me than what my father did. I think you done very right of not having a Wife & Children. Other ways would be dam coward like myself—If no Accident happens here I mean to go down to Canada in the winter rather Leisure times for me in the winter allways. [*Q. 43-2, pp. 784-785. PAC. Records of Niagara, Cruikshank, ed. Niagara Historical Society, no. 40, p. 92.*]

10 "THE MARCH OF THE CAMERON MEN": NANCY JEAN CAMERON WRITES FROM THE MOHAWK VALLEY THAT HER FAMILY IS FLEEING THE TAUNTING WHICH FOLLOWED IN THE WAKE OF WAR

Although John Cameron, a Scottish immigrant to the Mohawk Valley in 1773, never served in the British forces, he had passed on intelligence and helped scouting parties, particularly in 1777. He was characterized by Lieutenant Walter Sutherland, whom he had helped, as "an Honest Man, but very stupid."[1] His family tried to remain at Broadalbin near Johnstown after the war but their residence in the valley was attended by so much unpleasantness that in 1785 they determined to remove to New Johnstown (Cornwall), Canada. His wife, Nancy Jean Cameron, explains to Mrs. Kenneth Macpherson, her cousin in Perthshire, Scotland, their feelings on leaving the valley they had hoped would always be their home.

BROADALBIN, NEW YORK, MAY 15, 1785

℄ *My dear Margaret:—*

Our friends and neighbors, the Grants, will hand you this epistle for they are sailing for Scotland, and will visit their relatives in Blair Athol.

At last we are preparing to leave forever this land of my birth. The long weary years of war, followed by the peace years, that have been to us worse than the time of fighting, are over.

As soon as it is possible we shall set foot on our travels for a new land of promise. A settlement is to be made on the Northern Shore of the St. Lawrence River, some fifty miles from the town of Montreal.

Our lands are confiscated and it is hard to raise money at forced sales.

We expect the journey to be long and hard and cannot tell how many

[1] *Loyalist Transcripts,* vol. XXIV, p. 148.

weeks we will be on the road. We have four horses and John has made our big wagon as comfortable as he can. Through the forests we must trust to Indian guides.

Many of Scotch origin will form the band of travellers. The children little realize the days of hardship before them and long to start off.

I love friendship and neighborly kindness, and I am so glad that there will be no more taunting among the elders, no more bickering among the children. Bitter feelings are gone forever. Patriot or rebel we are what we see is right to each of us, conscience may make cowards.

When I leave this beautiful Mohawk Valley and the lands that I had hoped we would always hold, I shall hear no more the words "Tory" and "Parricide".

The McDonalds have with them their priest, Father McDonald, and hope to found in the new land a new Glengarry. The Glengarry will lack the mountains you see from your home.

Our grandparents little thought when they sought this new land, after the risings of Prince Charlie, that a flitting would be our fate, but, we must follow the old flag wherever it takes us. It is again "The March of the Cameron Men" and wives and children must tread the hard road.

We all send our love to you and Kenneth and when I know where we are to live you shall hear from us.

> Your affectionate cousin,
> *Nancy Jean Cameron*
> *(Mrs. John Cameron)*
> [*Private papers of Mrs. D. J. Macpherson,*
> *Wales, Ontario. Now in PAC.*]

11   JAMES MATRA PROPOSES NEW SOUTH WALES AS A REFUGE FOR THE LOYALISTS

It was in 1771 when Captain James Cook's *Endeavour* dropped anchor in Botany Bay and took possession of New South Wales for George III. On board was James Mario Matra (Magra), a midshipman born in New York, educated in England, and imbued with Cook's spirit of adventure. The necessity for Britain to occupy the country to make good her claim coincided with the need of the Loyalists for a place to settle and suggested to Matra a scheme for aiding the Loyalists and benefiting the government at the same time. With the assurance from fellow Loyalists in Nova Scotia that they would be willing to go to Australia, Matra laid his memorandum of August 17, 1783, before the Cabinet, giving an estimate of a maximum of £ 2,000 to cover the cost. It appears that the proposal was not given serious consideration by the Cabinet, although Matra discussed it with Lord Sydney (Thomas Townshend), Secretary of State under Pitt. The scheme died through procrastination as well as because of an alternate plan of promoting New South Wales as an asylum for criminals destined to be transported out of England. The number of prospective colonists also dwindled as they found more certain quarters in Nova Scotia. By 1786, Matra's plan was a dead letter. Nonetheless, his proposal below remains part of the Loyalist saga.

AUGUST 17, 1783

❡   I am going to offer an object for the consideration of our Government which may in time atone for the loss of our American Colonies.

By the discoveries and enterprise of our officers, many new countries have been found which know no sovereign and that hold out the most enticing allurements to European adventurers. None are more inviting than New South Wales.

The climate and soil are so happily adapted to produce every various and valuable production of Europe and of both the Indies, that with good management and a few settlers, in 20 or 30 years they may cause a revolution in the whole system of European commerce; and secure to England a monopoly of some part of it and a very large share in the whole. . . .

This country may afford an asylum to those unfortunate American Loyalists, whom Great Britain is bound by every tie of honour and gratitude to protect and support, where they may repair their broken fortunes and again enjoy their former domestic felicity. . . .

That the Ministry may be convinced that this is not a vain, idle scheme, taken up without due attention and consideration, they may be assured that the matter has been seriously considered by some of the most intelligent and candid Americans who all agree that, under the patronage and protection of the Government it offers the most favourable prospects that have yet occurred to better the fortunes and to promote the happiness of their fellow sufferers and countrymen. [*"The American Loyalists and Australia: Matra's Proposal," Journ. Royal Empire Society, vol. XXV, p. 471.*]

12 CAT ISLAND IN THE BAHAMAS ANSWERS THE EXPECTATIONS OF OSWELL EVE OF PHILADELPHIA

When the war began Oswell Eve had been a sea captain for thirty years, operating his ships so successfully that he had been able to become part owner of some twenty-five vessels and a shipping merchant of importance. He married in 1744, acquired a large family, and settled them on a 200-acre farm near Philadelphia. Business reverses led him and his two oldest sons to move in 1768 to the West Indies, where they carried on the family business for five years. Oswell Eve returned to his Pennsylvania family in 1773. During the Revolution he was given command of the British warship *Roebuck.* His daughter, Sarah Eve, who kept a journal during her father's absence, records in it her engagement to Dr. Benjamin Rush. She died, however, in 1774, a few weeks before her scheduled wedding.[1]

Oswell Eve's experience sailing and trading in the West Indies rendered him a reliable informant on prospects for favorable places of settlement in the Bahama Islands. Here he writes about Cat Island to Daniel Coxe, a former member of the New Jersey Council, whose property had been confiscated and who was seeking a new home. Cat Island was Columbus's San Salvador, so-called because cats which had been left there had multiplied so extensively. Although there was no permanent white settlement on Cat Island until the Loyalists came in 1783, five years later it accommodated forty heads of families and had 2,000 acres in cultivation.[2]

MAY 29, 1784

❡ As it may possibly be of service to you, as a Person interested in the Bahama Islands, to here any Thing that may tend to give a just Idea of their Value, I could not omit taking this Opportunity of informing you that

---

[1] "Extracts from the Journal of Miss Sarah Eve," *Penna. Mag. Hist. Biog.,* vol. V, pp. 19–20.

[2] Daniel McKinnen, *Tour through the British West Indies,* London: 1804, p. 201.

our Expectations are entirely answered in this Island. Indeed the Indolent and unsettled Lives of the Natives of these Islands possessed the World with an Opinion that they were of inconsiderable Value and only at best a fit Asylum for Pirates and Wreckers and those fond of a marine Way of living; but the World will soon have an Opportunity of being better informed. Within these six Years a Gentleman from Pennsylvania, who was reduced in his Circumstances and in Debt, retired from Providence to Long-Island which lays to Windward. His Situation required that he should do Something to retrieve his Fortune. With the Assistance of a Negro or two of his own & three or four that were lent him he took to the cultivating of Cotton and has by his Industry in that Line acquired a Fortune of Five or Six Thousand Pounds. This Gentleman has shewn the Bahama-ans their true Interest and Numbers; having followed his Example, have become Men of considerable Property. Cotton, it is true, was raised in these Islands long before this Period but by an indolent set of Men who never made it a first Object or properly attended to it. Tortola was once thought a barren rocky Island of no Value, but Experience having shewn how properly the Soil was calculated for raising Cotton, it immediately became of Note, and there is scarcely an Island in the Bahamas but will produce that Article equal to Tortola.

The Appearance of these Islands are very much to their Disadvantage, the Hills & Ridges being all covered with Rocks, in many Places very large, but they are generally found of a smaller size, loose, and piled in little Heaps by the Indians who formerly inhabited them; and it plainly appears by the Circumstance and other Relicks d[a]ily met with that the Inhabitants have been very numerous, as there is none or but very little Ground but what has been cleared and cultivated. Great Quantities of their Bones are to this Day found in different Cavities of the Rocks. All along the Sea Coasts and sandy Bays are found considerable Tracts of what is called white Land, which has been formed out of the Sea Wreck Land. In this Land there is not a Stone to be met with and it produces as good Indian Corn, Guinea Corn, with all Kinds of Vegetables, as any Land on the Continent and with a tenth Part of the Labour. Between many of the Hills or Ridges are found deep red, yellow or black Bottoms—the former of which will produce in great Perfection Sugar Cane, Plantains, Bananas, Pines or any of the most luxuriant Vegetables or Fruits the West Indies produces. The real Madeira Grape is a native of these Islands, and Grapes in general are found to thrive amazingly well. And not only the tropical but those Vegetables found to the Northward thrive equally well here.

The Hills and most rocky Ground is the best for Cotton—the rich Bottoms will by no Means answer. A Cotton Field will last several Years and is not an annual Plant, as some suppose it; it yields two Crops per Year, one in December, the other in May. The second and third Year afford the greatest Crops. The Timber on these Islands in general is very small owing to the Dry or Salt Seasons. Such happens once or twice a Year at which Time you are often without a Shower of Rain for 40 Days. Stock in general thrive very well, Poultry and Hogs perhaps much better than to the Northward. Wild Hogs and wild Fowl are pretty plenty and any Quantity of the best Fish may be had whenever the Breeze will admit of Fishing. The Character of this Country differs in the different Islands—Providence, being surrounded by the great Bahama Bank, which reflects an intense Heat which is carried by the predominant Winds over the Island, is from this Circumstance, and the Town being situated under a Hill, in Summer Time the most hot and unwholesome of all the Bahamas. Harbour Island and Iluthera has been inhabited these ninety Years; they now contain upwards of 2000 Souls. They have never had a Doctor on the Islands and hardly know what Sickness is.

How [Port Howe], being so near the Continent, has sometimes Frost in the Winter Season. This Island is much, in Respect to Climate, like Bermuda; it being so far distant from the Continent and having Ocean Water all around it occasions it to be very cool and healthful. Those from the Northward find the Weather as cool as they could wish and at this Season much cooler than in Pennsylvania. Two or three who were troubled with consumptive Complaints for several Years, who came with me, have since their Arrival found every Symptom removed. We have settled at the South End of the Island on a good Harbour for Vessels not exceeding 200 Tons, on one Side of which is a Hill better calculated than any I have seen on these Islands for a Town. Here I have laid out one which I have called Carlisle, the Harbour, Port Howe, after their Lordships. Six or Seven Thousand Loyalists are arrived and expected from St. Augustine. They principally centre at Exuma which has an excellent Harbour, capable of admitting a 50 Gun Ship. This probably will become the Seat of Government some future Day. So much for the Bahamas. [*PRO C.O. 23/26.*]

Expectations Soured,
Hopes Fulfilled

Younger and more vigorous expatriates embraced their new life in exile with resignation and with optimism—a mood expressed in the remark of Edward Winslow that the American states would envy them yet.[1] It was otherwise for older Loyalists well established before the war, whose homes and savings were gone, and whose age precluded a resumption of careers and old ways. These were the Loyalists who most longed to return and be good citizens, to live their last years in a familiar and, they hoped, a forgiving country. Thus the experience of the Loyalists in exile was a mixture of hopes fulfilled and expectations dashed.

England furnished a haven for some men of property and distinction and also for the retired, the pensioners of the Crown. Yet here, with a few exceptions, such as Hutchinson, who did not live beyond the war

[1] Raymond, Ed., *Winslow Papers,* p. 193.

years, or eligible daughters with a DeLancey name, refugees experienced the greatest souring of their expectations. The meager government compensation, one-third of their losses, was only a part of the disillusionment. A deeper hurt was their loss of place in society, demonstrated by the aloofness, even contempt, of Englishmen for exprovincials.

Robust and young men like Joel Stone and Stephen Jarvis saw the best opportunities in Canada. Even here expectations exceeded the cold realities, for which Shelburne became the grim illustration. While most of the experiences detailed below point out elements of disillusionment—failure of promised supplies, injustice to the black Loyalists and Indians, seigneurial tenure, trade restrictions, and the physical struggle with the wilderness—nonetheless the sturdier pioneers gripped these problems and worked out contented lives.

I MEMORIALS TO GOVERNOR PARR REVEAL UNNECESSARY HARDSHIPS

Governor John Parr wrote favorably to Lord North from Halifax (February 4, 1784) about progress in resettling the Loyalists in Nova Scotia: "Several towns are almost completely built with some exceeding good Houses. . . . The whole of the Loyalists (very few excepted) seem contented with their Situation and are well pleas'd and satisfied with the goodness and richness of the Land which proves in most places to be much better than was ever expected. If they continue the same Industry which they have hitherto shewn I have not a doubt but that in a few years this will become a great and flourishing Country. . . . I flatter myself the Province will become a happy Asylum to an unfortunate People whose greatest Crime has been their Loyalty to the best of Kings. . . ."[1] At the same time disillusioned settlers were complaining to Captain Robert Mathews. General Haldimand's aide, that their distress was so acute, especially at Shelburne, that wholesale desertion of the colony threatened. The memorial below of Robert Ross, Samuel Campbell, and Alexander Robertson, alarmed at the attempt of the Assembly at Halifax to impose excise taxes on them, peti-

---

[1] *Colonial Office Records, Nova Scotia.* M.G. 11, A-104 PAC.

tioned Governor Parr for relief, spelling out their grievances. Instead of a happy asylum, Shelburne declined steadily from 1785 on into a virtual ghost town.[2]

Complaints poured in from other areas as well. From Montreal Rudolph Ritzema, the son of the Reverend Johannes Ritzema of the Dutch Church in Sleepy Hollow, and a former British officer, wrote of the wretchedness which he had encountered in Lower Canada. On the other hand, Sir John Johnson, the most prominent Loyalist of the Mohawk Valley, established himself in Montreal as Superintendent of Indian Affairs and had the same rosy prospects for royal favors that his family had enjoyed in New York.

Disenchantment in Nova Scotia: Memorials of Robert Ross, Samuel Campbell, and Alexander Robertson

[1785]

❦ . . . Your Memorialists humbly beg leave to call Your Excellency's attention to the present alarming state of this settlement, the actual Distress of the Inhabitants and the Greivances which have occasioned that distress. It is now above six weeks since the Salt provisions provided for the use of the Loyalists have been expended, and now there remains no provisions of any kind in his Majesties Stores. Without an early supply the horrors of Famine must ensue. . . . Near two years are now elapsed since the first Establishment of this Colony, yet at this hour a large proportion of the Inhabitants are unprovided with Lands. Experience shows that the dilatory steps hitherto pursued are inadequate to the purpose of settling the Loyalists. The Provisions Granted by the bounty of Government have been expended and the property of the Colonist wasted in idle expectancy of his Rights; thereby the means of providing a future subsistance by Agriculture have been denied and the period approaches when it is apprehended the Royal bounty will cease. In this alarming situation Your Memorialists . . . humbly pray that Your Excellency will be pleased to make application to his Majesty's Ministers in their behalf and stating the cause of their dis-

---

[2] Parr estimated the Shelburne population in 1784 at 10,000 souls. In 1818 the *Acadian Recorder* estimated it at 300. T. Watson-Smith, "The Loyalists at Shelburne," Nova Scotia Historical Society *Collecs.*, vol. VI, p. 85.

tress solicit a further supply of Provisions. They also Pray that Your Excellency will direct some more expeditious mode of settling the Inhabitants on their lands, and as the speedy means of providing for a great number of Individuals and of rendering a most essential service to this Town they beg leave to propose that the very large quantities of reserved lands around and in the vicinity of Shelburne may be divided into small parcels and appropriated to that purpose. In fact, some measure of this kind is absolutely and immediately necessary to prevent the desertion of the Inhabitants of the above description, a great many of whom, tired out with fruitless expectation, have emigrated to other parts. [*Photostat in Misc. Mss. Shelburne, N.Y. Historical Society.*]

2   RUDOLPH RITZEMA WRITES CAPTAIN MATTHEWS HE IS
LEAVING THE CONTINENT OF AMERICA FOREVER

SEPTEMBER 15, 1783

❮   *Sir* [Captain Matthews]
    . . . I am sorry to inform you that I am wholly disappointed in them [my reasons for coming to Montreal] and that I shall be under the necessity of returning to the West Indies in the Course of next Month.

Least I should incur any Censure of Fickleness and be thought to want Firmness of Mind, my reasons for my Conduct are the following: Upon the whole I find this Country to the full as expensive as the West Indies. Next the Profession of the Law, if not in small repute, at least the law a Mixture of French and English, inasmuch that the most experienced cannot pronounce this or that to be the *Law*. The Laws of England are like her women, on a first View forbidding, but on a formed Acquaintance, heavenly and beyond Description. Lastly, there is nothing to be done to Effect in the Colonies; the rabble has still the sway among them; . . . the greatest outrages are dayly committed on the Persons of those who are only thought to favour the return of the Loyalists, and every avenue shut against the recovery of former Debts. I even despair of a Letter from my Father on Account of the many Enemies he has for his monarchical principles. The only hope left me is that when the Times become more calm my Friends may be enabled to glean a little of what I once had and what my Father must soon leave me and remit the same to me in the Islands I mean to bid adieu to the Continent of America forever. [*Haldimand Papers (M.G. 21, B-162) PAC.*]

3 SIR JOHN JOHNSON TELLS ROBERT WATTS THAT HIS
PROSPECTS FOR PREFERMENT AND COMPENSATION IN
CANADA ARE BRIGHT

NOVEMBER 26, 1785

❡ . . . Neither time, distance, nor the unhappy Revolutions that have
taken place can make me forget my friends or lessen in the least the sincere
regard I always had for you and your good Lady. Few Men, if any, have
greater reason to regret their Seperation from friends than myself, particularly as my fate puts an end to the prospect of our ever meeting in the same
happy Situation we once experienced. However, I have the Satisfaction to
assure you that my present Situation is far from being ineligible and that the
prospects before me are such as cannot but be Satisfactory to myself and
family—having the Approbation of my Sovereign and my Country, at least
of that part that is Worthy of esteem, for my conduct, with rewards and
prospects of future preferment and Compensation, the first at least adequate to my Merit, and I hope and have some reason to believe, the latter
will be little short of my pretentions. Thus Circumstanced in point of honor
and Emolument, with a good Stock of health, a partner I have the Sincerest
Affection for, and a fine growing young family as engaging as they are fine,
I think I would be unreasonable, notwithstanding my disappointments and
hopes, was I not contented and happy. [*Robert Watts Papers, Box II,
N.Y. Historical Society.*]

4 WARD CHIPMAN WRITES GLOOMILY OF BRITISH
RESTRICTIONS ON TRADE BETWEEN NEW BRUNSWICK
AND THE STATES

Ward Chipman was on the road to a distinguished legal career in Massachusetts Bay in 1774. He was living in Cambridge with Jonathan Sewall, the
Attorney General, when a mob attacked the house. He defended the place
with youthful zeal and as a result had to flee to the King's troops in Boston.
An Addresser to General Thomas Gage, he was further marked as a Loyalist and left Boston with the evacuation of the King's troops for Halifax.
However, early in the war, he signed over his real and personal property to
his mother and sister, who were permitted to enjoy it unmolested. In 1777,
he returned to New York to serve in the King's troops, in the Court of
Admiralty, and in time as Deputy Muster Master General.

In New Brunswick his postwar career was as distinguished as his earlier career was promising. He served as a member of the Assembly, Justice of the Superior Court, Council member, and finally President and Commander in Chief of the Colony of New Brunswick.[1]

One of the grievances of the American colonies had been the subordinate economic position that enforcement of the Navigation Acts imposed on them. Ward Chipman's letter to John Moore in New York attests to Britain's continuing enforcement of these mercantilistic restrictions on her colonies, which affected adversely the interests of Loyalists trading with the States.

JULY 4, 1785

❮ *My dear Sir* [John Moore]

. . . I feel most sensibly the inconveniences of your Situation and greatly regret that nothing offers in this Asylum for Loyalists to encourage your taking your chance with us. A New Country you know is ever attended with a thousand peculiar inconveniences & altho this is perhaps settled under as many, if not greater, advantages than any other has been, yet the rude face of nature cannot be polished in a day and the present poverty of the Inhabitants prevents any rapid advances to that state of improvement which alone affords opportunities of speculation in a commercial line or great exertion in any other.

The Policy of Great Britain is now restricting the commerce of these Provinces within narrower limits every day and I expect soon to see by regulations on one side or the other every communication with the States cut off. I enclose to you an extract from the last proclamation by which you will see how total the exclusion is of American Bottoms from the Ports here and how confined the trade even in British Vessels is rendered in some instances particularly the article of Naval Stores. I think we shall experience peculiar inconveniences from this regulation. Hitherto the attention of the Customhouse officers in Nova Scotia has been very much relaxed and almost every American Vessel might under some pretence or other have landed a cargo, but very severe reprehensions from home have taken place and of course an opposite extreme of conduct here. Every vessel is seized that is not bona fide *British built, wholly owned* by British Subjects

[1] *Loyalist Transcripts,* vol. XIV, p. 397 ff. James H. Stark, *The Loyalists of Massachusetts,* Boston: 1910, p. 432. Sabine, *Loyalists,* vol. I, p. 311.

& navigated with the master & three fourths of the hands British, agreable to the strict letter of the law, except under the Governor's proclamation in instances where Loyalists are *actually removing* with their effects to *settle* here, in which case they may bring in American Vessels such Articles as are not prohibited by law, that is, such as a British Vessel may bring from the United States. I need not after this add any opinion respecting the proposal you make of coming here with a cargo unless under the latter description, which I most sincerely wish it was your interest to do.

But the times must mend both in your Country and this and tho for the present the prospect is very gloomy, Countries with such natural advantages for commerce & so populous must afford favorable grounds for speculation in a short time. The Americans, I think, must be more and more convinced of the destructive tendency of their late Politicks and, tho I do not suppose a reunion with Great Britain can ever take place, they must yet in some way look up to & be dependent upon the lenient interference of that nation to save them from ruin, but the haughtiness of their temper & stile must first be greatly lowered, which will, I think, soon take place. The cruel severity of your quondam residence, New York, is beyond example and I with pleasure anticipate the day, which must come, when their pride, insolence, and injustice must give way to more rational principles of conduct. [*Gunther Collection, Courtesy Chicago Historical Society.*]

5 PATRICK McNIFF CONTENDS THAT HOLDING LAND UNDER A SEIGNEUR IS SLAVERY

Patrick McNiff, an Irish immigrant in 1764, was carrying on his business as a merchant and living in ease with his family in Saratoga at the start of the rebellion. The Committee of Safety considered him unfriendly to the rebel cause and sent him to Albany where he stayed until Burgoyne's surrender. When the rebels found out he was sending intelligence to Canada, he sought refuge within the British lines in New York. He soon built a house and opened a store at the Watering Place on Staten Island only to have it plundered two years later and to be taken prisoner himself. On his release at the close of the war he joined the trek of the Loyalists to

Canada, taking up residence at New Johnstown in eastern Canada.[1] Here, as his protest indicates, the Loyalists soon found out that they could not hold their lands in fee simple, but only under a seigneur.[2]

⟨ *To Stephen DeLancey, Inspector of Loyalists in Nova Scotia*
Sir,

We the Inhabitants of Township No. 3, being duly assembled in order to take into consideration the Governor's Proclamation of the 16th Ult. respecting the erecting of Grist Mills in the Different Townships, have to acquaint you that on perusal of the same we conceive it to hold out to us prospects the most distressing & disagreeable that the immagination can suggest. We, who from a state of ease and contentment, out of pure love for his Majesty and attachment to the British Government, abandoned our once happy abodes, nay, our Wives and tender offspring, sooner than brook to the userped authority of a rebellious faction, not only took refuge in this province, but also bore Arms, numbers of us for years, with a desire to support his Majesty & the British Constitution in the rebellious Colonies, until at length the ballance of Power, having determined the War in favor of the Rebels, left us, his Majesty's faithful subjects, to seek the means of subsistance in a howling Wilderness, where we have every imaginable hardship to encounter, in order to procure the common necessaries of life. Still with all these hardships we should endeavour to be content, did we but see the least prospect of enjoying the benefit of that mild & Lenient Government, for which we have so long & nobly contended & for which we have at least sacrifised our all.

Tis with the utmost astonishment & concern, that we see by said Proclamation that so little regard is paid to our loyalty or past services, but from all appearance every measure is taken to reduce us to the state of a conquered people who being born slaves cannot know what it is to be free. Is it possible that this can be meant as a reward for our fidelity & loyalty? NO! His Gracious Majesty never meant it, nor can we, consistant with our duty to our Posterity, Brook to such measures as tend in the least

---

[1] *Loyalist Transcrpts,* vol. XXX, p. 155; vol. XXI, p. 387. His memorial of September 6, 1783, appears in a series called "Memorials, etc." vol. VI, pp. 67–70.
[2] Until 1854, a seigneury in Canada was a landed estate held by feudal tenure.

to entail Slavery on them; in which State we consider such of the Canadians as hold Lands of Seigneurs to be. The numerous and cordial Invitations which many of our Friends & relations have lately received to return again to their places in the different States from whence they fled we doubt [not] will be by them embraced sooner than be reduced to the necessity of holding Lands in the manner lands are generally held by the Canadians. We whose Names are hereunto Subscribed therefore think it our duty to acquaint you that we will not directly or indirectly hold or possess any of these lands as under a Seigneur but will, as soon as the Spring opens, immediately depart the same, if we have not assurances that we shall hold them in fee Simple as we have hitherto held our Lands under the Crown. [*Canada East, Civil Secretary's Corresp., S. Series, (R. G. 4), PAC.*]

6 JOHN DESERONTYOU, A MOHAWK CAPTAIN, AND HIS INDIANS SETTLE ON THE BAY OF QUINTE BUT SOON FIND THAT THE AMERICANS THREATEN THEIR LANDS "LIKE A WORM WHICH CUTS OFF THE CORN"

At the close of the war a tract six miles square along the Grand River was purchased from the Mississauga Indians and granted by the British government to the Loyalist tribes of the Six Nations. Here the main body of the Mohawks and many of the Senecas and Cayugas settled. Joseph Brant, the Mohawk chief, himself lived on a farm on the Grand River near the town of Brantford, about twenty miles from the Canadian shore of Lake Erie. Another Mohawk chief, Captain John Deserontyou, who had served under Daniel Claus in expeditions to the Mohawk Valley, preferred not to settle with the rest of the tribe. He had led a small group of Mohawks from Fort Hunter on the Mohawk River to La Chine near Montreal in July 1775. In 1784, after land had been granted to Brant's Indians on the Grand River, General Haldimand and the Reverend John Stuart, former missionary to the Mohawks at Fort Hunter, made repeated efforts to persuade Deserontyou's Mohawks to join the rest of their nation, but they obstinately refused. They chose instead a tract on the Bay of Quinte near Cataraqui, which they bought from the Mississaugas also. Deserontyou describes it with satisfaction to Daniel Claus but a month later complains to Claus that the Loyalists are trying to take some of the Indians' lands, remarking: "It has come to pass as I thought, Major [Samuel] Holland [Surveyor] and his son were here yesterday for to get some land from us for the loyalists, but I could not spare of any. . . ."[1]

In September 1800, at a council fire, Deserontyou gave his reasons for settling his small band away from the main tribe: "I informed Colonel Claus I was not fond of going to the Grand River owing to their being so near the Americans, and I told him I thought I could not live in peace so near those people and made choice of this place as being at a greater distance from them. The Americans are like a worm that cuts off corn as soon as it appears."[2]

An elderly white woman, who had gone with the Indians at age fifteen and intermarried, passed down before her death an account of the landing on the Bay of Quinte of this small group of Mohawks. When they fled from the Mohawk Valley in 1775 they buried some precious communion silver, given them by Queen Anne in 1712, and after the war Captain John Deserontyou returned to Fort Hunter and retrieved it. On reaching their new home on the Bay of Quinte they overturned a canoe, covered one end with a communion cloth, laid out Queen Anne's silver, and conducted prayers and hymns with the canoe as altar. For a long time a cross and flagstaff marked the spot. Part of the silver may still be seen in the Mohawk Church near the present town of Deseronto.

JUNE 8, 1784

❦ *Sir* [Colonel Claus] I am glad to find such a good opportunity to write you this to acquaint you that we have found a place for to Setle &c. at the crook of Bay Quinty & also a good River Suitable for Saw & grise Miles; the land is So and So, we are now come down at Quataracauie I & Mr. Vincent with the Missisaguees and by thier desirs for to hear thier Speech, as they said; . . . we are expecting Sir John Johnson every day at our camp &c—for we have Sundries smal triful to petision for, such as cows horses Seeds &c—I send you a plan of the land which we are to have & likewise a little fawn, by 3 Canadiens to Mr. Gocheé at la Chine. We have freech [water] upon our land which you may see on the map. . . . remember Sir

---

[1] July 29, 1784. *Claus Papers.* M.G. 19, F 1, V, 4. PAC.
[2] S. Series, PAC. See M. E. Herrington, "Captain John Deserontyou and the Mohawk Settlement at Deseronto," *Bull. Dept. Hist.,* Queens University, Kingston, no. 41 (November 1921), p. 6.

that you promise me to answer my letters and to help me as much as possible; Should be very glad that you would assist us in mentioning these things to Sir John, and also to General Haldimand.

A blackSmith is wanted very much by us for all the Smal hatches are like lead.

Mr. Vincent's compliment to Colonel Claus and desir of him that he would [be] so kind as to Send him his brother in law to him, his name is Joseph Chalifan lives in St Laurance Suburbs, he was gone to winter in the woods some where among the Indians for Mr. Beaubien Desrivier Merchant in Montreal &c please Sir to send him up as soon as possible for his mother & sister want him very mush for they are a lone a mong us

I am Sir your humble Servan^t
John Deserontyou
[*Claus Papers (M. G. 19, F 1, IV).*]

7 BLACK LOYALISTS ARE BUFFETED ABOUT IN NOVA SCOTIA: THOMAS PETERS PETITIONS FOR REDRESS OF THEIR GRIEVANCES OR RESETTLEMENT ELSEWHERE

Among the 30,000 Loyalists who sought asylum in Nova Scotia was a corps of Negro soldiers, called the Black Pioneers, who were disbanded in Shelburne in 1783. On the list was a sergeant, Thomas Peters, age forty-five, a former slave of William Campbell of Wilmington, North Carolina. He left his master in 1776, served with the Black Pioneers for seven years of the war, and then tried to take up a grant of land in Nova Scotia which had been promised him, expecting also to work as a millwright. His disappointment with Nova Scotia and flight to Sierra Leone reflect the buffeting which most Negroes experienced at the close of the Revolution. Many of them, had they remained in Canada, would have been entitled, along with their descendants, to use the title of United Empire Loyalists after their names.[1]

---

[1] A United Empire Loyalist was defined by the government, November 9, 1789, as a Loyalist who joined the standard before the peace treaty. Any child or descendant was also permitted to use U.E.L. after his name. Over 500 Negroes were placed on the Honor Roll of U.E.L. Mrs. Denis Harvey, "The Negro Loyalists: Arrival and Departure," typescript, 1962, p. 9. PANS.

On June 30, 1779, Sir Henry Clinton had issued a proclamation promising to "every Negroe who shall desert the Rebel Standard full Security to follow within these Lines any Occupation which he shall think proper."[2] Under this promise of sanctuary, widely circulated in Loyalist newspapers, many enlisted as buglers, drummers, and common soldiers, until about two thousand were in British uniform. Others fled their masters and sought refuge behind the British lines. When Sir Guy Carleton learned that Article VII of the treaty of peace prohibited the carrying away of former slaves and required the return of those who had sought British protection, he faced a serious dilemma. Already former masters were abducting ex-slaves on the streets and sending chills of terror through the ranks of the black refugees. Carleton felt that Britain could not honorably default on Clinton's promise of 1779 and surrender them into servitude, "some possibly to execution and some others to severe punishment. . . ."[3] Instead, he proposed to Washington to take a census of those within the British lines on the basis of which an evaluation could be made to reimburse former owners. This arrangement was agreed on and a commission of three appointed which proceeded to register about three thousand blacks at Fraunces Tavern.[4]

The Black Pioneers who were evacuated to Nova Scotia were to be paid for their army service to October 1783 and were each to receive a town lot in Shelburne and about twenty acres in the vicinity, with a possible grant of a hundred acres farther away if the grantee qualified as a farmer. Others, who were not disbanded soldiers, but fugitives from their masters, were not entitled to claim anything from the British government beyond their freedom and personal protection.[5] Shiploads of this class also sailed from New York in the general evacuation, some of them "destitute of every

---

[2] Rivington's. *Royal Gaz.,* July 3 to Dec. 29, 1779, inclusive.

[3] Conference between Carleton and Washington, May 6, 1783, Fitzpatrick, *Writings,* vol. XXVI, p. 404.

[4] "Carleton's Book of Negroes Registered and Certified," April 23 to November 30, 1783. Books I and II contain 3,000 names; 1,336 men, 914 women, and 750 children. Original in Carleton Papers, vol. LV, PRO. Carleton wrote to Washington: "Had these Negroes been denied permission to embark, they would, in spite of every means to prevent it, have found various Methods of quitting this place, so that the former owner would no longer have been able to trace them, and of course would have lost in every way all chance of compensation." May 12, 1783, *Dorchester Papers,* vol. II, Military Correspondence no. 3, PANS.

[5] Sir Guy Carleton to Secretary of State Henry Dundas, December 13, 1791. W. O. Raymond, "The Negro in New Brunswick," *Neith Mag.,* St. John, vol. I, p. 27.

necessary of life."[6] These free Negroes were urged to indenture themselves to a Loyalist for a time in order to receive food and clothing and land or money on termination of the contract, but many were too old or too unwilling to work for someone else.

The Black Pioneers were given either thick pine-forest land or no land at all. Those who went to Shelburne were settled in a segregated area called Birchtown where conditions steadily deteriorated until in 1789 the Overseers of the Poor applied to the Magistrates of Shelburne for relief from the burden of trying to assist them.[7]

Thomas Peters waited six years for a fair allotment and then set off for London to present his grievances and those of his people to the British government and even to request resettlement in some other part of the British Empire. His memorial follows.

1791

❦ The humble Memorial and Petition of Thomas Peters, a free Negro, and late a Sergeant in the Regiment of Guides and Pioneers, serving in North America under the command of General Sir Henry Clinton, on be-

---

[6] Journal of Thomas C. Haliburton, *Historical and Statistical Account of Nova Scotia,* vol. I, p. 266. Benjamin Quarles points out that there were also many unregistered Negroes and estimates those leaving New York at 4,000, Savannah at 4,000, and Charleston at 6,000. Herbert Aptheker gives the figures as 5,000 from Savannah, and 6,500 from Charleston, evacuated in 1782–1783, and estimates that 100,000 slaves in all made good their escape during the Revolution. Quarles, *The Negro in the American Revolution,* Chapel Hill: 1961, p. 172; Aptheker, *The Negro in the American Revolution,* New York: 1940, pp. 19–20.

Mrs. Denis Harvey has estimated that 10 percent of the Loyalists who went to the Maritime Provinces and 7 percent of all those who went to Canada were Negroes. Blacks from Colonel Stephen Bluck's Black Pioneer companies, numbering one thousand five hundred and twenty-one men, women and children were mustered at Shelburne in the summer of 1784. She concludes that the attempt to settle them in the Maritime Provinces was unfortunate, that by temperament they were incapable of "sacrificing immediate pleasure for future benefit." "The Negro Loyalists . . ." p. 19.

[7] *Original Minute Book and Muster Book of the Free Blacks,* Port Roseway Associates. The Overseers of the Poor wrote: ". . . it is not in our Power to afford the Blacks the assistance which their present necessities loudly call for . . . It is evident that they become more and more Burthensome every Year. It appears incumbent upon us to apply to your Honours and submit their Case to your Consideration . . . some Mode may be adopted that may be favourable to the distressed Blacks and free this Infant Settlement from a Burden which it is by no Means in a Capacity to Bear," vol. I, p. 52, PAC.

half of himself and others, the Black Pioneers and Loyal Black refugees, hereinafter described;

Sheweth,

That your Memorialist and the said other Black Pioneers, having served in North America as aforesaid for the space of seven years and upwards during the late war, afterwards went to Nova Scotia, under the promise of obtaining the usual Grants of land and provisions;

That notwithstanding they have made repeated applications to all persons in that Country whom they conceived likely to put them into possession of their due allotments, the said Pioneers with their wives and children, amounting together in the whole to the number of 102 people, now remain at Annapolis Royal, having not yet obtained their allotments of land, except one single acre each for a Town lot, and though a further proportion of 20 acres each private man, viz: (a fifth part of the allowance of land that is due to them) was actually laid out and located for them agreeable to the Governor's order, it was afterwards taken from them on pretense that it had been included in some former grant, and they have never yet obtained other lands in lieu thereof, and remain destitute and helpless; that besides the said 102 people at Annapolis, who have deputed your Memorialist to represent their unhappy situation, there are also a number of the Black refugees, consisting of about 100 families or more at New Brunswick in a like unprovided and destitute condition, for tho' some of them have had a part of their allowance of land offered to them, it is so far distant from their Town lots (being 16 or 18 miles back) as to be entirely useless to them, and indeed worthless in itself from its remote situation.

That the said two descriptions of people, having authorized and empowered your Memorialist to act for them as their Attorney, he has at much trouble and risk made his way into this country in hopes that he should be able to procure for himself and his fellow sufferers some establishment where they may attain a competent Settlement for themselves and be enabled by their industrious exertions to become useful subjects to his Majesty;

That some part however of the said Black people are earnestly desirous of obtaining their due allotment of land and remaining in America, but others are ready and willing to go wherever the wisdom of Government may think proper to provide for them as free subjects of the British Empire.

Your Memorialist therefore, most Honored Sir, humbly prays that you will humanely consider the case of your Memorialist and the said other

Black people, and by Laying the same before His Majesty or otherwise as you shall deem most proper, that they may be afforded such relief, as shall appear to be best adapted to their circumstances and situation;

And your Memorialist shall ever pray, etc.

The mark of X Thomas Peters

[Clarkson, Journal, vol. I, Aug. 6, 1791–Mar. 18, 1792, N.Y. Historical Society.]

AFTERNOTE *Granville, Sharp, William Wilberforce, John Clarkson, and several others concerned in ending the slave trade were in London when Thomas Peters arrived. They were planning to form a company to run a settlement in Sierra Leone and had purchased twenty square miles for the colony. Already a group of 460 settlers, including 60 whites, had been sent out in 1787, but the severe climate, poor sanitary conditions, and unfavorable composition of the group, many of whom were prostitutes, promised poorly for the enterprise. Fever and black death struck; bands of savages preyed on the settlers; and their own indolent and loose ways undermined the community until the village burned and only 64 souls remained in 1791[1] Undeterred by this disaster, Sharp and his friends formed the Sierra Leone Company, raised $250,000, and prepared for another colonizing enterprise. The directors embraced Peters's cause and presented him to Sir Henry Clinton and other proper persons. Soon he found himself lionized by both press and philanthropists. He was sent back to Nova Scotia to gather recruits and bring them to Halifax for embarkation to Sierra Leone. The British government was to assume transportation costs. One thousand one hundred ninety blacks decided to join the expedition.*

The leadership was entrusted to John Clarkson, a young navy lieutenant, who agreed to charter the ships, secure provisions, wangle the necessary permissions to emigrate, and accompany the expedition as a volunteer. Fifteen ships finally sailed on January 16, 1792, only to be scattered by storm; sixty-five deaths occurred en route.[2] Peters, however, who sailed on the Venus *with his wife and children, wrote appreciatively*

[1] George Washington Williams, *History of the Negro Race in America from 1619 to 1880*, New York: 1883, vol. I, pp. 86–87.

[2] John Clarkson to Henry Dundas, March 1792. *Journal of John Clarkson*, vol. I, p. 469, N.Y. Historical Society B.V. "C."

to Henry Dundas, the Secretary of State, on his arrival: "The treatment we received on our passage was very good; but our provisions was ordinary; we was allowed Salt Fish four days in a week and one half of that was spoilt. Nevertheless we are satisfied if Government is not charged an extraordinary price. We also inform your Lordship that the Natives are very agreeable with us, and we have a grateful sense of His Majesty's goodness in removing us. We shall always endeavour to form ourselves according to His religion and Laws; and endeavour to instruct our children in the same."[3]

Despite Peters's optimistic report, troubles began to mount almost immediately on arrival of the settlers in Freetown—poor rainfall, tornadoes augmenting the Sahara dust, rampant dysentery and African fever, jealousies over white leadership, and quarrels over land allotment. In addition there was a menacing slave station opposite their site. Clarkson became ill and desired to return to England, but was induced to stay on as Governor to try to get the colony on its feet. Thomas Peters began working against Clarkson, stole some money, and was tried and rebuked. He attempted to have himself made Governor.[4] In the epidemic of fever which had sickened half the colony Peters succumbed and died on June 24, leaving behind a legend of his leadership in the founding of Sierra Leone.

Clarkson, dispirited, left after a year. A French siege in 1794 added to the ravages of African fever and the colony deteriorated. Essentially, however, it was the rebellious nature of the settlers which undermined the stability and growth of the colony[5]

---

[3] March 1792. See C. H. Fyfe, "Thomas Peters: History and Legend," *Sierra Leone Studies,* New Series no. 1, December 1953, pp. 8–9.

[4] *Clarkson Journal,* vol. II, "Clarkson's Mission to Africa, March 19–August 4, 1792," pp. 20–21; 81–88; 163–164; 222; 326.

[5] Williams, *History of the Negro Race,* p. 87. "Once more [after the French raid] an effort was made to revive the place. . . . Some little good began to show itself . . . but it was soon trampled under the remorseless heel of five hundred and fifty insurrectionary maroons from Jamaica and Nova Scotia."

8 "THE FIERCE SPIRIT OF WHIGISM IS DEAD": THE REVEREND
JOHN TYLER OF NORWICH, CONNECTICUT, WRITES TO SAMUEL
PETERS THAT IT IS SAFE TO RETURN

John Tyler, a graduate of Yale in 1765, was one of three Episcopal rectors
in Connecticut whose ministry was not interrupted by the war. In fact, he
was continuously rector of Christ Church parish for fifty-four years. When
his parishoners in April 1776 elected to close their church rather than
omit the prayer for the King, he continued the services in his own home
but was not subjected to violence, imprisonment, or even molestation.[1]
His church was permitted to reopen three years later after the congregation voted to omit from the liturgy prayers for the King and Parliament.
Tyler rationalized that "the cause of religion ought not to be annihilated
on a civil account, that public worship was of too much consequence to be
totally omitted on acc't. of a few words in a liturgy; that my obligations,
though binding at first, could not be so to use the whole Liturgy now, when
matters were so much altered. Christ's kingdom is not of this world and so
may exist without the civil powers: an obligation that becomes wrong, or
impossible to adhere to, is of course null and void. . . ."[2]

Other members of the Connecticut clergy, such as Samuel Peters,
considered such reasoning a compromise with conscience and submitted
to banishment rather than concede or rationalize the issue. Peters waited
twenty years before he tested Tyler's judgment on the dangers of returning
and then deemed it best to settle outside of Connecticut. He ended his
days in poverty and eclipse in New York.

DECEMBER 2, 1784

❡ . . . the vindictive Spirit of the Country is almost totally altered in
the space of one year past, and though, if you had returned last Spring,
some few Curs might have growled a little and I am confident that would
have been all; yet now I can assure you that the fierce Spirit of Whigism is
Dead; and it is the general Sense of the People of Connecticut, Rulers and

---

[1] James Shepard, *The Episcopal Church and Early Ecclesiastical Laws of Connecticut,*
New Britain: 1908, p. 83.
[2] E. E. Beardsley, *History of the Episcopal Church in Connecticut,* Boston: 1865, vol.
I, 320–321.

A portion of a page from the *Book of Negroes* which contained the names of 3,000 Negroes (1,336 men, 914 women, and 750 children) who took advantage of the proclamation of His Excellency Guy Carleton K. B. General and Commander-in-Chief. It granted freedom for

Inspection Roll of Negroes Continued.

Remarks.

anyone who had resided twelve months within British
lines. After registration and inspection, the Negroes
boarded vessels bound for Nova Scotia from the Port of
New York between April 13 and July 31, 1783. *Guy
Carleton Papers, vol. 55.* (Public Record Office, London.)

all, that the old Spirit of Bitterness is now the Worst of Policy. Not one word of Whig and Tory appears now in the Newspapers and even the fiery Darts at General Arnold, which lasted longest, are now tottally out of Fashion. Those heretofore call'd Tories, and who were treated with the greatest Bitterness, are now in as good Reputation as any. Doctor Johnson is chosen a Member of Congress, Mr. Semour Mayor of the City of Hartford, and Cpt Nathaniel Backus who was much harrassed in the War for being a bold Friend to Great Britain is now the Second Alderman of our City of Norwich. And if you should incline to return, I am sure that not one Dog would move his Tongue against you. And you would be much more at Peace here than you was even seven years before the War. *[Samuel Peters Mss. vol. II, no. 23. Microfilm N. Y. Historical Society.]*

9   THE ELTING BROTHERS PLAN THEIR RETURN HOME

Roelof and Josiah Elting, the tradesmen of New Paltz in Ulster County who were declared inimical to the Continental Congress in 1776 for refusing Congress money, had spent eight years away from their homes. After languishing some time in jail in New Hampshire they were officially banished from the state in 1778, but allowed to remove within the British lines. Even though absolved from their allegiance to Britain by the treaty of peace, the men had to await action by the Legislature relieving them from the Act of Banishment before they could venture back. Roelof's letter to his wife forecasts a favorable outcome of their petition to the Legislature.

ACQUACKNONCK, NEW JERSEY, JANUARY YE 11TH 1784

❡ *Loveing Wife*

I take this opportunity to acquaint you that I and Brother Solomon are, By the Blessing of God, in Good health and am in hopes to hear the Same From you and Family. I have wrote to you by Mrs. Colden a few Days ago in Which I have mentioned to you that I Expected I Would not be Able to Come home as Soon as I had Expected on account of the Definitive treaty not Being Published By authority, and not knowing as yet, weather the assembly have made a house or not. . . . Weather they Will or Can Do any thing for us Before the Definitive treaty is published By authority is a matter in Doubt With me. So that I am at a Loss at Present What to advise you about Comeing to See me. For I Expect it will not be Long Before the assembly Will meet and then if the[y] Will Do any thing in Behalf of us, We Will Soon Come home, and if not, We must Wait till they or the Definitive treaty gives us Liberty. And if it is not Done Soon, I am a Fraid it Will Be Some time Before I Will Be able to Come home. Therefore I must Leave it to You to take your oppurtunity to Come to me when you think Proper. If you undertake to Come I think it is Best to Come by the Way along Mr. Coldens and so trough the Clove, for I Expect to Come that Way When I Come. If you Donth Come Soon I Shall Expect that you Will Write to me By the first Oppurtunity. No more at Present. But Remember my Love to you and Family and all Friends. I am Your Loveing Husband

Roelof Josias Elting

To Mrs. Maria Eltinge in the New Paltz

P.S. Solomon Desires you would Bring his Whig or Pruke along or Send it With a Safe hand.
[*Elting Papers, Jean Hasbrouck Memorial House Collection, New Paltz, N.Y.*]

10   JOHN TABOR KEMPE, LAST ATTORNEY GENERAL OF NEW YORK PROVINCE, EXPERIENCES THE FRUSTRATION OF SECURING EVIDENCE FROM AMERICA TO SUPPORT HIS CLAIM FOR COMPENSATION

Illustrative of the Loyalists who had suffered substantial losses from confiscation and attainder and who sought redress from government was John Tabor Kempe, the last Attorney General and Advocate General of New York Province. Kempe estimated his losses for property at £ 65,656 sterling; thus, in 1775 he had been one of the wealthiest men in the Province.[1] The fact that Kempe, age twenty-four in 1759 when he succeeded his father in office, began with no fortune whatever, but rather liabilities—

---

[1] According to their claims, Frederick Philipse III's losses were £ 155,328 (received £ 51,660); Sir John Johnson's, £ 103,182 (received £ 38,995); General Oliver De-Lancey's, £ 78,066 (received £ 23,446); Colonel Beverly Robinson's, £ 68,784 (received £ 24,087); William Bayard's, £ 65,274 (received £ 19,397); and Colonel Roger Morris's, £ 61,891 (received £ 5,503). *Loyalists Transcripts,* vol. XI.

including his father's debts and an obligation to support his mother, four maiden sisters, and an impecunious half-brother—stirs wonder at his achievement. Amassing a fortune of such size, primarily in the pre-revolutionary decade, suggests the opportunities open to placemen who were important enough to receive timely information about land acquisition and to make the most of it. Kempe's rise from poverty to riches was not gained by illegal or fraudulent practices but through the advantages of office and through a fortunate marriage in 1766 to Grace Coxe of Trenton. Of the 168,000 or so acres which he listed in his memorial to the Crown, 36,000 came to his ownership by his marriage and the remaining 132,000 were acquired for nominal considerations, often just the fees involved and the cost of a survey.[2]

Through most of the war years Kempe continued to serve the Crown as Advocate General in New York. In 1783 he went with his family of eleven to London where he suffered the heartbreaking experience of seeing his fortune vanish and his hopes for just compensation evaporate. Only about one-tenth of his fortune was salvaged through compensation by the British government.[3] Excerpts from two of his letters to his old friend William Livingston, Governor of New Jersey, written when his case before the commissioners was still pending, indicate the frustration and disappointment experienced by most of the Loyalist petitioners to the Crown.

A third brief selection from Ann Watts Kennedy, another Loyalist refugee in London, to her brother, Robert Watts, in New York shows little sympathy for Kempe's dissatisfaction.[4]

John Tabor Kempe to William Livingston

NOVEMBER 6, 1787

❡ . . . Permit me Sir to repeat again of what immense Consequence it may be to me that the Remainder of my Lands be speedily sold. I am told

---

[2] Ibid., vol. XLVI, pp. 37–68.

[3] *Loyalist Transcripts*, vol. XI, p. 68. Kempe's total claim for loss of both property and income was £ 70,713 sterling. He received as compensation £ 5,546 for loss of property, plus £ 1,500 for loss of income, and a pension of £ 640 under the Act of June 9, 1788. The pension did not last long as Kempe was killed in 1791 when he was thrown from his carriage.

[4] Ann Watts Kennedy (Mrs. Archibald Kennedy) was a daughter of John Watts and a sister of Mary Watts Johnson, wife of Sir John Johnson.

that the Commissioners for examining our Claims will close their Business in a few Months. My Case must come on without fail on the 19 Instant and I am very indifferently prepared with Proofs of the actual Sale of my confiscated Estates in your State and that of New York. As to Vermont where I had a large Property, I cannot find whether they have confiscated my Estate or not, tho I have some Proofs that my Lands in that Quarter have all been granted by the Vermontese since they sat up for themselves, but they have done this without any mention of my Interest, or that the Lands were contained in any New York Grant; so that my Evidence is not by public Document, but by Affidavit.

I see by the Papers that your Convention has broke up after having digested a new System of Federation. . . .

JUNE 16, 1788

❡ . . . I . . . return you most sincere Thanks for the friendly Interest you have taken in my Concerns and for the indefatigable Pains you have bestowed in your kind Endeavors of furnishing me with the Proofs & Documents necessary to bring my Claims to a favorable Issue.

Partly for Defect of Proofs of Sale, but more I apprehend from the Principles which (tho not avowed, all Circumstances make apparent) the Commissioners have adopted in Liquidating the Claims and from the unpardonable Remissness of the Agents for managing the Affairs of the Claimants in not apprizing Parliament of the certainty of the greatest Inequality taking Place upon the System adopted by the Commissioners, I fear I shall be among those who will not receive one Tenth of the Value of their lost Property, while others, not better entitled to Consideration, will have their full Losses made up to them. This Reflection is still rendered more aggravating by the Persuasion (which Self Love perhaps makes me entertain) that I have deserved better Things.

The final Settlement respecting those whose Cases have been heard and reported upon has just been taken up in Parliament & the Bill will this Day pass the House of Commons for their Relief, so the Scene, I suppose, is closed with respect to me; however I understand that it yet remains a profound Secret, and is to continue so til January next at least, what Sum is allowed to the respective Individuals. To the Honor of the House of Commons I cannot but mention that without one dissenting Voice they acceded to every Proposition made by the Minister for our Benefit and never was there a stronger Appearance of a universal Desire of doing what-

[439]

ever was right and fit to be done upon the Occasion. With such a Disposition in the House it is manifest that, had they had the necessary Information before them to have enabled them to have done equal Justice, it most certainly would have taken Place. This very Consideration must heighten yet more the Affliction of the many Sufferers who I fear have been sacrificed by those whose Duty it was to have made the Necessary Representations to Parliament and which there is too must Reason to believe have been withheld from interested Motives.

Whatever my Fate may be, I hope I shall "learn therewith to be content" and in every Exigency shall remember your kind Offices at my Heart, assured that I have had your sincerest Wishes and best Endeavors for my succeeding as I ought to do. [*Livingston Papers, vol. II, Mass. Historical Society.*]

Ann Watts Kennedy to Robert Watts

DECEMBER 3, 1788

❡ I have just seen Mr. Kempe who is much dissatisfy'd with what Government has done for him. I have no patience with such people. They have given him five thousand pounds and Six hundred and fifty a year for life and he owns he made during the War enough to spend Eight hundred a year. If they had allow'd him to Continue in New York he would not have been in the receipt of anything and what would his Lands have brought him. He may now Save—but had he have staid he would have found it hard to live. I think we are much worse of[f]. What remittances do we get? . . . They wont give us a Six pence for what the British troops have demolished. I wish our Estate had been forfitted. We should then have got as Jones, etc.—[He] has thirty thousand and that in the funds would have look'd large and given our Children good Estates when we are call'd away. [*Robert Watts Mss., vol. IV, N.Y. Historical Society.*]

II   MARTIN GAY MEETS WITH A DISAGREEABLE RECEPTION
ON RETURNING TO BOSTON

Martin Gay, son of Ebenezer Gay, a Hingham minister, was an early and consistent Loyalist. A captain of artillery, deacon of West Church, warden of the town, prosperous merchant and coppersmith, he had built up, by 1773, a respectable place for himself in Boston. When the war broke out he signed as one of the Addressers of Governor Hutchinson, necessitating his departure with the British troops in 1776. He took his son Martin Jr. and his daughter Mary with him, stationing himself at Halifax. His brother, Jotham, had been a permanent settler of Cumberland, Nova Scotia, since 1764, becoming a member of the Assembly, and was thus able to handle family interests in lands and trade in the Maritime Provinces. Martin Gay's son Samuel, a Harvard graduate in 1775, had joined his uncle in Cumberland that same year, helping also to carry on the family interests in that part of the continent. Thus the way was already well prepared for Martin Gay. His wife, Ruth Atkins Gay, however, remained in Boston, separated from him for eight years. She was able thereby to salvage some of the Gay property, namely part of the house and shop on Union Street, Boston, which they had occupied. In 1779, she succeeded in having the Probate Court set off her dower third of the real estate of her absentee husband under provisions of the Act of the General Court for the disposal of estates of absentees.

Martin Gay was encouraged to return to Boston in 1784 but found such a cool reception, as his letters indicate, that he again departed the city.[1] On returning once more to Boston in 1792, he resumed his business as coppersmith and maintained his residence there until his death. While he told Joshua Winslow that he had lost £2,000 by bad debts through the Revolution, he nonetheless fared far better than most Boston Loyalists.

HALIFAX   MAY 5, 1784

❡   *To his wife, Ruth Atkins Gay*
   . . . I do now with a pleasing prospect hope that in a very short time there will be no occation of our Conversing togather at so great a distance, that a period will be put to our long unhappy Sepperation, by again meeting

[1] April 27, 1786, *Martin Gay,* Gay-Otis Collection, Columbia University.

and liveing with each other in the Injoyment of happy Conversation and dear Embraces, uninterrupted untill the Supreme Disposer of all Events in the course of his allwise Governing Providence make a final Sepperation of us by Death. The motives to induce me to make you a visit are so power-full, together with the incouragement you and our good friend, Mr. [Thomas] Walley, have given me that you apprehend no opposition or In-sult will be offered me, has determined me to go to you. . . .

BOSTON SEPTEMBER 15, 1784

❡ *To Benjamin Holmes*

. . . I now find that many Expressions I have made in the course of eight or nine years last past are known here (which I don't deny) and now made use of to my Prejudice. Tis now near six weeks since I arrived . . . it was night when I landed which I thought a favorable circumstance in some Respects. . . .

Early in the morning I sent for my friend Mr. Walley. He advis'd me to repare into the Country without delay. A favorable opporty soon offerd and in a few Hours was safe in my fathers House [Hingham], where I met Mrs. Gay, with my Father and famely all well in Helth.

. . . I returnd here, then Expected to see people and transact Business without the lest objection or opposition, but it seems there was so many informations against me for the wicked speaches I had made which cast reprochfull reflections on some high Charicters who are Esteemed the Saviour of the Country, which it seems were considerd by their Mighti-nesses as high Crimes and Misdemeners and it was a mear Chance a Vote was obtain (through the Interest of my Friend who attended the Council when my Case was taken up by them) to refer the further Consideration of it to their next meeting. . . . Thus I have Escaped for the presant an Order being served on me to depart this *State.* . . .

NOVEMBER 16, 1784

❡ *To Benjamin Holmes*

I am still advised not to Expose myself at present in the publick Streets of this Sacred and *remarcably Religious Town.* . . .

FEBRUARY 26, 1785

❡ *To Benjamin Holmes*

. . . my Dear friend, my present Situation in many respects is disagreeable and mortifying. To live in open view of my Buildings and other property occupied and made use of by Certin Charicters, with that apparent Exulting Insolence and not allowed even to ask for the lest Satisfaction is highly aggrevating.

I live retire[d] from Company. Though the necessary Expence of my small famely is but trifling, I have not been able to recover out of the Considerable sums due to me but a very little more then has Supported that Expence. However, I will not Dispare of seeing Better times and live in hopes that a Change of Situation and Circumstances is at no great Distance. . . .

APRIL 4, 1785

❡ *To Captain Samuel Haynes at St. Croix*

I return you my thanks for your friendly Congratulations to myself and famely on my return to my native Country. On this accasion, my good friend, you Judge very right, with respect to the happiness I have in my famely and particular friends, but with regard to the property I left in this Country, tis quite the reverse, being deprived of all of my real Estate. My wife keeps possession of a third part of the House I formerly lived in, set of[f] to her by *the powers that be* which affords a present Shelter for myself & famely. By means of the late *Revolution* I am really reduced, not only to Low but Mortifying Circumstances in life. My only dependence to support a Subsistence is the money due to me from privit persons, in the Colection of which I meet with much Difficulty. . . .

SEPTEMBER 7, 1785

❡ *To Captain Samuel Haynes*

To tell you the truth, my good friend, I am under very Disagreeable Circumstances in this Country and want to be gaun from it; tis now about twelve months since I returned here, in all which time it has not been in my power to accomplish but a small part of the Business I am here upon.

[I] live Entirely on the Expend[iture] of what little was saved of my property from the demands for it, without Earning a farthing in any way what-ever. . . .

❡ *To Benjamin Holmes*

. . . By the best observations I am Capable of making togather with what I am told by some of the most knowing the trade of this place is in a most Deplorable Situation, growing worse and worse every day. Such a Scarcity of money they say was never known amongst them which, togather with the restriction the British acts of parliment lay on their Navigation, deprive them of the Benifit they vainly bosted they should obtain by their glorious Independence are now seariously thought of. I will only make this one observation, that there is good reason to believe the generality of the people would rejoice to be restored to their former state under the British Government. [*Gay-Otis Collection, Martin Gay, Columbia Univ.*]

12 CHIEF JUSTICE RICHARD MORRIS SUGGESTS A SOLDIER'S DUTY TRANSCENDS THE DICTATES OF THE HEART IN A WARTIME MURDER CASE

In the spring of 1781 a sizable group of DeLancey's Cowboys swept into Northcastle, seized three rebels, and hanged one of them to get even for a rebel hanging. Four years later one of the party, John Griffin, a laborer from Bedford, was in turn about to be executed for murder when Chief Justice Richard Morris intervened with an appeal to Governor Clinton. Morris's argument has a present-day parallel, raising the questions of the primacy of military duty and the operation of law in a no-man's land in time of war. Governor Clinton did not pardon Griffin; it required an act of the Legislature to accomplish this.[1]

[1] *Laws of New York,* 1786, chap. 3, Jan. 31, 1786. An Act to Pardon John Griffin of the Felony Herein Mentioned.

NEW YORK JUNE 15, 1785

℄ *Sir* [Governor George Clinton],

The day before yesterday Ended the Court of Oyer and Terminer and General Goal delivery for the county of Westchester, at which one John Griffin, was Convicted of the Murder of John Strom. In the Indictment he was Charged with "being present, Aiding, helping, Abetting, Comforting, —Assisting, and Maintaining one Isaac Akerley Jun[r] to commit the Murder, and [it] then Concludes "And so the Jurors aforesaid do say that the said John Griffin and others—feloniously, willfully, . . . and of their Malice Aforethought, did Kill and Murder, etc." The proof to Support the Charge was that Isaac Akerley Jun[r], an Officer with a party of 17 or 18 men all of DeLanceys Corps, came out in the Spring of the year 1781 to North Castle or thereabouts, that they took three of our men prisoners, and on Phillipsburgh, about Six or Seven miles South of where they took the prisoners, Isaac Akerley fixed a Rope about the neck of John Strom, one of the prisoners, and Hung him, declaring he did it as a Retaliation for his brother, who had been Hung at Poghkeepsie. Griffin was one of the party and present at the Murder, but it did not appear on the Tryal he had in any Instance been an Actor in the Business. His presence at the time was proved by his own confession, and that also proved his Disapprobation of the Measure. He Appeared much Affected in the Course of his tryal, whether it was produced by his Situation or by a Sincear Contrition for his past life I am not able to determine. He is under Sentence of death and is Ordered to be Executed on fryday the 15th of July Next. May it not be proper to Observe to your Excellency that Akerley appeared the Officer of the party, and this Griffin one of the men? Might not his military duty as a Soldier be an Obligation to his presence in a Business his heart did not Approve?—Farther, this crime was committed at a time in a District of [a] Country in which our Own Conduct—by permitting crimes of Almost Every Kind to pass Unnoticed tacitly—declared the Law there to have little or no Operation.

These Observations I could not urge to the Jury. The Law makes all present at a Murder principals, unless they came by Accident, and tho the place and time may have weight with your Excellency, it could not be taken into Consideration by the Jury. Griffin has a wife and five Children in Westchester and some other Connections. Judge Tompkins and Justice Burling, who sat with me on his Tryal, I believe, mean to Recommend him to your Excellency. I mentioned to them that I should Report to you his Case very particularly. I have

> The Honor to be with Great Respect and Esteem Your Excl
> most Obed^t and very Hum^l Servt
> *R. Morris*
> > *[Private Papers of Frank Smith, Scarsdale, N.Y.]*

13 JAMES CLARKE WOULD GIVE HIS LIFE TO RESTORE RHODE ISLAND TO ITS FORMER HAPPY SITUATION

The domestic struggles of the new Republic during the first few years of peace under a weak Confederation were well known to the Nova Scotia refugees and reinforced their belief that independence was a grievous mistake. Rhode Island was particularly hard hit by the loss of the West Indies trade, by state tariff barriers, by monetary difficulties, and by the postwar depression. In 1785–1786, debtors, clamoring for unrestricted paper money, forced the legalizing of paper emissions. When merchants closed shops rather than accept depreciated paper and when creditors fled the state to avoid accepting payment, the Legislature set up a special nonjury court to deal with recalcitrant creditors. James Clarke, a Newport Loyalist, writes from Halifax to Miss Coggeshall in Newport, expressing his pity for his native Rhode Island.

FEBRUARY 5, 1786

❡ I hope Prospects brighten at Newport and that you begin to realize some of the many Benefits which Independence and a new Constitution were to give you. A whole Continent ruined to get rid of ideal Taxes— Without a Friend, unconnected with Great Britain, groaning under the severest Burthens, deprived of the Advantages of Commerce, and forsaken by all the World are Evils of so extensive a Magnitude and in their Consequences so Fatal that America must fall under its accumulating Pressure. My Attachment to our native Country is so fervent and sincere that I could freely give up my Life, and Ten Thousand more if I possessed them, could I restore dear Rhode Island to its former happy, happy Situation. You will begin to think me a perfect Enthusiast. [*Box 45, Folder 5, Newport Historical Society.*]

14 JOSEPH BRANT SENDS HIS SONS TO DARTMOUTH AND REQUESTS ATTENTION TO THEIR MORALS

Joseph Brant, Chief of the Mohawks and ravager of Cherry Valley and Wyoming, had received two years of education in 1761-1763 at Eleazar Wheelock's school in Lebanon, Connecticut. After the war, when he was living at Grand River, Ontario, he seized the opportunity offered by President John Wheelock and his brother, James Wheelock, to send his sons, Joseph and Jacob, to Dartmouth. In each of the letters to the Wheelocks, which follow, Brant expresses satisfaction that their behavior and morals would be "strictly attended to," even "with respect to dress and the cutting of their hair." Brant's unforgettable tragedy with his eldest son Isaac, a child of his first marriage, lay behind this stress on conduct. Isaac had developed an unmanageable temperament, prone to jealousy, inebriation, and tantrums, during which he had several times threatened the life of his father. During one seizure he had killed an innocent harnessmaker. In 1795, he made a drunken assault on his father, who drew a dagger and struck his son on the head. Isaac died from the wound a few days later. The case came before the Council of Sachems and Warrors, which exonerated Brant, saying: "The son raised his parricidal hand against the kindest of fathers. His death was occasioned by his own crime."[1] This indelible incident augmented Brant's disappointment when both his sons became dropouts after a year, one in the spring and one in the summer of 1801. Although the young Joseph explained his departure as occasioned by the constant bickering with his brother, the father laid it to "the imprudence of youth," adding: "I am full confident he could not have been in a better place."[2]

[1] William L. Stone, *Life of Joseph Brant, Thayendanegea*, New York: 1838, vol. II, pp. 465-466 and fn.
[2] Brant to James Wheelock, Mar. 10, 1802, *Misc. Mss B*, N.Y. Historical Society. Quoted Ibid., p. 476.

OCTOBER 3, 1800

❡ *To Mr. James Wheelock*
Dear Sir:

Although long since I have had the pleasure of seeing or corresponding with you, still I have not forgot there is such a Person in being. And now embrace the kind offer you once made me in offering to take charge of my Son Joseph who I certainly should at that time have sent out had it not been that there was apparently a jealousy exsisting between the British & Americans. However, I hope it is not yet too late. I send both my Sons, Joseph & Jacob, who I doubt not will be particularly attended to by my friends. I could wish them to be studiously attended to, not only as to their education but behaviur, as to their Morals in particular, this no doubt is needless mentioning as I know of old & from personal experience at your Seminary that those things are paid strit attention to. Let my Sons be at what schools soever, your overseeing them will be highly flattering to me. I should by this opportunity have wrote Mr. John Wheelock on the same subject, but a hurry of business at this time prevents me. But I shall hereafter take the first opportunity of dropping him a few lines untill when Please make my best respects to him & I earnestly solicit his friendship and attention to my Boys which, be assured of, I shall ever gratefully acknowledge. I am, Dear Sir, with wishing you & family health & happiness

Your Friend and Well Wisher
Jos. Brant
[*Vt. Historical Society, Quoted in Stone, Brant, vol. II, p. 469.*]

GRAND RIVER, FEBRUARY 9, 1801

❡ *Dear Sir* [James Wheelock]

It is sometime since I had the pleasure of receiving your kind letter of the 3rd of November 1800. It gives me unspeakable satisfaction to find that my boys are with you, as I am fully confident they would not have a better or more agreable situation. I am assured from the known reputation of the President that if they do not make a progress in their studies it will be owing to themselves. I therefore hope you will shew me the kindness to make free and be particular in exhorting them to exert themselves and to behave in a becoming manner. . . .

I yet add that I should wish them to be learnt that it is their Duty to be subject to the customs of the place they are in, even with respect to dress and the cutting of their hair. [*B. 735, Vt. Historical Society, Stone, Brant, vol. II, p. 471.*]

FEBRUARY 9, 1801

⊄ *To John Wheelock, President*
. . . For my part nothing can ever efface from my memory the persevering attention your ever revered father paid to my education when I was in the place my sons now are. Though I was an unprofitable pupil in some respects, yet my worldly affairs have been much benefitted by the instruction I there received. I hope my children may reap greater advantages under your care both with respect to their future as well as their worldly welfare. Their situation at your brother's meets with my highest approbation. Your goodness in having provided for them out of the funds far exceeds my expectations and merits my warmest thanks. The reason that induced me to send them to be instructed under your care is the assurance I had that their morals and education would be there more strictly attended to than at any other place I knew of. I am much pleased at the kindness you shew in pressing them to be familiar at your house. I beg you will be constant in exhorting them to conduct themselves with propriety. The character you give me of the worthy gentleman their Preceptor is extremely pleasing. From the whole I feel perfectly easy with respect to their situation and care taken of their education and am fully convinced that all now depends on their own exertions. [*Dartmouth College Library. Stone, Brant, vol. II, pp. 470-471.*]

15 "LEARN THIS OF ME, WHERE E'ER THY LOT DOTH FALL; SHORT LOT, OR NOT, TO BE CONTENT WITH ALL."—ROBERT HERRICK, *LOTS TO BE LIKED*, 1648

Among the Loyalists who found contentment as permanent settlers in Nova Scotia were Gideon White and Stephen Millidge. Despite a residue of bitterness from the treatment they had received in their former homes, they had the stamina to set the bitterness aside, adjust to a new life, and in time make significant contributions to their adopted provinces. Gideon

White of Massachusetts, a captain in the British forces when the war ended, settled in Shelburne in 1783 and founded a distinguished family there. He continued as a merchant and farmer in that town through its rise and decline, raising a family of nine children and becoming in time a member of the Assembly and Judge of the Court of Common Pleas. Michael Roberts, a friend, assured him that his choice was no mistake. Comparing the situation with that in New York, he wrote (March 30, 1785): "Our present Situation here is very unpleasant & our future prospects exceeding gloomy—what with the Imposts, Rents, enormous Taxes &c. we *poor Tories* have got to pay." Another friend, N. Ford, sojourning in Massachusetts, pointed with satisfaction to the disunity prevailing in the States, adding (September 23, 1786): "It is my most sincear prayer Shelburne may continue to Flourish . . . and a Speedy end put to and Total downfall to Satans Kingdom, those United States, which thank God is hastening. . . ."[1]

From the perspective of twenty years after the war Stephen Millidge, a New Jersey Loyalist, also a friend of Gideon White, reviewed the consequences to himself of his family's loyalty to the Crown. Although it had altered his life's plans, he concluded that he had lived "hitherto very happy in New Brunswick" and had no regrets.

JANUARY 2, 1803

❦ *Dear Sir* [John Milledge in Louisville, Georgia]
I also gave you a general account of our Family, and now for your amusement communicate a short one of my own Life.

My Father was not born in affluence. The Education therefore which he acquired, was owing to a naturally strong and inquisitive genius & great industry and application. He married pretty early in Life my Mother, a Woman whose fortune was not superior to his own, and whose mental powers are not inferior. I was their first, born in the year 1761. With a strong inclination to educate their children, I was sent early to a School in the Village of which I am a Native, and at the age of about 15 years was sent to a Gentleman of some eminence near the place of my Birth to study the art of Physic, and acquire a classical education, in the State of New Jersey. At the commencement of the Revolution in America, my Father

---

[1] *White Collection,* vol. IV, no's. 359 and 427. PANS.

adopted a part which did not coincide with the principles of the majority of his Countrymen and aided in embodying a Battalion, which he commanded as Major (the Colonel having been taken prisoner) a great part of the War. He directed his family to take shelter within the British lines. Being the eldest child and the only confidential friend and assistant to my Venerable Mother, and in obedience to my Fathers directions, I contrived means to abandon the paternal estate and by so doing lost a good Education and a moral Certainty of a very handsome support for the Family. We however arrived, with a little property, safely in New York, and being too young and ignorant for any other place, I was appointed Surgeons Mate to the Battalion already mentioned, and after some time was considered equal to the task of Paymaster, which I unluckily accepted. Being of a volatile disposition, possessing a passion for Gaiety and Mirth, and somewhat attached to the fishionable and prevailing View of Gambling, countenanced and in some measure introduced by Sr W. Howe, having much money at Command, I risqued more than belonged to myself, and with the usual luck of such adventures, lost more than I was able to pay. My Father very handsomely made up the deficiency, & in some measure discarded me.

Lands were promised the disbanded Troops, and I came to this Country with plenty of Cloaths and a "plentiful scarcity" of every other necessary. Here I ballotied for and drew—owing to its vicinity to the Seat of Government, a valuable tract of Uncultivated Land, which after a severe trial I found it impossible personally to till, and to hire I could not, and therefore sold it. With the money I explored the natural productions and Curiosities of the Country. This Sum being almost exhausted, some of my Friends near the Court (for even here we have a Court) mentioned to the Governor, to whom I had not made myself personally known, that two appointments were vacant in this County, that of High Sheriff and Land Surveyor. I obtained them and have thus continued since the year '86. In 1790 I married . . . a Miss Botsford, now the only daughter of a Gentleman who has been Speaker of the house of Assembly of this Province since the division of Nova Scotia took place. By her I have seven children and have lived hitherto very happy. About 7 years since, I commenced a Country Trader and have no reason to regret the honest undertaking in support of my Family. [*Crary, Misc. Papers.*]

16   THE REVEREND JOHN STUART, MISSIONARY TO THE
MOHAWKS, WRITES BISHOP WILLIAM WHITE OF
PENNSYLVANIA OF HIS CONTENTMENT IN KINGSTON

The final words of the Reverend John Stuart, who followed the Indians to
Ontario and became chaplain of the Kingston garrison carry a warning,
derived from the Loyalists' experience, that accounts cast for the short
term are subject to a different evaluation when weighed against the perspective of time.

NOVEMBER 26, 1798

❰   How mysterious are the ways of Providence! How short-sighted are
we! Some years ago I thought it a great hardship to be banished into the
wilderness and would have imagined myself compleatly happy could I have
exchanged it for a place in the delightful city of Philadelphia. Now the best
wish we can form for our friends is to have them removed to us.   [*O'Callaghan, Doc. Hist. New York, vol. IV, p. 321.*]

Bibliography

Anyone who has worked with Revolutionary materials has experienced the awesomeness aroused by their very volume and has confronted the mountainous task of compiling an exhaustive bibliography. Such an assignment, related only to Loyalist source materials, has been undertaken by the Program for Loyalist Studies and Publications under the direction of Professor Robert East of the Graduate Division of the New York City colleges, with publication by the American Antiquarian Society expected soon. Thus this bibliography has been strictly limited to sources from which excerpts have been taken or which have been mentioned in the editorial commentary. Many obvious and important sources which have been consulted have not been listed. Newspapers and collections of manuscript papers have been included in the general bibliography only when an excerpt from them has been quoted and needed to be identified.

Bibliography

MANUSCRIPTS, BOOKS, PERIODICALS, AND
HISTORICAL COLLECTIONS

Addison, Daniel D., *Life and Times of Edward Bass* (Boston: 1897).

Allen, Jolley, "An Account of Part of the Sufferings and Losses of Jolley Allen, a Native of London," *Minute Book March 1776,* American Antiquarian Society, Worcester. See *Massachusetts Historical Society Proceedings* (February 1878).

Allen Papers, Bailey Library, University of Vermont, Burlington.

Anderson, Joseph, *The Town and City of Waterbury Connecticut from the Aboriginal Period to the Year 1895,* 3 vols. (New Haven: 1896).

Anderson, Troyer, *The Command of the Howe Brothers during the American Revolution* (New York: 1936).

Aptheker, Herbert, *The Negro in the American Revolution* (New York: 1940).

Auchmuty, Robert, *Naval Historical Society Collection,* New York Historical Society.

Bakeless, John, *Turncoats, Traitors, and Heroes* (Philadelphia and New York: 1959).

Balch Papers, 1775-1782, Manuscript Division, New York Public Library. Astor, Lenox and Tilden Foundations.

Baldwin, Ernest H., *Joseph Galloway, The Loyalist Politician* (Philadelphia: 1902).

Barber, John W., and Henry Howe, *Historical Collections of the State of New York* (New York: 1841).

Barnum, H. L., *The Spy Unmasked* (New York: 1828).

Bates, Walter, "The Narrative of Walter Bates," W. O. Raymond, ed., *Kingston and the Loyalists of 1783* (St. John, New Brunswick: 1889).

The Battle of Brooklyn: A Farce of Two Acts As It Was Performed on Long Island on Tuesday 27th of August 1776 by the Representatives of the Tyrant of America Assembled at Philadelphia. Copy in the Boston Atheneum and New York Public Library (New York: Printed for James Rivington, 1776).

Baxter, the Reverend Simeon, *Tyrannicide Proved Lawful, From the Practice and Writings of Jews, Heathens, and Christians. A Discourse Delivered in the Mines at Symsbury . . . to the Loyalists . . . September 19, 1781* (London: 1782).

Beardsley, E. E., *The Life and Correspondence of the Right Reverend Samuel Seabury* (Boston: 1881).

——— *The History of the Episcopal Church in Connecticut* (Boston: 1865).

Blagden, Charles, *Blagden Letters,* Royal Society, London.

[Bloodgood, Simeon DeWitt], *The Sexagenary or Reminiscences of the American Revolution* (Albany: 1833).

Bolton, Robert, *History of Several Towns, Manors, and Patents of the County of Westchester* (New York: 1905).

Burgoyne, John, *A State of the Expedition from Canada as Laid Before the House of Commons* (London: 1780).

Bouton, Nathaniel, ed., *State Papers, New Hampshire Documents and Records, 1776-1783* (Concord: 1874), vol. VIII.

Brant, Joseph, *Miscellaneous Manuscripts B,* New York Historical Society.

Brant, Mollie, Manuscripts 1–443, Public Archives of Canada. Copies in Johnson Hall, Amsterdam.

Brown, Alan S., "James Simpson's Reports on the Carolina Loyalists 1779–1780," *Journal of Southern History,* vol. XXI (November 1955).

Brown, Wallace, *The King's Friends* (Providence: 1966).

Burnett, Edmund C., ed., *Letters of the Members of the Continental Congress,* 8 vols. (Washington, D.C.: Carnegie Institution of Washington, 1921–1936).

Burr, Nelson, *The Anglican Church in New Jersey* (Philadelphia: 1954).

Butterfield, Consul W., *History of the Girtys* (Cincinnati: 1890).

———, *Washington-Irvine Correspondence* (Madison, Wis.: 1882).

Cameron, Nancy Jean, to Mrs. Kenneth Macpherson, May 15, 1785, Public Archives of Canada.

Canada East, *Civil Secretary's Correspondence,* S Series (R.G. 4), Public Archives of Canada.

Caner, Henry, *Letterbook,* University of Bristol Library, England.

Canniff, William, *The Settlement of Upper Canada* (Toronto: 1872).

Carleton, Sir Guy, *Papers,* Public Record Office, London.

Cartwright, Richard, Jr., *Continuation of a Journal of an Expedition into the Indian Country, June 25-August 29, 1779.* Courtesy of Richard L. Cartwright, Port Hope, Ontario.

Carstairs, J. S., "Late Loyalists," *Annual Transactions, United Empire Loyalists Association,* vol. IV, 1901–1902 (Toronto: 1903).

Caruthers, E. W., *Interesting Revolutionary Incidents and Sketches of Character, Chiefly in the "Old North State"* (Philadelphia: 1854).

Bibliography

Chapman, G. T., *Sketches of Dartmouth College* (Cambridge: 1867).

Chesney, Captain Alexander, "Memoirs," British Museum. See *Tennessee Historical Magazine,* vol. VII (1921).

Chipman, Ward, *Papers, Gunther Collection,* Courtesy of the Chicago Historical Society.

Clark, Walter, ed., *North Carolina State Records,* vol. XIII (Winston: 1896).

Clarke, James, *Papers,* Box 45, Folder 5, Newport Historical Society.

Clarke, William, *Clarke Papers,* Diocesan Library, Boston.

Clarkson, John, *Journal August 6, 1791–March 18, 1792,* New York Historical Society.

Claus, Daniel, *Claus Papers,* MG 19, F 1, vol. 4, Public Archives of Canada.

Clinton, George, *Public Papers of George Clinton 1777–1795, 1801–1804,* vol. VIII, Hugh Hastings, ed. (Albany: 1904).

Clinton, Sir Henry, *Papers,* Clements Library, Ann Arbor, Mich.

Colden, Cadwallader, in *Calendar of Historical Manuscripts in Albany,* Revolutionary Papers I.

———, *Journal* (microfilm), New York Historical Society.

Commager, Henry Steele, and Richard B. Morris, *The Spirit of 'Seventy-Six* (Indianapolis: 1958).

Connecticut Superior Court Records, Jan. 23, 1777, Connecticut State Archives, Hartford, Conn.

Cooper, James Fenimore, *The Spy: A Tale of the Neutral Ground* (New York: 1821).

Crary, Catherine S., "The Tory and the Spy," *William and Mary Quarterly,* vol. XVI.

Craton, Michael, *History of the Bahamas* (London: 1962).

Crèvecoeur, Hector St. John de, *Sketches of Eighteenth Century America,* H. L. Bourdin, R. H. Gabriel, and S. T. Williams, eds. (New Haven: 1925).

Crèvecoeur, Robert de, *St. John de Crèvecoeur: Sa Vie et Ses Ouvrages* (Paris: 1883).

———, "The Grotto," H. L. Bourdin and S. T. Williams, eds. "Crevecoeur the Loyalist," *The Nation,* vol. 121 (Sept. 23, 1925).

Cruden, John, "Narrative of John Cruden," *South Carolina Loyalists, Ford Collection,* New York Public Library.

Cruikshank, E. A., ed., *Records of Niagara,* Niagara Historical Society, 1927, no. 38.

Curtis, Abel, to Levi Willard, Sept. 22, 1777. Vermont Historical Society, Montpelier.

Curwen, Samuel, *The Journal and Letters of Samuel Curwen, 1775-1783,* George A. Ward, ed. (Boston: 1864).

Custis, George W. Parke, *Recollections and Private Memoirs of Washington,* B. J. Lossing, ed. (New York: 1860).

Davies, Hanbury, "The American Loyalists and Australia," *Journal of the United Empire Society,* vol. XXV.

Dawson, Henry B., *Westchester County during the American Revolution* (New York: 1886).

Delafield, Martin, "William Smith, the Historian," *Magazine of American History,* no. 13 (1881).

DeLancey Papers, Misc. Private collection of Mrs. Norman Duffield, Buffalo, N.Y.

DePeyster, Arent S., to General Allan Maclean, July 8, 1783, *Magazine of History,* vol. VIII, no. 10 (1910).

Dexter, Franklin B., *Biographical Sketches of the Graduates of Yale* (New York: 1896).

Dorchesteer Papers II, Military Correspondence no. 3, Public Archives of Nova Scotia.

Draper, Lyman C., *King's Mountain and Its Heroes* (Cincinnati: 1881).

Drinker, Elizabeth, *The Journal of Elizabeth Drinker,* New York Historical Society.

Duane, James, *Duane Papers,* New York Historical Society.

Duane, William, ed., *Extracts from the Diary of Christopher Marshall . . . during the American Revolution, 1774-1781* (Albany: 1877).

Dunbar, Moses, *The Last Speech and Dying Words of Moses Dunbar Who Was Executed at Hartford on Wednesday the Nineteenth of March 1777 for High Treason Against The State of Connecticut,* see *The History . . . of Waterbury,* Joseph Anderson, ed. (New Haven: 1896), vol. I. (Original in the Morgan Library.)

Eager, Samuel W., *History of Orange County* (Newburgh: 1846-1847).

Eddis, William, *Letters from America, Historical and Descriptive, Comprising Occurrences from 1769 to 1777 Inclusive* (London: 1792).

Einstein, Lewis, *Divided Loyalties* (London: 1933).

Elliot, Andrew, *Papers Consisting of Fifty Letters, 1747-1777,* New York Historical Society.

Elting, Clarence J., "Lineage of the Elting Family," *Olde Ulster* (Kingston: 1907).

Elting Papers, Hugenot Historical Society, New Paltz, N.Y., Inc.

Elzas, Barnet A., *Leaves from my Historical Scrapbook* (Charleston: 1907–1908).

Eve, Oswell, to Daniel Cox, May 29, 1784, CO 23/26, Public Record Office, London. Copy in Public Library, Nassau, Bahama Islands.

Eve, Sarah, "Extraacts from the Journal of Miss Sarah Eve," *Pennsylvania Magazine of History and Biography,* vol. V.

Fanning, David, *A Journal of David Fanning's Transactions, 1775-1783* (Richmond: 1861).

Fitch, Asa, *Manuscript History of Washington County, New York, 1845-1847,* New York Genealogical and Biographical Library.

Fitzpatrick, John C., ed., *The Writings of George Washington, from the Original Manuscript Sources, 1745-1799,* 39 vols. (Washington: United States Government Printing Office, 1931-1944).

Force, Peter, ed., *American Archives: Fourth Series, Containing a Documentary History of the English Colonies in North America from the King's Message to Parliament of March 7, 1774, to the Declaration of Independence by the United States,* 6 vols. (Washington: M. St. Clair Clarke and Peter Force, 1837-1846).

——*American Archives: Fifth Series, Containing a Documentary History of the United States of America from the Declaration of Independence, July 4, 1776, to the Definitive Treaty with Great Britain, September 3, 1783,* 3 vols. (Washington: M. St. Clair Clarke and Peter Force, 1848-1853).

Ford, Paul L., ed., *Winnowings in American History* (Brooklyn: 1890-1891) no. 5.

Franklin, William, to William Strahan, May 7, 1775, Morgan Library.

Franks, Rebecca, to Mrs. Anne Harrison Paca, Feb. 26, 1778, *Pennsylvania Magazine of History and Biography,* vol. XVI (1892).

——, to Mrs. Abigail Franks Hamilton, Aug. 10, 1791, *Pennsylvania Magazine of History and Biography,* vol. XXIII (1899).

Frey, Samuel L., ed., *Minute Book of the Committee of Safety of Tryon County,* (New York: 1905), *Collections,* 1925, II, New York Historical Society.

Frost, Sarah, *Diary, Kingston and the Loyalists of 1783,* W. O. Raymond, ed. (St. John, New Brunswick: 1889).

Fyfe, C. H., "Thomas Peters: History and Legend," *Sierra Leone Studies,* New Series no. 1 (London: 1953).

Galloway, Grace, "Diary of Grace Growden Galloway," Raymond C. Warner, ed., *Pennsylvania Magazine of History and Biography,* vol. LV (1931). Original in Pennsylvania Historical Society.

[Galloway, Joseph,] *Historical and Political Reflections on the American Rebellion* (London: 1780).

Gamsby, Dorothea, *Dorothea,* Told to Belle Thorn, North Stratford, N.H. Courtesy of Mrs. John Downie, Kingston, Ontario.

Gardiner, David, *Chronicles of Easthampton* (New York: 1871).

Gardiner, Sylvester, *Gardiner Papers,* vol. II, Massachusetts Historical Society.

Gay, Julius, *Farmington in the War of the Revolution* (Hartford, Conn.: 1893), pamphlet, New York Historical Society.

Gay, Martin, *Gay-Otis Collection,* Columbia University, Special Collections.

Georgia Historical Society, *Collections,* vol. III (Savannah: 1873).

The Georgia Gazette, James Johnson, ed. (also called *The Royal Gazette*)

Gray, Colonel Robert, "Observations on the War in South Carolina," *South Carolina Historical and Genealogical Magazine,* vol. XI.

Hadaway, William S., ed., *The McDonald Papers* (White Plains: 1927), New York Historical Society.

Haldimand Papers, MG 21, B-162, Public Archives of Canada.

Haliburton, Thomas C., *Historical and Statistical Account of Nova Scotia,* vol. I (Halifax: 1829).

Halsey, F. W., *The Old New York Frontier, 1614-1800* (New York: 1901).

Hamilton, J. C. ed., *The Works of Alexander Hamilton,* 7 vols. (New York: 1850-1851), vol. 1.

Hamilton, John, Mar. 31, 1782, Public Record Office, H.O. 42,1.

Hammond, Otis G., "The Tories of New Hampshire," *New Hampshire Historical Society Proceedings,* vol. V.

Hancock, Harold B., "John Ferdinand Dalziel Smyth, Loyalist," *Maryland Historical Magazine,* vol. LV.

Hardy, John, *Valentine's Manual of the Corporation of the City of New York* (New York: 1870).

Harvey, Mrs. Denis, "The Negro Loyalists: Arrival and Departure," 1962 (typescript), Public Archives of Nova Scotia.

Heidgerd, William, and Ruth Heidgerd, *New Paltz* (New Paltz: 1955).

Herrington, M. E., "Captain John Deserontyou and the Mohawk Settlement at Deseronto," *Bulletin of the Department of History of Queens University, Kingston,* no. 41 (November 1921).

Hildeburn, Charles R., *Sketches of Printers and Printing in Colonial New York* (New York: 1895).

Historical Anecdotes Civil and Military in a Series of Letters Written from America in the Years 1777-8 to Different Persons in England, by a Loyalist (London: 1779).

Historical Manuscript Commission Report on American Manuscripts in Britain (London: 1904–1909).

Hoadly, Charles, ed., *Colonial Records of Connecticut, 1775-1776* (Hartford: 1890), vol. XV.

Hoople, Elizabeth L., *The Hooples of Hooples Creek* (Toronto: 1967).

Hufeland, Otto, *Westchester County during the Revolution 1775-1783* (White Plains: 1926).

Hulton, Ann, *Letters of a Loyalist Lady* (Cambridge: 1927).

Hulton, Henry, *Letterbook. Shepherd Manuscripts.* Manchester College Library, Oxford, England (copy).

Hutchinson, Peter O., ed., *Diary and Letters of Thomas Hutchinson* (London: 1883).

Ingraham, Hannah, *The Narrative of Hannah Ingraham,* October 1783 (Typescript edited by R. P. Gorham, June 1933), Folder 12, St. John Public Archives. Original in Public Archives Canada.

Jackson, John W., ed., *Margaret Morris: Her Journal with Biographical Sketches and Notes* (Philadelphia: 1949).

Jarvis, Stephen, *Journal of Stephen Jarvis Esq. . . . during His Service in the British Army in the American Rebellion, His residence in the Province of New Brunswick and in the Province of Upper Canada* (typescript), New York Historical Society.

Jarvis, Stinson, ed., "Reminiscences of a Loyalist," *Canadian Magazine,* vol. XXVI (February 1906).

Jay, William, *Life of John Jay,* vol. I (New York: 1833).

Jenkins, Stephen, *The Story of the Bronx* (New York: 1912).

Johnson, Joseph, *Traditions and Reminiscences of the American Revolution* (Charleston: 1851).

Johnston, Henry P., *The Campaign of 1776 around New York and Brooklyn* (Brooklyn: 1876).

Jones, Thomas, *History of New York during the Revolutionary War,* Edward F. DeLancey, ed. (New York: 1879).

Landrum, J. B. O., *Colonial and Revolutionary History of South Carolina* (Greenville: 1897).

Lindley, Jacob, "Narrative," *Friends Miscellany,* vol. II, quoted by E. A. Cruikshank, ed., *Records of Niagara,* Niagara Historical Society, no. 40.

Liscomb, A. A. and A. L. Bergh, *Writings of Jefferson,* vol. IV (Washington: 1903).

Livingston, William, *Livingston Papers,* vol. III, Massachusetts Historical Society.

Lossing, B. J., *Field Book of the American Revolution,* vol. II (New York: 1850–1852).

Loyalist Transcripts, *Transcript of the Manuscript Books and Papers of the Commission of Enquiry into the Losses and Services of the American Loyalists Held under Acts of Parliament of 23, 25, 26, 28, and 29 of George III preserved amongst the Audit Office Records in the Public Record Office of England. Examinations in London and New York, 1783-1790,* 60 vols; New York Public Library.

Lydekker, J. W., *Life and Letters of Charles Inglis* (London: 1936).

MacDonald, Allan R., *The Truth about Flora MacDonald,* Donald Mackinnon, ed. (Inverness: 1938).

MacKall, Leonard L., ed., *American Antiquarian Society Proceedings,* New Series, vol. XXX (April 1920).

MacKenzie, Roderick, *Strictures on Lt. Col. Tarleton's History "Of the Campaigns of 1780 and 1781, in the Southern Provinces of North America." Wherein Military Characters and Corps Are Vindicated from Injurious Aspersions, and Several Important Transactions Placed in Their Proper Point of View. In a Series of Letters to a Friend. To Which Is added, a Detail of the Siege of Ninety Six, and the ReCapture of the Island of New-Providence* (London: 1787).

M'Alpine, John, *Genuine Narrative and Concise Memoirs . . . Adventures of John M'Alpine, a Native Highlander, 1773-1779* (Greenock: 1780), New York Historical Society.

McCall, Hugh, *History of Georgia* (Savannah: 1812–1816), 2 vols.

McDonald, Herbert S., "Memoirs of Joel Stone . . . a United Empire Loyalist and the Founder of Gananoque," *Papers and Records,* vol. XVIII, Ontario Historical Society (Toronto: 1920).

McGrady, Edward, *The History of South Carolina, 1775–1780* (New York: 1901).

McKesson, John, *McKesson Papers,* New York Historical Society.

McKinnen, Daniel, *Tour Through the British West Indies* (London: 1804).

McLane, Allan, *McLane Papers,* New York Historical Society.

McLean, J. R., *Flora MacDonald in America* (Lumberton, N.C.: 1909).

McRee, Griffith J., *Life and Correspondence of Joseph Iredell* (New York: 1857–1858).

McReynolds, George, ed., *The New Doan Book* (Doylestown, Pa.: 1952).

The Massachusetts Spy (1774), New York State Library.

Mather, Frederic G., *The Refugees of 1776 from Long Island to Connecticut* (Albany: 1913).

Millidge, Stephen, to [John Millidge], Jan. 2, 1803, Crary miscellaneous papers.

Moody, James, *Narrative of His Exertions and Sufferings in the Cause of Government since the Year 1776* (London: 1783), in Charles I. Bushnell, *Crumbs for Antiquarians* (New York: 1865).

Moore, Frank, *Diary of the American Revolution,* 2 vols., (New York: 1860).

Moore, John, *John Moore Collection: 1755–1785,* Courtesy of the Chicago Historical Society.

Morris, Margaret, *Her Journal with Biographical Sketches and Notes,* John W. Jackson, ed. (Philadelphia: 1949).

Newport Gazette, Newport, R.I., John Howe, ed.

New York City during the Revolution (New York: Mercantile Library Association, 1861).

New York Gazette and Weekly Mercury, Hugh Gaine, ed., Feb. 27, 1775.

New York Gazetteer and Weekly Advertiser 1773–1783 (called *The Royal Gazette* in 1780), James Rivington, ed., Apr. 20, May 11, 1775.

New York in the Revolution, Supplement, Office of the State Comptroller (Albany: 1904).

New York, *Journal of the Provincial Congress of the State of New York*, Albany: 1842, vol. III.

———, *Minutes of the Council of Safety*, vol. I.

———, *Revolutionary Papers*, New York Historical Society *Collections*, vol. III.

———, *Minutes of the Commision to Investigate the Fire September, 1776, Miscellaneous Manuscripts*, Box XII (1776), New York Historical Society.

New York Morning Post (Nov. 7, 1783), copy in St. John Public Archives.

Noble, H. H., "A Loyalist of the St. Lawrence," *Ontario Historical Society Proceedings*, vol. XIV.

O'Callaghan, Edmund B., ed., *Documents Relative to the Colonial History of the State of New York: Procured in Holland, England, and France, by John R. Broadhead, Esq.*, 9 vols. (Albany: 1853–1858).

———, *Documentary History of the State of New York*, 4 vols. (Albany: 1849–1851).

Oliver, Peter, *Origin and Progress of the American Rebellion*, Douglas Adair and John Schutz, eds. (Stanford: 1961).

Onderdonk, Henry, Jr., *Revolutionary Incidents of Suffolk and Kings Counties* (New York: 1849).

Original Minute Book and Muster Book of the Free Blacks, Port Roseway Associates I, Public Archives of Canada.

Oxnard, Edward, "Diary of a Loyalist, 1775–1785," *New England Historical and Genealogical Register*, vol. XXVI (1872).

Parker, James, *Parker Papers*, Record Office, Liverpool, England.

Peabody, Nathaniel, *Papers*, New Hampshire Historical Society.

Peck, Epaphroditus, "Loyal to the Crown," *Connecticut Magazine*, vol. VII (1903).

Peirce Papers, The Atheneum, Portsmouth, N.H.

Pennsylvania Gazette (June 1, 1774) (called *Pennsylvania Ledger* during the British Occupation).

Peters, John, "Defense of the Provincials and Indians against Burgoyne's Charges," Dec. 9, 1779, *Peters Papers*, New York Historical Society.

———, "A Narrative of John Peters, Lt. Col. of the Queens Loyal Rangers" [1785], *Peters Papers, Miscellaneous Manuscripts P*, New York Historical Society.

[Peters, the Reverend Samuel], *A General History of Connecticut by a Gentleman of the Province* (London: 1782).

——, *Peters Papers,* Church Historical Society, Austin, Tex.

——, *Peters Manuscripts,* vol. II (microfilm), New York Historical Society.

Phelps, Richard H., *History of Newgate of Connecticut* (Hartford: 1844, 2d ed. 1860).

Philipse, Frederick, *Papers,* Sleepy Hollow Restorations, Irvington, N.Y.

Pickering, James H., "Enoch Crosby, Secret Agent of the Neutral Ground: His Own Story," *New York History,* vol. 47, January 1966.

Piper, John, to J. Vilett, July 19, 1783, Box 45, Folder 5, Newport Historical Society.

Pond, E. Leroy, *The Tories of Chippeny Hill Connecticut* (New York: 1909).

Preston, Richard A., ed., *Kingston before the War of 1812* (Toronto: 1959).

Protestant Episcopal Church, *Historical Magazine,* vols. II, X.

Quarles, Benjamin, *The Negro in the American Revolution* (Chapel Hill: 1961).

Rankin, Hugh F., *The American Revolution* (New York: 1964).

Rapelje, George, *A Narrative of Excursions, Voyages, and Travels* (New York: 1834), Easthampton Library.

Rawle, Anna, "Diary," *Pennsylvania Magazine of Biography and Geneology,* vol. XVI.

Raymond, W. O., "The Negro in New Brunswick," *Neith Magazine* St. John, vol. I.

——, *The River St. John* (St. John: 1910).

——, ed., *Winslow Papers* (St. John: 1901).

Reed, Joseph, *Papers,* vol. III, 1774–1775, New York Historical Society.

Remembrancer, The, London, vol. VI, copy in New York Historical Society.

Resco, Stephen, *Account Sent to Mr. Printer* (author unknown), no. 242, 8 E-18, Pocumtuck Valley Memorial Association, Deerfield.

Riker, James, *Memoria,* vol. XV *(Balch Papers),* New York Public Library.

Robinson, Beverly, *Papers,* New Brunswick Museum, St. John, New Brunswick.

——, *Examination of Beverly Robinson before the Committee of Safety,* Washington's Headquarters, Newburgh, N.Y.

Rogers, John P., *The Doan Outlaws or Bucks County's Cowboys in the Revolution* (Doylestown: 1897).

Romer, John L., *Historical Sketches of the Neutral Ground* (Buffalo: 1917).

Roth, Cecil, "A Jewish Voice for Peace in the War of America Independence," *American Jewish Historical Society Publications,* vol. XXXI (1928).

Ruttenberger, E. M., and L. H. Clark, *History of Orange County New York* (Philadelphia: 1881).

Sabine, Lorenzo, *Loyalists in the American Revolution,* 2 vols. (Boston: 1864).

Sanborn, F. B., "The Conversion of a Loyalist to a Patriot," Massachusetts Historical Society *Proceedings,* vol. L.

Sargent, Winthrop, *Life and Career of Major John André* (New York: 1861).

Scharf, J. Thomas, and Thompson Westcott, *History of Philadelphia* (Philadelphia: 1884).

Schaw, Janet, *Journal of a Lady of Quality, Being the Narrative of a Journey from Scotland to the West Indies, North Carolina, and Portugal in the Years 1774 to 1776,* E. W. Andrews, ed. (New Haven: 1921).

Scott, Kenneth, "A British Counterfeiting Press in New York Harbor," *New York Historical Society Quarterly,* 1955.

Shelburne, Miscellaneous Manuscripts (negative photostat), New York Historical Society.

Sheldon, George, *History of Deerfield* (Deerfield: 1895), 2 vols.

Shepard, James, *The Episcopal Church and Early Ecclesiastical Law of Connecticut* (New Britain: 1908).

———, "The Tories of Connecticut," *Connecticut Magazine,* vol. IV.

Sherwood, Justus, *Journal,* British Museum. See H. S. Wardner, "The Journal of a Loyalist Spy," *The Vermonter,* vol. XXVIII, no. 6.

Shipton, Clifford L., ed., *Sibley's Harvard Graduates* (Boston: 1968).

Siebert, Wilbur H., *Loyalists of Pennsylvania* (Columbus: 1894).

———, "Refugee Loyalists of Connecticut," Royal Society Ottawa *Transactions,* Series X.

———, *Legacy of the American Revolution to the British West Indies and the Bahamas* (Columbus: 1913).

Skinner, Stephen, *Letterbook, December 11, 1780–March 27, 1793,* BV, New York Historical Society.

Smith, Frank, Private Miscellaneous Papers, Scarsdale, N.Y.

Smith, J., ed., "Long Island's Counterfeiting Plot," *Journal of Long Island History*, vol. II (1962).

Smith, Jesse, *Orderly Book, Headquarters Morristown, February 21,-May 17, 1780*, New York Historical Society.

Smith, Mary M., "The Story of the Old Red House," *Town Historical Papers* (Washington, Conn.: 1905).

Smith, William, Jr., *Historical Memoirs*, vol. I, New York Public Library.

Smyth, John Ferdinand Dalziel, *Narrative or Journal of Captain John Ferdinand Dalziel Smyth*, written between Dec. 25, 1777, and Feb. 25, 1778. Courtesy of Mr. William Wright, Easthampton, N.Y.

Society for the Propagation of the Gospel, *Manuscripts*, vol. V.

Sosin, Jack M., *The Revolutionary Frontier 1763-83* (New York: 1967).

South Carolina, Historical and Geneological Magazine, vol. XXVII.

———, *The Royal Gazette*, Mar. 17, Sept. 7, 1782, Robert and John Wells, eds.

Spargo, John, *David Redding, Queen's Ranger* (Bennington: 1945).

Sprague, William B., *Annals of the American Pulpit* (New York: 1959), vol. V.

Stark, James H., *Loyalists of Massachusetts* (Boston: 1910).

Stedman, Charles, *The History of the Origins, Progress, and Termination of the American War* (London: 1794).

Stevens, B. F., *Facsimiles of Manuscripts in European Archives Relative to America, 1773-1783* (London: 1889-1895).

Stimson, F. J., *My Story: Being the Memoirs of Benedict Arnold* (New York: 1917).

Stoesen, Alexander R., "The British Occupation of Charleston, 1780-82," *South Carolina Historical Magazine*, vol. LXIII.

Stokes, I. N. P., *Iconography of Manhattan Island*, vol. IV.

Stone, Joel, *Narrative*, Caniff Papers, Department of Public Records and Archives, Ontario. See James J. Talman, *Loyalist Narratives from Upper Canada* (Toronto: 1946).

Stone, William L., *Life of Joseph Brant, Thayendanegea* (New York: 1838).

———, *The Campaign of Lt. General John Burgoyne and the Expedition of Lt. Col. Barry St. Leger* (Albany: 1877).

Story, D. A., *The DeLanceys: A Romance of a Great Family* (London: 1931).

Sullivan, Edward D., *Benedict Arnold: Military Racketeer* (New York: 1932),

Talman, James J., *Loyalist Narratives from Upper Canada* (Toronto: 1946).

Tatum, Edward H., Jr., ed., *The American Journal of Ambrose Serle, Secretary to Lord Howe, 1776-1778* (San Marino: 1940).

Townsend, Gregory, *Miscellaneous Mss. Townsend, G.,* New York Historical Society.

Trumbull, Jonathan, *Papers,* Connecticut State Library (photostat Easthampton Library, vol. V, pt. 1, no. 174).

Uhlendorf, Bernhard, *The Siege of Charleston* (Ann Arbor: 1938).

Updike, Wilkins, *History of the Episcopal Church in Narragansett* (Boston: 1907).

Vail, R. W. G., "The Loyalist Declaration of Dependence of November 28, 1776," *New York Historical Society Quarterly,* vol. XXXI, no. 2.

Van Doren, Carl, *Secret History of the American Revolution* (New York: 1941).

Varick, Richard, *Papers 1775-9,* New York Historical Society.

Vermont State Papers, Mary G. Nye, ed., *Vermont Historical Gazetteer,* A. M. Hemenway, ed.

Waite, Otis, *History of the Town of Claremont, New Hampshire, 1764-1895* (Manchester: 1895).

Walker, Mabel G., "Sir John Johnson, Loyalist," *Mississippi Valley Historical Review,* vol. III (December 1906).

Walker, Warren S., "The Prototype of Harvey Birch," *New York History,* vol. 37 (October 1956).

Ward, Christopher, *The War of the Revolution,* 2 vols., (New York: 1952).

Watson-Smith, T., "The Loyalists at Shelburne," *Collections,* vol. VI, Nova Scotia Historical Society.

Watts, Robert, *Papers,* Box II, New York Historical Society.

Webster, Henry S., "Dr. Sylvester Gardiner," *Historical Series* no. 2, Gardiner, Me.

White, George, ed., *Historical Collections of Georgia* (New York: 1854).

White, Gideon, *White Collection IV,* Public Archives of Nova Scotia.

Wilberforce, Samuel, *History of the Protestant Episcopal Church in America* (New York: 1846).

Bibliography

Williams, George, W., *History of the Negro Race in America from 1619 to 1880* (New York: 1883).

Wiswall, John, *Papers,* Acadia University, Wolfville, Nova Scotia (microfilm in Public Archives of Nova Scotia).

Woolsey, G. M., *Marlborough in the Revolution,* no. 4541, Senate House Museum, Kingston.

Worth, Gorham A., *Recollections of Albany 1800-1808* (Albany: 1866).

Younglove, Samuel, "Record of the Narrative of Dr. Moses Younglove, December 1777." See *Herkimer Family Portfolio,* New York State Library, Albany.

Index

Abingdon, Lord, 130
Act of Attainder (October 22, 1779), 44, 185
Acts of Trade, 53-54
Adams, John, 3, 135, 334, 341
Adams, Mrs. Nathaniel, 172-173
Adams, Sam, 125
Addison, Daniel, 109
Aitchison, William, 58-59
Alexander, General William (see Stirling, Lord)
Allaire, Lieutenant Anthony, 238-239
Allen, Eleanor (Nelly), 117
Allen, Eleanor Warren, 117
Allen, Ethan, 147, 258-265, 270, 326, 374
Allen, Ira, 258, 260-264, 326, 374
Allen, Jolley, 14-16, 113, 117-123
Allen, Levi, 258, 265-268, 326, 374
Allen, Lewis, 117
Allen, Thomas, 117
Alsop, John, 6, 388
Amherst, Lord, 131
André, Major John, 85, 315, 342-344

Andrews, Nicholas, 370, 372-373
Anglican clergy, 87-111
Anne, Queen of England, 426
Apthorpe, Charles Ward, 178, 179
Arbuthnot, Admiral Marriott, 275, 276
Armstrong, Major Thomas, 38
Arnold, General Benedict, 9, 147, 210, 244-247, 304, 338-344
Arnold, Peggy, 9, 388
Ashley, Reverend Jonathan, 214-215
Auchmuty, Caty, 334
Auchmuty, Robert, 92, 334-336
Austin, Major Jonathan, 171-173
Avery, Reverend Ephraim, 88n.

Babcock, Reverend Luke, 88n.
Backus, Captain Nathaniel, 436
Bacon, Jabez, 162
Bahamas, Loyalist emigration to, 10, 354-357, 390-391
Bailey, Francis, 387n.
Baker, John, 95
Balfour, Lieutenant Colonel Nisbet, 278

Index

Banyar, Goldsbrow, 158-161, 388
Barclay, Anna Dorothea, 150*n.*
Barnes, Captain John, 36-38, 176-177
Barnwell, Robert, 354
Bartlett, Enoch, 56*n.*
Barton, Reverend Thomas, 88
Bass, Reverend Edward, 89*n.*, 109-111
Bates, Walter, 81-82, 106
Bates, William, 81
Battle of Brooklyn, The (play), 300-302
Baxter, Reverend Simeon, 220-224
Bay of Quinte, Loyalist emigration to, 390, 405-410, 425-427
Bayard, William, 437*n.*
Beach, Enos, 96
Beach, Reverend John, 88*n.*, 92*n.*, 106-107
Becker, Carl, 3
Beckwith, George, 188-189, 368, 370
Bee, Thomas, 276
Belden, Mary, 162
Belknap, Jeremy, 4
Bell, Towers, 373
Benson, Egbert, 148, 149
Black Loyalists, 427-432
Black Pioneers, 427-431
Black slaves, treatment of, 270-274, 362
Blackwell, Robert, 89
Blagden, Sir Charles, 348
Blake, Robert, 38*n.*
Bloodgood, Simeon, 225
Bluck, Colonel Stephen, 429
Board of Associated Loyalists, 291
Boston, 296
    closing of port of, 4, 20-31, 97
    evacuation of, 112-113, 116
Boston Committee of Correspondence, 20, 24
Boston Port Act (May 12, 1774), 20-31, 95, 96
Boston Relief Fund, 21
Boston Tea Party (December 16, 1773), 5, 13-17, 20, 25, 47

Bosworth, David, 96
Boucher, Jonathan, 2, 336
Boyd, Colonel John, 238
Brant, Isaac, 447
Brant, Jacob, 447-449
Brant, Joseph, Chief of the Mohawks, 240
    military career of, 241, 247-248, 252-253, 255, 332
    post-war activities of, 407, 410-411, 425, 447-449
Brant, Molly, 9, 240, 242, 247-248
Breed's (Bunker's) Hill, Battle of (June 17, 1775), 47-49
Brewster, Caleb, 197
Breynton, Reverend John, 126, 128
Brinley, Mrs. Ed., 57
British East India Company, 13, 17
Brooklyn, Battle of, 84, 300-302
Brown, Prosper, 368, 370
Brown, Thomas, 256, 257
Browne, Mrs., 337
Browne, Monfort, 115
Browne, Thomas, 64-66
Brownson, Isaac, 94
Bucks County Treasury, 199
Buell, Reverend Samuel, 84
Buford, Colonel Abraham, 279
Buirtis, William, 209-211
Bunker's Hill, Battle of (June 17, 1775), 47-49
Burgoyne, General John, 4, 244, 294, 306-309
Burke, William, 14
Bush, Sam, 144
Butler, Colonel John, 73*n.*, 240-241, 252, 332, 406
Butler, Captain Walter, 240, 244, 245, 248, 252-255
Butler's Rangers, 240-241, 250, 252, 253, 406
Byles, Reverend Mather, 18, 126
Byles, Mather, Jr., 89*n.*
Byrd, William, III, 388

Caldwell, Captain William, 256
Cameron, Lieutenant Allan, 75
Cameron, John, 411
Cameron, Nancy Jean, 411–412
Campbell, Lieutenant Colonel Archibald,
    270
Campbell, Farquard, 64
Campbell, George W., 181n.
Campbell, Captain Robert, 118–123
Campbell, Samuel, 418–420
Campbell, William, 427
Canada Bill, 27
Caner, Reverend Henry, 17–19, 88n.,
    89n., 92–93, 109, 126–129
Captain Pipe (Delaware chief), 255
Carleton, Sir Guy, 40n., 169, 355, 356
    Black Loyalists and, 428, 434–435
    counterfeiters and, 383–385
    Loyalists in post-war period and,
        359n., 361–362, 367–374, 404,
        406
    military activities of, 348–349, 357
Carlisle, Abraham, 8, 236–237
Carlisle Peace Commission, 318–323,
    327
Carrington, Lemuel, 188–189
Carrington, Riverus, 188–189
Cartwright, Richard, Jr., 9, 252–255
Catlin, Seth, 214–215
Cayuga Indians, 247, 252, 425
Chabert, Marquis de, 274, 275
Chandler, Reverend Thomas B., 2, 90,
    294
Charleston, South Carolina, British loss
    of (May 12, 1780), 269, 270,
    275–281, 285
Charlie, Bonnie Prince, 50
Chase, Lieutenant, 184
Cherokee Indians, 65, 238, 355
Chesney, Alexander, 281–284
Chew, Benjamin, 389n.
Chickasaw Indians, 65
Chipman, Ward, 398n., 404, 421–423
Choctaw Indians, 65, 355

Claraco Sanz, Don Antonio, 355
Clark, George Rogers, 255
Clark, John, 194–195
Clark, Captain William, 184
Clarke, James, 446–447
Clarke, Dr. Joseph, 57–58
Clarke, Reverend William, 24–26
Clarkson, John, 431–432
Claudius Smith gang, 194–196
Claus, Colonel Daniel, 9n., 74, 240–243,
    247, 425–427
Clergy, Anglican, 87–111
Clinton, George, 176, 194, 227, 259,
    364–365, 444, 445
Clinton, Sir Henry, 130
    Black Loyalists and, 428, 429, 431
    military campaigns of, 149, 260, 323,
        332, 339, 341
    Southern theater campaigns of, 270,
        275–277, 280, 291, 292
Clinton, Brigadier General James, 253
Coercive Acts, 5, 21, 24, 97
Coggeshall, Miss, 446
Colden, Cadwallader, Jr., 80, 203–206,
    227–229, 298, 365
Colden, Cadwallader, III, 204, 365
Colden, David, 205, 365–367
Colden, Mrs. Richard Nicholls, 366
Cole, William, 194, 196
Coles, Abram, 181n.
Committee for Detecting and Defeating
    Conspiracies, 181–185, 204
Committee of Fifty-One, 20–23
Committee of One Hundred, 21
Committee of Sixty, 21
Committees of safety, 2, 55–86, 145n.,
    146, 147
    (See also committees for individual
        states and areas)
Common Sense (Paine), 135
Connecticut, Loyalist sentiment in, 4
Connecticut Assembly, 99–103
Connecticut Committee of Safety, 94,
    173, 216

Index

Connecticut Courant (newspaper), 21, 56, 231

Connolly, Lieutenant Colonel John, 75, 256n.

Continental Association, 2, 27, 29, 55–56, 146, 214

Continental Congress, 106, 136, 145, 155, 220–223

  First, 2, 4–5, 20–23, 26–28, 55, 135

  Second, 3, 5, 31–34

Cook, Captain James, 412–414

Cook, John, 364–365

Cooper, James Fenimore, 180–181, 184

Cooper, Myles, 90

Corbin, Richard, Sr., 388

Cornwallis, Lord, 282, 284, 295, 344, 346–347

Cossitt, Reverend Ranna, 64, 69

Counterfeiting activities, 382–386

Cowboys (military group), 173–174, 179, 369, 444, 445

Cowles, Martha, 56

Cowles, Solomon, 56

Coxe, Daniel, 414

Coxe, Grace, 438

Crawford, Colonel William, 255–257

Crèvecoeur, Hector St. John de, 189–194, 250–252

Crosby, Enoch, 181–185

Cruden, John, 291–293

Cruger, Ann DeLancey, 9, 179, 274–275

Cruger, Colonel John Harris, 9, 274, 346

Cumberland, Richard, 332

Cunningham, Captain, 45

Curtiss, Abel, 152–155

Curwen, Samuel, 2, 295, 309–311, 389n.

Customs officers, boycott of British goods and, 28–29

Cuyler, Abraham C., 253

Dartmouth, Lord, 62, 64

Dartmouth College, 447–449

Dashwood, Captain, 14

Dawkins, Henry, 382

Dayton, Colonel Elias, 78

De Borre, General Prudhomme, 225

Declaration of Independence (July 4, 1776), 2, 7, 135–136, 138, 155–158

Declaratory Act, 39

DeLancey, Charlotte, 129–131, 177–178

DeLancey, Cornelia Barclay, 270–274

DeLancey, Colonel James, 130, 173–176, 189, 393–395

DeLancey, Brigadier General Oliver, 129–131, 176–179, 274, 369, 372, 437n.

DeLancey, Phila Franks, 113, 129–131, 178

DeLancey, Stephen, 8, 253, 270–274, 424

Delaware, Loyalist sentiment in, 4

Delaware Indians, 255–258

De Peyster, Captain Abraham, 283

DePeyster, Major Arent S., 256–258, 379–381

Deserontyou, Captain John, 425–427

D'Estaing, Count, 270, 274, 275, 332

Deveaux, Lieutenant Colonel Andrew, Jr., 354–357

Devereux, James, 170–171

Diach, Alexander, 58, 59

Diamond (slave), 143

Dibble, Captain Charles, 60

Dibblee, Reverend Ebenezer, 92n., 107–108

Dibblee, Frederick, 108

Dickinson, John, 39, 40, 42n., 198–200

Dittrick, Jacob, 406, 409–410

Dittrick, Captain James, 406, 408–410

Doane, Aaron, 198–200

Doane, Abraham, 198–199

Doane, Israel, 198–199

Doane, Joseph, Jr., 198–199

Doane, Levi, 198–199

Doane, Mahlon, 198–199

Doane, Moses, 198-199
Dorman, Ezra, 188-189
Draper, Margaret, 234
Draper, Susanna DeLancey, 129, 131
Draper, General Sir William, 129, 131
Drinker, Elizabeth, 323
Duane, James, 20-23, 149, 159
DuBois, Peter, 298-299
Duché, Jacob, 90, 136, 155-158, 326, 389n.
Duer, Colonel William, 184
Dulany, Daniel, 389
Dunbar, Moses, 8, 88n., 187, 230-234
Dundas, Sir David, 129, 177n.
Dundas, Henry, 428n., 431n., 432
Dunmore, Lord, 75, 77, 374, 391

Eddis, William, 26-28
Eden, Robert, 389n.
Eden, William, 39n.
Elliot, Andrew, 52-54, 302-303
Elliot, Sir Gilbert, 52, 53, 297, 302
Elliot, Matthew, 256n., 257
Elmsley, Alexander, 342
Elting, Josiah, 436-437
Elting, Mrs. Maria, 436-437
Elting, Peter, 58, 82
Elting, Roelof J., 145-147, 436-437
Elting, Solomon, 146
Emmerick, Andreas, 176-177
Eve, Oswell, 390, 414-416
Eve, Sarah, 414
Executions of Loyalists, 224-239

Farmington, Connecticut, 21, 23
Fellowes, Captain Gustavus, 190n.
Ferguson, Major Patrick, 282-284
Fisher, George, 383
Fisher, John, 383
Fisher, Samuel, 145n.
Fisher, Thomas, 145n.
Fisher, William, 25

Fitch, Dr. Asa, 36, 38n.
Flanagan, Elizabeth, 180-181, 185
Fletchall's Party, 66
Floid, Colonel Benjamin, 165
Florida Rangers, 65
Floyd, Elizabeth, 177-178
Folliett, George, 382n.
Folliett, John, 382n.
Fonda, Major Jellis, 72-73
Fonda, John, 72
Ford, N., 450
Forward, Daniel, 383, 384n., 386
Foshay, Isaac, 369, 371-372
Foshay, William, 369, 371-372
Fowler, Jonathan, 100, 179, 182, 184
Franklin, Benjamin, 40n., 116, 209
Franklin, William, 56, 216
Franks, Moses, 130
Franks, Rebecca, 311-314
Fraser, Peter, 403
Freeman, E., 98
French Alliance, 295, 318, 323, 334-336
Frey, Colonel Henry, 241
Frey, Major John, 72, 241
Friends, Society of, 4, 21, 23-24, 145n., 345
Frisbey, Abel, 188-189
Frisbey, Levi, 188-189
Frost, Sarah, 395-397
Frost, William, 395

Gage, General Thomas, 130, 388, 421
  as Governor of Massachusetts, 25, 26, 31, 113
  military campaigns of, 48, 50, 112
Gaine, Hugh, 57
Galloway, Betsy, 323
Galloway, Grace, 323-326
Galloway, Joseph, 2, 6-7, 236-237, 258, 323, 326, 337-338
  reconciliation writings of, 39, 136-138

Index

Galwey, Phila DeLancey, 129-131
Gamsby, Dorothea, 47-49
Gardiner, Colonel Abraham, 84-85
Gardiner, Nathaniel (privateer
    commander), 206-208
Gardiner, Nathaniel (surgeon), 85-86
Gardiner, Dr. Sylvester, 18, 124-126,
    206, 336
Gardner, Henry, 31
Gay, Martin, 441-444
Gay, Ruth Atkins, 441
George III, King of England, 3, 36
Georgia:
    boycott of British goods in, 55
    Loyalist sentiment in, 4
Germain, Lord George, 113, 297, 307,
    320, 339, 347
Gilbert, Thomas, 81
Girty, Simon, 256-257
Glover, Amelia, 376, 377
Graham, Judge, 148
Graham, John, 269
Granby, Lord, 297
Grass, Captain Michael, 406, 407
Graves, Adam, 370, 372-373
Graves, John Georg, 370, 372-373
Graves, Reverend Matthew, 92n.
Graves, Ruth Jerome, 188
Graves, Stephen, 188
Gray, Robert, 278-280
Green Mountain Boys, 36
Greene, General, 274
Griffin, John, 444-446

Haldimand, General Frederick, 260, 262,
    375, 388, 425
Haliburton, Thomas C., 429
Halifax Journal (newspaper), 235
Hamilton, Abigail, 312, 313
Hamilton, Alexander, 225
Hamilton, General Henry, 255
Hamilton, Colonel John, 295, 346-347
Hamilton, Robert, 254

Hancock, John, 14
Hardenbrook, Captain Theophilus, 58,
    82, 83
Hardwicke, Lord, 360
Hart, Isaac, 196-197
Hart, John (Loyalist), 234-236
Hart, John (treasurer), 199
Hasbrouck, Judge, 230
Hassard, Thomas, 368, 370
Hatfield, Captain, 32, 33
Hathaway, Ebenezer, 217-219
Hauger, George, 179
Hayne, Colonel Isaac, 286
Haynes, Captain Samuel, 443
Hedges, Colonel Jonathan, 84
Herkimer, Lieutenant Colonel George,
    241
Herkimer, General Nicholas, 241
Herrick, Robert, 449
Herrick, Rufus, 364n.
Hewlett, Colonel Richard, 397
Highlanders, Scottish, in North Carolina,
    9, 50-52, 269, 281
Hill, John, 45
Hind, Reverend Richard, 89n., 97, 127,
    128, 168, 169
Hinman, Amos, 95
Hinman, Ebenezer, 95
Hinrichs, Captain James, 276
Holmes, Benjamin, 442-444
Honeywell, Israel, 369, 371, 372
Hooples, Brant, 241
Hooples, Francis, 241
Hooples, John, 241
Hooples, Jurgen, 241
Hopkins, John, 62-64
Hopkins, Jonathan, 184
Houston, Reverend John, 67
Howe, Lady, 130
Howe, John, 234-235
Howe, Admiral Richard, 82, 84, 136,
    138, 291, 336-338
Howe, Sir William, 82, 130
    Boston evacuation by, 48, 112, 296

Index

Howe, Sir William:
  military campaigns of, 8, 84, 158,
      270, 307, 332, 336-338
  peace missions of, 136, 138, 155
  Philadelphia protected by, 315-317,
      323
Hubbard, Reverend Bela, 100
Hubbard, Daniel, 398
Hulton, Ann, 29, 57
Hulton, Henry, 28-31, 116-117, 141
Humphreys, James, 236, 237, 389*n.*
Hunt, Theophilus, 393-395
Hunter, Jeremiah, 32*n.*
Hutchinson, Elisha, 13-14, 113, 114
Hutchinson, Peggy, 113-114
Hutchinson, Polly, 113, 114
Hutchinson, Thomas, 1, 13, 14, 31,
      113, 417
Hutchinson, Thomas, Jr., 13-14, 113
Hyde, Lord, 297

Indians, Loyalists and, 4, 65, 70-72,
      240-250, 252-258, 381,
      425-427
  (See also individual Indian peoples)
Inglis, Reverend Charles, 2, 89, 90,
      167-171, 258-259
Inglis, Samuel, 58
Ingraham, Hannah, 401-403
Iroquois Indians, 252-255

Jackson, John, 288
Jackson, Judith, 373, 374
Jackson, Thomas, 197
Jails, treatment of Loyalists in, 201-224
Jarvis, Stephen, 376-379, 418
Jay, John, 3, 40*n.,* 147-149, 227, 228,
      341
  Boston Port Act and, 20-23
  Committee for Detecting and Defeat-
      ing Conspiracies chaired by, 181,
      183

Jay, William, 40*n.*
Jefferson, Thomas, 135, 155
Jemison, Richard, 47
Jerom, Chauncey, 188-189
Jerom, Zerababel, Jnr., 188-189
Jessup, Edward, 404
John Barnes's Company, 36-38
Johnson, George, 319-320
Johnson, Guy, 2, 70-72, 240
Johnson, Colonel Henry, 311-312
Johnson, James, 65
Johnson, Sir John, 176*n.,* 240, 419
  compensation to, 421, 437*n.*
  military career of, 249, 298, 406
  Tryon County Committee of Safety
      and, 70, 72, 78-80
Johnson, Lady Mary Watts, 78-80
Johnson, Thomas, 40*n.*
Johnson, William, 73
Johnson, Sir William, 9, 73, 240, 241,
Johnson, William Samuel, 388
Jones, Reverend, 18
Jones, Nathanael, 188-189
Jones, Thomas, 39, 79-80, 177, 204,
      357-359
Joseph, Chief of the Mohawks, 240
  military career of, 241, 247-248,
      252-253, 255, 332
  post-war activities of, 407, 410-411,
      425, 447-449
Julius Caesar (Shakespeare), 18

Kemble, Peter, 388
Kempe, John Tabor, 437-440
Kennedy, Ann Watts, 438, 440
Kipp, James, 182, 184
Klock, Jacob, 73, 74
Kneeland, Reverend Ebenezer, 88*n.*
Knox, William, 9*n.,* 242, 247*n.*

Lafayette, Marquis de, 342
Laffin, Lieutenant Michael, 397-398

Index

Laurence, Henry, 319–320
Lawrence, Effingham, 363
Leaming, Reverend Jeremiah, 92n.
Lee, Deacon, 60
Lee, Arthur, 42n.
Lee, Major General Charles, 7, 46, 52,
    113
Lee, Colonel Henry, 285, 287–290
Lee, William, 135n.
Lefferty, Bryan, 202–203
Leonard, Daniel, 2, 57
Leslie, General Alexander, 274, 275,
    357
Lewis, Benjamin, 383
Lewis, Stephen C., 89n.
Lightbody, Mrs., 57
Lincoln, General Benjamin, 270, 275
Lind, John, 333
Lindley, Jacob, 406
Livingston, Henry B., 84
Livingston, William, 438
Long Island, Battle of, 166, 296, 298
Low, Isaac, 20–23
Loyal American Regiment, 149
Loyalist Declaration of Independence
    (November 28, 1776), 138–140

McAlpine, John, 306
McCleary, Colonel, 38
McClelland, Major John, 257
MacDonald, Major Allan, 50, 51
MacDonald, Brigadier General Donald,
    50
McDonald, Donald, Esq., 52
MacDonald, Flora, 9, 50–52
McDonald, John M., 393
MacDougall, Alexander, 20, 22–23
McGinn, Sarah Cass, 249–250
Machiavelli, Niccolò, 379, 381
McKee, Alexander, 256, 258
MacKenzie, Mrs. Alexander, 51
MacKenzie, Captain Roderick, 355
McLane, Allan, 328, 330

MacLean, Brigadier General Allan, 379
McLeod, Colonel Donald, 50
McNiff, Patrick, 423–425
McPherson, Mrs. Kenneth, 411
Malcolm, John, 28
Mansfield, Reverend Richard, 92,
    103-106
Marshall, Reverend John Rutgers, 93–
    97, 103, 105
Martin, Josiah, 50, 281
Martling, Abraham, 176
Martling, Isaac, 179–180
Maryland, Loyalist sentiment in, 4
Maryland Committee of Safety, 74–78
Maskelly, Hugh, 288–290
*Massachusetts Gazette and Boston
    Newsletter* (newspaper), 234–235
Massachusetts Provincial Congress, 29–
    31
Mathews, David, 216, 372
Mathews, John, 276
Mathews, Major Robert, 375, 407, 410,
    418, 420
Matra, James Mario, 412–414
Matthews, John, 188–189
Matthews, Nathan[1], 188–189
Maxwell, John, 390
May, William, 383, 385
Mechanics' Committee, 21
Midagh, Jacob, 8, 226–230
Millidge, John, 450
Millidge, Stephen, 449–451
Mississauga Indians, 425
Mitchel, John, 369
Mohawk Indians, 17
    military activities of, 240, 244, 250,
        252, 254
    post-war activities of, 407, 410–411,
        425, 427
Mohawk Valley, Loyalist sentiment in,
    240–241, 411–412
Moody, Lieutenant James, 208-213,
    225
Moore, John, 294, 422

Index

Moore's Creek Bridge, Battle at (February 29, 1776), 9, 50, 51, 269, 281
Morice, William, 109
Morris, Gouverneur, 34, 40, 202, 225
Morris, Lewis, 32, 33n., 34, 39, 40
Morris, Margaret, 9, 185–187
Morris, Richard, 444–446
Morris, Robert, 319n., 384, 386
Morris, Colonel Roger, 437n.
Motte, Rebecca, 285, 288–289
Moultrie, Colonel William, 275
Muirson, Heathcot, 197
Mulford, Colonel David, 84

Negro slaves, treatment of, 270–274, 362
Neutral Ground, 173, 180
New Hampshire Committee of Safety, 67, 68
New Jersey Province:
  Acts of Trade in, 54
  Loyalist sentiment in, 4
New Jersey Volunteers, 115
New Providence, Spanish loss of, 354–357
New York Assembly, 31–32
New York City:
  fire in (1776), 166–171
  Lee's invasion of (1776), 52–53
  Loyalists in, 4, 58, 138
New York Committee of Safety, 147–151, 298, 423
New York Council of Safety, 176
New York Gazetteer (newspaper), 328
New York Province, Loyalist sentiment in, 4, 20–21
New York Provincial Congress, 224, 226–227
Newport Gazette (newspaper), 234–236
Nichols, Reverend James, 57, 88, 92n., 187–188
Nicholson, Robert, 29, 116, 141

Noble, Samuel 23–24
Nooth, Dr. Mervin, 169, 170
North, Lord, 53
  Loyalists after independence and, 368, 418
  rebellion and, 65, 91, 126, 297, 347
North Carolina, Loyalist sentiment in, 4, 50–51
North Carolina Committee of Safety, 51
Nova Scotia, Loyalist emigration to, 10, 390, 398–405, 418–431
Nutting, Sir George, 47, 48

Odell, Dr. Jonathan, 9, 90, 185–187
Ogden, Isaac, 236
Ogden, Uzal, 89n.
Olive Branch Petition (July 5, 1775), 4, 5, 39–44
Oliver, Peter, 3, 14, 16–17
Oneida Indians, 244, 247–248, 252
Onondaga Indians, 247, 252
Oxnard, Edward, 295–297, 389n.

Paca, Mrs. Anne Harrison, 311
Paget, Lieutenant Henry, 360n.
Paine, Thomas, 135
Paine, Dr. William, 389n.
Palphrey, William, 14
Parker, James, 58–59, 315–321, 336, 342–344
Parker, Admiral Sir Peter, 275
Parker, Reverend Samuel, 89n., 111
Parr, John, 418–420
Parsons, General Samuel, 177
Patten, Joseph, 24, 25n.
Patterson, Brigadier General James, 278
Patterson, General John, 60
Payne, Lady, 131
Peabody, Nathaniel, 56n.
Peace treaty, 353–354
Peale, Charles Willson, 323–326
Peck, Jared, 188–189

Index

Pemberton, James, 23–24
Penn, John, 389*n.*
Pennsylvania, Loyalist sentiment in, 4
Pennsylvania Council, 198–200
Pennsylvania Gazette (newspaper), 23
Pennsylvania Packet (newspaper), 23
Peterites, abuse of, 90–92
Peters, Lieutenant Colonel John, 69–70,
    260, 304–309
Peters, Mrs. John, 304–306
Peters, Reverend Samuel, 69, 103, 107,
    216–217, 433
    harassment of, 90–92, 94, 97
    Loyalist activities of, 21, 23, 109
Peters, Thomas, 427–432
Philadelphia, British occupation of, 8,
    311–317
Philipse, Elizabeth Williams, 142–144
Philipse, Frederick, III, 32, 142–145,
    147, 176*n.,* 177*n.,* 437*n.*
Piper, John, 392–393
Platt, Zepeniah, 184
Poor, John, 383–386
Potts, John, 326–327
Potts, Captain William, 388
Powell, Brigadier General, 258
Power, John, 383–386
Prebble, J., 98
Preston, Captain Thomas, 334
Prevost, General Augustine, 270, 272,
    275
Prisons, treatment of Loyalists in,
    201–224
Privateers, Loyalists attempts to
    intercept, 291–293
Proclamation of Rebellion (August, 23,
    1775), 5, 135
Proud, Robert, 388
Pyle, Dr. John, 285

Quakers, 4, 21, 23–24, 145*n.,* 345
Quebec Act, 27, 95
Quincy, Josiah, 334

Rall, Colonel Johann, 198
Randolph, Edmund, 155*n.*
Randolph, John, 135*n.,* 155*n.*
Rapelje, George, 82–83
Rapelje, Rem, 58, 82–83
Rawdon, Lord, 286, 290
Rawle, Anna, 344–346
Redding, David, 224
Reed, Joseph, 7*n.,* 319*n.*
Resco, Stephen, 59–60
Reynell, John, 23–24
Rice, Abel, 188–189
Rice, Nemiah, 188–189
Richard, The Right Reverend, Bishop of
    London, 92
Ritzema, Rudolph, 419, 420
Rivington, James, 196, 280–281, 327–334
Roberts, John, 8, 236–237
Roberts, Michael, 450
Robertson, Alexander, 418–420
Robertson, General Archibald, 130,
    131, 343
Robinson, Beverly, 147–150, 184–185
Robinson, Colonel Beverly, Jr., 149–150,
    184–185, 260, 435
Robinson, Susanna Philipse, 147
Rochambeau, Comte de, 342
Rose, Jacobus, 8, 226–230
Ross, Major John, 406
Ross, Robert, 418–420
Royal Gazette (newspaper), 196, 280–
    281, 293, 333–334
Rush, Dr. Benjamin, 414
Russell, Eleazer, 67–68
Russell, Dr. George, 310
Rutherford, John, 60
Rutherford, Thomas, 64
Rutledge, Edward, 354
Rutledge, John, 40*n.*

Sackett, Nathaniel, 148, 184
St. Leger, Barry, 241, 242, 244–247
Sauer, Christopher, 389*n.*

Index

Schaw, Alexander, 61
Schaw, Janet, 60–62
Schuyler, Hon Yost, 244–247
Schuyler, Nicholas, 244, 246
Schuyler, General Philip, 72, 79, 80,
    202, 249
Scott, Samuel, 56
Scottish Highlanders in North Carolina,
    9, 50–52, 269, 281
Scovil, Reverend James, 92*n.*, 231, 389
Seabury, Reverend Samuel, 2, 90, 94,
    97, 99–103, 179, 389*n.*
Sears, Captain, 100–103
Sears, Isaac, 179*n.*
Seeber, Jacob, 74
Seeber, William, 73, 74
Segee, John, 369
Seminole Indians, 355
Seneca Indians, 247, 252, 254, 256*n.*, 425
Serle, Ambrose, 168
Sewall, Jonathan, 309, 310, 421
Shakespeare, William, 18
Shawanese Indians, 71
Sheldon, Captain Joseph, 184
Sherwood, Justus, 260–264, 374–375
Shippen, Edward, 388
Shippen family, 338
Shoemaker, Joseph, 6
Shoemaker, Samuel, 6, 326, 344, 389*n.*
Sierra Leone Company, 431
Simpson, James, 276–278
Simsbury copper mines, as prison, 201,
    216–220, 382
Six Nations (Indian people), 70, 247,
    249–250, 256*n.*, 425
Skene, Katherine Hayden, 38
Skene, Philip, 36–38
Skenesborough, seizure of (1775), 36–38
Skinner, Cortlandt, 112, 114–116, 362
Skinner, Stephen, 362–364
Skinner, Lieutenant Colonel William,
    115, 130
Skinners (banditti group), 174, 179–180,
    369

Slaves, treatment of, 270–274, 362
Smith, Claudius, 194–196
Smith, Reverend Isaac, 310
Smith, Levi, 285–290
Smith, Melancton, 148
Smith, Samuel, 56
Smith, Thomas, 217–219
Smith, William, 359, 364, 368
Smith, William, Jr., 39–44
Smyth, Frederick, 348–349, 389*n.*
Smyth, John Ferdinand Dalziel, 74–78
Society of Friends, 4, 21, 23–24, 145*n.*,
    345
Society for the Propagation of the
    Gospel (SPG), 18, 88–89, 106,
    107, 109–111
Solemn League and Covenant (June 5,
    1774), 24, 26, 27, 55, 69
Sons of Liberty, 21, 23, 55, 56, 62–65,
    304, 308
South Carolina, Loyalist activities in, 4, 8
Southern theater of battle, 269–293
Spy, The (Cooper), 180–181, 184
Stamp Act (1765), 96
Stedman, Charles, 166–167
Steele, Robert Johnson, 199
Steuart, Charles, 336, 338
Stirling, Lord (General William Alex-
    ander), 46, 115, 298, 300
Stone, Joel, 161–165, 400, 418
Stone, Leman, 161–162
Strahan, William, 56*n.*
Strong, Benajah, 197
Stuart, Reverend John, 425, 452
Sullivan, Major General John, 198, 253–
    255
Sutherland, Lieutenant Walter, 411
Swarthout, Colonel Jacobus, 148, 182
Sydney, Lord, 413
Sylvia (slave), 38

Taber, Pardon, 117
Talmadge, Major Benjamin, 197

Index

Tarleton, Banastre, 275, 279, 283, 285
Tarring and feathering as punishment,
 57-58
Tea Act (May 10, 1773), 1, 13
Thompson, Reverend Ebenezer, 88n.
Thompson, William, 65, 66
Thorn, Belle, 47, 49
Tiligman, Colonel Tench, 344
Tippet, Mrs. Henry, 401
Tippett, Martha, 173
Tomlinson, Henry, 96
Tomlinson, J., Jr., 400, 403
Tomlinson, John, 199
Townsend, Gregory, 398-399, 403
Townsend, Captain Micah, 183-184
Townsend, Samuel, 150-152
Trinity Church, New York, 167-168,
 170
Troutbeck, John, 109
Trumbull, Jonathan, 84, 85, 90-91,
 142-144
Tryon, William, 105, 108, 173, 177,
 274, 275
Tryon County Committee of Safety, 2,
 70, 72-73, 78, 249
Tuttle, Joel, 188-189
Tuttle, Simon, 188-189
Tyler, Reverend John, 433

Ulster County Committee of Safety, 203
Underhill, Nathaniel, 100, 179-180
United Empire Loyalists, 10, 427
Upper Creek Indians, 65

Van Schaack, Peter, 3, 336, 389n.
Van Tassel, Cornelius, 176-177
Van Tassel, Peter, 176-177
Varick, Captain Richard, 58, 202
Varnum, General James M., 235
Vaughn, General John, 204
Vermont, Allen brothers and, 258-264,
 374

Vetter, Lucas, 241
Vetter, Lucas, Jr., 241
Vetter, Wilhelm, 241
Viets, Reverend, 92
Viets, Captain John, 216, 220
Vilett, John, 393
Virginia, Loyalist sentiment in, 4

Wagg, Abraham, 318, 321-322
Walter, William, 89n.
Ward, Charles, 369
Warren, Dr. Joseph, 49
Washington, General George, 40n., 80,
 155-158, 220-223, 296
 Arnold affair and, 338, 342-344
 Loyalist expatriates and, 7, 113, 124,
  362, 428n.
 military campaigns of, 14n., 143,
  172n, 198, 323, 340, 349
 punishment of Loyalists and, 211,
  216, 220-223, 225
 Rivington's espionage and, 280,
  327-328
Washington, John A., 7n.
Waters, Abram, 188-189
Watts, John, 130, 176
Watts, Robert, 421, 438, 440
Wayne, General Anthony, 209, 304-
 305, 311-312
Weare, Meschech, 68
Wentworth, Mrs. Elizabeth, 126
Wentworth, John, 18, 19, 126
Wentworth, Joshua, 68
Wentworth, Paul, 39n.
Westchester Protesters against Second
 Continental Congress, 31-34
Wetherhead, John, 44-47, 169
Weymouth, Lord, 310
Wheelock, James, 447, 448
Wheelock, John, 447, 449
White, Alexander, 72-74
White, Catherine Chrysler (Crysdale),
 406-408

Index

White, Elizabeth, 72
White, Captain Gideon, 360*n.,* 449–450
White, Reverend William, 89*n.,* 452
White Eyes (Delaware chief), 255
White Plains, burning of (1776), 171–173
Wilberforce, William, 431
Wilkins, Isaac, 32, 34–35, 336–337, 389*n.*
Willard, Levi, 152–155
Williams, Elijah, 213–215
Williams, John, 213–215, 387
Williams, Reverend John, 213
Wilmington Committee of Safety, 60–62
Wilson, Lieutenant John, 390
Wilson, Joseph, 250–252
Winslow, Edward, 336, 403, 417
Winslow, Mary, 404

Wiswall, Elizabeth, 97
Wiswall, Reverend John, 97–99
Woodruff, Joseph, 96
Wormley, Ralph, 388
Worth, Gorham A., 158
Wright, Sir James, 62, 64, 270
Wyer, Edward, 127

Yerks, William, 181*n.*
Young, Joseph, 180, 182–183, 185
Younglove, Moses, 244
Youngs, Isaac, 382

Zeans, Isaac, 258
Zubly, Reverend John J., 6